RACISM AND ETHNIC RELATIONS IN THE PORTUGUESE-SPEAKING WORLD

PROCEEDINGS OF THE BRITISH ACADEMY • 179

RACISM AND ETHNIC RELATIONS IN THE PORTUGUESE-SPEAKING WORLD

Edited by
FRANCISCO BETHENCOURT
AND
ADRIAN J. PEARCE

Published for THE BRITISH ACADEMY
by OXFORD UNIVERSITY PRESS

Oxford University Press, Great Clarendon Street, Oxford OX2 6DP

Oxford New York

Auckland Cape Town Dar es Salaam Hong Kong Karachi
Kuala Lumpur Madrid Melbourne Mexico City Nairobi
New Delhi Shanghai Taipei Toronto

With offices in
Argentina Austria Brazil Chile Czech Republic France Greece
Guatemala Hungary Italy Japan Poland Portugal Singapore
South Korea Switzerland Thailand Turkey Ukraine Vietnam

Published in the United States
By Oxford University Press Inc., New York

First published 2012

British Library Cataloguing in Publication Data
Data available

Library of Congress Cataloging in Publication Data
Data available

Typeset by
Keystroke, Station Road, Codsall, Wolverhampton
Printed in Great Britain on acid-free paper by
CPI Antony Rowe, Chippenham, Wiltshire

ISBN 978–0–19–726524–6
ISSN 0068–1202

Francisco Bethencourt dedicates this work to the memory of
Vitorino Magalhães Godinho

Adrian Pearce dedicates this work to
Martin Pearce and Margaret Jennings

Contents

Figures and Tables

Figures

Tables

Notes on Contributors

Luiz Felipe de Alencastro is Professor of the History of Brazil at the Université de Paris, Sorbonne. His works include: (as editor) *História da Vida Privada no Brasil*, vol. 2, *Império (*São Paulo, 1997); *O Trato dos Viventes: Formação do Brasil no Atlântico Sul, séculos XVI e XVII (*São Paulo, 2000); 'Le versant brésilien de l'Atlantique Sud, 1550–1850', *Annales* 61:2 (2006); 'The Economic Network of Portugal's Atlantic World', in Francisco Bethencourt and Diogo Ramada Curto (eds), *Portuguese Oceanic Expansion, 1400–1800* (Cambridge, 2007); and 'Johann Moritz und der Sklavenhandel', in G. Brunn and C. Neusch (eds), *Sein Feld war die Welt: Johann Moritz von Nassau-Siegen 1604–1679* (Münster, 2008).

Francisco Bethencourt is Charles Boxer Professor of History at King's College London. His books include *The Inquisition: A Global History (1478–1834)* (Cambridge, 2009), after French, Portuguese, Spanish, Brazilian and Serbian versions. He co-edited *Portuguese Overseas Expansion, 1400–1800* (Cambridge, 2007); *Correspondence and Cultural Exchange in Europe, 1400–1700* (Cambridge, 2007); *L'empire portugais face aux autres empires* (Paris, 2007); and *História da Expansão Portuguesa*, 5 vols (Lisbon, 1998–9). He was Director of the National Library of Portugal (1996–8) and Director of the Gulbenkian Cultural Centre in Paris (1999–2004). He is preparing a new book on the history of Racism.

David Brookshaw is Emeritus Professor and Senior Research Fellow in Luso-Brazilian Studies at the University of Bristol. His books include *Race and Color in Brazilian Literature* (Metuchen, NJ, 1986), an extended version of the original in Portuguese, *Raça e cor na literatura brasileira* (Porto Alegre, 1983); *Paradise Betrayed: Brazilian Literature of the Indian* (Amsterdam, 1989); and *Perceptions of China in Modern Portuguese Literature* (Lewiston, NY, 2002). He is co-author of *The Postcolonial Literature of Lusophone Africa* (London, 1995), and co-editor of *Luso-Asian Voices* (Bristol, 2000). He is the editor of anthologies, including *Visions of China: Stories from Macau* (Hong Kong/Providence, RI, 2002), and of José Rodrigues Miguéis' *The Polyhedric Mirror: Tales of American Life* (Providence, RI, 2006).

Michel Cahen is Senior Researcher at the Centre de Recherches Pluridisciplinaires et Comparatistes 'Les Afriques dans le Monde', Bordeaux University. He has studied the history of the former Portuguese colonies in Africa, and the lusophone African countries of today, for thirty years. His research focuses primarily on issues of ethnicity, political democracy, and the state, and on personal identity within citizenship. He was founder and chief editor of *Lusotopie* (Leiden, 1994–2009), and his main books are: *Mozambique, la révolution implosée. Etudes sur douze années d'indépendance (1975–1987)* (Paris, 1987); *Vilas et Cidades: Bourgs et Villes en Afrique lusophone* (Paris, 1989); *Les Bandits. Un historien au Mozambique, 1994* (Paris, 2002); *La dialectique des secrets. Histoire et idéologie dans l'accouchement sous X et l'adoption plénière* (Paris, 2004); and *Le Portugal bilingue. Histoire et droits politiques d'une minorité linguistique: la communauté mirandaise* (Rennes, 2009).

Andrea Daher received her PhD from the École des Hautes Études en Sciences Sociales in 1995. She teaches at the Federal University of Rio de Janeiro, where she also coordinates the Research Laboratory of History of Literacy Practices. She is a researcher of the National Council of Scientific and Technological Development (CNPq). Her book *Les Singularités de la France Equinoxiale* was published in Paris in 2002, and, as *O Brasil francês*, in Rio de Janeiro in 2007. She directs research on cultural practices in the modern and contemporary eras at the Graduate Programme of Social History of the UFRJ. She holds the Chair of Social Sciences 'Sergio Buarque de Holanda' at the Maison des Sciences de l'Homme in Paris (2010 to 2014).

Antonio Sérgio Alfredo Guimarães holds a PhD in Sociology from the University of Wisconsin – Madison (1988). He is currently Professor of Sociology at the University of São Paulo, and occupies the Sérgio Buarque de Holanda Chair at the Institute d'Études Politiques at the University of Bordeaux. His research focuses on racial, national, and class identities, Black social movements, affirmative action, and Black intellectuals. He has published, among other books, *Preconceito Racial – Modos, Temas, Tempos* (São Paulo, 2008); *Classes, raças e democracia* (São Paulo, 2002); and *Racismo e anti-racismo no Brasil* (São Paulo, 1999; 2nd edn, 2005).

Miguel Bandeira Jerónimo is Research Fellow at the Institute of Social Sciences, University of Lisbon, and Visiting Professor at Brown University. He concluded his PhD in History at King's College London in 2008, with a thesis titled 'Religion, Empire, and the Diplomacy of Colonialism: Portugal, Europe, and the Congo Question, c.1820–1890'. In 2010 he published his first book, *Livros Brancos, Almas Negras. A 'Missão Civilizadora' do Colonialismo Português, c. 1870–1930* (Lisbon). His second book is *A Diplomacia do Imperialismo. Política e Religião na Partilha de África (1820–1890)* (Lisbon: Edições 70, 2012). He is co-editor of the academic book collection *História & Sociedade,* published by Edições 70.

Herbert S. Klein is Gouverneur Morris Professor Emeritus, Columbia University, and Research Fellow at the Hoover Institution, Stanford University. He is the author of twenty-four books, among which are four comparative studies of slavery in the Atlantic world: *Slavery in the Americas: A Comparative History of Cuba and Virginia* (1968); *The Middle Passage: Comparative Studies in the Atlantic Slave Trade* (1978); *The Atlantic Slave Trade* (2nd edn, 2010); and, as co-author, *African Slavery in Latin America and the Caribbean* (2006). He is also the co-author of *Slavery and the Economy of São Paulo, 1750–1850* (2003), *Escravismo em São Paulo e Minas Gerais* (2009), and *Slavery in Brazil* (2009).

Jean Michel Massing, FSA, is Professor in the History of Art and Fellow of King's College, Cambridge. He has published widely, most recently on the relationships between European and non-European cultures, especially Africa and the Pacific, with articles on the history of cartography, the representations of foreign lands and peoples, and the collection of exotic artifacts. He has had a leading role in important exhibitions, such as *Encompassing the Globe: Portugal and the World in the 16th & 17th Centuries*, held in Washington, DC in 2007, in Brussels in 2007–8, and in Lisbon in 2009. He has just completed a massive volume *From the 'Age of Discovery' to the Age of Abolition: Europe and the World Beyond* (*The Image of the Black in Western Art,* 3.2) (Cambridge, MA, 2011).

José Pedro Paiva is Professor at Coimbra University and a researcher at the Centro de História da Sociedade e da Cultura (FCT). He is the author of several books: *Bruxaria e superstição num país sem caça às bruxas: 1600–1774* (Lisbon, 1997); *Os bispos de Portugal e do império 1495–1777* (Coimbra, 2006); *Baluartes da fé e da disciplina. O enlace entre a Inquisição e os bispos em Portugal (1536–1750)* (Coimbra, 2011); and, as editor, *Religious Ceremonials and Images: Power and Social Meaning (1400–1750)* (Coimbra, 2002). He is currently Director of the Coimbra University Archives.

Maria Lúcia G. Pallares-Burke was Professor at the University of São Paulo and is now an associate of the Centre of Latin American Studies at the University of Cambridge. She has worked on the cultural history of the European Enlightenment and its reception in Latin America. She published a collection of interviews with a group of cultural historians, *The New History: Confessions and Conversation* (Cambridge, 2002), which has been translated into four languages. Her most recent books are about the Brazilian polymath Gilberto Freyre: an intellectual biography of his formative years (*Gilberto Freyre, um vitoriano dos trópicos*, 2005), and, with Peter Burke, an intellectual portrait concerned with his whole lifetime (*Gilberto Freyre, Social Theory in the Tropics*, 2008).

Adrian J. Pearce lectures in Latin American History at King's College London, where he is a member of both the Department of History and the Department of Spanish, Portuguese, and Latin American Studies. His research is concerned primarily with the political, economic, and cultural impact of Spanish and British colonialism on the peoples of the Andes and the Caribbean (both island and continental), above all in the eighteenth and early nineteenth centuries. Within this framework, he has published on Spanish rule in the viceroyalty of Peru; British trade with Latin America; and (a new topic) 'reindigenisation' in early-republican Peru and Bolivia.

Cicero Pereira is a researcher at the Institute of Social Sciences of the University of Lisbon. He received his PhD from the ISCTE – University Institute of Lisbon in 2007, with a thesis on the roles of social norms and legitimisation factors in the relationship between prejudice and discrimination. His research interests focus on the legitimisation mechanisms of racism, prejudice, and discrimination. His methodological interests involve measurement theory, methods and techniques of psychological research (correlational, experimental, quasi-experimental designs), and data analysis.

João de Pina-Cabral is Research Professor at the Institute of Social Sciences, University of Lisbon, and Director of the journal *Análise Social*. He was Founding President of the Portuguese Association of Anthropology (1989–91), President of the European Association of Social Anthropologists (2003–5), and President of the Scientific Council, ICS/Lisbon (1997–2005). He is a corresponding member of both the Royal Academy of Moral and Political Sciences (Madrid) and the Lisbon Academy of Sciences, and an Honorary Fellow of the Royal Anthropological Institute (Great Britain). His principal monographs are: *Sons of Adam, Daughters of Eve: The Peasant Worldview of the Alto Minho (NW Portugal)* (Oxford, 1986); *Os contextos da antropologia* (Lisbon, 1991); *Between China and Europe: Person, Culture and Emotion in Macao* (Oxford, 2002); and *O homem na família* (Lisbon, 2003).

Ricardo Roque is Research Fellow at the Institute of Social Sciences, University of Lisbon. He works on the relations between colonialism, human sciences, and indigenous cultures in the Portuguese empire in Asia and Africa. His publications include *Headhunting and Colonialism: Anthropology and the Circulation of Human Skulls in the Portuguese Empire, 1870–1930* (Basingstoke, 2010); *Antropologia e Império: Fonseca Cardoso e a expedição à Índia em 1895* (Lisbon, 2001); and *Engaging Colonial Knowledge: Reading European Archives in World History* (edited with Kim Wagner) (Basingstoke, 2012).

Jorge Vala is Research Professor at the Institute of Social Sciences of the University of Lisbon. He received his PhD in Social Psychology from the Catholic University of Louvain in 1984. His research focuses on socio-cognitive processes, namely in the field of social representations and ideologies, social norms, and social identities.

His present projects articulate socio-cognitive processes with the study of racism and prejudice, immigration issues, political attitudes, social justice, and the validation of everyday knowledge.

Peter Wade is currently Professor of Social Anthropology at the University of Manchester. His publications include *Blackness and Race Mixture* (Baltimore, 1993); *Race and Ethnicity in Latin America* (2nd edn, London, 2010); *Music, Race and Nation:* Música Tropical *in Colombia* (Chicago, 2000); *Race, Nature and Culture: An Anthropological Perspective* (London, 2002); and *Race and Sex in Latin America* (London, 2009). His current research focuses on issues of race and new genomic technologies. He is directing a project on 'Race, Genomics and *Mestizaje* (Mixture) in Latin America: A Comparative Approach', funded by the ESRC and the Leverhulme Trust.

Acknowledgements

The British Academy and the Portuguese Instituto Camões and Fundação para a Ciência e Tecnologia subsidised the crucial conference of 2009 that started the work leading to the preparation of this volume. Without their support this project would not have been brought to fruition. The British Academy also agreed to publish this volume in its prestigious series, thus guaranteeing the diffusion of carefully planned research enriched by discussion. The requirements for publication involved choices. The final texts certainly benefited from the discussion stimulated by Sir John Elliott, Richard Drayton, Nancy Naro and Jon Wilson. We would also like to highlight the input of Laura de Mello e Souza, Antonio Feros, Maria Conceição Neto, Abdoolkarim Vakil and Luisa Pinto Teixeira, participants in the conference. Finally, the editors benefited from the support of the external reviewer, Peter Burke, who played a major role in the final discussion of the texts.

Introduction

FRANCISCO BETHENCOURT

I

HOW DID RACISM EVOLVE in different parts of the Portuguese-speaking world? How should we evaluate the impact on ethnic perceptions of colonial societies based on slavery or the slave trade? What was the reality of inter-ethnic mixture in different continents? How has the prejudice of white supremacy been confronted in Brazil and Portugal? How should we assess the impact of recent trends of emigration and immigration? These were the key questions addressed by a group of historians, art historians, political scientists, anthropologists, literary scholars, sociologists and social psychologists at a conference held at King's College London in December 2009. These scholars were invited to present papers, engage in collective discussion and prepare an up-to-date volume providing new perspectives on these issues.

During the discussions that led to this book, the North American notion of race relations was seriously challenged as inadequate, since it contributes to reinforcing prejudices, although it was acknowledged that the noun race has been used by specific groups to express their identity. The nouns racist and racism were only coined in the 1890s and 1900s to designate promoters of racial theory and a hierarchy of races, while in the 1920s and 1930s these nouns took up the meaning of hostility against a racial group considered inferior. The antinomies antiracist and antiracism were coined in the 1930s and 1950s.[1] By contrast, race has been used as a noun since the late Middle Ages (*razza* in Italian, *raza* in Castilian-Spanish, *raça* in Portuguese and Catalan, *race* in French and English, *rasse* in German), but it shows far more semantic changes. Probably originating from the Latin *generatio* by aphaeresis, race designated varieties of breeding animals and plants, but also

[1] Alain Rey (ed.), *Dictionnaire historique de la langue française*, 3 vols (Paris: Le Robert, 1998), vol. 3, pp. 3,056–7.

Proceedings of the British Academy **179**, *1–14*.

social lineages (in North Italy from the twelfth to the fourteenth century), proceeding from the upper group of kings and noblemen (in sixteenth-century France and England) to vast communities believed to originate from the same ancestors. By the eighteenth century it represented the division of mankind into specific types supposedly sharing common descent; in early modern Europe it could be used to designate mankind or women; finally, by the late nineteenth and first half of the twentieth century, race was even equated with nation.[2] In the sixteenth-century Spanish and Portuguese world the noun started to designate minorities of violently converted Jewish and Muslim people; the same meaning of stained descent was quickly extended to black people and Native Americans.[3] In the Portuguese dictionary published by Bluteau in the early eighteenth century, race is equated with caste, designating species of animals (horses and dogs); it is said to always take the bad part of generations: to have race means to have the race of Moor or Jew (and Bluteau quotes the rules of the *Misericórdia*, a royal-sponsored confraternity, on purity of blood).[4] In the most recent dictionary of Portuguese, published in 2001, race is defined as a traditional and arbitrary division of human groups, expressing the ethnological consensus that cultural proximity is more relevant than physical features.[5] We can interpret this latest reference as the result of fifty years of discussion of the theory of races and rejection of its prejudiced foundations.[6]

The historical contamination resulting from the social uses of the noun race for defining hierarchies, labelling specific groups as inferior and targeting them for discriminatory action was taken into consideration when we discussed the title of the volume. Ethnic relations remains an ambiguous formulation, but it does not suffer from the same level of contamination as race relations; it can convey both racialisation and definitions of identity, while keeping on board the reference to ethnicity favoured by anthropologists. *Ethnicus*, in the Christian Roman world and medieval Latin, meant gentile or pagan, close to the modern notion of otherness.[7] Racism has a clear and stable content, which can be applied to periods

[2] J. A. Simpson and E. S. C. Weiner (eds), *Oxford English Dictionary*, 20 vols (Oxford: Clarendon Press, 1989), vol. 13, pp. 69–70; *Grande Dizionario della Lingua Italiana* (Turin: Unione Tipografica Editrice Torinese, 1990), vol. 15, pp. 586–8; Arlette Jouana, *L'idée de race en France au XVI*[e] *siècle et début du XVII*[e], 2nd edn, 2 vols (Montpellier: Université Paul Valéry, 1981).

[3] Joan Corominas, *Diccionario crítico etimológico castellano e hispánico*, 7 vols (Madrid: Gredos, 1981), vol. 7, pp. 800–2.

[4] Rafael Bluteau, *Vocabulario Portuguez e Latino*, 10 vols (Coimbra and Lisbon: Colégio das Artes, 1712–28).

[5] Antônio Houaiss *et al.* (eds), *Dicionário Houaiss da língua portuguesa* (Rio de Janeiro: Objectiva/Instituto Houaiss, 2001), p. 2,372.

[6] See the analysis of the debate launched by UNESCO from the late 1940s to the 1960s in Claudio Pogliano, *L'ossessione della razza: Antropologia e genetica nel XX secolo* (Pisa: Scuola Normale Superiore, 2005), ch. 4.

[7] *Thesaurus Linguæ Latinæ*, 8 vols (Lipsiae: E. B. Teubneri, 1931–53), vol. 5, pp. 923–4; J. C. Niermeyer and C. van De Kieft, *Mediæ Latinitatis Lexicon Minus*, 2nd edn, 2 vols (Leiden: Brill, 2002), vol. 1, p. 502.

of history before its coinage; as Lucien Febvre taught us, the idea can exist without the noun. Social psychology has defined racism as both prejudice and discriminatory action against specific human groups which are taken to share the same descent and the same attributes, transmitted from generation to generation.[8] The distinction generally used by historians between natural and cultural attributes[9] does not stand careful examination: those attributes – skin colour, shape of the body, forms of the nose and eyes, but also supposed patterns of behaviour, values or forms of intelligence – real or imaginary, were generally entangled in different periods of time and in different spaces.[10] This is why we retained racism in the title, since race relations is not a neutral and objective analytical framework, but rather has resulted from a historical accumulation of prejudices and discriminatory actions that we need to deconstruct. Finally, the notion of white supremacy, successfully used by George Fredrickson in the specific context of the United States and South Africa,[11] suggests a neutral stance, but it only concerns European dominance over non-white populations, leaving aside historical changes of prejudice and discriminatory action within Europe and raising problems of the definition of whiteness. In our view racism is always relational; it shapes changeable hierarchies of peoples, and cannot be understood from the single (even if crucial) angle of relations between white and black populations.

II

Decolonisation and postcolonial societies have reshaped ethnic relations around the world, due to the new system of values based on the formal international standard of human rights approved by the United Nations in 1948. The development of a global economy has become incompatible with hierarchies of peoples or ethnicities: white supremacy, based on imperial and national dominion, has been challenged by sophisticated international multi-ethnic elites sharing the same lifestyle and capitalist ethos, while the shock of the Holocaust, the liberation wars of independence and the Afro-American movement of civil rights all contributed to making anti-racism normative from the 1960s onwards. However, ethnic prejudice has not evaporated in the past forty years: racism has been evolving and adapting to the new norm under different guises. National and international

[8] James M. Jones, *Prejudice and Racism*, 2nd edn (New York: McGraw Hill, 1997).

[9] David Nirenberg, 'Was There Race Before Modernity? The Example of "Jewish" Blood in Late Medieval Spain', in Miriam Eliav-Feldon, Benjamin Isaac and Joseph Ziegler (eds), *The Origins of Racism in the West* (Cambridge: Cambridge University Press, 2009), pp. 232–64.

[10] See Peter Wade, *Race, Nature and Culture: An Anthropological Perspective* (London: Pluto Press, 2002).

[11] George M. Fredrickson, *White Supremacy: A Comparative Study in American and South African History* (Oxford: Oxford University Press, 1981), esp. pp. xi–xii.

traditions are also divergent: while France and parts of continental Europe refute the very notion of race as a by-product of racism, race identification in the United States and the United Kingdom is obligatory in many types of questionnaires; moreover, racial construction has became part of the identity of social groups. This means that the debate on the absence of a scientific basis for racial definition launched after the Second World War by UNESCO has been confronted by the daily use of the noun race by different ethnicities, such as Afro-Americans, to define their own identity. In sum, race is not a valid concept, but it exists in social perceptions.[12] Finally, the two divergent models of ethnic relations – the North American bipolar white/black system, without space for mixed-race people or racial mobility, against the Brazilian multiple or gradated system, in which the socially successful mulatto becomes white[13] – have been evolving. Recent affirmative action in Brazil adopted North American corrective mechanisms due to the equation of black people with social exclusion,[14] while in the United States the bipolar norm has been challenged by increased mixed-race relations.

The persistence of prejudice and discriminatory action in different parts of the world needs further research. The Portuguese-speaking world is an ideal case study that justifies our enquiry: there is no comparative and comprehensive work in this field ranging from early modern history to contemporary issues, although significant research has been carried out on the impact of the theory of races, lusotropicalism and racist attitudes.[15] This book concerns countries and communities spread through four continents historically shaped or touched by Portuguese colonialism in different ways. The variety of ethnic experiences in those countries before and after independence is also observed in Portugal, the centre of the old system, where constant emigration has been confronted in the past thirty years by significant immigration of African and Eastern European origin. Brazilian colonial society, structured by a minority of white people, presented an ethnic composition of the

[12] See the development of this line of argument in Sarah Daynes and Orville Lee, *Desire for Race* (Cambridge: Cambridge University Press, 2008).

[13] See the classical approach in Frank Tannenbaum, *Slave and Citizen: The Negro in the Americas* (New York: Vintage Books, 1946), already nuanced in Carl N. Degler, *Neither Black nor White: Slavery and Race Relations in Brazil and the United States* (New York: Macmillan, 1971).

[14] Carlos Alberto Steil (ed.), *Cotas raciais na universidade: um debate* (Porto Alegre: Universidade Federal do Rio Grande do Sul, 2006).

[15] Lilia Moritz Schwarcz, *O espectáculo das raças: Cientistas, instituições e questão racial no Brasil, 1870–1930* (São Paulo: Companhia das Letras, 1993); Yves Léonard, 'Salazarisme et lusotropicalisme: histoire d'une appropriation', *Lusotopie* (1997), pp. 211–26; Cláudia Castelo, *'O modo português de estar no mundo': O Lusotropicalismo e a ideologica colonial portuguesa* (Porto: Afrontamento, 1998); Lorenzo Macagno, 'Um antropólogo americano no "mundo que o português criou": Relações raciais no Brasil e em Moçambique segundo Marvin Harris', *Lusotopie* (1999), pp. 143–61; António Sérgio Guimarães, *Racismo e anti-racismo no Brasil* (São Paulo: FAUSP, 1999); Jorge Vala *et al.*, *Expressões dos racismos em Portugal* (Lisbon: Imprensa de Ciências Sociais, 1999); Patrícia Ferraz de Matos, *As cores do Império: Representações raciais no império colonial português* (Lisbon: Imprensa de Ciências Sociais, 2006).

population in which African slaves played a major role. By contrast, the Portuguese early modern society in Europe, although including an important number of African slaves – probably the most important black community in Europe – cannot be defined as a society based on slavery. The Portuguese enclaves in Africa did not produce a colonial society similar to the Brazilian one. Although they created a significant number of mixed-race people, they were surrounded by African societies. The decimation of Native Americans through epidemics, war and forced migrations contrasted with the resilience of African societies; the Portuguese could dominate chiefdoms in Guinea or in the Zambezi valley, but they were part of African societies. In Asia, the role of global society was also decisive: the Portuguese were dependent on local elites of Christianised people.

In postcolonial societies white supremacy was naturally reversed. The Brazilian case is a very interesting one, shaped by the pride of mixed-race people from the 1930s onwards. Recent affirmative action, already mentioned, produced a new dynamic, placing racial issues at the centre of the political debate. The freedom fight of African peoples against colonial rule came along with the assertion of blackness, which cemented African values. But postcolonial realities present unexpected outcomes, such as the geography of power in Mozambique, in which the ruling party Frelimo inherits the urban, coastal and southern areas privileged by the old colonial power, while the opposition party Renamo embodies the cultural resistance of rural central and northern areas.[16] In Angola, the native political elite (partly mixed-race) of Luanda managed to assert its power against the strong northern and central regional elites, while the enormous transfer of populations provoked by the civil war dramatically changed the political geography. Turning our attention to West Africa we could consider that the post-independence separation of the Cape Verde Islands and Guinea-Bissau is not immune to ethnic divisions, while the precocious establishment of democracy in Cape Verde could be related to the particular history of a multi-ethnic population.

Historical analysis has been complicated by the stereotype of Portugal as a backward but mild colonial power, more humane than other European empires. This background requires a double investigation of perceptions and realities. The traditional vision of the European colonies as reflecting essential virtues and defects of the colonisers is at stake here. This pervasive essentialist approach, developed by David Hume and widely accepted until nowadays,[17] supposes that the European powers projected onto other continents their laws, their manners, their ways of doing and thinking, without contradiction; native agency did not exist. This essentialist approach was coupled with national pride, a driving force of

[16] Michel Cahen, *Les bandits: Un historien au Mozambique, 1994* (Paris: Centre Culturel Calouste Gulbenkian, 2002).

[17] David Hume, 'On National Characters' (1741), in Stephen Copley and Andrew Edgar (eds), *Selected Essays* (Oxford: Oxford University Press, 1993), pp. 113–25.

historiography: Niall Ferguson boasts that the British colonial administration was remarkably cheap, efficient and non-venal.[18] This vision finds in the vast and complex Portuguese-speaking world a loud refutation, due to the obvious presence of native peoples' agency since the beginning of the colonial process, not to mention entirely different social formations, inter-ethnic relations and divergent paths defined by countries such as Brazil (independent since 1822) or Angola (independent since 1975). I believe that this refutation would be easy to verify in the other European colonial systems, but we need here to better understand the historical roots of variety and divergence in the Portuguese-speaking world.

III

> The Portuguese were more humane than the Dutch, Spanish and English. For this reason, it was easier in the coasts of Brazil than elsewhere for slaves to gain their freedom, and large numbers of freed Negroes were to be found in this region.[19]

This phrase was supposedly formulated in the 1820s by Hegel in his lectures on History published as *Die Vernunft in der Geschichte* (Reason in History). He was probably inspired by the contemporary publication of the travels in Brazil of Von Spix and Von Martius, who praised the mildness with which slaves were treated in that country.[20] We do not know whether Hegel elaborated on this statement, in which Spaniards are curiously placed at the same level as the Dutch and English. Hegel also stated that Spaniards had left their noble and magnificent character in Europe: Creoles (descendants of Spaniards born in America) would have merely exercised their pride against indigenous people. This contempt can better be explained by Hegel's bipolar approach to the history of America: the conquest of the South against colonisation of the North, the submissive spirit of the Catholics against the entrepreneurial spirit of the Protestants, rigid hierarchy based on the exploitation of the Indians against the freedom of the individual. The main stereotypes of the Northern European historiography, still reproduced to this day, were then defined by this sequence of oppositions, guided by the notion of essential national and religious characters projected onto the new world by the colonists. These contrasting pairs have become totally outdated as an interpretative framework; the general picture of colonial America is now extremely nuanced by massive evidence assembled by many researchers, most notably by John Elliott in his comparison of the Spanish and the British empires.[21]

[18] Niall Ferguson, *Empire: How Britain Made the Modern World* (London: Penguin, 2003), p. 370.

[19] Georg Wilhelm Friedrich Hegel, *Lectures on the Philosophy of World History. Introduction: Reason in History* (Cambridge: Cambridge University Press, 1975), p. 165.

[20] Johann Baptist Von Spix and Carl Friedrich Philipp Von Martius, *Travels in Brazil in the Years 1817–1820 . . .* (London: Longman, 1824), p. 179.

What matters for our argument here is the stereotype of Portuguese good nature in relation to African slaves and the rate of manumission (or slave emancipation). If we look at the work of Hegel's contemporary, Alexander von Humboldt, who travelled extensively in Spanish America between 1799 and 1804, and in the 1820s wrote a political essay on the island of Cuba, we find the same issue of manumission studied in an accurate way, this time involving the Spaniards. He pointed out that the freed coloured population in Cuba had reached 115,691 people in 1817, in contrast with 199,292 slaves, while Jamaica had only 35,000 freed coloured people against 380,000 slaves. Humboldt explained this discrepancy by reference to the ethic of the white inhabitants of Cuba and the Spanish legislation, '[which] favours liberty, instead of opposing it, like the English and French legislation'.[22]

Legal rules were indeed a major deterrent to manumission in the English and French cases: at the beginning of the eighteenth century in Virginia, for instance, it was forbidden by the colonial assembly to emancipate a slave, and in 1806 freed black men were expelled from the territory. In 1685, in the French colonies, the black code limited manumission, but in 1724 the code for Louisiana made emancipation virtually impossible, since it stipulated that slaves were not allowed to buy their own freedom. In the first decades of the eighteenth century, several French laws also prohibited marriage between white and black people. By contrast, Portuguese and Spanish legislation did not forbid inter-racial marriage or payment by slaves for their own manumission. By the end of the colonial period in Brazil, freed coloured people represented a significant part of the population: 28 per cent of the total, against an identical 28 per cent for white people, 38 per cent for slaves and 6 per cent for Indians.[23]

The colonists' ethic is a difficult topic to analyse: I prefer to discuss different models of managing slavery. Although modern historiography has highlighted the self-interested emancipation of old slaves by white people who did not want to maintain the 'burden' after using the energy of the slaves in their youth and maturity, the scale of manumission clearly indicates that it was not limited to old age.[24] In the Iberian case we have a model of management of slavery that included different mechanisms of control and regulation, such as the role of confraternities, the possibility of legal complaint to the king against unfair treatment, and individual manumission. It is true that the first two mechanisms, involving the Church and

[21] J. H. Elliott, *Empires of the Atlantic World: Britain and Spain in America, 1492–1830* (New Haven: Yale University Press, 2006).

[22] Alexander von Humboldt (Thomasina Ross, ed.), *Personal Narrative and Travels to the Equinoctial Regions of America during the Years 1799–1804* (London: George Routledge and Sons, 1895), vol. 3, pp. 236–7, 243.

[23] Dauril Alden, 'Late Colonial Brazil, 1750–1808', in Leslie Bethell (ed.), *Colonial Brazil* (Cambridge: Cambridge University Press, 1987), pp. 284–343, see p. 290.

[24] Herbert S. Klein and Francisco Vidal Luna, *Slavery in Brazil* (Cambridge: Cambridge University Press, 2010), esp. ch. 9.

the Crown, targeted excessive violence, but they did not change the foundations or the logic of the system. They might have deterred unusual practices of terror, helping to define the norm and avoid further disruption of the system by widespread marooning. These mechanisms certainly enhanced manumission: the confraternities of black people functioned as networks of solidarity, which in some cases lent money or guaranteed credit for members to obtain their freedom. However, Hegel's idea of humane treatment of slaves by the Portuguese is difficult to establish besides manumission. There is no significant difference of disciplinary methods concerning slavery in the French, British, Spanish and Portuguese colonies. In all cases of plantation systems, domestic women slaves were generally better treated and mixed-race slaves could be promoted for supervision work. These two groups were also favoured by the Iberian practice of manumission.

The Portuguese resisted prohibiting the slave trade as best as they could and they prolonged slavery for as long as they could. It is true that in 1761 Pombal had abolished the slave trade into Portugal, but not between the colonies, a decision followed by the abolition of slavery in the metropolis under certain circumstances – the famous law of the free womb, which became the template for the first wave of anti-slavery legislation in Iberian America, fifty or even one hundred years later.[25] However, as these decisions did not concern the colonies they remained without further consequences until the British political pressure of the 1810s. Portugal signed the convention of Vienna in 1815, which forbade the slave trade north of the Equator, but it required a systematic campaign by the British Navy against numerous Portuguese slave ships, many of them captured or even sunk, to obtain some action from the Portuguese authorities. In 1836 the total abolition of the slave trade was decreed but not implemented, even after the British imposed another treaty in 1842, in which the slave trade was equated with piracy. The practice was still continued, due to acceptance of the slave trade in Brazil and Cuba. Slavery in the Portuguese colonies in Africa was not touched until a series of convoluted laws abolished it in the 1860s and 1870s. Again, an ambiguous system of forced labour replaced old slavery. The situation in Brazil, independent since 1822, was no better: the slave trade was only formally prohibited in 1850, and slavery in 1888.[26] This prolonged resistance says a lot about the rooted interests of slave traders and owners in Portugal and Brazil, who were unwilling, until very late, to reinvest their capital or convert their plantations into a wage system. Slave traders were among the major capitalists in Portugal in the first half of the nineteenth century;

[25] Francisco Bethencourt, 'Race Relations in the Portuguese Empire', in Jay Levenson (ed.), *Encompassing the Globe: Portugal and the World in the 16th and 17th Centuries – Essays* (Washington, DC: Smithsonian Institute, 2007), pp. 45–56, 263–5.

[26] Leslie Bethell, *The Abolition of the Brazilian Slave Trade: Britain, Brazil and the Slave Trade Question, 1807–1869* (Cambridge: Cambridge University Press, 1970); Seymour Drescher, 'Brazilian Abolition in Comparative Perspective', in Rebecca J. Scott *et al.* (eds), *The Abolition of Slavery and the Aftermath of Emancipation in Brazil* (Durham, NC: Duke University Press, 1988), pp. 23–54.

they had infiltrated freemasonry and the radical liberal movement of Setembrismo. These facts raise doubts, not about the bipolar slave trade system between Brazil and Africa analysed by Luiz Felipe de Alencastro,[27] but about the real centre of operations of the slave traders and the core of their financial network. Political blockages are better explained by the study of the political influence of slave traders, as the widespread social interests involved in the slave trade explain the absence of an abolitionist movement in Portugal, as João Pedro Marques has pointed out.[28]

IV

The abolition of slavery did not change the racist system of prejudices and discrimination that had structured colonial (and metropolitan) society for centuries. We have been focusing here on prejudice against black people fuelled by the slave trade and slavery, but we have to keep in mind that in Iberia these prejudices were part of a system of relations including Jews and Muslims, labelled as New Christians and Moriscos after violent conversion, and supposed to carry with them imaginary physical and mental attributes transmitted from generation to generation. Prejudices against black people were projected onto different continents by Iberian expansion: Native Americans and Asian people were labelled as the 'blacks of the land' in the correspondence of captains, governors and authors of surveys concerning colonial settlements.[29] The disruption of political settings, including the impact of liberalism or decolonisation, contributed to change the relative position of these prejudices in the racial state:[30] the Jews, who were arguably at the top of ethnic contempt in the early modern Iberian world, were received back in Portugal and Spain in the second half of the nineteenth century and never persecuted again; the Muslims, traditionally targeted as the main enemies throughout Portuguese expansion in Africa and Asia, were discovered as possible allies in Guinea and Mozambique by the regime of Salazar before and during the colonial war; Muslims from North Africa have been migrating to Spain in recent decades, being targeted in some places by racist attitudes.

[27] Luiz Felipe de Alencastro, *O trato dos viventes: Formação do Brasil no Atlântico Sul, séculos XVI e XVII* (São Paulo: Companhia das Letras, 2000).

[28] João Pedro Marques, *The Sounds of Silence: Nineteenth-Century Portugal and the Abolition of the Slave Trade* (Oxford: Berghahn, 2006).

[29] John M. Monteiro, *Negros da terra: Índios e bandeirantes nas origens de São Paulo* (São Paulo: Companhia das Letras, 1994); Francisco Bethencourt, 'Low Cost Empire: Interaction between the Portuguese and Local Societies in Asia', in Ernst van Veen and Léonard Blussé (eds), *Rivalry and Conflict: European Traders and Asian Trading Networks in the 16th and 17th Centuries* (Leiden: CNWS, 2005), pp. 108–30.

[30] David Theo Goldberg, *The Racial State* (Oxford: Blackwell, 2002). The idea of a racially configured state, implicated in defining prejudices and implementing discriminatory actions, can be applied to the case of the Portuguese empire.

The notion of purity of blood, which was used in Iberia from the fifteenth century on to frame the exclusion of Christians of Jewish and Muslim descent by the statutes of confraternities, cathedral chapters, municipalities, military orders and religious orders, proved to be more pervasive and resilient in Spain than in Portugal. The distinction between Old and New Christians was abolished in Portugal in 1773, while it took two liberal revolutions in Spain to bring about its final abolition almost one century later. This notion of purity of blood contributed to define hierarchies of caste (or strata of mixed-race peoples) in Spanish and Portuguese America, a practice of classification that reached the highest point during the eighteenth century, expressed by series of paintings in Mexico and Peru.[31] Purity of blood still had some resonance in Iberia in the nineteenth and twentieth centuries, mainly with the assertion of nation as race during the regimes of Salazar and Franco, but it has faded away in the new democratic environment of the past thirty years.

The idea of white supremacy guided Brazilian policies of European immigration until 1930, while in Portugal this idea was only nuanced in the 1950s due to the obvious political handicap in the face of the tide of general decolonisation. Colonial statistics still classified respectively 95 per cent and 97 per cent of the population in Angola and Mozambique in 1959 as 'uncivilised indigenous'; it was only in 1960 that this embarrassing criterion was discontinued. In the 1930s and 1940s Gilberto Freyre played a major role in the re-foundation of Brazilian national identity based on the idea of the multiracial society,[32] while in Portugal his ideas were received as suspicious by the political elite of the Salazar regime, concerned about possible subversive impact on the colonial system. In 1950, challenged by decolonisation, Salazar saw the possibilities of recycling Freyre's theory of relatively mild Portuguese colonial rule; Freyre accepted the official invitation to visit the Portuguese colonies. In the 1950s and early 1960s, Freyre played a dubious role as supporter of the Portuguese colonial project.[33] From the Brazilian experience of miscegenation, he coined the idea of lusotropicalism and extended it to the Portuguese colonies, praising the specific Lusitanian ability to adapt to the tropics. Although Freyre had not denied racism in his first works on the 'world the Portuguese created', the books he produced for Salazar's propaganda largely avoided the issue.

The main challenge to Freyre's vision of a soft and specific Portuguese colonial rule came from Marvin Harris, who worked first in Brazil and then in Mozambique.[34]

[31] Ilona Katzew, *Casta Painting: Images of Race in Eighteenth Century Mexico* (New Haven: Yale University Press, 2004).

[32] Gilberto Freyre, *The Masters and the Slaves: A Study in the Development of Brazilian Civilization* (New York: Alfred A. Knopf, 1946). Originally published in 1933, this book was followed by others that asserted the multiracial approach.

[33] Léonard, 'Salazarisme et lusotropicalisme'; Yves Léonard, 'O ultramar português', in Francisco Bethencourt and Kirti Chaudhuri (eds), *História da expansão portuguesa*, 5 vols (Lisbon: Círculo de Leitores, 1998–9), vol. 5, pp. 31–50; Castelo, *'O modo português de estar no mundo'*.

He showed how racism was widespread in mid-twentieth-century Brazil and he exposed the extremely low level of miscegenation in Portuguese Africa: less than 1 per cent of the population in Angola and Mozambique were officially classified as mixed-race. Moreover, he proved that Mozambique was a society moving close, although without formal laws, to South African apartheid in the late 1950s. Harris's findings coincided with a new generation of Brazilian sociologists and economists, namely Fernando Henrique Cardoso and Octávio Ianni, who broke away from Freyre's relatively harmonious vision of a multiracial society.[35] In the meantime, Charles Boxer's book on *Race Relations in the Portuguese Colonial Empire, 1415–1825*, published in 1963, immediately after the outbreak of the colonial war in Portuguese Africa, demolished the propaganda of historical peaceful and cordial race relations with empirical data colony by colony.[36] Nowadays this book looks impressionistic and theoretically weak, unable to include native agency and forms of inter-ethnic negotiation at ground level, but it played a significant role in the debate on colonialism.

If in Brazil the issue had been how to build a modern society within a post-slavery social and cultural framework, in Portugal the issue was how to break away from the trap of a colonial society that wanted to perpetuate itself along with Salazar's dictatorship. The connection between the two realities that Salazar had skilfully woven to accommodate the alliance with the republican right wing showed its limits in the 1960s. The colonial war contributed to wiping out the last remnants of republican imperialist thought, creating a new set of left, extreme left and centre-right parties or associations that by the beginning of the 1970s agreed on the termination of both the regime and the colonies, although the solutions advocated for the latter were divergent. Finally a new spirit of emancipation broke into the declining regime of the *Estado Novo*, in which the decisive African liberation movements were celebrated in Portugal by the growing movements of the working class, students and new urban professionals.[37]

The democratisation of Portugal and the independence of the colonies encouraged a new spirit of cooperation between peoples who had been oppressed in

[34] Marvin Harris, *Town and Country in Brazil* (New York: Columbia University Press, 1956); Marvin Harris, 'Portugal's African "Wards": A First-Hand Report on Labor and Education in Mocambique', *Africa Today* 5:6 (1958), pp. 3–36.

[35] Fernando Henrique Cardoso and Octávio Ianni, *Côr e mobilidade social em Florianópolis: Aspectos das relações entre negros e brancos numa comunidade do Brasil Meridional* (São Paulo: Editora Nacional, 1960); Fernando Henrique Cardoso, *Capitalismo e escravidão no Brasil meridional: O negro na sociedade escravocrata do Rio Grande do Sul* (São Paulo: Difusão Européia do Livro, 1962); Octávio Ianni, *As metamorfoses do escravo: Apogeu e crise da escravatura no Brasil meridional* (São Paulo: Difusão Européia do Livro, 1962).

[36] Charles R. Boxer, *Race Relations in the Portuguese Colonial Empire, 1415–1825* (London: Oxford University Press, 1963).

[37] There is a vast bibliography on these subjects, namely by Kenneth Maxwell, Fernando Rosas and António Costa Pinto. See the latter's *O fim do império português* (Lisbon: Livros Horizonte, 2001).

different ways and degrees. But ethnic relations and racism remain unresolved, vexed issues, as major sociological enquiries have proved after the significant immigration from the former colonies in the final decades of the twentieth century. As a formal colonial power it would have been difficult for Portugal to score better than the European average in successive surveys. In Brazil, the debate over the black movement and affirmative action has drawn attention to the impasses of Freyre's deep-rooted multiracial harmonious vision. In Africa, the issue of blackness has been used in political debate, mainly during the civil war in Angola. Although some divisions are inherited from the colonial past, the new system of relations cannot be understood in terms of race. Postcolonial society has different meanings in Africa, Brazil, Portugal or East Timor, but the centrality of racism and ethnic relations in recent social debates is undeniable.

V

We decided to organise the volume in three parts: 'Present Issues', 'The Modern Framework', and 'The Long View'. We begin with contemporary issues, to search for their origins and evolution in the twentieth century and other configurations in a more distant period of time. The recent process of redefining identity and race in Brazil as a result of affirmative action provides an extraordinary case study of the impact of state policies, analysed by António Sérgio Guimarães. Moreover, Guimarães also reconstitutes the evolution of racist, racial and ethnic vocabulary since the abolition of slavery, showing the ambiguities of different usages between and within social groups. Peter Wade addresses the issue of race or ethnic relations in a comparative perspective involving both Colombia and Brazil. Different social formations and perceptions of racial issues are at stake in this chapter, which also offers a useful reflection on racial construction as involving representations of both nature and culture. Jorge Vala and Cícero Pereira analyse the main trends of racist attitudes in Portugal from the 1990s to the 2010s, based on successive enquiries they have undertaken. Their chapter also reflects on comparative European data and the theoretical development of this area of studies, showing how racism adapted as a 'virus in evolution'. Lastly, Luiz Felipe de Alencastro addresses the different expression, meaning, social status and destiny of mixed-race people in Brazil and Angola, from the seventeenth century to the present day. The issue of global society is at stake here, since the vast majority of mixed-race people were absorbed by African society in Angola, contrary to what happened in Brazil, due to social recognition and specific mobility. This analysis challenges lusotropicalism in both theoretical and empirical ways, since it shows how Portuguese colonial societies differed.

In the first chapter of the second section, discussing the modern period, João de Pina-Cabral places Charles Boxer's book *Race Relations in the Portuguese Colonial*

Empire in context. He highlights Boxer's project to work in the United States and rescue his previous work, stained by accusations of colonial complicity. Pina-Cabral likewise analyses the misunderstanding between the social sciences' tradition of race relations in the United States and the ideology of 'assimilation' developed both in Brazil and in Portugal, bringing the case of South Africa into discussion. Maria Lúcia Pallares-Burke then reconstitutes the ideological background of white supremacy and the whitening of the population against which Gilberto Freyre wrote *Casa grande e senzala*. The previous derision of mixed Brazil is highlighted, showing the extraordinary impact of Freyre's approach, which contributed to reshaping Brazilians' self-perception and national mythology. David Brookshaw next introduces an important survey of Afro-Brazilian literature throughout the twentieth century. This chapter brings to light the power of this literature, which has not been a central focus of literary criticism, expressing specific social conditions and intervening, in the long run, in the redefinition of identities and ethnicity. Michel Cahen analyses the legislation on indigenous labour from the 1870s to the 1960s, challenging the vision of forced labour as a continuation of slavery in Portuguese Africa, particularly in Mozambique, since he relates slavery to a plantation economy, itself quite limited in Africa. His chapter also questions the official ideology of native assimilation under the capitalist mode of production, since forced labour and deferred payment of salaries to the natives postponed the creation of an indigenous working class. Cahen regards racism and racial construction as the consequence of the colonial discrimination against natives, pointing out that the noun race was applied to black people, while the Portuguese were defined as a nation. Finally, forced labour is again tackled by Miguel Jerónimo, who focuses on the case of Angola. He discusses the ideological debate and the legislative production concerning slavery and forced labour at the centre of the Portuguese empire, involving the intervention of colonial governors and local administrators in his analysis. He highlights the persistence of cultural frameworks and compulsory methods in the transition from slavery to forced labour. The parallel between forced labour and racial construction is well captured by Goldberg's notion of racial state.

In the third and final section, 'The Long View', Ricardo Roque challenges the reifying notions of race and race relations that obscure the understanding of colonial societies and the agency of native people. This chapter focuses on indigenous elite marriage ties (*barlake*) in East Timor in the final third of the nineteenth century. The innovative notions of predatory, parasitic (Michel Serres) and mimetic relations help to analyse the strategies developed by missionaries, governors and colonisers, while native elites manipulated contrasting colonial behaviour for their own benefit. Herbert Klein addresses the issue of manumission in Brazil. The main trends are analysed with reference to a set of data never before collected so extensively. The key distinctive feature of Brazil among the societies based on slavery is brought into focus, opening the way for a serious comparative analysis with other American societies in the nineteenth century. Andrea Daher tackles language as an issue curiously absent from debates about racism and ethnic relations. She considers language as the main vehicle to understand the perception of American Indians and their shifting position in (and before) colonial society, from subordination, discrimination and segregation to forced integration. The different language policies are analysed over time, from the invention of the *língua geral* by the Jesuits using Tupi, based on the policy of secluded villages, to the offer of civil rights and free circulation by the government of Pombal (1750–77) in return for the abandonment of native languages, followed finally by the corrective policies of language and territory in the nineteenth century. José Pedro Paiva then provides a full survey of the divide between Old Christians and New Christians in Portugal and its empire. The impact of the notion of purity of blood is here discussed, as well as the ambiguous identities of the New Christians in time and space. Finally, Jean Michel Massing analyses the first images of East African peoples in Europe, showing the shifts and continuities from Marco Polo to the first Portuguese and German explorers at the beginning of the sixteenth century. This chapter underlines the importance of work on visual sources to understand perceptions, stereotypes and prejudices, based on the distinction between dressed/naked, sedentary/nomadic, and living in nature/living in society.

This volume, in sum, offers a complete review of the main themes linked to racism and ethnic relations in the Portuguese-speaking world, from the present to the distant past. It tackles the evolution of Brazilian multi-ethnic society in the last 200 years, seen from the point of view of sociology, history and literature, an interdisciplinary approach reinforced by the comparison with Colombian society. The same can be said about Portugal, in which social psychology is playing a crucial role in monitoring recent racist trends. The different colonial and postcolonial realities are approached through the contradictory colonial strategies and native agency around the *barlake* in East Timor, the divergent status and destiny of mixed-race people in Brazil and Angola, and the transition from slavery to forced labour and free labour in Mozambique and Angola. The ideological traps of Gilberto Freyre's notion of lusotropicalism and Charles Boxer's reconstitution of race relations are criticised and placed in context. We hope that this book will contribute to new theoretical and methodological approaches to racism and ethnic relations based on the deconstruction of different systems of classification, promoting the analysis of social, economic, cultural and political practices, in order to interrogate concrete colonial, native and postcolonial agency and interactions in everyday life.

Part I

PRESENT ISSUES

1

Colour and Race in Brazil: From Whitening to the Search for Afro-Descent

ANTÓNIO SÉRGIO ALFREDO GUIMARÃES

Brazil and the United States unquestionably constitute paradigmatic cases of the construction of post-slavery societies in the Americas. While the United States experienced exceptional and singular development, the Brazilian case can be generalised, with certain caveats, to other countries of Central and South America and the Caribbean, in terms of the incorporation of Afro-descendant and Amerindian populations into the free work regime, the formation of a class society, and the development of racial and national ideologies. Whereas in Brazil racial democracy was cultivated, in the United States segregation still presents a problem; whilst the former perpetuates pre-capitalist forms of exploitation and precarious employment, the latter provided for the formation of a modern black society, albeit separate from the rest of the nation. If in Brazil colour became the basis of a complicated symbolic system of status attribution, in the US race was built into a descent status group.

In this chapter I aim to clarify the ways in which Brazil has, since abolition, been developing a system of colour classification with regard to Afro-descendants. I seek to show not only how this system has developed over time, but also how it is shaped by the mobilisation of the black population around the notion of race – as a group sharing solidarity and common experiences of subordination and discrimination. My strategy is to trace the terms 'colour' and 'race' and their meanings through time, as used or systemised into classifications by the state, social movements and social scientists. Clearly, this remains a preliminary and incomplete study, but I hope that it can serve as a guide to future and more systematic research into specific periods, places and social agents.

From the 'class of men of colour' to the 'black race'

In colonial Brazil the Portuguese used the term *negro* not only to refer to people of darker skin, as was the case in Europe, but also to refer to slaves; Amerindians,

Proceedings of the British Academy **179**, *17–34*.

for example, were called *negros da terra* (blacks of the land), to differentiate them from blacks from Africa.[1] However the social meaning of the terminology of colour changed over time. Manuela Carneiro da Cunha tells us that in the first half of the nineteenth century,

> Three dimensions were used to internally classify this population [of free men]: 'colour', 'nationality' and 'legal condition'. The colour *negro* or *pardo* [dark or brown individuals], and intermediary graduations sometimes used to describe an individual, did not seem to be used for classification into subclasses. With regard to nationality there were Africans (with ethnic subdivisions not necessarily used, such as mina, angola, etc.) or *crioulos*, that is, those born in Brazil. With regard to their legal condition, one could either be *forro*, freed, or *ingênuo*, born free.[2]

João Reis observes, in the first half of the nineteenth century in Bahia, two main racial terms: *preto* [black], designating Africans, and *crioulo*, designating blacks born in Brazil. In the second half of the century, however, in the same province, there was a tendency to use the term *preto* to encompass both Africans and Afro-descendants. *Negro* therefore stopped designating 'colour' and gradually came to have a more pejorative meaning.[3]

Analysing the São Paulo state press during the abolitionist period, Lilia Schwarcz concludes that in São Paulo in the years prior to abolition, a time of many slave escapes and revolts as well as of ideological struggle between abolitionists and defenders of slavery, the term *negro* acquired an insulting connotation, as opposed to *preto*, which took on a more neutral meaning.[4] Schwarcz reproduces a text in which the word 'class' is used to refer to both masters and slaves.

Hebe M. Castro seems to agree with Schwarcz, as she transcribes a satirical poem, published in the newspaper *O Monitor Campista* in 1888, which suggests that during the post-abolition period, *negro* still carried an offensive meaning, as a reference to slaves, whereas *preto* was understood as a reference to colour and not social position:

[. . .] *Fui ver pretos na cidade.*	I went to look for *pretos* in the city
Que quisessem se alugar.	Who might want to be hired.
Falei com esta humildade:	I said to them humbly
– *Negros, querem trabalhar?*	– *Negros*, do you want to work?
Olharam-me de soslaio.	They looked at me slyly.
E um deles, feio, cambaio,	And one of them, ugly and bowlegged,

[1] John M. Monteiro, *Negros da terra: Índios e bandeirantes nas origens de São Paulo* (São Paulo: Companhia das Letras, 1994).

[2] Manuela Carneiro da Cunha, *Negros, estrangeiros: Os escravos libertos e sua volta à África* (São Paulo: Brasiliense, 1985), p. 22.

[3] João José Reis, 'De olho no canto: Trabalho de rua na Bahia na véspera da Abolição', *Afro-Ásia* 24 (2000), pp. 199–242, see p. 233.

[4] Lilia Moritz Schwarcz, *Retrato em branco e negro: Jornais, escravos e cidadãos em São Paulo no final do século XIX* (São Paulo: Companhia das Letras, 1987), pp. 195–6.

Respondeu-me, arfando o peito	Answered me, puffing out his chest:
– Negro, não há mais, não:	– There ain't no *negros* no more:
Nós tudo hoje é cidadão	We're all citizens now
O branco que vá pro eito.	The white man can go to the fields.[5]

During the 1920s those considered to be the pioneers of the present-day black movements referred to themselves – and constructed a certain social identity – with words, concepts and ideals inherited from the past. They called themselves 'men of colour' and *homens pretos* [black men], and referred to themselves collectively as a 'class'. At this time the words 'race' and *negro* were used in a very different way from how they are used today by black activists.

O Menelick, a black newspaper from 1916, called itself 'a monthly publication with news, literature and criticism dedicated to men of colour'. Note how it publicised a beauty contest: 'the contest is, of course, for the "class"' (with 'class' in speech marks).[6] *O Bandeirante* was 'a monthly publication for the defence of the class of men of colour'. In an editorial published in 1918, *Vencendo a encosta* ['Conquering the Mountain'], it stated that 'it fights for the interests of the class of black (*preto*) men', and again in 1919, it was a 'publication to fight for the general promotion of the class of men of colour'. *O Alfinete*, too, published in 1918, was 'dedicated to men of colour'. *A Liberdade* of 1919 was at first a 'publication dedicated to the class of colour [offering] criticism, literature and news', again describing itself in 1920 as a 'publication with criticism, literature and news dedicated to the class of colour'.

This does not mean that the expression *raça negra* [black race] was eschewed by those who wrote for these publications, but it carried unambiguously the nineteenth-century meaning of biological inferiority.[7] 'Race' was used in a biological sense, whereas 'class' and 'men of colour' had a social meaning. However, on occasion, 'race' was also already being used almost as synonymous with 'class'.

The pejorative and insulting meaning of the term '*negro*', as well as the peculiar meaning usually given to the word 'race', was clearly established in a small article published in *A Liberdade* on 28 December 1919:

> **Hypocrisy of colour**
> The reader should know how to appraise the horror contained within the word '*disdain*' as it is this word that breaks and pursues the unfortunate black (*negro*) man, or person of equivalent class; we know that the word *negro* is used carelessly, whereas more educated people use the expression '*moreno*' which I prefer. The black (*preto*) man is despised in everything, even in some societies where some dark-skinned people think themselves light; this is the same in many countries, especially in the

[5] Hebe M. Mattos Castro, 'A cor inexistente: Relações raciais e trabalho rural no Rio de Janeiro pós-escravidão', *Estudos Afro-Asiáticos* 28 (1995), pp. 101–28, see p. 110.
[6] *O Menelick*, 1 Jan. 1916, p. 4.
[7] See, for example, *Alfinete*, São Paulo, 3 Sept. 1918.

> land of civilization, in the United States; why make fun of the black (*preto*) man, when he is also a creature of God? He is a living being like any other, if there are some who act wrongly, there are people like this of all *colours*. Is it possible that in this endless world, only the *negro* is a contemptible being, almost abandoned by those who are their *equal in race*, as there are or seem to be in the societies of this earth formed by the group of *men of colour*? Do they forget that we all die and that we have only one judge who will not be making any allusions to *colour*? Let us leave behind the prejudice of those **equal in race**, and try to summon to the path of honour and duty those that have been led astray, so that we are able to leave the utopia in which we live, particularly in a wealthy and free country like ours, where there is prejudice, it is true, but in large part, by those of the same **race of *azeviches*** [black].

The ideology that underpinned the use of race can be itemised as follows. First, as I have already said, the term *negro* was considered pejorative and offensive, and was avoided in interpersonal relations and not claimed by 'men of colour'. Second, colour was claimed as an objective marker and real, though considered of little importance in assessing someone's value. Third, 'race' was only referred to in order to group all African descendants together; in particular the lighter-skinned ones, considered to be those who showed the most prejudice. Fourth, the expression *preconceitos de raças iguais* [prejudices of equal races] and the words 'utopia' and 'hypocrisy' were used with reference to the Brazilian situation. The meaning of these words and this expression is revealing: the black race lived in a utopia, pretending that races were equal, without paying attention to the inequality of their material, cultural and social situation. Fifth, 'those that were led astray', that is to say, *negros* of dubious morality, were responsible for the stigma that the word *negro* carried, even if this generalisation was at the same time considered incorrect, and 'those led astray' should be the reason for the mobilisation of 'those equal in race'. Sixth, 'race', therefore, was mobilised to establish equality between, on the one hand, those that could occasionally be mistreated as *negros* and were commonly referred to as *pretos* and *morenos* (this seen as attenuating racial difference) and, on the other, those who hypocritically considered themselves as whites. The idea of race, therefore, was not used to mobilise a social identity, but to break it up; to make those who were socially 'white' and 'those of colour' equal, as in each case either close or distant descendants of this 'race'. Seven, and finally, the word 'colour' in 'colour prejudice' also means that there was discrimination within the same race (for example amongst those with African blood); that is, it was precisely those of lighter skin (who considered themselves white) who discriminated against and despised those who were darker.

We should not forget, nevertheless, that the constant accusation of prejudice on the part of those lighter-skinned members of the 'race' was also a discursive strategy, designed to create solidarity and identity among both close and distant descendants of Africans; and that, therefore, implicitly, the idea of biological race was being employed to this end. But at the same time, this strategy strengthens the argument of whites that prejudice does not exist in Brazil and that the problems that black people face are their own fault, including discrimination.

A new meaning of 'race', however, began to become commonplace from the 1920s, together with self-denomination by the term *negro*. The negative, inferior and insulting connotations of the term were supplanted by a claim to a positive and regimenting meaning. *A Liberdade,* a newspaper well aware of the political movement among black Americans, was perhaps the first to register this change. It is probable, therefore, that the idea of 'historical race', as defined by DuBois, was already having some influence on Brazilians.[8]

The course of developments between 1921 and 1923 is less certain, since no journals are extant for these years in the collections I consulted (of Mirian Ferrara and Michael Mitchel).[9] But when *Elite*, *Clarim* and *Auriverde* appeared in 1924, the terms *negro* and *raça* [race] had begun to be used to refer to the collective formerly mainly designated 'men of colour' and 'class'.[10]

Terms such as 'class' and 'men of colour', then, were gradually to fall out of use in the press and in the movements which now called themselves *negros*, although 'class' would survive through to present times, with another meaning: to designate the absence of the idea of 'race' in the treatment of blacks in Brazil. But, even amongst those who, in the 1920s, started to call themselves *negros*, the change was gradual.

Self-defined race

Both 'race' and *negro* were words whose meanings became completely reversed through time. First used by Europeans to designate persons and peoples of darker colour, *negro* then became the designation of persons and peoples of inferior social status or supposedly biological constitution: slaves or submissive peoples. At a third stage, it was used to self-designate by these same peoples in colonial liberation movements and as a tool in building self-esteem.

The evolution of terms which occurred in Brazil with regard to black people's self-designation can, in part, be viewed under the aegis of the identity revolution by black people at a world level, which occurred from the end of the nineteenth to the middle of the twentieth century. The ideological bases of this revolution were founded on the re-appropriation and re-approximation of two scientific terms: 'race', a pretentiously biological concept of the nineteenth century, reworked to

[8] W. E. B. DuBois, 'The Conservation of Races', in *Writings* (New York: Library of America, 1986). See *A Liberdade*, São Paulo, 7 March 1920, p. 1, and 9 May 1920, p. 2.

[9] Both collections are available at the Instituto de Estudos Brasileiros library at the Universidad de São Paulo.

[10] See, for example, *Elite*, São Paulo, 20 Jan. 1924, p. 1; *O Clarim*, São Paulo, 2 March 1924, p. 3; or *Auriverde*, São Paulo, 29 April 1928, p. 1.

designate a historical and spiritual transnational community; and 'culture', re-appropriated as a near synonym of the former term, to designate a set of artistic and material manifestations of this transnational people. 'Negroes', 'nègres', 'negros': these were the words chosen – in English, French and Portuguese respectively – for self-designation by the community claiming to be part of this race. However, although worldwide this 'people' traced their roots back to Africa, they have not always, in their various adopted nationalities, claimed their own culture, whether black or African. The most extreme example of this occurs in Brazil, in fact, where only much later did black Brazilians claim themselves to be the producers of 'black culture', of African origin. We shall return to this issue hereafter. For now, we need briefly to address the way in which 'race' and 'culture' were appropriated by intellectuals who defined themselves as *negros*.

W. E. B. DuBois was one of the first authors to theorise about the 'black race', giving it a meaning that was not altogether biological, but was close to that which would be defined as 'culture' by Franz Boas (though still impregnated by German romantic thinking). In a talk he gave to the America Negro Academy in 1897, he insisted on the predominance of spiritual and cultural traces over physical traces in the definition of human 'races'. DuBois' objective was to advocate, in a clear and precise way, an autonomous and independent cultural evolution for black Americans.

Belief in the existence of a 'black culture', as an expression of the 'black soul', was shared by Americans and Europeans at the end of the nineteenth and beginning of the twentieth century. It was a belief that fuelled a profound sense of the differences between whites and blacks, a sense popularised during the same period by the discovery of 'black art' and 'African art' by cubist and modernist artists, and by the values attached to them. In the United States, the Caribbean, and Europe, the existence of a 'black culture' was never seriously questioned. On the contrary, it served to justify the struggle for the political emancipation of blacks, and fed the pan-Africanist nationalist ideal of many social movements. In literature and in politics this ideal was expressed in France and the Caribbean under the name of *négritude*.[11] In Brazil, in the 1950s, the ideal of cultural decolonisation and economic nationalism and social development would also be given the same name of *negritude*.[12]

We see, therefore, that overcoming the pseudoscientific classification of humanity into colours and races as a way of subordinating human diversity to egalitarian and individualist ideals of modern democracy could, and indeed did, concretely lead to different types of political-ideological attitudes.

[11] Aimé Cesaire, *Cahier d'un retour au pays* (Paris: Présence Africaine, 1956); Léopold Sédar Senghor, *Négritude, arabisme et francité: Réflexions sur le problème de la culture* (Beyrouth: Dar al-Kitab Allubnani, 1967); René Depestre, *Bonjour et adieu à la negritude* (Paris: R. Laffont, 1980); Kabengele Munanga, *Negritude: Usos e sentidos* (São Paulo: Ática, 1986).

[12] Alberto Guerreiro Ramos, 'O problema do negro na sociedade brasileira', in *Cartilha brasileira do aprendiz de sociólogo* (Rio de Janeiro: Andes, 1954). Abdias do Nascimento, *O negro revoltado* (Rio de Janeiro: Nova Fronteira, 1982).

Let us look at three of these. The first attitude is that of the denial of races and the re-reading of the differences between human peoples in terms of 'culture'; any mention of race is therefore seen as racist. The best example is the ideology of the French republic, which does not allow adult and healthy human beings to act in the public sphere from the vantage point of any particular racial or ethnic characteristic, be it individual or collective. The second attitude is the transformation of the old biological race into 'historical race', whose specificity is the experience of pan-Africanist or diasporic movements. In this case, racism is defined not in terms of the affirmation of physical or cultural differences between races, but in its hierarchisation and possible oppression. The political ideal is of multiracial and multicultural representation and recognition. Finally a third attitude preaches cultural hybridisation and biological miscegenation between peoples of original 'races', so as to constitute, in the future, one nation and a single mixed humanity, but of a variety of colours. This proposal takes on various forms, of which the main ones in Brazil were 'whitening' (based on the belief that the predominant colour would be white) and the Freyrean ideal of *mestiçagem* [race mixture], which like José Vasconcelos' 'cosmic race' in Mexico, argued that racial mixing would over time produce a single and general colour of humanity or of a nation.[13]

For Gilberto Freyre, in the 1960s, Brazil was already experiencing this phenomenon of loss of colour, the main symptom of which was the popularisation of the term *moreno*, an imprecise term that could mean dark white or light brown or even black. According to Freyre, the increased use of this word represented not only a semantic shift, but 'a growing trend in which not only the white *moreno* was considered *moreno*, as before, but also the *pardo* and even the *preto*, in various degrees of *morenidade* [the condition of being *moreno*], from light to dark, due to the effects of *mestiçagem*'. Freyre could only conclude:

> With this '*amorenamento*' [the turning of a people into *morenos*] (anthropological and sociological), to which can also be added, in the last few years, those whites who try to make themselves *moreno* in the tropical sun of Copacabana and other beaches, *morenidade* is asserting itself, in the case of the Brazilian Man, as a denial of race and an affirmation of a meta-race.[14]

The colours (or races?) of Brazilians

How are Brazilians classified and how do they classify themselves in terms of colour nowadays? We have two sources of data: sample surveys covering the whole of the Brazilian territory, and ethnographic research restricted to relatively small areas: a village, a neighbourhood, a city.

[13] José Vasconcelos, *La raza cósmica: Misión de la raza Iberoamericana* (1925; Mexico City: Espasa-Calpe, 1966).
[14] Gilberto Freyre, 'O homem situado no trópico, metarraça e morenidade', in *Gilberto Freyre: Seleta para jovens* (Rio de Janeiro: José Olympio, 1971), p. 120.

A number of major studies of colour, racism and discrimination have employed representative sample surveys.[15] Data relative to colour is also available from the *Pesquisa de Emprego e Desemprego* (Survey on Employment and Unemployment), conducted monthly in the main metropolitan regions of the country.[16] However, the most important colour statistics in Brazil are gathered by the *Instituto Brasileiro de Geografia e Estatística*, through the *Pesquisa Nacional por Amostra de Domicílios* (Brazilian National Household Sample Survey), and particularly the Demographic Census which officially registers the composition of the Brazilian population by colour every ten years. In censuses held up to 1980, the question was, 'What is your colour?' In the 1872 census, the alternatives presented to respondents were *branco* (white), *preto, pardo* and *caboclo* (of mixed Amerindian and white descent); in 1890, the *pardo* category was substituted by *mestiço* (mixed race); in 1940 the categories were *branco, preto, amarelo* ('yellow', or of East Asian descent), and 'others' (although the last category was grouped under the denomination *pardo*). In 1950 and 1980, respondents had a choice of four categories: *branco, preto, pardo* and *amarelo*. In 1960, a new term was added to those of 1950: *indio* ('Indian', or Amerindian). In 1991, there was a return to the 1960 categories, but the term *indio* was substituted by *indígena* (indigenous), and the question was also changed, to 'What is your colour/race?' Finally in 2000, the same question and categories used in 1991 were maintained.[17] We should add that until 1960 the census interviewer determined the colour of the interviewee, while from 1980 onward this became a matter of self-classification.

Ethnographic studies in Brazil in the 1950s preferred the term 'social races' to that of 'historical races'. This terminology is based on an uncontested fact: if the concept of human races does not form an empirical reality – that is, if there are no races in nature, but they continue to inhabit the imaginary of many human societies – it is because, far from being simple superstitions that can be exorcised by

[15] DataFolha, 1995, 300 anos de Zumbi (for which see C. Turra and G. Venturi (eds), *Racismo cordial: A mais completa análise sobre o preconceito de cor no Brasil* (São Paulo: Ática, 1995); DataFolha, Pesquisa sobre racismo, 2008; PESB, Pesquisa Social Brasileira [Brazilian Social Survey], Universidade Federal Fluminense, 2002; G. Venturi, *Discriminação racial e preconceito de cor no Brasil* (São Paulo: Fundação Perseu Abramo/Rosa Luxemburg Stiftung, 2003); Universidade Federal de Minas Gerais, Pesquisa da Região Metropolitana de Belo Horizonte, 2002. These databases are available from the *Consórcio de Informações Sociais* [Social Information Consortium], Universidade de São Paulo, at www.nadd.prp.usp.br/cis/index.aspx

[16] Differently from other surveys, the colour classification of the *Pesquisa de Emprego e Desemprego* is made by the interviewer and not by the interviewees themselves. See Departamento Intersindical de Estatísticas e Estudos Socio-Econômicos/Instituto Sindical Interamericano pela Igualdade Racial, *Mapa da população negra no mercado de trabalho – regiões metropolitanas de São Paulo, Salvador, Recife, Belo Horizonte, Porto Alegre e Distrito Federal* (São Paulo: INSPIR/Centro de Solidariedade AFLCIO/DIEESE, 1999).

[17] Melissa Nobles, *Shades of Citizenship: Race and the Census in Modern Politics* (Stanford, CA: Stanford University Press, 2000), p. 104.

enlightenment, they are social constructions and have a social function and reality. If this is the case, the criteria by which races are perceived change from one society to another, and even from era to era.

Charles Wagley, studying the formation of social races in the Americas, identified three different patterns or three types of classification systems, based on the criteria of (1) ancestrality or origin, (2) socio-cultural status, and (3) physical appearance.[18] In fact, Wagley systemised these discoveries from a series of anthropological and sociological studies regarding race relations in Latin America, from the 1950s and 1960s.

In Brazil, the majority of these studies were conducted under the auspices of UNESCO,[19] under an agreement between the State of Bahia and Columbia University,[20] or as academic theses in the Department of Sociology at the University of São Paulo.[21] In some of them, Brazilian racial classification, that is, how people in the country classified themselves into groups of colour or race, formed an important part of the research.

Perhaps it was Marvin Harris who best synthesised the specificity of colour classification in Brazil when he stressed that, contrary to what happened in the United States, there were no racial descent rules in Brazil: that is to say, children did not inherit the same racial status as their parents. In the United States, such a rule did exist, since children inherited the racial status of the progenitor with the lower prestige. For example, children of mixed marriages were classified according to the status of the partner with the lowest racial position (Harris called this 'hypodescent'). In Brazil, however, the colour of children was socially defined

[18] Charles Wagley, 'The Concept of Social Race in the Americas', in *The Latin American Tradition* (New York: Columbia University Press, 1968), pp. 155–74.

[19] Charles Wagley, *Race et classe dans le Brésil rural* (Paris: UNESCO, 1952); Thales Azevedo, *As elites de cor numa cidade brasileira: Um estudo de ascensão social & classes sociais e grupos de prestígio* (1953; Salvador: EDUFBA, 1996); Luis Aguiar Costa Pinto, *O negro no Rio de Janeiro: Relações de raças numa sociedade em mudança* (1953; Rio de Janeiro: Editora Nacional, 1998); Roger Bastide and Florestan Fernandes, *Relações raciais entre negros e brancos em São Paulo* (São Paulo: Anhembi, 1955); René Ribeiro, *Religião e relações raciais* (Rio de Janeiro: Ministério da Educação e Cultura, 1956).

[20] Marvin Harris, 'Les relations raciales à Minas Velha communauté rurale de la région montagneuse du Brésil Central', in Charles Wagley (ed.), *Races et classes dans le Brésil rural* (Paris: UNESCO, 1952); Marvin Harris, *Town and Country in Brazil* (New York: Columbia University Press, 1956); H. W. Hutchinson, 'Les relations raciales dans une communauté rurale du Reconcavo (État de Bahia)', in Wagley (ed.), *Races et classes dans le Brésil rural*; H. W. Hutchinson, *Village and Plantation Life in Northeastern Brazil* (Seattle: University of Washington Press, 1957); B. Zimermann, 'Les relations raciales dans la région aride du Sertão', in Wagley (ed.), *Races et classes dans le Brésil rural.*

[21] Florestan Fernandes, *A integração do negro na sociedade de classes* (São Paulo: Dominus, 1965); Fernando Henrique Cardoso and Octávio Ianni, *Cor e mobilidade social em Florianópolis: Aspectos das relações entre negros e brancos numa comunidade do Brasil Meridional* (São Paulo: Editora Nacional, 1960); Octávio Ianni, *As metamorfoses do escravo: Apogeu e crise da escravatura no Brasil meridional* (São Paulo: Difusão Européia do Livro, 1962); Fernando Henrique Cardoso, *Capitalismo e escravidão no Brasil meridional* (São Paulo: Difusão Européia de Livro, 1962).

individually and independently of the parents, where a black father, for example, could have a white or *moreno* child if this child had white phenotypical features. In other words, in Brazil it was physical appearance, physionomic and socio-cultural markers which counted in colour classification, and not origin or descent. For Harris, following earlier anthropologists, Brazilian colour groups did not constitute a 'race' as such, as hereditariness was absent from these groups, but only a 'class', that is, a socially open group (to which an individual does not belong by birth) even if constituted by markers which are not totally acquired. A group of colour, but not race; a class, but not a race.

Donald Pierson, the pioneer in race relations studies in Brazil, systemised this discovery thus:

> Of course, [colour] classification can be derived, in part, from physical appearance; but it is also derived from the possession of one or more criteria of social position; for example, personal, educational or occupational achievements, or an accumulation of economic resources.[22]

Harris's position with regard to the ambiguity of the system of racial classification in Brazil later became more radical, after field research conducted in the rural areas of the state of Bahia in 1962 led him to doubt even the existence of any system; that is, of a permanent structure giving meaning to the employment of colour terminology.[23] Harris's misgivings were further expressed in his strong criticism of the Instituto Brasileiro de Geografia e Estatísticas (IBGE), where he cast doubt on the results of successive censuses concerning the colour of Brazilians, deeming them lacking in objectivity. For Harris, the IBGE, which treated colour or race as objective characteristics, should simply put an end to its predefined colour categories (*branco*, *preto*, *pardo*, *amarelo*) and allow the interviewees to express themselves freely. For him, 'the Brazilian census [. . .] neither registers a subjective concept of social races nor the objective opinion of biologists'.[24]

Both the ideas of Harris and those of Freyre exerted considerable influence.[25] In the 1970s, at the height of the military dictatorship, the Brazilian state looked to review its racial policies, taking the 'colour' question out of the IBGE Demographic Census.[26] The justification given by the sponsors of this new policy was that the census colour categories were artificial and not used by the man in the

[22] Donald Pierson, *Negroes in Brazil: A Study of Race Contact in Bahia* (Chicago: University of Chicago Press, 1942); published in Portuguese as *Brancos e pretos na Bahia* (São Paulo: Editora Nacional, 1971); see the latter edition, p. 35.

[23] Marvin Harris, 'Racial Identity in Brazil', *Luso-Brazilian Review* 1:2 (1964), pp. 21–8, see p. 27.

[24] Harris, 'Racial Identity in Brazil', p. 22.

[25] See also Marvin Harris, 'Referential Ambiguity in the Calculus of Brazilian Racial Identity', *Southwestern Journal of Anthropology* 26:1 (1970), pp. 1–14.

[26] Robert Park, 'The Career of the Africans in Brazil', introduction to Donald Pierson, *Negroes in Brazil* (Chicago: University of Chicago Press, 1942).

street, where a plethora of designations prevailed. Under pressure from demographers and social scientists, however,[27] the IBGE decided instead to introduce an open question about colour (that is a question whose answer was not classified a priori) in the questionnaire for the 1976 National Household Survey, in order to measure empirically to what point its earlier colour classification was adequate. In this survey the IBGE collected 136 different answers to its question;[28] that is, 136 'colours', far in excess of the forty racial types found by Harris and Kotak in Bahia.[29]

What does this gamut of colours mean? On the one hand, it points to the importance of colour as a social marker. After all, a characteristic which was not very important would not be distinguished with so many names. But, on the other hand, if there are so many names, it also means that the demarcational power of these on their own is not very great. At best, one could argue, like Harris, that there cannot really be racial groups defined from a characteristic subjected to such great variation and ambiguity.

Nelson Valle Silva argued differently however. Of the 136 colours registered, 94 per cent 'of respondents spontaneously kept to the categories white, *claro* [light], *moreno claro*, *moreno*, *pardo* and *preto*, with the most dominant categories being *branco* (47%) and *moreno* (32% of answers)'. That is, census categories were in fact consistent and, therefore, demarcated groups. What the open question was measuring was a phenomenon of social identity different from that asked by the closed question, and not exactly racial, since it was outside a scale of colour. Silva believed, furthermore, that as the category *moreno* encompassed elements of all other census categories, it would not be possible to introduce it alongside other categories in a closed question, or for it to substitute for any of the other categories, without introducing enormous ambiguity in the scale, and making the results collected incomparable with those of earlier censuses.[30]

We should stress, however, that keeping the question about colour in the Brazilian census was, in large part, a victory achieved through political pressure on the part of black activists and researchers in the Brazilian Congress and the IBGE. It was a victory against the position championed by Gilberto Freyre who argued that Brazilians already constituted a metarace, of a *moreno* colour.[31] Melissa Nobles tells us how, despite the opposition of the management body of the IBGE,

[27] See, for example, Tereza C. N. Araújo Costa, 'O princípio classificatório "cor", sua complexidade e implicações para o uso censitário', *Revista Brasileira de Geografia* 36:3 (1974), pp. 91–103.
[28] Nobles, *Shades of Citizenship*, p. 114.
[29] Marvin Harris and Conrad Kotak, 'The Structural Significance of Brazilian Categories', *Sociologia* 25:3 (1963), pp. 203–8, see p. 203.
[30] Nelson Valle Silva, 'Distância social e casamento inter-racial no Brasil', *Estudos Afro-Asiáticos* 14 (1987), pp. 54–84; Nelson Valle Silva, 'Uma nota sobre "raça social" no Brasil', *Estudos Afro-Asiáticos* 26 (1994), pp. 67–80; Nelson Valle Silva, 'Morenidade: Modo de usar', *Estudos Afro-Asiáticos* 30 (1996), pp. 79–95.
[31] Gilberto Freyre, 'Brasileiro – sua cor?', *Folha de São Paulo*, 5 Dec. 1979, p. 3.

black activists and researchers were able to re-establish the colour question in the 1980 census, with the argument that it was only more refined statistical analyses that could yield knowledge about the social situation of blacks in Brazil.[32]

The fact is that anthropologists and sociologists returned to studying and thinking about Brazilian racial classification.[33] Moema Teixeira was one of the first to review the studies of the 1960s, in an attempt to keep her distance from the political writings of the black movement, which saw the fluidity of Brazilian racial classification as a form of alienating blacks and as an ideology imposed by whites.[34] Teixeira returned to the basic principles of sociological analysis of the forms of social classification, as established by Durkheim and Mauss,[35] to make two important observations about the Brazilian classification system: first, 'that categories, despite not being explicit, have as an ultimate reference the duality of whites and blacks'; and second, regarding the ambiguity of the colour categories (as already noted by Harris and Kotak).[36]

Fry and Maggie in a sense follow the same line of analysis, though pointing to the simultaneity of different forms of colour classification in Brazil, which operate in different social contexts. Fry talks of three types of classification which act

[32] Nobles, *Shades of Citizenship*, p. 117.

[33] Tereza C. N. Araújo Costa, 'A classificação de "cor" do IBGE: notas para uma discussão', *Cadernos de Pesquisa* (Fundação Carlos Chagas) 63 (1987), pp. 14–16; Charles Wood, 'Categorias censitárias e classificações subjetivas de raça no Brasil', in Peggy A. Lovell (ed.), *Desigualdade racial no Brasil contemporâneo* (Belo Horizonte: CEDEPLAR/FACE/UFMG, 1991), pp. 93–111; Marvin Harris *et al.*, 'Who Are the Whites? Imposed Census Categories and the Racial Demography of Brazil', *Social Forces* 72:2 (1993), pp. 451–62; Livio Sansone, 'Pai preto, filho negro: Trabalho, cor e diferenças de geração', *Estudos Afro-Asiáticos* 25 (1993), pp. 73–98; Edward E. Telles and Nelson Lim, 'Does It Matter Who Answers the Race Question? Racial Classification and Income Inequality in Brazil', *Demography* 35:4 (Nov. 1998), pp. 465–74; Lilia Moritz Schwartz, *Racismo no Brasil* (São Paulo: Folha Explica, 2001); José Luís Petruccelli, 'Raça, etnicidade e origem nos censos de EUA, França, Canadá e Grã-Bretanha', *Estudos Afro-Asiáticos* 24:3 (2002), pp. 533–62; Sérgio Costa, 'A construção sociológica da raça no Brasil', *Estudos Afro-Asiáticos* 24:1 (2002), pp. 35–61; Rafael G. Osório, *O sistema de classificação de 'cor ou raça' do IPEA*, working paper, no. 996, 2003.

[34] On the Brazilian Black Movement, see, among others, José Correia Leite, . . . *E disse o velho militante José Correia Leite* (São Paulo: Secretaria Municipal de Cultura, 1992); Márcio Barbosa (ed.), *Frente negra brasileira: Depoimentos* (São Paulo: Quilombhoje, 1998); Roger Bastide, 'A imprensa negra do Estado de São Paulo', in *Estudos Afro-Brasileiros* (São Paulo: Perspectiva, 1973); Miriam Nicolau Ferrara, *A imprensa negra paulista (1915–1963)* (São Paulo: FFLCH/USP, 1986); Regina Pahim Pinto, *O movimento negro em São Paulo: Luta e identidade* (São Paulo: FFLCH/USP, 1993); Josenilda Silva, 'A União dos Homens de Cor: Aspectos do movimento negro dos anos 40 e 50', *Estudos Afro-Asiáticos* 25:2 (2003), pp. 215–36; and Florentina da S. Souza, *Afro-descendência em Cadernos Negros e Jornal do MNU* (São Paulo: Autêntica, 2005). On the latter point, see, for example, Clovis Moura, 'A quem interessam as mulatas', *Versus* 19 (1978), pp. 39–40, p. 39.

[35] Emile Durkheim and M. Mauss, 'De quelques formes de classification – contribution à l'étude des représentations collectives', *Année Sociologique* (Paris) 6 (1903); published in Brazil as 'Algumas formas primitivas de classificação', in *Ensaios de Sociologia* (São Paulo: Perspectiva, 1981).

[36] Moema P. Teixeira, 'A questão da cor nas relações e representações de um grupo de baixa renda', *Estudos Afro-Asiáticos* 14 (1987), pp. 85–97.

simultaneously: the multiple mode (which can have up to a hundred terms) and census mode (closed-question categories such as 'What is your colour?'), present in the lower socio-economic groups, and the binary mode (blacks and whites), used by black activists, the media and intellectuals. Underlying Fry's analysis is the suggestion that the binary mode is being imposed on the lower socio-economic groups by politicians or intellectuals, as the census categories were imposed by the state.[37] Maggie, on the other hand, prefers to use three orders of social relations in which colour identities are constructed: culture, society and inter-group relations.[38]

Telles, using data gathered by DataFolha,[39] highlights the inconsistency between categorisation (classification by others) and self-classification in the census categories, coming to the conclusion that 'only approximately 1/5 of Brazilians in the sample are classified ambiguously'.[40] That is, for 79 per cent of Brazilians, the IBGE categories are those that are used on a daily basis to identify themselves and to be identified. For the remaining 21 per cent, however, these are not the terms they use to identify themselves or others.

Assessing the effects of affirmative action and ethnic mobilisation

With the adoption of affirmative policies, mainly quotas for blacks at Brazilian universities, some authors such as Bayle have argued that there will be a tendency for the Brazilian population to declare itself darker than it has done in the past.[41] Although Bayle's argument may sometimes lead to errors, such as his claim that universities adopt the bipolar system used by the black movements,[42] it seems right to suppose that the influence of black mobilisation in the media and the state creates actual material and symbolic incentives for the construction of black identity

[37] Peter Fry, 'O que a Cinderela Negra tem a dizer sobre a "política racial" no Brasil', *Revista da USP* (São Paulo) 28 (1995–6), pp. 122–36, see p. 131.

[38] Yvonne Maggie, 'Cor, hierarquia e sistema de classificação: A diferença fora do lugar', *Estudos Históricos* (Rio de Janeiro) 7:14 (1994), pp. 149–60; Yvonne Maggie, 'Aqueles a quem foi negada a cor do dia: As categorias de cor e raça na cultura brasileira', in Marcos C. Maio and Ricardo V. Santos (eds), *Raça, ciência e sociedade* (Rio de Janeiro: Fiocruz/Centro Cultural Banco do Brasil, 1996).

[39] Turra and Venturi (eds), *Racismo cordial.*

[40] Edward E. Telles, 'Racial Ambiguity among the Brazilian Population', *Ethnic and Racial Studies* 25:3 (2002), pp. 415–41, see p. 425.

[41] Stanley R. Bayle, 'Unmixing for Race Making in Brazil', *American Journal of Sociology* 114:3 (2008), pp. 577–614.

[42] In fact, the majority of universities use the IBGE classification, offering benefits to *pretos*, *pardos* and *indigenas* who have studied in secondary public schools. The term '*negro*' in the legislation only appears in a few universities, in states where this term is widely used by the population in general.

as an ethnic identity, or, at least, a colour one, and will lead to a change in the Brazilian statistics. Telles and Flores have also recently observed the decline of whiteness in Brazil, using data from the Americas Barometer.[43]

To assess this general trend, albeit tentatively, I will use some other available data. These data seem to indicate the direction which racial re-classification is taking. It should be kept in mind that the most ambitious affirmative action – quotas for blacks at public universities – was only adopted from 2003, and became generalised in the following years, involving up to seventy-one universities. Current data, therefore, can only vaguely reflect any strategies for racial re-classification this measure may have produced. However, they do reflect, in a general way, the large black political mobilisation of the last decades.

Let us start with census data. IBGE data show that the number of whites oscillated very little between 1940 and 1960, but since then has declined constantly as the *parda* population has increased; the data also indicate that the whitening trend of the Brazilian population has stopped, with a small increase in the number of people who declare themselves to be *pretos* (see Figure 1.1). Alternatively, if we take the *Pesquisa Nacional por Amostra de Domicílios*, also by the IBGE, to obtain the latest official data, the number of whites falls four percentage points between 1995 and 2005, while there is also a relative increase in the numbers of *pardos* and *pretos* (see Table 1.1).

Unofficial current data, collected using a different methodology, from representative sample surveys by DataFolha of the over-16 urban Brazilian

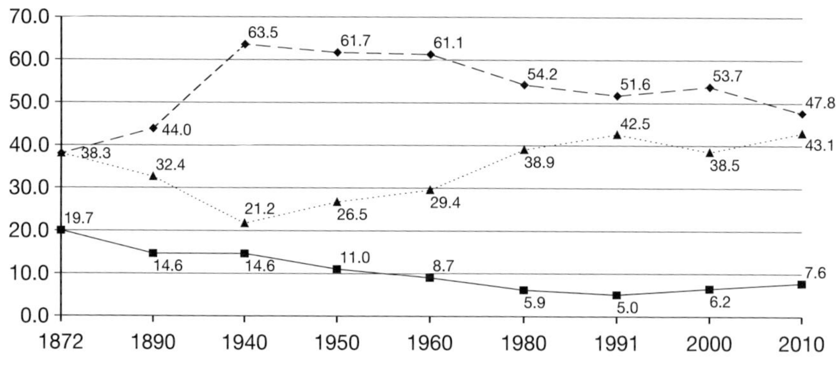

Figure 1.1. Brazil: population by colour, 1872–2010 (%)

Source: IBGE, Brazil demographic censuses, 1872–2010.

[43] Edward E. Telles and R. Flores, 'Not Just Color: Whiteness, Nation and Status in Latin America', *Hispanic American Historical Review* (forthcoming).

Table 1.1. Brazil: population by colour, 1995–2008 (%)

Year	*Total*	*Colours*			
		Branca	*Preta*	*Parda*	*Amarela/Indígena*
1995	151,922,545	54.5	4.9	40.0	0.6
2005	181,000,608	50.5	6.3	42.5	0.7
2008	189,995,300	48.8	6.5	43.8	0.9

Source: *Pesquisa Nacional por Amostra de Domicílios*, IBGE 1995, 2005, 2008.

population, show more accentuated changes. DataFolha, in two surveys in 1995 and 2008 about racial prejudice in Brazil, gathered data on colour in two different ways. One was through the open question, 'What is your colour?', and the other used the same category alternatives as the IBGE. Because they are more detailed and recent, the comparison using these data can move us closer to a better understanding of how Brazilians today define their colour.

As the data are very detailed in terms of the demographic and socio-economic characteristics of the respondents, and as I have only been able to use cross-tabulations, without being able to access the database for more refined statistical analyses, I will attempt to make a synthesis in order to describe more closely the colour groups that concern us here – *branco*, *pardo* and *preto* – comparing changes apparent in their composition (see Tables 1.2 and 1.3).

Table 1.2. 1995: self-classification by colour in open and closed questions

Colour in open question	*Colour in closed question (%)*					
	Branca	*Parda*	*Preta*	*Amarela*	*Indigena*	*No declaration*
Branca	92.1	6.5	2.9	40.7	5.0	28.6
Morena	5.5	26.7	11.7	15.2	56.5	11.1
Parda	0.2	55.8	1.3	2.3	8.9	9.5
Negra	0.1	3.0	64.9	2.3	9.9	14.3
Preta		0.3	13.0			
Amarela		0.1		27.9		1.6
Other	0.4	4.1	3.3	2.3	9.0	3.2
No declaration	1.7	3.5	2.9	9.3	10.7	31.7
Total %	100	100	100	100	100	100

Source: DataFolha 1995.

Table 1.3. 2008: self-classification by colour in open and closed questions

Colour in open question	*Colour in closed question*			
	Branca	*Parda*	*Preta*	*Other*
Branca	82	2	1	4
Morena	11	44	25	73
Parda	1	46	2	2
Negra		3	41	2
Preta	0	1	28	1
Amarela	1	1	0	8
Other	4	2	3	9
No declaration	1	1	0	1
Total %	100	100	100	100

Source: DataFolha 2008.

Branco (white)

In 1995, the tendency of this group was to declare themselves spontaneously 'white' (92.1 per cent). Only residually did they declare themselves *morenos* (5.5 per cent) or not declare their colour (1.7 per cent). The terms *pardo*, *negro*, *mestiço*, *mulato* and *moreno escuro* only appeared in insignificant numbers. It could be said, then, that only 8 per cent of Brazilians who were officially white, within this social group, had any doubts with regard to their racial identity.

In 2008, however, this group was less sure of itself: 83 per cent spontaneously declared themselves to be 'white', whereas 11 per cent preferred *moreno*. Other colours declared in the open question were *pardo*, *amarelo*, and *claro* (1 per cent each). Seventeen per cent of the group therefore doubted their whiteness.

Pardo (brown)

In 1995 this was a category that fewer people chose. Only 55.8 per cent declared themselves spontaneously to be *pardo*. They preferred to call themselves *moreno* (26.7 per cent), or 'white' (6.5 per cent) and *pardo claro*, when they wanted to whiten themselves, or *negro* (3 per cent) and *preto* to become blacker. This was the colour category where the largest number of people looked for alternative names, such as *claro*, *amarelo*, *mulato claro*, *mulato*, *misto* [mixed], *castanho* [chestnut brown], *mestiço*, *marron* [brown], *mulato escuro* [dark *mulato*], *moreno médio* [medium *moreno*], *branco brasileiro*, or *mulato médio*; 3.5 per cent did not declare their colour spontaneously.

In 2008, *pardo* was chosen by even fewer people (45 per cent), while an equal number preferred to identify themselves spontaneously as *moreno* (44 per cent) or *mulato*. Some who self-declared themselves *negro* (3 per cent), 'white' (2 per cent), or *amarelo* (1 per cent) also declared themselves *pardo* in the closed question.

Preto (black)

In 1995, this category was less accepted: only 13 per cent classified themselves spontaneously as *preto*, 64.9 per cent preferred to call themselves *negro*, and 11.7 per cent preferred the denomination *moreno*. The number of those who called themselves 'white' (2.9 per cent) or did not declare their colour (2.9 per cent) is interesting. Both spontaneous declarations, in this case, seemed to denote a denial of the official categories, in the first case through an inversion game, in the second by a refusal to answer. There were other answers such as *moreno claro*, *escuro* [dark], *mestiço* and *moreno escuro*.

In 2008, the number who spontaneously declared themselves *preto* increased substantially (to 27 per cent). The majority of those who chose this category in the closed question had previously classified themselves as *negro* (40 per cent) or *moreno* (25 per cent). Other designations used were 'white' (1 per cent), '*pardo*' (2 per cent), '*moreno claro*' (1 per cent), '*mulato*' (15 per cent), and '*moreno escuro*' (1 per cent).

Seen as a whole, the classificatory movement seems to have gone from white towards black, in the following way: first, the tendency to call oneself *moreno* increased (Table 1.4), probably as those who used to declare themselves white started to call themselves *moreno* (that is, accepting a darker skin colour); secondly, more people spontaneously classifying as *pardo* in 1995 preferred to declare

Table 1.4. Changing classification in the open question ('What is your colour?'), 1995–2008

Colour in open question	*1995*	*2008*	*Change*
Branca	50	32	–18
Morena	15	33	18
Parda	20	17	–3
Negra	7	7	0
Preta	1	4	3
Other	3	6	3
No declaration	4	1	–3
Total %	100	100	0

Source: DataFolha 1995 and 2008.

Table 1.5. How those self-defining as *morenos* reclassified themselves using census categories, 1995–2008

Year	*Branca*	*Parda*	*Preta*	*Other*	*Total %*
1995	14	62	7	17	100
2008	10	50	12	28	100
Change	–4	–12	5	11	

Source: DataFolha 1995 and 2008.

themselves *preto* in 2008. People who earlier used to classify themselves spontaneously as *moreno*, and who, when forced to choose between the census colours, tended to choose white or *pardo*, more recently have tended to declare themselves *preto*, *amarelo* or *indígeno* – clearly demonstrating social valorisation. Table 1.5 shows the shift of the spontaneous declaration of *moreno* colour to the closed census categories. Whereas in 1995, 14 per cent of *morenos* moved towards white, in 2008 this number fell to 10 per cent; the displacement of *pardos* decreased 12 percentage points, whereas the shift towards *preto* (5 per cent), *amarelo*, and *indígeno* (11 per cent) grew.

In conclusion, there is strong evidence that the Brazilian population is using darker colours to classify itself racially. This change can be attributed to a range of factors and conditions that I cannot develop here. They range from demographics (the decline in European immigration since the 1950s) to the political (increased black mobilisation in recent decades); from the cultural (exposure of lower-class Brazilians to other systems of race classification as emigration towards Europe and the United States soared at the end of the twentieth century) to the representational (as the Brazilian media modified its secular misrepresentation of blackness); from the psychological (the development of self-esteem and even a certain pride in being black) to the institutional (the recent establishment of affirmative action creating material rewards for the assumption of Afro-descent). The fact is that if Brazil ever had a unique system of race classification, that system is today under stress from other competing systems.

2

Brazil and Colombia: Comparative Race Relations in South America

PETER WADE

Introduction

IN THE LAST TWENTY YEARS OR SO, there has been an explosion of scholarly research into what might be called 'blackness' in Latin America, involving studies of Afro-descendants, black people and race relations.[1] The tendency has been towards country-based studies, and comparison, where it has taken place, has mostly followed the well-worn path of placing Brazil in relation to the United States. Some important work has questioned the terms of this standard contrast, challenging the 'methodological nationalism'[2] that it entails and highlighting how such case-study comparisons can erase the dynamic dialogues and exchanges that take place between the 'cases' and that, in some sense, actually constitute the cases as such.[3] Other work has pointed out the ongoing and longstanding exchanges and dialogues that link Brazil to Africa across a more southerly version of Gilroy's Black Atlantic.[4] Less work has sought to make comparisons within Latin America.

[1] George Reid Andrews, 'Afro-Latin America: Five Questions', *Latin American and Caribbean Ethnic Studies* 4:2 (2009), pp. 191–210; Peter Wade, 'Afro-Latin Studies: Reflections on the Field', *Latin American and Caribbean Ethnic Studies* 1:1 (2006), pp. 105–24; Peter Wade, *Race and Ethnicity in Latin America*, 2nd edn (London: Pluto Press, 2010).

[2] Andreas Wimmer and Nina Glick Schiller, 'Methodological Nationalism and Beyond: Nation-State Building, Migration and the Social Sciences', *Global Networks: A Journal of Transnational Affairs* 2 (2002), pp. 301–34.

[3] Micol Seigel, *Uneven Encounters: Making Race and Nation in Brazil and the United States* (Durham, NC: Duke University Press, 2009); see also Ann Laura Stoler, 'Tense and Tender Ties: The Politics of Comparison in North American History and (Post) Colonial Studies', *Journal of American History* 88:3 (2001), pp. 829–65.

[4] Paul Gilroy, *The Black Atlantic: Modernity and Double Consciousness* (London: Verso, 1993); J. Lorand Matory, *Black Atlantic Religion: Tradition, Transnationalism, and Matriarchy in the Afro-Brazilian Candomblé* (Princeton: Princeton University Press, 2005); J. Lorand Matory, 'The "New World" Surrounds an Ocean: Theorizing the Live Dialogue between African and African American

cont.

Proceedings of the British Academy **179**, *35–48*.

Some of the work that has tackled this line of enquiry comes out of political science, where a common mode of enquiry compares different political systems with a view to finding out the key variables that influence political outcomes.[5] In this direction, Juliet Hooker has recently outlined some useful broad categories with which to think about how different countries have dealt with black and indigenous minorities in the context of a region-wide shift, which has occurred since about 1990, towards the official adoption of multiculturalist policies and definitions of national identity.[6] She identifies a first category of countries in which indigenous and black groups have come to be seen as basically the same and have been incorporated into national legislation on more or less the same basis, as equivalent ethnic minorities. This category includes Guatemala, Honduras and Nicaragua, countries where the Afro-descendant population is strongly represented by Garifuna populations, which have managed to define themselves as indigenous-like, autochthonous minorities – although not without competing discourses making reference to a more cosmopolitan blackness.[7] Nicaragua is a more complex case, due to the presence in the Atlantic coastal region of black creole people, who have a rather different history from the Garifuna.

Hooker identifies a second category of countries where indigenous peoples are accorded a number of rights (to land, cultural autonomy, bilingual education, and so on), while black people are more or less ignored in legislative terms. Venezuela and Mexico are currently examples of this category. Finally, a third category consists of countries where indigenous peoples are seen as ethnic minorities, with certain, often quite substantial rights, at least on paper, while black people are seen as what Hooker calls 'cultural groups' and 'racial groups', which may get some land rights, although less than those of indigenous peoples, and may also be the beneficiaries of some institutional actions designed to combat racism and/or its effects. In this category, Hooker places Brazil, Colombia, Ecuador and Peru.

This categorisation puts Brazil and Colombia together as similar cases and, indeed, they share some common traits. However, it also masks some important

Cultures', in Kevin Yelvington (ed.), *Afro-Atlantic Dialogues: Anthropology in the Diaspora* (Santa Fe, NM: School of American Research Press, 2006), pp. 151–92; Kevin Yelvington (ed.), *Afro-Atlantic Dialogues: Anthropology in the Diaspora* (Santa Fe, NM: School of American Research Press, 2006).

[5] Juliet Hooker, 'Indigenous Inclusion/Black Exclusion: Race, Ethnicity and Multicultural Citizenship in Contemporary Latin America', *Journal of Latin American Studies* 37:2 (2005), pp. 285–310; Donna Lee Van Cott, *The Friendly Liquidation of the Past: The Politics of Diversity in Latin America* (Pittsburgh: University of Pittsburgh Press, 2000).

[6] Juliet Hooker, *Race and the Politics of Solidarity* (Oxford: Oxford University Press, 2009), pp. 137–8.

[7] Mark Anderson, *Black and Indigenous: Garifuna Activism and Consumer Culture in Honduras* (Minneapolis: University of Minnesota Press, 2009). Garifuna (also known as Garinagu and Black Caribs) are the descendants of a process of mixture between Africans and Carib indigenous populations exiled in the eighteenth century from St Vincent, a British colony in the eastern Caribbean, to islands off the coast of Honduras, whence they spread along the coasts of Honduras, Guatemala, Belize, and Nicaragua.

divergences, as I will show below. Furthermore, the reference to Afro-descendants as both 'cultural' and 'racial' groups points to, but leaves unexplored, the complexity and ambiguity of the 'black' category and the way its definition has ambivalently shifted between different kinds of criteria.

In this essay, I will focus on Brazil and Colombia in the context of the official multiculturalism which both countries have adopted. I will look primarily at 'blackness' but will necessarily make reference to the category 'indigenous', as this is an inherent part of the processes by which identities come to be reckoned, defined, claimed and contested in both countries. I will map out how blackness in each country wavered and oscillated between 'ethnic' and 'racialised' definitions, both from an official and social movement point of view, and how oscillation was related to different contexts, race-ethnic relations and political conjunctures. In brief, in Colombia, we can see a move between 1991 and 2009, from a very 'ethnic' definition towards a more explicitly 'racialised' one, while in Brazil, we can see a move from a pre-1988 racial definition, towards a more ethnic one, which however coexists with a more racial definition. Clearly, these are not opposed trajectories – or even separate 'cases' which are unrelated to each other. Instead they should be seen as variations on a theme of changing, overlapping and often conflicting definitions, all of which are taking place in a transnational, indeed globalising, context of post-colonial identity politics and struggles for human rights and, sometimes, reparative justice.[8] Brazil and Colombia together highlight the fundamental ambiguity of blackness in the Latin American context: black people have long been (dis)located as both the same as and different from other people in the nation; perhaps culturally distinctive, perhaps just ordinary (if in practice second-class) citizens; as marginal to, but also at the heart of the nation.

Colombia

Before the constitutional reform of 1991, black people in Colombia figured in various ways in the national imaginary.[9] Despite some academic claims made that Afro-Colombians had been made entirely 'invisible' in the nation, there were some conditional spaces for blackness. *Los negros* was a generalised race/class term used by many people to refer to people identified as 'looking black', in Colombian terms, and used by the middle and upper classes to refer generically to the lower classes,

[8] Claudia Mosquera Rosero-Labbé and Luiz Claudio Barcelos (eds), *Afro-reparaciones: Memorias de la esclavitud y justicia reparativa para negros, afrocolombianos y raizales* (Bogotá: Universidad Nacional de Colombia, 2007).

[9] Peter Wade, *Blackness and Race Mixture: The Dynamics of Racial Identity in Colombia* (Baltimore: Johns Hopkins University Press, 1993); Peter Wade, *Music, Race and Nation:* Música Tropical *in Colombia* (Chicago: University of Chicago Press, 2000).

seen as generally rather 'dark', without much attention to specific features of appearance and ancestry. *Negro* was, and still is, a racial category in popular usage, as were *blanco*, *indio* and other race/colour terms such as *moreno* (brown). An individual person might be nicknamed *el negro*, perhaps because he or she was the darkest one of the family, without necessarily being very African-looking; a man might call his romantic partner *mi negra*, as a term of endearment – one which, however, evoked a history of sexualised racial domination in which black (and indigenous) women were relatively accessible to whiter, higher-status men.[10]

Another instance of the presence of blackness was the irruption of music from the Caribbean coastal region of the country – styles such as *cumbia* and *porro* – onto the national popular music scene of the 1940s and 1950s, where it was identified as 'black', even though it was rapidly undergoing a process of whitening as part of its entry into middle- and upper-class social clubs.[11]

The most obvious manifestation of blackness in ideas about the nation, however, was in the delineation of a regional geography for the country, stemming in large part from a number of nineteenth-century expeditions to map the nation and its human and natural resources, such as the Comisión Corográfica of the 1850s. The nation was described as comprising a number of distinct provinces and/or 'natural regions',[12] which were geographically, climatically, culturally, and racially distinctive. The division of the country by province or region varied by classifier and over time, but in broad terms a mode of categorisation solidified in which the Andean interior was the seat of government, wealth, urbanity and whiteness. The Caribbean coastal region was much more black and indigenous, but it was the Pacific coastal region which figured as the black region *par excellence*, while also being the poorest, the least healthy and the area least conducive to progress and modernity. In fact, then, as now, black people lived in large numbers in many areas of the country, including in areas of the interior of the country, but this did not prevent the Pacific (and to a lesser extent the Caribbean) region from signifying blackness within the nation. This, in turn, also tended to constitute blackness as rather marginal in the nation – geographically and developmentally.

Despite the popularity of Caribbean coastal music, blackness was never included in representations of the nation in quite the same way as in Cuba or Brazil: in this sense blackness was indeed 'invisible'. Colombian elites might recognise the mixedness of their nation, but the preferred image of the country was a very whitened mestizo – a trend that arguably continues today with such national figures as the pop stars Carlos Vives and Shakira, and the emblem of Colombian coffee, 'Juan Valdez', a branded construct which represents a generic Colombian highland coffee farmer.

[10] Peter Wade, *Race and Sex in Latin America* (London: Pluto Press, 2009).

[11] Wade, *Music, Race and Nation*.

[12] Francisco Vergara y Velasco, *Nueva geografía de Colombia*, 3 vols (1901; Bogotá: Banco de la República, 1974).

In the 1970s and 1980s, when a few anthropological voices began to contest the definition of Colombian anthropology as the study of indigenous peoples – a bias in which Colombia followed other Latin American countries – the status of the Pacific coastal region as *the* black region of the country became consolidated, as anthropologists focused on blackness as 'other', as culturally distinctive, as linked through antique roots to a non-Western history (Africa), in short as an ethnic minority.[13] These anthropologists did, in fact, study blackness in other areas of the country as well, but the Pacific coast was already pre-constructed to amplify any attention paid to it as a black area.

At the same time, there emerged the beginnings of a black social movement, fomented by university students, mainly from the Pacific coastal region, who had gone to the universities of the large cities of the interior to study.[14] They were inspired more by transnational exemplars of blackness – Martin Luther King, Malcolm X, Léopold Senghor, Aimé Césaire – than by local figures, but the fact that they themselves came from the Pacific coastal region helped cement its predominance as the symbol of blackness in the country. This black movement began to adopt the imagery of the runaway slave, the maroon or *cimarrón* – imagery used in the Caribbean and also in Brazil (the *quilombo*) – and in fact this highlighted the key role of a small village in the Caribbean coastal region, called Palenque de San Basilio, where descendants of a maroon slave settlement lived and spoke a unique creole language.[15] But the Pacific coastal region, where colonial and republican governance had always been weak and patchy, was also reputed to have been home to many runaway slaves and palenques,[16] so the overall relationship between the Pacific and blackness remained powerful.

In 1991, Colombia underwent a constitutional reform, similar in many ways to the processes of reform that were taking place elsewhere in the region.[17] In the

[13] Jaime Arocha, *Ombligados de Ananse: Hilos ancestrales y modernos en el Pacífico colombiano* (Bogotá: Universidad Nacional de Colombia, 1999); Nina de Friedemann, 'Contextos religiosos en una área negra de Barbacoas, Nariño', *Revista Colombiana de Folclor* 4:10 (1966–9), pp. 63–83; Nina de Friedemann, '"Troncos" among Black Miners in Colombia', in T. Greaves and W. Culver (eds), *Miners and Mining in the Americas* (Manchester: Manchester University Press, 1985); Nina de Friedemann and Jaime Arocha, *De sol a sol: Génesis, transformación y presencia de los negros en Colombia* (Bogotá: Planeta, 1986).

[14] Peter Wade, 'The Cultural Politics of Blackness in Colombia', *American Ethnologist* 22:2 (1995), pp. 342–58.

[15] Nina de Friedemann, *Ma Ngombe: Guerreros y ganaderos en Palenque* (Bogotá: Carlos Valencia, 1980); Armin Schwegler, *Chi ma nkongo: Lengua y rito ancestrales en El Palenque de San Basilio (Colombia)*, 2 vols (Frankfurt and Madrid: Vervuert Verlag Iberoamericana, 1996).

[16] William Sharp, 'Manumission, Libres and Black Resistance: The Chocó 1680–1810', in Robert Toplin (ed.), *Slavery and Race Relations in Latin America* (Westport, CT: Greenwood Press, 1974).

[17] Van Cott, *The Friendly Liquidation of the Past*; Donna Lee Van Cott, 'Constitutional Reform in the Andes', in Rachel Sieder (ed.), *Multiculturalism in Latin America: Indigenous Rights, Diversity and Democracy* (Basingstoke: Palgrave Macmillan, 2002); Deborah Yashar, *Contesting Citizenship in Latin America: The Rise of Indigenous Movements and the Postliberal Challenge* (Cambridge: Cambridge University Press, 2005).

elections to the constituent assembly, indigenous delegates managed to gain a foothold, while no black candidates were elected. An indigenous delegate from the Pacific coastal region undertook to represent the interests of both black and indigenous people in the area. Several measures were included in the new constitution which protected and expanded the rights of indigenous peoples. A short transitory article related to rural black communities in the Pacific coastal region was included at the last minute and, two years later, became Law 70 of 1993. This is not the place to assess this legislation; the point I want to emphasise here is that Law 70 privileged the Pacific coastal region as the location of blackness in Colombia. The law addressed the black communities of Colombia (*comunidades negras*) as 'an ethnic group', but at the same time focused explicitly on rural, riverine, black communities occupying state-owned land in the Pacific coastal region and their prospective land rights. Even though it said that rural, riverine, black communities occupying state land in other regions of the country were also covered by the legislation, in practice this caveat had virtually no impact. Thus the law consolidated the idea of the historically and ethnically distinctive black community located in the Pacific coastal region. The legislative category of *comunidad negra* was an emergent one, created to a significant degree by the very law that claimed to be recognising it, yet it also built on existing, and especially anthropological, conceptions of blackness in the Pacific coastal region. Rather like the anthropological conception, it was also a clearly indigenising category: it made black communities look, especially in the eyes of the state, like indigenous communities. The definition of black community in the law makes this very plain: it is 'the set of families of Afro-Colombian descent which possess their own culture, share a history and have their own traditions and customs [. . .] which reveal and maintain an awareness of identity which distinguish them from other ethnic groups'.[18]

Law 70 had significant effects in the region. By 2005, collective land titles for black communities numbered 132, with an area of 4.7 million hectares, representing about 4 per cent of the national territory.[19] By comparison, in 2005 indigenous *resguardos* (land reserves) numbered 710, with an area of about 34 million hectares, representing 30 per cent of the national territory. These figures need to be seen against the results of the 2005 census which showed that Afro-Colombians formed 10.5 per cent and indigenous people 3.4 per cent of the national total (although, of course, most of these Afro-Colombians did not live in rural, riverine communities on state-owned land – on the contrary, most of them lived in cities).

[18] 'Es el conjunto de familias de ascendencia afrocolombiana que poseen una cultura propia, comparten una historia y tienen sus propias tradiciones y costumbres dentro de la relación campo-poblado, que revelan y conservan conciencia de identidad que las distinguen de otros grupos étnicos' (Ley 70 de 1993, Article 2).

[19] Departamento Administrativo Nacional de Estadística (DANE), *Colombia una nación multicultural: Su diversidad étnica* (Bogotá: Departamento Administrativo Nacional de Estadística, 2006).

In the 2000s, while the *comunidad negra*, the ethnic community, and rural land claims remain central, there has been a discernible shift of attention towards urban black populations, a more racial definition of blackness, and issues of racism. As indicated above, the 2005 census showed most blacks living outside the Pacific coastal region and in cities; this was a key moment in giving some institutional space to blackness. In the 1993 census, a new question had been included asking people if they belonged to a *comunidad negra* and, if so, which one. The question was a failure as only 1.5 per cent of people ticked this box, which hardly seemed to represent the presence of blackness in the nation. After lengthy negotiations, involving the state, academics and black activist organisations, and sponsored in part by the World Bank and the Inter-American Development Bank, a much more inclusive question appeared on the 2005 census form.

The urban presence of blackness was also being increasingly recognised by academics who began to include city contexts as well as rural ones in their studies of Afro-Colombians.[20] Meanwhile, black social movements, which for obvious reasons had been working hard in the Pacific coastal region, where land rights were at issue,[21] also began to look towards cities and urban issues of racism in the labour and housing markets, as well as black culture construed more in terms of cosmopolitan, commodified black style than 'traditions and customs'.[22] Furthermore, the issue of land titles in the Pacific coastal region had, by chance or by design, coincided with the massive incursion of paramilitary forces into the area, displacing large numbers of black (and indigenous) people into the cities of the interior.[23] While black social movements protested about displacement and the take-over of land by capitalist interests, they also began to address issues related to the displaced populations in the cities.

[20] Michel Agier *et al.*, *Tumaco: Haciendo ciudad* (Bogotá: Universidad del Valle, 1999); Olivier Barbary and Fernando Urrea (eds), *Gente negra en Colombia, dinámicas sociopolíticas en Cali y el Pacífico* (Cali and Paris: CIDSE/Univalle, IRD, Colciencias, 2004); Claudia Mosquera Rosero-Labbé, *Acá antes no se veían negros: Estrategias de inserción de migrantes del Pacífico colombiano en Bogotá* (Bogotá: Observatorio de Cultura Urbana, 1988); see also Wade, *Blackness and Race Mixture*.

[21] Libia Grueso, Carlos Rosero and Arturo Escobar, 'The Process of Black Community Organizing in the Southern Pacific Coast of Colombia', in Sonia Alvarez, Evelina Dagnino and Arturo Escobar (eds), *Cultures of Politics, Politics of Cultures: Re-Visioning Latin American Social Movements* (Boulder, CO: Westview, 1998), pp. 196–219.

[22] Olivier Barbary, Héctor F. Ramírez and Fernando Urrea, 'Identidad y ciudadanía afrocolombiana en el Pacífico y Cali', in Barbary and Urrea (eds), *Gente negra en Colombia*, pp. 245–82; Peter Wade, 'Working Culture: Making Cultural Identities in Cali, Colombia', *Current Anthropology* 40:4 (1999), pp. 449–71.

[23] Oscar Almario, 'Dinámica y consecuencias del conflicto armado colombiano en el Pacífico: Limpieza étnica y desterritorialización de afrocolombianos e indígenas y "multiculturalismo" de Estado e indolencia nacional', in Eduardo Restrepo and Axel Rojas (eds), *Conflicto e (in)visibilidad: Retos en los estudios de la gente negra en Colombia* (Popayán: Universidad del Cauca, 2004); Arturo Escobar, *Territories of Difference: Place, Movements, Life, Redes* (Durham, NC: Duke University Press, 2008); Mieke Wouters, 'Ethnic Rights under Threat: The Black Peasant Movement against Armed Groups' Pressure in the Chocó, Colombia', *Bulletin of Latin American Research* 20:4 (2001), pp. 498–519.

Lastly, the question of racism began to receive more attention, not only from the black social movements, but also from the state. One of the main black organisations, the Proceso de Comunidades Negras (PCN), based in the southern Pacific coastal region, which in 1996 saw racism as a theme with 'little audience',[24] by 2008 had declared as one of its aims the struggle against racism; its website has a link to the Racial Discrimination Observatory, established in 2007 at the private and elite Universidad de los Andes to monitor racism.[25] In May 2009, the first National Campaign Against Racism was launched with support from the Vice-President.

In sum, although the definition of blackness in terms of localised communities, defined by ancestral occupation and cultural traditions, has by no means disappeared and remains a powerful legislative category, there has undoubtedly been a shift towards a more racialised understanding of blackness. This does not mean that 'culture' has been replaced by 'biology', as 'race' is always about the relationship of those two things, or more broadly of nature and culture.[26] It does mean that the notion of blackness has expanded beyond a narrow notion of ethnic particularity, derived from the particular history of Colombia's Pacific coastal region, and begun to encompass blackness as a category that is rooted in a colonial history of the enslavement of Africans.

Brazil

While similar in many respects to Colombia, in terms of its ethnic and racial structures and relations, Brazil diverges from Colombia, first insofar as blackness and the idea of Africa formed a more salient element in public representations of national identity, prior to any shifts towards official multiculturalism that took place in the late twentieth century. Slavery was abolished in Brazil in 1888 and slaves had been imported in large numbers into Brazil from Africa until at least 1860.[27] In contrast, slavery was already a weak institution in Colombia when it was

[24] Alvaro Pedrosa *et al.*, 'Movimiento negro, identidad y territorio: Entrevista con la Organización de Comunidades Negras', in Arturo Escobar and Alvaro Pedrosa (eds), *Pacífico: ¿desarrollo o biodiversidad? Estado, capital y movimientos sociales en el Pacífico colombiano* (Bogotá: CEREC, 1996), pp. 245–65, see p. 251.

[25] See the PCN website, www.renacientes.org/ (accessed 6 May 2010). See also the Observatory site, http://odr.uniandes.edu.co/ (accessed 6 May 2010); and César Rodríguez Garavito, Tatiana Alfonso Sierra and Isabel Cavelier Adarve, *Informe sobre discriminación racial y derechos de la población afrocolombiana: Raza y derechos humanos en Colombia* (Bogotá: Universidad de los Andes, 2009).

[26] David Theo Goldberg, *Racist Culture: Philosophy and the Politics of Meaning* (Oxford: Blackwell, 1993); Peter Wade, *Race, Nature and Culture: An Anthropological Perspective* (London: Pluto Press, 2002).

[27] Philip Curtin, *The Atlantic Slave Trade: A Census* (Madison: University of Wisconsin Press, 1969), p. 234.

abolished in 1851, and relatively few slaves had been imported from Africa in the preceding decades. After abolition, black people, by any measure, formed a much larger proportion of the population in Brazil than in Colombia, and they were distributed differently too. Although certain areas (such as Salvador) were strongly associated with blackness, and with relative poverty and 'backwardness', an area such as Rio de Janeiro, which was unequivocally central to the nation, also had a substantial black population.

This demographic reality underlay the representation of Brazil by intellectuals in the 1930s as a highly mixed country, with important black/African components. Writers such as Arthur Ramos and Edison Carneiro focused scholarly attention on Afro-Brazilians in ways unparalleled in Colombia at the time, while Gilberto Freyre famously recast Brazil's mixture as a positive trait, against the grain of the eugenic thought popular in Latin America, Europe and North America in the period. Granted this view of Brazil was very assimilationist and in fact perpetuated some of the whitening ideologies of previous decades, but it was still a much more forceful embracing of mixture, including its component of African ancestry, than one could find in Colombia during these decades.[28]

An interesting comparison is that between Brazilian samba and Colombian cumbia. The two genres had rather similar trajectories, in starting out as nominally 'black' musical styles and becoming national icons, having been significantly whitened along the way; but samba began this journey much earlier than cumbia and yet arguably retained more of a black image than cumbia did, at least when considering their urban, commercial, popular musical forms.[29] Clearer yet is the difference between the two countries in terms of social movements seeking to redress racial inequalities and promote equal rights for black people: Brazil's black press, centred on São Paulo in the 1910s and 1920s, and the short-lived Frente Negra Brasileira founded in 1931, have no equivalent in Colombia.[30]

In terms of scholarly attention to race, there is a tradition of studying race relations in Brazil that goes back to the 1950s and the well-known UNESCO studies which sought to understand Brazil's reputed 'racial democracy' in the wake of Nazi racism. These early studies were mainly urban,[31] and focused on discrimination against a racialised category of citizens who were culturally very similar to everyone else. While some studies focused on the culturally distinctive patterns of Afro-

[28] Jan Hoffman French, *Legalizing Identities: Becoming Black or Indian in Brazil's Northeast* (Chapel Hill: University of North Carolina Press, 2009), p. 156; Jeffrey D. Needell, 'Identity, Race, Gender, and Modernity in the Origins of Gilberto Freyre's *Oeuvre*', *American Historical Review* 100:1 (1995), pp. 51–77; Thomas Skidmore, *Black into White: Race and Nationality in Brazilian Thought* (New York: Oxford University Press, 1974); see also the essay by Guimarães, in this volume (Chapter 1).

[29] Hermano Vianna, *The Mystery of Samba: Popular Music and National Identity in Brazil* (Chapel Hill: University of North Carolina Press, 1999); Wade, *Music, Race and Nation*.

[30] See also Guimarães, this volume.

[31] Although see Charles Wagley (ed.), *Race and Class in Rural Brazil* (Paris: UNESCO, 1952).

Brazilian religion,[32] the main focus was on race, capitalism and social change. These themes have proved durable and, although scholarly work on race in Brazil has diversified, there is still a strong leaning towards race relations, racism and racial politics, usually in an urban context, which contrasts markedly with the situation in Colombia, where the culture of black communities, especially those of the Pacific coastal region, seen as distinctive, was the key focus until much more recently.[33]

It is in this context that we have to understand Brazil's 1988 constitutional reform, which opened the door to land claims by so-called *remanescentes das comunidades dos quilombos* (remnants, remainders or survivors of *quilombo* communities), in a legislative move that looks rather similar to Colombia's Law 70. Of course, one difference is the explicit mention of maroon communities in the Brazilian case, but in fact the two trajectories run along parallel or converging lines.

Initially, the Brazilian constitutional clause had very little impact. There was little debate about it in the constituent assembly, compared to the lobbying carried out by indigenous delegates and organisations. Contrast Colombia where, although issues around indigenous peoples similarly took precedence over those about Afro-Colombians, there had also been a good deal of debate about whether black communities should be recognised in any way, and black organisations had mobilised and occupied buildings such as the Haitian Embassy in Bogotá. French argues that the *quilombo* clause made it into the constitution partly because the black social movement had long adopted the famous *quilombo* of Palmares as a key symbol, but also because the state saw old *quilombos* as a kind of national patrimony, which symbolised the struggle of all Brazilians against colonial domination.[34] The target of the clause was rather ill-defined: compared to the Colombian case, where Law 70 was clearly aimed at rural, riverine communities in the Pacific coastal region, it was not very clear how much ground was potentially being ceded in Brazil (although the assumption seems to have been that it was not much).

After 1988, not a great deal happened until the mid-1990s, when definitions of *quilombo* began to change.[35] Until 1994, there had been quite a strict adherence to the need to prove that the community making a land claim actually descended from a historical *quilombo*; this was despite arguments from the black social movements that a more inclusive definition was needed. In 1994, the Palmares

[32] E.g. Roger Bastide, *The African Religions of Brazil: Towards a Sociology of the Interpenetration of Civilizations* (Baltimore: Johns Hopkins University Press, 1978).

[33] Antonio Sérgio Guimarães, *Racismo e anti-racismo no Brasil* (São Paulo: Editora 34, 1999); Michael Hanchard (ed.), *Racial Politics in Contemporary Brazil* (Durham, NC: Duke University Press, 1999); Rebecca Reichmann (ed.), *Race in Contemporary Brazil: From Indifference to Inequality* (University Park, PA: Pennsylvania State University Press, 1999); Robin E. Sheriff, *Dreaming Equality: Color, Race, and Racism in Urban Brazil* (New Brunswick, NJ: Rutgers University Press, 2001).

[34] French, *Legalizing Identities*, p. 94.

[35] French, *Legalizing Identities*, pp. 95–8.

Foundation, created in 1988 to, among other things, administer the *quilombo* land claims process, began to shift its ground towards a broader definition that included rural black communities (a category already established in academic studies since the 1980s), populated by people who were presumed to descend from slaves, who lived at a subsistence level and whose cultural practices were linked to the ancestral past in a way that was interpreted as constituting a history of resistance, even if there was no particular history of insurrection or rebellion. There was no need to establish a specific link to fugitive slaves, to African-derived culture. Increasingly, *remanescentes de quilombos* were recognised as emergent phenomena: people could re-discover their *quilombola* identity,[36] often prompted by outsiders such as priests and legitimated by experts such as anthropologists.

As a result of this change in criteria for recognition, there has been a great increase in the number of communities claiming *quilombo* status: by November 2003, 743 had been recognised, representing some 30.6 million hectares of land or 3.6 per cent of the national territory, of which however only seventy-one had received land titles. Another sixty titles were issued between 2003 and 2008, giving a total titled land area of about 1.25 million hectares.[37] As of January 2009, 1,305 had been recognised by the Palmares Foundation and some estimates put the figure at 2,000–3,000 communities.[38] As in Colombia, where at least one 'black community' was recognised in the city of Santa Marta (although land title was not given), some claims have also emerged for urban *quilombos* in Brazil.[39]

The role of colour here was ambiguous. On the one hand, the people claiming *quilombola* status were often mixed-race peasants, who by no means identified straightforwardly as *negros* and might even reject such a label. On the other hand, the presumption of a generalised descent from slaves suggested that colour (darkness of skin, some phenotypical traits associated with *negros*) could be a marker of membership of a potential *quilombola* community.

French interprets this mid-1990s shift as a move from race to ethnicity, from ideas of descent to ideas of culture and territory. I am not sure the shift is quite so clear. Although removing the need to prove descent from a historical *quilombo* clearly

[36] José Mauricio Andion Arruti, 'A emergência dos "remanescentes": Notas para o diálogo entre indígenas e quilombolas', *Mana. Estudos de Antropología Social* 3:2 (1997), pp. 7–38; José Mauricio Andion Arruti, 'Comunidades negras rurais: Entre a memória e o desejo', *Tempo e Presença* 298 (1998) pp. 15–18.

[37] See www.nead.org.br/index.php?acao=princ&id=6&id_prin=46 (accessed 7 May 2010); *Notícias Agrárias*, 24–30 November 2003, no. 212, www.nead.org.br/boletim/boletim.php?boletim=212¬icia=891 (accessed 12 May 2010); and www.palmares.gov.br/003/00301015.jsp?ttCD_CHAVE=2702 (accessed 7 May 2010).

[38] See www.palmares.gov.br/003/00301009.jsp?ttCD_CHAVE=1853 (accessed 7 May 2010).

[39] For Colombia, see Peter Wade, 'The Colombian Pacific in Perspective', *Journal of Latin American Anthropology* 7:2 (2002), pp. 2–33, see p. 18; for Brazil, see Lourdes de Fátima Bezerra Carril, 'Quilombo, território e geografia', *Agrária* 3 (2006), pp. 156–71, www.geografia.fflch.usp.br/revistaagraria/revistas/3/8_carril.pdf (accessed 7 May 2010).

broadens the definition, the idea of slave descent and the ambiguous role of colour and racialised appearance seem to indicate that race did not disappear as a criterion, especially if one bears in mind that race is always about culture as well as nature.

This aside, I would argue that the shift parallels the longer-term Colombian shift towards seeing blackness as a cultural phenomenon located in the Pacific coastal region. There too, issues of descent and appearance did not disappear, as the black people of the Pacific mainly fitted into Colombian stereotypes of what a *negro* looked like, but the point is that all other such *negros* in the country were effectively left out of this categorisation. In both Brazil and Colombia, black communities were effectively assimilated to dominant images of what an indigenous community looked like, while at the same time criteria of ethnicity (culture) and race (descent, appearance) intertwined and blurred. This, I think, responds to the ambiguous status of blackness in these Latin American contexts: are black people culturally different and 'other', like indigenous people; or are they simply citizens, culturally the same as everyone else, but marked by an inherited phenotype that acts as a stigma?

Meanwhile, the previous image of blackness in Brazil as a racial category – referring mainly to urban black people, identified principally by inherited phenotype, located disadvantageously in residential and labour markets, subject to racism and struggling for equality – was by no means displaced by the *quilombo* clause in the way that Colombia's Law 70 had consolidated the definition of blackness as a marginal, regional culture and, for a time, more or less displaced a more racialised and inclusive definition of blackness. On the contrary, it could be argued that, however fast the *quilombo* land movement is growing, the real ground for black identity and politics in Brazil is still firmly in urban areas and not related to land titles. It is this that has underlain the emergence of controversial affirmative action policies in Brazil in ways that are still incipient – and as yet remarkably uncontroversial – in Colombia. The heated debates over the imposition of programmes of racial quotas for entry into federal universities, the creation of SEPPIR (Secretariat for Policies for the Promotion of Racial Equality) and the proposed Statute of Racial Equality, which would spread the coverage of affirmative action and racial quotas much further – all these are testament to the racial nature of blackness in Brazil. These measures are seen to strike at the heart of ideas of Brazilian national identity and to differentiate the notion of 'citizen' in ways that the affirmative action of Colombia's Law 70, directed at a regional ethnic group, did not.

The urban, racial character of blackness in Brazil, compared to Colombia, is also evident in the gradual emergence of a black middle class, which overtly identifies with notions of *beleza negra* (black beauty) and consumption of fashion and style based on a black aesthetic, especially of the body.[40] While this may still

[40] Peter Fry, 'Estética e política: Relações entre "raça", publicidade e produção da beleza no Brasil', in Mirian Goldenberg (ed.), *Nu e vestido: dez antropólogos revelam a cultura do corpo carioca* (Rio de Janeiro: Record, 2002); Livio Sansone, *Blackness Without Ethnicity: Constructing Race in Brazil* (Basingstoke: Palgrave Macmillan, 2003).

not be a very powerful trend in Brazil, it is certainly more noticeable there than in Colombia, partly because the Colombian black middle class is smaller, but also because the urban presence of blackness, particularly of middle-class blackness, is more muted.

Comparative lessons

Juliet Hooker's characterisation of Colombia and Brazil as recognising blacks as both 'racial groups' and 'cultural groups' may appear confusing, but it actually directs us to a central feature of both countries and, arguably, of Latin America more widely. In both places, legislation and multiculturalist policies have shifted between, on the one hand, ideas that emphasise racialised, inherited appearance, perhaps with some acknowledgement of an African origin, and which refer to black people as a national category (and indeed a transnational one); and, on the other hand, ideas that emphasise local, cultural histories and bounded community territories, often assimilating these to images of the indigenous community, and which construct black people as a category that does not traverse the nation. These emphases are not mutually exclusive, but overlap and shade into each other: pointing to inherited appearance can also entrain ideas about local histories, and vice versa. As Guimarães argues (in this volume), a racial classificatory binary can coexist with multiple other categories of identity. Still, one can see the political effects of relying on one emphasis more than the other. In Colombia, the effect of Law 70 in limiting the whole issue of blackness to the Pacific coastal region has been evident.

However, a more ethnic-cultural emphasis – and the modelling of black rights after indigenous rights which it often entrains – while constrictive at first sight is not as simple as it seems. French argues that, in Brazil, the flexibility with which the same people can opt to make claims as indigenous or as black works to open up options.[41] Both options rely on an ethnic-cultural emphasis, but they multiply the overall possibilities for engagement and mobilisation. Taking a different tack – which also nuances the difference between Hooker's first and second categories – Anderson thinks that, for Honduras, a discourse of ethnic rootedness can coexist quite easily with a discourse of urban cosmopolitan blackness.[42] Again, more options are better than fewer.

The Colombian and Brazilian cases indicate that a focus on cultural difference and ethnic distinctiveness may be useful in the struggle for local land rights, but it is also necessary to complement this with a focus on racism (as it affects housing, employment and aesthetics). If Law 70 had closed down the debate and restricted

[41] French, *Legalizing Identities*.
[42] Anderson, *Black and Indigenous*.

it only to land rights in the Pacific coastal region, this would have been a negative effect. In fact, it arguably opened up new horizons for talking about blackness in other, more inclusive ways, which begin to converge with a Brazilian-style discourse about blackness.

Whether Colombia should follow Brazil towards racial quotas as a mechanism to address racism is a more difficult question. Quotas seem to have a positive effect in publicising and naming the problem of racial inequality, but it is also the case that many black Brazilian students want to avoid using racial quotas, because they suggest the student unfairly obtained a university place and is not up to scratch academically. The same students are much less allergic to public school quotas, which preferentially admit students from public schools, and which should carry the same stigma as the racial quotas. This seems to suggest that (a) the fact of being black and thus subject to racism is not seen as worthy of reparation, compared to the fact of having been poor and only able to attend public school, and (b) it is the possibility of being *identified* by skin colour as the beneficiary of a racial quota that makes the students uncomfortable. Both suggestions indicate that quotas are actually needed in order to force into the open discussions about the moral worthiness of racially oriented reparation.

In Colombia, thus far, affirmative actions have not caused controversy. They have consisted of small-scale and assistentialist measures (special grants and places are available to black students, but there are no quotas to fill, which *looks* less ‘unfair’ towards non-blacks) and/or they have comprised indirect actions, which target whole regions, rather than individuals. My hunch is that Colombia’s convergence with Brazil will stop short of the kind of quota systems that have been put in place there. There is no indication that Colombia’s political elites will take this kind of (apparently) radical action; instead it seems likely that they will prefer less controversial and more tokenistic measures.

3

Racism: An Evolving Virus

JORGE VALA AND CÍCERO PEREIRA[1]

THIS CHAPTER PRESENTS A SERIES OF HYPOTHESES and empirical results associated with some questions that have guided our research into racial beliefs and racial prejudice: first, does it make sense to talk about racism in contemporary democratic societies? Secondly, if it does, how is it possible to explain the durability of racial prejudice and discrimination based on belief in the idea of race in formally anti-racist democratic societies? And thirdly, what possible peculiarities are displayed by social attitudes in Portugal in relation to people who are seen to belong to different racial or cultural groups?

We will attempt to answer these questions by revisiting some of the results of our previous studies and by presenting new empirical evidence that supports the hypothesis that we have developed: namely, that racist beliefs and racial prejudice persist and are publicly expressed in contexts in which the anti-racism norm is not prominent, or in which processes of legitimisation are invoked and preserve a self-concept defined as non-prejudiced. We are thereby adopting a psychosocial level of analysis rooted in social representations, inter-group relations, legitimating and normative principles, and self-concept construal.

We begin by briefly presenting an overview of psychosociological research into racism in the USA and in Europe. It is within this context that we situate our own investigation, carried out in Portugal, the main analytical lines of which are described in the second part of the chapter. In the third part, we present new data that allow better understanding of the evolution of racial prejudice in Europe and in Portugal within the context of migratory processes. Finally, adopting a psychosociological analytical framework, we present new empirical evidence of the evolution of racial beliefs and their impact on attitudes to immigrants and to black people.

[1] This research was partially supported by a grant from the Fundação para a Ciência e Tecnologia awarded to the first author (PTDC/PSI/69009/2006). We would like to thank Rui Costa-Lopes and Denis Sindic for comments on an earlier draft of this manuscript.

Restructuration of racial beliefs and racial prejudice in the post-war period

In the 1990s, a series of studies published in the USA revealed that negative attitudes towards black people were decreasing significantly.[2] Thirty years after the struggle for civil rights and the institutionalisation of equal rights between whites and blacks in the USA, it was becoming clear that beliefs, stereotypes and negative attitudes towards black people were changing.

It was also in the 1990s that a theoretically oriented analysis of the results of the 1988/Autumn Eurobarometer, by Pettigrew and colleagues, revealed that Europeans had rearranged their beliefs concerning immigrants (Turks in Germany; North Africans and Asians in France; Surinamese and Turks in the Netherlands; West Indians and Asians in Great Britain).[3] These beliefs were structured into a single pattern that opposed traditional or *blatant racial prejudice* (i.e. attribution of racial inferiority and expression of the feeling that the 'purity of the ingroup' is under threat) in favour of a more *subtle racial prejudice* rooted in a belief in the cultural inferiority of immigrants from countries perceived to be ethnically different (the highlighting of cultural differences; the attribution to these groups of inferior values and skills to those of Europeans). At the same time, the results of the research of Pettigrew and Meertens showed that the interviewees in the four European countries expressed more *subtle racial prejudice* than *blatant racial prejudice*, the latter corresponding to common-sense appropriations and transformations of ideas diffused by the so-called scientific or biological racism and by formalised racist ideology.

These European findings came in the wake of studies in the USA which, since the 1980s, had shown that racial prejudice based on beliefs in biological inferiority were becoming reoriented towards beliefs in cultural inferiority.[4] In fact, these studies showed that a new type of anti-black prejudice was emerging, based on the belief that blacks did not share the values of meritocratic individualism and threatened the 'cherished values' on which American success was founded. Significantly, these new types of belief were seen not as prejudice but as legitimate reasons for maintaining a social distance with respect to black people.

[2] J. F. Dovidio and S. L. Gaertner, 'Aversive Racism', in M. P. Zanna (ed.), *Advances in Experimental Social Psychology* (San Diego, CA: Academic, 2004), vol. 36, pp. 1–51; R. Brown, *Prejudice* (Oxford: Blackwell, 1995).

[3] T. F. Pettigrew and R. W. Meertens, 'Subtle and Blatant Prejudice in Western Europe', *European Journal of Social Psychology* 25 (1995), pp. 57–75; T. F. Pettigrew *et al.*, 'Outgroup Prejudice in Western Europe', *European Review of Social Psychology* 8 (1997), pp. 241–73.

[4] D. R. Kinder and D. O. Sears, 'Prejudice and Politics: Symbolic Racism versus Racial Threats to the Good Life', *Journal of Personality and Social Psychology* 40 (1981), pp. 414–31; D. O. Sears and P. J. Henry, 'The Origins of Symbolic Racism', *Journal of Personality and Social Psychology* 85 (2003), pp. 259–75; J. B. McConahay and J. C. Hough, 'Symbolic Racism', *Journal of Social Issues* 32 (1976), pp. 23–45.

How can this rearrangement of the bases of racial prejudice and its public expression be explained? We believe that a normative explanation, as proposed by Pettigrew, could provide clarification.[5] In fact, after the Second World War and the confrontation with the consequences of racist ideology, it was difficult to defend biological racism and its justifications publicly. It is true that the apartheid regime in South Africa was founded after the Second World War, in 1948, and that twenty long years, dominated by protests and struggle, passed between the end of the war and the passing of the Civil Rights Act (1964) and the Voting Rights Act (1965) in the United States. But it is also true that these struggles and the legislative changes to which they gave rise progressively created an anti-racist social norm whose impact on individual and collective attitudes is, in our opinion, demonstrated by the aforementioned studies.

Individuals' relationships with social norms can assume different modalities. Using a typology proposed by Pettigrew and Meertens, and inspired by Kelman's ideas on normative social influence, we would say that these modalities can be designated as: rejection, compliance, and interiorisation of the norms.[6] Thus, the expression of traditional blatant racism would correspond to the rejection of the anti-racism norm, while the expression of subtle or cultural racism would imply a formal acceptance of that norm accompanied by hidden expressions of racial prejudice which do not involve self-identification as a prejudiced person. Only egalitarianism (rejection of cultural and traditional racism) would correspond to the interiorisation of the anti-racism norm. The transformation of biological racism into cultural racism would thereby grant continuity to basic racist beliefs without the anti-racism norm being questioned.

The possibility that biologically based racism might be transformed into culturally based racism was raised by Lévi-Strauss[7] and has given rise to an extensive range of literature that is historical,[8] theoretical-reflexive,[9] or more empirical.[10] It is in the context of this debate that the expressions 'new racisms' or

[5] T. F. Pettigrew, 'Normative Theory in Intergroup Relations: Explaining Both Harmony and Conflict', *Psychology and Developing Societies* 3 (1991), pp. 3–16.

[6] Pettigrew and Meertens, 'Subtle and Blatant Prejudice'; H. C. Kelman, 'Two Phases of Behavior Change', *Journal of Social Issues* 8 (1952), pp. 81–8.

[7] C. Lévi-Strauss, *Race and History* (Paris: UNESCO, 1958); C. Lévi-Strauss, 'Préface', in L. Frois (ed.), *Européens et Japonais* (Paris: Chandeigne, 1998).

[8] E.g. G. M. Fredrickson, *Racism: A Short History* (Princeton: Princeton University Press, 2002).

[9] E.g. M. Wieviorka, *Le racism: Une introduction* (Paris: La Découverte, 1998); M. Barker, *The New Racism* (London: Junction Books, 1981).

[10] Pettigrew and Meertens, 'Subtle and Blatant Prejudice'; I. Walker, 'The Changing Nature of Racism: From Old to New?', in M. Augoustinos and K. J. Reynolds (eds), *Understanding Prejudice, Racism, and Social Conflict* (London: Sage, 2001), pp. 24–42; Jorge Vala, C. Pereira and R. Costa-Lopes, 'Is the Attribution of Cultural Differences to Minorities an Expression of Racial Prejudice?', *International Journal of Psychology* 44 (2009), pp. 20–8.

'new expressions of racism' were coined.[11] 'New racism' refers to a phenomenon that is highly complex because it is manifested indirectly and ubiquitously and because it involves different behaviours and beliefs which have at least two characteristics in common: they are not perceived as being anti-normative, and they imply more than 'ethnocentrism' or the simple glorification of the ingroup. 'New racism' evokes a series of diffuse beliefs and sentiments that involve the perception of 'profound differences between human groups', the 'essential' nature of these differences and a belief in the hierarchised organisation of human groups. While these beliefs are ever more ubiquitous, they are not inevitable. As was stated above, the prominence of the anti-racism norm could reduce their expression.

But just as social contexts that affirm egalitarian values, the basis of anti-racism, can reduce prejudice, so the expression of racism can increase in social contexts in which values promoting a hierarchical organisation of people in society prevail, such as meritocratic individualism. This hypothesis follows one of the central arguments in Gunnar Myrdal's 1944 study, *An American Dilemma*.[12] In fact, the tension between the values of egalitarianism and meritocracy was first stated by Myrdal in his analysis of racism in the USA. Myrdal analysed racism in the context of the conflict between a belief in humanistic egalitarianism, the pressure of personal interests, and the belief in meritocratic individualism. According to Myrdal, the 'American Dilemma' was that, even though the USA promoted humanistic egalitarianism, racism was still frequent because of the importance of meritocratic individualism. Later, Katz and Hass developed the hypothesis that the tension between egalitarianism and meritocratic individualism was the foundation for ambivalent attitudes towards black people in the USA, and showed that, when egalitarianism is prominent in a given social context, people express less or no racism; however, when the values of meritocratic individualism, associated with the legitimacy of social hierarchies, are prominent, then racist beliefs are expressed more easily.[13] Moreover, as Schwartz would show, the conflict between the values of egalitarianism and meritocracy and power is not specific to American society, and those values may therefore be relevant in explaining racism in other social and cultural contexts, as shown by several authors in a wide range of national contexts.[14]

[11] E.g. Vala *et al.*, 'Is the Attribution of Cultural Differences to Minorities an Expression of Racial Prejudice?'

[12] G. Myrdal, *An American Dilemma: The Negro Problem and Modern Democracy* (New York: Harper & Bros., 1944).

[13] I. Katz and R. G. Hass, 'Racial Ambivalence and American Value Conflict: Correlational and Priming Studies of Dual Cognitive Structures', *Journal of Personality and Social Psychology* 55 (1988), pp. 893–905.

[14] S. Schwartz, 'Value Priorities and Behavior: Applying a Theory of Integrated Value Systems', in C. Seligman *et al.* (eds), *The Psychology of Values: The Ontario Symposium* (Mahwah, NJ: Lawrence Erlbaum Associates, 1996), vol. 8, pp. 1–24; see also D. Spini and W. Doise, 'Organizing Principles of Involvement in Human Rights and Their Social Anchoring in Value Priorities', *European Journal of Social Psychology* 28 (1998), pp. 603–22; Jorge Vala *et al.*, 'Social Values, Prejudice and Solidarity

cont.

Racial prejudice in Portugal: analytical paths

It was in the theoretical context just described that, in 1995, we began a research programme whose initial results were published four years later.[15] Surprised by the fact that, at the time, the social sciences in Portugal had not yet produced systematic analyses of expressions of racism in the country, specifically with regard to immigration from the ex-colonies and the widespread manifestation of opposition to this immigration, we outlined a research project that aimed to diagnose and identify the correlates of racism and racial prejudice in Portugal. In the meantime this research project was extended, and the new working hypotheses to which it gave rise now assumed a much broader scope that is not confined to the Portuguese socio-political context.

The correlational empirical research on which our project was based allowed us to conclude that racial prejudice towards black people was framed in Portugal in accordance with the same patterns of beliefs that Pettigrew and Meertens had described for other European countries (Germany, the United Kingdom, France and the Netherlands).[16] In other words, there was a *blatant* model, rooted in biological racism, and a so-called *subtle* model associated with cultural differentiation. The oft-invoked conjecture that the racial attitudes of the Portuguese displayed a certain particularism or specificity was not supported.

The examination of the factors underlying the patterns of racial prejudice revealed that its relationship with individual economic income was very weak. It was also shown that levels of education were found to correlate with blatant prejudice but not with subtle prejudice. We interpreted this result as stemming from the greater ability of more educated people to identify blatant prejudice as being anti-normative.

The examination of the correlates of these two types of prejudice (*blatant* and *subtle*) also revealed that the key underlying psychosociological factors are the feeling of negative interdependence between whites and blacks, racial identity, and moral conservatism.[17] The importance of perceptions of negative interdependence associated with feelings of threat, as well as identity-related factors, in the origin of racial prejudice is not surprising as these findings are in line with current results

in the European Union', in W. Arts and L. Halman (eds), *European Values at the End of the Millennium* (Leiden: Brill, 2004), pp. 139–63; A. Ramos and J. Vala, 'Predicting Opposition towards Immigration: Economic Resources, Social Resources and Moral Principles', in A. Gari and K. Mylonas (eds), *Quod Erat Demonstrandum: From Herodotus' Ethnographic Journeys to Cross-Cultural Research* (Athens: Pedio Books, 2009), pp. 245–64; C. Pereira *et al.*, 'From Infra-Humanization to Discrimination: The Mediation of Symbolic Threat Needs Egalitarian Norms', *Journal of Experimental Social Psychology* 45 (2009), pp. 336–44.

[15] Jorge Vala, R. Brito and D. Lopes, *Expressões dos Racismos em Portugal* (Lisbon: Imprensa de Ciências Sociais, 1999).

[16] Pettigrew and Meertens, 'Subtle and Blatant Prejudice'.

[17] These conclusions are based on results of a multiple regression model, and therefore the effect of each variable is controlled for the whole set of variables included in the model.

obtained in other countries.[18] However, the prominence of 'moral conservatism' (independently of 'political conservatism' and political identification) as a facilitator of prejudice does constitute a surprise, which calls for a revisiting of the studies carried out by Adorno and his colleagues in the United States.[19]

Moreover, as we know, a significant correlation between right/left-wing identification and racial prejudice has been confirmed in the majority of European countries,[20] although in Portugal this correlation has not been consistently found. In fact, while the first sets of data collected in Portugal (in 1995) did not show any significant correlation between right/left-wing identification and racial prejudice, and while the same was true of data gathered in 1999,[21] this phenomenon has nevertheless undergone changes. In fact, while data collected in 2002 continued to show that racial prejudice in Portugal did not clearly correlate with right/left-wing identification, the perception that immigrants constitute a threat in symbolic and economic domains showed a significant correlation with political identification.[22] We believe that the political and public debate on immigration that has begun in the meantime is now leading, in Portugal, to the construction of the traditional ideological pattern in which right and left occupy opposing positions with regard to immigration, xenophobia, and racial prejudice.

Where the predictors of racial prejudice are concerned, we were also surprised by the absence in our first research of any significant correlation between prejudice and national identification in Portugal. This fact, which we have frequently identified in subsequent studies, led us to explore the possibility of an implicit association between national identification and lusotropicalistic ideology, and the likelihood that this association constitutes a buffer to the expression of traditional racism, but not to cultural, or more veiled, racism.[23]

From hetero-ethnicisation to racial beliefs

> For white people, the black man is a saint or a devil, moving from innocence to wickedness without passing through the human.
>
> Andaré, in Mia Couto's *Vinte e Zinco*

Particularly stimulating for the understanding of contemporary racial prejudice was the fact that the data from our first investigation allowed us to maintain that the

[18] Pettigrew *et al.*, 'Outgroup Prejudice in Western Europe'.

[19] T. W. Adorno *et al.*, *The Authoritarian Personality* (New York: Harper and Row, 1950).

[20] E.g. Pettigrew and Meertens, 'Subtle and Blatant Prejudice'.

[21] Vala *et al.*, 'Social Values, Prejudice and Solidarity'.

[22] Jorge Vala, C. Pereira and A. Ramos, 'Racial Prejudice, Threat Perception and Opposition to Immigration: A Comparative Analysis', *Portuguese Journal of Social Sciences* 5 (2006), pp. 119–40.

[23] Jorge Vala, D. Lopes and M. Lima, 'Black Immigrants in Portugal: Luso-Tropicalism and Prejudice', *Journal of Social Issues* 64 (2008), pp. 287–302. A new theoretical approach to this problem was recently proposed in a study on national identity and attitudes to social exclusion, by Jorge Vala *et al.*, 'Atitudes Face à Imigração e Identidade Nacional', in J. Sobral and J. Vala (eds), *Identidade nacional: Inclusão e exclusão* (Lisbon: Imprensa de Ciências Sociais, 2010), pp. 191–210.

mere perception of strong cultural differences between a national ingroup (for example, the Portuguese) and an outgroup that has been the subject of explicit racial inferiorisation constitutes an indirect manifestation of racial prejudice. In other words, the attribution of cultural differences to a group that has been racialised in the past is not an antecedent of prejudice against this group, as traditionally proposed, but an expression of prejudice. We have named this expression of prejudice *hetero-ethnicisation*. Several studies that we have led have shown that the simple attribution of cultural differences in important areas of life strongly correlates with traditional racism, with explicit cultural inferiorisation and orientation to behavioural discrimination. More importantly, our studies have also shown that black people's meta-perceptions that they are seen as culturally different correlate with the expression of feelings of discrimination.[24] These results led us to study the relationship between *hetero-ethnicisation*, and *ontologisation* and *infra-humanisation*.

Ontologisation was defined by Moscovici and Pérez as the attribution to members of an outgroup (for example, black people) of more personological traits that evoke nature (e.g. intuitive, spontaneous) than traits that evoke culture (e.g. honest, creative, intelligent).[25] This categorisation of personological traits into *cultural* vs. *natural* is implicit; it is consistently found in Western languages and is recurrently used in daily life. Moreover, it acquires a strong sense of latent inferiorisation when it is used in the context of relations between social groups, namely, when a dominant ingroup opposes an outgroup that has been racially inferiorised in the past.[26]

In turn, Leyens and colleagues studied a very particular, and also veiled, form of group inferiorisation within the plane of the emotions.[27] They call this *infra-humanisation*. In fact, they verified that common sense distinguishes between primary emotions (e.g. contentment, excitement, anger, irritation) and secondary emotions or feelings (e.g. compassion, hope, bitterness, regret); and they also showed that while primary emotions are attributed both to humans and to animals, secondary emotions or feelings are considered to be exclusively human. The results of studies carried out in very different countries have confirmed that people attribute greater ability to express (negative or positive) secondary emotions to their group than they do to other groups, particularly racialised outgroups.

Following the hypotheses of the studies that we have just mentioned, recent work (see Figure 3.1) carried out in Portugal has shown that the representation of

[24] Vala *et al.*, 'Black Immigrants in Portugal'.

[25] S. Moscovici and J. A. Pérez, 'Prejudice and Social Representations', *Papers on Social Representations* 6 (1997), pp. 27–36.

[26] J. A. Pérez *et al.*, 'The Taboo Against Group Contact: Hypothesis of Gypsy Ontologization', *British Journal of Social Psychology* 46 (2007), pp. 249–72.

[27] J.-P. Leyens *et al.*, 'The Emotional Side of Prejudice: The Attribution of Secondary Emotions to In-Groups and Out-Groups', *Personality and Social Psychology Review* 4 (2000), pp. 186–97; Pereira *et al.*, 'From Infra-Humanization to Discrimination'.

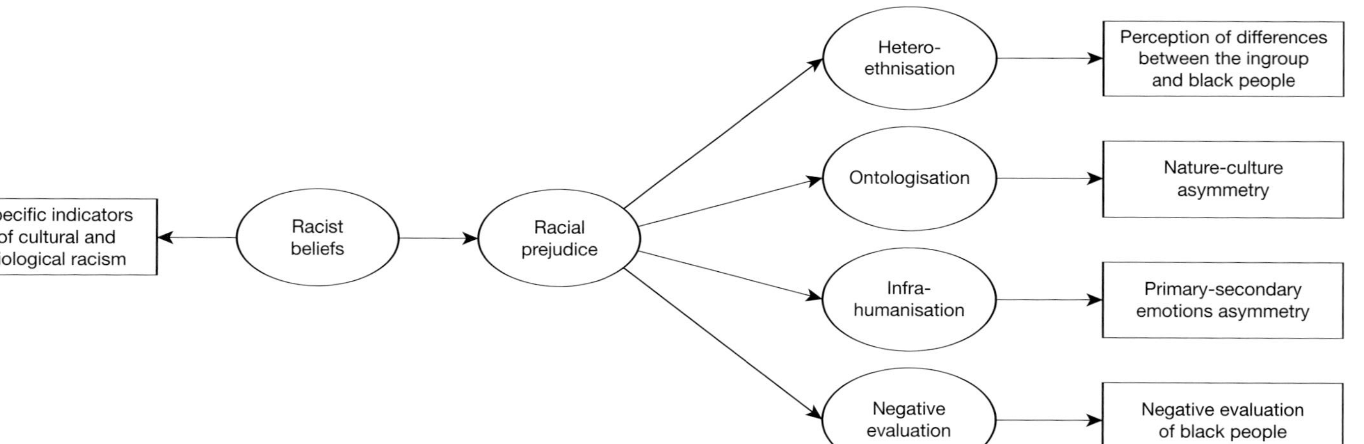

Figure 3.1. Structural relations between racist beliefs and dimensions of racial prejudice

black people involves not only hetero-ethnicisation but also ontologisation and infra-humanisation.[28] It shows how, in an indirect way, when black people are implicitly represented as being culturally different and inferior they are also seen as being closer to nature than to culture; less capable of expressing specifically human emotions (secondary emotions); and are more negatively evaluated. Our results also show that these perceptions constitute a 'latent factor' of racial prejudice. More importantly, this latent factor is predicted by explicit racial beliefs associated with biological and cultural racism.[29]

This analytical path and the empirical studies carried out show not only the ubiquity of contemporary racism but also the diversity of its explicit and veiled expressions.[30] The non-apparent racist nature of many of these expressions proves that the anti-racism norm is effective and that many people are genuinely concerned with the construction of a non-prejudiced self-concept.[31] On the other hand, the series of studies presented also shows that racism has moved from the biological plane to the plane of culture.[32] These transformations in racial beliefs imply clarifications to which the following point aims to contribute.

A conceptual statement

In contemporary societies, diverse modalities of racism coexist. Is it possible to identify some theoretical principles underlying the diversity of the phenomenon and, simultaneously, to distinguish it from racial prejudice? Indeed, definitions of racism in the plane of social representations or collective beliefs are more ambiguous, less consensual and thus more problematic than the definition of racial prejudice. In fact, with very few exceptions,[33] most studies have conceptualised and operationalised

[28] Vala *et al.*, 'Is the Attribution of Cultural Differences to Minorities an Expression of Racial Prejudice?'

[29] Figure 3.1 is a highly simplified presentation of the test of a model based on Structural Equation Modelling; see R. B. Kline, *Principles and Practices of Structural Equation Modelling* (New York: Guilford, 1998). The results indicate that this model fits very well to the data and that it is better than alternative theoretical models.

[30] Several empirical studies carried out in Portugal have contributed to explore this perspective deeply; see e.g. R. Cabecinhas, *Preto e Branco: A naturalização da discriminação racial* (Porto: Campo das Letras, 2007); M. F. M. Mendes, *Imigração, identidades e discriminação: Imigrantes russos e ucranianos na área metropolitana de Lisboa* (Lisbon: Imprensa de Ciências Sociais, 2010).

[31] M. B. Monteiro *et al.*, 'The Development of Intergroup Bias in Childhood: How Social Norms Can Shape Children's Racial Behaviours', *International Journal of Psychology* 44 (2009), pp. 29–39.

[32] For a discussion of the subject see, among others, P. A. Taguieff, *La force du préjugé: Essai sur le racism et ses doubles* (Paris: Éditions La Découverte, 1987); Fredrickson, *Racism*; and Barker, *The New Racism*. For a critical position on this hypothesis, see F. L. Machado, 'Contextos e percepções de racismo no quotidiano', *Sociologia Problemas e Práticas* 36 (2001), pp. 53–80; and P. M. Sniderman and P. E. Tetlock, 'Symbolic Racism: Problems of Motive Attribution in Political Analysis', *Journal of Social Issues* 42 (1986), pp. 129–50.

[33] E.g. D. Operario and S. T. Fiske, 'Racism Equals Power plus Prejudice: A Social Psychological Equation for Racial Oppression', in J. L. Eberhardt and S. T. Fiske (eds), *Confronting Racism: The Problem and the Response* (Thousand Oaks, CA: Sage, 1998), pp. 33–53.

racism as a set of negative beliefs and attitudes against black people (or other specific outgroups), that is to say, racism has been studied as a particular example of prejudice (a negative evaluation against a specific target).[34] We propose a distinction between racism and prejudice or racial prejudice, specifying that the former is not a simple negative evaluation of a specific target-group, although it may be related to negative attitudes (racial prejudice) toward outgroups. We propose racism as a general representation about the nature of humanity based on the following core aspects:[35] categorisation (belief that humanity is organised into racial or ethnic groups); differentiation (belief that the people categorised into groups are deeply different); hierarchy (belief that some groups perceived as different are better than others); essentialisation (belief that perceived differences between people categorised into groups are fixed, natural and immutable); 'radical-alterity' (belief that not all groups have the typical 'human essences'). We also propose that racism can be organised in two dimensions: biological racism – when people organise their representation of humanity based on the idea of 'race', that is to say, that human beings can be categorised into racial groups; and cultural racism (or ethnicism) – when people organise their representation of humanity based on the idea of 'ethnicity' (i.e. that human beings can be categorised into ethnic groups).

A study inspired by this conception of racism will be presented later. However, in order to contextualise that study, we will now offer a longitudinal analysis of European attitudes towards immigrants perceived as belonging to a different ethnic group.

Attitudes of Europeans towards immigration of people perceived as ethnically different, 2002–10

The data that we have presented so far refer to published studies and aim to show the different dimensions of racial prejudice and its connection to racist beliefs in Portugal, as well as the significant parallel that exists between the structural organisation of racial prejudice in Portugal and the structure that exists in some other European countries.

The question to which we now turn concerns the way that racial prejudice has changed (or not) in Portugal and Europe as a whole. We do not have data of sufficient quality to allow us to answer this question directly. However, to address this issue, albeit indirectly, we can make use of the European Social Survey (ESS) data.[36] In fact, the analysis of the ESS indicator regarding opposition to immigration

[34] This was the theoretical orientation adopted in our research published in 1999. The current chapter is based on a very different conceptual approach.

[35] See Fredrickson, *Racism*, for a historical approach.

[36] The European Social Survey (ESS) is a biennial study of social attitudes which is academically oriented and based on probabilistic samples and highly rigorous methodologies. This makes it different from other European surveys and has made this open database a reliable source for academic researchers.

cont.

in European countries by people perceived as belonging to 'a different race or ethnic group' could constitute a proxy for discrimination based on race or ethnicity. In addition, the fact that we can compare results obtained in Portugal with those from other countries allows us to test once again our hypothesis concerning the non-specific nature of racial prejudice in Portugal.

Opposition to immigration

As can be seen in Table 3.1, the different European countries that participate in the ESS express moderate opposition to immigration, contrary to the message that is habitually circulated in the media. Greece and Hungary are the countries that most openly express opposition to immigration, and Sweden is the country that expresses least opposition.[37]

From a longitudinal point of view, small changes occurred between 2002 and 2010, and the response pattern was maintained. If we compare the countries present in all of the rounds with the answers involving all of the countries, regardless of their involvement in a given wave, we can also confirm that the response pattern is maintained.

In Figure 3.2, we compare Portugal with Europe as a whole, taking 'Europe' to mean the European countries involved in all of the rounds. The results show greater opposition to immigration in Portugal than in these countries taken together. These differences are statistically significant despite the fact that the *effect size* is small. In other words, although a tendency towards greater opposition to immigration is found in Portugal, it lies within the same response pattern as that of the group of 'European' countries. It should also be noted that throughout the decade (2002–10) anti-immigration attitudes remained steady, even after the financial crisis broke out in September 2008.[38]

Immigration and economic and cultural threat perceptions

The literature has shown that threat perception, specifically the perception of economic threat and the threat to cultural identity, underlies negative attitudes to immigration.[39]

The study involves a minimum of 1,500 statistically valid interviews in each country. The questions are designed by experts in their respective fields and the data collected are subject to a demanding validation plan. The ESS began in 2000, and the first wave of data was collected in 2002. At that time, as now, the debate on immigration was highly contentious. For this reason, it was a central topic in the first edition of the ESS. Some of the questions asked in 2002 were incorporated into subsequent ESS waves (2004, 2006, 2008).

[37] The indicator is the following: 'To what extent do you think [country] should allow people of a different race or ethnic group from most [country] people?' 1. Allow many to come and live here; 2. Allow some; 3. Allow few; 4. Allow none.

[38] The 2008 data were collected between September 2008 and February 2009.

[39] V. M. Esses *et al.*, 'The Immigration Dilemma: The Role of Perceived Group Competition, Ethnic Prejudice, and National Identity', *Journal of Social Issues* 57 (2001), pp. 389–412; Vala *et al.*, 'Racial Prejudice, Threat Perception and Opposition to Immigration'.

Table 3.1. Opposition to immigration of people perceived as belonging to a different ethnic group (ESS data)

Countries	*2002*	*2004*	*2006*	*2008*	*2010*
Austria	2.69	2.54	2.64		
Belgium	2.52	2.59	2.50	2.44	2.58
Bulgaria			2.38	2.18	2.17
Switzerland	2.27	2.36	2.40	2.32	2.35
Czech Republic	2.60	2.74		2.79	2.84
Cyprus			3.17	3.17	
Germany	2.40	2.57	2.54	2.27	2.31
Denmark	2.49	2.54	2.44	2.38	2.29
Estonia		2.87	2.85	2.72	2.65
Spain	2.42	2.43	2.58	2.67	2.56
Finland	2.66	2.65	2.62	2.52	2.67
France	2.53	2.55	2.51	2.45	2.47
United Kingdom	2.61	2.53	2.63	2.55	2.62
Greece	3.12	3.08		3.12	
Hungary	3.06	3.01	3.16	3.11	3.06
Ireland	2.32	2.32	2.26		
Luxembourg	2.65	2.68			
Netherlands	2.45	2.53	2.54	2.32	2.36
Norway	2.41	2.39	2.35	2.27	2.25
Poland	2.44	2.34	2.16	2.12	2.11
Portugal	2.83	2.92	2.94	2.85	2.82
Sweden	1.93	1.91	1.85	1.81	1.75
Slovenia	2.49	2.46	2.50	2.40	2.39
Slovakia		2.34	2.34	2.45	
Total	2.49	2.58	2.57	2.56	2.50
Europe*	2.49	2.52	2.52	2.42	2.44

* Only countries that have participated in all rounds: Belgium, Switzerland, Germany, Denmark, Spain, Finland, France, United Kingdom, Hungary, Netherlands, Norway, Poland, Portugal, Sweden, Slovenia.

But if the association between economic threat perception and negative attitudes towards immigration is an old one in the common sense, the association between cultural threat and immigration is more recent. This association has been reinforced by the Islamist attacks on the USA of 11 September 2001, and diffused by the media. But in so-called 'cultivated' thought, too, this association is an object of dissemination. For instance, Huntington, after the 'Clash of Civilizations' in 1996, published a book on the 'challenges to the American national identity' in which he presents Latin American immigration as a force against the 'American credo'.[40] In this vein, we will now assess the impact of threat perceptions on attitudes to immigration. To do so, we begin by describing the prominence of threat perceptions.

[40] S. P. Huntington, *Who Are We? The Challenges to America's National Identity* (New York: Simon and Schuster, 2004).

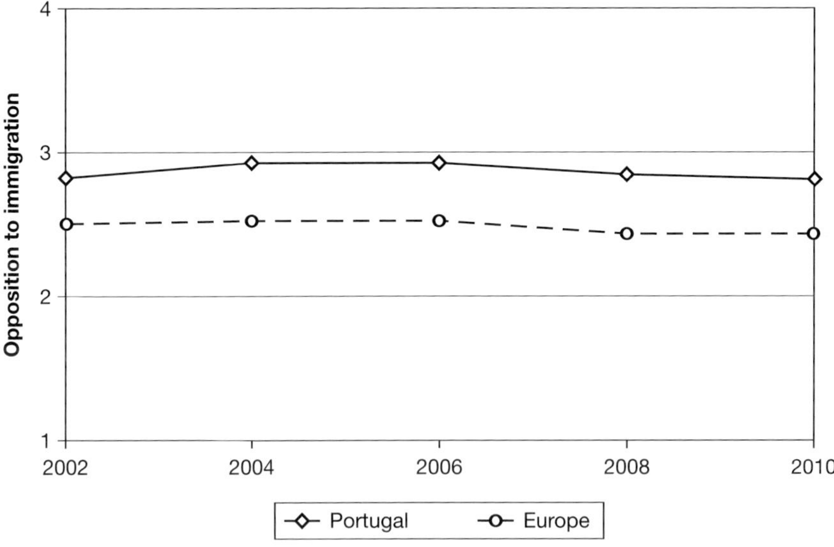

Figure 3.2. Opposition to immigration of people perceived as belonging to a different ethnic group in Portugal and in Europe as a whole

Figure 3.3 compares the degree of perception of economic threat in Portugal and in Europe as a whole.[41] We therefore confirm that the response patterns are similar and that they lie above the mid-point on the scale.[42]

With regard to the cultural threat attributed to immigrants,[43] it is much lower than the perception of economic threat, but reaches slightly higher values in Portugal than in the other European countries that participated in all rounds of the ESS (see Figure 3.4).

We can now take a new step in the analysis, exploring the hypothesis that threat perception is an important factor that underlies the expression of opposition to the immigration of people perceived as being racially or ethnically different. The data presented in Table 3.2 show very clearly that threat perception is much more

[41] The indicator of economic threat is the following: 'Would you say it is generally bad or good for [country]'s economy that people come to live here from other countries?' 0 – Bad for the economy; 10 – Good for the economy.

[42] The response means lie significantly above the mid-point on the scale ($p < .001$). In this part of the chapter, when we state that the differences are significant, we are taking as a reference point the $p < .001$. Due to the size of the samples one should devote more attention to the value of the *effect size*. In this case, despite the fact that the threat perception attributed to immigrants in Portugal is statistically higher than in other European countries, the value of the *effect size* is small and we can consider that, in social terms, we are faced with very similar values of economic threat in Portugal and in the other European countries.

[43] Indicator of cultural threat: 'Would you say that [country]'s cultural life is generally undermined or enriched by people coming to live here from other countries?' 0 – Cultural life undermined; 10 – Cultural life enriched.

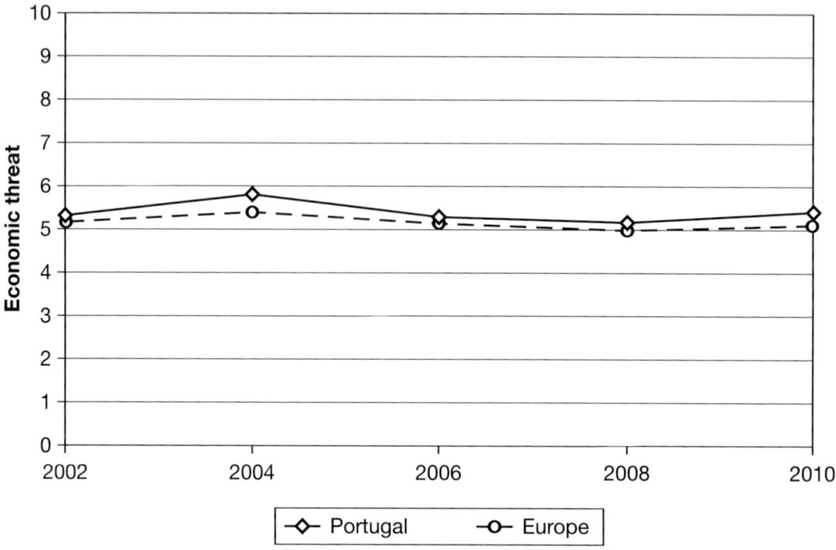

Figure 3.3. Perception of immigration of people perceived as belonging to a different ethnic group as an economic threat in Portugal and in Europe as a whole

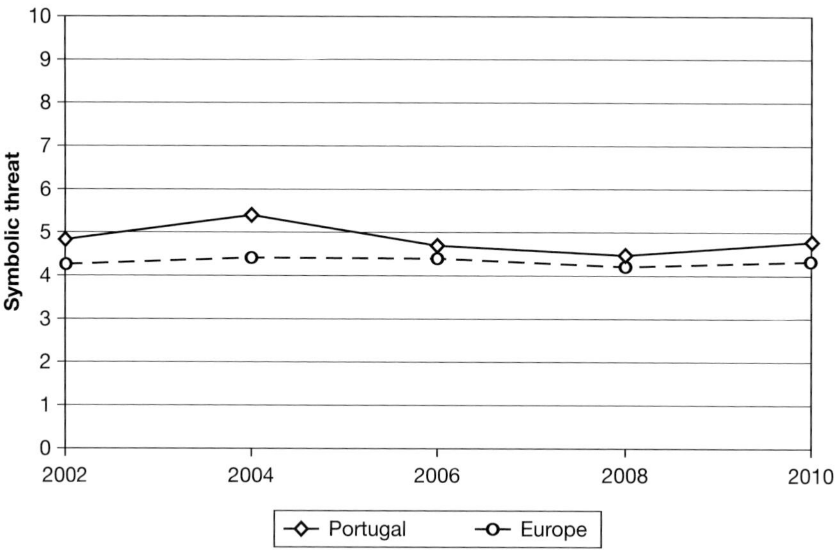

Figure 3.4. Perception of immigration of people perceived as belonging to a different ethnic group as a cultural threat in Portugal and in Europe as a whole

Table 3.2. Predictors of opposition to immigration of people perceived as belonging to a different ethnic group (for Portugal and Europe as a whole)

	2002		2004		2006		2008		2010	
Predictors	*PT*	*Europe*	*PT*	*Europe*	*PT*	*Europe*	*PT*	*Europe*	*PT*	*Europe*
Control variables										
Gender	.03	.02*	–.04	.00	–.03	.00	–.03	.01	.01	.01
Age	.07	.09*	.07	.08*	.02	.09*	.06	.08*	.07	.09*
Education	–.08	–.11*	–.02	–.08*	–.11*	–.09*	–.08	–.09*	–.14*	–.09*
Left–right	.07	–.09*	.02	.07*	.04	.07*	.02	.07*	–.02	.07*
Threat perceptions										
Economic threat	.27*	.27*	.37*	.31*	.37*	.33*	.28*	.33*	.38*	.32*
Cultural threat	.24*	.26*	.22*	.29*	.19*	.26*	.27*	.27*	.13*	.28*
R^2 Adjusted	.26*	.30*	.30*	.35*	.30*	.35*	.29*	.36*	.27*	.36*

Standardised regression coefficients (Betas). Gender (0 = female; 1 = male). Education = years of full-time education completed. Left-right = 0 (left) to 10 (right).
*p < .001.

important in determining oppositional attitudes to immigration than educational level, age or political identification.[44] These results occur in Portugal and in Europe (as a whole) and reveal a considerable degree of stability throughout the decade. It was within the framework of these conclusions that Pereira and co-authors proposed and showed that threat perception is a factor that legitimates discrimination against immigrants and facilitates the transition from prejudiced feelings to discriminatory action.[45]

In sum, the series of data presented reveal that Europeans' opposition to immigration of people perceived as being ethnically different is not as high as is frequently stated. They also establish that economic and cultural threat perceptions are important predictors of opposition to immigration, particularly as far as economic threat is concerned. Although many studies in different countries have shown the need for immigrants and their relevant contribution to the economy,[46] the threat perception associated with immigration is confirmed as one of the most important factors in determining oppositional attitudes to immigration and the legitimisation of this opposition.

The increase in immigration classified as illegal, discussions concerning it in social communication, and political measures taken to prevent immigration have created the social ambience to expand and renovate racist beliefs and their veiled or manifest expression. The next section in this chapter analyses this hypothesis within the framework of the assumptions about the conceptualisation of racial beliefs stated above.

Racist beliefs, anti-black racism and opposition to immigration

In a study carried out by the European Community in 2008 on discrimination experienced by so-called ethnic minorities, it was found that the Roma reported the most episodes of discrimination, followed by sub-Saharan Africans.[47] These

[44] A recent study shows that threat perception remains an important predictor of opposition to immigration, even when socio-cultural factors such as the number of immigrants, the increase in immigration flows, and legislation on immigration are included in a *multilevel analysis*: A. Ramos, J. Vala and C. Pereira, 'Racial Prejudice and Opposition to Anti-Racist Policies in Europe: Individual and Contextual Predictors', paper presented at Annual Conference of the European Survey Research Association, Prague, 2009.

[45] C. J. Pereira *et al.*, 'From Prejudice to Discrimination: The Legitimizing Role of the Perceived Threat in Discrimination against Immigrants', *European Journal of Social Psychology* 40 (2010), pp. 1231–50.

[46] In the case of Portugal, see the study by E. S. Ferreira, H. Rato and M. J. Mortágua, *Viagens de Ulisses: Efeitos da imigração na economia portuguesa* (Lisbon: Alto Comissariado para a Imigração e Minorias Étnicas, 2004); also A. Almeida, *Impacto da imigração em Portugal nas contas do Estado* (Lisbon: ACIDI, 2003).

[47] See the report at http://fra.europa.eu/fraWebsite/attachments/eumidis_mainreport_conference-edition_en_.pdf

data are in accordance with other data collected by us which show that the Roma are not protected by the social norm of anti-racism, which makes them easy targets for prejudice and discrimination. It is also clear that black people, despite being protected by this norm, continue to be a target of discrimination. These data show that, in the EU as a whole, discrimination affects immigrants of various origins, but black immigrants feel themselves to be the most frequent targets of discrimination. This is why we will now analyse new data on 'anti-black racism' and opposition to immigration, exploring more deeply our hypothesis concerning the changes of expression of racism, from a phenomenon based on beliefs in biological differences between people categorised as social groups, to a phenomenon based on beliefs in deep cultural differences.[48]

The data presented in Figure 3.5 show a response pattern that is common to all countries.[49] The principles of cultural racism are more easily expressed than those of biological racism, and anti-black racism is less easily expressed than both biological and cultural racist beliefs. In all of the countries, and in accordance with our analytical model, biological racism correlates to cultural racism. In accordance with the theoretical hypotheses stated at the beginning of the chapter, these results could signify that the anti-racism norm affects prejudice against black people in the first place, biological racism in the second place, and, to a lesser

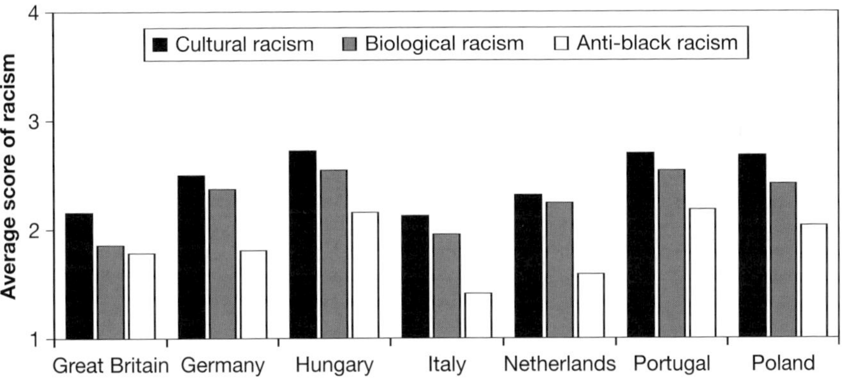

Figure 3.5. Mean values of racism measures in different European countries

[48] This study, 'Group Focused Enmity', was led by Wilhelm Heitmeyer and Andreas Zick of the University of Bielefeld. In Portugal it was coordinated by Cicero Pereira, ICS, University of Lisbon. The study was conducted in eight European countries: France, Great Britain, Germany, Hungary, Italy, the Netherlands, Poland and Portugal.

[49] Measures used: *Cultural racism*: 'Some cultures are clearly superior to others'; 'We need to protect our own culture from the influence of other cultures'. *Biological racism*: 'Some races are more gifted than others'. Responses vary from 1 (strongly disagree) to 4 (strongly agree).

degree, culturally based racism.[50] Note that the questions we are using to identify approval of racist beliefs do not associate these beliefs, as is usual, with specific targets (for instance black people). Two further conclusions can also be drawn: racist beliefs play an active role in social opinion, but only in some countries are they above the midpoint on the scale: Hungary, Portugal, and Poland.

Continuing our argument, it is now necessary to determine whether biological and cultural racism are significantly related to anti-black racism and opposition to immigration. In other words, do those who believe that profound biological and cultural differences exist between human groups, and that these differences are associated with stable hierarchies, tend to oppose immigration and to believe that blacks, specifically, are an inferior group?

In order to answer this question, we have used multiple regression models. These models assess the effects of racial beliefs on anti-black racism[51] and opposition to immigration[52] once the effects of sex, age, education, and political identification have been statistically controlled.

Our results confirm that in the case of anti-black racism, both in Portugal and in the other countries, biological and cultural racism are important factors in the emergence of anti-black racism. In other words, our model, which separates 'untargeted' racist beliefs from racism aimed at a specific group, is reinforced by this analysis. At the same time, it is shown that cultural as well as biological racist beliefs, rather than being simply organisers of social perception or categorisation principles, are antecedents of a 'radical alterity', the consequence of which is the infra-humanisation of certain social groups (black people, in the case in question). Concerning opposition to immigration, the results are similar. We can therefore conclude that, rather than the other factors that are habitually considered, it is racist beliefs that motivate people to oppose immigration.[53]

[50] See Figure 3.5. In each country means are statistically different: $F_{\text{Great Britain}}(2, 940) = 39.05$, $p < .001$, $\eta^2p = .08$; $F_{\text{Germany}}(2, 898) = 135.40$, $p < .001$, $\eta^2p = .23$; $F_{\text{Hungary}}(2, 828) = 51.01$, $p < .001$, $\eta^2p = .11$; $F_{\text{Italy}}(2, 882) = 133.85$, $p < .001$, $\eta^2p = .23$; $F_{\text{Netherlands}}(2, 924) = 184.48$, $p < .001$, $\eta^2p = .29$; $F_{\text{Portugal}}(2, 924) = 141.89$, $p < .001$, $\eta^2p = .24$; $F_{\text{Poland}}(2, 827) = 99.59$, $p < .001$, $\eta^2p = .19$. Multiple comparisons also indicate differences between means in each country, $p < .05$ (LSD).

[51] *Anti-black racism*: 'There is a natural hierarchy between black and white people'; 'Blacks and Whites should rather not get married'. Responses vary from 1 (strongly disagree) to 4 (strongly agree).

[52] In order to measure opposition to immigration two indicators were used. Participants were asked to indicate to what extent they thought their country 'should allow people of a different race or ethnic group from most [country nationality] people to come and live here?' (OI-item 1) and 'should allow people from the poorer countries outside Europe to come and live here?' (OI-item 2). The answers were registered on a scale ranging from 1 (allow many to come and live here) to 4 (allow none).

[53] For each dependent variable we estimated three regression models. In the first model we estimated the effect of the controlling variables (i.e. sex, age, education, and political identification). In the second model we added biological racism, and in the third we added cultural racism as a predictor. Looking at the effects on anti-black racism, the results of the first model explain 14 per cent of the variance in Portugal and 5 per cent of that in Europe. Biological racism explained 7 per cent of the variance in anti-black racism in Portugal and 9 per cent of that in Europe over and above the variance explained

cont.

Conclusions

This chapter addressed the meanings of racism in contemporary democratic societies and the possible peculiarities of racism in Portugal. With regard to the first question, we put forward hypotheses and empirical results in support of the idea that racism has undergone 'adaptive transformations', an expression derived from the evolutionary metaphor that inspired us. These transformations allowed the essential aspects of traditional racial ideology to be maintained, and could be described as an adaptive response to the normative pressures that have been exerted on racism since the end of the Second World War. In fact, the use of the metaphor of racism as an evolving virus helps to see it as a series of dynamically structured beliefs that are capable of undergoing adaptive transformations. The 'mutations' that have taken place permit derogatory attitudes and behaviours towards people perceived as being different and inferior, in spite of the force of the anti-racism norm.

It was within this framework that we analysed the emergence of 'subtle racial prejudice' in contrast to 'blatant racial prejudice', and proposed the hypothetical construction of 'cultural racism', highlighting the way in which it retains the same essential characteristics as traditional biological racism, while protecting the individual from being seen by him/herself or by others as prejudiced or racist. Explicit cultural racism has also been subjected to the anti-racism norm and is now often expressed in veiled forms, of which we described just three: 'hetero-ethnicisation', 'ontologisation', and 'infra-humanisation'. Normative pressures and processes related to the representation of the self are therefore central to the analysis of the changes which racism has undergone.

It is within this analytical context that several medium-range theories analyse the mechanisms that legitimise prejudice and discrimination and that allow social thinking to develop apparently non-racist justifications for racist behaviours and attitudes. These justifications resolve possible social and psychological conflicts arising from the tension between the need to show compliance with egalitarian values and, at the same time, congruence with racist attitudes and beliefs.

Understanding the contemporary dynamics of racial beliefs requires a distinction between racial prejudice and racism. The former is particularly associated with a negative evaluation of a group based on the idea of race or ethnic differences, and

by the controlling variable, while cultural racism explained 3 per cent of the variance in Portugal and 7 per cent of that in Europe. Significantly, both biological and cultural racism are the best predictors of anti-black racism both in Portugal and in Europe. A similar pattern was obtained concerning opposition to immigration. Controlling variables explained 4 per cent of the variance in Portugal and 3 per cent of that in Europe. Biological racism totalled 5 per cent of the variance in both Portugal and Europe, while cultural racism explained over 7 per cent of the variance in Portugal and 10 per cent of that in Europe. Significantly, both biological and cultural racism were the best predictors of opposition to immigration, with cultural racism presenting the stronger effects.

largely corresponds to the traditional content that has come to be known as ethnocentrism.[54] Racism, however, is now a common-sense theory about the organisation of human groups based on a belief in profound differences between these groups and their hierarchical organisation. It also involves the belief that not all groups share human 'essences' or 'characteristics' to the same degree. Appropriating a conceptual proposal made by Doise, prejudice is close to ethnocentrism, while racism expresses a feeling of 'radical alterity', to the extent that differences perceived between groups, based on biological or cultural criteria, are represented as profound or based on essential traits in a way that transforms the Other, perceived as different, into someone less human.[55]

The new wave of immigrants who have come to Europe in the last twenty years have lent a new acuity to the study of racism, racial prejudice, and the changes that it has undergone. In fact, in response to European countries' unacknowledged needs of more workforce and a compensation of their demographic imbalances, new immigrants from Eastern Europe, Asia, Africa and Latin America have sought better living conditions in the European Union. However, the arrival of such immigrants has given rise to an increasing sense of threat in the political-institutional discourse and in the minds of many Europeans. We therefore analysed fear of immigration and the perception of threat associated with immigration in order to better understand contemporary expressions of racism and its consequences. We were thereby able to confirm that opposition to immigration derives not only from the perception of economic threat but also from the perception of cultural threat, both in Portugal and in other EU countries. In the case of Portugal, these feelings of economic threat are widespread despite the studies that show the benefits to economic development that result from immigration.

In the final stage of the paper, we took black immigrants as the object of our analysis. Studies in Europe have shown this group to be one of the most likely to be subjected to discrimination. Thus we developed an empirical analysis of the relationship between biological racism, cultural racism, and anti-black racism, within the framework of the assumptions stated above concerning contemporary racisms. This analysis also assumes that the pressure of the anti-racism norm is exerted differently on beliefs that uphold biological racism, on beliefs that uphold cultural racism, and on the application of these different types of racial beliefs to specific targets, such as black people. As has been shown, the anti-racism norm exerts a stronger pressure on the application of racist beliefs to specific targets, such

[54] W. G. Sumner, *Folkways: A Study of the Sociological Importance of Usages, Manners, Customs, Mores, and Morals* (Boston: Ginn and Co., 1906). Sumner not only introduced the concept of ethnocentrism but also associated it with the distinction between 'we-groups' and 'other-groups'.

[55] W. Doise, 'Préface', in M. Sanchez-Mazas and L. Licata (eds), *L'autre – Regards psychosociaux* (Grenoble: PUG, 2005).

as black people. In turn, and also in accordance with our normative hypothesis, biological racism has fewer adherents than cultural racism. It is perhaps normative pressure, which protects black people, that underlies the fact that in Portugal, black people are targeted with less prejudice than Brazilian and Eastern European immigrants, as other studies show.[56] The following results must also be highlighted: both biological racism and cultural racism correlate with opposition to immigration and with anti-black racism. Thus, cultural racism is as consequential as biological racism.

With regard to the differences that lie behind the structure and salience of racist beliefs in Portugal and in the other European Union countries, the results strongly contradict the hypothesis of Portuguese singularity. This hypothesis is often present in common sense and in political discourse, and has also been repeated in academic discourse. However, different results stemming from broad and diversified samples taken at different times do not show any traces of this oft-invoked Portuguese singularity. It is therefore worth examining the reasons for the persistence of such a hypothesis.[57] As a tentative explanation, we propose that a systematic study of the collective memory of the Portuguese regarding the discoveries, the Empire, colonialism, and decolonisation should be carried out. Few studies have empirically addressed the collective memory regarding such subjects. Above all, no study to date has analysed the relationships between such memories and the contemporary representations that uphold cultural and biological racism as well as anti-black racism.[58] We believe that there is an urgent need to develop this field of research and to analyse the hypothesis that such collective memories function as a legitimising factor of contemporary prejudice and racism.

We know that the development of our understanding of contemporary racism must involve the study of representations of the relations between European countries, ex-colonies, decolonisation, and the recruitment of workers from ex-colonies in order to stimulate post-war European development. But one other field of research awaits a new impulse. We are referring to the link between social events and the cognitive processes involved in the construction of racial prejudice and the changes which it undergoes.

In fact, the conceptual hypothesis that we propose regarding racism and its

[56] We are referring to the recent study by António and Policarpo, carried out by CESOP of the Universidade Católica Portuguesa for the FCG: J. António and V. Policarpo, *A imigração em Portugal aos olhos dos portugueses* (Lisbon: Universidade Católica Portuguesa, 2011).

[57] Note, however, the complex relationship between racism, national identification and political ideologies in Portugal: Vala *et al.*, 'Black Immigrants in Portugal'.

[58] Some exceptions should be mentioned, particularly Valentim Alexandre, 'O Império e a ideia de raça, séculos XIX e XX', in Jorge Vala (ed.), *Novos Racismos* (Oeiras: Celta, 1999), pp. 133–44; Claudia Castelo, *'O modo português de estar no mundo': O Luso-tropicalismo e a ideologia colonial portuguesa, 1933–1961* (Porto: Afrontamento, 1998); and C. Sá and P. Castro (eds), *Memórias do descobrimento do Brasil* (Rio de Janeiro: Museu da República, 2005).

adaptive transformations involves an analysis of their historical, cultural and socio-economic correlates, but also requires an understanding of how those transformations are fed by the basic principles governing the functioning of the cognitive system. We therefore draw attention to the need to undertake research addressing not only the relationship between social and ideological processes, social prejudice, and categorisation, but also to investigate whether there exists a relationship between the hierarchised architecture of categorisation systems and the hierarchised representations of social groups. The known link between social categorisation and 'value' must be associated with this process. Thus, the process by which profound differentiation and 'value' hierarchisation are established in relation to human groups is a phenomenon that stems from social processes, but which is fed by the cognitive processes of categorisation and essentialisation of social categories, as well as by the relationship between these processes and the social 'value' of categorised objects.

4

Mulattos in Brazil and Angola: A Comparative Approach, from the Seventeenth to the Twenty-First Century

LUIZ FELIPE DE ALENCASTRO

To Alfredo Margarido

FROM THE LAST QUARTER OF THE SIXTEENTH CENTURY until 1850, most of Brazil and Angola formed a South Atlantic system sustained by an intercolonial trade that complemented, albeit often contradictorily, exchanges between these regions and Portugal.[1] Bilateral trade and the movements of merchants, militiamen, royal servants and missionaries fostered relations between the Portuguese enclaves on either side of the South Atlantic. Typically, ships from Lisbon travelling to and from Angola called at Brazilian harbours, and during this period, Bahia, Rio de Janeiro and Pernambuco were in practice closer to Luanda and Benguela than to Maranhão and Pará. In fact, thanks to winds and maritime routes, the former three captaincies were socially, economically and geographically closer to Angola than they were to the Brazilian territories to the north of Cape São Roque (in the modern state of Rio Grande do Norte), comprising the *Estado do Grão Pará e Maranhão*.

Therefore, to compare colonial Brazil and Angola is to bring together two parts of a social space also shared (in South America) with Amerindians. Both regions were also slave societies, such that Portuguese and African cultures collided and mingled in both. Nevertheless, as is well known, settlement patterns were distinct on either side of the Atlantic, and Brazil's colonial population and territory were far greater than those of other Portuguese colonies.[2] *Mulattos* never exceeded

[1] The notion of a South Atlantic system unifying slave production areas in Portuguese America and slave reproduction areas in Portuguese Africa is not new. Referring mainly to Angola, Oliveira Martins states in 1880, '[Portuguese] Africa was [. . .] almost until today, a dependency of Brazil [. . .] the two colonies [*sic*] formed a system'; O *Brasil e as colónias portuguesas*, 3rd edn (1880; Lisbon: Livraria Antonio Maria Pereira, 1888), pp. vi–vii.

[2] Up to 1900, only one-tenth of Angola's current territory was occupied by the Portuguese: Luanda, the strip of the Cuanza River, N'dalantando-Malange, Benguela, Moçamedes (now Namibe), Novo Redondo (now Sumbe), and a few other places.

Proceedings of the British Academy **179**, *71–96*.

2 per cent of the Angolan population prior to the 1970s,[3] while 200 years earlier, in São Paulo and Minas Gerais, they already accounted for 19 per cent and 24 per cent of the population respectively, and probably made up similar proportions in other well-populated Brazilian captaincies.[4]

In spite of the paucity of data, Gerald Bender collected and analysed population figures that demonstrate some of these disparities (see Tables 4.1 and 4.2).[5] Even a cursory examination shows that the *mulatto* population was rather marginal in the other Portuguese colonies, with the exception of the Cape Verde islands.[6] Put in demographic and social perspective, there is no comparison between *mulatto* populations in Brazil and Angola. And yet Luso-Brazilian miscegenation eventually became the bedrock of Lusotropicalism: an essential component of Portugal's colonial ideology in the second half of the twentieth century, particularly in Angola. A large spectrum of politicians and intellectuals see miscegenation as characterising the Portuguese presence in Africa and Asia as well as America.

Table 4.1. Racial composition of the Angolan population

Year	*White*		*Mulatto/mestiço*		*Black*		*Total*
	Number	*%*	*Number*	*%*	*Number*	*%*	
1777	1,581	–	4,043	–	–		–
1845	1,832	0.03	5,770	0.10	5,378,923	99.9	5,386,525
1900	9,198	0.20	3,112	0.06	4,777,636	99.7	4,789,946
1920	20,700	0.48	7,500	0.18	4,250,000	99.3	4,278,200
1940	44,083	1.20	28,035	0.75	3,665,829	98.1	3,738,010
1950	78,826	1.90	29,648	0.72	4,036,678	97.4	4,145,266
1960	172,529	3.60	53,392	1.10	4,604,362	95.3	4,830,449
1970	290,000	5.10					5,673,046

Source: Gerald J. Bender, *Angola under the Portuguese: The Myth and the Reality* (Berkeley: University of California Press, 1992), pp. 20–1; research completed by the Instituto Brasileiro de Geografía y Estatística Brazilian Census of 1980.

[3] More recent data show the following racial distribution in Angola: Ovimbundu 37%, Kimbundu 25%, Bakongo 13%, *mestiço* (mixed European and native African) 2%, European 1%, other 22%; Central Intelligence Agency, World Factbook, December 2010, available at www.cia.gov/library/publications/the-world-factbook/geos/ao.html

[4] Dauril Alden, 'The Population of Brazil in the Late Eighteenth Century: A Preliminary Study', *Hispanic American Historical Review* 43:2 (1963), pp. 173–205, see p. 196.

[5] Gerald J. Bender, *Angola under the Portuguese: The Myth and the Reality* (Berkeley: University of California Press, 1992), pp. 20–1.

[6] Contrary to current ideas, miscegenation and the population of *mulattos* in São Tomé is quite circumscribed. The 1950 census registered only 7 per cent *mulattos* in the island, and recent research shows that some of them came from other Africans regions; Gil Tomas *et al.*, 'The Peopling of Sao Tome (Gulf of Guinea): Origins of Slave Settlers and Admixture with the Portuguese', *Human Biology* 74:3 (2002), pp. 397–411. The only exception to this rule is Cape Verde (for which see below).

Table 4.2. Racial composition of the Brazilian population

Year	*White*		*Mulatto/Pardo*		*Black*		*Other*	*Total*
	Number	*%*	*Number*	*%*	*Number*	*%*		
1818	1,000,000	27	500,000	13	2,000,000	53	250,000 (Indian)	3,750,000
1872	3,787,289	38	4,188,737	42	1,954,543	20		9,930,569
1890	6,302,198	44	5,934,291	41	2,097,426	15		14,333,915
1940	26,171,778	63	8,744,365	21	6,035,869	15	242,230	41,194,332
1950	32,027,661	62	13,786,742	27	5,692,657	11	329,082	51,836,142
1980	59,713,405	56	33,073,567	31	8,867,360	8	4,163,268	105,818,600

Source: Gerald J. Bender, *Angola under the Portuguese: The Myth and the Reality* (Berkeley: University of California Press, 1992), pp. 20–1; research completed by the Instituto Brasileiro de Geografía y Estatística Brazilian Census of 1980.

To understand these paradoxes we must examine, beyond the demographic figures, the historical processes framing *mulattos* as a group on both sides of the South Atlantic. As we will see, miscegenation is a necessary but insufficient condition for the growth of a *mulatto* population.[7]

Ever since the turn of the seventeenth century, Africans had been understood as a constitutive element of the colonial system in South America. Ambrósio Fernandes Brandão, a planter and merchant with extensive knowledge of Iberian overseas territories, then living in northeastern Brazil, stated that the study of African peoples and cultures was essential to understand the country.[8] This interpretation was not uncontroversial. Following the black and *mulatto* rebellions that destroyed sugar plantations on the island of São Tomé in the second half of the sixteenth century, the Jesuit Pero Rodrigues – an expert on the South Atlantic system – warned of the dangers of a slave uprising in Brazil. In his view, the Crown and settlers should preserve alliances with Indian tribes to protect themselves against the Africans, their 'main enemies' in Portuguese America.[9]

Ambivalence towards the African presence in Brazil, then, was explicit: blacks and *mulattos* were a part of the colonial settlement in South America, but also a threat to it.

[7] I discussed some of these issues in 'Géopolitique du Métissage', in 'Symposium', *Encyclopaedia Universalis*, Paris, 1984, pp. 969–77.

[8] Ambrósio Fernandes Brandão, *Diálogos das grandezas do Brasil* (1618; Rio de Janeiro: Dois Mundos, 1943), p. 99.

[9] Father Pero Rodrigues was chief Jesuit in Brazil (1594–1603) and director of missions in Angola (1593). His report to the Crown is dated 1597; Serafim Leite, *História da Companhia de Jesus no Brasil, 1549–1760*, 10 vols (Lisbon and Rio de Janeiro: Livraria Portugália/Civilização Brasileira, 1938–50), vol. 2, p. 358. It also noteworthy that the intensification of the Atlantic slave trade accelerated the destruction of Indian tribes in Brazil.

Towards the later 1600s, Portuguese America had about 100,000 colonists, the majority of them *mulattos* and *mestiços*.[10] Some 113,000 Africans were disembarked there in the sixteenth century, and 850,000 in the seventeenth century.[11] The disparity between African and European migration to Brazil narrowed after the gold rush to Minas Gerais, the settlement of inland territories, and agricultural development in the maritime captaincies.

Social reproduction of *mulattos* in Angola and Brazil

Contemporary writings suggest that *mulattos* were seen as a distinct group in colonial Brazil. Deported to Bahia in 1657–8, Dom Francisco Manuel de Melo wrote a book on Portuguese America, now lost, entitled *Paradise of Mulattos, Purgatory of Whites and Hell of Blacks*.[12] The quote is a variant of proverbs relating to social life in England and France, probably known to Dom Francisco, a refined writer and a well-travelled man.[13] Fifty years later, the proverb was taken up again and significantly adapted by the Tuscan Jesuit Andreoni (known as Antonil), who likewise lived in Bahia: 'Brazil is the hell of the Blacks, the purgatory of the Whites, and the paradise of Mulatto men and Mulatto women.'[14] Antonil's addition of the *mulatto* women may well be related to the cultural habitus that inspired the famous erotic poems, most debased, on *mulatto* women written by the Luso-Bahian poet Gregorio de Matos in previous years.[15] In essence, Dom Francisco and Antonil adapted an aphorism of British and French origins to the peculiarities of Bahia's slave society in the seventeenth and eighteenth centuries.

Aware of *mulattos*' social and demographic significance in Brazil, Francisco Inocêncio de Sousa Coutinho, governor of Angola from 1764 to 1772, emphasised

[10] Including 30,000 whites and 70,000 black *mulattos* and Indian *mestiços*; see the sources and discussion in Instituto Brasileiro de Geografía e Estatística (IBGE), 'Apêndice: Estatísticas de 500 anos de povoamento', in *Brasil: 500 anos de povoamento* (Rio de Janeiro: IBGE, 2000), p. 221.

[11] Trans-Atlantic Slave Trade Database, available at www.slavevoyages.org/tast/index.faces (accessed October 2010).

[12] D. Francisco was deported to Salvador in 1657–8; E. Prestage, *D. Francisco Manuel de Melo – esboço biographico* (Coimbra: Imprensa da Universidade, 1914), p. 291.

[13] Bonaventure des Periers, *Nouvelles Recréations*, 1558: 'Paris c'est le paradis des femmes, l'enfer des mules, et le purgatoire des solliciteurs'; J. Florio, *Second Fruits*, 1591: 'England is the paradise of women, the purgatory of men, and the hell of horses'; *Oxford Dictionary of Proverbs*, available at www.answers.com/topic/england-is-the-paradise-of-women-the-hell-of-horses-and-the-purgatory-of-servants (accessed 21 October 2010).

[14] 'O Brasil é o inferno dos negros, o purgatório dos brancos, e o paraíso dos mulatos e mulatas'; A. J. Antonil, *Cultura e opulência do Brasil*, 3rd edn (1711; São Paulo: Editora Itatiaia, 1982), p. 90.

[15] See for instance the poem 'Mulatinhas da Bahia'. Several other of Gregorio de Matos's poems offer degrading descriptions of *mulattas*; his writings thus portray the misogyny common to other contemporary poets. See João Adolfo Hansen, *A sátira e o engenho, Gregório de Matos e a Bahia do século XVII*, 2nd edn (Campinas: Unicamp, 2004), pp. 65, 198, 221, 348, 411–22, 499.

their role in his plans to extend settlement and diversify economic activities in Central Africa. In a report to the Crown, he underlined the 'lack of [colonist] residents' and the 'disorder' existing among those who lived in Angola, who 'neither could form a society nor help themselves to improve trade and agriculture'. The reason for such disorder, he wrote, was the failure of the colonists to multiply, since 'even when they had children with the African women [. . .] after the death of their fathers [these children] move to the savannah (*sertão*) with their mothers'. Accordingly,

> notwithstanding this country has been somewhat peopled by Europeans and Brazilians, it never had sufficient residents, nor did the Crown benefit from those born here. For sure, if those Mulattos lived in society, marrying each other [. . .] they would have built, in this long period of two centuries, a great number of settlements (*povoações*).[16]

Actually, Sousa Coutinho describes here the kinship pattern of the Mbundu peoples. Once the ties with the colonist disappeared, the native mother and her sons moved to her family village and assumed their African status and culture. Belonging to matrilineal communities, the sons lived with their maternal family in the mother's brother's home. Previously, governor Antonio Vasconcellos had already observed in 1759 that most of the residents of Massangano, a town close to Luanda, moved to the African villages; as he put it with some exaggeration, 'they jump into the bush almost straight from the cradle'.[17]

An earlier text, a poem written in Luanda in the last decades of the seventeenth century, also described the reafricanisation of *mulattos* in Angola, from colonial to native status:

> Here where the son is Brown
> And almost Black the grandson
> And all Black the great-grandson
> And everything is dark[18]

In another dispatch to the Crown, Sousa Coutinho referred to the prostitution of slave women. He remarked that the children of prostitutes were victims of 'destruction' in their early years and that *mulatto* children who survived were simply

[16] Francisco Inocêncio de Sousa Coutinho to Francisco Xavier de Mendonça Furtado, Luanda, 24 Nov. 1768, in A. de Albuquerque Felner, *Angola – Apontamentos sôbre a colonização dos planaltos e litoral do Sul de Angola* (Lisbon: Agência Geral das Colônias, 1940), vol. 1, doc. 3, pp. 160–2.

[17] 'Quase do berço saltam para o mato'; quoted by Catarina Madeira Santos, 'Um governo "polido" para Angola. Reconfigurar dispositivos de domínio (1750 – ca. 1800)', unpublished PhD thesis, Universidade Nova de Lisboa, 2005, p. 187. The question of *mulattos* and Sousa Coutinho's reports, mentioned here, is also discussed on pp. 187–97.

[18] 'Aqui onde o filho é fusco / e quase negro o neto, / e todo negro o bisneto, / e tudo escuro.' With forty-eight strophes that describe the evils of Angola and the sufferings of Europeans there, the poem was written before 1680 by an author who was probably a Portuguese exiled convict (*degredado*). Literary critics and literature manuals wrongly attribute this poem to the Bahian Luso-Brazilian poet Gregorio de Matos; see Luiz Felipe de Alencastro, *O trato dos viventes: Formação do Brasil no Atlântico Sul, séculos XVI e XVII* (São Paulo: Companhia das Letras, 2000), pp. 335–45, p. 465, n. 60.

neglected. To solve these problems and to promote the growth of the population, he proposed 'general freedom for Mulattos', for the benefit of both Crown and colony. Following the emancipation of 'Mulattos, Brown or Grey-Brown', the colonial administration should focus on developing their skills. This would lead to the emergence of 'industrious couples' of *mulattos*, thus saving the Crown the expense of transporting Portuguese couples to colonise Angola.[19] For the same reasons, another governor, the Baron of Mossamedes, again in 1784 sought freedom for *mulattos* in Angola (again unsuccessfully).[20]

Sousa Coutinho's analysis drew on internal and external processes to highlight the atrophy of the *mulatto* population. First, he explained the decline in the social reproduction of *mulattos*, as a result of reafricanisation in villages outside the areas of Portuguese control.[21] Secondly, he pointed to the factors inhibiting the reproduction of *mulattos* inside colonial townships.

In fact, Sousa Coutinho was pragmatic enough to also promote the arrival of new colonists from Madeira and to initiate new economic activities in Angola. The failure of these experiments has been analysed by many authors and will not be discussed here.[22] Nonetheless, his plans shed light on the obstacles arising in the colony through the prevalence of the slave trade, as well as on circumstances acting to curb the social reproduction of *mulattos*. Linda Heywood and Roquinaldo Ferreira have analysed and emphasised the role played by *mulattos* in Angola.[23] And yet they

[19] He referred to the 'Mulatos, Fuscos ou Pardos'; Francisco Inocêncio de Sousa Coutinho, Luanda, 13 Sept. 1769, Instituto Histórico e Geográfico Brasileiro (hereafter, IHGB), DL81, 02.14, fols 46–7. Sousa Coutinho was Governor and Captain-General of Angola; the letter is surely adressed to Francisco Xavier de Mendonça Furtado, the Overseas Minister.

[20] Santos, 'Um governo "polido" para Angola', p. 193.

[21] I have adapted here the concept elaborated by Orlando Patterson who defines 'social reproduction' of a slave population by taking into account both biological reproduction and non-natural factors (i.e. manumissions and emigration/immigration rates) which create a 'social leakage' of that population; Orlando Patterson, *Slavery and Social Death: A Comparative Study* (Cambridge, MA: Harvard University Press, 1985), pp. 132–3.

[22] Sousa Coutinho's government has been studied by many historians; the most recent work is Santos' doctoral thesis, 'Um governo "polido" para Angola'. Yet this important thesis underestimates the significance of Sousa Coutinho's actions in developing the slave trade in Angola. Since Santos barely analyses Angolan trade, she misses an important issue: during 1766–70, West African (mainly Angolan) slave exports rose 19 per cent, reaching the highest five-year figure since the arrival of the Portuguese. Sousa Coutinho improved conditions (including food stocks on slave ships and regulation of the inland trade) and made possible the historical peak of 152,000 Africans exported during this period (a figure only surpassed in 1781–5, when the Brazilian plantation economy began to grow again). Research still to be done should focus on the ways Sousa Coutinho's enlightened administration combined with this expansion of the slave trade in Angola.

[23] Linda Heywood, 'Portuguese into African: The Eighteenth-Century Central African Background to Atlantic Creole Cultures', in Linda Heywood (ed.), *Central Africans and Cultural Transformations in the American Diaspora* (Cambridge: Cambridge University Press, 2002), pp. 91–114, see pp. 92–6; also Roquinaldo Ferreira, 'Transforming Atlantic Slaving: Trade, Warfare and Territorial Control in Angola, 1650–1800', unpublished PhD thesis, University of California, Los Angeles, 2003, pp. 159–71.

do not accord enough attention to the constraints restricting the *mulatto* population, miscegenation notwithstanding. Ferreira refers to baptism records from the parish of Remédios, in Luanda, which show a large number of children of Portuguese fathers and African mothers.[24] It is likely that the *mulatto* children were still more numerous, given that many whites and *mulattos* had several African wives.[25] Even so, the Mbundu matrilineal culture reduced the statistical significance of these interracial unions. As observed above, part of their mixed-race progeny, often illegitimate, became embedded in their mothers' culture and thus reafricanised.[26]

A wide array of interactions between colonists and natives took place during colonial times, and Angola, like other regions of Portuguese Africa, underwent processes that generated extensive creolisation. Nevertheless, in this text we focus specifically upon miscegenation and its crux, the growth of the *mulatto* population.

In fact, the regular presence of *mulattos* from São Tomé and Brazil in Luanda and particularly in Benguela, as well as persistent requests by local authorities for more of them, and the frequent deportation of vagrant free *mulattos* from Brazil to Angola, suggests that the endogenous growth of the *mulatto* population fell short of official expectations of managing Luso-Angolan '*mestiços*' as an intermediate tier.[27]

In 1800, the governors of Angola and Benguela again asked for free *mulattos* from Brazil to colonise the region; Linda Heywood mentions that the latter official specified that they should count as many as eighty couples.[28] Thus, Brazilian *mulattos* were transported to Angola, alongside other immigrant families, to bolster colonial dominion. And the foreignness of Brazilian *mulattos* in Portuguese Africa was underscored after 1822, as the news of Brazil's independence reached the

[24] The comparative status of *mulattos* in Brazil and Angola is also discussed in Rafael de Bivar Marquese, 'A dinâmica da escravidão no Brasil: Resistência, tráfico negreiro e alforrias, séculos XVII a XIX', *Novos estudos – CEBRAP* 74 (2006), pp. 107–23; and Flávio Gomes and Roquinaldo Ferreira, 'A miragem da miscigenação', *Novos estudos – CEBRAP* 80 (2008), pp. 141–60.

[25] Jill Dias states that polygamy was common between colonists up to the end of the nineteenth century; Jill Dias, 'Angola', in Valentim Alexandre and Jill Dias (eds), *O Império Africano, 1825–1890*, vol. 10 of *Nova História da Expansão Portuguesa* (Lisbon: Estampa, 1998), p. 511.

[26] Analysing the Imbangala and Tshokwe trades in Angola during the nineteenth century, Isabel de Castro Henriques writes that in mixed couples, even when whites married African women, except for the father's presence, *mulatto* children were 'entirely entrusted to their African maternal parenthood'; *Commerce et changement en Angola au XIXe siècle: Imbangala et Tshokwe face à la modernité*, 2 vols (Paris: L'Harmattan, 1995), vol. 2, p. 33.

[27] Ferreira indicates that most of the political and criminal exiles deported from Brazil to Angola in the eighteenth century were *mulattos*; 'Transforming Atlantic Slaving', p. 165. On Brazilian *mulattos* in Benguela, see José C. Curto, 'Americanos', in 'Angola: The Brazilian Community in Benguela, c. 1722–1832', unpublished paper, 2003.

[28] Heywood quotes an urgent call by Benguela's governor in 1800 for eighty couples of *mulattos* from Rio de Janeiro for use as colonists; 'Portuguese into African', p. 97.

slaving Atlantic, and they were denounced as separatists and pro-Brazil plotters in Benguela and Mozambique.[29]

The contrast in the situation of *mulattos* on either side of the South Atlantic deepened as settlement expanded in Brazil. With the onset of gold production in Minas Gerais, Goiás and Mato Grosso, the slave trade and African slavery spread into the inland territories. As settlement increased in the gold and diamond mining areas, so too urban slavery grew, eventually leading to unexpected problems of social control. A great number of Portuguese with little experience of slavery and African culture arrived in Brazil, and troubles arose as fresh settlers faced slaves, blacks and *mulattos* in urban and rural settings, leading to an enforcement of security laws and practices against slave runaways and rebellions. 'Bush captains' (*capitães do mato*) in charge of capturing maroons, on duty since the first decades of the seventeenth century in Bahia and Pernambuco, had their general regulations (*regimento*) for Portuguese America published in 1724. Issued after the war against the maroon villages (*quilombos*) of Palmares, a royal order of 1699 exempted colonists who killed any maroon (or *quilombola*) from punishment.

What was more, a royal decree of 1741 prescribed that a group of five runaway slaves should be considered a *quilombo*.[30] A family of free blacks or *mulattos* living in the countryside, then (such as a father, mother and three children), could be considered a *quilombo*, and its members killed, imprisoned, or sold as slaves unless they could prove their status as free or freed persons. Such repressive practices threatened autonomous families and isolated persons of African descent. Free and freed blacks were obliged to maintain links with former owners or institutions (brotherhoods, churches) who could confirm they were not runaways. Hence, free and freed blacks would remain inside colonial enclaves, thus locking in the social stratification of mixed families and *mulattos*. Besides miscegenation, the social reproduction of *mulattos* thus came about mainly as a result of racial constrictions generated by Luso-Brazilian slave society.

Racist laws and attitudes permeated Brazilian colonial society, and the image of the *mulatto* in literature and historical narratives was mostly undignified.[31] Even so, despite or perhaps because of the arbitrary conditions imposed upon them, quantitative data demonstrate that *mulattos* enjoyed better conditions than did blacks and Africans.[32] Stuart Schwartz calculates that *mulattos* represented just 10 per cent

[29] Ferreira, 'Transforming Atlantic Slaving', p. 171, n. 102; João Manuel da Silva (Governor of Mozambique) to Manuel Gonçalves de Miranda, n.p., Dec. 1824, IHGB, Docs África/Moçambique, DL88, 04.26.01.

[30] Perdigão Malheiro, *A escravidão no Brasil – Ensaio jurídico, histórico, social*, 2 vols (1866; Petrópolis: Vozes, 1976), vol. 1, pp. 50–1.

[31] See the thesis of Raimundo Agnelo Soares Pessoa, analysing texts from 1633 to 1824: 'Gente sem sorte: Os Mulatos no Brasil colonial', unpublished PhD thesis, Universidade Estadual Paulista, 2007.

[32] As Marc Bloch stated, 'arbitrariness is an essential element of the slavery notion'; Bloch, *La société féodale* (1939; Paris: Albin Michel, 1982), p. 245.

of the slave population of Bahia in 1648–1745, while they benefited from 45 per cent of manumissions. Likewise, *mulattos* accounted for less than 6 per cent of slaves in the sugar mills analysed during this period, but held 20 per cent of domestic and skilled jobs. By contrast, blacks worked mainly in the sugar cane fields.[33] Vidal Luna and Klein found the same trends favouring *mulattos* in Minas Gerais and São Paulo in 1750–1850.[34] Their most recent book confirms the pattern, while also demonstrating *mulattos*' social cohesion, given that their marriage rates were higher than those of free blacks.[35]

Turning again to the South Atlantic perspective, then, we may observe that, in contrast to Angola, conditions outside Portuguese enclaves in Brazil were more adverse for free and freed *mulattos*, just as conditions inside colonial townships were more favourable to them.

While colour prejudices permeated the whole of Brazilian society, historical studies have established the importance of Catholic brotherhoods (*irmandades*), namely those of Our Lady of the Rosary (*Nossa Senhora do Rosário*), in the Americanisation of Africans and people of African descent.[36] It is also interesting to observe that in the sixteenth and early seventeenth centuries, missionaries in Brazil taught the cult of *Sumé*, an Indian epitome of Saint Thomas (*São Tomé*) who allegedly lived with the tribes before the arrival of the Europeans. This Indian association with Catholicism, however, did not blend with the religious beliefs of those times.[37] Of greater religious appeal in Brazil was the later cult of São Benedito, a black saint sometimes presented as a native Angolan from Kisama.[38]

[33] Stuart B. Schwartz, *Sugar Plantations in the Formation of Brazilian Society: Bahia 1550–1835* (Cambridge: Cambridge University Press, 1985), pp. 137, 278.

[34] Francisco Vidal Luna and Herbert S. Klein, *Slavery and the Economy of São Paulo, 1750–1850* (Stanford, CA: Stanford University Press, 2003), pp. 165–7.

[35] Herbert S. Klein and Francisco Vidal Luna, *Slavery in Brazil* (Cambridge: Cambridge University Press, 2010), pp. 263, 276.

[36] Since the pioneering book of Fritz Teixeira Salles, *Associações religiosas no ciclo do ouro: Introduçao ao estudo do comportamento social das irmandades de Minas no século XVIII* (Belo Horizonte: Universidade Federal de Minas Gerais, 1963), the connections between *irmandades* and slavery and Afro-Brazilian culture have been extensively studied. See for instance Mariza de Carvalho Soares, *Devotos da cor: Identidade étnica, religiosidade e escravidão no Rio de Janeiro, século XVIII* (Rio de Janeiro: Civilização Brasileira, 2000); Mary Karash, 'Construindo comunidades: As irmandades de Pretos e Pardos no Brasil colonial e Goiás', paper presented at conference on 'American Counterpoint: New Approaches to Slavery and Abolition in Brazil', Yale University, October 2010.

[37] Fray Vicente do Salvador, *História do Brasil, 1500–1627*, 7th edn (*c*. 1627; São Paulo: Editora Itatiaia, 1982), p. 112; Simão de Vasconcellos, *Crônica da Companhia de Jesus*, 2 vols (1663; Petrópolis: Vozes, 1977), vol. 1, pp. 83, 123–4.

[38] Antônio de Oliveira de Cadornega, *História geral das guerras angolanas*, 3 vols (1681; Lisbon: Agência Geral do Ultramar, 1972), vol. 3, p. 27. On the cult of São Benedito in Brazil, see Julita Scarano, *Devoção e escravidão – A Irmandade de Nossa Senhora do Rosário dos Pretos no distrito diamantino no século XVIII*, 2nd edn (São Paulo: Companhía Editora Nacional, 1978), pp. 38–9; Anderson J. M. de Oliveira, *Devoção negra: santos e catequese no Brasil colonial* (Rio de Janeiro: FAPERJ, 2008).

It was an Afro-Brazilian variant of Our Lady of the Immaculate Conception that became the main Catholic cult in Brazil. Later declared the patron saint of the country, a statue of *Nossa Senhora Aparecida* was found in the Paraíba valley, a major route into Minas Gerais, in the early eighteenth century, when African and black slaves were brought in great numbers to this region. The Brazilian national cult of the Black Patroness thus contrasts with Latin American countries of distinct colonial background, where the Holy Virgin took an Indian face: in Mexico, the Virgin of Guadalupe; in Ecuador, Our Lady of Gualupo; in Peru and Bolivia, Our Lady of Copacabana; in Argentina, the Holy Virgin of Lujan; and in Paraguay, Our Lady of Caacupe. Ultimately, the cult of *Nossa Senhora Aparecida* endorses the *mulatto*, and not the Indian *mestiço*, as the central element of colonial peopling in Brazil.

The social and economic significance of Brazil's *mulattos* was further highlighted during a controversy arising from the enforcement of a Sumptuary Law of 1749, of which one clause denied free and freed coloureds the right to wear silk clothes or jewels. Criticising this law, a statement by the Lisbon merchant guild (*Mesa do Bem Comum*) argued that 'in America *mulattos* constitute the largest group, and it seems that this inferior condition they are born with should not deprive them of the credit and the esteem they acquire'.[39] Approving the merchants' arguments, the Crown lifted the prohibition some weeks later.[40]

Of course, restrictions against *mulattos* persisted. But their class status could clear the way to 'whitening'. This metamorphosis is described by the well-known remarks of Henry Koster, a British merchant who lived in Pernambuco in the early nineteenth century:

> In conversing on one occasion with a man of colour who was in my service, I asked him if a certain *capitão-mor* (militia commander) was not a *mulatto* man. He answered, 'He is, but is not now', I begged him to explain, when he added 'Can a *capitão-mor* be a *mulatto* man?'[41]

First highlighted by Ferdinand Denis in 1839, and taken up by generations of authors, and notably by Gilberto Freyre in his study on the social ascent of *mulattos* in the nineteenth century, the quote came to be regarded as emblematic of a Brazilian racial classification based on social and economic status rather than on physical

[39] 'Na república da América são os mulatos os que constituem o maior corpo e parece que esta inferior condição com que nasceram os não deve privar do crédito e estimação de que se fazem credores'; 'Representação da Mesa do Bem Comum de Lisboa contra a Pragmática de 1749', in Íris Kantor, 'Pacto festivo em Minas colonial: A entrada triunfal do primeiro bispo na Sé de Mariana, 1748', MA dissertation, Universidade de São Paulo, 1996, p. 113.

[40] 'Alvará porque V. M. ha por bem [. . .] ordenar que por hora não tenha efeito o cap° 9 da Pramatica de 24 de Mayo a respeito dos negros, e mulatos das Conquistas', Lisbon, 20 Sept. 1749, Arquivo da Universidade de Coimbra, Colecção Conde dos Arcos, v. 9, [347v] no. 420.

[41] Henry Koster, *Travels in Brazil*, 2 vols (London, 1817), vol. 2, pp. 209–10.

appearance. Like any reiterated quote, Koster's words became self-explanatory, obscuring the problematic nature of the *mulattos*' condition.[42]

Closer to the Brazilian than to the Angolan context, Cape Verde, and to a lesser extent São Tomé, illustrates the role of desocialisation in the transformation of Luso-African communities in a *mulatto* society. Although slavery was not so widespread in Cape Verde as in São Tomé, Africans were regularly taken from their continental communities and exported to both archipelagos – first as slaves, and later as contracted labourers – to work under the control of colonists and Portuguese authorities.

In Cape Verde, the first census of 1731 already showed the racial distribution that characterised society over the following decades: an important number of *mulattos*, followed by blacks and a small number of 'whites of the land' (*brancos da terra*), defined 'properly as *mulattos*' by a royal officer in 1800.[43] The higher proportion of *mulattos* in Cape Verde compared with São Tomé was the result of several factors, as recent research has demonstrated.[44] São Tomé had a real plantation system, and imported 100,000 Africans as malaria and yellow fever restricted the inflow of Portuguese settlers. The Cape Verde islands, by contrast, had only 25,000 African slaves and presented a less severe disease environment for Europeans.[45]

We should also note that in Cape Verde a creole language arose, considered today the national idiom alongside Portuguese (the official language). In Brazil, excluding the lexical systems formed by the inhabitants of *quilombos* or the Afro-Brazilian religious cults (*lingua-de-santo*), there is no general creole language. According to the Brazilian ethnolinguist, Yeda Pessoa de Castro, the proximity between the 'archaic' (sixteenth to eighteenth centuries) Portuguese and the Bantu languages melted creole dialects into a *mestiço* Portuguese that today differentiates Brazilian from European Portuguese.[46]

Hence, linguistic trends in Brazil broke down the social fragmentation generated by African languages and dialects and ensured that the dominant cultural and racial pattern permeated Afro-Brazilian communities. These processes thus also facilitated

[42] Fréderic Mauro considered Ferdinand Denis the first French Brazilianist; see Denis, *Histoire et description du Brésil* (Paris: Didot Frères, 1839), p. 147; Gilberto Freyre, *Sobrados e Mucambos* (1936; São Paulo: Global, 2006), ch. 12 ('Ascent of the University Bachelor and the Mulatto'), p. 727.

[43] André Pinto de Sousa Dias Teixeira, *A ilha de São Nicolau de Cabo Verde nos séculos XV a XVIII* (Lisbon: Universidade Nova de Lisboa, 2004), pp. 159–80.

[44] Maria Jesus Trovoada *et al.*, 'Insights from Patterns of mtDNA Variation into the Genetic History of São Tomé e Príncipe', *International Congress Series* 1,261 (2004), pp. 377–9; Rita Gonçalves *et al.*, 'Y-Chromosome Lineages in São Tomé e Principe and Cabo Verde Islands: Different Input of European Influence', *Forensic Science International: Genetics Supplement Series* 1:1 (2008), pp. 210–11.

[45] Tomas *et al.*, 'The Peopling of Sao Tome'.

[46] Yeda Pessoa de Castro, *Falares africanos na Bahia* (Rio de Janeiro: Academia Brasileira de Letras/Topbooks, 2005), pp. 117–20.

mulattos' social reproduction. In Angola, the official language has been strongly shaped by recent Portuguese immigration, and there is no creole language either.[47] The duality separating the elite's European Portuguese speech and the national languages reflects the racial duality of the Angolan culture.

Mulattos in Brazil and Angola in the nineteenth century

After independence, the Brazilian Constitution of 1824 introduced a two-stage system of electoral suffrage. Any male citizen older than 25 years of age – including freedmen – with 100,000 réis of annual income could vote at the first level (as *votantes*), electing municipal councilmen as well as second-level electors (or *eleitores*). With a minimum 200,000 réis of annual income, those *eleitores* then voted for office holders at the provincial and national levels.

Freedmen were not permitted to be second-level electors. Nevertheless, the scarcity of whites who fulfilled the criteria for first-level voters – when each second-level elector needed thirty votes from *votantes* – left *eleitores* (landowners, merchants, civil servants, and free professionals) dependent on black and *mulatto* voters.[48] Provided they complied with suffrage requirements as first-level voters, then, free and freed blacks and *mulattos* enjoyed a political status unique in New World slave societies.[49] In addition, in contrast to the situation in most towns in the United States, and in Rio de Janeiro in Brazil, blacks and *mulattos* did not experience competition from European immigrants in urban centres prior to the twentieth century.[50]

[47] Bender shows that only 28 per cent of the Portuguese colonists living in Angola in 1970 were born in the colony; Bender, *Angola under the Portuguese*, p. 227.

[48] For the same reason, planters allowed service tenants (*agregados* and *moradores*) to live on and exploit parcels of land on their property. Of these *agregados*, Richard Graham writes, 'we can reasonably conclude that most *agregados* were black or *mulatto*. Outside the few Brazilian cities, voters in the first state of electoral process were generally *agregados*'; Graham, 'Free African Brazilians and the State in Slavery Times', in Michael Hanchard (ed.), *Racial Politics in Contemporary Brazil* (Durham, NC: Duke University Press, 1999), pp. 30–58, see p. 38.

[49] Free blacks and freedmen were largely denied the right to vote in the United States before abolition. As Engerman and Sokoloff observe, when the Civil War broke out, only 'New York (where a property requirement of $250 was applied to them alone) and five New England states (where those of African descent were exceptionally rare) had extended the franchise to blacks'. In the 1890s and the first decade of the twentieth century, poll taxes and literacy tests were introduced in Southern states to restrict suffrage by African Americans. Analysing Latin American countries, the authors do not mention the franchise extended to free blacks and freedmen in nineteenth-century Brazil; Stanley L. Engerman and Kenneth L. Sokoloff, 'The Evolution of Suffrage Institutions in the New World', *Journal of Economic History* 65:4 (2005), pp. 891–921.

[50] In Rio de Janeiro, then the Brazilian capital and the most important town in South America, with 260,000 inhabitants in 1850, Portuguese immigrants took jobs previously occupied by slaves and free coloureds; Luiz Felipe de Alencastro, 'Prolétaires et esclaves: Immigrés portugais et captifs africains à Rio de Janeiro 1850–1872', *Cahiers du CRIAR* (Rouen) 4 (1984), pp. 119–56.

The independence of Brazil also altered Lisbon's African policy. Facing British pressure to halt the slave trade, and the loss of Portuguese America, in 1836 Sá da Bandeira, the Portuguese Prime Minister, proposed a profound change in African policy. In the bill issued to abolish the Atlantic slave trade, he stated, 'India, first, and Brazil later made us set aside Africa, our most natural field of work.' Instead of being sold abroad, Africans should be employed to work within Portuguese Africa. In his view, bearing the rising cost of slaves following the end of the slave trade, Brazilian planters would lose markets for tropical products grown in the remaining Portuguese colonies. European colonisation of the African territories should be promoted by the Crown.[51]

These ideas were endorsed by many political leaders and colonial officers. Another imperial reformer, Sebastião Xavier Botelho, perhaps inspired by his direct knowledge of Brazilian slavery, suggested gradual protection for slaves born on settlers' properties (*escravos crioulos*), to reinforce colonial enclaves in Angola and Mozambique and ultimately extinguish slavery. Like Sá da Bandeira, Botelho believed Brazilian agricultural exports would decline after the ending of the slave trade, opening new prospects for Portuguese plantations in Africa.[52] Brazilian slavery eventually became a point of reference for labour systems to be implemented in Africa. Thus, governor of Angola Calheiros e Menezes (1861–2), emphasising the impairment of Africans' resistance following their desocialisation from their original communities and their enslavement in Brazil, proposed the transfer of natives from Angola to Mozambique and vice versa, to enforce coerced labour in both colonies.[53]

Notwithstanding the growth of the *mulatto* population in Luanda around 1850 – due, as José Curto shows, to the arrival of migrants from the hinterland, attracted by jobs created with the end of the slave trade and the increase of legitimate commerce – no plan or official concerns arose based on their specific situation in Angola.[54]

Ultimately, the end of the slave trade split the colonial spatial matrix of the South Atlantic and brought new issues to Angola, Portugal and Brazil. Increased

[51] Sebastião Lopes de Calheiros e Menezes, *Relatório do Governador Geral da Província de Angola* (Lisbon: Imprensa Nacional, 1867), pp. 364–5.

[52] Sebastião Xavier Botelho lived in Brazil in the 1810s and was Appellate Judge (*Desembargador*) in Rio de Janeiro. Later he became successively Captain-General of Angola and Mozambique; *Escravatura: Benefícios que podem provir às nossas possessões d'África da prohibição daquelle tráfico* (Lisbon: Typographia de José B. Morando, 1840), pp. 30–5, 40.

[53] Letter to Ministro do Ultramar, Luanda, 31 Jan. 1862, in Menezes, *Relatório do Governador Geral*, pp. 82–7.

[54] José C. Curto, 'The Anatomy of a Demographic Explosion: Luanda, 1844–1850', *International Journal of African Historical Studies* 32:2–3 (1999), pp. 381–405. In fact, the *mulatto* population of Luanda had decreased during the first decades of the nineteenth century; José C. Curto and Raymond R. Gervais, 'The Population History of Luanda during the Late Atlantic Slave Trade, 1781–1844', *African Economic History* 29 (2001), pp. 1–59.

emigration to Brazil raised an important debate in Lisbon over whether the government should let citizens move to Rio de Janeiro, or rather redirect them to Luanda. The issue was discussed by the Overseas Council, which stated in 1852 that emigration from Portugal to British Guyana and Brazil should be redirected to Portuguese Africa. As remittances from migrants grew, the subject came to involve considerable financial benefits to Portugal. Thereby, colonial strategies conflicted with economic interests in Lisbon, and especially in Porto, whence most migrants embarked for South America. Taking into account the remittance money, Alexandre Herculano, who debated these issues for decades and whose opinion was influential in Lisbon, considered emigration to Brazil more profitable to Portugal than sending settlers to Africa. In a few well-chosen words, later famous, he wrote: 'since it ceased to be our colony, Brazil became our best colony'.[55] The rising value of migrants' remittances from Brazil was matched by concerns that the African and overseas possessions were too costly to be settled, exploited and sustained by Lisbon.

In this way, Brazil appeared to present obstacles to Portuguese colonisation in Angola. The problem was hardly new. In 1655, responding to repeated Crown instructions that cotton and sugar cane were to be cultivated there 'as it is done in Brazil', the municipal council of Luanda explained that production costs in Angola, and above all the South Atlantic trading system, rendered the whole economic scheme unviable.[56] Two centuries later, the project to create 'a new Brazil' in southern Africa, advocated by Sá da Bandeira and endorsed by authorities intending to send settlers to Angola, was once more thwarted by Brazil, which drew most of Portugal's emigrants.[57]

Another leading politician and intellectual, Andrade Corvo – regarded by Calvet de Magalhães as 'one of the most remarkable Portuguese statesmen', and by Valentim Alexandre as the leading imperial reformer of his times – also offered a

[55] Around 233,000 Portuguese (including those from the Azores and Madeira) disembarked at Rio de Janeiro between 1844 and 1878, a number only reached in Angola a century later; Alencastro, 'Prolétaires et esclaves'.

[56] The Luanda Chamber explained that the enterprise foundered amid local difficulties (including lack of firewood and the bad quality of African sugar cane). Furthermore, given the area's trade routes, with little direct transportation to Lisbon and a high level of activity in the slave trade to Brazil, the cotton and sugar eventually produced in Angola had to stop over at Brazilian ports before sailing on to Portugal. The freight costs caused Angolan produce to arrive in Lisbon at a higher price than its Brazilian equivalent; Consultation to Overseas Council, 21 June 1655, Arquivo Historico Ultramarino, Angola, box 6/18.

[57] The question of whether Portuguese emigration to Brazil and abroad should be redirected to Angola was recurrent, and was discussed in Lisbon until the 1950s. Except for the years 1943–5, the Portuguese emigrating abroad always exceeded those who went to the colonies; Claudia Castelo, 'A migração de metropolitanos para Angola e Moçambique 1945–1974', paper presented at the VIII Congresso Luso-Afro-Brasileiro de Ciências Sociais, Coimbra, September 2004 (available at www.ces.uc.pt/lab 2004/pdfs/ClaudiaCastelo.pdf); Claudia Castelo, *Passagens para Africa: O povoamento de Angola e Moçambique com naturais de metrópole 1920–1974* (Porto: Afrontamento, 2007).

global analysis of colonial problems. In 1875, as foreign and overseas minister, he outlined his plans to the Lisbon Parliament.[58] On Angola, he emphasised the training of native troops to secure the colony's defence, and analysed the conflicting interests that restrained metropolitan and island emigration to the colony. More generally, he viewed Angola through the duality colonists/colonised, Portuguese/Africans, and made no reference either to *mulattos* or to Luso-African culture. Setting out – in a rare and remarkable declaration – the non-racist policy that Lisbon should follow in Africa, and the values of freedom and justice that must transform Angolans into an 'integral part' of the Portuguese nation, Andrade Corvo nevertheless did not envisage interracial marriages, miscegenation or the *mulattos*' ascent in Angola as components of colonial policy.[59]

Overseas issues are also well addressed in Oliveira Martins' *O Brasil e as colónias portuguesas* (1880), arguably the most important book on the Portuguese colonial questions of the time.[60] To Oliveira Martins, Angola and Mozambique, still regarded as factories, might develop into plantation colonies provided the authorities achieved an effective system of coerced labour: '[Portuguese] Africa should be exploited and not colonised'. Underlining Herculano's aphorism, cited above, Oliveira Martins was 'absolutely' (*terminantemente*) against redirecting migrants aiming to establish themselves in Brazil, to Angola. He contended that the future of Portuguese Africa was not in the hands of the whites, but rather in the hands of the blacks: Africans had to work efficiently under the control of a few metropolitan managers. Otherwise, the country's colonies should be sold off or rented.

Reflecting on Brazil as an independent and stable nation, under the same ruling dynasty as Portugal – during troubled times in most of the American republics – Oliveira Martins stated proudly that, contrary to the Dutch companies, organised

[58] João de Andrade Corvo (1824–90), Foreign Minister of Portugal between 1871 and 1878, was also Overseas Minister from 1872 to 1877. An important writer and political reformer, Andrade Corvo is an author who deserves to be better known; see José Calvet de Magalhães, 'Portugal e Inglaterra: De D. Fernando ao mapa cor-de-rosa (II)', *Janus* 1999–2000, 10 Dec. 2010, available at www.janusonline.pt/1999_2000/1999_2000_1_25.html#1; Valentim Alexandre, 'A questão colonial no Portugal oitocentista', in Joel Serrão and A. H. de Oliveira Marques (eds), *Nova História da Expansão Portuguesa* (Lisbon: Editorial Estampa, 1998), vol. 10, pp. 101–8.

[59] 'Our colonies' system shall not, even remotely, look like those of other nations where racial dominance seems to prevail over all other feelings'; *Relatórios do Ministro e Secretário d'Estado dos Negócios da Marinha e do Ultramar* (Lisbon: Imprensa Nacional, 1875), pp. 64, 174–83.

[60] Influenced by Leroy-Beaulieu, he describes three categories of overseas possessions: the simple factories, the plantation domains (*fazendas*) and the colonies. Leroy-Beaulieu's book was authoritative in his time and is quoted by Oliveira Martins and by Portuguese parliamentarians. Analysing the Second European Expansion, the French economist defines two categories of colonies: 'colonies d'exploitation' and 'colonies de peuplement'. Differently from Brazilian historians, like Caio Prado Júnior, who uncritically adopted Leroy-Beaulieu's ideas, Oliveira Martins appropriately considers also another category, the 'factoreries' (*feitorias*), which is more pertinent to Portuguese and European history in Asia and Africa before the nineteenth century; Paul Leroy-Beaulieu, *De la colonisation chez les peuples modernes* (Paris: Guillaumin et Cie, 1874).

to plunder overseas peoples, Portugal 'created nations, and [. . .] gave birth [. . .] to new overseas countries'. Quoted and endorsed by Jaime Cortesão and other Portuguese authors, these remarks inspired the idea of Portugal's 'colonial exceptionalism', which would be taken up again by Gilberto Freyre and his Lusotropicalist followers.[61] However, Oliveira Martins, too, made no reference to the *mulattos* in Angola. As a matter of fact, he disapproved of Portuguese miscegenation in Africa and advised the Brazilian government to avoid black or Asian immigration so as not to 'bastardise' Brazil's population.[62]

By design or default, Portuguese America's evolution and independence (the 'loss of Brazil') remained the major point of reference for nineteenth-century colonial projects.[63] And yet neither Andrade Corvo – an inspired and liberal reformist – nor any other political thinker or overseas administrator advocated miscegenation or the improvement of the situation of *mulattos* as a step in consolidating the peopling of Angola. Nothing similar to Sousa Coutinho's 1770s plans regarding Angolan *mulattos* was conceived throughout the 1800s.

Eventually, the 'Scramble for Africa' and the British ultimatum of 1890, which forced a Portuguese military retreat from southern African territories claimed by Lisbon, led to a national movement to preserve the integrity of the colonies.[64] Colonial policy changed as the Portuguese settlements in Angola grew in geopolitical significance. Henceforth, the overseas territories were to be strengthened and peopled by Portuguese, and foreign immigration avoided.[65] This shift in colonial policy had an impact on the *mulatto* community in Luanda.

[61] 'Acusem-nos de termos instalado na América um sistema feudal, acusem-se os vícios da nossa administração colonial; mas o fato é que ela criou nações, fez germinar e nascer as sementes de novas pátrias ultramarinas, ao passo que as Companhias dos Holandeses jamais criaram coisa alguma, a não ser um sistema hábil de rapinar o trabalho indígena, depois de terminado o período das rendosas piratarias. Saquear e entesourar, eis aí o propósito destas instituições, exclusivamente nascidas dos espírito mercantil'; Martins, *O Brasil e as colónias portuguesas*, p. 41; see also Jaime Cortesão, *O Ultramar português depois da Restauração* (Lisbon: Portugalia, 1971), p. 115.

[62] In fact, Martins also proposed social and land reform in Portugal to avoid emigration and improve the country's economy: '[Today] Brazil is a better colony to us than Africa, nevertheless the best of all our colonies would be the Kingdom itself'. He also thought that Brazilian government should prefer European immigrants, so as to turn the country into 'a European and not a Mestiço Nation'; *O Brasil e as colónias portuguesas*, pp. 175–6, 233–56, 287–8.

[63] For an essay on this issue, see Gabriel Paquette, 'After Brazil: Portuguese Debates on Empire, c. 1820–1850', *Journal of Colonialism and Colonial History* 11:2 (2010). It would be interesting to undertake research on this theme for the period 1850–90.

[64] As Valentim Alexandre demonstrates, Oliveira Martins followed the nationalist mood which 'sacralized the Empire', and reconsidered his views on the uselessness of overseas possessions; Alexandre, 'Questão nacional e questão colonial em Oliveira Martins', *Análise Social* 31:1 (1996), pp. 183–201.

[65] See for instance, the Parliamentary debate of 1912, on a project on Angola's colonisation by Jewish Russians, when Freitas Ribeiro, Minister for the Colonies, declared, 'We need to save Angola by peopling it with the Portuguese'; *Diário da Camara dos Deputados*, session of 21 May 1912 (available at www.primeirarepublica.org/portal/images/stories/sa_049_1912_05_21.pdf). Direct threats in Angola came from Boer and German southwest African moves in the Cunene River and on the Huila Plateau.

cont.

As several researchers had shown, in the second half of the nineteenth century, a Luso-African elite in Angola formed of educated blacks and *mulattos*, as well as *filhos da terra* (old colonists), expressed nationalist opinions, with some of its members publishing their demands in the Luanda press.[66] Meanwhile, reacting to European threats to the borders of its territories in Africa, Lisbon tightened metropolitan control of the Angolan administration. Increased Portuguese immigration, press censorship, and educational restrictions obscured the Luso-African elite's activities into the first decades of the twentieth century.[67] There also occurred a simultaneous decline of Luso-African oligarchies living in the hinterland (Massangano, Golungo Alto, Ambaca, Caconda) who produced Angolan agricultural exports. Coping with competition from immigrants and new administrative restrictions, these families lost most of their economic and political status.[68] Another important intermediate group, the *ambaquistas* – African inland traders and peasants who connected Luba-Lunda societies with maritime networks, used written documents and a Luso-Kimbundu language (the *ambaca*), and identified themselves as Christians – likewise suffered the impact of the nineteenth-century transformations.[69] In fact, their importance lessened with the influx of metropolitan merchants, the introduction of steamships on the Kwanza River, and the growth of Angolan trade with industrialised countries.[70]

See the debate in the National Constituent Assembly, 25 July 1911, 7 Aug. 1911, and 16 Aug. 1911, *Diario da Assembléia Nacional Constituinte*, Lisbon, and 10 March 1916 and 6 Aug. 1918, in Congresso da Republica (available at http://debates.parlamento.pt/?pid=r3).

[66] The 'filhos da terra' were also referred to as 'filhos do país'; see Anon., *Catalogo dos Governadores de Angola* (1825); Anon., *Colleçao de noticias para a historia das nações ultramarinas* (Lisbon: Academia Real das Sciencias, 1826), vol. 3, part 2, p. 427.

[67] Douglas L. Wheeler, '"Angola Is Whose House?" Early Stirrings of Angolan Nationalism and Protest, 1822–1910', *African Historical Studies* 2:1 (1969), pp. 1–22; Marcelo Bittencourt, 'A resposta dos "Crioulos Luandenses" ao intensificar do processo colonial nos finais do século XIX', in *A África e a instalação do sistema colonial (c.1885 – c.1930)*, Actas da III Reunião Internacional de História da África, 1999 (Lisbon: IICT, 2000), pp. 655–71; Marcelo Bittencourt, *Dos jornais às armas: Trajectórias da contestação angolana* (Lisbon: Vega, 1999); Aida Freudenthal, 'Voz de Angola em tempo de ultimato', *Estudos Afro-Asiáticos* 23:1 (2001), pp. 139–69.

[68] Jill Dias, 'Mudanças nos padrões de poder do "Hinterland" de Luanda: O impacto da colonização sobre os Mbundu (c.1845–1920)', *Penélope. Fazer e desfazer a história* 14 (1994), pp. 43–91.

[69] In the nineteenth century, the word *ambaquista* was employed for any African Kimbundu speaker with Portuguese dress or behaviour; Dias, 'Mudanças nos padrões de poder', pp. 51–2, 77, n. 30. On written documents in Angolan societies, see Catarina Madeira Santos and Ana Paula Tavares, *Africae Monumenta. A apropriação da escrita pelos Africanos, t. 1, Arquivo Caculo Cacahenda* (Lisbon: Instituto de Investigaçao Científica Tropical, 2002); and Catarina Madeira Santos, 'Écrire le pouvoir en Angola', *Annales. Histoire, Sciences Sociales* 64:4 (2009), pp. 767–95.

[70] Beatrix Heintze, *Pioneiros africanos: Caravanas de carregadores na África Centro-Ocidental (entre 1850–1890)* (Lisbon: Caminho, 2004); Beatrix Heintze, 'Between Two Worlds: The Bezerras, a Luso-African Family in Nineteenth Century Western Central Africa', in Ph. J. Havik and Malyn Newitt (eds), *Creole Societies in the Portuguese Colonial Empire* (Bristol: University of Bristol, 2007), pp. 127–53; see also the review by Jean-Luc Vellut, 'New Perspectives on the Ambaquista Network', *Journal of African History* 45:2 (2004), pp. 327–9.

At this point, *mulattos* and Luso-Africans became economically and socially less significant, as whites for the first time outnumbered mixed-race inhabitants. According to overall population data, the *mulatto* population actually fell. In Angola, in 1845, *mulattos* numbered 5,770, while whites numbered 1,832. In 1900, these figures were respectively 3,112 and 9,198. Certainly, the colony was afflicted by famines and epidemics in the late nineteenth century, and its black population also registered a decrease, albeit in smaller proportions, during the same period.[71] However, the sharp drop of 46 per cent in *mulatto* inhabitants (compared to an 11 per cent drop in the black population) could plausibly have been provoked by other restrictions on the social reproduction of *mulattos*. Indeed, the growing arrival of *petits blancs* from Portugal toughened both status competition and colonist hostility towards the middle racial group.[72] Perhaps these moves impelled more *mulattos* to live with their mothers' families, embedding themselves within African communities.[73]

In addition, the authorities were generally negative to interracial relations, fearing the uneven effects of miscegenation. They also attempted to avoid *cafrealisation*, that is, poor whites' immersion into their African wives' communities. Contradicting colonialist beliefs on cultural and racial domination, cafrealisation jeopardised the social reproduction of the Portuguese settlers and thwarted effective territorial expansion.[74] Even if we may distinguish cafrealisation (the 'social leakage' of whites into African communities) from reafricanisation (*mulattos*' incorporation in their mothers' kinship system), both processes illustrate the elusive and contentious phenomena underlying the concept of race and its derivatives.[75]

As Claudia Castelo states, to prevent cafrealisation, Lisbon controlled metropolitan and island departures to Angola up to the 1960s, opposing travel by poor migrants and encouraging the emigration of families. Thus, from the 1940s on, families outnumbered single colonists entering Angola.[76] Ultimately, the momentum of *mulatto* and Luso-African ascendancy in colonial Angola faded at the

[71] Jill Dias, 'Famine and Disease in the History of Angola, c. 1830–1930', *Journal of African History* 22:3 (1981), pp. 349–78.

[72] Like many other researchers, I consider the Portuguese immigrants arriving in Angola as colonists.

[73] *Mutatis mutandis*, in the United States, as Aaron Gullickson suggests, the hostility of poor whites also contributed to the decline of *mulattos* as a distinct group at the beginning of the twentieth century. The *mulatto* category 'was visible enough to be granted official recognition on the U.S. census from 1850 to 1920 (with the exception of 1900)'; Aaron Gullickson, 'Racial Boundary Formation at the Dawn of Jim Crow: The Determinants and Effects of Black/Mulatto Occupational Differences in the United States, 1880', *American Journal of Sociology* 116:1 (2010), pp. 187–231.

[74] See the comments of Alfredo Margarido, 'Littérature et Nationalité', *Politique Africaine* 29 (1988), pp. 58–70.

[75] I rely here on the thoughtful essay by Loïc J. D. Wacquant, 'For an Analytic of Racial Domination', *Political Power and Social Theory* 11 (1997), pp. 221–34.

[76] Claudia Castelo, interview for *Observatório da Emigração*, 30 June 2010 (available at www.observatorioemigracao.secomunidades.pt/np4/1878.html).

beginning of the twentieth century.[77] Flawed to begin with, the idea of transforming Angola into 'another Brazil' now stood beyond the realm of possibility.[78]

It is well known that European mass migration and theories of social Darwinism adopted by some influential intellectuals transformed the status of *mulattos* in Brazil. In contrast to the post-slavery context in the United States, no legislation forbade interracial marriages.[79] But public prejudice and indirect legal restrictions brought discrimination, as shown in the outcome of the electoral law. Up to 1882, if they met the annual income criteria, illiterate male adults could vote in Brazilian elections. A literacy requirement for suffrage issued that year, in the context of reforms leading to the abolition of slavery in 1888, to target blacks and *mulattos*, then excluded poor Brazilians, whether blacks, *mulattos*, or whites, from citizenship. And since the percentage of illiterate blacks and *mulattos* was (and remains) higher than the percentage of illiterate whites, African-Brazilians endured this denial of their citizenship rights on a larger scale.[80]

In view of the particularities and contingencies summarised above, the contrast between the two sides of the South Atlantic was patent at the beginning of the twentieth century. Certainly, an observable *mulatto* group and culture existed in Angola. However, *mulattos* were effectively a more durable entity and a more stable historical subject in Brazil.

The divide of the twentieth century

Following the abolition of the slave trade and slavery in Portuguese Africa, the government made several attempts to regulate native labour in Angola and the other

[77] Douglas Wheeler states, 'As the *assimilado* was beginning to achieve a higher status and position, the increase in European immigration from Portugal and the islands wiped out the numerical superiority enjoyed up to 1890. The Europeans now began to compete for jobs, and government policy, though claiming to practice no discrimination, began to restrict entry into certain jobs in the bureaucracy by raising educational requirements'; Wheeler, '"Angola Is Whose House?"', pp. 12–13.

[78] Nevertheless, up to 1950, the *Movimento Democrático de Angola* (MDA), an autonomist organisation formed by liberal whites, sustained the project of transforming Angola into 'another Brazil'; see Juliana Marçano Santil's important thesis, '"Ce métis qui nous trouble"; Les représentations du Brésil dans l'imaginaire politique angolais: L'empreinte de la colonialité sur le savoir', unpublished doctoral thesis, Université de Bordeaux IV, 2006, pp. 256–7; also Fernando Pimenta, 'Ideologia nacional dos brancos angolanos (1900–1975)', paper presented at the VIII Congresso Luso-Afro-Brasileiro de Ciências Sociais, Coimbra, September 2004.

[79] It must be noted that many municipal and association rules indeed included racial clauses against blacks and *mulattos* in the twentieth century. For instance a 1906 rule of São Paulo's municipal guard forbade admission of blacks and *mulattos* to its ranks; Carolina Vianna Dantas, 'O Brasil cafe com leite. Debates intelectuais sobre mesticagem e preconceito de cor na primeira republica', *Tempo – Revista do Departamento de Historia da UFF* 1 (2009), available at www.thefreelibrary.com/O+Brasil+cafe+com+leite.+Debates+intelectuais+sobre+mesticagem+e. . .-a0207745037

[80] The literacy requirement was lifted only in 1985.

colonies.[81] The relevant legislation often drew on post-slavery and immigration laws and procedures adopted by other countries in the Americas and in Africa. From our perspective, it is interesting to recall the similarities between the social and identity issues in Brazil and Portugal during this time.

The concept of 'civilisation' – a key component of the second Western expansion – was instrumental in Brazil on a large scale (most likely for the first time in a colonial society) after the Marquis of Pombal expelled the Jesuits and issued the Code on Amerindians: the *Directorio* of 1759. Throughout the nineteenth century, the *Directorio*'s 'civilising' ideas – the distinction between 'domesticated' (*mansas*) and 'undomesticated' (*bravas*) tribes, the teaching of Portuguese to the Indians, legal tutorship over the tribes, and progressive assimilation of Indians into the national community – remained deeply rooted in deliberations on native peoples in Brazil. Aptly, these ideas were also present in Andrade Corvo's reflections on the natives' evolution in Angola.

Luso-Brazilian intellectual exchange continued, as Portuguese and Brazilian abolitionists partook of the same political agenda during the struggle to end slavery and its after-effects in Brazil and Portuguese Africa.[82]

In the meantime, Portugal became a republic too (in 1910), and ties between Rio de Janeiro and Lisbon were strengthened by cultural transfers and significant Portuguese immigration. Amid accusations of massacres of tribes by ranchers in the state of Santa Catarina, in the same year the Brazilian government created the Indian Protection Service (SPI), the first national agency designed to administer Indian affairs.[83] Referring to the Indians, as well as to the evolving status of freed slaves, immigrants, and particularly Japanese families arriving in São Paulo, press and parliamentary debates on civilisation, nationality, and citizenship combined the new social diversity with old hierarchies.[84] Sociological Positivism, with its comparative and historical references, was equally influential in Brazil and Portugal

[81] Maria Paula G. Meneses, 'O "indígena" africano e o colono "europeu": A construção da diferença por processos legais', *e-cadernos CES* (Coimbra) (2010), pp. 68–93.

[82] In January 1881, the Brazilian abolitionist leader Joaquim Nabuco visited and was honoured by the Assembly in Lisbon. In his presence, parliamentarians voted in a law intended to eliminate corporal punishment in Portuguese Africa; Joaquim Nabuco, *O Abolicionismo* (1883; São Paulo: Publifolha, 2000), p. 78, n. 10.

[83] Although the SPI's first director, General Candido Rondon – a soldier of Bororo descent, learned Indian expert, and Positivist – conceived of the Brazilian tribes as 'autonomous Nations with whom we should establish friendly relations', the thrust of most public and government opinion was much more unambiguous regarding control and economic exploitation of Indian territories; Mércio Pereira Gomes, 'Por que sou rondoniano', *Estudos Avançados* 23:65 (2009), pp. 173–91.

[84] On reactions hostile to the arrival of Japanese and foreign blacks in Brazil, see Jair de Souza Ramos, 'Dos males que vêm com o sangue: As representações raciais e a categoria do imigrante indesejável nas concepções sobre imigração da década de 20', in Marcos Chor Maio and Ricardo Ventura Santos (eds), *Raça, ciência e sociedade no Brasil* (Rio de Janeiro: FioCruz, 1996), pp. 59–82.

in issues regarding natives peoples' status and rights.[85] After 1902, the learned Brazilian jurist and Positivist João Mendes Júnior wrote about the concept of *indigenato*, a traditional and legitimate Indian settlement, as distinct from *colonato*, a settlement founded by colonists.[86]

At that time, mass migration to Brazil encouraged elite hopes of 'whitening' the Brazilian population through European immigration.[87] In this context, and contrary to prevailing racist ideas, Gilberto Freyre published his *The Masters and the Slaves* (1933),[88] the seminal book that instated miscegenation at the core of Brazilian history, and blacks and *mulattos* as an essential component of the nation.[89]

Such debates were conflated in Lisbon with issues of European policies in Africa, and particularly the expansion of settlement in South Africa and Algeria. Most notably, in Algeria, the *Décret Crémieux* of 1870 granted French citizenship to the Algerian Jews, while the *Code de l'Indigenat* of 1881 differentiated between French citizens and 'subjects' (natives of the French colonies) and empowered colonial administrators with extensive authority over native communities.[90] Ensuing discussions focused on the different status of the colonies' inhabitants and the making of a middle racial tier able to play an interstitial role so as to reinforce settler and metropolitan dominance.[91]

Thus, Portuguese, Brazilian, American and European colonial practices paved the way towards appearance of the *assimilado* category in 1926 and the Colonial

[85] On Positivism and Republican ideas in Portugal, see Fernando Catroga, 'A importância do positivismo na consolidação da ideologia republicana em Portugal', *Biblos* 53 (1977), pp. 283–327.

[86] João Mendes Júnior, *Os indígenas do Brazil: Seus direitos individuais e políticos* (São Paulo: Hennies Irmãos, 1912), pp. 58–64. This book includes a series of papers given by the author in previous years.

[87] On immigration, national identity and related issues, see Jeffrey Lesser, *Negotiating National Identity: Immigrants, Minorities, and the Struggle for Ethnicity in Brazil* (Durham, NC: Duke University Press, 1999); and the comments of Jair de Souza Ramos, 'Afinal, o que é preciso para ser "brasileiro"? Leitura de um texto que fala sobre as lutas por esta e outras identidades', *História, ciência e saúde – Manguinhos* 7:1 (2000), pp. 197–204.

[88] On racism and immigration policies in Brazil during this period, see Endrica Geraldo, 'O "perigo alienígena": Política imigratória e pensamento racial no governo Vargas (1930–1945)', unpublished PhD thesis, UNICAMP, 2007. There is an extensive bibliography on *The Masters and the Slaves* and the other works of Freyre; for a recent and important book, see Peter Burke and Maria Lúcia G. Pallares-Burke, *Gilberto Freyre: Social Theory in the Tropics* (Oxford: Peter Lang, 2008).

[89] It should be noted that in 1946, when the American translation of Freyre's book was published, more than half of the United States had statutes which prohibited racial intermarriage; Irving G. Tragen, 'Statutory Prohibitions against Interracial Marriage', *California Law Review* 32:3 (1944), pp. 269–80. Such laws, still existing in nine states in 1967, were overturned that year by the Supreme Court; Ewa A. Golebiowska, 'The Contours and Etiology of Whites' Attitudes toward Black-White Interracial Marriage', *Journal of Black Studies* 38:2 (2007), pp. 268–87.

[90] Isabelle Merle, 'De la "légalisation" de la violence en contexte colonial. Le régime de l'indigénat en question', *Politix* 17:66 (2004), pp.137–62.

[91] Laure Blévis, 'Les avatars de la citoyenneté en Algérie coloniale ou les paradoxes d'une catégorisation', *Droit et Société* 48 (2001), pp. 557–80.

Act of 1930.[92] This Act and its connoted issues have already been studied and will not be discussed here.[93] Yet, in the light of our previous remarks, the *assimilado* categorisation has considerable significance. Lisbon's decision to create *assimilados* by law as a 'buffer class' exposes the absence of social or demographic conditions enabling mixed-race groups to achieve an intermediate social rank. Actually, any metropolitan project for managing control by means of miscegenation or transethnic kinship was impracticable, indeed structurally unviable, in Angola.[94] That is when Lusotropicalist ideas began to gain momentum in Portuguese colonialist circles.

The invention of Luso-Brazilian miscegenation as a Portuguese pattern

As is well known, after being frowned on or ignored, Freyre's ideas on Luso-Brazilian miscegenation and Portugal's colonial specificity were increasingly adopted by the Lisbon government in the 1950s and the 1960s.[95] A browser search of Parliamentary debates held in the Lisbon National Assembly suggests that Freyre's works were quoted only five times between 1935 and 1974.[96] In 1944, they were cited in connection with issues concerning Portuguese language and institutions, and in 1953, for praising the alleged absence of racism in Portugal's overseas possessions. Later, in 1962, in connection with the loss of Goa the previous year, a parliamentarian emphasised – for the first and only time – Freyre's concept of Lusotropicalism. Also in 1962 there appeared the first and only meritorious

[92] 'The assimilated were indigenous people who had to undergo a probation period and exams in order to prove that they were Christian, that they dressed in European fashion, that they were monogamous, and that they spoke Portuguese. They never amounted to more than 1% of the colonial population'; Miguel Vale de Almeida, 'Portugal's Colonial Complex: From Colonial Lusotropicalism to Postcolonial Lusophony', paper presented at Queen's Postcolonial Research Forum, April 2008 (available at http://site.miguelvaledealmeida.net/wp-content/uploads/portugals-colonial-complex.pdf).

[93] Christine Messiant, *1961. L'Angola colonial, l'histoire et la société, les premises du mouvement nationaliste* (Basel: P. Schlettwein, 2006), pp. 105–17; Henriques, *Commerce et changement en Angola*, vol. 1, pp. 29–30.

[94] As Marcelo Bittencourt states, the premise of *assimilado* status was the idea that the Luso-African entitled to it had entirely abandoned African culture. Analysing the *ambaquistas*, Beatrix Heintze employs the term 'transethnic kinship' to define 'certain phenomena normally or allegedly associated to ethnicity, claiming the ethnic ties or barriers vis-à-vis other ethnic groups are, at least temporarily or partially, dissolved, transcended or minimalised'; Heintze, 'Translocal "Kinship" Relations in Central African Politics of the 19th Century', *Global Studies in Global Social History* 4 (2010), pp. 179–204, p. 187, n. 18.

[95] For a Brazilian point of view, see Waldir José Rampinelli, *As duas faces da moeda – as contribuições de JK e Gilberto Freyre ao colonialismo português* (Florianópolis: UFSC, 2004), pp. 59–64. For a Portuguese approach, see Claudia Castelo, *'O modo português de estar no mundo': O Luso-tropicalismo e a ideologia colonial portuguesa, 1933–1961* (Porto: Afrontamento, 1998).

[96] The Parliamentary website is available at http://debates.parlamento.pt/?pid=mc (accessed November 2010).

reference to an African *mulatto* (encountered in southern Africa in the 1850s by David Livingstone) as a faithful subject of the government and a truly Portuguese character.

Indeed, in 1961 and 1962 a series of setbacks affected Lisbon's overseas policy. In addition to the storming of Goa by the Indian army, the independence of the French colonies in Sub-Saharan Africa, the intensification of the Algerian war, and the tragedies of decolonisation in the Belgian Congo exposed Portuguese Africa's vulnerability. Brazil, an important and traditional backer of Portugal's colonial policy, voted in the UN session of 1961 against Lisbon's control of Angola.[97] More critically, the first large military attack launched by a nationalist movement (the UPA, later FNLA) struck northern Angola in 1961.

Lisbon's decision to extinguish the *assimilado* category that same year appears as a response to the UN charges of racial discrimination, but also as an admission of the failure to create a buffer class in Portuguese Africa.[98] In 1960, black *assimilados* in Angola, including women and children, amounted to some 41,000, most of whom lived in Luanda. Put together, *mulattos* and *assimilados* made up 8.9 per cent of the capital's inhabitants. This is not a trivial number, but neither is it a transformative one.[99]

Yves Léonard has shown that Adriano Moreira, then the overseas minister, promoted Freyre's Lusotropicalist theories as a 'substitution ideology' for Portuguese colonialism.[100] Christian Geffray asks why the Lusotropicalist ideology was born in Brazil – and why nothing similar appeared in Hispanic America? Why was there no 'hispanotropicalism'?[101] The answer lies in the depth of the Portuguese overseas crisis, after decolonisation by the British, French and Belgians. Freyre's efforts to propose a normative meaning for his interpretation of Luso-Brazilian

[97] On the reaction of the Lisbon government against Brazilian diplomats sympathetic to Portuguese-African independence, see the book by the first Brazilian ambassador in Angola in 1975: Ovídio de Andrade Melo, *Recordações de um removedor de mofo no Itamaraty* (Rio de Janeiro: Fundação Alexandre de Gusmão, 2009), p. 86.

[98] Gilberto Freyre disliked the '*assimilado*' status, which he considered 'inept'. He also attacked the apartheid established by Diamang, owned by the British multinational De Beers, in the Lunda province of Angola. After Angola's independence, he made the unlikely assertion that these criticisms showed that he condemned Portuguese colonialism in Africa; 'O Brasil em face das Áfricas Negras e Mestiças', paper presented at a conference held at the Gabinete Português de Leitura, 10 June 1962, in *Edição de um grupo de amigos e admiradores portugueses para distribuir gratuitamente às escolas* (Lisbon, 1963), pp. 10, 13–14, 19. See Freyre's interview in *O Estado de São Paulo*, 9 July 1979, in Bernardo Ricupero (ed.), *Gilberto Freyre* (Rio de Janeiro: Beco do Azougue Editorial, 2010), pp. 174–5.

[99] Whites, with 58,256 people, represented 16.7 per cent of the Luanda population, '*Mestiços*' (mostly *mulattos*) 14,719 or 4.3 per cent, *assimilados* 15,576 or 4.6 per cent, and '*Indígenas*' or natives 258,156 or 74.3 per cent; Messiant, *1961. L'Angola colonial*, pp. 313–16, table 12.

[100] Yves Léonard, 'Salazarisme et lusotropicalisme, histoire d'une appropriation', *Lusotopie* (1997), pp. 211–26.

[101] Christian Geffray, 'Le Lusotropicalisme comme discours de l'amour dans la servitude', *Lusotopie* (1997), pp. 361–72.

society, and his willingness to support Portuguese colonialism, also played a decisive role in the adoption of Lusotropicalism by Lisbon. And this Luso-Brazilian convergence of history and ideology is witnessed again during this period, albeit in a different sense, when the writings of Jaime Cortesão on the *bandeirantes* reassured the regionalist pride of *Paulistas*.[102]

Political and scholarly criticism of Freyre's ideas on Portuguese colonisation and Luso-African miscegenation, and its biological corollary the *mulatto*, became more frequent in the late 1950s. As data from the 1960s Angolan census were published, showing that the percentage of mixed-race persons was 1 per cent, much less than the 9 per cent rate observed even in apartheid South Africa, Freyre played down the importance of *mulattos*. In 1966, in an article significantly entitled 'Eurotropical Interaction: Aspects of Some of Its Several Processes, Including the Lusotropical', he referred to the census and dismissed the 'statistical simplicity' that failed to take account of the larger populations in Angola and Mozambique who were 'socially and culturally *mestiços*'. Whereas in 1962 Freyre considered miscegenation the 'main feature' of Portuguese colonialism, he now relocated his reflections in a European perspective ('Eurotropical interaction') and described the broader phenomena of acculturation occurring across European possessions in tropical Africa. Yet he continued to describe the 'Lusotropical style' of 'conviviality between Europeans and Non-Europeans' as the way to preserve Portuguese Africa from the (supposedly uncertain) destiny of the Belgian, French, British and Dutch colonies.[103]

Dematerialised in this new exegesis of Lusotropicalism, the *mulatto* turned into an issue of factionalism in Portuguese Africa. Indeed, as the influx of metropolitan and island colonists rose in Angola, many *mulattos* and *assimilados* joined the anti-colonial rebellion. Much of this shift favoured the MPLA (*Movimento Popular de Libertação de Angola*), although UNITA (*União Nacional para a Independência Total de Angola*) also numbered many *assimilados* and *mulattos* among its ranks.[104] In any case, UNITA and FNLA (*Frente Nacional de Libertação de Angola*)

[102] Indeed, Cortesão's aversion to 'Fascist Iberism', a historical revisionism stimulated by the Franco-Salazar friendship, made him frame the *bandeirante* raids on the Jesuit missions in Paraguay in the 1630s and early 1640s as part of the anti-Hispanic offensive leading to the Restoration in the 1640s and to the war for Portugal's independence from Spain. This edifying reinterpretation of slaving expeditions for Indian captives was adopted by *paulista* elites, whose self-esteem, knocked by defeat in the 1932 rebellion against the Vargas government, found comfort in Cortesão's writings. Charles Boxer criticised Cortesão's benevolence on the *bandeirante* raids; Alencastro, *O trato dos viventes*, pp. 334–5, 443, n. 228.

[103] Gilberto Freyre, 'Interação Eurotropical: Aspectos de alguns dos seus varios processos, inclusive o lusotropical', *Journal of Inter-American Studies* 8:1 (1966), pp. 1–10; Freyre, 'O Brasil em face das Áfricas Negras', p. 10.

[104] Quoting Leon de Costa Dash Junior, Clarence-Smith writes that around 10 per cent of UNITA's troops in the 1970s were *mestiços*; W. G. Clarence-Smith, 'Class Structure and Class Struggles in Angola in the 1970s', *Journal of Southern African Studies* 7:1 (1980), pp. 109–26.

propaganda attacks, whether inspired or not by colonial security services, targeted the alleged *mulatto* ascendancy within the MPLA.[105] Today, Angolan opponents criticise the MPLA regime through racist insults aimed at its *mulatto* members.[106]

In Brazil, the identity of *mulattos* has also undergone changing perceptions in recent decades. Echoing the quotation from Henry Koster, cited above, the story of Robson, a *mulatto* football player in the Fluminense team in the mid-1950s, illustrates the enduring belief in the process of 'whitening'. Asked by a journalist if another player was not 'too black' to be popular, Robson answered: 'I was a black once, and I know what it's like'![107]

Meanwhile, the reintroduction of racial criteria in Brazilian census and demographic surveys in the late 1970s prompted new approaches to racial classifications.[108] In fact, most recent research offers a more complex analysis of the 'whitening' process. On the one hand, some data demonstrate that, at a certain social level, *mulattos* enjoy a better social status than do blacks. To mention just one aspect, research on infant mortality indicates that among children born to poor illiterate mothers, mortality is 95 per 1,000 for whites, 110 per 1,000 for *mulattos* ('*pardos*'), and 120 per 1,000 for blacks ('*pretos*').[109] On the other hand, there is no difference between the situations of *mulattos* and blacks at higher social levels, as shown by the 2000 census data regarding persons aged 25–64 years entering universities. The percentage of whites in this group is 13.4, while the percentage for *mulattos* is 4.0, the same as for blacks.[110] As Edward Telles states, 'the overall effects of whitening by education are not as great as previously suggested and, in the case of the darkest males, there are almost no effects'.[111]

[105] On the MPLA and *assimilados*, see Christine Messiant, 'Sur la première génération du MPLA: 1948–1960 – Mário de Andrade, entretiens avec Christine Messiant (1982)', *Lusotopie* (1999), pp. 185–221; Messiant, *1961. L'Angola colonial*, pp. 109–18, 313–50.

[106] See for instance the attacks of the Angolan opposition weekly *Agora* against *mulattos* allegedly supporting president José Eduardo dos Santos: 'Os Mulatos do Zé Du', 25 March 2006, in Petra Kátia Amaral Catarino, 'Sociedade civil angolana. Contributos para a democracia, paz e desenvolvimento', Masters dissertation, Universidade Técnica de Lisboa, 2006, p. 123, n. 173 (available at www.adelinotorres.com/teses/Petra%20K%C3%A1tia%20Amaral%20Catarino_Sociedade%20Civil%20Angolana.pdf). Harsher racist insults against Angolan *mulattos* can be found in comments in online papers dated January 2011, available at http://angonoticias.com/full_headlines_.php?id=16075

[107] 'Eu já fui preto e sei o que é isso'; Mário Filho, *O Negro no futebol brasileiro*, 5th edn (1947; Rio de Janeiro: Faperj, 2003), p. 318.

[108] On the Brazilian census and Afro-Brazilian demography, see Elza Berquó, 'Demografia da desigualdade. Algumas considerações sobre os negros no Brasil', *Novos Estudos – CEBRAP* 21 (1988), pp. 74–84.

[109] This research, by Estela Garcia Tamburo, is quoted in Berquó, 'Demografia da desigualdade', table 2, p. 76.

[110] Marcelo H. R. Tragtenberg, 'Programa de Ações Afirmativas da UFSC: Fundamentos e resultados preliminares', quoting research by Edward Telles (available at www.stf.jus.br/portal/cms/verTexto.asp?servico=processoAudienciaPublicaAcaoAfirmativa).

[111] Edward E. Telles, 'Racial Ambiguity among the Brazilian Population', revised version of a paper presented at a Brown University Sociology Department colloquium, September 1998 (available at

cont.

Ultimately, a web of racialised practices and institutions interlock to form a specific system of racial domination in Brazil.[112] In this system the status of *mulattos* remains largely dependent on the arbitrariness of the dominant order.[113] We might end, then, by paraphrasing the famous sentence of Simone de Beauvoir, in *The Second Sex* (1949): in Brazil, one is not born a *mulatto*, but rather becomes one.[114]

www.sscnet.ucla.edu/soc/faculty/telles/Paper_RacialAmbiguityBrazil.pdf). See also the same author's important book, *Race in Another America: The Significance of Skin Color in Brazil* (Princeton: Princeton University Press, 2004).

[112] See Wacquant, 'For an Analytic of Racial Domination', p. 230.

[113] Several analyses of racial issues and affirmative actions in Brazil are available on the website of the *Supremo Tribunal Federal*: www.stf.jus.br/portal/cms/verTexto.asp?servico=processoAudienciaPublicaAcaoAfirmativa

[114] De Beauvoir's quotation, is, of course, 'One is not born a woman, but rather becomes one.'

Part II

THE MODERN FRAMEWORK

5

Charles Boxer and the *Race Equivoque*

JOÃO DE PINA-CABRAL[1]

CHARLES BOXER'S BOOK *Race Relations in the Portuguese Colonial Empire, 1415–1825* was published in 1963 – nearly half a century ago – and has continued to be read to this day. In contrast to his other works, this short essay has found a readership beyond the circle of those who are interested in the history of the Portuguese expansion. In fact, it constitutes a singular piece of analytical debate in the work of a writer who saw himself chiefly as a descriptive historian, bibliophile and archivist and who studiously avoided political posturing. The 1963 essay, however, was conceived from the start in a polemical mode and, according to his biographer, Boxer was perfectly conscious of the impact it would have as he produced it. The essay starts with a direct and explicit rebuttal of the more ideological formulations on race by the then Portuguese dictator António de Oliveira Salazar in support of his fascist and colonialist policies.

The furious response to the book from some of Boxer's former Portuguese and Brazilian colleagues is well known – chief among them, Armando Cortesão, a very close friend and collaborator, who felt deeply betrayed by Boxer's implicit distancing. There were also less extreme cases, such as that of Virgínia Rau, who responded with quiet sadness to Boxer's declaration of distance. Less well known, however, is that Boxer also touched nerves to the north of the Rio Grande. Many North American colleagues felt troubled about Boxer's obvious interest in, and even sometimes outright appreciation for, aspects of the history of the Portuguese empire. Even as late as the mid-1970s, Boxer's work was being rejected by American publishers on the grounds that editors (and I quote from a referee report) 'found themselves troubled by what appears to be a kind of defence of the

[1] This chapter was written during my stay as Tinker Visiting Professor at the University of Chicago in 2009. I am grateful to the Tinker Foundation, the Department of Anthropology, the Centre for Latin-American Studies, and the Reggenstein Library, as well as to Kesha Fikes and to Dan Borges. I am grateful to Raffaella D'Intino and Omar Ribeiro Thomaz for their discussions of this topic with me.

Portuguese empire-builders. In view of subsequent events, particularly the dissolution of the empire, they felt this might strike some readers as a discordant note.'[2] This was not an isolated instance, according to Dauril Alden's detailed personal biography, to which I am indebted for the following biographical notes.

The historical context to Boxer's *Race Relations*

The circumstances of the writing of Boxer's book, therefore, deserve our attention. To my mind, they highlight in an interesting manner how the work constituted an almost unavoidable response both to deep changes in the life of the author and to the major ideological changes that were taking place all around him. Boxer was a third-generation descendant of British military men who had given their lives at a young age in the struggle for the attainment of world hegemony by the British empire. The whole first part of his life was very much guided by his sense of participation in the project of empire – he reached the rank of major in the British army and was closely associated with Japanese militarist circles during the pre-war years, at a time when the Japanese military were immersed in the violent colonial occupation of Korea and northern China.

It was the deeply troubling experience of the Second World War, and the lapse into irrelevance of the earlier forms of imperialism based on extensive territorial administration, that led Boxer to rethink his earlier views of empire – as happened with so many British intellectuals of his generation. In fact, in Boxer's case, the change was gradual and was marked by deeply formative experiences shortly before and during the Japanese occupation of Hong Kong, in which he played a prominent and public role, first as a member of the British intelligence and, subsequently, as a military prisoner in Canton, having been convicted for attempted escape.

In Boxer's case, his relationship with an American writer, Emily Hahn, his second wife, and his eventual stay in the United States during an important period of his creative life, were marked influences. In fact, as Emily herself wrote to a friend as early as 1947, 'Charles is madly in love with America'. When his appointment at King's College as Camoens Professor was coming to an end in the early 1960s, it became possible for him to contemplate acting upon his dream of moving to the United States, where his wife was by then a permanent resident in Manhattan (they kept house apart for long periods of their marriage). It is significant, for example, that right to his final days he kept to the habit of offering a party to friends and associates on Pearl Harbour Day, to celebrate the entry of the United States into the war.

[2] Dauril Alden, *Charles R. Boxer: An Uncommon Life: Soldier, Historian, Teacher, Collector, Traveller* (Lisbon: Fundação Oriente, 2001), p. 568.

From 1962 he started carrying out regular and extended lecture tours in the United States. In 1964, he started formal negotiations concerning the sale of his valuable collection of books and manuscripts about the European expansion to the Lilly Library in the University of Indiana, Bloomington, with a view to an appointment there. He moved to Bloomington in 1967.[3] Earlier on, in 1964, he had been a candidate for a post at Harvard which he lost to a specialist on a topic felt to be less contentious by the appointment committee: Spanish imperial history. He was to keep his association with Bloomington until the middle of the following decade, even though he held a prestigious position as Professor of the Expansion of Europe Overseas from the Fall of 1969 to 1972 at the University of Yale. During his stay there, he acted as Master of Saybrook College for a year, which happened to be one of the especially intense years of student riots. In particular, he was forced to adjudicate in complex and violent student confrontations due to 'Black/White tension', as he described it. He returned to Indiana in 1972 where he stayed until 1979 when, on turning 75, he finally retired to his house in southern England.

This information is of concern if we see that *Race Relations* accompanied him right throughout this period in a very significant way. The first glimpses of the argument emerged in the second of a set of three lectures on the Portuguese expansion that Boxer delivered in 1960 at the University of Witwatersrand in Johannesburg (my own *alma mater*), entitled 'The Clash of Colour. Caste and Creed in the Sixteenth Century'. Jorge Dias was to deliver a set of lectures there the following year.[4]

That the lectures were delivered in Johannesburg in 1960 is not an irrelevant fact. That year, two events occurred that called attention to the need to rethink earlier approaches to the subject: first, in March of that year, as a sequel to public protest against the 'pass laws' which constituted the principal instrument of enforcing racial segregation in South Africa, a massacre by the police took place in Sharpeville, which marked the transformation of the apartheid regime into an international pariah and led to an important exodus of white opponents from the country; secondly, at the end of the year, the Portuguese government, feeling that it was in need of boosting its international credit, organised a major academic and political event in honour of Prince Henry the Navigator, where Boxer was one of the principal speakers and where Brazil's President, Juscelino Kubitschek, played an important and visible role. These were, in fact, troubled days internationally, not only in Africa but also in the United States and Brazil – where, for example, the students of the newly formed National University of Brasilia went on strike.

Indeed, the winds of change had already been blowing for a number of years. In 1955–6 the famous bus boycott took place in the United States out of which

[3] Alden, *Charles R. Boxer*, pp. 454–62.

[4] Jorge Dias, *Portuguese Contributions to Cultural Anthropology* (Johannesburg: Witwatersrand University Press, 1961).

Martin Luther King Jr. emerged as a national leader and which ended legal segregation in public transportation in the United States. The year 1963, which saw the publication of *Race Relations*, was the year of King's major success, the Peaceful March on Washington, where he delivered the speech about his dreams of an egalitarian future that all of us have heard and learnt from.

Elsewhere, in April 1955, the Bandung conference had been convened in Indonesia. There, leaders such as Nehru and Zhu Enlai assumed centre stage internationally, taking a forceful stand against territorial colonialism. India's pressure on Portugal to abandon the *Estado da Índia* (its colonial possessions in the sub-continent) started to mount after 1958 and, in 1961, India assumed control of the territories unilaterally by military means. The liberation movements in the Portuguese African colonies were also gaining strength during the late 1950s from their base in Algiers. The actual colonial war started in Angola in 1961, to be followed in subsequent years by the other anti-colonial movements. In 1961 also, Henrique Galvão and his associates staged the internationally famous hijacking of the liner *Santa Maria*.

There is little to surprise us in the fact that, in 1960, in the middle of all this, the odd combination of contrast and similarity between the Portuguese colonial regimes in southern Africa and the South African and Rhodesian regimes should present itself to Boxer as an intellectual and ethical challenge, forcing him to address openly the matter of race relations in the Portuguese empire. Peter Fry's recent essays on the topic, in his book *A persistência da raça*, and the polemics that accompanied it, show beyond any doubt that we are far from having exhausted the theme.[5] As it happens, the debate was hardly virgin territory, as Fry has argued in his article on the meanings of race in Brazil published in *Daedalus* in 2000:

> since the days of slavery, well before modern globalization, 'race relations', real or imagined, in Brazil and the United States, have been held as contrasting models that in a sense have come to define for many the two national identities.[6]

In his book, Boxer globalised the debate in a clear and timely response to what was happening all around him. His innovations were, on the one hand, to include a third party in the race debate (Africa), and on the other, that he cast the race issue in terms of the whole history of Portuguese expansion.

The essay itself started to take its final shape in November 1962 when Boxer delivered a set of lectures on race relations at the University of Virginia. He then proceeded to lecture on the same topic at Cornell and Harvard in the same year. According to his biographer, the lectures caused a sensation in Harvard. This led

[5] Peter Fry, *A persistência da raça: Ensaios antropológicos sobre o Brasil e a África Austral* (Rio de Janeiro: Civilização Brasileira, 2005).

[6] Peter Fry, 'Brazil: The Burden of the Past; the Promise of the Future', *Daedalus* 129:2 (2000), pp. 83–118, see p. 84.

to his being invited to apply for the Gardiner professorship, and eventually also to his not receiving the appointment, as we have seen.[7] Clearly, it was the topic of the day. Throughout his stay in the United States in the 1970s – at Bloomington, then Yale, later Virginia, and Bloomington again – the lectures on race formed the core of his teaching engagements.

If we set *Race Relations* – the book – against this backdrop, we see how it constituted an indispensable intellectual tool for its author. It provided Boxer with a much needed instrument of mediation between what he knew of the history of the Portuguese expansion and the upcoming discourse on race that was becoming hegemonic internationally and that was so deeply marked by the emergent black struggle in the United States. In the course of the 1950s, and then suddenly with enormous impact in 1960–1, a new race discourse forced itself on the international scene which made nonsense of the background assumptions that had underwritten the history of European imperialism until the Second World War and that the Portuguese authorities had wanted to salvage by means of the commemorations of Prince Henry the Navigator. These were no longer the days of the 1940s, when the imperial celebrations in Belém produced such a favourable impact internationally.[8]

The sympathy towards the early Renaissance empire builders that had characterised British elite attitudes in the heyday of the British empire, and which had been the principal driving force behind Boxer's own youthful fascination with Dutch and Portuguese naval bravery, became utterly untenable in the light of the dominant opinion in the United States in the early 1960s. If he was to carry his scholarship to the world's leading intellectual centres, Boxer had to produce a mediating mechanism that allowed for the ideological transformation of his earlier historical engagements into contemporary discourse. This he did notably well in his 1963 essay, both to his profit and his honour.

There was a price to pay, however, on both sides of the mediation. At the same time as he demonstrated that the history of Portuguese expansion had indeed been marked by racism, he was also led to state repeatedly that this was of a less marked nature than other forms of imperial racism and was characterised by greater ambiguity of race classification. He found it hard to hide his fascination and respect for many of the historical figures he described. To many in the United States, this was seen as a problematic position to assume. For his American contemporaries, racism was conceived both as of a single piece and as an evil, which was more easily dealt with in its purest form – somewhat on the lines of what Christian Geffray defended in *Lusotopie* much later.[9] The argument is implicit in practically all writings on the issue by North American colleagues right up to our day.

[7] Alden, *Charles R. Boxer*, p. 454.

[8] See Omar Ribeiro Thomaz, *Ecos do Atlântico Sul: Representações sobre o Terceiro Império Português* (Rio de Janeiro: Universidade Federal do Rio de Janeiro, 2002).

[9] Christian Geffray, 'Le Lusotropicalisme comme discours de l'amour dans la servitude', *Lusotopie* (1997), pp. 361–72.

This is how Talcott Parsons famously put it in 1969:

> Relatively sharper polarization clearly favours conflict and antagonism in the first instance. Providing, however, other conditions are fulfilled, sharp polarization seems in the longer run to be more favourable to effective inclusion than is a complex grading of the differences between components, perhaps particularly where gradations are arranged on a superiority-inferiority hierarchy. To put cases immediately in point, I take the position that the race relations problem has a better prospect of resolution in the United States than in Brazil, partly because the line between white and Negro has been so rigidly drawn in the United States and because the system has been sharply polarized.[10]

Note that, in this quote, he writes 'white' with a small letter and 'Negro' with a capital letter – a point that will later become relevant in my argument.

On the other side of the polemics, however, Boxer's mediation implied the painful loss of some of his closer intellectual allies. By then, as it turns out, he had no choice if he was to avoid becoming an anachronistic monument to a bygone age of empire. His resigned response to Armando Cortesão's fury on being betrayed reveals that Boxer was fully conscious that time was on his side. He had to find the way to transport himself to the new language of empire that had become globally dominant in the post-war period with the onset of the Cold War and, particularly, around the youth struggles that accompanied the Vietnam War. These essays on race relations, therefore, were the lectures that he delivered to his students in the American campuses at Yale, Virginia and Bloomington precisely during those mutinous years. After all, he was to move from Bloomington to Yale the year after Martin Luther King Jr. was killed. There was no way he could have lived there and avoided the issue.

It is probably necessary at this point to state clearly that, as read in terms of mid-twentieth-century Anglo-American views about race (what it constitutes and what it implies), the claim by the Portuguese dictator and his collaborators in the 1960s that the Portuguese were not historically prone to practise acts of racism made little or no sense at all. Thus, I want to leave no doubt that, as far as I can see, Boxer's claims in 1963 were, on the whole, correct. Moreover, his essay is based on a thorough knowledge of the history he surveys, as he was at the time the foremost historian of the subject.

Why, then, are we revisiting his arguments in this volume? Again, to my mind, there does not seem to be much evidence to overturn the observations he makes about his material. Rather, it seems necessary to set his writing in historical perspective, simply because the world and its hegemonies have changed and the context that gave relevance to his lectures is now a thing of the past – much as the

[10] Talcott Parsons, 'The Problem of Polarization on the Axis of Color', in John Hope Franklin (ed.), *Color and Race* (Boston: Beacon Press, 1969), pp. 349–73, see pp. 352–3; quoted in Fry, 'Brazil: The Burden of the Past', p. 95.

hegemony of colonialist ideologies of empire that had ruled up to the 1930s had become a thing of the past when he wrote his own essay in the early 1960s.

Cross-cultural mis-readings

What had Boxer come to discover then that his earlier close friends and collaborators in Portugal, Brazil and India had not discovered? What were the new facts that caused their distancing? It would seem that the answer is: none. There was nothing new that Boxer now unearthed and that Cortesão, Rau or their Brazilian colleagues had not known before.[11] Contrary to what global hegemonic trends at the time made it appear, it was not the Portuguese who were newly engaged in a major error of judgement in the 1960s; rather, it was Boxer and his Anglo-American colleagues who, in the course of the post-war decade, had changed their minds. Their world-view had changed aspect, bringing further into focus the previously less noticeable fact that Portuguese and Brazilian discourses of power were not compatible with the new language of power that had become dominant during the Cold War period.

The difference of opinion, however, was not a recent or a simple thing. Manifestations of cross-cultural mis-readings had made their impact for a very long time. They simply had not assumed the historical centrality that they did at the time of Portuguese late-colonialism – 1961 to 1974. Much like the case of South Africa, whilst the Portuguese colonial regime in Africa was still sustained by American military and financial support as part of the Cold War strategy, its ideological framework had become untenable in terms of dominant American public opinion.

By mid-century, the need for a mediating mechanism was not felt uniquely by Boxer. Even the Portuguese regime saw that it required a new ideological framework to respond to this new cause of embarrassment. Under the inspiration of the then youthful Adriano Moreira, the regime elected to pick on Gilberto Freyre's work from the 1920s in order to attempt to regain its legitimacy. It failed miserably in this, however, for a number of reasons which are, on the whole, beyond the reach of the present essay. To my mind, however, the most prominent of these was the fact that internal fascist repression in Portugal stunted the mid-century generation, forcing the livelier members to migrate, and thus preventing it from carrying out the vigorous renegotiation of positions that would have allowed for a decisive and creative political evolution both in Portugal and in Africa.

The source of the mis-reading, however, long antedates the mid-twentieth century. The 1920s were the period when American attitudes concerning race

[11] Francisco Bethencourt has called my attention to the fact that Armando Cortesão was by then one of the few remaining allies of Salazar within the Republican right wing, due to his earlier engagements in the colonial project.

started to be exported globally. This happened very importantly even within the British empire. For example, the intellectual mould that produced the apartheid regime in South Africa in the 1930s was not primarily German Nazi ideology, as has so often been assumed. To the contrary, the decisive influence on apartheid's main ideologue, Henrik F. Vervoerd, were the Carnegie Foundation and sociologists T. Sorokin from Harvard and Charles Coulter from Ohio, as well as their social psychologist colleagues then engaged in developing what they called 'social engineering'.[12] Again, leaving out of the debate developments in Africa and Asia would seriously reduce the possibility of understanding what was at stake. It is to Boxer's credit that he saw this plainly.

On the western side of the Atlantic, the emergence of a growing divergence of opinion between North American and Brazilian activists and intellectuals can be traced through the pages of the São Paulo 'Black press' from the end of the First World War.[13] Speaking of an article by José do Patrocínio Filho written in 1923, Micol Seigel writes,

> this clear-sighted critique of the idea of racial democracy, fully aware of its differential significance abroad and in Brazil, predates by ten years [Freyre's book] that would supposedly introduce this myth [. . .]. Afro-Brazilians generated the idea of racial democracy right alongside its critique.[14]

Even as the author notes this fact, she is engaged in a play of words that turns Patrocínio's argument into a case of blatant false consciousness. She goes on to state, 'today most observers see the idea of racial democracy as a reactionary erasure of racism and social inequality, but in the twenties its final violence was far from clear'.[15] Again, the ambiguity of the word 'idea' allows for a play of meaning where the difference between an observation of fact and a political ideal to fight for is comfortably erased.

In fact, whether in the 1920s, the 1950s, or today, no informed observer ever doubted that racism based on colour and culture played an important role in Brazil or, as a matter of fact, throughout the other contexts of Portuguese expansion in Asia or Africa.[16] Boxer's use of Salazar's speeches in his essay was but a rhetorical gesture, much, indeed, as were the speeches themselves. By the mid-twentieth century, even people like Boxer or Henrique Galvão who, in the 1920s, had been close to Portuguese right-wing circles, came to realise that the Portuguese dictator

[12] Roberta B. Miller, 'Science and Society in the Early Career of H. F. Vervoerd', *Journal of Southern African Studies* 19:4 (1993), pp. 634–61.

[13] See Micol Seigel, *Uneven Encounters: Making Race and Nation in Brazil and the United States* (Durham, NC: Duke University Press, 2009).

[14] Seigel, *Uneven Encounters*, p. 194.

[15] Seigel, *Uneven Encounters*, p. 209.

[16] See Ricardo Ventura Santos *et al.*, 'Colour, Race and Genomic Ancestry in Brazil: Dialogues between Anthropology and Genetics', *Current Anthropology* 50:6 (2009), pp. 805–6.

meant no good by his paternalistic claims of love for his subjects. Galvão's writings from his Brazilian exile after 1947 leave amply clear that Portuguese colonialism at mid-century was racist, immoral and economically deleterious both for Portugal and for the territories it administered in Africa.[17]

Speaking of the black activists in the São Paulo press of the 1920s, Seigel finds that there is 'a paradox of a nationalist denial of a Brazilian racism by an anti-racist Afro-identified subject'.[18] But the paradox is purely a matter of perspective: that is, Seigel's *own* incapacity or unwillingness to rise above North American definitions of race as blackness and of ethnicity as based on Diaspora. It would be immediately resolved should she attempt seriously to reconstitute her subject's perspectival difference. Indeed, it might seem incoherent or absurd that, and I quote again, 'alongside every profession of patriotism and praise for Brazil's lack of racism ran denunciations of perfectly concrete instances of prejudice'.[19] It would indeed be incoherent if the background assumption were Talcott Parsons' kind of segregationist ideal. But if, on the contrary, the background assumption were a legal and religious tradition based on assimilationist ideals, the paradox immediately vanishes. In both cases, either Parsons and Seigel, or Patrocínio and Freyre, it is less a question of what is than of what should be; not a matter of ideas but of ideals.

Brazilian race activists and intellectuals in the 1920s and 1930s felt that they had to protect the important political capital that the assimilationist legal tradition constituted. As Peter Fry reminds us,

> in Brazil, racial discrimination is and has been illegal since the inauguration of the republican regime in 1890. In the United States, 'race' was, until the civil rights movement of the 1960s, a legal construct that divided the population along 'racial' lines in all spheres of social life.[20]

Indeed, this is the sentiment that guided Gilberto Freyre's thesis presented at the University of Columbia as a student of Franz Boas and written in the late 1920s – which formed the basis of *Casa-grande e senzala*.[21] Much like Vervoerd's wholehearted adoption of American conceptions of social engineering in sociology and social psychology, Freyre's book must also be read as a response to the growing global impact of American intellectual opinion during that period (in his case a far more humane version of it, as enshrined in American anthropological theory). Whoever has read the book surely cannot forget that the formative experience that is at the root of its writing is one of painful confrontation with an instance of

[17] See João de Pina-Cabral, 'Galvão among the Cannibals: The Emotional Constitution of Colonial Power', *Identities* 8:4 (2001), pp. 483–515.

[18] Seigel, *Uneven Encounters*, p. 191.

[19] Seigel, *Uneven Encounters*, p. 192.

[20] Fry, 'Brazil: The Burden of the Past', p. 86.

[21] Gilberto Freyre, *Casa-grande e senzala; Formação da família brasileira sob o regimen de economia patriarchal* (1933; Rio de Janeiro: Editora Record, 1998).

collective subalternity. The band of Brazilian sailors whom Freyre saw in Manhattan and whose blatant 'inferiority' as a specimen of humanity was so painful to him, forced him to question the mould that made him feel that way. In order to do so, he had to bypass the hegemony of white supremacy and the racial binarism that shored it up. In fact, had he known it, he would have had to recognise that the history of the Brazilian navy during that period displayed signal and courageous instances of direct struggle against racist violence.[22]

In short, after nearly a century of systematic misunderstanding, it would seem that Boxer's solution in pointing to the fact that Salazar was wrong that there was no racism and discrimination in the history of the Portuguese expansion will not resolve the issue. Perhaps the solution does not lie even in study of the evidence that points to the existence of racial prejudice and discrimination in Lusophone countries, or to the existence of a legal and religious system that favours assimilationism as opposed to one that favours segregationism as in the United States. If either of these solutions were sufficient, they would already have yielded results and there would be no matter to debate presently. In the polemics that have recently re-emerged in the pages of *Current Anthropology* (Ventura Santos *et al.*) or in books such as Micol Seigel's, it seems amply evident to me that the problem lies in our very dependence on the North American emic concept of 'race' as the definitional axis of a comparison that breaches two very distinct intellectual and religious traditions. This furthers cross-cultural mis-reading rather than resolving it.

A plurality of 'races'

It should be clear by now, then, that since the 1920s, all of these debates have been marked by an increasingly dominant semantic shift in the use of the word 'race'. We should be alerted to this, for example, by Talcott Parsons' use of words in the quotation above. There, he writes 'Negro' with a capital but 'white' with small letters, thus implying that Negro is being used as a proper noun – that is, the label of an ethnic group – whilst 'white' is used adjectivally to describe a skin type.

Whilst the category 'race' presents itself definitionally as describing all kinds of human biological and/or cultural difference, the word in fact is used more appositely when it describes the condition of a specific 'people': blacks or Negroes, as they were then called. In turn, these are taken to be a distinct ethnic group with clearly determined collective interests. Moreover, as an ethnic group, they are defined by a myth of origin: their ancestry of slaves coming from a generalised Africa. Finally, the debates always focus on the United States in relation to another single country (usually Brazil or South Africa, but more recently in the writings

[22] See '*a revolta da chibata*' ('the revolt of the lash'); Maria Inês Roland, *A Revolta da Chibata* (São Paulo: Editora Saraiva, 2000).

of psychologists also China)[23] rather than triangulating the gamut of differences as Charles Boxer had shown to be necessary. This was the category to which Boxer necessarily had to adapt his argument if he was going to be able to teach in the United States.

The best formulation I know of this point is the famous debate between Cornel West, a professor at Harvard who has made a name for himself as a race activist and scholar, and Jorge Klor de Alva, again a prestigious university professor who is a spokesperson for Latino identity in the United States. The debate started when the latter questioned the former as to whether he was indeed 'black'. West's response was:

> I think when I say I am a black man, I am saying first that I am a modern person, because black itself is a modern construct, a construct put forward during a particular moment in time to fit a specific set of circumstances. Implicit in that category of 'black man' is American white supremacy, African slavery and then a very rich culture that responds to these conditions at the level of style, mannerism, orientation, experimentation, improvisation, syncopation – all of these elements that have gone into making a new people, namely, black people.[24]

The collective category 'black man' is being used here in an ethnic sense – at least that is how an anthropologist would see it[25] – not in a racial sense, and that is why it makes no sense for Cornel West that Klor de Alva should contest that, going by his skin, he would not be black in Africa. That surely is not the point for him. We are here reminded of Livio Sansone's book on black identity in Brazil where, after a lengthy study of the material available, he concludes that there is indeed such a thing as black identity in Brazil (*negritude*, as he calls it), but it does not shape itself into an ethnic category, since there is no single ethnic group that is formed by it.[26] Sansone's argument remains valuable today even though one might disagree with him concerning the presumption that all ethnicity is necessarily formed in terms of clearly delineated interest groups; in terms of a 'people' of some sort.

Later on in the published report of the debate between West and his Latino conversant the following interaction occurs, which I think highlights what is at stake:

> **Klor de Alva:** [. . .] We have in the United States, two mechanisms at play in the construction of collective identities. One is to identify folks from a cultural

[23] See D. J. Kelly *et al.*, 'Development of the Other-Race Effect during Infancy: Evidence toward Universality?' *Journal of Experimental Child Psychology* 104 (2009), pp. 105–14.
[24] Cornel West, *The Cornel West Reader* (New York: Basic Civitas Books, 1999), p. 500.
[25] See Thomas Hylland Eriksen, *Ethnicity and Nationalism: Anthropological Perspectives* (London: Pluto Press, 1993).
[26] Livio Sansone, *Negritude sem etnicidade: O local e o global nas relações raciais e na produção da cultura negra do Brasil* (Salvador and Rio de Janeiro: EDUFBA/Pallas, 2004).

perspective. The other is to identify them from a racial perspective. Now, with the exception of black-white relations, the racial perspective is not the most critical for most folks. The cultural perspective was, at one time, very sharply drawn, including the religious line between Catholics and Protestants, Jews and Protestants, Jews and Catholics, Jews and Christians. But in the course of the twentieth century, we have seen in the United States a phenomenon that we do not see any place else in the world – the capacity to blur the differences between these cultural groups, to construct them in such a way that they become insignificant and to fuse them into a new group called whites, which didn't exist before.

West: Yes, but whiteness was already in place. I mean, part of the tragedy of American civilization is precisely the degree to which the stability and continuity of American democracy has been predicated on a construct of whiteness that includes the subordination of black people, so that European cultural diversity could disappear into American whiteness while black folk remained subordinate.[27]

West was referring here indirectly to the arguments he developed in his essay on 'A Genealogy of Modern Racism' which has been so widely read and quoted in the United States.[28] There, he argues in favour of a historicist perspective on racial domination. He traces the history of modern racism to the sixteenth century, but he insists that it must be understood in terms of a neo-classical recovery of Greek models of beauty and of human perfection. I find the argument persuasive but it seems to me that there is a dangerous side to it, since it hides a complex series of local conditioning factors. These need illuminating if we are going to make sense of the contemporary global significance of the concept of 'race'.

Indeed, models of corporeal 'whiteness' have been with the European imperialists since the very beginning. Thus, for example, one of the reactions of the Portuguese who arrived in China in the mid-sixteenth century, after over half a century of commercial and military expansion across the coast of Africa and India, was fascination at the relative whiteness of Chinese and Japanese women. Due to this, such women were fetching higher prices in the Asian slave market at the time.[29]

This example might suggest that Cornel West is correct in his opinions concerning the centrality of Greco-Roman classical values of corporality at the onset of the modern era. Matters, however, are far more complex. Much like what happened with African religion, the Portuguese response to these questions was hardly one of imperial distance and rejection – as was to be the case, a little later, with eighteenth- and nineteenth-century Protestant empire builders – but rather one of negotiated creolisation. We have evidence of this type of response both from the period of initial contact (see Sansi-Roca's interestingly new history of the use

[27] West, *The Cornel West Reader*, p. 504.

[28] Cornel West, *Prophesy Deliverance! An Afro-American Revolutionary Christianity* (Philadelphia: Westminster Press, 1982), pp. 47–68.

[29] See João de Pina-Cabral, *Between China and Europe: Person, Culture and Emotion in Macao* (New York: Continuum/Berg, 2002), p. 114; P^e^ Manuel Teixeira, *O comércio de escravos em Macau/The So-Called Trade in Slaves in Macao* (Macau: Imprensa Nacional, 1976).

of 'fetish' on the West Coast of Africa)[30] and from seventeenth- and eighteenth-century Brazil – where James Sweet, for example, amply demonstrates that 'the impact of Christianity on Africans was no greater than the impact of African beliefs on Christians'.[31]

In fact, in matters of skin colour in South and Southeast Asia (as much as in Brazil), things did not turn out to be as linear as one might have thought. Portuguese men of the period apparently preferred as conjugal partners the darker-hued pre-Islamic Malay women, on the supposition that Chinese women, albeit whiter, had much greater difficulty in adopting Christianity. This, incidentally, is held to explain why, over four centuries later, Macanese Eurasian cuisine is still so deeply marked by Malay cooking styles.

Now, when we compare South African attitudes to 'race' with American attitudes, one major difference should immediately be recognised – one that we can only choose to disregard at the peril of reproducing large areas of hegemonic shadow. To put it as simply as possible, in South Africa, 'blackness' was not the issue, but rather 'whiteness', for the simple reason that black people were too diverse and the category included people who were not necessarily African (such as 'Coloureds' – who were supposed to have a large percentage of Malay ancestry; Indians – who were not African at all; and even other kinds of Africans – such as Khoi-San peoples). Africanness and blackness, furthermore, could not be conjoined and that is what the term *Afrikaans* (to describe those who, in Spanish America, would have been called *criollos*) was meant to imply. What was at stake was a dispute over Africa, not a matter of skin colour, and there was, furthermore, no implication of slavery and dislocation. Thus, 'non-whiteness' was the prevailing metaphor.

In the United States, on the other hand, 'blackness', slavery and dislocation conjoined. Whiteness, as we have seen, was a hold-all produced out of a dispersed set of categories that supposedly mirrored an ever increasingly certain blackness. The discourse of Africanness, it should be remembered, was a response to this, and emerged coevally with the hold-all whiteness to which Klor de Alva and West refer in their debate. It had to be intellectually constructed at mid-century when it became clear that the 'melting-pot' was not going to include the blacks – precisely at the same time as American intellectuals were becoming more influential abroad. Africanness had to be fought for in the United States and some (such as Frazier, the most eminent Afro-American sociologist of the time) did not feel it deserved support; thus it created rifts among the different contenders in the United States

[30] Roger Sansi-Roca, 'The Fetish in the Lusophone Atlantic', in Nancy Naro, Roger Sansi-Roca and David Treece (eds), *Cultures of the Lusophone Black Atlantic* (New York: Palgrave Macmillan, 2007), pp. 19–39.

[31] James H. Sweet, *Recreating Africa: Culture, Kinship, and Religion in the African-Portuguese World, 1441–1770* (Chapel Hill: University of North Carolina Press, 2003), p. 230.

itself. The apparent transparency of many concepts that have become common parlance today – such as Seigel's 'Afro-diasporic identity', which she retro-projects to the opinions of her subjects in the 1920s – relies on specific processes of ideological production that were never consolidated until much later. Some of the complexities that the definition of blackness by reference to African Diaspora throws up are well delineated, for example, in a recent text by Stanford Carpenter, a young black American anthropologist,[32] and it is significant that, according to his biographer, Charles Boxer knew Melville Herskovits and was influenced by him at the time of his American stay.

In fact, one notes again that the silent contender, the unstated referential background that gives the point to the arguments of recent books like James Sweet's on the cultural legacy of African slaves in Brazil or Micol Seigel's on early twentieth-century black activists, is the American-specific category of 'race'. To sum up, first, the category shapes itself as applying specifically to blacks rather than to other racial groups; secondly, blacks are seen to be an ethnic group with defined collective interests; and thirdly, they are defined by a generic origin in Africa.

Whilst Boxer found in the race discourse an instrument of mediation that allowed him to continue to develop his favoured topics of research in the United States in the 1960s and 1970s, then, the polemic that the book met with does not seem to have been resolved. It is perhaps possible today to throw new light on what caused such a longstanding cross-cultural mis-interpretation.

[32] See his interesting self-biographical account: Stanford Carpenter, 'What We Bring to the Table: The Means of Imagination in an African American Family', in James Faubion (ed.), *The Ethics of Kinship: Ethnographic Inquiries* (Oxford: Rowman and Littlefield, 2001).

6

Gilberto Freyre and Brazilian Self-Perception

MARIA LÚCIA G. PALLARES-BURKE

AT FIRST SIGHT it seems that so much ink has been spilt on the topic, that there is nothing especially new to be said about the intellectual construction and negotiation of this elusive entity, Brazilian self-perception. Nevertheless, the aim of this chapter is to make a small contribution to the subject by means of an explicitly comparative approach, linking foreign (especially American) views of Brazil to Brazilians' views of themselves, and placing Freyre's impact in this wider context.

During the competition to host the 2016 Olympic Games, President Lula made a speech that included the following extremely revealing comments:

> We are a people in love with sports, in love with life. Our men and women come from every continent; we're all proud of our origins, but even more proud of being Brazilian. We are not only a mixed people, but a people who likes very much to be mixed. That is our identity.

This passage offers a recent example of the official use of Freyre's idea of Brazilian identity; in the service of a particular aim, of course, but taken for granted, as if everyone in the country agreed with the description of Brazil as a land composed of a joyful and cheerful people, 'in love with life'; where everybody lives in harmony and is friendly with one another, showing these feelings with open smiles and affectionate gestures (as the film made for the occasion repeatedly shows); who, in short, are proud and happy to be the mixed people they are.

Of course one could raise the issue of the elusive quality of what it means to be Brazilian, or English or French (for instance), and indeed ask if such a question should even be posed, as the protesters against the present national discussion about what it means to be French, launched by the Minister for Immigration and National Identity, suggest. After all, since the publication of Benedict Anderson's acclaimed book, *Imagined Communities*, and Eric Hobsbawm and Terence Ranger's *The Invention of Tradition*, it has become accepted wisdom that a nation is a construction, that it does not have an essence forever fixed, but undergoes a process

Proceedings of the British Academy **179**,*113–132*. © The British Academy 2012.

of building or even 'inventing' in which the collective imagination or shared images are powerful elements.[1]

On this occasion it is sufficient to accept the idea that the concept of national identity is marked by transience and precariousness, since it is always a cultural product built up over time, and not constructed in a vacuum. The case of Brazil in particular shows that its 'identity' – or one of its most powerful identities, since people and nations can be said to have multiple identities[2] – has been linked to its heterogeneous racial origin, including indigenous peoples, Portuguese colonisers, and the African slaves who arrived in the country in greater numbers than in any other in the Americas.

The view of Brazil that Lula presented as 'our identity' (despite being periodically denounced in Brazil itself as pure idealisation) is not confined to the country, but has become part of the public imagination abroad as well. Browsing through the international press and talking to foreigners, again and again one finds the association of Brazil with carnival, football, sun, beaches and sex, but perhaps most of all with cultural hybridity, racial mixture and lack of discrimination on the grounds of colour.

One example that illustrates this last association very well is the case of the African-American pop singer Dionne Warwick, who in an interview in the *Observer* explained why she lived in Brazil and had decided to make that country her home. Among the reasons for this move she mentions family values, music and, above all, the freedom to be whoever you are – black and female – without being stigmatised. 'For me Brazil is paradise. It really is. I think that is where God lives', she says.[3] Recently I heard a similar view of the country from a taxi driver in New York, in an experience that I know is shared with many others when abroad. As soon as he found out that I was Brazilian, he gave a broad smile, saying: 'Ah, Brazil, that's where I'd love to live. I've been thinking a lot about going to Salvador' – which, interesting enough, is the same place chosen by Warwick to be her new home.

How could he have arrived at this view? That is the question that puzzled me then, and one of the possible ways to answer it is to look at a long tradition of views about Brazil abroad, in which Freyre plays only a part, albeit an important one.

I

This positive image of Brazil is undoubtedly controversial, especially because it is connected with the idea that the 'rainbow of colours' that characterises the

[1] Benedict Anderson, *Imagined Communities* (1983; New York: Verso, 1991); Eric Hobsbawm and Terence Ranger (eds), *The Invention of Tradition* (Cambridge: Cambridge University Press, 1983).
[2] Amartya Sen, *Identity and Violence: The Illusion of Destiny* (New York: W. W. Norton, 2006).
[3] *Observer*, 14 July 2002.

population is proof that the country is a paradise of race relations – an association that has been progressively challenged in the last few decades.

My aim here is to reflect on the reception of this idea and its intriguing resilience, a resilience that has been both pleasing and exasperating for Brazilians and foreigners over the course of its history. What I will attempt to do is to follow the suggestion that in discussing race relations, it is important to distance the analysis from a purely national approach, by incorporating transnational connections. Even in the case of national identities and of people's self-perceptions, one cannot overlook the fact that these are often the result of the 'transnational flow of ideas, images, practices and institutions'; in other words, of a 'complex dialogue' between various interlocutors.[4] The development of the concept of racial democracy as the positive social consequence of miscegenation, for instance, so central to Brazilian identity, or one of its identities, cannot be properly understood if the dialogue between Brazilians and North Americans is not taken into account. In what follows, I will simply draw attention to a few examples from many possible ones in a rich field full of opportunities for more thorough research.

There is a virtual consensus, at least among scholars, that a dramatic change in the self-perception of Brazilians took place in the early 1930s, and that the 'arch-ideologist' of this new perception was Gilberto Freyre.[5] The change was so great that one can say that Brazil was reinvented and that the low national self-esteem, which was so deeply ingrained, suffered a big blow. Both Freyre's critics and his admirers talk of him as the 'inventor' of Brazil and he himself at least once called himself a second Pedro Álvares Cabral, the Portuguese explorer who 'discovered' the country in 1500. This description has its merits, for the positive view of race mixing which Freyre is supposed to have inaugurated would have been impossible to find until the early 1930s. Until then, the mixture of races and cultures was generally viewed negatively, by Brazilians and foreigners alike. Created by the miscegenation of 'three sad races' – when miscegenation was believed to imply degeneration – the country was thought to lack an identity of its own. Abroad, the Swiss scientist established in the USA, Louis Agassiz, was an authority frequently quoted on the theme of racial mixing: 'Let anyone who doubts the evil of the mixture of races, and is inclined from mistaken philanthropy to break down all the barriers between them, come to Brazil. He cannot deny the deterioration consequent upon the amalgamation of races [. . .]'[6]

[4] George Reid Andrews, 'Brazilian Racial Democracy, 1900–90: An American Counterpoint', *Journal of Contemporary History* 31:3 (1996), pp. 483–507.

[5] David Cleary, 'Race, Nationalism and Social Theory in Brazil: Rethinking Gilberto Freyre', David Rockefeller Center for Latin American Studies, Harvard University, working paper WPTC-99-09.

[6] Louis Agassiz, as quoted in Lothrop Stoddard, *The Rising Tide of Color against White-World Supremacy* (1920; Brighton: Historical Review Press, 1981), p. 210.

According to the prevalent view, laziness, indolence, intellectual weakness, immorality and corruption were associated with miscegenation, and were thought to explain much of what was wrong with the country or hindered its future development. As a result of hybridity, the country was supposed to suffer from lack of spirit, an inferiority complex and a certain sadness, which a well-known writer, Paulo Prado, considered part of the Brazilian character. His famous book of 1928, *Retrato do Brasil* (Portrait of Brazil), which refers to the 'vices of our mestiço origin' and to Brazil as 'the kingdom of mixing', *starts* like this: 'In a radiant country lives a sad people'. Described at the time as an 'essay about the deep frustration of being Brazilian', Prado's book represented the country as full of unfulfilled promises, and one that did not progress but only 'lives and grows up like a sick child'.[7]

In this context, one possible solution envisaged was the whitening of the population, defended by, among others, the Brazilian sociologist Oliveira Vianna, who put forward his ideas at a time when mass immigration from Europe was transforming the south of Brazil. He welcomed this process as a much needed 'aryanisation' of the country, the only way to set it on the right road to development and civilisation – as Argentina was already wisely doing.

So, when Freyre put forward his ideas about *mestiçagem* in *Casa-grande e senzala* (1933 – henceforth *Casa-grande*), turning the conventional wisdom upside down, these views were unusual, and either shocking or fascinatingly subversive and welcome. Following essays by Vianna, Prado and others, Freyre's intervention in the debate on interpretations of Brazil inevitably represented a sharp break with the pessimism that prevailed.[8]

His emphasis on the interpenetration of three cultures (Amerindian, African and Portuguese), which he saw as enriching and powerful, and on the special importance of African traditions in the shaping of Brazilian culture, in what he described as the 'civilising mission' of this so-called inferior people (according to the then triumphant 'science of race'), shocked part of the Brazilian public. When, soon after, he also expressed this view in the Afro-Brazilian Congress that he organised in Recife in 1934, some critics even described the Congress as 'Bolshevist' and demanded that it be closed down.[9]

Particularly shocking was the famous affirmation which opens a chapter in *Casa-grande*, that 'Every Brazilian, even the light-skinned fair one, carries about with

[7] Paulo Prado (Carlos A. Calil, ed.), *Retrato do Brasil: Ensaio sobre a tristeza brasileira* (1928; São Paulo: Companhia das Letras, 1997); compare Olavo Bilac's slightly earlier reference to Brazilian music as the 'loving flower of three sad races', quoted in David T. Haberly, *Three Sad Races: Racial Identity and National Consciousness in Brazilian Literature* (Cambridge: Cambridge University Press, 1983), p. 1.

[8] For a general intellectual portrayal of Gilberto Freyre, situating him in national and international contexts, see Peter Burke and Maria Lúcia G. Pallares-Burke, *Gilberto Freyre: Social Theory in the Tropics* (Oxford: Peter Lang, 2008).

[9] Richard M. Levine, 'The First Afro-Brazilian Congress', *Race* 15 (1973), pp. 185–93.

him in his soul, when not in soul and body alike [. . .] the shadow, or at least the birthmark, of the native or the Black.' It was because of such an open praise of miscegenation that Freyre's ideas were rejected on occasion as 'a new kind of racism: mulatto racism' – a criticism still made today.[10]

The description of the patriarchal system in general and of the sexual activities of the planters in particular as benign, and as the source of the relative social harmony that became part of the country's character, has been another major focus of criticism, and Freyre has often been accused of offering an idealised picture of colonial Brazil and of producing myth rather than history.[11] In fact, particularly important from the perspective of Brazilian self-perception is the much employed but also much criticised idea of 'racial democracy', an idea that might be said to be implicit in *Casa-grande*, but did not originate with Freyre, though he refined and developed it.[12]

Far from being generally accepted, Freyre's essay was inevitably criticised from almost every possible point of view, from both the Right and the Left. Some readers believed the author to be a Marxist, but Marxists rejected him as a reactionary. Some critics faulted Freyre for his lack of attention to economic factors, others for his excessive materialism, and so on.

On the other hand, many reviewers and early readers were enthusiastic about the book. Freyre's friends reported that it was becoming known in Rio as the 'Ulysses' of Pernambuco. The 'educational hour' on a very popular national radio channel had a programme dedicated to the presentation of the book nationwide. It was compared to 'Halley's comet' and to an 'earthquake' which 'shook a whole generation', changing the views that Brazilians had of their culture. It was described as a 'revolution' in national development for having revealed 'ourselves to ourselves', as the writer Monteiro Lobato put it. 'Without *Casa-grande* we would not be what we are', concluded the respected anthropologist Darcy Ribeiro in the 1970s, in perhaps the most eloquent praise the book ever received. 'Freyre, so far as culture is concerned, founded Brazil in the same way as Cervantes founded Spain, Camões, Portugal, Tolstoy, Russia and Sartre, France.'[13]

[10] R. Ghioldi, 'Freyre, sociologo reaccionario', in *Escritos*, 4 vols (Buenos Aires: Anteo, 1975–7), vol. 4, pp. 16–44; Evaldo Cabral de Mello, 'O "Ovo de Colombo" Gilbertiano', in J. Falcão and R. M. Barboza de Araújo (eds), *O Imperador das idéias* (Rio de Janeiro: Topbooks, 2001), p. 24.

[11] Fernando Henrique Cardoso, 'Livros que inventaram o Brasil', *Novos Estudos* 37 (1993), pp. 21–36.

[12] On the history of the idea, see Levy Cruz, 'Democracia racial', www.fundaj.gov.br/tpd/128.html. Critical discussions include Emilia Viotti da Costa, 'The Myth of Racial Democracy', in *The Brazilian Empire: Myths and Histories*, rev. edn (Chapel Hill: University of North Carolina Press, 2000), pp. 234–46; Michael G. Hanchard 'Racial Democracy', in *Orpheus and Power: The* Movimento Negro *of Rio de Janeiro and São Paulo, Brazil, 1945–1988* (Princeton: Princeton University Press, 1994), pp. 43–74; Hermano Vianna, 'A meta mitológica da democracia racial', in Joaquim Falcão and Rosa Maria Barboza de Araujo (eds), *O Imperador das idéias*: *Gilberto Freyre em questão* (Rio de Janeiro: Topbooks, 2001); and Antonio Sergio Guimarães, 'Democracia racial', www.fflch.usp.br/sociologia/asag/Democracia%20racial.pdf

[13] On the reception of *Casa-grande*, see Burke and Pallares-Burke, *Gilberto Freyre*, pp. 89–94.

The success of *Casa-grande* was not confined to the literati, and the general public were sufficiently interested to take part in celebrations like the ball organized by the French Embassy on the theme of 'The Big House and the Slave Quarters', at which everyone attending was required to dress as a character inspired by the book. Throughout the years, *Casa-grande* enjoyed a popular success that few history books can match, appealing to both an academic and a wider public, and its author, as a critic put it, 'attained the status of a popular icon'.[14] Besides more than forty editions, and translations into nine languages, it has been translated into a comic book and a television mini-series, it was used as a theme for carnival floats and parades, its name was given to a hotel in the northeast, while two directors (one of them Roberto Rossellini) planned to turn it into a film.

It also inspired novels and music, and these different media conveyed to a much wider public a set of ideas that would otherwise be confined to a far smaller group. Many of the novelist Jorge Amado's works, for example, may be seen as a translation into fiction of themes that are central to *Casa-grande*, notably sex, miscegenation and African traditions. *Tent of Miracles* (1969), for instance, fictionalises the debate over *mestiçagem*, while the author defended the idea that 'there is only one solution for the racial problem, the mixture of blood. No other solution exists, only this one which is born from love.'[15]

It has been well said that one reason for the success of *Casa-grande*, over the long term if not immediately, was that it told the Brazilian public 'something that it wanted to hear'.[16] After all, Freyre's emphasis on *mestiçagem* turned what had been perceived as a problem into a solution, claiming that being mixed was not an obstacle to the development of a Brazilian identity, but rather was that identity. Even when an awareness of Freyre's role in the construction of this particular Brazilian identity is lacking, it only proves that his ideas have become part of one important way Brazilians see themselves. In other words, Freyre has been, so to speak, a 'victim' of his own success. He is, in fact, the 'hidden interlocutor' to whom critics and enthusiasts for the view of Brazil that Lula portrayed before an international committee always turn, whether to support or criticise it.[17]

II

But the sharp break with the past that Freyre seems to represent would not be accurate unless the complex dialogue with foreign discourse on Brazil is taken

[14] Cleary, 'Race, Nationalism and Social Theory'.

[15] Jorge Amado, 'Meu país é uma verdadeira democracia racial', *O Estado de São Paulo*, 9 Oct. 1971.

[16] David H. P. Maybury-Lewis, preface to reprint of the English translation of *Casa-grande* (Berkeley: University of California Press, 1986), p. lxxxvi.

[17] Manolo Florentino, 'Da atualidade de Gilberto Freyre', in Peter Fry *et al.* (eds), *Divisões perigosas: Políticas raciais no Brasil contemporâneo* (Rio de Janeiro: Civilização Brasileira, 2007), p. 91.

into account. And if we try to understand the resilience of Freyre's view, one of the things we have to consider is the role played by the outsider, in other words, the dialogue between local and foreign discourses on Brazil. By widening the frame of reference, as we suggested before, it becomes clear that a conversation about racial issues has been taking place for almost two centuries between the United States and Brazil, and that both countries have, at different moments, defined themselves in contrast to each other.

The dialogue between the US and Brazil, with the latter seen as embodying a completely different and enviable reality, becomes quite visible after the American Civil War, when the so-called 'race problem' demanded solutions other than segregation and the violence of the age of Reconstruction. However, it has been shown that, even earlier, abolitionists in both countries 'constructed little by little the image of Brazil as a society immune to racial violence'. As early as the 1830s, the North American abolitionist imagination had absorbed the idea that the USA had the cruellest slaveholders in the entire history of both modern and ancient slavery, and the contrast between the 'American racial hell and the Brazilian racial paradise' was established. Such a rosy view of Brazil seems to have been part of a huge effort to inculcate in the southern slaveholders and their allies in the north a sense of shame for their 'double sin, of slavery and racism'. And when the Brazilian abolitionist movement developed later, it took over much of what was said abroad about Brazil.[18]

In a speech in New York in 1858, the black leader and ex-slave Frederick Douglass, for instance, contrasted the Brazilian and North American situations, noting, not without irony, that

> even a Catholic country like Brazil – a country that we, in our pride, stigmatise as semi-barbarian – does not treat its people of colour, free or slave, in the unjust, barbarous and scandalous way we treat them [. . .] Democratic and Protestant America would do well to learn a lesson of justice and freedom from Catholic and despotic Brazil.[19]

Years earlier, in 1848, Douglass had already cited Brazil as proof that enslavement of coloured people did not necessarily imply race prejudice. The fact that free blacks and *mulattos* held 'important positions in the state, church and army' gave ample evidence of the difference between Brazil and the United States.[20]

So, it was not necessary to wait for the Civil War for Brazil to become what China or Persia were for the contemporaries of Montesquieu, and to serve as the

[18] Celia M. Marinho de Azevedo, *Abolicionismo: Estados Unidos e Brasil, uma história comparada (século XIX)* (São Paulo: Annablume, 2003), pp. 37–8, 87–8, *passim*.

[19] Cited in Celia M. Marinho de Azevedo, 'O abolicionismo transatlântico e a memória do paraiso racial brasileiro', *Estudos Afro-Asiáticos* 30 (1996), pp. 7–40.

[20] David J. Hellwig, 'Racial Paradise or Run-Around? Afro-North American Views of Race Relations in Brazil', *American Studies* 31:2 (1990), pp. 43–60, see p. 44.

pattern against which the evils of their own world could be measured. Throughout the history of what we might call the 'the cult of Brazil', some admirers came only a little short of saying, as Leibniz said of China to the Europeans in the eighteenth century, that the Americans had so much to learn about racial problems, that it was 'almost necessary' that Brazilian missionaries should be sent to the USA in order to enlighten them.[21]

Brazil was viewed then as a possible refuge for former slaves who found conditions in the US unbearable, and schemes for emigration to that country appeared in the late nineteenth century, continuing until at least the first half of the twentieth – as the American black press offers ample witness – or indeed till this day, if the individual examples of Dionne Warwick and the taxi driver from New York are in any degree representative.

As early as 1852, the black leader and polymath Martin Delany argued that there was no future for the advancement of coloured people in the United States. Emigration was the only solution, as indisputable a condition for their development as the Exodus from Egypt had been for the Jews. Having become disillusioned with the Liberian option, he came to the conclusion that 'we must not leave this continent; America is our destination and our home'. But not Canada in the North, which could easily be annexed by the United States. Instead, 'Central and South America *must be our future homes*', he argued. But 'our oppressors will not want us to go there', and would try to prevent coloured people from fulfilling their main objective: 'to become elevated women and men [. . .] the worthy citizens of an adopted country'. He went on to point out that in Central and South America there was never any 'inequality on account of race or color'. According to Delany's eloquent plea,

> this vast number of people, our brethren [. . .] stand ready and willing to take us by the hand – nay, are anxiously waiting, and earnestly importuning us to come, that they may make common cause with us [. . .] Will we go? Go we must, and go we will, as there is no alternative. To remain here in North America, and be crushed to the earth in vassalage and degradation, we never will.[22]

With the end of the Civil War, not only former slaves considered Brazil a possible refuge for what were felt to be unbearable conditions in the United States. Well acquainted with the country through 'the circulation of compelling first-person accounts published in Southern newspapers and widely read books', the defeated Confederates also saw the southern slave society as an ideal place of retreat for those who were 'fully resolved never to submit to nigger rulers', as one of them

[21] Cited in Arthur O. Lovejoy, 'The Chinese Origin of a Romanticism', in *Essays in the History of Ideas* (New York: Capricorn Books, 1960), pp. 99–135, see p. 106.

[22] Martin Delany, *The Condition, Elevation, Emigration, and Destiny of the Colored People of the United States* (1852; Project Gutenberg Ebook, www.pgdp.net).

put it.[23] As early as March 1866, a poem published in a New Orleans newspaper sang the glory of this South American refuge:

> Oh, give me a ship with sail and with wheel
> And let me be off to happy Brazil
> I yearn to feel her perpetual spring
> and shake by hand Don Pedro, her king
> Kneel at his feet – call him 'My Royal Boss'!
> And receive in return 'Welcome, Old Ross'.[24]

In fact, the Confederate colony in Brazil, which attracted from 2,000 to 4,000 white emigrants, is considered the most successful among many others formed at the invitation of different governments, from Mexico and Peru to England and Egypt.[25]

For African Americans, on the other hand, the violence in the South and the general disappointment with the social and economic promises of the North of the country determined renewed interest in the promised land that Delany and others had located in another America, even while slavery had not been abolished there.[26]

In *The Crisis* – the official magazine of the National Association for the Advancement of Colored People (the NAACP) founded in 1910 by the black leader W. DuBois – African Americans could, once again, hear about an alternative society in which they could find what they could not at home. As R. W. Merguson's 'Glimpses of Brazil' put it in November 1915,

> for [the] ambitious and intelligent colored man, in quest for fairer fields for expansion and growth, for an atmosphere not tainted or permeated by the endless varieties and forms of race prejudice to be found in the United States, it might be well to turn his attention in the direction of Brazil.[27]

Similar flattering remarks about Brazilian race relations – sometimes made by authoritative black leaders like DuBois – could be found in different organs of the American black press throughout the early decades of the twentieth century.[28] And during the heyday of the Harlem Renaissance, in the 1920s, Brazil and Latin America represented 'an embodiment of America's romantic, cinematic fantasies',

[23] Zita Nunes, *Cannibal Democracy: Race and Representation in the Literature of the Americas* (Minneapolis: University of Minnesota Press, 2008), p. 102.

[24] *New Orleans Daily Picayune*, 18 March 1866, cited in Lawrence F. Hill, 'The Confederate Exodus to Latin America', *Southern Historical Quarterly* 39:2 (1935), pp. 100–34.

[25] Nunes, *Cannibal Democracy*, p. 102.

[26] See Edwin S. Redkey, *Black Exodus: Black Nationalist and Back-to-Africa Movements, 1890–1910* (New Haven: Yale University Press, 1969), p. 176; Randall B. Woods, *A Black Odyssey: John Lewis Waller and the Promise of American Life, 1878–1900* (Lawrence: Regents Press of Kansas, 1981), p. 115.

[27] Quoted by Valerie Popp, 'Where Confusion Is: Transnationalism in the Fiction of Jessie Redmon Fauset', *African American Review* 43:1 (2009), pp. 131–44.

[28] Hellwig, 'Racial Paradise or Run-Around?'

contradicting the view that writers and artists affiliated to the movement were inspired mainly by Africa at the expense of other places.[29]

The publication of Roy Nash's *The Conquest of Brazil* in 1926 is believed to have greatly contributed to stimulating the 'enviable reputation' of the country as a nation without colour prejudice.[30] Written in a journalistic rather than an academic style, it was reviewed by the *New York Times* in the most praiseworthy terms. It was presented as an original and long-awaited book 'worth reading from cover to cover', since it offered a faithful picture of Brazil, presenting the society of this 'United States of South America' (as the reviewer chose to call the country) as a 'melting-pot' model that America should follow.[31]

With such a good reputation, it is no wonder that 'many nationalists of the post World War I period looked to Brazil as a potential base for the establishment of a proud black homeland', and that 'a number of schemes [. . .] to promote emigration' were proposed in the 1920s – although none of them succeeded.[32] On the other hand, Brazil was also pictured in this period as the place not to go if one felt comfortable with life in a segregated society. As a character of an important 1928 novel who had made a fortune in Brazil put it, the country would be nice, but only if 'they ever get the niggers out of it'.[33]

In the 1930s, as the Second World War approached and Nazi anti-Semitism was discussed in the American black press, the journalists often compared the discrimination that the African Americans suffered with what the Jews were suffering in Nazi Germany, arguing that even if the Germans were more brutal to their minority than the Americans to theirs, the similarity between them was embarrassing to the country. It was in this context that references were made to South America in general as a safe haven where African Americans could feel protected if their situation deteriorated even more. 'I believe we should prepare ourselves to be absorbed into South America so when the tide turns to us as it has on the German Jews, we may have some protection and some place to go.'[34] As the Second World War went on and the prospect of German defeat became stronger, one heard once again the plans of black veterans to make Brazil especially, or Latin America in general, their chosen home. 'When Johnnie comes marching home he mustn't be marching back to a broom or a cotton sack', and he might very well decide to look for good jobs in Brazil, where 'there are no Jim Crow signs and

[29] See Popp, 'Where Confusion Is'.

[30] Roy Nash, *The Conquest of Brazil* (New York: Harcourt, Brace & Co., 1926); see also Roy Nash, 'Is Race Prejudice on the Increase in Brazil?', *The Crisis*, April 1951, pp. 247–54, 287, 290.

[31] H. Armstrong, '"Brazil – Immense, Fantastic": Mr. Nash Portrays the Melting-Pot of South America', *New York Times*, 4 July 1926, cited in Popp, 'Where Confusion Is'.

[32] Hellwig, 'Racial Paradise or Run-Around?'

[33] Jack Kendry, in Nella Larsen's *Passing*, cited in Nunes, *Cannibal Democracy*, p. 136.

[34] 'US Discrimination as Bad as Germany's; Suggests Migration to South America', *The Afro-American*, 21 Jan. 1939, p. 2.

where one of its greatest presidents, Nilo Peçanha, was a negro', said an article of May 1944. Addressing the piece especially to American companies, like the Ford Motor Company, the writer argued that they could sponsor the training of Negro veterans who, when in Latin America, would have a 'chance not only to better themselves [. . .] but also to better the other coloured people who are their blood and spirit'.[35] The desire to spare their children the humiliating experience of fighting 'in this Jim Crow Army', was also one of the reasons mentioned for the move. 'Even dogs and cats leave home when they are mistreated', wrote a correspondent from Kansas City to *The Chicago Defender*.[36] Soon after the end of the Second World War, the editor of the *Los Angeles Sentinel* published the newspaper's replies to the 'several Negro servicemen' who had written to the newspaper showing a desire to move to Brazil 'once they have their discharge papers' and asking for information about job conditions and passport requirements.[37]

In short, visitors' observations, travellers' reports, the black press, and even films and literature in the US produced over the decades a picture of Brazil as a country with a similar background, with a common history of slavery, but a country that did not have a colour line and the violence and racial hatred which segregation entails. A society, as some admirers put it, in which 'a black man is an artist, writer or scientist', whereas in the 'United States he is always a "Negro artist" or "Negro scientist"'; in short, a place where the Negro could be at the same time Negro and Brazilian, or better still, one in which he 'first of all is a Brazilian'.[38] An updated version of this same compliment can be found in a recent issue of *The Economist*, where Brazil's melting pot is described as 'more successful than America's. There is no such thing as a hyphenated Brazilian', it is claimed.[39]

And the explanation always given for these positive Brazilian qualities was the great miscegenation that was part of the country's history. The colour line, the source of so many evils in the USA, simply could not be drawn in Brazil because miscegenation had made it impossible, since 'in many instances it would cut across many of the families', explained an observer.[40] 'Infiltration of Negro blood' could be seen from Manaus to the south of the country, declared another enthusiastic traveller. 'The whites are more than unconscious of any racial difference. They are totally oblivious of it. They have actually forgotten that any demarcation ever existed.'[41] The fraternal result of this phenomenon was evident, according to

[35] H. Preece, 'The Negro in Latin America', *New York Amsterdam News*, 20 May 1944.

[36] R. Lawrence, 'Disagrees with Critic of Russia', *The Chicago Defender*, 20 Oct. 1945.

[37] 'Negro in Latin America', *Los Angeles Sentinel*, 21 March 1946.

[38] E. Franklin Frazier, 'Brazil Has No Race Problem', *Common Sense*, 11 Nov. 1942, in David J. Hellwig (ed.), *African-American Reflections on Brazil's Racial Paradise* (Philadelphia: Temple University Press, 1992), pp. 121–30, see p. 126.

[39] 'A Special Report on Business and Finance in Brazil', *The Economist*, 14–20 Nov. 2009, p. 17.

[40] 'Dr. Frazier Discusses Brazil's Race Problem', *The Pittsburgh Courier*, 28 March 1942.

[41] 'Traveller Finds No Color Line Drawn in Brazil', *Chicago Sunday Tribune*, May 1942.

visitors, in the friendly atmosphere they could observe all around, a confirmation, as they tended to note, that, contrary to what was happening in their country, the emancipation of the slaves had not left a trail of hate and resentment among Brazilian compatriots. An illustration of this was the fact that in Brazil, 'all celebrate Emancipation day together. It is a national holiday like our Fourth of July', as a bewildered visitor put it.[42]

Sometimes the determination to see Brazil as a true democracy, instead of the 'mock democracy' which existed in the USA, was so great that visitors and observers were prepared to contradict any facts that suggested the opposite, as in the case of the series of apologetic reports on Brazil published in 1923 in the *Chicago Defender* – the country's most widely read black periodical – by Robert Abbot, the newspaper's founder. The series of articles on Abbot's trip to Brazil, described as the 'realization of a long dream cherished', are a moving example of the determination of some African Americans to find abroad what they lacked at home. When his Brazilian experiences contradicted his 'long cherished' dreams, he accused the 'American colour prejudice' of infecting the country, as in the case when he was denied rooms in hotels in Rio de Janeiro and São Paulo. 'Even here we are met by that incubus monster ['American colour prejudice'] who, like a legendary sea serpent, it seems, has trailed our course down the South Atlantic way and proposes to find an abode in Brazil.'[43]

Years later, when black men who had fought in the Second World War were considering making Brazil their home, one hears once again the complaint that 'Anglo-Saxon' influence was corrupting Brazil and that 'the growing color consciousness' had much to do with American influence.[44] For the new African-American arrivals, the prospect of good jobs could be threatened because the new Brazilian industries, largely controlled by American capitalists, were being infected by their odious segregation: 'Americans who control the money, largely control the country'.[45]

Focusing his eyes only on what confirmed the country to be in a 'state of absolute harmony', Abbot, like so many other visitors from the USA, pointed out 'the influence of the social milieu on the mind'. Ironically, as some observers pointed out, even the Confederates who had fled from 'the rule of the niggers' to take refuge in the Brazilian slave society and founded a 'Villa Americana' were eventually brazilianised. As Abbot put it, in Brazil 'slavery has left no inconveniences for the

[42] 'Wonderful Opportunities Offered in Brazil for Thrifty People of All Races', *Tulsa Star*, 11 Dec. 1920, in Hellwig (ed.), *African-American Reflections*, pp. 40–3, see p. 42.

[43] Robert S. Abbot, 'My Trip through South America', in Hellwig (ed.), *African-American Reflections*, pp. 55–81, see p. 61.

[44] 'Dr. Frazier Discusses Brazil's Race Problem', *The Pittsburgh Courier*, 28 March 1942.

[45] G. Schuyler, 'Brazil's Negroes', *The Pittsburg Courier*, 10 Oct. 1942; 'Negro in Latin America', *Los Angeles Sentinel*, 21 March 1946.

negro' and 'the white sons and daughters of these former slave holders have intermarried and mixed freely with those who are the descendants of slaves'.[46]

To Roy Nash, already mentioned as author of one of the most important books about Brazil in the 1920s (*The Conquest of Brazil*), the American Confederates 'made small mark upon Brazil, but Brazil certainly put her stamp upon them and their descendants'. Nevertheless, diaries and documents related to these emigrants show that some of them did not allow this assimilation to happen and 'came, saw and returned'. They were not only surprised, but stupefied and even horrified when they realised that they had come to a country 'in which the criterion of color was not the dominant one in social classification' and that negroes and *mulattos* occupied so called 'high positions', and because of that were not considered negroes any more. One Mr McCollun, for instance, who arrived in Brazil only to leave it for good soon after, expressed his indignation very clearly, saying that the Old South was better, even with 'the damned yankees'.[47]

The refusal of the Brazilian Consulates in the USA to grant visas to black Americans in the 1920s was another occasion in which the immense desire to preserve the rosy view of Brazil can be observed. As if they had become prisoners of their dreams, instead of seeing this refusal as suspicious, Abbot and other Brazilophiles like Roy Nash saw it as 'the result of propaganda from the US Government and as the usurpation of Brazil's rights to oversee migration'.[48] Another visitor to Brazil published a series of eloquent reports in the *Chicago Defender* with the aim of persuading his fellow black countrymen to 'send our children as things grow blacker and blacker, harder and harder here in this country' with the assurance that they 'will be permitted to grow, to expand, to reach out to the fullest extent of their ability to become men and women'. As to race prejudices, he could not say they did not exist, but those that existed were taken to Brazil by the American people who were determined, as he argued, to carry them 'into whatever country they go'. While among the Brazilians, he says, 'I did my best to find some trace of prejudice' among them;

> kept my eyes and ears open for it and went out of my way to look for it. But I failed to find it. It is not there, it is not there socially, it's not there economically, it is not there politically. It is not there at all [. . .] They have Coloured captains, and generals in their army and navy, they have had Coloured presidents and they now have Coloured senators and governors.[49]

[46] Abbot, 'My Trip through South America', pp. 65, 74.

[47] J. Arthur Rios, 'Assimilation of Emigrants from the Old South in Brazil', *Social Forces* 26:2 (1947), pp. 150–1.

[48] Nunes, *Cannibal Democracy*, pp. 126–7; Abbot, 'My Trip through South America', p. 58; see Teresa Meade and Gregory Alonso Pirio, 'In Search of the Afro-American "Eldorado": Attempts by North American Blacks to Enter Brazil in the 1920s', *Luso-Brazilian Review* 25:1 (1988), pp. 85–110.

[49] E. R. James, 'Brazil as I Found It', *Chicago Defender*, 4 June 1921 (other articles were published on 28 May and 11 June); in Hellwig (ed.), *African-American Reflections*, pp. 47–50.

In spite of all that could contradict the idyllic picture of Brazil, the message which kept being put forward in articles in the press, speeches and literature was that Brazil could provide a solution for North American racial problems, either by serving as a model of a society that, by promoting miscegenation, avoided discrimination; or by being a 'land of promise', a place which offered African Americans 'a vision of freedom and opportunity beyond' their 'wildest dreams', and to which they could emigrate, as an article from the *Baltimore Afro-American* in 1916 eloquently put it.[50] The later view of Roy Nash can be said, therefore, to be part of a long tradition. Deeply disappointed in 1951 with news of an increase in race discrimination in the country he claimed to know so well, and shocked to hear that important African Americans had been refused entry to high-class hotels in Brazil, he nevertheless made the following confession to the readers of *The Crisis*: 'I would rather be a Negro in Brazil than anywhere else in the world.' And his explanation for this 'increasing discrimination' was the importation of foreign values to Brazil: 'when you get to importing cultural values, the bad comes along with the good'. Besides, the hotels in question were far from representative of the country; they were so exclusive 'that only the very rich of any nationality can patronize them'.[51]

III

Considering this earlier history of the Brazilian image in the United States, the 1946 publication of Freyre's *Casa-grande* in English cannot be said, therefore, to introduce a completely new idea. At least among a certain circle, perhaps mainly of African Americans, Brazil was already clearly pictured as a unique and heavenly place in their popular magazines and newspapers, and was even an important theme in at least two novels of the Harlem Renaissance in the late 1920s: *Passing* by Nella Larsen and *Plum Bun* by Jessie Fauset. In these novels, Brazil appeared as a complex symbol of escape from racism and of utopian desire for a place where race was erased.[52] What it is reasonable to say, therefore, is that Freyre's work developed and formalised the popular view or myth of Brazilian harmonious miscegenation and racial relations – or the wisdom of the 'Brazilian Solution', a common phrase for decades – giving it the 'legitimacy of a social scientist's stamp'.[53]

[50] Nunes, *Cannibal Democracy*, p. 120; 'Opportunities in Brazil: South American Country Offers First Hand Knowledge of the Solving of the Race Question', *Baltimore Afro-American*, 29 Jan. 1916, in Hellwig (ed.), *African-American Reflections*, pp. 35–6.

[51] Nash, 'Is Race Prejudice on the Increase in Brazil?', pp. 251, 254, 290.

[52] Nunes, *Cannibal Democracy*, pp. 139–42.

[53] Rebecca Reichmann (ed.), *Race in Contemporary Brazil: From Indifference to Inequality* (University Park, PA: Pennsylvania State University Press, 1999), p. 24; Edward E. Telles, *Race in Another America: The Significance of Skin Color in Brazil* (Princeton: Princeton University Press, 2004), pp. 33–6.

If at the popular level Brazil was known as an alternative model for race relations, at the academic level knowledge of the country was thought to be very thin. Professor William Shepherd, an important historian of Latin America during the first part of the twentieth century – and who, coincidentally, had been Freyre's supervisor at Columbia University in the early 1920s – wrote in 1933, just before Freyre's book was launched, about this void in historical studies of Brazil. Urging 'a comprehensive and altogether adequate treatise of its past', Shepherd mentions the uniqueness of the country's achievement in race relations: 'The inhabitants of Brazil have solved the problem of racial amalgamation as no other nation has ever done [. . .] Brazil has proceeded farther than any other nation in harmonizing racial differences and dispelling the prejudices associated with them.'[54] So it is not too far-fetched to say that the positive reception of Freyre's work – a work that was also the result of a complex dialogue and had some of its roots in the author's experience of segregation in the USA – had been prepared for a long while.[55]

In Brazil, Freyre's ideas were taken over by the Vargas regime and made into a semi-official ideology to be propagated in public proclamations, schools and the national media. In a similar way, there was an attempt in the United States in the early 1940s to use Freyre's work to raise awareness in the country about the importance of Brazilian cooperation against the dangerous influence of the Germans in Latin America, and it is very likely that the translation of *Casa-grande* was the result of this official or semi-official concern. Newspapers frequently referred to the new situation created by the war, and an article in the periodical *Common Sense* in 1942 explained it quite bluntly: 'Our Chief allies today are among the colored peoples of Asia, Africa', the West Indies, Latin America and Brazil. 'These people are watching us with suspicion' and our relation with them has been affected by 'our treatment of the American Negro and our attitude toward colored people'. In short, it is as if there was a possibility of the war between the nations becoming a war for racial equality.[56] Already in 1938, the foreign policy of the US had been unmasked as flawed, for condemning as barbaric the way the Jews were being treated in the Third Reich, at a time 'when the Congressional Act to make the crime of lynching a federal crime was defeated'.[57]

During the 1942 debates in the House of Representatives about the 'importance of Brazil and the Negro to the hemisphere unity and defense in this crisis which menaces the security of all the Americas', it was argued that the USA could not hope 'for the destruction of Naziism in the Old World while retaining race prejudice

[54] W. R. Shepherd, 'Brazil as a Field for Historical Study', *Hispanic American Historical Review* 13:4 (1933), pp. 428–36.

[55] On Freyre's early intellectual trajectory and the importance of his years in the United States, see Maria Lúcia G. Pallares-Burke, *Gilberto Freyre, um vitoriano dos trópicos* (São Paulo: UNESP, 2005).

[56] Franklin Frazier, 'Brazil Has No Race Problem'.

[57] 'Foreign Policy of US Flawed', *The Pittsburgh Courier*, 10 Dec. 1938.

in the new'. It was in this context that Freyre's 'monumental works' were mentioned as works that should be urgently translated into English. Not only would they be 'a signal contribution to the United States-Brazilian understanding', but their ideas about the crucial importance of the 'negro to the life, culture and defense' of both countries would have great impact. 'Americans', the congressmen were told, all

> have much to learn from Brazil in how diverse races and cultures can live together in harmony and contribute jointly to the development of a new civilization, rich in its production of the arts and the things of the spirit.

Recalling the 1940 census in Brazil, which contrary to the one in the United States in the same year did not include any 'specific questions [. . .] on race', the attention of the congressmen was drawn to what well illustrated 'Brazil's fascinating three-way blending' and the fact that it 'accepts her citizens of Negro descent without worry'.[58]

The publication of the English translation of *Casa-grande*, as *The Masters and the Slaves*, in 1946 strengthened the positive view North Americans had of Brazil, since it gave rise to academic works which legitimised what had already been in the air, in certain circles, for so long. Some of Freyre's fellow-students of Brazil followed the idea: not only American anthropologists and historians, like Donald Pearson, Charles Wagley, and Frank Tannenbaum, but Brazilians as well. The writer Jorge Amado, for instance, wrote that 'my country is a true racial democracy'.[59] Even Florestan Fernandes, well known as a sharp critic of Freyre on this issue as on others, began by suggesting that racial democracy in Brazil was an ideal rather than a practice 'which is still being developed and refined', a point with which Freyre would not have disagreed.[60]

Of course, the reception of Freyre's ideas and what from this time on was described as 'the semi-official orthodoxy' about Brazil's identity was far from unanimous. Some representatives of the Afro-Brazilian press supported the idea of Brazilian social harmony in the 1920s, while others, especially from the 1930s, argued that 'in Brazil, racial equality is a lie'. Comparing Brazilian reality with the existence of African-American institutions of various kinds, from schools and colleges to civic organisations, which Brazil lacked, one article of 1931 in the Brazilian press even raised the possibility that 'blatant open prejudice is a stimulus to black competence and ability'. The positive reports published by Robert Abbot in the *Chicago Defender*, mentioned earlier, had already been strongly criticised

[58] Congressional Record, Proceedings and Debates of the 77th Congress, Second Session, 2 Oct. 1941; 30 March 1942.

[59] Amado, 'Meu país é uma verdadeira democracia racial'; see also Amado, *Tenda dos milagres*, 45th edn (Rio de Janeiro: Record, 2006), pp. 105, 164, 287.

[60] Fernandes, preface to Fernando Henrique Cardoso and Otavio Ianni, *Cor e mobilidade social em Florianópolis: Aspectos das relações entre negros e brancos numa comunidade do Brasil Meridional* (São Paulo: Editora Nacional, 1960), pp. xix, xvi.

by a few members of the black Brazilian intelligentsia at the time, who considered Abbot's views a complete distortion of reality. Nevertheless, in spite of the critics, what came to be known as 'Freyre's paradigm' kept its hegemony until at least the early 1950s, especially because, as a scholar put it, criticism 'took place well outside the boundaries of mainstream intellectual, academic, and official discourse'.[61]

Ironically enough, it was probably in response to Freyre's ideas that UNESCO decided to sponsor research on race relations in Brazil as a possible model for other nations. When the fieldwork was carried out, however, the researchers (including Fernandes, Roger Bastide, Octávio Ianni and Fernando Henrique Cardoso, at that time a young sociologist at the University of São Paulo) reached conclusions contradictory to Freyre's. Fernandes, studying the city of São Paulo between 1880 and 1920, stressed the lack of hope among African-Brazilians there, while the book on contemporary São Paulo that he wrote with Roger Bastide stressed race prejudice. Cardoso and Ianni emphasised prejudice and discrimination in their study of social relations between blacks, whites and *mulattos* in Florianópolis in the mid-1950s. Summing up this work, Fernandes criticised what he now called 'the myth of Racial Democracy'.[62]

The challenge to the picture of Brazil as a paradise or quasi-paradise of racial relations has continued to come from many quarters: from research on race relations carried out by academics of various origins, from Brazilians' own experiences and visitors' comments about their Brazilian experience, from exchange between the American and the Brazilian black press, or from the development of the Brazilian black consciousness movement (a movement that Freyre once described as 'non-Brazilian'), all of these being definitely marked by the American Civil Rights and Black Power movements of the 1960s which had an impact on racial issues throughout the world.

In this new context, a movement of counter-hybridity grew stronger, miscegenation being now strongly denounced as a way 'to get rid of the blacks', in a process that some even called 'ethnic lynching' or 'white lynching'.[63] Hence, we might say that in one important respect, Freyre's theory of *mestiçagem* has changed its meaning. In 1933, the author had to defend *mestiçagem* against the prevailing ideology that emphasised the need to whiten Brazil. More recently, it is against black separatism that Freyre's supporters have to defend his theory, as miscegenation is criticised as a denial of the separate cultural identities of indigenous peoples and African Americans who have had an insidious history of discrimination.

[61] Reid Andrews, 'Brazilian Racial Democracy', pp. 489–94.

[62] Roger Bastide and Florestan Fernandes, *Relações raciais entre negros e brancos em São Paulo* (São Paulo: Anhembi, 1955); Florestan Fernandes, *A integração do negro na sociedade de classes*, 3rd edn, 2 vols (1965; São Paulo: EDUSP, 1978), vol. 1, pp. 249–69.

[63] Richard L. Jackson, 'Mestizaje vs. Black Identity: The Color Crisis in Latin America', *Black World*, 24 July 1973, in Hellwig (ed.), *African-American Reflections*, p. 217.

In similar fashion, the idea of racial democracy has been denounced as hypocrisy or mystification, as a mask which 'institutionalizes the negation' of white racism; or as part of Brazil's 'huge experience in being dishonest', according to an editor of *Newsweek*.[64]

In short, in the late twentieth century, the 'Brazilian solution', praised for so long in the USA as a source of pride for Brazil, became a target and a source of shame, instead of an ideal to follow. As an American critic wrote, the Brazilian solution indicated 'how not to guide our own struggle'.[65] Nevertheless, to the despair of many American critics, even after 'one discovers the Brazilian experience to be one long tale of cruelty, racial atrocities [. . .] the benign image remains', as one of them complained, while putting much of the blame on the black press, which has fashioned the image that 'most blacks' have of Brazilian race relations.[66]

Freyre too was held responsible for the benign image of Brazil, at least among a better-informed public. As one African-American scholar put it in the 1970s,

> if you're like me, you've probably read Gilberto Freyre [. . .] or watched a couple of CBS reports, paged through *Holiday* or some comparable journal. Perhaps you've talked to a Brazilian or two. If you've done any of these things, you know already that 'no racial problem exists in Brazil'.[67]

And in Brazil itself, Freyre's praise of miscegenation and his myth of racial democracy – usually simplified and stripped of its nuances – have become in certain circles the challenge to be confronted, the target at which to aim. This was the case in the 1950 National Congress of the Negro and it was still the case fifty-eight years later in the Congresso Nacional de Negras e Negros do Brasil, according to one of the leaders of the black movement, Edson França, who recently emphasised 'two worrying phenomena: the strength and the rootedness of Brazilian racism and the lack of political efficacy of the Black Consciousness Movement'.[68]

As a historian puts it, Freyre's arguments about the positive value of miscegenation were (and perhaps still are) appealing for those who were interested 'in creating a Brazilian identity'. These arguments were therefore transformed in 'the most fully elaborated object of investment' from the age of Vargas to that of the military regime, 'explaining how Brazil should think itself, love itself and describe itself'.[69]

[64] Jackson, 'Mestizaje vs. Black Identity', p. 217; Edson França, 'Uma breve reflexão sobre o Congresso Nacional de Negras e Negros do Brasil', *Vermelho* Online, 15 April 2008; 'Race Relations in Brazil, South Africa, and the United States', Common Ground radio programme, aired 24 June 1997.

[65] Jackson, 'Mestizaje vs. Black Identity', pp. 216–17; Niani (Dee Brown), 'Black Consciousness vs. Racism in Brazil', *The Black Scholar* 11 (1980), in Hellwig (ed.), *African-American Reflections*, p. 226.

[66] Cleveland Donald, Jr., 'Equality in Brazil: Confronting Reality', *Black World*, 22 Nov. 1972, in Hellwig (ed.), *African-American Reflections*, pp. 198–202.

[67] Leslie B. Rout, Jr., 'Brazil: Study in Black, Brown and Beige', *Negro Digest*, 19 Feb. 1970, in Hellwig (ed.), *African-American Reflections*, p. 182.

[68] França, 'Uma breve reflexão sobre o Congresso Nacional'.

[69] Florentino, 'Da atualidade de Gilberto Freyre', p. 97.

We could also claim that one reason for the resilience of this way of thinking is that it is flattering to the self-image and self-esteem of a substantial proportion of Brazilians, as to the post-military governments who, one might say, have done their best to keep that view of Brazil alive.

The 'molecular portrait of Brazil' (*Retrato molecular do Brasil*) produced by a team of geneticists from Belo Horizonte in 2000, showing that a high percentage of Brazilians who look white are actually mixed (a point that the anthropologist Melville Herskovits, a former student of Franz Boas, had made about whites in general in the 1920s), contributed to the debate about Brazil's true identity, not least because it has been interpreted in some quarters as a means of 'bringing new blood to the dying myth of racial democracy'.[70] Described in the press as 'the scientific proof of what Gilberto Freyre formulated in sociological terms', the portrait was taken by the dissidents as an 'imitation science', which could be used to maintain the status quo of inequality.[71]

This research, together with the decree of July 1999 by which the then President of Brazil Fernando Henrique Cardoso (the sociologist who was once one of Freyre's leading intellectual opponents) declared the year 2000, the centenary of Freyre's birth, to be the 'National Year of Gilberto Freyre', seemed to represent the peak of Freyre's fortune, in a career that can be described as oscillating over the decades between 'canonisation' and 'excommunication'.

The President seemed to have had two ideas in mind. One was to trump the Portuguese celebrations of their discovery of Brazil in 1500 by focusing attention on a Brazilian discovery of Brazil. The other was to reaffirm the Freyrian definition of Brazilian identity. Cardoso even gave an interview in which he declared that although the idea of racial democracy contains an element of mystification, 'it also contains an element of truth'.

Returning to the speech by Cardoso's successor as President, Lula da Silva, mentioned at the beginning of this chapter, it is known that Sepp Blatter, the head of FIFA (the International Federation of Football Associations), declared himself deeply moved: Lula's 'speech went into my skin', he said.[72] But what about the Brazilians? I have carried out an informal survey and asked a few Brazilians about their reactions on hearing the President's description of 'our identity'.[73] Whether or not they associated that description with Freyre, those who are not connected to

[70] Ricardo Ventura Santos and Marcos Chor Maio, 'Qual "Retrato do Brasil?": Raça, biología, identidades e politica na era da genômica', *Mana* 10:1 (2004), pp. 61–95.

[71] Sergio Pena, 'Retrato molecular do Brasil', in Falcão and Barboza de Araújo (eds), *O Imperador das idéias*, pp. 283–300; Ricardo Ventura Santos and Marcos Chor Maio, 'Race, Genomics, Identities and Politics in Contemporary Brazil', *Critique of Anthropology* 24 (2004), pp. 347–78.

[72] Karolos Grohman, 'Fifa's Blatter Moved by Lula's Rio 2016 Rio Bid Speech', Reuters, 2 Oct. 2009, in.reuters.com/article/idINIndia-42868420091002

[73] I am very grateful to the people who answered my questionnaire, and I am especially indebted to Diva Moreira for introducing me to members of the *Movimento Negro* across Brazil.

the black movement agreed, with few exceptions, that the country is mixed, and proudly so, and that people's relations tend to be warm. However, they also accepted the fact that zones of fraternisation, in sports and carnival, for example, coexist with zones of discrimination, such as employment. In other words, they accepted the fact that 'racial harmony' coexists with inequality, which they explain – like Freyre – by class, and not by colour or race.[74]

Among those connected with the black movement, on the other hand, the reaction was mainly negative and inflamed. While a few agreed that miscegenation 'constituted what we are, and gives the direction to what we would like to be and do', the great majority did not agree at all with Lula's representation of 'our identity', arguing that it was either pure mystification or one-sided. Let me offer a few quotations: 'Lula repeats what the first colonisers did. Mixes together all cultures in one, so that it becomes easier to dominate and administer. We cannot accept that.' Again, 'the elite does not like to mix. The stimulus for miscegenation is found only among people of low income.' And yet again: in contrast to the 'North American logic of "separated but equal", we are "together but unequal"'; 'all this is nothing more than mystification, mere manipulation'. 'The people always believe in fairy tales that the elite tell them, like this one that we are all equal, of one mixed race, happy, friendly', much of this 'on account of Freyre's legacy of fantasy'.

So, if the impact of Freyre's ideas on Brazilian self-perception is undeniable, these ideas have changed their meaning since 1933. What was once shocking has become official or semi-official, and what was defined against whitening is now defined against black consciousness.

[74] See Antonio Sergio Guimarães, 'Racial Democracy', in J. Souza and W. Sinder (eds), *Imagining Brazil* (Lanham, MD: Lexington Books, 2005), pp. 119–40.

7

Writing from the Margins: Towards an Epistemology of Contemporary African Brazilian Fiction

DAVID BROOKSHAW

THERE IS NO SPECIFICALLY BLACK LITERARY TRADITION in Brazil, as there is in the United States. Names such as James Baldwin, Richard Wright and, more recently, Alice Walker and Toni Morrison have no equivalents, as household literary names, in Brazilian narrative fiction. The reasons for this are as varied as they are complex, and can be attributed to the sociological reality of Brazil, as well as to the way Brazilians perceive themselves in terms of race. In the former category, the reduced level of literacy and educational opportunities among black Brazilians over the last century or so (ever since the abolition of slavery) has meant quite simply that there are fewer writers and readers. Black cultural traditions and black concerns, and even resistance, have been expressed in non-print ways, such as in music, oral tales and religious ritual. If there is some truth to this, the same, of course, could be said of North America, where music and song as expressions of an African-American identity preceded literary production. Moreover, the existence of a black press in Brazil ever since the beginning of the twentieth century and the emergence of a black Brazilian poetic voice, at least since the 1930s, suggest that we should treat the argument surrounding literacy with caution.

On the other hand, the idea of a black literature or even black writers in Brazil suggests that there is a clear distinction in that country's social culture between people of African and non-African descent. This, of course, goes against one of the founding principles of Brazilian nationalism, one of whose sacred cows is the notion that the long tradition of miscegenation has created an authentically *mestiço* nation with an integrated cultural identity. Even now, and certainly since the administration of Fernando Henrique Cardoso first introduced policies geared towards affirmative action, many have articulated their resentment against the imposition of what is seen as a North American solution to Brazil's problems of social inequality and discrimination; a solution, it is argued, that is both unnecessary and contrary to Brazilian national tradition. Critics claim that it is impossible to tell who is black in Brazil. However, what the defenders of Brazilian *mesticismo*

Proceedings of the British Academy **179**, *133–147*. © The British Academy 2012.

forget is that the balm of race mixture coexists with and is contradicted by another Brazilian tradition: that of *branqueamento*, the whitening ethic that has traditionally encouraged black Brazilians to aspire to escape their origins by marrying lighter-skinned partners, and by implication abandon African or Afro-Brazilian cultural practices. It is this uneasy coexistence of miscegenation and whitening that has allowed the emergence, down the years, of writers who are of clear Afro-Brazilian descent (or at least they would be to North Americans), but who have been considered, or have considered themselves, white. Whether we are talking of Machado de Assis, or Mário de Andrade, or more recently João Ubaldo Ribeiro, they have all joined the pantheon of great national novelists.

This ambiguity in Brazil has meant that writers of Portuguese or mixed descent, but who consider themselves white, have identified themselves as culturally *mestiço*, or, it might be claimed, have appropriated Afro-Brazilian culture and made it their own.[1] This has led to the assumption by the general Brazilian public, as well as consumers of Brazilian culture outside, that black Brazilians are somehow spoken for: Jorge Amado's long literary career and his defence of Afro-Bahian cultural values is a demonstration to many that Brazil is a culturally integrated nation where social position, more than colour, defines what little prejudice and discrimination there is. In such a scenario, the idea of a black Brazilian literature, that is, a type of Brazilian negritude in which black writers become the agents of literary production rather than literary objects, is seen as profoundly un-Brazilian and in itself racist. Yet the emergence of a black literary voice over the last half-century, including that of a number of fiction writers, suggests not an emerging black racism but a questioning of the myth of their country's racial democracy. Black Brazilian poetry and fiction, and to a lesser extent drama, is a testimony to as well as a critique of the contradictions mentioned above: *mesticismo* but *branqueamento*.

Having established the existence and even the concept of *uma literatura negra*, a number of questions need to be asked. First, can a white author write as if he or she were black, with any degree of credibility? With regard to Brazil, we have already seen that writers who consider themselves white have done so, and it would be a racist assumption to suppose that this was impossible, in the same way that it would be sexist to assume that a male author could not put himself into the mindset of a female, or socially divisive to assume that a middle-class writer could not imagine him or herself as working-class. The answer here is, perhaps, one of cultural formation, and beyond that, the notion that a balance needs to be drawn between the celebration of difference and the acceptance of a common humanity. Maggie

[1] The concept of Brazil as a culturally '*mestiço*' nation goes back to the nineteenth century and the writings of Sílvio Romero, but in the modern period, its greatest and most influential spokesman was Gilberto Freyre, from his classic *Casa-grande e senzala* through to his development of 'Lusotropicalism'. For a recent interpretation of race and culture in Brazilian literature, see Alexandra Isfahani-Hammond, *White Negritude: Race, Writing, and Brazilian Cultural Identity* (New York: Palgrave Macmillan, 2008).

Gee, a white British female novelist, has written convincingly about racism in contemporary urban Britain, in *The White Family* (2002). On the other hand, the black *paulista* writer, Oswaldo de Camargo, as we shall see later, probably finds it marginally easier to write about the concerns of the Afro-Brazilian urban middle class in his city than he does about the inhabitants of the *favelas*. Looking at other parts of the Lusophone world, one could hardly deny the Mozambican and Angolan pedigree of white writers like Mia Couto or Pepetela, any more than we can deny the British (English) identity of contemporary novelists like Zadie Smith and Courtia Newland. What we can say about Afro-Brazilian authors whose work reflects an African Brazilian experience, is that these are voices that need to be heard, even if they address uncomfortable truths.

The second question to consider is whether one can talk about a black Brazilian literary tradition in the same way that one can talk about a supposedly 'white' one. Histories of Brazilian literature are, of course, no more than narratives themselves that take us through, say, the evolution of the Brazilian novel, from the great domestic romances of the nineteenth century through to the linguistic, cultural and social concerns of the modernists and regionalists of the first half of the twentieth century, and the transgressional regionalism, new women's fiction, and contemporary urban novels of the latter half of the century. None of these histories pay particular heed to the ethnic origin of writers or to a black literary history. Indeed, with the exception of Oswaldo de Camargo's homespun *O negro escrito* (1987), published to coincide with the centenary of the abolition of slavery, and the special edition of the North American review, *Callaloo* (1995), devoted to African Brazilian writers, little has been done to categorise a black Brazilian literary tendency.[2] The questions that then arise are when black fiction begins, whether there is an awareness on the part of its authors of belonging to a black literary history and therefore playing a part in the formation of a black narrative canon, and if not (or even if so), what its relationship is to 'mainstream' Brazilian fiction, that is, to the wider Brazilian narrative canon.

The first novelist to write openly about the effects of colour prejudice and to even posit the need for a *literatura negra* was Lima Barreto, who, like his elder contemporary, Machado de Assis, was a man of Afro-Brazilian descent from the suburbs of turn-of-the-century Rio, and who felt the full weight of the post-abolition backlash against people of African ancestry because they seemed to serve as a

[2] Interestingly, literature by contemporary black Brazilian writers has become the subject of study and translation by African-American scholars in North American universities. See, for example, the studies by Niyi Afolabi, Esmeralda Ribeiro and Márcio Barbosa, *The Afro-Brazilian Mind: Contemporary Afro-Brazilian Literary and Cultural Criticism* (Trenton, NJ: Africa World Press, 2007), and *Cadernos Negros – Black Notebooks. Contemporary Afro-Brazilian Literature* (Trenton, NJ: Africa World Press, 2008).

[3] As writers of Afro-Brazilian descent, both Machado and Lima Barreto illustrate the correlation between class and colour in their different approaches towards Brazil's social problems in their writing. Both

cont.

visible reminder of the country's slave past.[3] Literary scholarship since the 1960s has elevated Lima Barreto into the Brazilian mainstream, and he is now generally considered an important precursor to the modernists. However, the emergence of a more consistent form of black literature, and, within this, black prose fiction, really only began to gather pace after the Second World War. There are, of course, political and historical reasons for this, which it is important not to lose sight of. The long dictatorship of Getúlio Vargas from 1930 through to 1945 severely hampered intellectual activity and political debate, including that of an incipient black urban middle class that had begun to discuss specifically black issues in the press in the 1920s and 1930s. It is also probably true to say that Vargas's channelling of Brazilian cultural nationalism for his own purposes, and his currying of support among the urban working class of the country's large southern cities, provided at least emotional compensation for the absence of political freedoms that Afro-Brazilians had never really experienced anyway. The return of civil freedoms after 1945 witnessed a revival in the debate about race issues among urban Afro-Brazilians, and this was heightened by one high-profile incident of racial discrimination, when the black North American dancer and actress, Katherine Dunham, was barred from a hotel in São Paulo, an occurrence that helped fuel the passage of the Afonso Arinos law in 1951, which outlawed racial discrimination. At the same time, as the civil rights movement in North America was re-ignited, interest in Brazilian race relations produced UNESCO-sponsored research that in fact, rather than confirming the country's racial democracy, began to discover its contradictions.[4] The novel that synthesised this debate was Romeu Crusoé's *A maldição de Canaan*, first published in 1951, significantly re-edited in 1955, and then forgotten.

Crusoé was born in 1915 in Petrolina, a town on the Pernambuco bank of the São Francisco river opposite the Bahian town of Juazeiro. By the time he wrote his only novel, he was living in Rio, having also authored a number of plays for Abdias do Nascimento's Teatro Experimental do Negro. The first thing to say about *A maldição de Canaan* is that it relates intertextually to a number of twentieth-century Brazilian novels that could be considered as belonging to the country's narrative canon. It could be seen, for example, as an African Brazilian's ironic reply to Graça Aranha's overtly racist turn-of-the-century novel, *Canaã* (1902), which extolled the role of European immigrants in Brazil at the onset of the Old Republic and looked forward to the time when the mass of the country's population would have been lightened through mixture between European immigrant male and Brazilian *mestiça*, while the immediate descendants of the recently freed slaves

satirised Brazilian society, but Machado, who rose into the high bourgeoisie of Rio, did so with great sublety, while Lima Barreto, rooted in the suburban *petite bourgeoisie* of the Federal capital, was more open in his denunciation of colour prejudice.

[4] Initial findings were published in the UNESCO *Courier* 5:8–9 (1952), pp. 6–15.

would have succumbed to the effects of poverty. Equally, Crusoé's novel could be seen as a literary riposte to exponents of the northeastern regionalist novel of the 1930s, most notably Jorge Amado's novel *Jubiabá* (1935), whose main protagonist, the young black Antônio Balduino, suffers from racial prejudice but finds salvation in the labour movement; and Lins do Rego, whose novel *O moleque Ricardo* (1935) recounts the experiences of a young black plantation boy as he migrates to the city of Recife and also becomes involved in urban proletarian politics. There is an echo of Lins do Rego's black hero in Crusoé's similarly named narrator, Ricardo, while Balduino's fixation with the upper-class white girl, Lindinalva, is also reflected in Ricardo's obsession with Maria Alice in *A maldição de Canaan*. Moreover, Lindinalva's fall into prostitution, which reduces her to the level of Balduino, is repeated in Crusoé's novel, when Ricardo re-encounters Maria Alice, who had previously spurned him, in a brothel. However, any comparison between the heroes of Amado and Lins do Rego and Crusoé's narrator/protagonist ends there.

To begin with, *A maldição de Canaan* is written in the form of a confession, in which the issue of racial discrimination is central to the theme, taking precedence over any evocation of region, specific geographical location (in spite of certain clues), or historical period (although there are oblique references to the political upheavals of the 1920s). The deliberate absence of place names is explained in the narrator's introductory statement that life has taught him that 'a humanidade é igual a si mesma em todos os quadrantes da terra'.[5] The purpose of the confession is therefore to lay bare, through the experiences of this black everyman, the insidious nature of racial prejudice in Brazil generally. Reminiscent in many ways of the Iberian picaresque, we follow the narrator's life through a series of spatial dislocations, from interior to coastal capital and back to the interior, and through a series of relationships contracted with white women, all of which serve to bring out complexes in the hero that, it is stressed throughout, are the product of the formative social influences upon him and his lovers. As in the picaresque, Ricardo's is a story of material success, graduating as he does from poverty through the humiliations of finding employment in a racist society to relative prosperity as an independent dealer in the skin trade with employees of his own. His upward social mobility is offset at every stage by his inability to settle down to a committed relationship with any of the women with whom he lives. Forsaking as he does the possibility of love with his childhood friend, the black Nair, Ricardo's obsession with white women (and by implication *branqueamento*) is destined to failure, simply because he is made conscious at every turn that his relations, first with Laura, then with Solange, and finally with Maria Alice, are only possible because these women have in some way been outcast and reduced to his level in the social pecking order. This knowledge corrodes his capacity to show any commitment, much less

[5] Romeu Crusoé, *A maldição de Canaan*, 2nd edn (Rio de Janeiro: Irmãos di Giorgio, 1955), p. 20.

confidence in the stability of such a relationship, which in turn causes suffering to himself and his love partners. Ultimately, the humiliation suffered in everyday life is visited upon the female, as it is indeed in Alice Walker's *The Color Purple* (1982), except that here the female is white.

The first-person narration along with its inevitable tone of self-analysis and introspection gives Crusoé's Ricardo far greater depth of character than Lins do Rego's namesake, or Amado's Balduino. A further, crucial difference is that the drama of Crusoé's hero is that of a man with social and educational pretensions far beyond those of the other two characters. He pays to go to night school, he aspires to learn languages, he becomes financially independent. His drama is that of a social riser, a member of an emergent black middle class that white writers could hardly imagine black Brazilians belonging to, much less understand the hardships and humiliations which such ambitions might produce. For most white writers, their first and sometimes only encounter with their black compatriots had been as servants and subalterns, and as for problems of prejudice, whites were the main exponents of the Brazilian nationalist myth that skin colour was not an impediment to social advance in their country.

We must not, of course, misinterpret the reasons why *A maldição de Canaan* was consigned to oblivion after its second edition. It is clearly a thesis novel and its message occasionally overstated, but its absence from histories of Brazilian fiction may also be explained by the fact that Crusoé withdrew from literary life, as if he had no more to say. On the other hand, it is equally significant that criticism did not seem to link it to the northeastern regional models it was clearly responding to, but rather to more militant black models such as Lima Barreto and Richard Wright. Perhaps its message, and above all its contestation of the national myth were too hard to stomach, too near the bone for it to be included in the national literary pantheon. Whatever the case, Romeu Crusoé was not beyond reconciliation with the notion of Brazil's fundamentally *mestiço* identity. What he criticised was what he saw as a pandering by the white Brazilian elite to foreign racist tendencies, and there is a suggestion that, possibly because of greater European immigration, the situation of Afro-Brazilians was considerably worse in the large southern cities than in the northeast. Whatever the weakness of this particular argument, it is a cue for us to turn our attention to black literary activity in São Paulo, which resurfaced in the 1950s and 1960s.

During the course of the 1950s, São Paulo once again assumed a role as centre of the black movement in Brazil which it had held in the 1920s and 1930s. Inspired to some extent by African-American writers, but also by the poets of French negritude, Carlos Assumpção (the author of one iconic poem), Eduardo de Oliveira, and Oswaldo de Camargo became the poetic voices of their generation of black *paulistanos*. But it was Camargo who was to translate some of the themes and emotiveness of his poetry, published between 1959 and 1962, into prose fiction, through a first collection of short stories entitled *O carro do êxito* (1972) and a novella, *A descoberta do frio* (1979). By the time of the publication of the latter, Camargo was something of an elder statesman among black writers in São Paulo, lending his support to a new generation of writers that began to emerge in the late 1970s, coinciding with the *abertura política* following years of military dictatorship, and who began to produce collections of poetry and short fiction in a new series, entitled *Cadernos Negros*, that appeared regularly between 1978 and 2004. The author who emerged as the most prolific and versatile writer of this next generation is undoubtedly Cuti, the sobriquet of Luiz Silva, who has published various collections of poetry, short stories, plays and essays. One could say that Cuti did for black writing in São Paulo in the 1980s and 1990s what Camargo had done in the 1960s and 1970s. Cuti's work, when read alongside that of the older writer, demonstrates how the nature of black fiction has changed, reflecting not only changing socio-economic circumstances (years of recession and economic disparity), but also the way narrative themes and techniques have shifted over those years to reflect such changing circumstances.

Camargo was born in Bragança, in upstate São Paulo, in 1936, the son of coffee plantation workers. He was educated in a seminary, learned to play the organ, developed an interest in church music, and worked for many years as a copy editor in the offices of the *Estado de São Paulo*. His collection of short stories, *O carro do êxito*, was a first major breakthrough by a black writer into mainstream publishing. In general, the stories, some of which are masterpieces of irony, focus on the black community in the city of São Paulo during the 1950s, round about the time of the seventieth anniversary of abolition, and chronicle the activities of an aspiring young black intelligentsia, as it strives to create the organisational structures and symbols (cultural associations, magazines) of its journey along the road to success in the 'carro do êxito' (the car of success). Camargo evokes the contradictions within and among black *paulistas* in terms of their self-image, and the incompatibilities that emerge when ethnic categorisations are superimposed on class difference – for example, when the aspiring young black intellectual discovers that his black taxi driver has no interest in negritude, and has never heard of the black poet to whose book launch his passenger is going; or, in the same story, when the invited Nigerian ambassador fails to turn up at the book launch because he is still visiting the ranch of the white owner of the house in which the launch is taking place, and where the black poet's mother used to work as a cook;[6] or in another story, when the middle-class white woman asks her black maid, whose son plays the oboe, whether it is an instrument used for playing samba.[7]

If various of Camargo's stories underline the dependence of young blacks upon whites, such as 'Por que fui ao Benedito Corvo' or 'Civilização',[8] perhaps the

[6] 'Esperando o Embaixador', in Oswaldo de Camargo, *O carro do êxito* (São Paulo: Livraria Martins Editora, 1972), pp. 77–83.

[7] 'Oboé', in Camargo, *O carro do êxito*, pp. 11–19.

[8] In Camargo, *O carro do êxito*, pp. 35–9 and 63–71 respectively.

most poignant illustration of the black experience is one with which Camargo could identify deeply on a personal level, and that was the issue of cultural dualism. In Camargo's chronicles of *afro-paulistano* life, there are those who have been brought up rooted in a sense of black community. In *O carro do êxito*, this is enshrined in the figure of the young Benedito. But there are others who have lost any attachment to black cultural roots, a predicament embodied by Deodato, the adopted son of white parents, whose sense of alienation is such that it eventually leads to his destruction. He returns to his adoptive mother, D. Aurora, in the small town in the interior of São Paulo to die of tuberculosis, the ultimate disease of ennui. Benedito, with his concern to express his Afro-Brazilian identity, and Deodato, who nevertheless exerts some fascination over Benedito, Deodato, the lover of classical music, the reader of Bernanos and Dostoievski, are really extensions of Camargo's own psyche, Camargo, with his taste for baroque music, but his identification with the black movement and with the poetry of negritude. These two characters represent the two sides of Camargo's personality and, by extension, many black *paulistas* with an upbringing similar to Camargo. Indeed, the theme of black exile in a white world, so much a feature of Camargo's poetry, is also the central focus of his second work of fiction, *A descoberta do frio*, which attests to the difficulty the author had in resolving the cultural conflict within himself.

The depictions of the city offered by Camargo and Cuti are to some extent a measure of how urban life has changed over the last half-century. The São Paulo of Oswaldo de Camargo is not the alien, violent environment it is for Cuti's characters. Camargo's characters live near the centre and frequent the downtown streets and bars; the *Associação Cultural do Negro*, the main black organisation in the city during the 1950s in which the author was active, is situated near the Anhangabaú. Benedito is attracted to the city lights: the city represents progress and freedom by contrast to the small town where he was brought up. He therefore contemplates the city with optimism: 'Achegava-me à janela da sala maior e olhava, à noite, as costas dos edifícios vizinhos, enormes na sua vasta quietude. Gostava sobretudo de contemplar o Vale do Anhangabaú e sorver o bulício dos homens, respirar sobre a cidade.'[9] It is strange to think that Camargo's fictitious Benedito was mesmerised by the lights of São Paulo, at about the same time, perhaps, as an obscure inhabitant of Canindé, one of the city's favelas, was writing a diary that depicted a very different side to urban life. Carolina Maria de Jesus's *Quarto de despejo*, written throughout the second half of the 1950s, was 'discovered' by a white journalist and first published to national and international acclaim in 1960.[10] It is a black single mother's account of the drudgery of everyday existence in trying to feed and keep her growing children out of trouble. It is also an evocation of life

[9] Oswaldo de Camargo, *A descoberta do frio* (São Paulo: Edições Populares, 1979), p. 102.

[10] The diary was edited by Audálio Dantas, a journalist on the *Folha de São Paulo*, selling 10,000 copies in the first week, and becoming a publishing sensation.

in the favela, its violence but also little examples of solidarity, the relationships among its inhabitants and between them and those of the neighbouring brick houses, with more than a few wry comments about the exploitation of the *favelados* by local and national politicians during the Kubitschek years. And yet it is also a testimony to the power of the human spirit: Carolina is determined to write, largely in order to get out of the favela, and her reputation within the community as a writer, the chronicler of favela life, gives her a certain power over her less literate, or indeed illiterate neighbours. Exceptional though she was, Carolina de Jesus, and Oswaldo de Camargo, are reminders that expressions of African Brazilian sensitivities, whether these relate to Afro-Brazilian culture or to the everyday issues of discrimination and prejudice, are inflected by the social class to which the writers belong as well as by such formative influences as region.

That said, it is probably true to say that Cuti's stories contribute to bridging the gap between Camargo's aspiring black *paulistana* middle class and Carolina's world of unremitting poverty. Cuti's São Paulo of the final decades of the twentieth century is a far cry from that of the 1950s, reflecting as it does an urban violence that is the product of continuing metropolitan expansion and the maintenance of abysmal social inequalities. In literary and cultural terms too, Cuti belongs to a generation of writers that emerged with the *abertura política* of the 1970s. Cuti's city is the urban jungle first evoked in literary terms in the brutal neo-naturalistic fiction of Rubem Fonseca, in such stories as 'Feliz ano novo', and later portrayed on screen in films such as *Pixote*, *Central do Brasil*, and more recently, of course, *Cidade de Deus*.

Stories such as 'Tentativa', in which an ex-drug dealer's attempt to reform for the sake of his baby daughter comes too late when the police, on another case, torture and kill him; 'Dupla culpa', in which a man who has killed a shopkeeper in an argument is himself shot by police in connection with another crime he has not committed; 'Vida em dívida', which centres on a case of mistaken identity in a contract killing; or finally, 'Um lapso', the confession by a *malandro* who had killed his best friend over an affair with his girl, also killed and buried under the floor of his home – all bear witness to the arbitrary and random way in which violence is meted out on its victims, either by the agents of authority or by the criminalised population. And if, in 'Avenidas', violence is avoided at the end, it is only because the wife of the perpetrator of this violence has taken the bullets out of the gun he intends to use on the man he has seen and followed through the city, convinced that he was the same person who had previously robbed him on a bus. His pursuit takes place against the backdrop of a city that is vast and labyrinthine, an environment where people struggle to make ends meet, and where latent violence waits to be unleashed against any potential victim. Cuti's city is far from the romanticised notion of a carnavalesque country of mild, hedonistic and unprejudiced people.

Cuti's subliminal message for blacks emerges in stories in which black men and women are exploited or discriminated against in sexual relationships. While

'Preto no branco' evokes the rather more predictable racism and hypocrisy within the family of a 'mulata' who is being courted by an upwardly mobile 'preto', and 'Desencontro' centres on an affair between a pillar of the black community and a 'mulata' who has advertised her sexual services in an erotic magazine, and which leads to his wife leaving him, other stories highlight in more grotesque fashion the lack of agency among African Brazilians in São Paulo. In 'Toque-te-me-toque', a black woman sits in a bar alone, in dialogue with the dead white man who had simultaneously been her lover and that of Suzy, a white woman with whom she had also had a lesbian relationship. The suggestion, therefore, of a double exploitation by two white partners is only alleviated at the end of the story by the arrival in the bar of a black male friend, an implied new partner with whom she may form a lasting and equal relationship. The story is, in many ways, a mirror image of 'Entreato', from Cuti's first collection, *Quizila*, in which a black man is in an abusive and failed relationship with a white woman, who appears to embody the cold cynicism of a white world, and is eventually saved by her suicide and the arrival of his true love in the form of a black woman.

The unnatural, exploitative, and unsatisfactory (not to mention unsatisfying) sexual relationships between blacks and whites is the theme of another story, 'Vitória da noite', in which the focus is on a young black poet, Eduardo Santos, an elderly professor, Mendes Fontoura, and Maria Inês, a woman in her forties and member of an older generation of black poets, protégés of the professor. The sexual servicing of Fontoura by Inês, who fulfils his vague fantasies about black women, is an ironic comment on the mutual sexual dependence between blacks and whites, which is an extension of the relationship of power of whites over blacks in the socio-economic hierarchy. Here again, the suggestion of a more romantic and more emotionally fertile and satisfying relationship between the young black male poet and the black female is conveyed in the conclusion to the story, when the drunken Fontoura and Santos pass each other at the entrance to Inês's apartment.

The sexual dimension to racial stereotyping is, of course, not new in Brazil. Indeed, it could be said to form one of the foundation stones of white portrayals of black people in literature and other cultural forms down the years. Cuti's stories contain a counter-stereotype, reminiscent, to some extent, of the portrayal of American innocence in the face of cynical European exploitation that characterised the work of romantics like Gonçalves Dias. White involvement with blacks is corrupting because it is manipulative and self-serving. Black pride must lie in black solidarity, which begins in the family – the black couple. In a very indirect way, Cuti is suggesting in stories like 'Vitória da noite' what the black *paulista* poet of the 1930s, Lino Guedes, stated openly.[11] Perhaps more importantly, Cuti is claiming

[11] Lino Guedes (1897–1951) was a popular black poet of the 1920s and 1930s, whose work reflected a desire that black Brazilians should adopt middle-class family values in order to counter the negative

cont.

that black Brazilians must break away from the cultural structures (the stories) that have made them object rather than subject. Only by telling their own story will they gain some sort of agency, which explains his devotion to the cause of a black Brazilian literature over the last twenty-five years.

The same period has witnessed the emergence of a small but significant number of black women writers in Brazil. Like their male counterparts, there is a greater tendency towards poetry, the major exponent being Miriam Alves. But others, such as Conceição Evaristo, have written short stories, which focus on the experiences of black women in an urban environment. However, for the purpose of this chapter, I wish to concentrate on two writers whose work represents another facet of the African experience in Brazil. The work of one, rather like that of Romeu Crusoé, is based on region, migration, and the interface between urban and rural Brazil, and I refer to Marilene Felinto's quasi cult novel of the early 1980s, *As mulheres de Tijucopapo* (1980). The other work I refer to is Geni Guimarães's short novel, *A cor da ternura* (1989), about growing up in the rural and small-town interior of São Paulo.

Marilene Felinto was only just over 20 years of age when she wrote *As mulheres de Tijucopapo.* It is a raw, passionate novel, addressed to the narrator's mother, and based closely on the author's life, in that it contains early memories of Recife, where Felinto was born, of migration to São Paulo, which Felinto's family, along with thousands of other impoverished northeasterners, undertook in the 1960s, and of her upbringing in Brazil's greatest metropolis. The novel is about the reassertion of origins and an affirmation of female independence by Rísia, the main protagonist, born in the northeast but brought up in São Paulo in a situation of relative poverty. In leaving the city and returning to the mythical village of Tijucopapo where, she claims, her mother had been born, she sets out on a quest to redeem her mother for her resignation in the face of an authoritarian, brutal and unfaithful father. Tijucopapo, the mythical village associated with a group of Amazon-like women who had resisted the Dutch invasions in the seventeenth century, serves as a metaphor for some sort of pre-patriarchal utopia. It is therefore a novel about shame, and in particular the shame a young female felt towards her mother's acceptance of her father's tyranny; but it is also a novel of rejection of the city and its corruptive influences, and of a return to origins, including an implied return to an Afro-Indian past of resistance to alien oppression. In this sense, it echoes a number of traditional themes in Brazilian literature and culture, as expressed by such canonical texts of modernist and regionalist fiction as *Macunaíma* (attraction to and rejection of the city) and *Vidas secas* (a type of inversion of the migration evoked by Graciliano Ramos, a writer admired by and written about by Felinto), and by the Hollywood road movie tradition, with its Brazilian manifestations such as *Bye bye Brasil* and *Central do Brasil.*

stereotypes of blacks held by whites. See David Brookshaw, *Race and Color in Brazilian Literature* (Metuchen, NJ and London: Scarecrow Press, 1986).

More recently, Conceição Evaristo has returned to the theme of urban migration and return to rural roots in her novel, *Ponciá Vicêncio* (2003), which rather in the manner of Felinto's novel is a testimony to the power and rootedness of black women of her mother's generation. Like Crusoé's novel, it is a kind of de-regionalised novel, in the sense that the city that is evoked has no name, while the village Ponciá migrates from and finally returns to is only by implication based on Evaristo's native region, the interior of Minas Gerais.

Guimarães's novel, *A cor da ternura*, classified as '*literatura infanto-juvenil*', is an autobiographical narrative about a young girl growing up on a coffee *fazenda* in rural São Paulo. She is made conscious at an early age of her colour, and white attitudes towards it, and she goes through a period of self-hatred as a result. But it is also a novel about social ascent, and escaping the fate normally assumed to be that of blacks. In this sense, it contains some of the pride and positive images that can be detected in immigrant narratives: the main character becomes a teacher, the first in her family to receive an appropriate level of education for this. It is therefore a life-affirming book about overcoming the impediments of social conditioning and prejudice, and its harmonious ending contrasts with the ironies and brutalities of Cuti's stories. But this is a writer who has stayed close to her roots in the rural interior of São Paulo. Absent are the difficulties and dramas of migration. Moreover, the fact that the book has gone through twelve editions since it was first published is an indication of its value as an educational tool and of its message, which is one that heralds the slow but inevitable erosion of age-old prejudices (including the internalised prejudices that impede people from breaking down the barriers to opportunity in the social world, and which have been erected by the prejudices of others). It is no coincidence that its success has occurred during the years since Brazil returned to democratic government, a period that has witnessed a greater willingness to address the race question.

If African Brazilian narrative fiction is determined to a large extent by regional cultural background, then there remains one crucial region that we have not yet looked at. Bahia, the cradle of African Brazilian civilisation, is also the birthplace of Muniz Sodré, an anthropologist and specialist in media and mass communications at the Federal University of Rio de Janeiro, but also the author of short stories and novels. Of particular relevance to us here is his collection of tales, *Santugri* (1988), which have as their central motif *capoeira*, the mixture of martial art and ring dance perfected by the slaves on the plantations of Brazil in the colonial period, which has spread from its original Bahian heartland throughout the world. There is an appeal in the circular nature of *capoeira*, which serves as metaphor for a cultural process that has neither beginning nor end, and which has an endless capacity to re-invent itself, absorbing new influences while never losing the identity of its original cultural roots. Moreover, in its aesthetics as both dance and form of self-defence (demonstrated in a number of the stories as being more effective and less destructive than firearms), it possesses a flexibility, a multi-faceted identity, expressed in its interdisciplinary nature: it is a dance but also a fight. In short, the *capoeira* ring is a borderland, a space where hybridity occurs.

'Ancestral' is set among a community of slave descendants on the rural island of Itaparica. The young boy, Bino, is living the mythical time of childhood, but he has the curiosity about the outside world that portends his crossing of the threshold into adulthood. This outside world is brought to him by a group of *capoeiristas* from the city, who have absorbed new influences into their performance. Through them, Bino begins to learn about improvisation, while not losing one's base, but equally, through the figure of Tio Marco, the *preto velho* and harbinger of ancient African customs enshrined in *candomblé*, he learns about the inter-relationship of life and death and ancestral wisdom. At the end of the story, Bino has undergone an initiation which enables him to reconcile the old and the new, the ancestral and that which comes from outside, and which is absorbed into ancestrality, breathing new life into it: 'Jogou capoeira, incorporando os golpes novos com tanta tranquilidade e mandinga, que o espírito do jogo renascia, o novo vinha reforçar a tradição, assim como Tio Marco subsistia em Bino.'[12]

In 'Comer jabuticabas', on the other hand, the closed circle of dance and confrontation is an elevator rather than a *capoeira* ring. A black *capoeirista* takes a luxury flat after winning the lottery, and a white resident's irritation latches onto the way he eats *jabuticabas* from a bag while he travels in the elevator. This becomes the area of confrontation, but also the locus where borders are crossed. The white eventually accosts him, slapping him on the cheek, but rather than return the blow, the *capoeirista*, using the time-honoured tactic of surprise, turns the other cheek, forcing the ashamed white out of the ring, and consigning him to the servants' elevator at the rear of the building. The clash of opposites has produced an exchange of places, a crossing over.

Muniz Sodré's evocation of an African Brazilian-centred learning about the world is extremely important because it has the effect of cutting out the all-powerful middleman in the form of Western European (or white North American) culture. It is visible, for example in the story 'Iamada-San', which is a tale about an individual's capacity to transform and re-invent himself, as a former black Bahian *capoeirista* travels the world and returns to Brazil as a Buddhist monk. Two opposites are thus joined, with an emphasis on pluralism rather than assimilation within a fixed hierarchical structure. Iamar crosses from one ethnic minority culture to another as part of his life's journey and not as a process of upward social mobility. Something similar is experienced by a black nightclub singer in Bahia who finds himself singing with the voice of Otis Redding on the very night that the famous rhythm and blues singer was killed in an air crash. Once again, another identity is

[12] Muniz Sodré, *Santugri* (Rio de Janeiro: Livraria José Olympio Editora, 1988), p. 14.

assumed through an affiliated sense of rhythm and soul. But it is also about crossing borders, and re-inventing oneself:

> Manuelzinho jamais ouvira falar de Redding, tudo que sabia e sabe é entrar no ritmo, inventar sons, brincando de gringo, ou então desenhar círculos com passinhos em torno da dama no meio da pista [. . .] sente, assim, sem que precisasse ouvir de ninguém, que a força existe, que fronteira não há para a força, axé![13]

By way of conclusion, I now return to the title of this chapter. Is it desirable or even possible to create an epistemology of African Brazilian writing? The libraries are full of general histories of Brazilian literature which have organised literary activity into an ongoing narrative, based perhaps inevitably on the response of Brazilian writers to Western cultural movements, and their adaptation to (and transformation by) Brazilian social and cultural reality. Occasionally, regional literatures have been catalogued in similar, but essentially parallel fashion. The question arises, then, as to whether something similar can be done for a literary tradition based on a particular ethnic group. Regardless of what we have said about the difficulty of ethnic categorisation in Brazil (because of mixture, cultural tradition, etc.), it has to be said that a work such as Oswaldo de Camargo's *O negro escrito*, a chronological account of the work of African Brazilian writers accompanied by an anthology, relates as much to the politics of race as it does to literature itself; if indeed the two can be separated. It gives the impression that accepted skills have been handed down from one generation to another. It contributes to a sense of a community – an imagined community, or at the very least an intellectual vanguard for such a community. And yet, as we have seen, these writers emerge from within the concrete social and cultural context of a region. Marilene Felinto is a *paulista*, but she is not a participant in the black literature of São Paulo. Perhaps she does not identify with the group, or maybe she feels more of a northeasterner (and a reading of Carolina Maria de Jesus reveals the rifts between *paulistas* and northeastern migrants in her favela). Or it may be that, as a product of migration, she feels displaced, nomadic (as evinced in some of her short stories). Muniz Sodré's celebration of what one might call a black-based pluralism, comes closer in its ethics to what was propounded by the *antropófagos* of Brazilian modernism: an ability to appropriate and transform, and by so doing transform oneself; identity as process rather than a fixed state. Once again, Muniz Sodré's work may be attributed to region: Bahia and its cultural background explored previously by the black writer, Deoscoredes do Santos, and the white, Jorge Amado. If what unites all these writers is a response to the top-down oppressiveness of enslavement to '*branqueamento*', or at the very least to a 'white *mesticismo*' masquerading as assimilation, regional background is what explains their differing approach to the problem. If, for example, one were writing about Brazilian literature

[13] Sodré, *Santugri*, p. 54.

of Italian or Lebanese immigration, one would have to take into account that José Luís Pozenato is an Italian-Brazilian from Rio Grande do Sul and that Milton Hatoum is a Lebanese-Brazilian from Manaus. This is what they write about, and while their experiences may bear similarities with those of other Italian and Lebanese descended writers in Brazil, it is region that gives their work its own particular social and cultural context. Finally, herein lies the analogy with African Brazilian literature: these voices from the margins help to unwrite the nation, to question the sacred cows of establishment cultural identity, even as they throw into question the false cohesion of establishment Brazilian nationalism. If, in the cause of pluralism, we set store by cultural identity as being an unending process, creative in its adaptability and its predisposition towards re-invention, then perhaps it is not desirable to attempt to create epistemologies.

8

Indigenato Before Race? Some Proposals on Portuguese Forced Labour Law in Mozambique and the African Empire (1926–62)

MICHEL CAHEN

WHEN ASKING '*INDIGENATO* BEFORE RACE?', my purpose is quite obviously not to conclude that Portuguese colonial law organised only *social* discrimination and therefore was not racist. One need only read the successive Native Statutes and the Colonial Act to be convinced to the contrary. Nor is the aim to answer the question of the function of Portuguese colonial racism: it is very easy to point out that it was an ideological tool to define who was native (and was to be compelled into forced labour up to 1962) and who was not. People were black and *therefore* native or 'not civilised' (with the small exception of *assimilados*), or white and *therefore never* native and always 'civilised', even when completely illiterate. Nevertheless, these realities do not suffice to show exactly how it all worked.

But let me digress for a moment. Is it correct to translate the Portuguese *indígena* as *native* in English (in particular American social sciences English)? One first problem is that *indígena* in Portuguese is at the same time a noun and an adjective, whereas 'indigenous' is only an adjective in English: this implies translating *um indígena* as 'a native' and, in general terms, this will probably run. But in old Portuguese African colonies, there were whites and mixed-race or black Luso-Africans, sometimes since generations earlier. Were they 'native'? It was obvious to everybody that they were not *indígena*. They were 'Angolan' or 'Mozambican', that is to say white, mixed-race or black *Portuguese* from Angola and Mozambique, but not *indígena*. Would it, in the case of completely black Luso-Africans, be the same in English: would those blacks really *not* be natives? Moreover, in the Portuguese African empire, *indígena* became a legal status within the juridical

I thank Maria da Conceição Neto (University Agostinho Neto, Luanda) for her remarks and criticism, which drove me to change or better qualify some aspects of the original version. That does not mean she will agree with all my final proposals.

Proceedings of the British Academy **179**, *149–171*.

duality imposed on the colonised (*indígenas*, or 'not-civilised', versus *cidadãos*, or 'civilised'). In that sense, *indígena* might be translated by '[colonial] subject', but it would thus embrace the whole of the local colonised population, when *assimilados* were (officially) full Portuguese citizens, as well as the Indians of Goa and the Chinese of Macao – and when the Cape Verdeans were neither *indígena* nor *assimilados* (citizens) and enjoyed an intermediary status. Maria da Conceição Neto points out 'the absurdity [which] could be seen at São Tomé where "the natives" (*indígenas*) were not those born locally but those brought there as "contract workers" (*contratados*) from Angola and Mozambique', since the very São Toméan natives were not compelled to forced labour and therefore not called *indígenas*, but *forros*.[1] In this text, I will translate *indígena* (adjective) as 'native' when it refers to the legal status or the condition of living within this legal status ('native policy', 'Native Code', etc.), and as 'indigenous' when it refers to the fact of being *historically* from that place ('indigenous customs and habits', but a locally born European or Goan will not be an 'indigenous' because his origin lay abroad), with some special cases (I will translate *imposto indígena* as 'hut tax'). Often, I will simply use the Portuguese words, in italics. Furthermore, it is impossible to translate *indigenato* (the legal status and the social category) as 'indigenousness', which would be an *indigenidade* which does not exist in Portuguese.

Even if the Portuguese noun *indígena* had been used before,[2] among many other words, to refer to African peoples (*cafres*, *gentio*, *selvagens*, *pagãos*, i.e. kaffirs, horde, savages, pagans), its generalisation as a concept in order to refer to colonised native peoples in Portuguese continental Africa (and probably elsewhere) is more recent. Such a generalisation was linked to Lisbon's effort to produce a systematic legislation for its new empire, from the beginning of the last quarter of the nineteenth century and above all after 1885. Before then, in the days of the slave trade in the first age of colonisation, it is well known that the coloniser concluded alliances with some African states to secure the capture of slaves in other states. Arab or Swahili slave traders did the same. That meant that not all black people were to become slaves: it depended on the alliances. In contrast, under colonial capitalism, *all* black people became natives (*indígenas*), unless they succeeded in extracting themselves from their race. In Portuguese colonies, this was done with a remarkable degree of systematisation.

The concepts *indígena* and *indigenato* as a legal category[3] are therefore more or less contemporary with the implementation of colonial capitalism. It could be

[1] María da Conceição Neto, personal communication, 8 May 2011.

[2] Francisco Bethencourt points out that, in the first edition of Morães, *indígena* already exists with the modern meaning, and it may have existed before (António de Moraes Silva and Rafael Bluteau, *Diccionario da lingua portugueza composto pelo padre D. Rafael Bluteau; Reformado, e accrescentado por António de Moraes Silva natural do Rio de Janeiro* (Lisbon: Officina de Simão Thaddeo Ferreira, 1789).

[3] Ana Cristina Nogueira da Silva, 'A cidadania nos Trópicos. O Ultramar no constitucionalismo monárquico português (1820–1880)', unpublished PhD thesis, Universidade Nova de Lisboa, 2004, pp. 4–42.

said that this was a logical consequence of the victory of abolitionism,[4] indirectly linked with the expansion of capitalism, and it could also be said that *indigenato* and forced labour replaced slavery. But it is this very notion of 'replacement' that needs to be discussed. Situations differ greatly according to whether we are looking at the French Caribbean before 1848, Brazil before 1888, the creole Portuguese archipelagos of Cape Verde or São Tomé, or the continental colonies of the Portuguese empire before 1878. The key is whether, in all these places where slavery occurred, there was or there was not a slave plantation economy, a plantation complex.[5] The result of abolition was obviously different according to each case. It is well known that in the South of the United States, Brazil, the French Caribbean, and Réunion, the plantation economic system declined quickly after the end of the multiple extensions of time granted to the former owners of slaves in order to oblige the 'freed' slaves to stay. With obvious differences from one place to another, the majority of former slaves did not stay and preferred to become labourers in industrial cities, smallholders in the mountains, or even landless peasants, engendering a massive *plebe* that was poorly integrated into the capitalist production process. Nevertheless, that scenario does not seem to fit the case of São Tomé and Principe – the 'Caribbean' island of Portugal in equatorial Africa.

São Tomé and Principe

São Tomé and Principe seem to be an exception, a case of the lingering survival of a closed system of slavery in a plantation economy (the cocoa *roças*) up to the Second World War. This may be explained by the peculiar history of the genesis of creole society,[6] which prohibited the imposition of forced labour on the natives (*filhos da terra*, or *forros*)[7] and required the late and growing importation of slave

[4] Since the new uniqueness of human kind needed the codification of its categories.

[5] Philip D. Curtin, *The Rise and Fall of the Plantation Complex: Essays in Atlantic History* (Cambridge: Cambridge University Press, 1990). In this chapter, when I speak about 'plantation', it will always be 'large plantations' and not the peasant self-subsistence agriculture which, nevertheless, may be very intensive in some areas.

[6] I am calling 'creole' not only the colony-born whites, but all the colonial (not colonised) social milieus produced by, or at the margins of, the imperial state apparatus. The longevity of the Portuguese first age of colonisation made it peculiar; Isabel Castro Henriques, *São Tomé e Príncipe: A invenção de uma sociedade* (Lisbon: Véga, 2000); Elisabetta Maino, 'Le kaléidoscope identitaire. Anthropologie historique de São Tomé e Príncipe', unpublished PhD thesis, École des Hautes Etudes en Sciences Sociales, Paris, 2004, pp. 7–12; Augusto Nascimento, 'S. Tomé e Príncipe no século XIX: Um espaço de interpretação das mudanças sociais', in Valentim Alexandre (ed.), *O Império Africano (Séculos XIX e XX)* (Lisbon: Edições Colibri, 2000), pp. 95–116; Valentim Alexandre, *Poderes e quotidiano nas roças de S. Tomé e Príncipe, de finais de oitecentos a meados de novecentos* (Lousã: author, 2002).

[7] The last attempt to impose forced labour on the *forros* provoked the 'war of Batepá' in 1953; Gerhard Seibert, 'Le massacre de février 1953 à São Tomé, raison d'être du nationalisme santoméen', *Lusotopie* 4 (1997), pp. 173–92.

manpower (named *serviçais* from the end of the nineteenth century) due to the insularity and small size of the archipelago, as well as the violence of the colonial state of a weak metropolitan capitalism. However, even in this case, the growing difficulties of maintaining the system led to its 'criminalisation': in the 1950s, being sent from Mozambique to São Tomé was not a question of forced labour for indigenous people, but very often of penitentiary labour for native convicts.

In other words, São Tomé represents one case of a slave plantation complex, and the fact that this complex needed a few decades more to die than was the case in the Americas does not change anything. Thus, it must not be understood as a transition where slavery was slowly substituted by forced labour; rather, forced labour was tried, but never successfully.[8] Historically speaking, in São Tomé, there was no transition: there was an attempt to continue slave exploitation, and afterwards, the convulsions of its decline. Social improvements for *serviçais* after the Second World War in order to stabilise them were concomitant with the crisis of this single-crop farming and of its profitability.[9] Deep convulsions occurred too in the Americas: the difference is that in São Tomé, capitalism hardly replaced slavery. It was the transition from slavery to nothing.

The problem the social sciences face today is that the analysis of forced labour in Portuguese continental Africa has been and remains excessively influenced by the case of São Tomé, which fed famous scandals and abolitionist protests from the end of the nineteenth century up to 1925.[10] The issue was always that forced labour was no more than modern slavery, and forced labour in Angola and Mozambique was seen as forming part of other plantation complexes as early as the nineteenth century or beginning of the twentieth.[11] Obviously, slavery is literally a kind of forced labour. But this does not mean that twentieth-century forced (officially indentured) labour was 'modern slavery', at least if seen from the viewpoint of the mode of production and its historical path.

[8] See the first chapter of Gerhard Seibert, *Comrades, Clients and Cousins: Colonialism, Socialism and Democratization in São Tomé and Príncipe* (Leiden: University of Leiden, 1999), pp. 18–49.

[9] Alexander Keese, 'Early Limits of Local Decolonisation: Forced Labour, Decolonisation and the "Serviçal" Population in São Tomé and Príncipe, from Colonial Abuses to Post-Colonial Disappointment, 1945–1976', *International Journal of African Historical Studies*, forthcoming.

[10] In particular the famous Nevinson and Ross Reports: Henry W. Nevinson, *A Modern Slavery* (London: Harper and Brothers, 1906); Edward A. Ross, *Report on Employment of Native Labour in Portuguese Africa* (New York: Abbott Press, 1925). For a recent anlysis, see Miguel Bandeira Jerónimo, *Livros Brancos, Almas Negras: A 'missão civilizadora' do colonialismo Português c. 1870–1930* (Lisbon: Imprensa de Ciências Sociais, 2009), esp. chs 2 and 5.

[11] See the unambiguous title of the famous book by James Duffy, *A Question of Slavery* (London: Oxford University Press, 1967).

Late but extensive slave trade; weak slavery; modern forced labour

What was the situation in the Portuguese colonies on the continent? With few exceptions, the former slave traders, being white, *mulatto* or black, did not become planters. Some managed to find their place among the very small urban elites – in Luanda, Benguela or Moçâmedes in Angola, or Quelimane, Moçambique or Ibo Island in Mozambique. But the new plantation companies were generally not theirs, and were a new phenomenon stemming from foreign or metropolitan capital, and in any case *external capital.* Even the descendants of the *prazeiros* of Great Zambezia in Mozambique, who could have been best placed to transform their *prazos* into *latifundios*, failed to do so, first for military reasons: they sought to defend their freedom to be slave traders too long and too late, and they had to be defeated by metropolitan Portugal.[12] With the very tiny exception of the Mossuril peninsula facing Moçambique Island – the so-called *terras firmes* where slave plantations existed – and a few places in the hinterland of Luanda in Angola, Portuguese (and also Swahili) slavery in these areas was domestic and above all for exportation. Obviously, domestic slavery did include some slaves working in *quintas* (small plantations), but I believe it is right to emphasise that the slave trade never produced a *plantation economy* in continental Portuguese Africa comparable to that in Latin America. The first reason for this was a military one: in order to create those plantations, it would have been necessary to defeat a number of African states, some small and some larger, in order to dominate large areas of land directly. It was far more profitable to export slaves, all the more since Brazilian production (even after independence) answered to the needs of legitimate trade in tropical commodities.[13] This effective conquest occurred very late, which is to say, at the very moment when abolition was actually implemented, between the Berlin Congress and the First World War. Even if they had wanted to do so, the former slave exporters had no more time to develop slave-worked plantations.

In the Portuguese African empire, forced labour and *indigenato* were *not* implemented to maintain former slaves on the plantations (or in the mines), for

[12] Allen Isaacman, *Mozambique: The Africanization of a European Institution: The Zambezi* Prazos, *1750–1902* (Madison: University of Wisconsin Press, 1972); Allen Isaacman and Barbara Isaacman, 'Os prazeiros como trans-raianos: Um estudo sobre transformação social e cultural', *Arquivo* (Maputo: Arquivo Histórico de Moçambique), 10 (1991), pp. 5–48. About the last period of the *prazos*, see Leroy Vail and Landeg White, *Capitalism and Colonialism in Mozambique: A Study of Quelimane District* (London: Heinemann, 1980); René Pelissier, *Naissance du Mozambique: Résistance et révoltes anticoloniales (1854–1918)*, 2 vols (Orgeval: Ed. Pélissier, 1984); and Sérgio Chichava, 'Le "Vieux Mozambique": L'identité politique de la Zambézie', unpublished PhD thesis, Université de Bordeaux, 2007.

[13] Gervase Clarence-Smith, *The Third Portuguese Empire, 1825–1975: A Study in Economic Imperialism* (Manchester: Manchester University Press, 1985).

such plantations or mines scarcely existed (with the exception, as we have seen, of São Tomé, probably up until the Second World War).

As is known, the first Portuguese law against the institution of slavery was the decree of the Marquês Sá da Bandeira ordering the end of transatlantic trade in 1836, which became effective only in 1850 when Brazil issued a similar decree. Obviously, this supposed end of the transatlantic slave trade was not the end of slavery. The same Marquês Sá da Bandeira issued a series of anti-slave laws between 1854 and 1858, freeing some slaves and establishing 1878 as the final date for abolition. In 1869, the slaves were made *libertos* and in 1875 the ex-*libertos* had to stay in the service of their former masters for two more years (1876–8). These twenty years were thought of in Lisbon as a period of gradual abolition and orderly transition from slavery to free labour: the Portuguese government visibly hoped that slaves who could no longer be exported would therefore stay with their owners, who would then be able to create plantations and transform their slaves into wage-earning workers. But in the great majority of cases, these plantations would be new ones, and not former *latifundios* full of former slaves. Unlike in Brazil or the French Caribbean colonies, the twenty-year intermediate period conceived in Lisbon was not to give time to slave-based plantation owners, but to allow a transition to a new, capitalist economy. The key point in the 1875, 1878 and 1899 legislation was that (with some hesitation and contradictory minor changes between these first three Portuguese native labour codes) the prohibition of 'forced labour' – referring to the former slavery – was enacted alongside the vagrancy clause under which the 'non-productive' African could be judged a vagrant and made to contract for his services. It amounted to no less than the creation of *modern* forced labour.

But this is not the same thing as slavery.[14] On the moral level and that of day-to-day life, similarities can easily be found between slavery and forced labour (above all before the 1950s); and it was on these grounds that Portugal was denounced by anti-slavery movements throughout the first half of the twentieth century. But historically speaking, forced labour and *indigenato* were not the product of a long process of the decline of slavery: they were the direct consequence of the new age of colonialism, meaning the colonial capitalism now made possible

[14] Portuguese has two separate words: *escravatura* for the slave trade, and *escravidão* for slavery in plantations, mines, and so forth. When I refer here to slavery it is to *escravidão*. Portuguese colonial literature in the 1930s sometimes distinguished *escravidão,* used specifically for domestic slavery of Africans by Africans (excluding any reference to forced labour) from *escravismo* (or *esclavagismo*) for the European system and doctrine. When the World Trade Organization was investigating 'forced labour', the Portuguese authorities understood this voluntarily as 'slavery' – indeed in the colonial official vocabulary, *trabalho forçado* refers to slavery – and answered that there was no longer such *escravismo* but there was some *escravidão* remaining, which they were fighting against; Maria Emilia Madeira Santos and Vítor Luís Gaspar Rodrigues, 'No rescaldo da escravatura. As ciências sociais chamadas à iça nos anos 30 (século XX)', *Africana Studia* (Porto) 8 (2005), pp. 259–73.

by effective military conquest of the land and the defeat of the former social groups based on the economy of war and the slave trade. Between slavery and forced labour and *indigenato*, there was no continuity or even transition; there was a break. It was a matter of a change in production modes, which could now concern the whole African population, thanks to military conquest, while slaves had been only a minority of the African population. Military campaigns were not only a conquest of land, they very often involved the violent destruction of the former colonial economic system based on coexistence of an indigenous economy and long-distance trade by Luso-Brazilians, Portuguese, Luso-Africans (in Mozambique, in particular the *prazeiros*), Indians, Swahilis, or (obviously) African trade caravans, themselves linked with African states further into the hinterland. This point is very important.

The peculiarity of the Portuguese break with slavery

Nevertheless, it can be said that the continental Portuguese empire in Africa was not the only one where there was no European-owned slave plantation complex, but almost exclusively slave trade exports, and therefore *de facto* no transition from enslaved manpower to forced labour manpower on European plantations.[15] But this simply provides a further reason to revise the history of this 'transition'.

Moreover, in this short chapter it is impossible to discuss important cases of development of domestic slavery within African societies, and even production in market-oriented slavery in some African pre-colonial states, both stimulated by legitimate and illegitimate colonial trade on the coast. But even in the latter case, which indeed represented a first means of capitalist penetration within African states, its social formation prevented its possible use by new direct European imperialism to develop large forced labour plantations.[16] First, the African cases of market-oriented slavery very often did not produce a plantation complex, the slaves being spread among the local population as captives or forming special villages, but not working in plantations. Secondly, in the few (albeit important)

[15] See for example Emmanuel Terray, *Une histoire du royaume abron du Gyaman: Des origines à la conquête coloniale* (Paris: Karthala, 1995); Robin Law, *Ouidah: The Social History of a West African Slaving 'Port', 1727–1892* (Athens, OH: Ohio University Press, 2004); Kristin Mann, *Slavery and the Birth of an African City: Lagos, 1760–1900* (Bloomington and Indianapolis: Indiana University Press, 2007).

[16] That does not mean that nothing in African slavery could be used by new European plantations. For example, the plantations in Zambezia sometimes recovered the old *ensacas* of the *prazos* as forced workers. *Ensaca* here must not be confused with the same word in the Portuguese of Brazil or Portugal (packing into sacks or bags) but refers to the *nsaka*, the ten- to twelve-slave soldier squads which were the local structure of the Achikunda (the slave soldiers of the *prazos*). One can immediately see that such a use of *ensacas* for a rural gang forced labour system was based on the military defeat and humiliation of the Achikunda who, as proud slave soldiers, desperately resisted against their 'liberation' by the Portuguese trying to indigenise them.

cases where a full plantation complex occurred, as in the Caliphate of Sokoto (in modern northern Nigeria, based on cotton) or in the kingdom of Dahomey (based on palm oil), the colonial conquest provoked their disintegration: slaves fled from the plantations due to the colonial conquest, or the social planters' milieu was militarily defeated and broken up. The European plantations had therefore to be new ones, with another organisation, and other social relations of domination. The only exception could be the case of the formation of a plantation complex based on cloves in Zanzibar (fully developed by the 1840s) and part of the Swahili East African coast, which English and German colonisers had partially conquered.[17] But this must be considered as only a partial exception, since it represented conquest by new colonisers of former colonisers, the Arabs of Oman, and not of an indigenous planter class.

In the space occupied today by Mozambique, market-oriented slave production by Africans seems scarcely (if at all) to have existed;[18] but going further into the hinterland, the case of the Lunda empire is well known and covered part of eastern twentieth-century Angola and the Belgian Congo. The Lunda empire made intensive use of slaves in production tasks, but not within a plantation complex.[19] Generally speaking, these African social formations based on slavery had to be defeated – with the exception already noted.

But even comparing the neighbouring Portuguese Angola and the Belgian Congo, or other European empires in Africa, there are huge differences. In the Portuguese empire, unlike in other European empires, but similar to what occurred in Latin America, there were old creole elite nuclei dating from the first age of colonisation. One might have expected them to have developed slave plantations and then passed to forced labour (and later wage-earned) manpower, thus leading the 'transition'. But as in other European empires, and unlike in Latin America, there was no transition. The thesis of a transition from slavery to forced labour in Portuguese Africa is thus based first on a wrong understanding and generalisation of the São Tomé case, and second on misinterpretation of the reaction of pre-existent old elites when the age of modern imperialism dawned.

The peculiarity of the continental Portuguese empire thus lies not only in the very absence of any 'transition' – which is, with the exception already noted, the

[17] Frederick Cooper, *Plantation Slavery on the East Coast of Africa* (1977; Portsmouth, NH: Heinemann, 1997); Frederick Cooper, 'The Problem of Slavery in African Studies', *Journal of African History* 20:1 (1979), pp. 103–25; Jan-Georg Deutsch, *Emancipation without Abolition in German East Africa c. 1884–1914* (Oxford: James Currey, 2006).

[18] Malyn D. D. Newitt, *Portuguese Settlement on the Zambezi* (London: Longman, 1973); Allen F. Isaacman and Barbara S. Isaacman, *Slavery and Beyond: The Making of Men and Chikunda Ethnic Identities in the Unstable World of South-Central Africa, 1750–1920* (Portsmouth, NH: Heinemann, 2004).

[19] Isabel Castro Henriques, *Percursos da modernidade em Angola: Dinâmicas comerciais e transformações sociais no século XIX* (Lisbon: Instituto de Investigação Científica Tropical/Instituto da Cooperação Portuguesa, 1997).

general case within the new European imperialism in Africa – but in the fact that there was no transition *in spite of* the existence of old social colonial milieus for whom Sá da Bandeira had legislated from the 1850s because they were expected to produce such a transition.

There is another way to approach the same Portuguese peculiarity. For other European countries, Africa was a case of 'New Colonies' – the 'Old Colonies' being those in the Americas and Caribbean – and there were no, or insignificant, creole populations.[20] In the Portuguese case, the New Colonies were conquered *from* the Old ones and with territorial continuity. The Old Colonies lay *within* the New ones – the '*Le temps long dans le temps court*' of Fernand Braudel – with the decline but survival of their old elites within the new social context.

It is worth noting one further aspect, in particular with regard to the Congos or French West Africa: between the end of slave exports and the generalisation of forced labour, forty years or so[21] elapsed in the Portuguese empire, whereas France and Belgium developed harsh and massive forced labour *immediately*.[22] Although the legislation was all ready, and forced labour was expanding after the First World War, the 1929 crisis and the rigorous financial policies of Salazar slowed down economic growth and so the need for indigenous forced manpower on plantations, which cannot much have exceeded 100,000 people in each of Angola and Mozambique in the middle of the 1930s. Thus, the generalisation of forced labour (in plantations, fisheries, and harbours, as well as in regions of forced peasant production)[23] actually did not occur before the end of the 1930s and during the Second World War. In the Portuguese empire, then, this chronological gap stresses even more forcefully the *rupture* between slavery and forced labour as distinct historical periods.

Nevertheless, this assessment does not include the compulsory use of native people as porters (*carregadores* freely furnished by pro-Portuguese or subdued traditional chiefs) for Portuguese traders up to the 1920s, or for building roads or other public works, all of which was highly disruptive for the social life and production process of the Africans. In Angola, this was the case particularly under the rule of Norton de Matos as Governor (1912–14) and *Alto-Comissário* (1921–3).[24]

[20] I do not tackle here the very specific cases of Sierra Leone and Liberia.

[21] Only twenty years in the case of diamond exploitation in the Lunda region (Angola).

[22] Adam Hochschild, *King Leopold's Ghost: A Study of Greed, Terror and Heroism in Colonial Africa* (Boston: Mariner Books, 1999); Crawford Young, *The African Colonial State in Comparative Perspective* (New Haven: Yale University Press, 1994).

[23] For cotton and rice, there were generally not European-owned plantations (as there were for tea, copra, coffee, sugar cane, or coconuts), but concession areas where companies heavily organised and pressured the Africans to cultivate such crops at the expense of their food production.

[24] Maria da Conceição Neto, 'Nas malhas da rede: O impacto económico e social do transporte rodoviário na região do Huambo c. 1920 – c. 1960', in Beatrix Heintze and Achim von Open (eds), *Angola on the Move: Transport, Routes, Communications and History/Angola em movimento: Vias de transporte, comunicações e história* (Frankfurt: Otto Lambeck, 2008), pp. 117–29.

Is it possible, then, to view these practices as filling the aforementioned gap of forty years between the end of the slave trade and the generalisation of forced labour, and therefore as constituting a 'transition'? There could be good grounds for thinking so, since the use of *carregadores* for the traders and small coffee plantations of the hinterland, and of forced native workers for the 'development' of Angola as dreamed by Norton de Matos, was systematic, harsh, and violent.[25] Such a use of compelled recruits may indeed surely be considered as a lingering legacy of slavery, for some natives; even if it was now 'part-time slavery', since they were no longer sold when arriving on the coast or in the cities (except for those sent to São Tomé, but not specifically recruited from the *carregadores*).

Nevertheless, I do not share this historical interpretation, for three main reasons. First, even if some legacy of slavery may be found in the guise of the *carregadores*, this did not equate to preparation for modern forced labour. During the same period, the continuing export of *serviçais* to São Tomé plantations did not prepare for any change in the archipelago, but was the tendency of lingering slavery. *Carregadores* were slaves up to 1878 (and after), and then forced workers, and did indeed represent the main case of 'sector-based transition', since they carried out the same activity, probably for the same traders or their immediate descendants. But this is rather an exception. Were the latter transformed, two or three decades later, into forced labour-based plantation owners or shareholders of concession companies of forced cotton production? Had they been able to keep their former slaves to work on the new plantations? Generally speaking, I do not think so. Even if some managed to become 'modern traders', or even medium-sized planters (*fazendeiros*), in no way did their social milieu become the dominant one in twentieth-century Mozambique and Angola. The major plantations represented a new period, with new people and a new process. It comes as little surprise that during several decades, slavery continued in declining forms, while forced labour appeared and developed alongside it; but the simultaneity of both does not at all mean that the first was *producing* the second, economically and socially. Rather, this was the competition of two historical ages.

Secondly, the quantitative aspect is also a qualitative one. Except in the case of São Tomé, the half-slave/half-forced-labour regimes of the 1890s, 1910s, and 1920s cannot be compared with the systematic recruitment of any native male for forced labour in plantations, fisheries and mines, and the forced production of cotton and rice, in the 1940s and 1950s. Now, rather than thousands of people a year, hundreds of thousands were implicated (see below).

Third, and linked to the first point, the development of huge estates (Portuguese-owned or not, chartered or not), very often created from the end of the nineteenth century but fully developed by the end of the 1930s, or even the spreading of many

[25] Maria da Conceição Neto, personal communication, 8 May 2011.

medium-sized settler-owned plantations in the 1950s (with the settlers often recent arrivals), is a completely distinct social phenomenon from the families, the capital and even the culture of the former slave traders of the nineteenth century.

We now come to a new contradiction: it was indeed forced labour that allowed capitalist domination of Mozambique, Angola and areas of Guinea (and of other empires), but forced labour is *not* really a mode of capitalist *exploitation*. We will have to return to this contradiction. But first it is necessary to go into the detail of the workings of the Statute governing *indigenato*.

The social significance of *indigenato*

In this chapter, my analysis will not begin with the colonial labour legislation of 1875, 1878, 1899 or even 1914, but will start directly with the legislation of 1926–8, since it was between 1926 and 1942 that all the main legislation concerning the 'national-colonialism' of the *Estado Novo* was issued, shaping the whole system until 1962 and partially up to 1974. But once again, one must emphasise that the new legislation was not brought in to discipline and govern huge crowds of post-slavery forced workers. The forced labour legislation of 1926–9 must therefore be analysed as 'developmentalist', with a forward-looking view of what Angola and Mozambique *should* become: a general work camp for Africans.

Who was who?

It may seem strange to remark that before 1926, there was no rule to define clearly who was native or 'not civilised' and who was 'civilised'. One was 'notoriously recognised' as being *gentio* or *assimilado*. As Jill Dias has shown, self-definition as 'Angolan' or even 'African' within the African elite of Luanda and its hinterland, Benguela, or Moçâmedes, was not at all similar to being 'gentio' or indigenous up to the late nineteenth century.[26] The liberal monarchy during its last years maintained this absence of a definition. In 1917 (at least in Mozambique), a first text required former *assimilados* to obtain an *alvará* (certificate) from the court certifying their assimilation. After 1926–7, terms for obtaining the assimilation certificate became more and more restrictive: henceforth, the aim of legislation was clearly to define who would not be exempted from forced labour. Since James Duffy, Douglas Wheeler, René Pélissier, Gerald Bender, Malyn Newitt and other more recent researchers have already studied the content of such legislation, I would like to only stress some specific aspects.

[26] Jill Dias, 'Uma questão de identidade: Respostas intelectuais às transformações económicas no seio da elite crioula da Angola portuguesa entre 1870 e 1930', *Revista Internacional de Estudos Africanos* (Lisbon) 1 (1984), pp. 61–94.

Who did work?

The *Estatuto Político, Civil e Criminal dos Indígenas de Angola e Moçambique*, issued on 23 October 1926, and extended to Guinea in 1929, definitely established the principle that metropolitan and colonial law must be different, in spite of the unity of the Nation.[27] It precisely defined natives as 'individuals of black race or being descended from them, who, by the way of their instruction and customs, do not distinguish themselves from the common people of this race' (article 3). According to this *Estatuto*, colonial governments had to define who would be native by a special diploma in each colony. In Mozambique, for example, the *Diploma legislativo definindo as condições especiais que devem caracterizar os indígenas ou não indígenas* performed this role.[28] There were slight differences between the different colonial diplomas or their successive versions in 1927, 1931, and so on, regarding conditions for becoming 'assimilated', but three conditions were always included: first, to have completely abandoned 'indigenous habits and customs'; second, the ability to speak Portuguese; and third, to 'practise a profession, trade or industry' or to 'own goods being enough for their subsistence' (article 1). In the 1931 Angolan *diploma*, this third condition was more precise: 'practise a profession [. . .] compatible with European civilisation'.[29]

The issue here is: what was more segregationist in this law – serving as a tool of discrimination – and what was more socially structuring? Even if the questions of knowledge of Portuguese and having abandoned indigenous customs and habits would obviously lead to a huge range of arbitrary judgements by local administrators, my hypothesis is that the third point, regarding 'profession', was by far the worst. Actually, knowledge of the Portuguese language extended to very few people at the time, but living in a city, or within a mission, or working for a company could give rise to such an ability. But what is understood by 'profession' is only an activity fully integrated within the monetarised economy and on a permanent basis: a native person working in his field for his own subsistence, or a native person working in a European company on a two-year contract, did not have a 'profession'. In Mozambique, 'owning goods being enough for their subsistence' was defined, for example, as having 100 head of cattle or five hectares of land on a private basis. The meaning is very clear: the definition of indígena is *any (black) person not directly integrated into the capitalist economy.* This is a mixture of what I will call 'literal racism', or even 'racial racism' (because it dealt only with blacks), and

[27] Decree no. 12,533, 23 Oct. 1926, *Boletim Oficial de Moçambique* (Lourenço Marques), 1st series, 28, 27 Nov. 1926.

[28] *Diploma legislativo* . . ., no. 36, 12 Nov. 1927, *Boletim Oficial de Moçambique* (Lourenço Marques), 1st series, 46, 22 Nov. 1927.

[29] *Diploma legislativo* . . ., no. 237, 26 May 1931, art. 1, quoted by Elisabeth Ceita Vera Cruz, *O estatudo do indigenato e a legislação da discriminação na colonização portuguesa: O caso de Angola* (Coimbra: Novo Imbondeiro, 2005), p. 106.

'social racism' (not only social discrimination), since it deals with the whole category of people not living within capitalism. The two types of racism form a whole, but the second is far more effective: actually, since the 1899 Labour Code had introduced a vagrancy clause, any person 'not working' was a vagrant and could therefore be obliged to choose 'freely' his employer. The whole people was made vagrant, in an early kind of clash of civilisations.

Within the context of the scandal provoked by the Ross Report on São Tomé, Angola and Mozambique in 1925, it might be noted that the vagrancy clause disappeared in the 1926–9 legislation on native labour (*Estatuto* and *Código*). In the same way, the 'obligation, moral and legal' of working returned to the pre-1899 formulation of 'moral obligation'. Was this new legislation less harsh than the former one? It has been suggested that it was, but I very much doubt it: at the same time, the *coup d'état* of May 1926 ended the Republic with the mute approval of the British government, and supporters of open forced labour came to power.[30] If they did so, it was because any change in the labour regime could be merely cosmetic. The reason is that the colonial administration no longer needed such precise clauses; the simple fact of not considering as 'work' the traditional activity of the indígenas had been sufficient to put them under the 'moral obligation to work' (*dever moral do trabalho*), which could allow (and actually allowed) for administrative intervention. African people perhaps were no longer vagrant, but since their day-to-day self-support activity was not recognised as labour, this was irrelevant. From 'vagrant people' to 'not relevant people', no progress was made at all.

Late but massive forced labour

Many years ago, during my doctoral research on Mozambique, I calculated that in the 1940s and 1950s, *all* males who could be recruited for forced labour – that is to say, any male between the ages of 15 and 60, not serving in the army or rural (native) police, a traditional chief, a domestic in a European family, or a permanent worker in a harbour or on a railway, and who had not emigrated – had in fact been recruited, for six months a year or one year in two in companies, or permanently in forced food production. Indeed, in 1940, when Mozambique had a population of 5 million, of 1,197,028 native males aged between 15 and 60, some 533,780 were *chibalo* (forced) workers in plantations (*latifúndios* of tea, copra, coffee, sugar cane, or coconuts), railways and ports, mines, and so on, 331,000 were forced cotton producers, and 60,000 forced rice producers, for a grand total of 924,780 people; that is to say, 117 per cent of the legal number of males liable for legal recruitment

[30] The legislation on forced cotton growing was published at this very moment.

(who should have numbered 793,370).[31] It is worth stressing that these figures were calculated *a minima*, do not include women, who were legally not to be recruited but who were very often as forced as their husbands to produce cotton, rice and castor oil, and do not include day-to-day forced work on roads or for other public tasks (in Mozambique this 'invisible forced labour' was legalised as the *contribuição braçal*, the 'arm drudgery').

The situation became still worse after 1947, and the number of forced labourers by the end of the 1950s became very large, even though it was at this very moment that the internal economic crisis of colonisation began. What was more, 'vagrant/ not relevant people' were prohibited from entering the 'civilised occupations'; particularly from the 1940s, these occupations were open only to those holding a professional card issued by white trade unions. The tiny number of *assimilados* in Mozambique – 4,353 out of 5,733,000 black inhabitants in 1950, or 0.008 per cent – was thus the product not of direct racist measures against black individuals, but of large-scale forced labour among a whole people that had been made vagrant or not relevant. When someone was subjected to forced labour, it became almost impossible to change their situation, except by illegal emigration. Forced labour, not direct racist behaviour, was the reason for the weakness of the African elite in Mozambique – but obviously, forced labour is *per se* a racist process, against a whole way of life. In Angola, the number of *assimilados* was tiny too, but far greater than in Mozambique – 30,089 *assimilados* out of a black population of 4,036,687 people, or 0.75 per cent – because of the persistence of old social milieus stemming from the nineteenth century or even before, and not at all a product of the twentieth century.

This is the general framework, but regional differences were important. Indeed, forced labour created strong contradictions within colonial society: for example, it prevented Africans from producing on their own and selling their products to Portuguese merchants. According to Manuel Loff, in 1943 white traders blocked a train transporting *contratados*, 'on the grounds that these emigrations were excessive and injurious to their trade'.[32] Maria da Conceição Neto stresses that, in

[31] That is to say, the total number of indigenous males aged from 15 to 60, minus the categories of other labour status listed *supra*. Personal calculations from data in: Missão de Inquérito Agrícola, *Recenseamento agrícola de 1930–1940: Contribuição para o recenseamento agrícola mundial* (Lourenço Marques: Imprensa Nacional de Moçambique/Repartição Técnica de Estatística, 1944); Nelson Saraiva Bravo, *A cultura algodoeira na economia do Norte de Moçambique* (Lisbon: Junta de Investigações do Ultramar, 1963); Armando Lourenço Rodrigues, 'A produção no sector indígena de Moçambique', BA dissertation, Instituto Superior de Estudos Ultramarinos, Lisbon, 1960; and Armando Castro, *O sistema colonial português em África (meados do século XX)* (Lisbon: Editorial Caminho, 1978), which was written but not published in 1959.

[32] 'The Labour Shortage in Angola', 15 Nov. 1950, by Scott (Assistant Information Officer of the British Embassy in Lisbon), National Archives, London, Foreign Office 371/80861, JP2183/2, quoted by Manuel Loff, 'As colónias portuguesas de África entre a II[a] Guerra Mundial e a Guerra colonial: A visão anglo-americana', in Adriana Pereira Campos (ed.), *Trabalho forçado africano: Experiências coloniais comparadas* (Porto: Campo das Letras, 2006), pp. 395–442, see p. 432.

spite of forced labour laws, in some regions of central and south-central Angola, forced labour (in the form of work on plantations or in fisheries) was never completely imposed on peasants, in order to allow them to grow and sell a significant surplus of cereals to the Portuguese, even if 'invisible forced labour' was imposed on *all*.[33] Malyn Newitt has recently published part of the diary of Charles Spence, the British director of a trading company in Lourenço Marques, who made a tour of Mozambique in 1943. In the north, local Indian traders were all complaining that 'trade in native products had more or less come to a standstill on account of the emphasis imposed by the government on cotton growing'. Since the Nyassa Company's charter had come to an end, 'direct administration of the region had changed priorities from a focus on commercial activity (principally in African grown crops) in the imposition of a systematic administration and the commercial control of the cotton and rice monopoly concessionaires'.[34]

In Mozambique, during the Second World War, when forced labour recruitment was widespread, Portuguese law also made it possible, in exceptional instances, to escape forced labour laws. The *Estatuto do Agricultor Indígena* (Statute on African Agriculturalists) exempted some peasants from the *contrato* to allow them to develop their own farms, in full contradiction of the *Estatuto dos Indígenas*. Thus, if any peasant had not 'distinguished himself from the common people of his race' by owning private land or 100 head of cattle, he must be native and subject to the 'moral obligation' of labour.[35] If he had so 'distinguished himself', he must become an *assimilado*. But this special statute, introduced to authorise a very few Africans to plant large amounts of cash crops, simply allowed small Portuguese traders to buy products at native prices, that is to say below the officially fixed prices of the direct white settlers. The allocation of this status remained at the discretion of the *administrador da circunscrição* (district colonial officer) and was obviously a question of *política indígena* discussed at the highest level in the province. Moreover, since it allowed several thousand Mozambican peasants to avoid seasonal forced labour, it alleviated one important contradiction of the system. But it must be noted that this very special statute undermining the *Código dos Indígenas* categories was itself undermined, since peasants on concessions for forced production of cotton and rice were often considered *agricultores africanos* and therefore exempted from forced labour (seasonal work), to be compelled to work on forced crop growing. This was particularly the case in the Nampula

[33] Maria da Conceição Neto, personal communication, 27 April 2011.

[34] Malyn Newitt, 'Uma viagem pelo Norte de Moçambique durante a Segunda Guerra Mundial', in P. Havik, C. Saraiva and J. A. Tavim (eds), *Caminhos cruzados em História e Antropologia: Ensaios de homenagem a Jill Dias* (Lisbon: Instituto de Ciênças Sociais, 2010), pp. 143–58. Quotations are from the original manuscript in English; I thank Malyn Newitt for sending me this document.

[35] *Estatuto do agricultor indígena, aprovado pelo diploma legislativo no. 919, de. 5 de Agosto de 1944* (Lourenço Marques: Imprensa Nacional, 1944).

province of Mozambique in the 1950s, as a way to disguise the statistics of forced cotton growing. Marvin Harris had already remarked that for the south of the colony:

> According to the 1950 census, the active male population between the ages of 15 and 55 years in the regions south of Zambezi – roughly the *distritos* of Tete, Beira, Inhambane, Gaza and Lourenço Marques – numbered 593,834 men. Of this group, 33,766 were listed as exercising the 'profession' of agriculturalist. Of the latter, it is not clear what percentage held the certificate of *agricultor africano*. There is no doubt, however, that most of these officially recognised agriculturalists were merely engaged in the production of cotton under the government's forced planting program.[36]

How not to proletarianise: gendering and subalternising

What has to be stressed immediately, following these quantitative thoughts, is that forced labour did not in any way produce a process of local integration within the capitalist production process. On the contrary, the Portuguese administration resolutely fought any tendency towards the formation of a proletarian class. Sá da Bandeira's old dream of seeing former slave traders become employers of permanent employees was soon abandoned. This was not only for political reasons – fear of a proletarian mass – but above all because it was far more profitable *not to have* a proletarian class. A proletarian person must be paid at the cost of his social reproduction, and this was still too expensive. The *Código do Trabalho dos Indígenas nas colonias portuguesas de África*, the Labour Code of 1929, was very clear on this.[37] Contracts were never permanent ones, because Africans had to 'rest' and return home. 'Salary' was not calculated in relation to the value of work, but in relation to the amount of the hut tax;[38] actually, 'salary' was no such thing, but rather a payment calculated under the cost of social reproduction of the worker. It did not generate any native market. This is why the worker had to return home to his family and lineage, not to 'rest', but to help reconstitute the domestic economy that was weakened in his absence, in spite of the relentless work of the women. We have here one of the two most basic features of the forced labour system: its highly gendered structure. It was this domestic economy that would make up the shortfall between the 'payment' by the forced employer and the social cost of

[36] Marvin Harris, 'Portugal's African "Wards": A First-Hand Report on Labor and Education in Mocambique', *Africa Today* 5:6 (1958), pp. 3–36, p. 18. www.cultural-materialism.org/portugalsafricanwards.pdf

[37] República Portuguesa, *Código do Trabalho dos Indígenas nas colónias portuguesas de África, aprovado pelo decreto no. 16:199 de 6 de Dezembro de 1929* (Lourenço Marques: Imprensa Nacional, 1929).

[38] Article 197 specifies that the monthly wage must be 25 to 40 per cent of the *imposto indígena*, which means that the indigenous must work *at least* 2.5 to 4 months a year only to pay the tax; possibly more, since it is not clearly indicated if the wage is only the monetary part of income, or includes the value of food, blankets, and so forth.

reproduction. Therefore, there was no local economic basis for such a system that was cheaper than proletarianisation, except colonial violence to ensure it.

Nevertheless, no system can endure and rely solely on violence, above all a colonial system like the Portuguese one, where the forces of coercion were very weak: a *chefe de posto* had just six *cipaios* (native police) under his command, with guns from before the First World War. In order to understand how such a forced labour system could work, one has to remember three factors. First of all, the collaboration of some of the traditional chiefs – but this collaboration was efficient only when these chiefs were the legitimate ones. Linked to this first point, it is necessary to remember that, in the 1930s and even the 1940s and 1950s, only one or two generations had passed since the military conquest of the land. As René Pélissier has clearly demonstrated, this conquest was very violent and deadly; memories of it were still very present in communities, and any chief, any indigenous person, knew that although there might be only six *cipaios*, other stronger forces could be quickly sent.[39] But recruitment was not the only problem: it was necessary also to prohibit the indigenous from staying in the harbours or cities or on the plantations, where they would begin to become proletarianised. For that purpose, the Portuguese administration used a very efficient tool, the *pagamento diferido* or deferred payment: at least half of the 'salary' had to be paid not in the workplace, but after returning home.[40]

This system had several colonial functions: first, the native had to come back home to the domestic production sphere where he had been registered in the census; second, the hut tax was deducted without any problem from the deferred payment, since the company sent the money through the administration; third, local Portuguese traders demanded that this petty money should not be spent only in the big companies' shops; and last but not at all least, this tiny amount of money became essential – in particular in the 1950s when the amount slowly rose – precisely because of the weakening of the domestic economy. Forced labour had partly succeeded in creating its own necessity, when it moved slowly at the end of the 1950s and 1960s towards seasonal migrant work: the weakened domestic economy was no longer able to sustain many families.

The main issue is to understand that deferred payment was the 'mark' or the 'brand' of an economic process that needed a combination of colonial constraint and the maintenance of the domestic economy in order to be globally profitable for the colonial institution. This process did not integrate natives into a fully capitalist production process and capitalist social relationships system, but it did operate to submit them to capitalist *domination.* That is to say, we have here a legal expression of what Marxist anthropologists and historians conceptualised

[39] René Pelissier, *Les campagnes coloniales du Portugal, 1844–1941* (Paris: Pygmalion, 2004).

[40] Article 203, República Portuguesa, *Código do Trabalho . . .*, p. 54.

from the 1960s and 1980s as the unequal articulation of modes of production:[41] deferred payment was the very practical demonstration that workers were paid under the cost of social reproduction, which implied their regular return to the sphere of a maintained and subalternised domestic economy. We have here the second basic feature of the forced labour system: its very existence not as a whole but as one branch of a very authoritarian articulation of modes of production. On the ideological level, it is what I have before called the 'social racism' of Portuguese colonialism.

The last but not the least

On 20 May 1954, decree-law 39,666 was published, that is, a new *Estatuto dos Indígenas portugueses das províncias da Guiné, de Angola e Moçambique*; a new Native Statute.[42] The constitutional reform of 1951 had replaced the former 'colonies' by 'overseas provinces', reviving the old concept of liberal monarchy.[43] Thus, the unity of the Nation was politically reinforced: there was no longer one metropole and colonies belonging to the same empire, but only one Portugal. Everybody was therefore *directly* Portuguese, which implied the existence of different personal statuses within the same Nation and political constitution. Therefore, the new 1954 Statute aimed to respond to a situation in which the number of 'detribalised natives' was growing: it created, for example, the possibility of special native private ownership (urban and rural) which could prevent a few of them from being recruited for forced labour. But it answered above all to the need to prohibit a growing number of natives from becoming 'assimilated', when, in fact, a great number of urban Africans could have been considered as having abandoned native habits and costumes, as speaking Portuguese fluently, and so forth. On the other hand, some Portuguese employers preferred to engage skilled black workers, paying them as natives. But this would have represented unacceptable competition with petty-white workers in the cities.[44]

[41] Pierre-Philippe Rey, *Colonialisme, néo-colonialisme et transition au capitalisme* (Paris: Maspéro, 1971); Claude Meillassoux, *Femmes, greniers et capitaux* (Paris: Maspéro, 1982); Bruce Berman and John Lonsdale, *Unhappy Valley: Conflict in Kenya and Africa. 1. State and Class* (London, Nairobi and Athens, OH: James Currey/Heinemann/Ohio University Press, 1992); see too the retrospective, by Emmanuel Terray, of his research, 'Dernière séance', *Cahiers d'études africaines* (Paris) 50:198/199/200 (2010), pp. 529–44.

[42] *Diário do Governo* (Lisbon), 1st series, no. 110, 20 May 1954, pp. 560–5.

[43] *Constituição política da República portuguesa, actualizada de harmonia com a Lei no. 2.048 de 11 de Junho de 1951* (Lisbon: Assembleia Nacional, 1952).

[44] On this aspect and the activity of (white) labour unions aimed at protecting white manpower, see my article, 'Corporatisme et colonialisme: Approche du cas mozambicain (1933–1979)', *Cahiers d'études africaines* (Paris) 92 (1983), pp. 383–417, and 93 (1984), pp. 5–24.

Contrary to what has sometimes been written, the 1954 Statute did not soften the conditions of assimilation, but actually worsened them, and even endangered the very situation of being an *assimilado*:

- First, the status of *indigenato* or assimilation was now made strictly individual throughout the entire Nation:[45] the wife and children of an *assimilado* would no longer automatically become *assimilados*, as before; they could apply for this status if they were living with the husband and father, and if they fulfilled the second and third conditions (see below).[46] Since it was necessary to be over 18 years of age to apply for assimilation (paragraph A, article 56), that meant that sons of an *assimilado* could be obliged to go to native missionary schools instead of going to better state schools; because of the unity of the Nation, a native migrating to metropolitan Portugal would remain a native there.
- Second, it was not only necessary to speak Portuguese, but from now on also 'accurately'.[47]
- Third, it was necessary to display 'good behaviour' (for example, not to participate in an African Ethiopian, Zionist or Tocoist church) and to have acquired 'the instruction and habits required for the integral application of public and private law of Portuguese citizens' (paragraph D, article 56). Community ownership, and polygamy, including being a chief, were therefore incompatible with assimilation.
- Fourth, the stipulations regarding the 'profession, trade or industry' or ownership of 'goods being enough for their subsistence' (paragraph C, article 56) remained exactly the same as in 1926–9. Very significantly, this new Native Statute was not followed by a new Labour Code: the 1929 *Código do Trabalho dos Indígenas* remained, without any change and without any step towards authorisation of the formation of a permanent working class. With few exceptions, the only existing permanent working class was that of *assimilados* and *mulattos*, a very tiny one since the great majority of black *assimilados* and *mestiços* did not work as industrial workers, but in services.

For all these reasons, I consider the 1954 Native Statute to be the last archaic type of effort by the Portuguese administration in the middle of the 1950s, as the

[45] A point unique to Article 1: 'The statute of the Portuguese native people is personal and must be honoured in any part of the Portuguese territory where the individual who enjoys it is found.'

[46] Article 57: 'The native woman who is married to an individual who obtains citizenship [. . .] and the legitimate children or illegitimate children who are legitimated, and who are less than 18 years old, and who live under the direction of the father as of the date of said acquisition, may also obtain it, as long as the requirements in Paragraphs (b) and (d) of Article 56 are met.' Furthermore, the new code did not contemplate or allow for the case of a native single woman, or even a separated woman, who applied for citizenship, or for a married woman to apply independently of her husband.

[47] Paragraph (b) of Article 56: 'Falar correctamente a língua portuguesa'.

economic and political crisis of colonisation approached. Actually, this new Statute never really worked. In Mozambique, Africans were no longer even trying to become *assimilados*: the most violent period of forced labour was now disappearing (except in forced labour cotton-growing areas), and it was slowly becoming a seasonal migrant activity. In urban areas, to be an *assimilado* would mean more of a problem in getting jobs, since Portuguese employers would be obliged to pay the same as for whites and would therefore prefer to employ whites. The number of applications for *assimilado* status was strongly decreasing in the second half of the 1950s.

From native to rural: an answer to the Third-Worldisation of the colonies?

Does all of this mean that Portugal no longer wanted to avoid the formation of a permanent proletariat which must be paid at the cost of its social reproduction? Not at all, because, as we have noted, the Labour Code of 1929 remained the same. But the economic crisis in forced cotton growing at the end of the 1950s, and the beginning of the armed anti-colonial liberation struggle in 1961, led Salazar to authorise his Overseas Minister, Adriano Moreira, to take some important reformist measures. On 6 September 1961, decree-law 43,893 revoked the Native Statute of 1954.[48] The concept of indígena officially disappeared, but the same day, decree 43,897 recognised 'local habits and customs' and integrated them globally within Portuguese written private law.[49] Legal hybridism became, in a way, official. Assimilation applications were replaced by a mere declaration, since 'any individual may submit to [Portuguese] written private law, by the way of a mere formality at the registry office', and his descendants would automatically be included in this written law (article 3). Urban Africans were considered under written law (article 5). Traditional chiefs could, with the approval of their council, authorise private appropriation of land by individuals (article 8).

As there were no longer natives (indígenas), therefore, could the two separate spheres be managed: those of 'qualified professions' and 'undifferentiated masses'? First, the 1929 Labour Code remained in force for one more year, being revoked in turn on 27 April 1962, when Adriano Moreira issued his *Código do trabalho rural* (Rural Labour Code) by way of decree 44,309.[50] What is interesting is to understand the meaning of 'rural' as defined in articles 1 and 2:

[48] *Boletim Oficial de Moçambique* (Lourenço Marques), Supplement, 1st series, 14 Sept. 1962.
[49] *Boletim Oficial de Moçambique* (Lourenço Marques), Supplement, 1st series, 14 Sept. 1962.
[50] *Diário do Governo* (Lisbon), 1st series, no. 95, 27 April 1962 (Supplement); José de Albuquerque Sousa, *Código do trabalho rural do Ultramar. Edição revista, com indices alfabético e sistemático* (Coimbra: Coimbra Editora, 1962).

1. Manual workers without a defined profession, occupied in activities related to agricultural exploitation of land or gathering of produce, are considered rural workers [. . .]
2. For the implementation of the present Code [. . .] those workers whose duty is reduced to mere provision of manpower, not classified because of the nature of the service in any categories of employees or workers specifically qualified, are equivalent to rural workers [. . .]

That means that a European managing a modern farm in the bush was not a rural worker, but an urban African on a building site or road works or a street tradeswoman would always be classed as a rural worker. The vagrancy clause (official or implicit) had disappeared but the ideological 'watertightness' between the two spheres of social life remained intact. Therefore, article 69 could stand, that 'for equal work will always be attributed an equal salary', since this was *within* the rural sphere. Last but not least, article 80 completely reproduced the deferred payment system: 50 per cent of the earnings would be given to the worker after his return home. That meant that until 1974, the key institution of work paid under the social cost of reproduction remained current. Adriano Moreira had not invented the concept of 'rural labour', but had taken it from post-slavery Brazil. Anyway, the system no longer worked with all these details conceived by the Portuguese legal mind. During the 1960s and the beginning of the 1970s, Mozambique and Angola were already very much Third World countries. But there is no doubt that the duration of forced labour and the existence of an alleviated form of it up to the end of the 1960s, with the corresponding existence of a large community of petty whites occupying almost all qualified jobs, were the main obstacle to the formation of an African working class and elite.[51]

The new 1962 Labour Code was no longer a forced labour Code, but it was still a Native Code, now called 'rural', with two officially different spheres of social life. It must be understood as a desperate attempt to combine the economic developmentalism of the 1960s with the will to slow down the proletarianisation of African workers, as antagonistic to the profitability of colonial enterprise. The 1962 Rural Code never worked well either: the two spheres of social life did not need a detailed and bureaucratic Code to exist, since Angola, Mozambique, and Guinea were entering the situation of 'normal' Third World countries, in which the massive urban informal sector and plebeian social milieus were the ones Adriano Moreira once wanted to make 'rural'.

[51] That does not mean that no working class existed, as studied by Jeanne-Marie Penvenne, *African Workers and Colonial Racism: Mozambican Strategies and Struggles in Lourenço Marques, 1877–1962* (Portsmouth, NH, Johannesburg and London: Heinemann/Witwatersrand University Press/James Currey, 1995).

The ideology of petty-white colonialism within a weakened old capitalism

This was obviously the reverse of the officially proclaimed doctrine of assimilation, even when reinforced by the capture of neo-lusotropicalism of an increasingly dated Gilberto Freyre. But while Freyre's original lusotropicalism praised the process of racial mixing as the achievement of a new civilisation, Salazarist lusotropicalism saw it as a path to the racial and cultural whitening of African society – by the way remaining assimilationist. But the huge contrast between ideology and reality does not mean that the doctrine of assimilation was mere propaganda or mere cynicism. An ideology does not exist to 'serve' a political design; it is only *a posteriori* that the historian may analyse it in those terms. Ideology expresses the habitus of a social milieu, of the hegemonical group within a nation: it serves this group or nation to speak to itself, to represent itself in its own eyes, to imagine its own future. The question is therefore not to analyse assimilation as an inefficient process or cynical propaganda, but as the *sole ideology* possible and operating for a colonial capitalism short on capital and facing, thanks to masses of petty whites, political danger from abroad and foreign investment.

Codification of the two spheres of social life in Portuguese colonial labour law (capitalist or 'civilised' versus traditional or 'vagrant'; 'integral application of public and private law of Portuguese citizenship' versus 'rural') is no more than one expression of the existence of non-capitalist forms of capitalist domination, at the periphery of capitalism. As Immanuel Wallerstein showed, capitalism has always preferred non-capitalist forms of domination or exploitation, since it avoids paying for social reproduction at its cost;[52] and this was made possible in all the frontier areas of capitalist expansion where indigenous societies still survived. As we have seen, the deferred payment system is one trademark of this specific economic process.

Portuguese colonisation was obviously a racist system and produced a highly racialised society. We have seen that the founding texts of the colonial system are based on the notion of race – more exactly, 'race' was used almost exclusively to designate black people, while the Portuguese were a *nation*.[53] But black colour was never officially mentioned for direct discriminatory purposes against individuals:

[52] Immanuel Wallerstein, *Le capitalisme historique* (Paris: La Découverte, 2002).

[53] This does not mean that the concept of race was never used to designate Portuguese people: for example, the *Dia da Raça* (the 'Day of the Race') was a national day in Portugal up to 1974. But within the colonial legislation, race is used exclusively to name the Africans. This is understandable: the 'normal law' was the one in Portugal, and in Portugal, law need not specify the race of the inhabitants. Therefore, the 'normal law' in the colonies was for a tiny minority of the population (the 'civilised' people), while the 'exceptional' law devoted to a *specific race* was for the huge majority. The race of the (white) nation need not be named, since it was the whole of the nation – with the *not relevant* massive exception of the Africans.

it was mentioned to designate the whole of a people – the 'vagrant people' – which in turn would have the greatest consequences for individuals. It is what I have called 'social racism', a racism that defined Otherness *not only* by the skin colour of individuals, but *as much* by the definition of the non-capitalist sphere of social life of a whole people, even if petty whites and natives could live side by side in some neighbourhoods.[54] In certain ways, social racism transformed native people into something closer to a caste than a race; a kind of 'professional stratum'. In that way, in its social consequences, *indigenato* was far more important than blackness. It was *indigenato* more than blackness that prohibited the social formation of a black elite, expressing the 'proximity racism' of petty whites in Portuguese colonialism, different from the 'distant racism' of other more capitalised forms of colonialism.

[54] In order to avoid possible misunderstanding, I will stress that, obviously, all of this is 'capitalist' (forced labour is perfectly integrated in the capitalist world-system). But all of it does not work under the capitalist *mode of production*. It is a founding feature of capitalism to need such an articulation of modes of production, in order to nullify the contradiction of having to sell its products to the same persons it directly exploits.

9

The 'Civilisation Guild': Race and Labour in the Third Portuguese Empire, *c.* 1870–1930

MIGUEL BANDEIRA JERÓNIMO

THE GRADUAL, COMPLEX AND CONVOLUTED 'TRANSITION' (as James Duffy termed it) from the Luso-Brazilian imperial configuration to an African-oriented imperial venture was significantly marked by the continuity and the resilience of slavery and other modes of forced or compulsory labour.[1] Contrary to what was and still is recounted by the persisting narratives, primarily based on a legalistic reasoning, which focus on the abolition of the slave trade as a major landmark in the transformation of the political and moral economy of the Portuguese colonial empire, the coercive use of the African workforce continued to be a crucial element in the new colonial economy, and indeed endured as a major foundation stone of the overall imperial project. The new imperial political imagination of colonial rule in the 'decadent fragments' of a ruined and almost non-existent empire ('invaded and conquered by African Negroes', as Sá da Bandeira stated) also preserved the longstanding racial ideologies that legitimised the secular existence of slavery as an institution, a mode of production, and the central element of a nefarious transatlantic trade.[2] The political and economic assessments which aimed to

[1] See, above all, James Duffy, *A Question of Slavery: Labour Policies in Portuguese Africa and the British Protest, 1850–1920* (Oxford: Oxford University Press, 1967), esp. pp. 60–101; Miguel Bandeira Jerónimo, Livros Brancos and Almas Negras, *A 'missão civilizadora' do colonialismo português (c.1870–1930)* (Lisbon: Imprensa de Ciências Sociais, 2010).

[2] For the idea of imperial political imagination see Frederick Cooper, 'States, Empires, and Political Imagination', in *Colonialism in Question: Theory, Knowledge, History* (Berkeley: University of California Press, 2005), pp. 153–203; and a report by Sá da Bandeira, in *Memorial Ultramarino e Marítimo*, no. 1 (March 1836), pp. 13–18. For a summary of the role of *racial* issues in Portuguese imperial history, see Francisco Bethencourt, 'Race Relations in the Portuguese Empire', in Jay A. Levenson (ed.), *Encompassing the Globe: Portugal and the World in the 16th and 17th Centuries. Essays* (Washington, DC: Smithsonian Institution, 2007), pp. 45–53; as well as Valentim Alexandre, 'O império e a ideia de raça (séculos XIX e XX)', in Jorge Vala (ed.), *Novos racismos: Perspectivas comparativas* (Oeiras: Celta, 1999), pp. 133–44. For slavery as an institution and as a mode of production see, among others, the classic statement of M. I. Finley, 'Slavery', in *International Encyclopedia of the*

cont.

conceive and develop a *new Brazil* – a new imperial economy and polity that could replicate the golden years of the previous imperial configuration – were significantly conditioned by a persistent ideology of slavery that would continue to determine the conception and formulation, and the growing legal framing, of native labour policies, and that would persist within abolitionist discourses and eventually evolve into a proclaimed doctrine of the *civilising mission* of Portuguese colonialism.[3]

As a consequence, the enduring influence of racialised pro-slavery stances in the metropolitan and colonial societies must be constantly acknowledged in our efforts to understand the rise, the maintenance and the eventual demise of the third Portuguese empire.[4] Among many other aspects, the acknowledgement of this influence is fundamental to any endeavour that strives to understand the historical transition from slave systems based on the transatlantic trade, to slave systems (or analogous sets of organic socio-economic relationships and institutions)[5] connected to the commercialisation of agriculture and the rise of African plantation economies, that is, the rise of 'legitimate commerce'.[6] This recognition is also crucial to any attempt to historicise and contextualise the social, political, economic and legal production of *free* and *unfree* labour, highlighting the spectrum of techniques and historical circumstances in which coerced labour systems originated (including

Social Sciences, vol. 14 (New York: Macmillan, 1968), pp. 307–13, esp. p. 310; James L. Watson, 'Slavery as an Institution: Open and Closed Systems', in James L. Watson (ed.), *Asian and African Systems of Slavery* (Oxford: Basil Blackwell, 1980), pp. 1–15; and Paul Lovejoy, *Transformations in Slavery: A History of Slavery in Africa* (1983; Cambridge: Cambridge University Press, 2000), pp. 10–12, 276–80. For a recent and masterful comparative appraisal of abolitionist processes and trajectories, see Seymour Drescher, *Abolition: A History of Slavery and Antislavery* (Cambridge: Cambridge University Press, 2009).

[3] For the ideology of slavery in Portugal (and Brazil), see Maria do Rosário Pimentel, *Viagem ao fundo das consciências: A escravatura na época moderna* (Lisbon: Colibri, 1995), esp. pp. 161–94, 262–78; and João Pedro Marques, *The Sounds of Silence: Nineteenth-Century Portugal and the Abolition of the Slave Trade* (Oxford: Berghahn Books, 2006), pp. 15–22. For a classical approach see the trilogy by David Brion Davis, *The Problem of Slavery in the Western World* (Ithaca, NY: Cornell University Press, 1966); *The Problem of Slavery in the Age of Revolution, 1770–1823* (Ithaca, NY: Cornell University Press, 1975); and *Slavery and Human Progress* (Oxford: Oxford University Press, 1984).

[4] The best collective undertaking is the one provided in Francisco Bethencourt and Kirti Chaudhuri (eds), *História da expansão portuguesa: Do Brasil para África*, vols 4 and 5 (Lisbon: Círculo de Leitores, 1998). For a general, colony by colony appraisal, see also Valentim Alexandre and Jill Dias (eds), *O império africano, 1825–1890* (Lisbon: Estampa, 1988); and A. H. de Oliveira Marques (ed.), *O império africano, 1890–1930* (Lisbon: Estampa, 2001).

[5] For a definition of the slave system as a social system, see Enrico Dal Lago and Constantina Katsari, 'The Study of Ancient and Modern Slave Systems: Setting an Agenda for Comparison', in Enrico Dal Lago and Constantina Katsari (eds), *Slave Systems: Ancient and Modern* (Cambridge: Cambridge University Press, 2008), pp. 3–31, esp. p. 5.

[6] The academic disputes over the validity of the expression 'legitimate trade', or 'legitimate commerce', point to an important fact that is frequently neglected in the legalist perspective over abolition: the slave trade continued to be a 'legitimate' trade within and between African societies after the legal abolition. See, for instance, Robin Law (ed.), *From Slave Trade to 'Legitimate' Commerce: The Commercial Transition in Nineteenth-Century West Africa* (Cambridge: Cambridge University Press, 1995); and also Lovejoy, *Transformations in Slavery*, pp. 165–90, 276–89.

the potentially coercive nature of wage labour) and assessing the role of the *state apparatus* in their deployment.[7] Appreciation of the historical resilience and impact of racialised pro-slavery standpoints in the development of imperial and colonial projects – an aspect obscured by analytical proposals that overvalue the signposts of the *political* and *legal* abolition of slave trade and slavery – is also decisive to understanding the emergence of new forms of legitimation of the imperial and the colonial ventures, namely the formulation of the doctrines and policies of the *civilising mission*, either by the empire-state (in both the metropole and the colonies) or by the Church and respective missionary bodies.[8] This chapter will address these issues and sustain these arguments, demonstrating how they are useful to the study of the third Portuguese empire, and suggesting that they should be tested by an in-depth investigation of the local realities of native labour – a crucial analytical approach that lies beyond the scope of the chapter, but is an understudied aspect of the Portuguese colonial empire of the nineteenth and twentieth centuries.[9]

A civilising mission to colonise

Longstanding racialised outlooks fostered, sustained and constantly legitimised the formulation of a *civilisational* rhetoric and reasoning that became the most powerful political and ideological tool that justified the new imperial endeavour at large. This

[7] See, for instance, Robert J. Steinfeld, *The Invention of Free Labor: The Employment Relation in English and American Law and Culture, 1350–1879* (Chapel Hill: University of North Carolina, 1991); Robert J. Steinfeld, *Coercion, Contract and Free Labor in the Nineteenth Century* (New York: Cambridge University Press, 2001); Robert J. Steinfeld and Stanley L. Engerman, 'Labor – Free or Coerced? An Historical Reassessment of Differences and Similarities', in Tom Brass and Marcel van der Linden (eds), *Free and Unfree Labour: The Debate Continues* (Bern: Peter Lang, 1997), pp. 107–26; Stanley L. Engerman (ed.), *Terms of Labor: Slavery, Serfdom, and Free Labor* (Stanford, CA: Stanford University Press, 1999); Stanley L. Engerman, 'Slavery, Serfdom and Other Forms of Coerced Labour: Similarities and Differences', in M. L. Bush (ed.), *Serfdom and Slavery: Studies in Legal Bondage* (London: Longman, 1996), pp. 18–41.

[8] A comparative study on the formulation and employment of the doctrine and policies of the *civilising mission* is still to be done. Nonetheless, see, for the French case, Alice K. Conklin, *A Mission to Civilize: The Republican Idea of Empire in France and West Africa, 1895–1930* (Stanford, CA: Stanford University Press, 1997); James P. Daughton, *An Empire Divided: Religion, Republicanism, and the Making of French Colonialism, 1880–1914* (Oxford: Oxford University Press, 2007); and Dino Costantini, *Mission civilisatrice: Le rôle de l'histoire coloniale dans la construction de l'identité politique française* (Paris: La Découverte, 2008). For the British case, see Catherine Hall, *Civilising Subjects: Metropole and Colony in the English Imagination, 1830–1867* (Chicago: University of Chicago Press, 2002); and Harald Fischer-Tiné and Michael Mann (eds), *Colonialism as Civilizing Mission: Cultural Ideology in British India* (London: Anthem Press, 2004). For a broader approach, see the collective contribution in Boris Barth and Jürgen Osterhammel (eds), *Zivilisierungsmissionen: Imperiale Weltverbesserung seit dem 18. Jahrhundert* (Konstanz: UVK, 2005). For the Portuguese case, see Miguel Bandeira Jerónimo, 'Os missionários do alfabeto nas colónias portuguesas (1880–1930)', in Diogo Ramada Curto (ed.), *Estudos de sociologia da leitura em Portugal no século XX* (Lisbon: Fundação Calouste Gulbenkian, 2006), pp. 29–67.

[9] For some examples see Jerónimo, *Livros Brancos, Almas Negras*.

same rhetoric and reasoning was especially fundamental to the organisation of the colonial economy and to the creation of a system of labour relations, marked by coercion and compulsion, that replaced slavery from a legal point of view, but prolonged its institution, forms and practices well into the twentieth century. The catalogue of arguments used by Bishop Azeredo Coutinho to legitimise the continuation of slavery due to the 'secondary natural law' – which postulated the doctrine of the *lesser evil* in the analysis of slavery (slavery as circumstantial for the greater good, which was claimed to be the withdrawal of Africans from putative barbaric conditions and the consequent salvation of souls) – persisted, even if adapted to new historical and ideological contexts.[10] The racialisation procedures mobilised during empire building after the disintegration of the Luso-Brazilian imperial configuration replicated ancient ideologies and justified the continuation of old practices.[11] As Frantz Fanon repeatedly indicated, and many have confirmed, the co-constitution of the imperial and colonial economic and racial orders must be acknowledged. The racialisation of thought concurred with the constitution (and the cultural and political, including the diplomatic, legitimation) of the imperial and colonial polity and economy.[12] The imperial and colonial institutions were a by-product of the ways in which historical forms of *practical* and *ideological* racialisation were formed and evolved, being as they were social, political, scientific, cultural, legal and economic spaces in which those forms were produced and reproduced in a dynamic way.[13]

[10] José Azeredo Coutinho, *Ensaio economico sobre o commercio de Portugal e suas colonias* (Lisbon: Typografia da Academia Real das Sciencias, 1794); *Analyse sobre a justiça do Commercio do Resgate dos Escravos da Costa de Africa, novamente revista e acrescentada por seu author* (Lisbon: Nova Officina de João Rodrigues Neves, 1808); and *Concordância das leis de Portugal e das Bullas Pontifícias, das quaes humas permittem a escravidão dos pretos d'Africa, e outras prohibem a escravidão dos Indios do Brazil* (Lisbon: Nova Officina de João Rodrigues Neves, 1808). See also Pimentel, *Viagem ao fundo das consciências*, pp. 262–78; Marques, *The Sounds of Silence*, pp. 20–2; and Alexander Keese, *Living with Ambiguity: Portuguese and French Colonial Administrators, Mutual Influences, and the Question of Integrating an African Elite, 1930–1963* (Stuttgart: Steiner, 2007).

[11] For the concept and problematic of *racialisation* – successor to *race relations* and *racism* – and its mechanisms and processes, see Franz Fanon, *The Wretched of the Earth* (Harmondsworth: Penguin, 1967); Michael Banton, *The Idea of Race* (London: Tavistock, 1977); Robert Miles, *Racism* (London: Routledge, 1989), pp. 73–4; and Kenan Malik, *The Meaning of Race: Race, History and Culture in Western Society* (London: Macmillan Press, 1996). For a recent genealogical effort on the historical use of the concept of racialisation, see Rohit Barot and John Bird, 'Racialization: The Genealogy and Critique of a Concept', *Ethnic and Racial Studies* 24:4 (2001), pp. 601–18. For a recent collective overview based on conceptual and empirical investigations, see Karim Murji and John Solomos (eds), *Racialization: Studies in Theory and Practice* (Oxford: Oxford University Press, 2005), especially their 'Introduction: Racialization in Theory and Practice', pp. 1–27, and Michael Banton, 'Historical and Contemporary Modes of Racialization', pp. 51–68.

[12] Fanon, *The Wretched of the Earth*; and Franz Fanon, *Black Skin, White Masks* (New York: Grove Press, 1967).

[13] For the concept of practical and ideological racialisation, see Frank Reeves, *British Racial Discourse: A Study of British Political Discourse about Race and Race-Related Matters* (Cambridge: Cambridge University Press, 1983), p. 174.

It is therefore fundamental to understand the imperial and colonial endeavours as racial formations and to explore the role played by the empire-state in the promotion of ideologies of racism and institutional practices of racial definition of political, social and economic imperial and colonial policies. The empire-states and the colonial states were racial states. The production of racialised forms of differentiation, classification and management of colonial populations and the formulation and application of racialised methods of political, social, cultural and economic organisation and administration of colonial territories were integral to the overall imperial *modus operandi* and its mechanisms and institutions of incorporation and exclusion.[14]

The third Portuguese empire constitutes an excellent field for the scrutiny of these assertions. The gradual consolidation of racialised forms of labour that promoted slavery or analogous forms of coerced or forced labour was a product of the consolidation of a civilisational rhetoric and reasoning with strong racialised overtones. The developmental plans that aimed to transform the role and the function of the overall Portuguese African imperial venture – in which the formulation of effective and efficient policies of native labour had a crucial place, especially after the formal and legal abolition of the slave trade and slavery – were always conditioned by a racialised doctrine of the civilising mission.

On the one hand, this was clear in plans to devise a new colonial economy given the loss of the Luso-Brazilian empire and the progressive decline of the slave trade, based on efforts to support the development of a plantation economy in São Tomé, Angola and Mozambique, but also on efforts to enhance colonial sovereignty through a new geography of taxation in each colony. The latter was absolutely crucial in colonies (Angola and Mozambique) whose territorial vastness required more resources and personnel and entailed a more strategic approach regarding local powers and interests. Side by side with other 'gentle civilizers of nations' that formed the classic 'standards of civilization', the tentative organisation and regulation of a colonial market was promoted as a civilisational imperative.[15]

[14] For the notion of racial formation, see the path-breaking contribution of Michael Omi and Howard Winant, *Racial Formation in the United States: From the 1960s to the 1980s* (1986; London and New York: Routledge, 1994). For the idea of a racial state, see David Theo Goldberg, *The Racial State* (Oxford: Blackwell, 2002); and his 'Racial States', in David Theo Goldberg and John Solomos (eds), *A Companion to Racial and Ethnic Studies* (Oxford: Blackwell, 2002), pp. 233–58. For the best available study on the specificities of the colonial states, see Crawford Young, *The African Colonial State in Comparative Perspective* (New Haven: Yale University Press, 1994); and John L. Comaroff, 'Reflections on the Colonial State, in South Africa and Elsewhere: Fragments, Factions, Facts and Fictions', *Social Identities* 4:3 (1998), pp. 321–61.

[15] For the catalogue of mechanisms and 'standards' of civilisation, see Martti Koskenniemi, *The Gentle Civilizer of Nations: The Rise and Fall of International Law, 1870–1960* (Cambridge: Cambridge University Press, 2002), esp. pp. 98–178; Antony Anghie, *Imperialism, Sovereignty and the Making of International Law* (Cambridge: Cambridge University Press, 2007), esp. pp. 32–114; and Gerrit W. Gong, *The Standard of 'Civilization' in International Society* (Oxford: Clarendon Press: 1984). For

cont.

In the Portuguese case it was to a large extent the *sine qua non* of the empire. The need for a new geography of taxation in the Portuguese empire was clearly associated with purposes of territorial expansion and was simultaneously justified by the necessary pacification, stabilisation and routinisation of commercial exchange and trade (via legal, technological, communicational and military means), which was conceived as a blessing of civilisation. The legacy of the proposals of David Livingstone, and the slogan of civilisation, commerce and Christianity as fundamental colonising instruments, were clearly active. The Ambriz affair in the 1850s and the planned triangle of strategic territorial occupations of Ambriz–Bembe–São Salvador, which marked an important phase in the renewal of Portuguese administrative, military and ecclesiastical colonial efforts in Angola, are telling examples of this.[16]

On the other hand, the pronounced relationship between a racialised doctrine of a civilising mission of the Portuguese imperial and colonial venture and its developmental plans was also clear in the reasoning that guided the Portuguese diplomacy of imperialism, focused either on political issues (such as the ones that led to the famous Berlin West African Conference of 1884–5) or on religious aspects (such as those that opposed Catholic and Protestant interests from 1865 onwards – that is, the under-studied and under-appreciated religious scramble for Africa, which had a fundamental role in the consolidation of several civilising mission doctrines within colonial powers, while at the same time justifying their worldly outlooks and prospects). The political and the ecclesiastical imperial and colonial expansions, not entirely coincidental and not necessarily allied in their plans and purposes, were guided and legitimised by these doctrines, which were noticeably bolstered by racial and cultural prejudices.[17]

the market and the civilising mission, see Niels P. Petersson, 'Markt, Zivilisierungsmission und Imperialismus', in Barth and Osterhammel (eds), *Zivilisierungsmissionen*, pp. 33–54; and Brett Bowden and Leonard Seabrooke, 'Global Standards of Market Civilization', in Martin Hall and Patrick Thaddeus Jackson (eds), *Civilizational Identity: The Production and Reproduction of 'Civilizations' in International Relations* (New York: Palgrave Macmillan, 2007), pp. 119–33.

[16] See Miguel Bandeira Jerónimo, 'Religion, Empire, and the Diplomacy of Colonialism: Portugal, Europe, and the Congo Question, ca. 1820–1890', unpublished PhD thesis, University of London, 2008, pp. 23–33, 58–63. For the slogan, see Brian Stanley, 'Commerce and Christianity: Providence Theory, the Missionary Movement, and the Imperialism of Free Trade, 1842–1860', *Historical Journal* 26:1 (1983), pp. 71–94; and Andrew Porter, 'Commerce and Christianity: The Rise and Fall of a Nineteenth-Century Missionary Slogan', *Historical Journal* 28:3 (1985), pp. 597–621.

[17] See Jerónimo, 'Religion, Empire, and the Diplomacy of Colonialism'. For the Berlin West African Conference, see S. Förster, W. J. Mommsen and R. Robinson (eds), *Bismarck, Europe, and Africa: The Berlin Africa Conference 1884–1885 and the Onset of Partition* (Oxford: Oxford University Press/German Historical Institute of London, 1988). For the most convincing demonstration of the variety and the complexities of the relationship of politics and religion in imperial and colonial contexts, see Andrew Porter, *Religion vs. Empire? British Protestant Missionaries and Overseas Expansion, 1700–1914* (Manchester: Manchester University Press, 2004).

The whole debate over the principles and purposes of the *civilising stations* that started at the Geographical Conference, held in Brussels in 1876 under the auspices of King Leopold II, adds to this line of reasoning. The likes of Henry Rawlinson (a member of the Royal Geographical Society), Baron de la Roncière Le Noury (president of the Paris Geographical Society) and Sir Bartle Frere (vice-president of the Indian Council), among others gathered together in Leopold II's palace, saw the *civilising stations* as logistical platforms for civilisation via the promotion of trade, science and, to a lesser extent given the *kulturkämpfe* in Europe and in the colonial worlds, also religion. As Frere defined it, 'white man's superiority' should be the core of 'civilising focus' at the *civilising stations*, a term coined by Émile Banning, Leopold II's main counsellor on African affairs.[18]

In Portugal, the Lisbon Geographical Society (LGS), formed in 1875, appropriated the expansionist leaning set forth in Brussels and strove to turn the idea of *civilising stations* into its own creation, aiming to assert itself as a pivotal imperial institutional actor, both domestically and internationally. In relation to the *civilising stations*, the Portuguese tried to affirm their precocious colonial imagination, just as they tried to promote their colonialist ancestry: the ancient system of *presídios* was considered a path-breaking example of *civilising stations*, as stated in the LGS *Boletim* of 1881. In the same year the Portuguese *civilising stations* were legally created, following the constitution of the LGS *African Fund* in 1877, and the strategy of re-occupation of African soil was boosted by a public subscription, accompanied by an 'appeal' to the population, with a view to finance the new imperial endeavours and also to *imperialise* the nation – in one of the first massive moments of what would become an inextricable connection between nationalism and imperialism in Portuguese society.

As a consequence, on 18 August 1881, Júlio Vilhena (Minister of the Navy and Overseas Affairs) issued a decree that determined the main purposes of these 'civilising stations', the 'most practical and humanitarian way that experience and science suggest' of controlling the 'component and *adjacent* territories' of Portuguese overseas possessions. The Portuguese territorial stations aimed to civilise the native populations, to 'help them with the benefits of science', propagating the Christian religion and morality, in order to 'transform their barbarian behaviour', protect the Europeans, and promote commerce. The 'stations' should

[18] Auguste Roeykens, *Léopold II et la Conférence Géographique de Bruxelles (1876)* (Bruxelles: Académie Royale des Sciences Coloniales, 1956), pp. 200–1, 208–11, 217; and Auguste Roeykens, *Le dessein africain de Léopold II: Nouvelles recherches sur sa genèse et sa nature (1875–1876)* (Bruxelles: Académie Royale des Sciences Coloniales, 1956), pp. 120–212; for the proceedings see *Conférence Géographique de Bruxelles* (Bruxelles: Hayez, 1876), esp. pp. 8–11. For the European *kulturkämpfe*, see Christopher Clark and Wolfram Kaiser (eds), *Culture Wars: Secular-Catholic Conflict in Nineteenth-Century Europe* (Cambridge: Cambridge University Press, 2003). For an analysis of the context, interests at play, and consequences of these issues, see Jerónimo, 'Religion, Empire, and the Diplomacy of Colonialism', pp. 114–15, 117–19.

be used to promote the use and vulgarisation of the Portuguese language and to study 'the indigenous vocabularies, their grammars, their legends, their traditions and customs'. The stations should be centres of information gathering and colonial vigilance. They should also be centres of cultural *modernisation* that would operate according to the principles of a racialised economic, social and cultural division of the colonial world that governed their constitution.[19]

In all these historical processes, the self-proclaimed historical purposes of the *civilising mission* that presumably guided the Portuguese imperial venture assumed a crucial place: as the fundamental political and ideological resource that was constantly mobilised to further Portuguese interests in the competitive imperial and colonial environment of the scramble for and the partition of Africa. The constant political and diplomatic efforts made by the Portuguese to attain international recognition of their alleged *coast-to-coast* sovereignty rights (the *rose-coloured* imagined map that united Angola with Mozambique) – themselves a corollary of other territorial claims such as those to the north of Angola that led to the *Congo question* – were persistently and insistently enforced by civilisational premises and intent.[20] The wide-ranging series of developmental schemes that addressed imperial and colonial politico-administrative, military, religious or moral problems – which throughout the nineteenth century remained mostly projects, with few real accomplishments – were always framed and legitimised by *civilising* principles and prospects, as we have exemplified with the case of the *civilising stations*. Portugal needed to expand territorially in order to *civilise* trade (to turn commerce into a *legitimate* taxable enterprise) and with a view to create the institutional conditions necessary to *civilise* African populations. The expansion of colonial sovereignty was justified as the expansion of the conditions of and for civilisation. The suppression of the slave trade and the reduction of contraband, the rationalisation of economic circuits and the control of the economic agents (especially the native *brokers*), or the establishment of a minimum degree of infra-structural power of the colonial state (essentially projected on fiscal, military and judicial structures), were seen as the fundamental institutional conditions to *civilise* trade and the African populations.

[19] *Boletim da Sociedade de Geografia de Lisboa* (1877 and 1881), pp. 23–7, 391–2; *Ao Povo Português em Nome da Honra, do Direito, do Interesse e do Futuro da Pátria a Comissão do Fundo Africano Criada pela Sociedade de Geografia de Lisboa para Promover uma Subscrição Nacional Permanente Destinada ao Estabelecimento de Estações Civilizadoras nos Territórios Sujeitos e Adjacentes ao Domínio Português em África* (Lisbon: Imprensa Nacional, 1881). For the civilising stations see also *Diário do Governo*, 18 Aug. 1881.

[20] For the general context, see Eric Axelson, *Portugal and the Scramble for Africa* (Johannesburg: Witwatersrand University Press, 1967). For the Congo question, see Jerónimo, 'Religion, Empire, and the Diplomacy of Colonialism'; F. Latour da Veiga Pinto, *Le Portugal et le Congo au XIXe Siècle: Étude d'histoire des relations internationales* (Paris: Presses Universitaires de France, 1972). For the British involvement, see Roger Anstey, *Britain and the Congo in the Nineteenth Century* (Oxford: Clarendon Press, 1962).

Among these factors, the administration, rationalisation and control of native labour within and between the Portuguese colonies stood out as one of the most important requirements. The creation of a new model and the regulation of a new system of *indigenous* labour – funded, coordinated and legitimised by the state – was the most important factor in the formulation of a new imperial economy. It was also fundamental in the definition of the aspirations and methods of the mandatory *effective occupation* or colonisation, following the terms established by the Berlin Act of 1885. The establishment and consolidation of a new imperial polity depended on it. The formulation of labour policies – a constant concern of Portuguese metropolitan and colonial authorities – was closely connected to political, diplomatic, and economic integrated motives and aspirations. The formation and administration of a new system of *indigenous* labour, after the formal abolition of the slave trade and slavery, was one of the vital instruments in the overall catalogue of programmes and policies that aimed to *nationalise the empire*, and was therefore one of the most important colonial and imperial assets.[21]

A civilised transition? Race, labour and imperial modernisation

Several aspects combined to push the native labour question to the forefront of Portuguese domestic and imperial politics and policies. The first of these was the need to devise an alternative to the longstanding predominant trade in the Portuguese imperial world – the slave trade – a process that would simultaneously entail the transformation of the nature and the characteristics of the colonial economies and the transformation of the socio-political structures of the colonial societies. The rationale of the famous 1836 report made by the Secretary of State of the Navy and Overseas Affairs, Sá da Bandeira, could not be clearer in this respect: only the profound transformation of the economic nature and role of native labour could be the basis for any type of imperial and colonial development after the loss of Brazil.[22]

The second aspect, as we noted above, was the need to promote new sources of revenue that could enhance the chronically debilitated colonial finances, exhausted by malpractices and affected by an ineffective fiscal and tributary machine

[21] For the notion of infra-structural power of the state, see Michael Mann, 'The Autonomous Power of the State: Its Origins, Mechanisms, and Results', *Archives Européennes de Sociologie* 25 (1984), pp. 185–213. For the political, cultural and economic processes of *nationalisation of the empire* in the nineteenth century, see Miguel Bandeira Jerónimo, 'Empire-Rebuilding, State-Remaking and Nation-Reformation: The Case of Nineteenth-Century Portugal', unpublished typescript. See also Valentim Alexandre, 'Nação e império', and Jorge Pedreira, 'O Sistema de Trocas', in Bethencourt and Chaudhuri (eds), *História da expansão portuguesa*, vol. 4, pp. 90–142 and pp. 214–99.

[22] See Sá da Bandeira, 'Relatório do Secretário de Estado dos Negócios da Marinha e Ultramar', *Arquivo das Colónias* 1 (1836), pp. 13–18.

(associated with a weak colonial administration), via the development of new economic and commercial activities. From 1 December 1869, an administrative reform, devised by Rebelo da Silva, greatly reduced the financial dependence of the colonies on the metropole, ending direct subsidies. Although designed to meet other purposes (for instance, to reduce the costs of the empire in a period of imperial retrenchment), this brought about other consequences, since each colony had to find other strategies to guarantee a certain level of public revenues. This reduced the chances of a completely new moral and economic order in the imperial and the colonial worlds, certainly contributing to the variety of reasons that the abolitionist process in the Portuguese empire was a convoluted and protracted one.[23]

A third aspect lay in the need to counterbalance the shortage of emigrants (traditionally restricted to the contingent of exiled convicts, or *degredados*) who were supposed to embrace the new *el dorado* and carry on the much needed agricultural revolution that could promote the rise of 'legitimate commerce'. Only native labour, then, could sustain the great transition. Finally, the mobilisation of native labour also constituted the sole way to meet the need to develop infrastructures and communications that could assure the political and military enhancement of colonial sovereignty and sustain the logic of colonial expansionism that prevailed from the 1850s up to the pacification campaigns of the late nineteenth century (with the exception of the retraction period of the 1860s and early 1870s).[24] Moreover, the particularities and specific circumstances of the colonial world, for instance the lack of a native labour force in São Tomé and its 1875 labour crisis or the high cost of native labour due to the competitive intercolonial native labour market, added to the strong reasons that compelled the Portuguese authorities to highlight native labour as the most pressing and decisive question in the overall transformation of the new imperial configuration.[25]

From Acúrsio das Neves to Sá da Bandeira, from José Lopes de Lima to Andrade Corvo, and many other colonial experts, the formulation of an effective (that is, effectively controlled by the colonial state) and efficient (that is, able to meet the needs of public and private European, mainly Portuguese, colonial interests) system of recruitment and employment of native labour was a *sine qua non* of the imperial renaissance during the nineteenth century. According to Acúrsio das Neves in his *Considerações politicas, e commerciaes sobre os descobrimentos, e possessões dos Portuguezes na Africa, e na Asia* of 1830, for instance, the imperial renaissance relied on the systematic use of the abundant native workforce, following the rise

[23] See *Carta Orgânica das Instituições Administrativas nas Províncias Ultramarinas. Annotada por J. A. Ismael Gracias* (Nova Goa: Imprensa Nacional, 1894).

[24] For the waves of colonial expansionism, see Alexandre, 'Nação e império', pp. 90–111.

[25] For São Tomé and the 1875 labour crisis, see Augusto Nascimento, 'São Tomé e Príncipe', in Alexandre and Dias (eds), *O império africano*, pp. 269–318; and 'A "crise braçal" de 1875 em São Tomé', *Revista Crítica de Ciências Sociais* 34 (1992), pp. 317–29.

of international pressures against the continuation of the slave trade. This argument was shared by Sebastião Xavier Botelho, who produced one of the most solid pleas for the suppression of the slave trade (not slavery) in order to develop the new imperial project.

For Acúrsio das Neves, though 'indolent and lazy', the 'black class' could be led towards a productive position with 'stimulus conveniently exercised'. Their lack of ambition for ownership and economic independence, their lack of 'moral education' that turned them into a 'degenerate species of the human type', their 'limited intelligence' (a condition that could nonetheless be improved), and their physical capacities (which should be trained in order to 'fortify' them) were the factors adduced by Acúrsio das Neves to sustain his reasoning. The need for a widespread mercantile and economic reformulation of Portuguese colonial administration was undeniable, and the ability to transform the economic function of native labour was the key element in that challenge; an aspect equally underlined by Lopes de Lima in his multi-volume appreciation of the Portuguese imperial world after the loss of Brazil, entitled *Ensaios sobre a statistica das possessões Portuguezas na Africa Occidental e Oriental*. Published between 1844 and 1862, this work was turned into policy by Sá da Bandeira through multiple legal instruments, starting with a decree that aimed (but manifestly failed) to forbid and suppress the slave trade, dated 10 December 1836. As the latter clearly stated, the great *transition* depended on *real* abolition, given that without effective suppression it would be 'useless to legislate (for the colonies) [. . .] to promote the cultivation of the lands' and to try to direct any type of investment to Angola, Mozambique and the other poles of the empire. Again, side by side with an ethnocentric perspective, a racialised *civilisational* rhetoric was present as a crucial element in the overall modernising project, legitimising its foundations and purposes.[26]

The example of Andrade Corvo's important *Estudos sobre as províncias ultramarinas* (1883–7) is revealing in this respect. The *imperial modernisation* programme that Corvo tried to implement as Minister of Foreign Affairs (1871–8) and also as head of the Ministry of the Navy and Overseas Affairs (1872–7) entailed clear *civilisational* guidelines marked by racialised conceptions that accepted the gradual transformability of African cultures and societies, but were essentially

[26] See José Acúrsio das Neves, *Considerações politicas, e commerciaes sobre os descobrimentos, e possessões dos Portuguezes na Africa, e na Asia* (Lisbon: Impressão Régia, 1830), esp. pp. 202–6, 235–9, quotations at pp. 236 and 204; Sebastião Xavier Botelho, *Escravatura: Beneficios que podem provir ás nossas possessões d'Africa da prohibição daquelle trafico* (Lisbon: Typographia de José B. Morando, 1840), pp. 13–33; José Joaquim Lopes de Lima, *Ensaios sobre a statistica das possessões portuguezas na Africa Occidental e Oriental; na Asia Occidental; na China, e na Oceania* (Lisbon: Imprensa Nacional, 1844–62); Sá da Bandeira, 'Relatório do Secretário de Estado', pp. 13–18; Sá da Bandeira, *O Trabalho Rural Africano e a Administração Colonial* (Lisbon: Imprensa Nacional, 1873), esp. pp. 47–70. For the decisive role of Sá da Bandeira, see João Pedro Marques, *Sá da Bandeira e o fim da escravidão: Vitória da moral, desforra do interesse* (Lisboa: Imprensa de Ciências Sociais, 2008).

reduced to the promotion of 'commerce and productive labour', suspicious as they were of the immediate benefits of a religious civilising mission. The gradual diffusion of Darwinian principles within European and Portuguese socio-political imperial analysis, noticeable in Corvo's emphasis on the different degrees of 'degenerescence' of the 'African type'[27] or in A. F. Nogueira's learned *A raça negra sob o ponto de vista da civilisação da África* (1880) – in which he wrote that 'the whole matter of civilization in Africa comes down to a question of labour' and that the natives were 'the active instrument of labour' – reinforced the position of those interested in keeping the *status quo* regarding the real local circumstances under which the imperial economy was sustained and developed, characterised by slavery and other types of forced labour. The reasoning changed, the terminology varied and laws proliferated, but the continuities with secular practices of enslavement persisted and these became justified and legitimised by *civilising missions* and by *scientific* principles.[28]

The emergence in Portugal of critical approaches to the humanitarian, *civilisational* and developmental outlooks that effloresced in the Western world was epitomised by the work of Oliveira Martins, namely in his *O Brasil e as colónias portuguesas* (1880), *Elementos de antropologia* (1880) and *As raças humanas* (1881), the latter used later by the likes of William Sumner, a renowned social Darwinist and social scientist, in his *Folkways*. The 'philanthropy' that insisted 'that the bible [. . .] will convert the savages, and that the ferule of the headmaster will turn them into men like us' was constantly criticised via *scientific* demonstration made possible by anthropological and archaeological *data*, as well as by the contribution of the natural sciences. According to Oliveira Martins, what was expected of the 'mystical alliance of the Bible with textile production' had never been attained in the past by 'the bells and the crucifixes, the music and the incense of the catholic cult, either in America or in Africa'. The 'poetic plan of education of the negroes' and the 'chimera of civilisation of the savages' were

[27] Closely influenced by the works of William Winwood Reade (1838–75), namely *Savage Africa* (1864) and *African Sketch-Book* (1873). See João de Andrade Corvo, *Estudos sobre as Províncias Ultramarinas* (Lisbon: Typ. da Academia Real das Sciencias, 1883–7), esp. vol. 3, 'Civilização Africana', pp. 23–8 and 64–71, at pp. 71 and 25. For the reception of Darwin's ideas in Portugal, see Ana Leonor Pereira, *Darwin em Portugal. Filosofia. História. Engenharia social (1865–1914)* (Coimbra: Almedina, 2001). For Reade, see Felix Driver, *Geography Militant: Cultures of Exploration and Empire* (Oxford: Blackwell, 2001), pp. 90–116. For *Anglophone* conceptions on Africa and the Africans, see Philip D. Curtin, *The Image of Africa: British Ideas and Action, 1780–1850* (Madison: University of Wisconsin Press, 1964). For a general appraisal of racialised thoughts and images in Western culture at the time, see Jan Nederveen Pieterse, *White on Black: Images of Africa and Blacks in Western Popular Culture* (New Haven: Yale University Press, 1992), esp. pp. 76–101. For the most comprehensive analysis of the rise of *social Darwinism*, see Mike Hawkins, *Social Darwinism in European and American Thought, 1860–1945: Nature as Model and Nature as Threat* (Cambridge: Cambridge University Press, 1997).

[28] A. F. Nogueira, *A raça negra sob o ponto de vista da civilisação da África* (Lisbon: Typographia Nova Minerva, 1880), pp. 10, 209.

denounced as another of the various 'naive superstitions' of the time. The 'idea of the education of the negroes' was considered to be 'absurd, not only given History, but also given the mental capacities of those inferior races', that could never understand 'the metaphysics of the Verb and the dogma of Trinity'.[29]

Despite the clear doubts about the real possibilities of cultural change brought about by religion, an aspect Oliveira Martins shared with many in a context of turbulent church–state relations (especially concerning its imperial and colonial projection), what was at stake was the *scientific* justification of the imperative for a more pragmatic approach to colonisation. The idea should be to replicate the Dutch way, 'without scruples, preconceptions, or chimeras', that is, turning the colonial world into a large *fazenda*. The alternative would be to negotiate its own existence with a more industrious power. The *laws* of scientific racialism were closely combined with utilitarian, pragmatic evaluations of the past and present of the Portuguese colonial empire in order to devise a future model of colonisation that would have forced labour at its basis, as Oliveira Martins and many others maintained or argued.[30]

The nature and direction of *progress* of the imperial world that Acúrsio das Neves, Lopes Lima, Sá da Bandeira and Andrade Corvo envisaged (notwithstanding differences of historical context, personal and political trajectory, and ideological outlook) collided with other perspectives. One of the fundamental texts about the crucial role of native labour in the projected imperial renaissance of the country, Sá da Bandeira's *O trabalho rural Africano e a administração colonial*, aimed to counterbalance a well-rooted divergent perspective, one that blended longstanding

[29] For J. P. Oliveira Martins and his views, see *O Brasil e as colónias portuguesas* (1880; Lisbon: Guimarães Editores, 1978), pp. 253–7, at 254–5; also *Elementos de antropologia* (1880; Lisbon: Guimarães Editores, 1954); and *As raças humanas e a civilização primitiva* (1881–3; Lisbon: Guimarães Editores, 1955). For appraisals of his colonial thought, see, among others, Valentim Alexandre, 'Questão nacional e questão colonial em Oliveira Martins', *Análise Social* 31:1 (1996), pp. 183–201, esp. pp. 195 ff. For Sumner, see his *Folkways: A Study of the Sociological Importance of Usages, Manners, Customs, Mores, and Morals* (Boston: Ginn and Co., 1907), p. 334; Robert C. Bannister, Jr., 'William Graham Sumner's Social Darwinism: A Reconsideration', *History of Political Economy* 5:1 (1973), pp. 89–109; and Edward Caudill, *Darwinian Myths: The Legends and Misuses of a Theory* (Knoxville, TN: University of Tennessee Press, 1997), pp. 64–78.

[30] Oliveira Martins, *O Brasil e as colónias portuguesas*, p. 257. The defence of a model of colonisation essentially based on a model of agricultural exploration organised around *fazendas*, and completely dependent on native labour, was widespread in Portugal from the middle of the nineteenth century. For an overview since 1864 and a programmatic outline, see Fernando Emygdio Garcia, *Colonização e colónias portuguesas, 1864–1914* (Coimbra: F. França Amado, 1915). For the *fazendas* as a solution for colonisation in Africa, compared to other 'types of colonies', see, among others, the coeval assessment of Oliveira Martins, *O Brasil e as colónias portuguesas*, pp. 180–8. For an overview on the debates on forms and purposes of colonisation, see Rui Ramos, 'Um novo Brasil de um novo Portugal: A história do Brasil e a ideia de colonização em Portugal nos séculos XIX e XX', *Penélope* 23 (2000), pp. 129–52. For the *positivist* critical appraisal of the role of religion in the overall imperial venture in the 1870s and 1880s, see Jerónimo, 'Religion, Empire, and the Diplomacy of Colonialism', pp. 160 ff.

elements of the ideology of slavery with pragmatic evaluations in a context of transformation of the imperial economy and polity. In June 1872, the Lisbon Commercial Association sponsored an opuscule, entitled *Algumas palavras sobre a questão do trabalho nas colonias portuguezas da Africa, especialmente nas ilhas de S. Thome e Principe*, which conveyed serious doubts about the advantageous consequences promised by the decrees of 29 April 1875 and 1878. As happened with the tentative suppression of slavery of 25 February 1869, this institution contested the documents that legally suppressed servile labour and the official tutelage of the *libertos* in the imperial world. Echoing the pro-slavery precepts of Bishop Azeredo Coutinho, and based on the promotion of mandatory and forced labour as a civilisational gift and an economic imperative, this opuscule prolonged a systematic opposition to the very few who wanted to associate the end of slavery or analogous conditions with imperial and colonial modernisation and development. As the Minister of the Navy and Overseas Affairs, Mendes Leal, stated in Parliament on 12 April 1864, 'work can be obligatory without being enslaved; it can be imposed without being inflicted'. One day later he added that the 'natural transition' that governed historical evolution should not be tentatively obstructed in a colonial context: 'from slavery to servitude, that is, from enslaved work, or penal, to obligatory work, or duty'.[31]

Side by side with recognition of the vital need of a native workforce in the reorganisation of the colonial empire, the majority of the Portuguese political and economic elites endorsed the essential continuity between native labour systems. The putative *uneconomic* nature of Portuguese imperialism is hardly tenable in face of the multiplicity of economic interests that conditioned the formation of the new imperial economy, which should be based on forced labour, as was clearly stated in the above-mentioned opuscule. The constant delay of abolition was a major aim. As Sá da Bandeira pertinently stressed, the movement headed by the Commercial Association, representing colonial political and economic interests (some of them with important influence within political parties and inside the cabinets), expected the maintenance of a 'practice that represents the state of slavery, against the spirit and the letter of the laws that abolished it'. Philanthropic leanings were criticised as they were seen to endanger the future of the empire, an aspect that was reinforced by the difficulties that periodically affected São Tomé in the 1860s and 1870s, as well as those which permanently characterised the economic development of Angola and Mozambique. Sá da Bandeira's efforts to prohibit forced labour in 1874 were refused by the Chamber of Deputies, not even deserving a debate, and the *serviçais* system became predominant as a system of forced

[31] For the political context in which the legislation mentioned was critically received, see João Pedro Marques, 'O retorno do escravismo em meados do século XIX', *Análise Social* 180 (2006), pp. 671–92, esp. pp. 687–90; and Valentim Alexandre, *A questão colonial no Parlamento (1821–1910)* (Lisbon: Dom Quixote, 2008), pp. 126–34, at 132–3.

migration from Angola to São Tomé based on slavery and the slave trade that could, although not without difficulties, foster the plantation economy in the latter. The organisation and maintenance of a system of recruitment and employment of native labour based on slavery and analogous conditions was a critical component of the *new Brazil*. It would also become a pivotal element in the empire's development and consolidation in the twentieth century, contrary to the narratives of abolition and of emancipation.[32]

The combination of factors such as the internationalisation of colonial legitimate commerce and of overall imperial and colonial affairs (both related to the causes and effects of the scramble for Africa) increased the relevance of the African labour question. To control the availability and circulation of native labour was seen as a pre-condition for internal (colonial) development and external (inter-imperial) competitiveness. Portuguese authorities facing serious and manifold competitive disadvantages in international and imperial contexts – from the chronic scarcity of economic and financial means, to the recurring debilities in the infrastructural capacities of the colonial administration, including the frequently insurmountable resilience of the backbone of the colonial *ancien régime* – had to assure the constant availability of a native labour force, especially in a model of economic development almost exclusively based on a plantation economy, requiring an intensive use of labour.[33] Like many other powers, the Portuguese imperial venture depended on the efficient functioning of a system of native labour based on recruitment at low cost. Forced labour was proclaimed to be unacceptable as an exchange commodity but became acceptable as a mode of production of legitimate goods. As Paul Lovejoy argued, 'European rhetoric pushed in the direction of abolition and emancipation; European experience encouraged complicity and often openly supported slavery on the pretext that "domestic slavery" was different from slavery elsewhere', or, we might add, from the old slavery. The Portuguese case reinforces the soundness of this evaluation.[34]

[32] Bandeira, *O Trabalho Rural Africano e a Administração Colonial*, esp. pp. 11–45, quotation at p. 217. For the debate on the economic nature of the third Portuguese empire, see Richard J. Hammond, *Portugal and Africa, 1815–1910: A Study in Uneconomic Imperialism* (Stanford, CA: Stanford University Press, 1966), and 'Uneconomic Imperialism: Portugal in Africa before 1910', in L. H. Gann and Peter Duignan (eds), *Colonialism in Africa, 1870–1960* (Cambridge: Cambridge University Press, 1969), pp. 352–82; and the exemplary works by William Clarence-Smith, *The Third Portuguese Empire, 1825–1975: A Study in Economic Imperialism* (Manchester: Manchester University Press, 1985), and 'The Myth of Uneconomic Imperialism: The Portuguese in Angola, 1836–1926', *Journal of Southern African Studies* 5:2 (1979), pp. 165–80. For a critical appraisal, see also Adelino Torres, *O império português entre o real e o imaginário* (Lisbon: Escher, 1991), esp. pp. 121–200.

[33] For the issue of emigration see the coeval appraisal by Luís Schwalbach Lucci, *Emigração e colonização: Tese para o concurso de lente substituto da 2ª cadeira da escola colonial* (Lisbon: Typ. Do Annuario Commercial, 1914); and also Jerónimo, *Livros Brancos, Almas Negras*, pp. 142–52.

[34] Lovejoy, *Transformations in Slavery*, p. 254.

The economic and political viability of the Portuguese colonies in a context of internationalisation of African affairs was a priority. As a consequence – and despite the intensification of criticism towards its workings, characterised by a shift of focus by the vigilantes of empire from the slave trade to slavery and its multiple disguises – the systems of colonial development depended on a native labour force, reinforcing forms of coerced labour analogous to slavery, if not in fact slavery itself.[35] The anti-slavery movements, namely those associated with the British Anti-Slavery Societies, and the *crusade* against slavery ingeniously promoted by Charles-Martial-Allemand Lavigerie that converged in Brussels in 1889 apropos of the anti-slavery conference, proved incapable of controlling the terms of the great *transition*, still governed by the use of a compulsory African labour force.[36] As a consequence, and despite the widespread tentative *modernisation* of the overall colonial endeavour associated with the *new imperialism* – which elevated civilisational rhetoric to the major legitimating instrument and turned Law into the main (though scarcely effective) tool for moral regeneration and putative racial and social progressivism, both at an international and national-colonial level – the emergence of a newly legitimised international imperial economy and polity was paralleled by the rise of forms of alleged contracted labour. These were legal expedients for reproducing forms of coerced and compulsory labour and servile conditions throughout the African continent, processes connected with widespread forms of forced migration within and between imperial powers.[37] The nature and the procedures of labour recruitment and employment that emerged or were

[35] By far the best account of the historical evolution of the interest devoted by *vigilantes of empire*, mainly of British extraction, to the Portuguese empire is still James Duffy's *A Question of Slavery*. It is extremely revealing that this work and its implications were virtually ignored by Portuguese historiography focused on imperial issues. See also Jerónimo, *Livros Brancos, Almas Negras*, pp. 68–88. For an interesting collection of essays that address these issues in a historical perspective in the twentieth century, with an emphasis on the mandate systems and the United Nations Trusteeship Council, see R. M. Douglas, Michael D. Callahan and Elizabeth Bishop (eds), *Imperialism on Trial: International Oversight of Colonial Rule in Historical Perspective* (Lanham, MD: Lexington Books, 2006).

[36] For anti-slavery agitation in the Catholic world and the associated *civilising* purposes, see Jerónimo, 'Religion, Empire, and the Diplomacy of Colonialism', pp. 114–52; and François Renault, *Lavigerie, l'esclavage africain et l'Europe, 1868–1892*, 2 vols (Paris: Boccard, 1971). For the anti-slavery conference, see Suzanne Miers, *Britain and the Ending of the Slave Trade* (London: Longman, 1975), pp. 236–314.

[37] For several case studies, see the collective contributions in Suzanne Miers and Richard Roberts (eds), *The End of Slavery in Africa* (Madison: University of Wisconsin Press, 1988), and Suzanne Miers and Martin Klein (eds), *Slavery and Colonial Rule in Africa* (London: Frank Cass, 1999). For indentured labour and forced migration, see Colin Newbury, 'Labour Migration in the Imperial Phase: An Essay in Interpretation', *Journal of Imperial and Commonwealth History* 3 (1974–5), pp. 234–56; P. C. Emmer (ed.), *Colonialism and Migration: Indentured Labour Before and After Slavery* (Dordrecht: Martinus Nijhoff Publishers, 1986); and David Northrup, *Indentured Labor in the Age of Imperialism, 1834–1922* (Cambridge: Cambridge University Press, 1995). For a comparative assessment of forced and free migration on a global scale, see David Eltis (ed.), *Coerced and Free Migration: Global Perspectives* (Stanford, CA: Stanford University Press, 2002).

reinforced after the successive formal declarations of the *end* of the slave trade and slavery were, from some perspectives, scarcely distinguishable from the ones that characterised the forms and justification of enslavement in the nefarious trade.[38]

The Brussels anti-slavery conference nonetheless created the conditions for an increasing vigilance over the imperial *modus operandi*, especially in relation to alcohol, arms and munitions importation and traffic with the native populations, which had already been addressed in Berlin in 1884–5 and were considered to be fundamental causes of the persistence of the longstanding slave systems in African societies and in the colonial empires. In exchange, the proclaimed intensification of measures against these trades was presented as being completely reliant on European territorial expansion and on the strengthening of competitive colonial sovereignties. Only the consolidation of an administrative, military, religious and judicial state *apparatus* in the colonies, always backed by purposes of economic regulation and control, could enhance the declared intent to *moralise* and *civilise* the imperial world.

Obviously, the consolidation of sovereignty in the colonies would turn into the most important obstacle to an effective transformation of the moral and political economies of colonial rule.[39] In the first session of the conference, one of the members of the Portuguese delegation in Brussels, Augusto Castilho, presented a *memorandum* entitled *Memóire sur l'abolition de l'esclavage et de la traite des Noirs sur le territoire portugais*, which, accompanied by another document entitled *Liste des stations officielles que le Portugal possède en Afrique*, aimed to establish these precise arguments. Extremely interested in using the gathering to continue their aggressive foreign policy focused on colonial issues, the Portuguese representatives expected to bring territorial aspects to the forefront of the debate. The presentation of the list of *civilising stations*, with a catalogue of examples that putatively demonstrated the precedence and effectiveness of the country's abolitionist efforts, had territorial goals, especially related to the Anglo-Portuguese quarrels in the Zambezi.[40] But this strategy also revealed the assertion of a new strategy of imperial legitimation, based on a *civilisational* reasoning. Only the network of *civilising stations*, considered as proofs of the country's commitment

[38] For strong statements of this argument, see, among others, Hugh Tinker, *A New System of Slavery: The Export of Indian Labour Overseas, 1830–1920* (London: Oxford University Press, 1974); François Renault, *Libération d'esclaves et nouvelle servitude: Les rachats de captifs africains pour le compte des colonies françaises après l'abolition de l'esclavage* (Dakar and Abidjan: Nouvelles Editions Africaines, 1976); Monica Schuler, 'The Recruitment of African Indentured Labourers for European Colonies in the Nineteenth Century', in Emmer (ed.), *Colonialism and Migration*, pp. 125–61. For a more moderate approach see, for instance, Stanley L. Engerman, 'Contract Labor, Sugar, and Technology in the Nineteenth Century', *Journal of Economic History* 43:3 (1983), pp. 635–59.
[39] Suzanne Miers, *Britain and the Ending of the Slave Trade*, pp. 251–6; also Miers, 'Humanitarianism at Berlin: Myth or Reality?', and L. H. Gann, 'The Berlin Conference and the Humanitarian Conscience', both in Förster *et al.* (eds), *Bismarck, Europe, and Africa*, pp. 333–45, 321–31.
[40] See Malyn D. Newitt, *The History of Mozambique* (London: C. Hurst & Co., 1995), pp. 337–55.

to the humanitarian *zeitgeist*, could ensure the great historical civilising missions of the Portuguese empire: to suppress the slave trade and slavery, develop 'legitimate commerce', and civilise the African populations under a new, more *civilised* and *modern* colonial sovereignty. After decades of systematic condemnation of the involvement of the Portuguese authorities in the promotion and development of the slave trade and slavery, the constant proclamation of the civilisational virtues and the modernising capacity of Portuguese colonialism was an imperative.[41]

'On the difficulties to make the natives work': the legalisation of forced labour

The aftermath of the Berlin and Brussels conferences brought the beginning of effective colonisation, in the Portuguese third empire bolstered by *pacification* campaigns that aimed to effectively define the new colonial sovereignty. The imperative of territorial consolidation of the imperial frontiers certainly added force to pragmatic tendencies in relation to the colonial world. The *civilisational* rhetoric was not abandoned but it became acceptable only insofar as it legitimised the expansionist manoeuvres and the overall colonial policies, especially those related to the military pacification of local sources of insurgency (for instance, the *ngoni* kingdom of Gaza, Mozambique, led by the well-known Gugunhama, in 1895) and to the ongoing political and legal operations that aimed to settle and regulate the native forced labour market. The 1890s was a decade of administrative, mainly military, territorial consolidation. It was also a decade in which the *política indígena* (native policy) became more and more consistent, especially in what concerned the most pressing issue: how to organise a colonial economy based on compulsory native labour.

The majority of colonial experts, many of them the military men who *pacified* the resistance of the natives or their disinclination to accept the terms of colonial rule, and future colonial administrators, shared Oliveira Martins' conceptions and proposals. Personalities such as António Enes, Mouzinho de Albuquerque, Aires de Ornelas, Freire de Andrade, Eduardo Ferreira da Costa and Henrique da Paiva Couceiro – the so-called *generation of 1895* – replicated and developed many of Oliveira Martins' *realist* precepts of colonisation, and perfected the racialised conception of the entire imperial venture that he promoted so vigorously and

[41] For the details see Jerónimo, *Livros Brancos, Almas Negras*, pp. 31–6. For the sessions and the memorandum presented by Augusto Castilho, as well as the Lista de Estações Oficiais, see *Conférence Internationale de Bruxelles. Protocoles et Acte Final* (Paris: Imprimerie Nationale, 1891), pp. 10, 16–45, 53–62; see also Augusto de Castilho, *Memoria Ácerca da Extincção da Escravidão e do Trafico de Escravatura no Territorio Portuguez* (Lisbon: Publicação do Ministério da Marinha, 1889).

stridently. Sharing similar occupational trajectories and common imperial vistas, and benefiting from an atmosphere that promoted an imperial nationalism to the forefront of domestic politics, especially after the 1890 *ultimatum*, these were the most important imperial ideologues and practitioners. In both conditions they were the main promoters of a racialised conception of forced labour and its justification as the cornerstone of the imperial polity and economy. The consolidation of racialised conceptions of the colonial population was, simultaneously, the justification for a system of compulsory labour, as it was one of the key elements in the gradual formation of the colonial state, which would in its turn promote, via the legal expedient, a racialised conception of the colonial administration.[42]

The process of racialisation of the colonial world, both at the level of ideas and at the institutional level, was therefore closely related to the process of establishment of the colonial economy. And this was particularly so in the organisation of a system of native labour that included the massive transportation and trade of slaves and forced labourers within the imperial configuration. The ideas and intents that backed the promulgation of the decree of 9 November 1899, which regulated the use of native labour, were illuminating in this regard. Based on Enes' views, the decree's terms inexorably led to the legalisation of forced labour due to economic and *civilisational*, humanitarian reasons. If slavery was conceived as the *lesser evil*, forced labour entailed similar *noble* motivations and purposes. As Enes declared, 'the economic interests recommended that the legislator should draw on and preserve the habits of work that [slavery] imposed on the negroes' but the 'dangerous social doctrines' that dictated 'laws and statutes that constituted a sort of declaration of the negroes' rights' had led to a situation in which 'no one had the obligation to work'.

According to Enes, the 'liberal and humanitarian excited proclamations did not respect the code and the moral, the sense of balance and economic necessities', and therefore promoted and recognised the 'sacred right to idleness' within African communities. This was unacceptable. Encouraging the active collaboration of native chiefs in all process, and legalising old practices of corporal punishment (only abolished in 1911), the 1899 Code provided a catalogue of legal expedients that enabled the emergence of a system of native labour based on compulsory mechanisms. Only through work or labour could the native populations aspire to enter the 'civilisation guild', which would obviously be presided over by the Portuguese.

[42] For the pacification campaigns see René Pélissier, *História das campanhas de Angola: Resistência e revoltas, 1845–1941* (Lisbon: Estampa, 1986), and *História de Moçambique: Formação e oposição, 1854–1918* (Lisbon: Estampa, 1987–8). For the reception, not entirely positive, of Oliveira Martins' colonial thought in Portugal, see Carlos Maurício, *A invenção de Oliveira Martins: Política, historiografia e identidade nacional no Portugal contemporâneo (1867–1960)* (Lisbon: Imprensa Nacional-Casa da Moeda, 2005), pp. 92–9.

The formal abolition of the slave trade and the official abolition of slavery on 29 April 1875 created new problems and required new solutions.[43]

In a statement that encapsulated the common racialised perspectives of imperial ideologues and experts but also corresponded with the reality of a past, present and future *civilising mission*, Enes declared that

> labour was the best moralising mission, the most instructive school, the most disciplinable authority, the conquest less prone to revolts, the army that can occupy the intractable interior, the only police that will repress slavery, the religion that will combat Mohammedanism, the education that will turn brutes into men.

In conclusion, again against the religious leaning of some doctrines of the civilising mission, Enes added that if Africa would see the arrival of 'a messiah [. . .] the good news of his evangel would be a message of work'. Following Oliveira Martins' critical appraisal of the possible role of religion and education in colonial contexts, and participating in the late nineteenth-century debate about the social and political role that missionaries should play within the empire – see for instance the missionary-geographer proposed by Luciano Cordeiro, another major imperial ideologue – Enes argued that missionaries wanted 'to abruptly convert a savage into a saint, a beast into a martyr', and imagined that education was 'sufficient to overcome racial characteristics and to neutralise social and climacteric circumstances'. Setting the terms of colonial policies, the missionaries' role would only be accepted if they were able to articulate 'the merciful venture of saving souls to god' with efforts to 'educate bodies to work', as the only way to liberate the native from the 'tenebrous moral and social condition' in which they were imprisoned.[44]

In a broader context of imperial and colonial projects characterised by militarised, despotic conceptions of the overall imperial and colonial administrations, contrary to any form of assimilation – such as the influential proposal made by Eduardo Ferreira da Costa in *Estudo sobre a administração civil das nossas possessões africanas*, a work presented to the First Colonial Congress in 1901 – the outright downplay of education and evangelisation was related to a major desideratum: the constant promotion of labour as the single civilising tool in colonial policies. This process also included denial of the right of proprietorship to the native populations, side by side with the absolute political and economic deprivation that marked the latter. The racialisation of the colonial world and its respective populations, a process in which the empire-state and the colonial administration

[43] António Enes, *Moçambique: Relatório apresentado ao governo* (1893; Lisbon: Imprensa Nacional, 1971), pp. 70–1. For the decree, see *Diário do Governo*, no. 262, 18 Nov. 1899. For an analysis of its terms and implications, see Jerónimo, *Livros Brancos, Almas Negras*, pp. 58–62.

[44] Enes, *Moçambique*, pp. 75, 213, 217. See also Luciano Cordeiro, 'Primeiro Relatório Apresentado à Comissão de Missões do Ultramar' and 'Segundo Relatório Apresentado à Comissão de Missões do Ultramar', in *Questões coloniais* (Coimbra: Imprensa da Universidade, 1934), pp. 109–34, 135–59, at 112–13; and Jerónimo, 'Religion, Empire, and the Diplomacy of Colonialism', p. 160.

played a pivotal role, was central to the imperial and colonial *modus operandi*, defining the distribution of rights and resources. Again echoing Oliveira Martins, who had in his own view asserted 'in an irrefutable manner the dangerous and great mistake' that would be made if the 'civilised European and the savage inhabitant of the African interior' were 'considered equal before the law', Costa argued that the 'anthropological reasons, social reasons' that revealed the 'disparity of ethnic character, of uses and instincts' and demonstrated the 'manifest inferiority of the savage' recommended 'different systems of government' in the colonies and suggested an effective system of tutelage of the native populations, in which their civilisation via labour, compulsory if necessary, was a major element.

The elevation of the 'habit to work' to 'imperative social law', as a fundamental 'life reason, and as hygiene of spirit and body', entailed the promotion of forced labour, as the Governor-General of Angola between 1907 and 1909, Paiva Couceiro, neatly stated. Accordingly, Paiva Couceiro strongly supported the *serviçais* system that intimately connected Angola and São Tomé, through 66,000 Angolans transferred between the two territories between 1876 and 1904.[45] As the *Cadbury affair* (or *slave cocoa affair*) demonstrated, the prevalence of racialised outlooks and economic utilitarian principles, 'without scruples, preconceptions, or chimeras', as Oliveira Martins suggested, led to a systematic *civilised savagery* that would last until the 1940s, as Henrique Galvão's *Relatório sobre problemas nativos nas colónias portuguesas* (1947) established, revealing how the scarcity of labour and racial prejudices constantly led to forced labour. As Galvão stated, 'only the dead' were 'really exempt from forced labour'.[46] The *modern slavery* uncovered by Henry

[45] Eduardo da Costa, *Estudo sobre a Administração Civil das nossas Possessões Africanas. Memória Apresentada ao Congresso Colonial* (Lisbon: Imprensa Nacional, 1903), pp. 8–13, 37–9, 57–86, at 60; Martins, *O Brasil e as colónias portuguesas*, pp. 283 ff.; Henrique de Paiva Couceiro, *Angola. Dois anos de governo (Junho 1907–Junho 1909): história e comentários* (Lisbon: Tipografia Portuguesa, 1948), pp. 224–32, 252–8, at 226. For the issue of political and social rights in the Portuguese empire since the 1800s, see Ana Cristina Nogueira da Silva, *Constitucionalismo e império: A cidadania no Ultramar português* (Coimbra: Almedina, 2009).

[46] Jerónimo, *Livros Brancos, Almas Negras*, pp. 64 ff. See also Kevin Grant, *A Civilized Savagery: Britain and the New Slaveries in Africa, 1884–1926* (New York: Routledge, 2005), pp. 109–34; and William Clarence-Smith, 'Labour Conditions in the Plantations of São Tomé and Príncipe, 1875–1914', in Michael Twaddle (ed.), *The Wages of Slavery: From Chattel Slavery to Wage Labour in Africa, the Caribbean, and England* (London: Frank Cass, 1993), pp. 149–67. Henrique Galvão's *Relatório Sobre Problemas Nativos Nas Colónias Portuguesas* (a 52-page unpublished report on conditions in Angola, Mozambique and Guinea-Bissau) was presented to the National Assembly in a secret session of the *Comissão das Colónias*. A major colonial ideologue since 1927, Galvão was, like many others, a defender of compulsory labour in the past. See his *Santa Maria: My Crusade for Portugal* (Cleveland, OH: World Publishing Co., 1961), pp. 57–71, at 63; and *Huíla: Relatório de governo* (V. N. de Famalicão: Tipografia Minerva, 1929), pp. 160–1. See also Gerald Bender, *Angola under the Portuguese: The Myth and the Reality* (London: Heinemann, 1978), pp. 143–4; and Douglas Wheeler, 'The Galvão Report on Forced Labor (1947) in Historical Context and Perspective: Trouble-Shooter Who Was "Trouble"', *Portuguese Studies Review* 16:1 (2009), pp. 115–52.

W. Nevinson was a reality and once again exposed the nature of the Portuguese empire as contrary to the putative humanitarian, civilising zeal that was constantly mobilised by the Portuguese at international venues in a series of 'justificatory memoranda', and that was celebrated in the copious stream of legislative documents about native policies, especially those which aimed to regulate native labour.[47]

The *legalisation* of forced labour was the key component of Portuguese native policies; and the *ideology* of forced labour, akin to the ideology of slavery, especially as regarded the racialised outlooks that presided at its foundation, was a subject that also occupied the emergent class of *colonial scientists*, increasingly invoking rational principles of administration of the colonial world and its populations. In the geographical insights of Luciano Cordeiro and in the Ratzelian geopolitical evaluations of Silva Teles, in the anthropological schools of Oporto and Coimbra, in colleges devoted to colonial affairs – the School of Tropical Medicine (1902) and the Colonial School (1906) – in the sessions of colonial congresses (organised since 1901), and in the syllabi of university courses on colonial administration, geography, economy and law, the most important imperial themes became progressively addressed outside the political and economic milieus.

Moreover, they gradually became fundamental to the formulation of imperial and colonial policies. Colonial pragmatism became scientific.[48] As was argued in a report made by a commission of *Studies of Colonial Problems* of the Lisbon Geographical Society in 1913, only a 'practical' and 'scientific' approach to the colonial issues could sustain an 'overseas resurgence' and, at the same time, provide the 'best way to react to detractors' of the imperial venture. Obviously, the question of native labour stood out as one of the key subjects that should be submitted to scientific reasoning, especially so far as the rationalisation of its use and the legalisation of its nature were concerned.[49]

[47] Henry W. Nevinson, *A Modern Slavery* (London: Harper and Brothers, 1906). For the most important memoranda on native labour issues, used at a diplomatic level, see *O Trabalho Indígena nas Colonias Portuguesas. Memoria Justificativa* (Lisbon: Imprensa Nacional, 1906), and *Portugal e o Regime do Trabalho Indigena nas suas Colonias. Memoria Justificativa* (Lisbon: Imprensa Nacional, 1910). For an overview of the legislation focused on native labour, see J. M. Silva Cunha, *O trabalho indígena. Estudo de direito colonial* (Lisbon: Agência Geral do Ultramar, 1954).

[48] There is no study about the emergence and historical transformation of colonial science in Portugal. For an example to follow, see Emmanuelle Sibeud, *Une science impériale pour L'Afrique: La construction des savoirs africanistes en France, 1878–1930* (Paris: École des Hautes Études en Sciences Sociales, 2002). Luciano Cordeiro, 'Portugal e o movimento geográfico moderno' (1877), in *Questões coloniais*, pp. 1–29. For Francisco Silva Telles, see, for instance, 'A partilha de África', *Anais do Clube Militar Naval* (1890), pp. 302–7, 384–8, 421–4, 457–66, 547–61; or his take on 'racial' issues, 'La dégénérescence des races humaines' (1900). On the anthropological schools, see Ricardo Roque, *Antropologia e império: Fonseca Cardoso e a expedição à Índia em 1895* (Lisbon: Imprensa de Ciências Sociais, 2001); and Gonçalo Duro dos Santos, *A Escola de Antropologia de Coimbra, 1885–1950* (Lisbon: Imprensa de Ciências Sociais, 2005). For the colonial schools see João Carlos Paulo, 'Da "educação colonial portuguesa" ao ensino no Ultramar', in Bethencourt and Chaudhuri (eds), *História da expansão portuguesa*, vol. 5, pp. 304–33.

Replicating the old *corpus* of representations over the 'psychology' of the indigenous populations, over their cultural and social 'stages of development', this work of rationalisation and codification of colonial affairs, essentially political and economic in nature, was noticeably undertaken by figures such as Marnoco e Souza (the first professor of the course on Colonial Law created in the University of Coimbra in 1905), Rui Ennes Ulrich, and Sampayo e Mello, to name only the most influential figures. Indeed, and despite differences of perspective, their lectures and manuals crystallised Portuguese imperial thought and colonial projects at the beginning of the twentieth century, including the pressing question of native labour, always framed by racialised conceptions of the social and economic realities of native populations. The institutionalisation of racism was a crucial element in the institutionalisation and legal legitimation of forms of compulsory labour throughout the colonial world. In his *Política indígena* (1910), Sampayo e Mello, who would become a distinguished professor at the Colonial School from 1926 onwards, approved the traditional classification of the native populations as belonging to a backward 'social condition', and despite disagreeing with the exclusively utilitarian precepts of Oliveira Martins and with the pro-slavery stances of the influential Aspe Fleurimont – side by side with Paul Leroy-Beaulieu, Arthur Girault and Paul S. Reinsch, the great foreign influences on Portuguese imperial and colonial thinking – clearly elected labour as the fundamental colonial problem to be solved by new forms of imperial and colonial reasoning. Every one of these *colonial scientists*, well connected with international associations such as the Institut Colonial International, addressed at length the issue of native labour and formulated detailed proposals for its rationalisation and legalisation.[50]

[49] *Relatório ácerca do Estudo dos Problemas Coloniaes* (Lisbon: Sociedade de Geografia de Lisboa, 1913), pp. 3, 5–8.

[50] For a general appraisal of 'psychological' definitions of natives in Western culture at large, see Gustav Jahoda, *Images of Savages: Ancient Roots of Modern Prejudice in Western Culture* (New York: Routledge, 1998), esp. pp. 63–74 and 129–63. José Ferreira Marnoco e Souza, *Administração colonial. Prelecções feitas ao curso do 4.° anno juridico do anno de 1905–1906* (Coimbra: Tipografia França Amado, 1905); Ruy Ennes Ulrich, *Ciência e administração colonial* (Coimbra: Imprensa da Universidade, 1908), and *Política colonial. Lições feitas ao curso do 4.° anno juridico no anno de 1908–1909* (Coimbra: Imprensa da Universidade, 1909); and Lopo Vaz de Sampayo e Mello, *Política indígena* (Porto: Magalhães e Moniz Editores, 1910). For Lucien Aspe-Fleurimont, see his 'La colonisation française', *Revue Internationale de Sociologie*, tom. X, pp. 614 ff., and *La colonisation française avec des observations spéciales sur l'Afrique Occidentale* (Paris: V. Giard and E. Brière, 1902). For Leroy Beaulieu, *De la colonisation chez les peuples modernes* (1874; Paris: Guillaumin et Cie, 1882), esp. pp. 574–638. For Arthur Girault, 'La main d'oeuvre aux colonies', *Revue d'économie politique* 10 (1896), p. 147 ff, and *Principes de colonisation et de législation coloniale* (1895; Paris: Librairie de la Société du Recueil J.-B. Sirey, 1907). For Paul S. Reinsch, 'The Negro Race and European Civilization', *American Journal of Sociology* 11:2 (1905), pp. 145–67, and *Colonial Administration* (1905; London: Macmillan Co., 1912), esp. pp. 358–91. For the Institute's contribution to the native labour question, see *Le règime et l'organisation du travail des indigènes dans les colonies tropicales* (Bruxelles: Etablissements Généraux d'Imprimerie, 1929).

One of the most important efforts to create a model for action, especially important in a context of continued accusations over the nature and *modus operandi* of the Portuguese colonial administration and economic interests (such as the *slave cocoa affair*), was provided by Augusto Freire de Andrade, another key colonial expert, who was also governor of Mozambique (1906–10). Refuting the accusations made by William Cadbury throughout the process that led to a boycott of São Tomé cacao, and rebutting the strong criticism made by John H. Harris in his *Portuguese Slavery: British Dilemma* (1913), Freire de Andrade produced a typology of methods that could enable the colonial administrations to overcome the 'difficulties to make the natives work' (significantly, the title of a chapter of his book, *Relatório feito pelo Director-Geral das colónias acêrca do livro Portuguese Slavery escrito pelo Sr. John H. Harris*). Closely related to the contributions of Marnoco e Souza and Sampayo e Mello, Freire de Andrade considered the putative native resistance to organised forms of labour a major obstacle to civilisation, reinforcing known socio-cultural and psychological representations of the *indígena*, considered to be dominated by laziness and condemned to vagrancy. A series of legal mechanisms should impose an effective and efficient set of 'direct or indirect' mechanisms, models and programmes of socialisation via labour, at all times justified by the civilisational rhetoric defined in the nineteenth century and perfected under new circumstances. Labour was a mechanism of civilisation, and civilisation was an obligation, which was inevitable, given the stage of social evolution of colonial populations. This circular logic was a constant in Portuguese imperial and colonial thought, and was evidently adequate to the perceived political and economic necessities and requirements of the *new imperialism*. It was also extremely useful to counterbalance external criticism from the vigilantes of the empire.[51]

The acknowledgement of the 'difficulties to make the natives work' entailed new models of recruitment, organisation and regulation of the *trabalho indígena*. It was fundamental to 'force the native to work for his own sake and for the sake of civilisation, using humane, fair and legal processes', that is, to break down his 'natural inclination' to idleness and unproductive vagrancy. Again devaluing the role of religion or of education, even the purely technical or agricultural one, Freire de Andrade evoked a declaration of Joseph Chamberlain in the House of Commons, in May 1898, in which he considered that the necessary inducement of the natives to work would never be attained by preaching, and should rest on different means, of 'stimulus and pressure'. The same quotation had been used by Sampayo e Mello years earlier to justify the use of forced labour in the Portuguese colonies.

[51] Augusto Freire de Andrade, *A questão dos serviçaes de S. Thomé. Carta de A. Freire D'Andrade* (Lisbon: Edição da Agência Colonial, Typografia do Anuário Comercial, 1913), and *Relatório feito pelo Director-Geral das colónias acêrca do livro Portuguese Slavery escrito pelo Sr. John H. Harris* (Lisbon: Imprensa Nacional, 1913), esp. pp. 4–24. See also his *Relatórios sobre Moçambique*, 6 vols (Lourenço Marques: Imprensa Nacional, 1909–10).

A comprehensive catalogue of direct and indirect techniques and methods to make the natives work, against idleness towards civilisation, had to be devised. Among direct means, there were two solutions: the re-establishment of slavery and the imposition of forced labour. Among indirect means, there were several possibilities: taxes upon natives; laws against vagrancy; the development of native 'necessities'; contracted labour; and professional education. The reintroduction of slavery was seriously evaluated. As Freire de Andrade stated, the Portuguese, 'being opportunistic' in what regarded the nature of the colonial situation (for instance, the spread of 'domestic slavery'), should consider the possibility of associating the reintroduction of slavery with the goals of civilisation. The proclaimed native resistance to work, the pivotal instrument of the civilising mission, was thus crucial. In the end, defence of the system of forced labour prevailed, due essentially to recognition of the 'spirit of the age', the pondering of the economic consequences of the process, and also the calculated effects that it could have on the *social equilibrium* of colonial societies. But what was important was to understand that the ultimate rationale – the guarantee of a native workforce necessary to public and private undertakings throughout the empire, via coercive and compulsory means (the *corvée* and other forms of requisition of labour) – was similarly accomplished. The indirect means were auxiliary to the direct ones.[52] The Cadbury, the Ross Report (1925) and the Galvão affairs constitute excellent examples of a pattern of continuous promotion of forms of coerced labour based on a colonial pragmatism that had strong racial overtones and was systematically justified by an imperialism of obligation and inevitability, legal and civilised.[53]

Conclusion

The rhetoric of a *civilising mission* based on a global project of societal transformation – the propagation of faith; the diffusion of the Portuguese language and

[52] Andrade, *Relatório feito pelo Director-Geral das colónias*, pp. 4–5, 11, 25, 62 ff.; Mello, *Política indígena*, pp. 239–43. See also, for details of the debates, Jerónimo, *Livros Brancos, Almas Negras*, pp. 154–63.

[53] For the Ross report, see Jerónimo, *Livros Brancos, Almas Negras*, pp. 211–49. For the concepts of imperialism of *obligation* and *inevitability*, see Andrew Porter, *European Imperialism, 1860–1914* (London: Macmillan Press, 1994), pp. 20–9. For analysis of the two main colonies, see Linda M. Heywood, 'Slavery and Forced Labor in the Changing Political Economy of Central Angola, 1850–1949', in Miers and Roberts (eds), *The End of Slavery in Africa*, pp. 415–36; Douglas Wheeler, 'The Forced Labor "System" in Angola, 1903–1947: Reassessing Origins and Persistence in the Context of Colonial Consolidation, Economic Growth and Reform Failures', in Adriana Pereira Campos (ed.), *Trabalho forçado africano: Experiências coloniais comparadas* (Porto: Editora Campo das Letras, 2006); and Jeanne Marie Penvenne, *African Workers and Colonial Racism: Mozambican Strategies and Struggles in Lourenço Marques, 1877–1962* (Portsmouth, NH, Johannesburg and London: Heinemann/Witwatersrand University Press/James Currey, 1995).

culture; the colonial education; or the spiritual and material betterment of the 'standards of existence' of African communities under imperial and colonial domination – was in reality reduced to one single civilising apparatus in the third Portuguese empire. It was reduced to decrees, codes, political and social mechanisms and institutions devoted to the legalisation of forced labour and based on enduring racialised perspectives. The laws of the empire were laws of race relations, as the case of those formulated to regulate native labour reveals, while constituting the key mechanism to civilise the colonial native populations. Civilisational nurture depended on forms of forced and compulsory labour. Only labour could make the natives enter the 'civilisation guild', an expression that was frequently used by the ideologues and advocates of empire since its declaration by António Enes.[54] Only labour could seriously oppose the natives' putative predisposition towards idleness.

It was no coincidence that the natives' alleged predisposition towards vagrancy was constantly mentioned as a justification for their forced inclusion in the imperial commercial and labour systems. Side by side with active policies of land expropriation, the vagrancy and idleness clauses in the successive colonial labour codes were the fundamental techniques that sustained the *legalisation* of forced labour.[55] More than education or religion (or both combined), the Portuguese civilising mission rested upon the promotion of native labour, whether contracted, compulsory, forced or hard to distinguish from old slavery practices. The importance of 'redemptive labour', as the colonial expert Marnoco e Souza stated in 1905, had never 'penetrated in the rudimentary and timid brain of the savage negro' throughout history.[56]

As a consequence, to force the native to work was promoted as the major goal of the imperial and colonial endeavour. The ways in which Freire de Andrade addressed the League of Nations' efforts to suppress slavery, at its *Commission on Slavery*, could not be clearer: whatever the details and terminology, the general guiding principle of labour, forced if necessary, as the foremost civilising tool should not be questioned; the entire civilisation and development of Africa depended on it. As James Duffy demonstrated, the rhetoric of an institutionalised doctrine of a civilising mission was more a precept than a practice, more an expediency than a policy, and this reality continued until the end of the imperial venture.[57] The historical context of formation, the nature and the terms of the

[54] Enes, *Moçambique*, p. 71.

[55] Only in 1926 and 1928 did the legislative frame of native labour suppress the vagrancy clauses (but it inserted another mechanism of compulsion: the natives were obliged to work in case of 'pressing public interest', which included private agricultural enterprises); see, among others, Bender, *Angola under the Portuguese*, p. 141.

[56] Souza, *Administração colonial*, p. 557.

[57] For the debates at the League of Nations see Diogo Ramada Curto, 'Políticas coloniais e novas formas de escravatura', *Preface* to Jerónimo, *Livros Brancos, Almas Negras*, esp. pp. 23–8. For the best appraisal of the question of slavery in the League of Nations see Suzanne Miers, *Slavery in the Twentieth-Century:*

cont.

essential pieces of legislation that gave substance to the Portuguese *política indígena* until 1975 demonstrate the resilience, with variations in formulation and specification, of the racialised outlooks *legalised* in the Native Labour Code of 1899. The *Regime do Indigenato* that was formed by the combined legislation of 1926, 1929 and 1954 continued the tradition of legalisation of native forced labour (which retained many similarities with previous slave systems), and institutionalised and legitimised the production and administration of social, political and economic differentiation within the colonial societies; processes always shaped by enduring forms of practical and ideological racialisation.[58] The history of the mutual constitution of all these historical processes is the fundamental aspect of the third Portuguese empire. Unfortunately, this integrated history, including local manifestations and variations (historical and geographical), remains to be done.

The Evolution of a Global Problem (Walnut Creek, CA: Altamira Press, 2003), esp. pp. 58–173; James Duffy, *Portuguese Africa* (Cambridge, MA: Harvard University Press, 1959), pp. 289–328, at 89.

[58] The Estatuto Político, Civil e Criminal dos Indígenas das Colónias de Angola e Moçambique of 1926; the Native Labour Code in Portuguese African Colonies of 1928; the Colonial Act of 1930 (the 'Colonial Constitution'); the Organic Charter of the Portuguese Colonial Empire of 1933; and the Estatuto dos Indígenas das Províncias da Guiné, Angola and Mozambique of 1954, before its suppression in 1961, the year that saw the beginning of the colonial wars in Angola.

Part III

THE LONG VIEW

10

Marriage Traps: Colonial Interactions with Indigenous Marriage Ties in East Timor

RICARDO ROQUE

THIS CHAPTER EXPLORES A KEY THEME in the study of racism and ethnic relations in the Portuguese empire: intermarriage. In addressing this theme, it is the potential conveyed by the idea of *relations*, rather than the connotations of the category *race*, that I intend to explore.[1] I am interested here in tracing marriage as a form of relation between Portuguese men and indigenous women; but I am also – and especially – interested in tracing the varied *relationships* that the Portuguese established, in practice, with the marriage customs they encountered *in loco*. The topic of this chapter, then, is twofold: it concerns intermarriage as a colonial mode of relating to indigenous societies, and the colonial modes of relating to marriage ties as indigenous reality. The discussion of intermarriage will be expanded to include the colonisers' varied practices of establishing associations with local or indigenous marriage relations. Accordingly, the conventional notion of *inter*marriage in the colonial context – embedded in the notions of race and miscegenation, and associated with the idea of inter-racial sexual interactions – does not adequately convey the object of this chapter.

In modifying the idea of intermarriage so as to incorporate colonial interactions with indigenous marriage traditions, this chapter proposes a relational approach that expands on conventional treatments of this theme in Portuguese-speaking contexts, and perhaps elsewhere. To shift the focus from categories to relations may be a fruitful way to avoid the traps of the use of 'race' as an analytical term, a trap in which Charles Boxer's seminal work on race relations in the Portuguese

[1] An earlier version of this chapter was presented at the symposium on 'Race Relations: The Portuguese-Speaking World in Comparative Perspective', held at King's College London in December 2009. This essay is an output of the project *Colonial Mimesis in Lusophone Asia and Africa*, funded by the Foundation for Science and Technology, Portugal (PTDC/CS-ANT/101064/2008). Francisco Bethencourt, Judith Bovensiepen and Kelly Silva read an earlier version of this text and offered many generous comments and criticisms. Thanks are also due to Ângela Barreto Xavier and Frederico Rosa for comments and help with references. I have translated into English all passages originally in Portuguese.

colonial empire was caught.[2] Due to its often contested meaning and ideological burden, race remains a problematic category to be employed as a heuristic and explanatory device in historical and anthropological analysis. The term 'racial' in 'intermarriage' – either explicitly as a prefix, or tacitly as embedded construct – additionally misleads. For these reasons, the expression 'marriage relations' will here be preferred as an operational term. 'Intermarriage' confines our understanding of marriage practices in the colonial context to issues of miscegenation, hybridity, creolisation, or *métissage*, and, consequently, to the categories (*mestiço*, *mulatto*, *creole*) that express the composite products of inter-racial sexual interactions.[3] As such, the use of the conventional notion of intermarriage risks exposing in our analysis an underlying obsession of the Western colonisers – an obsession at its height in the Victorian period – with the 'purity of blood' and the social, cultural, and biological degeneration that could result from the creation of mixed or hybrid offspring caused by sexual intercourse between individuals of different races or species.[4] Consequently, in another fundamental sense, the emphasis on the race vocabulary in historical writing may lead to a reductionist view that overlooks the fact that, in many instances, race (even in the late imperialist period) did not decisively operate as an organising principle in the practical dealings of social actors. Race was certainly one of several aspects or frameworks that affected the way Europeans and indigenous people related to each other, but it was not necessarily the defining aspect. The colonial pragmatics of government, for example, as this text will observe with respect to parasitic interactions with *barlake*, were determinant in configuring colonial relationships with marriage, regardless of the colonisers' racist or non-racist feelings or ideas.

In the context of Portuguese studies, the shift proposed here acquires additional significance. In contrast with its ordinary pejorative meaning in racialist colonial

[2] Charles R. Boxer, *Race Relations in the Portuguese Colonial Empire, 1415–1825* (Oxford: Clarendon Press, 1963). See João de Pina-Cabral, 'Charles Boxer and the *Race Equivoque*' (Chapter 5, this volume).

[3] In this vein, considerable historiographical attention has been paid to 'mixed-race' categories, as the basis of hybrid cultures and creole societies in the colonies. Recent works have reinstated this imagery, calling attention to the importance of 'mixed-race' communities in the preservation of the Portuguese empire; see Malyn Newitt, *A History of the Portuguese Overseas Expansion, 1540–1668* (London: Routledge, 2005); Malyn Newitt and Philip Havik (eds), *Creole Societies in the Portuguese Colonial Empire: Proceedings of the Charles R. Boxer Centenary Conference* (Bristol: Seagull/Faoileán, 2007); Francisco Bethencourt, 'Low Cost Empire: Interaction between Portuguese and Local Societies in Asia', in Ernst van Veen and Leonard Blusse (eds), *Rivalry and Conflict: European Traders and Asian Trading Networks in the Sixteenth and Seventeenth Centuries* (Leiden: CNWS, 2005), pp. 108–30.

[4] For an overview of the themes of hybridity and race in colonial imageries, see Robert J. Young, *Colonial Desire: Hybridity in Theory, Culture and Race* (New York: Routledge, 1995); Annie Coombes and Avtar Brah (eds), *Hybridity and Its Discontents: Politics, Science, Culture* (London: Routledge, 2000). Compare with Boxer's observations about the Portuguese fixation on the concept of *purity of blood*: Charles Boxer, *The Portuguese Seaborne Empire, 1415–1825* (London: Hutchinson, 1969), ch. 11. See also Ângela Barreto Xavier, *A invenção de Goa: Poder imperial e conversões culturais nos séculos XVI e XVII* (Lisbon: ICS, 2008), ch. 7.

discourse, (inter)marriage has gained an anti-racist celebratory connotation in the study of Portuguese colonisation. From the 1950s, an allegedly unique Portuguese tendency to inter-racial marriage has been infamously used to support lusotropicalist ideological readings of the Portuguese empire. A special inclination to marry, or to simply interact sexually with, indigenous people of distinct cultural, racial and ethnic backgrounds, and consequently a tendency to produce harmonious mixed-race communities, has since been argued by advocates of the benevolence and exceptional nature of Portuguese colonisation as a demolisher of racial barriers.[5] In the 1960s, Charles Boxer's influential critique of this lusotropical imagery emphasised the persistence of colour prejudice, racism, violence and power relations.[6] The grounds of his critique have been restated and re-examined by critical historiography of the Portuguese empire.[7] Perhaps explored to a much lesser extent, however, have been the virtues (and the difficulties) entailed in Boxer's implicit suggestion that the complexity of colonial relations in the Portuguese empire cannot be reduced to essentialist readings, *lusotropical*, anti-racist, or any other. Portuguese relations with local societies and customs – including marriage – were complex, historically contingent and greatly varied. Boxer's erudite collection of miscellaneous cases of Portuguese associations (some more, some less violent or 'prejudiced') with local groups in Africa and India demonstrates such heterogeneity and contingency. Yet, Boxer does not introduce conceptual order in his kaleidoscopic and sometimes contradictory sample of episodes. In the end, he presents readers with an empiricist collection that seems basically to serve the author's academic-political purpose of denouncing racism and refusing universality and benignity to the idea of a Portuguese inclination to mix up with locals. Dominated by his otherwise very valuable critique of the biases of lusotropicalist ideologies, Boxer's overarching reading of 'race relations' in the Portuguese colonial empire is full of conceptual obscurity.

It is my purpose in this chapter to compensate for some of this conceptual obscurity. In order to follow in Boxer's wake, we need to strive for a finer conceptualising of colonial interactions, and make a few critical departures. We

[5] A number of valuable critical studies of Gilberto Freyre's *luso-tropicalismo* have been appearing; see for example Cláudia Castelo, *'O modo português de estar no mundo': O Luso-tropicalismo e a ideologia colonial portuguesa, 1933–1961* (Porto: Afrontamento, 1998).

[6] See Boxer, *Race Relations*; Boxer, *The Portuguese Seaborne Empire*, ch. 11.

[7] See Francisco Bethencourt, 'Race Relations in the Portuguese Empire', in Jay A. Levenson (ed.), *Encompassing the Globe: Portugal and the World in the Sixteenth and Seventeenth Century* (Washington, DC: Smithsonian Institution, 2007), pp. 45–53; especially with reference to Asia, M. N. Pearson, *The Portuguese in India* (Cambridge: Cambridge University Press, 1987), ch. 4; Bethencourt, 'Low Cost Empire'. An example of a recent critique of the lusotropicalist trope of intermarriage (from a statistical and quantitative perspective) is Maria Eugénia Mata, 'Interracial Marriage in the Last Portuguese Colonial Empire', *E-Journal of Portuguese History* 5:1 (2007), pp. 1–23. An overview of racial representations in the Portuguese empire is provided by Patrícia Ferraz de Matos, *As cores do império: Representações raciais do império português* (Lisbon: Imprensa de Ciências Sociais, 2006).

should, as argued above, escape the traps of 'race' in 'race relations' and of 'racial' in marriage relations; we should avoid these qualifications as working concepts in our approaches to European-indigenous interactions. In addition, it is necessary to look at these relations in their ethnographical specificity, with the help of analytical tools that allow us to overcome simplistic and homogenising definitions, and disentangle the empirical diversity of colonial interactions in the Portuguese-speaking world. My intention, then, is to concentrate on the implications of *inter-actions* and social ties, rather than on the cultural or identity claims that might have followed the history of these connections – certainly a relevant cross-cultural dimension of the 'intermarriage' trope, but one that is beyond the scope of this essay.

It might suffice to point out that these varied interactions with the Portuguese have remained central to the imagination, identity, and self-perception of social groups in Portuguese Asia. In Goa, for instance, where blood and purity of lineage were important local assets in structuring caste, status and lineage hierarchies, variations on the theme of miscegenation constituted a powerful device in identity struggles over time. They have nourished distinct or contradictory claims to 'Portuguese ancestry' (such as the purist claims of the *descendentes* to Portuguese racial purity and white genealogy), or claims to clear-cut differentiation (as in the case of the Brahmins of Goa).[8] In East Timor, Timorese claims to Portuguese genealogy, kinship, or identity could appear in association with some lineages, or even communities. Elizabeth Traube, for example, has famously observed the inclusion of the Portuguese colonisers as 'outsider-brothers' (therefore as Timorese kin) in Mambai mythic accounts.[9] In Timor, the indigenous appropriation of signs of 'Portugueseness' – including language, etiquette, Christian religion, and material objects – also mattered importantly in socio-political struggles for the constitution of status and authority, especially as regards the formation of indigenous hierarchies within the politico-jural realm of power and authority.[10]

[8] On the Goan *luso-descendentes*, see Ricardo Roque, '"Portugueses da Índia": Germano Correia e a antropologia dos luso-descendentes de Goa', in *VI Congresso Luso-Afro-Brasileiro de Ciências Sociais* (Porto: Fac. Letras Porto, 2002), pp. 339–46; Cristiana Bastos, 'Um luso-tropicalismo às avessas: Colonialismo científico, aclimação e pureza racial em Germano Correia', in M. C. Ribeiro and A. P. Ferreira (eds), *Fantasmas e fantasias imperiais no imaginário português contemporâneo* (Porto: Campo das Letras, 2003), pp. 227–53. On the Portuguese and the Goan Brahmins' claims, see Ângela Barreto Xavier and Catarina Madeira Santos, 'Nobreza per geração. Os descendentes dos Portugueses na Goa seiscentista', *Cultura – História e Teoria das Ideias* 25 (2007), pp. 89–118; Ângela Barreto Xavier, 'David contra Golias na Índia seiscentista e setecentista. Escrita identitária e colonização interna', *Ler História* 49 (2005), pp. 107–43.

[9] See Elizabeth Traube, *Cosmology and Social Life: Ritual Exchange among the Mambai of East Timor* (Chicago: University of Chicago Press, 1986); Ricardo Roque, *Headhunting and Colonialism: Anthropology and the Circulation of Human Skulls in the Portuguese Empire, 1870–1930* (New York: Palgrave Macmillan, 2010), ch. 2.

[10] See Roque, *Headhunting and Colonialism*; Ricardo Roque, 'The Colonial Command of Ceremonial Language: Etiquette and Custom-Imitation in Nineteenth-Century East Timor', in Laura Jarnagin (ed.),

cont.

New analytical concepts will here be essayed as a means to explore the different ways of relating with indigenous marriage ties, in their manifold expressions and meanings, in the colonial situation and with regard to definite historical materials. From this viewpoint, the research questions that I am interested in addressing are the following. What role did marriage relations and relationships with marriage play in the distinct projects of colonisation? What was their significance for European colonial communities, for indigenous societies, and for the effectiveness or ineffectiveness of the different enterprises of colonialism (missionary conversion, trade, administration, and so on)? What kind of connections did colonisers maintain with indigenous institutions of marriage? How did indigenous people (re)act upon these colonial connections and give them shape? Did the Portuguese tend to cohabit, sexually interact, or marry with indigenous women in accordance with either European codes of behaviour or, instead, 'the native ways'? Did colonisers allow indigenous marriage customs to develop freely; or did they impose external types of marriage institutions (for example, Catholic matrimony)? Were distinct strategies incompatible, or could they coexist in colonial practice?

Social forms of interaction with marriage ties: the case of *barlake*

This chapter explores these broader questions in the context of the Portuguese colonisation of Asia – and of East Timor, in particular – in the late imperialist period. The territories encompassed by the designation 'Portuguese Asia' have been providing historians with a rich research field for discussing marriage relations in the Portuguese-speaking world. This has occurred more often with regard to Goa and the *Estado da India* in the early modern period. In effect, in addressing the theme of 'intermarriage' one is immediately struck by a well-known narrative about the foundation of the Portuguese establishment in Asia. Following the conquest of Goa in the early sixteenth century, the success of Portugal's colonial presence has been partly attributed to Afonso de Albuquerque's policy of encouraging the marriage of the victorious Portuguese soldiers and officers – thereafter designated *casados* – with local women, who then presumably converted to Christianity. The lusotropicalist view that this moment stood for the essence of Portuguese colonialism as an enterprise of racial tolerance has recently been under criticism. Recent historiography about early modern Goa has shown the complexity and

Portuguese and Luso-Asian Legacies in Southeast Asia, 1511–2011, vol. 2, *Culture and Identity in the Luso-Asian World: Tenacities and Plasticities* (Singapore: Institute of Southeast Asian Studies, 2012), pp. 67–87. See also Janet Gunter, '*Kabita-Kaburai, de cada dia*: Indigenous Hierarchies and the Portuguese in Timor', *Portuguese Literary and Cultural Studies* 17/18 (2010), pp. 281–301.

contradictions of Albuquerque's policy of mixed marriages, including political opposition to this policy by the Portuguese king and nobility, and the 'racist' prejudices entailed therein.[11] Nevertheless, the symbolic weight of this narrative in the imagination of the Portuguese empire remains considerable, and it has perhaps prevented scholars from exploring other directions of the trope of marriage relations in different Asian settings. In fact, other, seemingly more marginal, colonies, such as Timor, as well as later moments of empire-building, have been left largely unexamined in this regard. Boxer's analysis of 'race relations', for example, did not include examples from Timor, let alone reference to *barlake*. I propose here to fill this gap, exploring colonial interactions with indigenous marriage customs in the Portuguese colony of Timor, in a specific historical context – the late decades of the nineteenth century. I will do so in relation to a specific marriage practice: the complex social institution that, in Timor, was designated as *barlake* (a term of Malay origin integrated into Tetum) or, alternatively, after the Tetum expression, *fetosaan-umane*; or even *vassau umane*, this latter Tetum term often being preferred by many colonial authors of the historical period covered by this essay.[12]

Barlake was a mode of marriage exchange based on the ritual gifting of women and the exchange of wealth between the families of the bride and the groom. This was of critical importance for the constitution of kinship ties and ritual and political alliances throughout East Timor – mainly amongst the indigenous elites. In this essay, I will articulate the colonial descriptions of *barlake* with my own reading of what social anthropologists have described as the patterns of marriage exchange relationships between lineages or 'houses'.[13] My interest here lies in the entangled

[11] See Francisco Bethencourt, 'The Political Correspondence of Alburquerque and Cortés', in Francisco Bethencourt and Florike Egmond (eds), *Correspondence and Cultural Exchange in Europe, 1400–1700* (Cambridge: Cambridge University Press, 2007), pp. 219–73; Ângela Barreto Xavier, 'Dissolver a diferença: Mestiçagem e conversão no império português', in Manuel Villaverde Cabral *et al.* (eds), *Itinerários: A investigação nos 25 anos do ICS* (Lisbon: Imprensa de Ciências Sociais, 2008), pp. 709–27. The classic treatments of the subject along these lines are to be found in Boxer, *Race Relations*; Boxer, *The Portuguese Seaborne Empire*.

[12] *Fetosaan-umane* is the Tetum term most currently adopted by contemporary social anthropologists. Yet, in referring to *barlake*, Portuguese colonial authors also used the term *vassau umane*, claiming that this was an expression of indigenous usage. Thus, eventually, both expressions – *fetosaan umane* and *vassau umane* – could be acceptable, depending on the *reino* or region, in the nineteenth-century colonial period. The Tetum expression *hafoli* (to marry) could also be used as synonymous with *barlake*. According to Luís Costa, the term *barlake* (spelt *barlaque* in most colonial sources) originates in the Malay phrase *bere laki* (meaning 'to take a man'), and initially also stood for marriage (with or without dowry): Luís Costa, *Dicionário de Tetum-Português* (Lisbon: Colibri, 2001), pp. 50, 106.

[13] East Timorese marriage institutions (including, but not exclusively, the *barlake*) were studied in ethnographic detail by structuralist-minded anthropologists in the 1960s–1970s, but with little or no concern for their connections to colonial history. See for example: James Fox (ed.), *The Flow of Life: Essays in Eastern Indonesia* (Cambridge, MA: Harvard University Press, 1980); Louis Berthe, 'Le mariage par achat et la captation des gendres dans une société semi-féodale: Les Buna' de Timor central', *L'Homme* 1:3 (1961), pp. 5–31; and Brigitte Renard-Clamagirand, *Marobo: Une société Ema de Timor*

cont.

history of Timorese marriage institutions and Portuguese colonialism, and my ethnographic elaborations on *barlake* marriage contracts thus largely depend on the virtues and limitations of colonial accounts. Accordingly, I will leave out a number of aspects that have been discussed by later social anthropologists. The world created by these marriage patterns is of great complexity and variety, and thus simplistic readings of *barlake* must be avoided. Colonial accounts (with some exceptions) tended to suggest that *barlake* was widespread and common throughout East Timor, thereby homogenising important differences and variations as regards indigenous conceptions and relations of marriage and exchange, across and within the many different ethnic and cultural groups that constituted the territory. Yet *barlake* should not be crystallised as *the* unique 'traditional' mode of marriage within East Timor. A number of other marriage forms existed. Professional ethnographers – but also some sensitive Portuguese colonial authors – have identified different names for, and types of, marriage relations and, consequently, different categories of alliances. Thus *barlake* was not a closed system, it was not historically static, and it cannot be homogeneously generalised to all Timorese classes and communities, but constituted a specific kind of marriage tie and alliance that, as I shall suggest, was dominant amongst Timorese royalty and aristocracy in the late imperial period.

I will thus deal with colonial materials that allow us to address Portuguese interactions with Timorese *barlake* at a particular historical moment. Yet, my intention is to develop a wider relational approach that aims at bringing out broader analytical concepts and connections. Relations with *barlake* in Timor involved tensional and heterogeneous social, cultural, and political arrangements. Notwithstanding their empirical variety, these ways of performing arrangements of social ties may be grouped conceptually into a limited set of social forms of interaction. My suggestion is that we can approach these different colonial relationships with marriage as modes of relating which, in the manner of Georg Simmel, we may treat as abstract social forms of interaction (and as such are of potential application to other colonial contexts and historical periods).[14] In this vein, I propose to analytically distinguish three types of colonial modes of relating to indigenous marriage ties – *predatory*, *parasitic*, and *mimetic*. These distinct forms of interaction could be dominantly, though not exclusively, associated with the activity of distinct types of colonial agents and with their particular colonising

(Paris: SELAF, 1982). But for relevant recent critical reassessments of this early literature on marriage relations in the wider context of eastern Indonesia, see for example Valerio Valeri, 'Buying Women But Not Selling Them: Gift and Commodity Exchange in Huaulu Alliance', *Man*, new series 29:1 (1994), pp. 1–26; Janet Hoskins, 'Slaves, Brides and Other "Gifts": Resistance, Marriage and Rank', *Slavery and Abolition* 25:2 (2004), pp. 90–107.

[14] Elsewhere I have also argued for the virtues of this approach. Roque, *Headhunting and Colonialism*, pp. 216–25; see Georg Simmel (Donald Levine, ed.), *On Individuality and Social Forms: Selected Writings* (Chicago: University of Chicago Press, 1971).

ethos, interests, projects, and agendas.[15] Thus, in Timor, as we shall see, depending on their condition as either missionaries, officers or settlers, the Portuguese tended to establish distinct (even opposed) relations with the Timorese *barlake*.

Predatory, parasitic, and mimetic forms of interaction can be briefly defined in abstract as follows (in the course of the chapter, I expect to illuminate them empirically). *Predatory* interactions concern destructive relations with indigenous marriage, including intrusive attempts towards their modification and replacement by Western/Christian institutions. *Parasitic* interactions, by contrast, concern interference, use and abuse of indigenous marriage relations by colonial agents. These interferences take place without basically (or only minimally) changing the pre-existing system, for they are orientated to exploit its original mechanics.[16] Parasitic relationships seek to derive some type of advantage from the indigenous institutions as they are found *in situ*, to the extent that the very subsistence of certain colonial collectives cannot be possible without their continuance. Transformation and replacement of indigenous marriage customs for European institutions is not, then, a primary objective – this is, in fact, contradictory to the nature of parasitic action. For, while predatory strategies endorse absolute moral standards and are, in logical principle, opposed to conventional inter-racial marriage, parasitic approaches disregard rigid *a priori* principles and operate on a pragmatic basis that accommodates local systems.

Mimetic relations, finally, refer here to forms of association with marriage ties established through the copying or adoption of indigenous marriage institutions. In other words, they concern what is usually seen as 'going native': the actions of marrying native women in accordance with native ways.

These are conceptual formations, and therefore require historical and empirical specification. Different combinations of these social forms may be identified in relation to different historical moments, colonial settings, or practical activities. Yet, in abstract terms, these forms of interaction might be said to have a tendency to establish different relations between them. For instance, if parasitism and predation seem to follow *opposite* paths in colonial practice, the same is probably not true about mimetic and parasitic approaches. Colonial parasitism and mimicry can more easily blur and/or occur in productive association with the activities of colonisers.[17]

[15] This perspective follows on from previous positions in anthropology and postcolonial studies which have convincingly argued for a more sensitive approach to the tensions and heterogeneities of colonialism. For example: Frederick Cooper and Ann Stoler, *Tensions of Empire: Colonial Cultures in a Bourgeois World* (Berkeley: University of California Press, 1997); Nicholas Thomas, *Colonialism's Culture: Anthropology, Travel and Government* (Princeton: Princeton University Press, 1994).

[16] This notion builds on previous elaborations on colonial parasitism. For my critical reading of Michel Serres's theory of parasitism and proposal of the notion of mutual parasitism, see Roque, *Headhunting and Colonialism*, ch. 1; also Michel Serres, *Le parasite* (Paris: Hachette, 1997).

[17] Parasitic and mimetic associations in particular can be difficult to disentangle in practice, because

cont.

In applying these notions, I will focus principally on their significance for the European colonial projects of religious conversion and political governance. However, it should be made clear, first, that these forms of interaction can appear in connection with other colonial projects;[18] and, second, that to understand these forms of interaction one needs to take indigenous agency and meanings into account. Colonial interactions with local marriage ties had an indigenous significance that, although difficult to ascertain in historical materials, needs to be considered. When adopted by Asian peoples, Christian customs (including marriage) were also means to enhance indigenous power and status, thereby interfering with locally meaningful issues of political, symbolic, and social order. They were thus not mere responses to the 'colonial' presence. The Portuguese intersections with local marriage customs could, too, be used creatively by local groups, and serve indigenous interests. For instance, the predatory and parasitic connections to marriage ties in Timor often succeeded only to the extent that the indigenous classes perceived an advantage in either embracing Christian mores, or using the Portuguese officers as mediators in their arrangements. The Timorese elite could actively seek the mediations of Portuguese officers in their marriage contracts and decide to circulate women to the Portuguese with a view to taking advantage of the latter's position within the *barlake* circuits. They could lead European outsiders to establish commitments later to be used strategically to gain access to further political, military, economic, or symbolic resources. Although this mutually parasitic aspect of these relations is not explored at length in this essay, the materials discussed herein hint at its manifestation.

My purpose is to emphasise the fissured and *tensional* relationships between predatory and parasitic interactions with marriage customs that emerged in East Timor in the 1870s to 1900s. Thus, for reasons of space and argumentation, I do not develop in detail empirical aspects associated with mimetic practices. I will argue that, in East Timor, Catholic missionaries, army officers, and governors developed contrasting approaches to Timorese traditional marriage. In the late nineteenth century, the colonial relationships with Timorese *barlake* were critically marked by a very tensional coexistence between, on the one hand, the predatory model followed by the Catholic missionaries; and, on the other hand, the parasitic model of mediation and exploitation of indigenous marriage ties, customarily practised by the officers and governors. My suggestion, finally, is that parasitic practices were particularly significant for the kind of colonial governmentality followed by the Portuguese military administrators in Timor. The parasitic practices were especially effective in the exercise of colonial government and jural

imitation or mimicry could be used as strategies by colonial parasites. Research on these connections is currently being developed by the author.

[18] The complicity between parasitism and commerce, or slavery, can be examples; see Roque, *Headhunting and Colonialism*, pp. 216–20.

administration, at the same time leading to smoother and more mutually convenient articulations with the indigenous aristocracies and their self-interest in perpetuating marriage alliances. The missionary strategy of predation met with doubtful success; mimetic appropriations of *barlake* were episodic, followed by a few Portuguese settlers, such as deportees. What I call parasitic mediation, in contrast, seems to have been a systematic and consequential approach of government agents on the spot.

The analysis takes as its main point of departure the discourse of the Portuguese Catholic missionaries on *barlake* in Timor. The first section will look at the predatory programme of the missionaries in the 1870s to 1880s. I will then explore the parasitic approach of the army officers and governors, including brief reference to mimetic interactions and their hypothetical significance for white settlers.

Predatory interactions: missionaries against *barlake*

In the mid-1870s, the Catholic Mission in Timor was reorganised with metropolitan-trained Portuguese priests filled with evangelical spirit, patriotic love, and unbending civilising will. In 1877, Father António Joaquim de Medeiros landed in Dili to take up his position as the new Superior of the Timor Catholic Mission, at the head of a team of ten priests trained at the seminary of Sernache do Bonjardim, in Portugal.[19] The situation of Christendom in Timor, as described by Father Medeiros after a visit to the country in 1875, had prompted the bishop's decision to reform the mission.[20] The 'primitive' and 'immoral' state of family and marriage ties amongst the indigenous caused special concern. A Christian family – monogamous, grounded in the institution of Catholic matrimony – was conceived of as a moral pillar of society, and a sign distinguishing civilised from savage human communities. But in Timor no signs of any such 'family' existed: 'They don't know about family ties', the Bishop of Macao wrote in 1875, 'the simplest principles of Natural and Moral Law, the social relationships that create a family amongst men: everything is ignorance, everything is misery amongst these unfortunate people.'[21]

[19] The team included also one Chinese priest from Macao. The Portuguese missionary settlement in Timor was under the control of Dominican friars in the seventeenth and eighteenth centuries. The extinction of the religious orders in Portugal in 1834 led to their removal and to the creation of an allegedly small and feeble mission led by Goanese priests, whom Medeiros and his team were to replace; compare Artur Teodoro de Matos, *Timor Português 1515–1769: Contribuição para a sua história* (Lisbon: IHIH, 1974), pp. 45–77; Manuel Teixeira, *Macau e a sua Diocese. Missões de Timor* (Macao: Tip. Missão do Padroado, 1974).

[20] See A. J. Medeiros to Bishop of Macao, 3 June 1881, Lisbon, Arquivo Histórico Ultramarino (hereafter AHU), Macau and Timor (hereafter MT), ACL_SEMU_DGU_1R_002_Box 2, 1881.

The civilising programme endorsed by the new missionaries allowed no concessions to indigenous institutions perceived as 'superstitious' or 'immoral'. 'Destruction', 'elimination', 'hunt', 'combat' were ordinary terms in the missionaries' discourse alluding to the nature of their relationship with the 'native' world. Accordingly, missionary action was orientated to actively chasing native superstitions and 'anti-Christian' institutions, razing them to the ground, and installing in their place Western and Christian models. Missionary work in Timor, in this respect, became a fervent predatory activity. This attitude prevailed, too, in relation to the indigenous forms of marriage and kinship ties – above all the *barlake*. 'The devil', Father Simões da Silva observed,

> always seeking the loss of souls, besides infusing the spirits of these poor natives with endless and varied superstitions, also sought to destroy the family at its foundation, inspiring them to show the highest indifference for the Catholic marriage, which they replace by the abominable *vassau humâni*, or *barlaque* [. . .] They are blinded by an abominable [economic] interest, and do not get tired of making business with their own flesh, with a view to getting richer and to becoming relatives.[22]

Barlake was understood as a fundamental threat to the integrity of Timorese Christendom. It was thus pejoratively described by the missionaries as a 'contract' guided mainly by devilish material interests, pre-arranged between the families of the bride and the groom; a contract in which the woman was treated as mere commodity as she was given away in exchange for considerable amounts of local valuables. Worse, *barlake* encouraged man and woman to fall into the deadly sins of 'polygamy' and 'concubinage'. These were seen as a generalised custom that gained particular visibility amongst the Timorese traditional elites and ruling lineages, the *liurais* who acted as traditional jural rulers of the socio-political units designated as *reinos* (kingdoms), and who as kings or *régulos* were simultaneously acknowledged by the colonial administration as legitimate holders of jural authority in the indigenous world. The woman with whom men first contracted *barlake* could be considered, some observers noted, as the 'legitimate' spouse, gaining relative ascendancy in the house over later wives and concubines.[23] Yet, men were not only allowed to establish *barlake* with more than one woman, they could simultaneously maintain as many concubines as they wanted in other residences, outside their house. 'Polygamy', one priest observed,

> was the law amongst the Timorese magnates. The *régulo* had many wives besides the first whom he married through *barlaque*, and who was considered the real

[21] D. Manuel Lourenço de Gouvea to Minister of the Navy and Overseas Affairs, 23 Sept. 1875, Lisbon, AHU, MT, ACL_SEMU_DGU_RM_005_Box 44, 1875.

[22] Elias Simões da Silva, 'Relatório de visita à contra-costa', *Annaes das Missões Ultramarinas* (hereafter *AMU*) 1:1 (1889), p. 117.

[23] João dos Reis Martins, 'Relatório do Padre João dos Reis Martins, respectivo à missão de Oekusse e Ambeno', *AMU* 3:3 (1891), p. 47.

> wife; one *régulo* in Timor had twenty or so, and the usual was between three and four [wives].[24]

On the assumption that commoners would imitate their leaders, the missionary strategy of cultural transformation and religious conversion was directed primarily at the Timorese royal and noble lineages. Consequently, the missionaries rapidly identified the *barlake* custom that prevailed amongst the ruling houses as the greatest obstacle to their project. 'With regards [to *barlake*], the exhortations of the missionary get lost very often', one missionary regretted in 1887. 'This is the greatest obstacle that we come across everywhere, the one I have fought most insistently, and which has brought me most disillusionment and fewest results.'[25] Instructions issued by the Mission Superior emphasised the need to celebrate baptisms and Catholic marriages first of all among members of the Timorese ruling classes. In 1879, two separate male and female schools were established in Lahane (near Dili) to teach the 'children or relatives of the *régulos*'. 'A very special purpose of these two colleges', Father Medeiros revealed, 'is to give both sexes equal education, afterwards *promoting among them the Catholic matrimony* and thereby the family unity in the districts. The peoples model their actions on the actions of their chiefs and, therefore, they tend to follow their examples.'[26]

Demonised by the Portuguese priests as the greatest obstacle to the expansion of Christendom, the *barlakes* of the Timorese ruling houses were selected as principal objects of predatory action. However, what the missionaries saw as a highly immoral and anti-social custom was a core East Timorese institution, a critical device for the construction and preservation of the political and social ascendancy of the Timorese royal and noble lineages.

The ruling houses and the indigenous significance of *barlake*

The transfer of women and the exchange of presents between wife-giving and wife-taking houses (from the same or from different *sukus* and kingdoms),[27] including the collective ceremonies that followed marriage, were of great importance in holding together the social and symbolic order within colonial East Timor. They had special significance for holding together the status, power and authority of the

[24] Manuel Alves da Silva, 'Relatório do Reverendo Padre Alves, Missionário de Timor, 1 de Maio de 1887', *AMU* 1:1 (1889), p. 110.

[25] Elias Simões da Silva, 'Relatório. 1 Maio 1887', *AMU* 2:2 (1890), p. 117.

[26] António Joaquim de Medeiros, 'Missões de Timor. 27 Junho 1887', *AMU* 2:2 (1890), p. 105 (my emphasis).

[27] *Sukus* and *reinos* were the indigenous collective units treated by the Portuguese as the main administrative units of jural administration in the indigenous world. In this historical period, colonial administration described the *reinos* as usually composed of a number of different *sukus* in the Tetum-based societies. It should be pointed out, however, that *suku* was a Tetum term and Tetum form of social organisation, and thus not homogeneously present across the country.

Figure 10.1. '*Noivos Timorenses*' (Timorese bride and groom), *c.* 1900. A Timorese couple are depicted in European costume, in a setting that includes fundamental items of the indigenous material culture of marriage exchange (the Timorese *tais*, fabrics). The picture possibly tentatively articulated the success of the missionaries' strategies of conversion as regards the embracing of Catholic marriage by the Timorese (from Carlos Leitão Bandeira's photograph album).

Source: Leitão Bandeira's family archives. Courtesy of António Bandeira.

Timorese ruling houses who took part in jural administration. The *barlake* represented one of the local forms of exogamous marriage involving the gifting of women along with the ritual exchange of reciprocally important presents, carrying precise symbolic and gendered value, and expressing significant wealth. This circulation of women and object gifts from 'wife-giving' houses (designated as *umane*) to 'wife-taking' houses (ordinarily designated as *fetosaan*, or, according to colonial authors, also as *vassau*) created between the houses a powerful and in theory unbreakable bond of ritual and political mutual obligations – the *fetosaan umane*, or *vassau umane*, alliance. Preference should go to marriage with former allies, as a means to preserving social standing. Coming generations of family members were thus obliged to care for an inherited network of kinship alliances through the celebration of further *barlakes* between members of the same lineages, following exchange circuits of wife-giver/wife-taker, previously established by the house ancestors. Marriage contracts were the cement of this network. Father Alves da Silva – a sensitive missionary observer – explained in 1887:

> In Timor there is a word [*barlake*] that originates in the Malay [language], and which expresses the alliance and the ties that connect the *suku* and the kingdom through kinship, turning them into true friends and relatives, so as to help each other on every critical occasion and circumstance of life. This tie or alliance is motivated by the woman who in her person and duties changes residence from one *suku* or tribute to another *suku* or tribute, or from one kingdom to another kingdom.[28]

Timorese social order depended on the continuity of the bonds generated by *fetosaan umane*. This was of special significance for the ruling houses of the *régulos* and *principais*, whose higher rank and status particularly depended on the formation and reproduction of *fetosaan umane* relations with formerly allied ruling houses, or with other new houses of equal or higher standing, from different *sukus* and kingdoms. In fact, as various colonial accounts seem to suggest – and although other ways of establishing alliances through exogamous marriage existed in East Timor – royalty and aristocracy eventually sought social and symbolic distinction from commoners by celebrating *barlakes*, in which significant amounts of wealth were put into circulation and ostentatious ceremonies were performed. Indeed, true *barlakes*, according to colonial observers, were the marriages involving either the so-called *régulos*, or their relatives. In 1884, Major José dos Santos Vaquinhas explained that *barlake* was used to refer to marriage contracts between *régulos*; in contrast, he remarked: 'Between the men of the people there is another species of *barlaque*, which they call marriage, because it stipulates what they have to satisfy.'[29]

[28] Silva, 'Relatório do Reverendo Padre Alves', p. 109.

[29] J. S. Vaquinhas, 'Timor. Usos – Superstições de guerra', *Boletim da Sociedade de Geografia de Lisboa* 4 (1884), p. 484. Afonso de Castro in 1867 had distinguished two types of Timorese marriage – *barlake* and *cabin* – in which similar alliances were forged but the practice of which was specific to different social strata: 'the *cabin* is accurately the marriage between poor people, the feasts are poorer; frequently

cont.

'*Bassau umâne. Fetò sauumanè. Fet oan. Nai-hun*', Father Laranjeira explained in the 1900s, 'These are the names given to the marriage contracts of the *régulos* or of the *principais*.'[30] *Barlakes* were by definition the 'royal marriage'; while other, lesser or poorer types of marriage contracts prevailed only among the commoners, and could bear different indigenous designations.[31]

In the light of the crucial significance of *barlake* in the Timorese communities, it is no wonder that the attempts to annihilate *barlake* most often met with resistance or led to relative failure – especially when, as a rule, the first targets of evangelical predation were the marriage customs of the ruling houses. Moreover, in most instances, *barlake* did not involve a rejection of Christian matrimony, as the Timorese aristocracy did not perceive it as incompatible with the adoption of Christian rites. Virtually every time a *régulo* agreed to celebrate Catholic marriage, the juxtaposition or accumulation of Christian matrimony *with* former or future *barlake* marriage ties was the rule amongst the nobility. *Barlake* was an indigenous practice that even conversion to the Christian religion was unable to eradicate. For it was practised both by those Timorese who rejected Christianisation and were classified as 'pagans' *as well as* by those self-declared Timorese Christians who showed deference to the missionaries and to the Church: 'So solid is polygamy established amidst this people,' the Mission Superior noted, 'that it is not rare to see the same Christians legally united to many women, according to the customs of the country.'[32]

However, for the Portuguese Catholic missionaries, the problem with *barlake* in Timor was not just a matter of indigenous resilience. The difficulties confronted by the Mission in its wars against *barlake* did not include 'indigenous' agents alone. They also concerned the active participation of the Portuguese colonial officers in the indigenous marriage relations. Having in mind the tensions with the predatory programme, let us now look at the parasitic approach of the Portuguese officers to *barlake* and the problems of government that it was aimed at resolving.

Parasitic interferences: *barlake* in government praxis

In 1887, D. António Joaquim de Medeiros – former Superior of the Timor Mission and then Bishop of Macao – described the principal troubles faced by the Portuguese

in fact there are no feasts at all'; Afonso de Castro, 'Résumé historique de l'établissement Portugais à Timor, des us et coutumes de ses habitants', *Tijdschrift voor Indische Taal-, Land- en Volkenkunde* 11 (1862), p. 483.

[30] Father Laranjeira, quoted in Alberto Osório de Castro, *Flores de Coral*, in his *Obra Poética* (António Osório, ed.) (Lisbon: INCM, 2004), vol. 1, p. 494.

[31] Bento da França, *Macao e os seus habitantes. Relações com Timor* (Lisboa: Imprensa Nacional, 1897), p. 234.

[32] A. J. Medeiros to Bishop of Macao, 30 Oct. 1881, Lisbon, AHU, MT, ACL_SEMU_DGU_1R_002_Box 2, 1881.

missionaries in Timor. In his view, a main reason for the Mission's frequent failure in the substitution of Catholic marriage for *barlake* was the complicity of the Portuguese colonial authorities in the indigenous marriage customs, namely whenever aristocratic and ruling classes were involved. This complicity meant more than indifference or non-intervention in indigenous affairs; it meant an *active engagement* of these authorities – all of whom were military officers – with the continuity of *barlake*. The bishop then explained:

> In Timor there circulates as a commonplace the idea that the authorities are forced to respect the manners and customs of the natives, and therefore they have nothing to do with the pagan marriages between Christians. If they would simply do this, it would be not too bad, because the missionaries would rectify in practice such an absurd error; however, cases have occurred that demonstrate with clear evidence the very intolerable abuses of some hinterland authorities who fight against Catholic matrimony between Christian natives.[33]

It was thus not simply the case that many *régulos* were unwilling to abandon the practices of *barlake* and polygamy. The Portuguese army officers who served as representatives of the colonial government in the wild interior – 'military commandants' heading districts that comprised several kingdoms – protected and instigated the Timorese marriage customs, in obedience to the local traditional laws. Because it promoted 'polygamy amongst Christians', this was to be denounced as a crime, a violation both of the Catholic religion and of Portuguese law.[34] Unless the Portuguese colonial authorities were willing to change this unacceptable behaviour and stop 'interfering with acts that belong to religion and the missionaries', all efforts at the progress of Christianity and civilisation in Timor would be condemned to failure.[35] In support of his statements, D. António reported an episode that offered evidence of the colonial officers' characteristic manners of intervening directly in Timorese *barlakes* and overtly *against* the Mission efforts – or sometimes even against the will of some *régulos*:

> One missionary in Timor, the current Bishop of Cochim [João Gomes Ferreira], was sent by me on a mission to visit the interior districts. There, he joined through matrimony the current *régulo* of Vemasse, D. Domingos da Costa, and a woman, *principal* [noble] of the kingdom, by whom the *régulo* already had some children. The zealous missionary went on afterwards to other kingdoms, happy to have given another effective boost to missionary works in Vemasse, which consisted of getting the *régulo* of that place legitimately married, whose example began to be followed by the *principais* who surrounded the chief. But soon afterwards he was told, to his astonishment and pain, that the commandant of Vemasse had arranged a new marriage between that *régulo* and the widow of the former regent of Vessaçú, in order to meet, so the [Portuguese] authority of the Tore garrison claimed, the *estilos* [consuetudinary

[33] Medeiros, 'Missões de Timor', p. 105.
[34] Medeiros, 'Missões de Timor', p. 105.
[35] Medeiros, 'Missões de Timor', p. 105.

> law] of the kingdom. The *régulo*, although poorly educated, initially opposed this authority, but then he gave in to the insidious observations he had received [. . .] Unfortunately, in Timor, cases like this occur, and others even more hideous and revolting.[36]

The missionary suggests that the officers in charge of the districts could interfere significantly with the Timorese marriage relations as *mediators* who actually enabled (or sometimes impeded) the arrangement of *barlakes* between specific aristocratic houses. He further suggests that this colonial way of relating to *barlake* was common in Timor; indeed, it appeared to the missionaries as the dominant mode of relating to *barlake* followed by the Portuguese colonial authorities. The officers' pernicious complicity in the customs of *barlake* was a constant theme of missionary discourse, including the idea that this complicity was 'officially recognised' and 'considered licit' by the colonial state, and by the governor himself.[37] In the late 1870s, the missionaries' and the officers' distinct modes of relating to *barlake* fed on highly tensional relationships within the Portuguese colonial community, as well as between the Portuguese and the representatives of Timorese ruling houses.

The strain between the missionaries, the military authorities and some Timorese lineages concerning the disparate colonial approaches to *barlakes* between *régulos* was to become one chief reason behind the violent political and military conflicts associated with the 'war of Laleia', which lasted in Timor from 1878 to 1881.[38] The animosity that then grew between the imperial agents resonated in Macao and Lisbon. In 1881, the head of the Timor Mission (António de Medeiros) accused the military of 'spreading doctrines contrary' to the Catholic religion, blocking missionary endeavours, and exercising authoritarian control over the celebration of baptisms and Christian marriages.[39] The animosity between the missionaries and officers – including even the governor – was so strong that the Mission Superior even considered terminating the Mission. The missionaries, wrote the same priest in conclusion,

> cannot baptise or marry even one *régulo* without, for this reason, suffering threats from the military and *even from the Governor*; because of all this they [the missionaries] beg Your Excellency to order their withdrawal from Timor and their return to Portugal. As for myself I beg the same, and my wish is to accompany them and go away.[40]

[36] Medeiros, 'Missões de Timor', p. 105.
[37] Medeiros, 'Missões de Timor', pp. 106–8; João Gomes Ferreira, 'Relatório, March 1884', *AMU* 1 (1889), p. 76.
[38] On the Laleia war, see Roque, *Headhunting and Colonialism*, ch. 7.
[39] António Joaquim de Medeiros to Bishop of Macao, 30 Oct. 1881, Lisbon, AHU, MT, ACL_SEMU_DGU_1R_002_Cx 2. 1881.
[40] António Joaquim de Medeiros to Bishop of Macao, 30 Oct. 1881 (my emphasis).

This sense of outrage revealed the coexistence in Timor of contradictory colonial relationships with indigenous marriage ties. By the 1870s to 1880s, they had come into dramatic collision. The intensity of the collision is also revealing of the centrality of *barlake* in the pragmatic orientation of government followed by the Portuguese military and governors in this specific historical context. The missionary project indeed contrasted with the parasitic form of interaction endorsed by officers and governors; that is, a form of relating that, through fine mediations and interferences, aimed at productively taking advantage of the indigenous marriage relations as they stood, without significantly modifying them – and in this manner strengthening colonial authority whilst, simultaneously, stimulating the continuance of the indigenous institutions.

The colonial politics of Timorese marriage alliances

The parasitic approach to *barlake* was fundamental to the colonial form of ceremonial government and to the Portuguese way of participating in the wider indigenous patterns of social affiliation.[41] As noted above, the kinship ties created through *barlake* implied a set of reciprocal obligations, including mutual support in case of war. These 'obligations' were perceived as dangerous liaisons for the ruling ambitions of the Portuguese. Over the centuries the Timorese elites had always made convenient use of their marriage alliances to fight the Europeans, including the Dili government. In the nineteenth century, because the *régulos* allied with the Portuguese could be relatives of *régulos* at war with the government, they would feel obliged to fulfil their *barlake* duties against the Portuguese enemy *whilst also* aiding the colonial government, according to the obligations of colonial vassalage. This caused great distress and uncertainty as to the outcome of battles, in situations of warfare. '[T]he *régulos* cannot be truly trusted,' explained captain Garcia in 1870, 'even those who consider themselves vassals, because all of them are connected, some by *barlaques* (marriages) and others by blood-oath, and when they give 200 men to the government, they give an equal or higher number of men to the enemy.'[42]

It comes as no surprise, then, that over time *barlakes* turned into matters of dramatic diplomatic and military significance for the Portuguese. Knowledge of Timorese alliances and the state of *barlake* connections throughout the country was an important device of colonial rule, especially in wartime. Accordingly, the

[41] I elaborate on the praxiology of Portuguese ceremonial government in Roque, *Headhunting and Colonialism*, ch. 2. On colonial rule and the kingdoms of Timor, see also Ricardo Roque, 'Os portugueses e os *reinos* de Timor no século XIX/The Portuguese and the Kingdoms of Timor during the Nineteenth Century', *Oriente* 20 (2011), pp. 91–111.

[42] António Joaquim Garcia to Governor of Macao and Timor, 9 Oct. 1870, Macau, Macau Historical Archives, AC, P-64.

governors took pains to gather intelligence on the state of existent and projected *barlakes* between ruling houses in order to be able either to *counter* the alliances created or actually to *take advantage of* the commitments and kinship ties that they generated between specific Timorese houses.[43] Attempts could also be made at manipulating the marriage contracts of the Timorese, inducing some marriages to take place. Positioned in between the Timorese exchange circuits of women, the officers could exert their influence so that certain convenient marriages between specific ruling houses were performed. In this light, the mediation of *barlakes* by the military as denounced by the Catholic missionaries in the 1870s to 1880s represented a strategy of colonial rule grounded in the exploitation of kinship ties. Rather than destroying the *barlake* circuits, the Portuguese officers wormed their way into the Timorese kinship networks and marriage ties, with a view to parasitically interfering, subtly and conveniently, with their functioning. Accordingly, the army officers offering resistance to the intrusions of the missionaries in the kingdoms might have been fighting to avoid the spoiling of their marriage manoeuvres, and struggling to maintain their own mode of colonial influence and authority within the marriage games of *barlake* – where they, too, were dynamic players.

Mimetic arrangements

Parasitism was a principal way of relating to the indigenous mores, especially by the officers and governors. At least for the period covered by this chapter, there is little evidence suggesting that the official representatives of the colonial government – Portuguese governors and army officers – sought overtly or systematically to take part in Timorese marriage contracts by joining with the indigenous royalty or nobility by means of *barlake*. However, on occasions this might have occurred. First, sexual interactions between officers, governors, or even missionaries, and Timorese women could happen with more frequency. Secondly, *barlake* and its polygamous elements might have been imitated by the Portuguese administrators within the colonial community. And, finally, there is evidence that, in some cases, Portuguese unofficial agents (usually deportees and former soldiers) established themselves through *barlake* in the indigenous communities as traders, planters, or mere residents. These variations in involvement with women point to the presence in Timor of yet another form of colonial interaction with indigenous marriage customs: a mimetic mode of relating that implied the actual bodily and practical adoption of Timorese customs, rather than just the mediation and exploitation of indigenous marriage circuits. As regards *barlake,* the Portuguese, too, could go native.

[43] See Celestino da Silva, *Instruções para os comandantes militares* (Macau, 1896), p. 8.

Local varieties of 'marriage ties' and Portuguese-Timorese traffic of women could occur. Sexual interactions between some governors and Timorese women also became a matter of colonial as well as indigenous lore in East Timor.[44] Governor Celestino da Silva, for instance, came to gain the reputation of allegedly maintaining sexual affairs with Timorese women (the 'daughters, wives or relatives of *régulos*') in order to obtain intelligence about the conspiracies of his indigenous enemies, or the misbehaviour of his subordinate colonial officers.[45] The sexual involvement of the military with indigenous women – often with the complicity of some Timorese nobles and *principais* – was observed by Father Medeiros in 1881. Medeiros denounced the rape, in Viqueque, of two young girls by the military commandant and a Timorese noble; he further accused this military officer of 'giving orders to [Timorese] family chiefs to present him with their daughters, or to the native authorities to lead to the garrison the virgin young girl they had seen in the church and who pleased him'.[46] The missionary suggested, moreover, that at Manatuto, the local missionary was chased by the army officer because he had reprehended a father who had given his daughter away to the commandant.[47]

Given the mutual hostility between missionaries and military commandants in the late nineteenth and early twentieth centuries, it comes as no surprise that this involvement was reported as improper and orgiastic – an abusive and violent appropriation of indigenous women, and an intolerable violation of the moral principles that should have guided the action of the Portuguese representatives. The accusation was that officers took advantage of their standing as colonial authorities to 'force' lineage leaders to give up their daughters for sexual intercourse. The violence this might have represented to indigenous women should not be discounted. But it is possible that some Timorese houses willingly gifted their young women to the army officers (and governors) in the expectation of a Portuguese counter-gift. This, moreover, was a situation to which the missionaries, too, might not have been immune. Some priests were possibly also involved in the transfer of women, and/or gave themselves up to sexual desire. For instance, comparable accusations of 'immoral' sexual involvement of certain priests with women

[44] In the 1970s, from indigenous recollections of colonial history, the anthropologist Sheppard Forman took note of piquant accounts about the sexual involvement of former Portuguese governors with Timorese princesses amongst the Makassai. See Sheppard Forman, 'East Timor: Exchange and Political Hierarchy at the Time of the European Discoveries', in Karl L. Hutterer (ed.), *Economic Exchange and Social Interaction in Southeast Asia: Perspectives from Prehistory, History, and Ethnography* (Ann Arbor: CSSAS/University of Michigan, 1977), pp. 97–111, see p. 109, n. 8.

[45] In the colonial literature, this romanticised version of Celestino da Silva's life appeared particularly in the works of Teófilo Duarte, also a governor of Timor in the 1920s; see Teófilo Duarte, *Timor (Antecâmara do Inferno?!)* (Famalicão: Tip. Minerva, 1930), pp. 73–4; Teófilo Duarte, *O Rei de Timor* (Lisbon: A. M. Pereira, 1931).

[46] A. J. de Medeiros to Bishop of Macao, 30 Oct. 1881, Lisbon, AHU, MT, ACL_SEMU_DGU_1R_002_Box 2. 1881.

[47] A. J. de Medeiros to Bishop of Macao, 30 Oct. 1881.

affiliated with the Timorese ruling houses were voiced by Governor Celestino da Silva in the 1890s to 1900s. According to Teófilo Duarte, this governor then denounced to the Mission Superior in Dili and to the Bishop of Macao a number of 'scandalous' cases involving the priests. He accused the missionaries of Vemasse and Funar of having 'seduced' young girls and of maintaining sexual affairs with the daughters or wives of the local *régulos*.[48] This kind of participation of the Portuguese in the indigenous circulation of women might have been more or less violent, and might, or might not, have respected the rules of *barlake* exchanges. But in some instances it probably generated mutual obligations and affiliations between specific Portuguese agents and specific Timorese houses. For the Timorese, too, could try to parasitically (ab)use the position of the army officers (or the missionaries), for their own benefit, getting the Portuguese to fall into their marriage traps.

However successful in either copying or appropriating the circulation of women, it is nonetheless likely that true *barlakes* were not usually performed with passing officers and governors, even if other varieties of 'marriage' or concubinage arrangements were made. The position of Portuguese outsiders as executives of jural government seems not to have been conducive to *barlakes*. In contrast, if Portuguese strangers appeared to be unrelated to the colonial administration, *barlakes* were more likely to occur. In this period, army officers and governors were often sent to Timor from Lisbon or Macao on commission for fairly short periods of time. To establish *barlake* would perhaps represent a commitment to community membership that was not mutually convenient. The formation of *fetosaan umane* alliances between European outsiders and Timorese insiders took place more often when foreigners actually settled in the local communities. In 1878, for instance, a Portuguese under the name of Manoel Joaquim was established in Lacló through *barlake* with the queen of this kingdom; his local influence was to be instrumental to Portuguese interests in the Laleia war of 1878–81.[49] A later source of the early 1940s lists virtually all the Portuguese deportees – in contrast with the government officers and officials – as being married to Timorese women, with whom they had children.[50]

The significance of these settlers' practice requires further investigation. Yet it can be hypothesised that the celebration of *barlake* between the Portuguese and the Timorese was most commonly associated with the few white settlers – deportees, former soldiers, traders – who occasionally established themselves in

[48] Celestino da Silva to Bishop of Macao [unknown date], cited in Duarte, *Timor*, pp. 77–8. These accusations, published by the former governor Teófilo Duarte in the 1930s, caused the immediate indignation and reaction of the missionaries. See Pe. Abílio José Fernandes, *Esboço histórico e do estado actual das missões de Timor . . .* (Macau: Tip. Mercantil, 1931).

[49] Manuel Salvador dos Remédios to Governor of Timor, [x] 1881, Lisbon, AHU, MT, ACL_SEMU_DGU_1R_002_Box 2.

[50] Cf. [Portuguese evacuees from Timor], Canberra, National Archives of Australia, A373.

the interior districts. There, the Portuguese would marry Timorese women according to *barlake* rules, thereafter turning into active local members of the communities. It needs to be noted, however, that this situation was not exclusively (and perhaps not predominantly) associated with Portuguese agents. Trade in Timor was dominated by the long-established Chinese community. Many Chinese traders in the interior had settled in the Timorese communities through *barlake*. In the 1890s, for example, to the despair of the Portuguese rulers, the Chinese traders and their mixed offspring (Chinese-Timorese *mestiços*) exerted a determinant influence upon the political and commercial affairs of the Maubara and Fatumean kingdoms – a consequence of *barlakes* celebrated between the Chinese and the local lineages over the years. The kinship ties and alliances thus forged by the Chinese in these kingdoms were a problem for the Portuguese during the wars of Maubara in 1893 and Cová-Fatumean in 1895–6.

Conclusion

The example of Goa has nourished the traditional imagery of marriage relations (in its strict sense of Luso-Asian mixed marriages, interbreeding, or sexual relationships) as a central feature of the historical identity of the Portuguese empire. By drawing on materials from another Asian colonial region – East Timor in the late imperial period – this chapter has been expanding our understanding of this trope in the Portuguese colonial empire. Here, a threefold shift has been proposed in our approaches to 'intermarriage'. First, I have argued for an approach that privileges relations, rather than bounded categories, as the unit of analysis. This, I believe, avoids some of the traps set by the racialist and colonial connotations of the conventional intermarriage notion. Relations, in fact, have been the starting-point from which to reconsider the theme of marriage in the context of the Portuguese expansion. As such, (inter)marriage has been seen here as *more* than simply European-indigenous sexual interactions and 'mixed-race marriages'; it has, instead, been conceptualised as a sociological field in which multiple ways of relating to marriage institutions, to women, and to sexual relationships have to be considered. Thus, secondly, this chapter has developed a historical ethnography of colonial interactions which expanded the analysis to encompass the colonisers' varied ways of interacting with the local circulation of women and with indigenous marriage customs. This perspective takes note of the heterogeneity and historical contingency of marriage in colonial relationships. But it also enables us to introduce some conceptual clarity into this diversity of modes of relating. Thirdly, then, I have argued for a conceptualising of colonial relations with marriage according to three forms of interaction: predatory, parasitic, and mimetic. The missionaries', governors', officers', and settlers' different modes of connecting to the Timorese social institution of *barlake* have provided the empirical grounds for the exploration of these notions – especially, in the case of this chapter, as regards the tensional coexistence of the parasitic and predatory varieties, in colonial government and missionary action respectively.

The case of East Timor usefully suggests that we can grasp the turbulence and heterogeneity of marriage relations in the Portuguese empire as a manifestation of the colonial nature of local interactions. On many occasions, colonial agents aimed for the elimination of indigenous marriage systems and their replacement by Christian marriage. However, on other occasions, colonial agents followed rather distinct strategies, sometimes historically simultaneous. This was clearly the case in East Timor in the late decades of the nineteenth century. Marriage contracts between Timorese *régulos* were a political affair of the highest importance to the indigenous societies. They were likewise critical to Portuguese efforts to exercise colonial power and authority, in politico-jural affairs as well as in spiritual-religious dealings. But, unlike the missionaries who, typically, sought to behave as destructive predators of indigenous customs, the governors and officers sought to exploit the local systems as they found them, with minimal changes. As parasites placed in between the circuits of marriage exchanges, the Portuguese tried to mediate indigenous marriage in ways that were to their own benefit. Parasitic relationships were dominant among colonial officers and governors in Timor, who followed parasitism as governmental praxis in their dealings with the indigenous authorities. The use and abusive exploitation of indigenous marriage relations (including the *barlake*), through which women were exchanged and socio-political bonds created, then became a critical aspect of jural government. It may be, for example, that parasitic and mimetic forms of interaction gained greater expression in other nineteenth-century situations where the presence of Europeans as settlers, traders, or administrators continued to be relatively feeble, such as in many hinterland colonial settings in Africa; and that the predatory strategy may have found wider resonance in the civilising strategies then also heartily adopted by many Western colonial missionaries in Asia, Africa, or the Pacific. It is not my intention to examine these comparative hypotheses here, as they call for further research. Yet in embracing this task, the exploration of these concepts in other settings and periods will require the ethnography of colonialism to look not just outside Timor, but also beyond the historical and geographical boundaries of the 'Portuguese colonial empire'.

11

The Free Afro-Brazilians in a Slave Society

HERBERT S. KLEIN

IN THE HISTORIOGRAPHY OF SLAVERY, little attention has been paid to freed slaves and their descendants before final emancipation. Much of the work comparing the major slave regimes in the New World has underestimated their importance, largely because they were only a minor part of the English-speaking slave societies. But in fact they were a crucial group within most Latin American slave regimes and their integration into free society before the end of the slave period presaged the eventual integration of all Afro-Americans into their respective societies. There is little question that Portuguese America produced the largest free coloured class under slavery in the Americas. Long before the abolition of slavery or even the abolition of the slave trade, free coloureds outnumbered slaves in Brazil. By the time of the first census of 1872 they numbered 4.2 million persons, compared to 3.5 million whites and 1.5 million slaves. Free coloureds could be found in every province of the empire and in every municipality, from the most urban to the most rural. In many northeastern provinces they formed the majority of the population and even in new frontier areas such as São Paulo they resided everywhere. The aim of this chapter will be to describe how this class of persons was created, how they evolved, their social and economic characteristics, and the role which they played within Brazilian slave society.

The growth of a free coloured class from the beginning was not unique to Portuguese America. A free coloured class developed in every American slave society virtually from the first days of colonisation. But all such populations grew slowly in the sixteenth and seventeenth centuries and all faced some type of restriction on their freedom. All societies began with a fairly active level of manumission, as masters piously freed their slaves – or fathers their children – or faithful service was rewarded with freedom. In all societies, from early on there developed self-purchase arrangements for slaves. The major differences among American slave societies began to appear only after the first several generations, when the Iberians not only continued to accept and support the traditional patterns

Proceedings of the British Academy **179**, *227–254*.

of manumission, but also actively accepted and codified the route of self-purchase. This further encouraged the growing number of freedmen, who in turn gave their support to increasing levels of manumission.

The non-Iberian societies began in this manner, but, as the number of free coloureds began to grow, so too did the fear of those freedmen. Though they had the same restrictive legislation as the Iberian societies, the whites of the Anglo-Saxon colonies, for example, became less and less trustful that these prohibitions would guard their privileges. They therefore began to attack the whole manumission process, making it more costly to both the master and the slave. Just as the Iberian regimes were legitimising self-purchase, the North Americans were restricting it, if not prohibiting it altogether.[1] This fundamental opposition to manumission effectively began to curtail the numbers of freedmen in these societies, which remained relatively limited until the final years of slavery.

In Brazil, the free coloured population grew at an ever more rapid rate over the course of the eighteenth and nineteenth centuries. In eighteenth-century population registers of various kinds, the free coloureds were already an important element of the population everywhere, but they did not exceed the slaves. The increasing arrival of African slaves in the nineteenth century did not slow the pace of growth of the free coloureds. Rather, their numbers grew even more rapidly in the first half of the century, so that by 1850, when the slave trade finally ended, the free coloureds had already passed the total number of slaves. This dominance of the free coloureds in the total coloured population increased with every passing year. By the time of the first national census in 1872, they accounted for 43 per cent of the 10 million Brazilians.[2] All this was more than a decade before the abolition of slavery and just before the first partial emancipation laws.

There was, of course, some variation in the regional patterns. In the northeast, the free coloureds were already dominant in the first part of the nineteenth century. Pernambuco in 1839 had 127,000 free coloureds to half that number of slaves, and this ratio appeared to be typical of Bahia and Maranhão as well.[3] In contrast, the province of Rio de Janeiro was unique in still having more slaves than free coloureds in 1872, whereas both Minas Gerais and São Paulo had many more freedmen than slaves by this time. São Paulo had only attained this balance quite recently, but

[1] Equally restrictions on the geographic and economic mobility of the ex-slaves were universal from the eighteenth century onward. See John Codman Hurd, *The Law of Freedom and Bondage in the United States*, 2 vols (Boston: Little Brown & Co, 1858–62), vol. 2; Ira Berlin, *Slaves without Masters: The Free Negro in the Antebellum South* (New York: W. W. Norton, 1974); and Franklin Johnson, *The Development of State Legislation Concerning the Free Negro* (New York, 1916).

[2] Diretoria Geral de Estatística, 'Imperio do Brazil: Quadro geral da população escravo . . .', in *Recenseamento Geral do Brazil de 1872* (n.p., n.d.).

[3] Joaquim Norberto de Souza e Silva, *Investigações sobre os recenseamentos da população geral do império . . .* (1870; São Paulo: IPE-USP, 1986), pp. 56–7.

Minas Gerais probably had more freedmen by the 1820s.[4] Though the free coloureds were probably most numerous in the northeast, they were well represented everywhere. Thus the two largest states where they resided in 1872 were Bahia with 830,000, and Minas Gerais – also the largest slave state – with 806,000 freedmen.

In contrast to the United States, the rigid class structure, and the elaborate caste and colour distinctions, may have provided Brazilian whites with a relative sense of security against free coloured competition, which made them more willing to accept the manumission process. This acquiescence of elite whites led to both public and private commitment to manumission from the beginning to the end of slavery. Recent studies have shown that manumission was a complex process that involved both voluntary and involuntary manumission on the part of the master class, and both passive and active intervention on the part of the slaves themselves.

Although it was sometimes argued that the masters were primarily freeing their old and infirm slaves,[5] this was not the case. Every study done of large samples of manumission records for Brazil (and Brazil is the best studied country on this theme) shows that the manumitted were primarily young, native-born and women, with the subset of self-purchased slaves being more male and more African than those voluntarily freed without remuneration.

The data available for most regions of Brazil show a high incidence of children and young adults and a correspondingly low incidence of the elderly. Although there is wide variation by region and period, overall children under 15 represented between one-fifth and two-fifths of all persons manumitted.[6] Moreover, the few studies which give detailed information on the ages of the manumitted slaves show that mean ages were quite low. In Porto Alegre in Rio Grande do Sul in the period 1858–72, the average age of the manumitted slaves was 21 years,[7] and in the port city of Santos between 1811 and 1877, it was 20 years for men and 22 years for women.[8] That these average ages well reflect the reality of the manumitted group can be seen in the fact that most studies find relatively few elderly persons manumitted in Brazil. In fact, the majority of slaves manumitted were in the working-age categories. In some twelve *municipio* (or county) samples currently available

[4] As early as the census of 1829–30, free coloureds represented 43 per cent of the total coloured population and 21 per cent of the total population, estimated at 128,000 persons; Herbert S. Klein and Francisco Vidal Luna, 'Free Colored in a Slave Society: São Paulo and Minas Gerais in the Early Nineteenth Century', *Hispanic American Historical Review* 80:4 (2000), pp. 913–41, table 1.

[5] See Jacob Gorender, *O escravismo colonial*, 4th edn (São Paulo: Editora Ática, 1985), p. 355.

[6] For the sources on the age of the emancipated slaves, see Herbert S. Klein and Francisco Vidal Luna, *Slavery in Brazil* (Cambridge: Cambridge University Press, 2009), pp. 255–6, n. 12.

[7] Moreira, *Faces da liberdade, máscaras do cativeiro*, tabela anexo 6, p. 91.

[8] Ian William Olivo Read, 'Unequally Bound: The Conditions of Slave Life and Treatment in Santos County, Brazil, 1822–1888', unpublished PhD thesis, Stanford University, 2006, table 8.5.

for which age of manumitted slaves is given, the average proportion of elderly, usually defined as 40 years of age or more, was 13 per cent of the total persons being freed.[9]

In the twenty-one *municipio* samples where the sex of the manumitted slaves is given, the sex ratio averaged just 74 males per 100 females.[10] The dominance of women in the letters of freedom (*cartas de alforria*) records is also reflected in census reports of the free coloured population. Thus in the Minas Gerais parish of São José d'El Rey in 1795, the sex ratio among the 1,411 resident *alforrias* (or manumitted slaves) was 84 males per 100 females,[11] and in the census of 1872, the sex ratio for the 355,745 freed persons of colour for the province of São Paulo was 79 males per 100 women. This compared to a sex ratio of 125 men per 100 women among the slaves, and 99 men per 100 women among the whites. Given that this class was relatively new due to the late participation of São Paulo in importing African slaves, this was probably the norm for most of the eighteenth-century provinces. In the empire as a whole, with a population of free coloureds of longer duration and size than in São Paulo, the sex ratio among the 4.2 million free coloureds was more balanced, but even so the free coloureds had the lowest ratio of men of any group in the society, being 102 males per 100 females, compared to 109 males per 100 females for the whites and 115 males per 100 females for the slaves.[12]

As could be expected, native-born slaves were more likely to obtain their freedom than African-born slaves, though there was great variation by time and region. Of course, many of these figures would be influenced by the origin of the resident slave population, which differed considerably across Brazil, and by the time period selected, with Africans progressively declining over time. It would seem that on average about a third of the slaves being freed were of African origin.[13] Moreover, not only would the importance of Africans differ by time and place, but there would be major differences by the type of manumissions.

There were three major types of manumission: voluntary without condition (*grátis*), in which the slave was immediately freed and had no obligations whatsoever to his master; voluntary with conditions (which might involve continued service, special work, or even formal acts of respect and piety), which was given the general term of *oneroso*; and self-purchase, which also often appears in the

[9] See Herbert S. Klein and Francisco Vidal Luna, *Slavery in Brazil* (Cambridge: Cambridge University Press, 2010), p. 257, table 9.2.

[10] Klein and Luna, *Slavery in Brazil*, p. 258, table 9.3.

[11] Douglas Cole Libby and Clotilde Andrade Paiva, 'Alforrias e forros em uma freguesia mineira: São José d'El Rey em 1795', *Revista Brasileira de Estudos de População* 17:1–2 (2000), pp. 17–46, tabela 1, p. 22. It has been suggested that if children were removed from the *forro* class the female domination would be even greater; personal communication of Stuart B. Schwartz, 4 Nov. 2008.

[12] Diretoria Geral de Estatística, 'Imperio do Brazil'.

[13] Klein and Luna, *Slavery in Brazil*, p. 260, table 9.4.

documents as *oneroso*, since the slave had to pay for his or her freedom. This has led some historians to assume that the last two types were identical.[14] But in fact, self-purchase was the only one of the three types of manumission initiated by the slave, and once agreed upon by the master and the courts, involved a fundamental change in status. *Coartado* slaves, as they were called, paid off their purchase price in instalments that could vary from months to years, they could hold funds on their own, make contracts, and could not be sold without their permission. All legal documents recognised their special status and carefully named any slaves who held this status.

While there was a surprising consistency in terms of age and sex among the manumitted slaves across all regions and in both urban and rural settings, the same was not the case with types of manumission which varied quite considerably.[15] In some regions, self-purchase was dominant, in others, it was voluntary and unconditional manumissions, and in others, it was voluntary and conditional. In general, voluntary manumissions dominated in most regions, and in only a few did self-purchase represent a majority.

There was some variation by origin of slaves. Creoles, or native-born slaves, tended to be more important in voluntary manumissions of whatever type, and African-born slaves tended to be more important among the self-purchasing slaves.[16] Due to their higher representation among self-purchased slaves,[17] African-born slaves were represented among the free coloured in roughly the same ratio as in the total slave population. Thus in a large sample of 16,729 manumissions in Rio, Africans made up 47 per cent of all slaves emancipated, but they were 50 per cent of the self-purchasers and made up only 36 per cent of the conditional and voluntary grants.[18] Finally, one of the few studies giving the occupations

[14] Lima, 'Trajetórias de crioulos', tabelas 10 and 11.

[15] The studies which include information on manumission include the works cited above in note 6.

[16] A recent study of manumissions in São João del Rei for 1774–1848 found that 58 per cent of the creoles freed (881) were given their freedom unconditionally, compared to only 43 per cent of the Africans (431) who were unconditionally freed: Sheila de Castro Faria, 'Aspectos demográficos da alforria no Rio de Janeiro e em São João Del Rey entre 1700 e 1850', *XVI Encontro Nacional de Estudos Populacionais, ABEP, de 2008*, quadro 4, p. 10. Note that this and all other papers cited in this chapter that were given at the annual meetings of the Associação Brasileira de Estudos Populacionais (ABEP) will be found at www.abep.org.br/usuario/GerenciaNavegacao.php?caderno_id=649&nivel=1

[17] One major survey of manumissions concluded that Africans were over-represented among the self-purchase and under-represented among the voluntary manumissions: see Eduardo França Paiva, *Escravidão e universo cultural na colônia, Minas Gerais, 1716–1789* (Belo Horizonte: Universidade Federal de Minas Gerais, 2001), p. 181. A smaller sample from the Bahian towns of Salvador da Bahia and Santo Amaro in the nineteenth century also found this same pattern of Africans' over-representation among the self-purchased *libertos*, with *pardos* being over-represented among the unconditional *alforrias*: see Arnold Kessler, 'Bahian Manumission Practices in the Early Nineteenth Century', paper delivered at the American Historical Association, 29 Dec. 1973, table IX, pp. 19–20.

[18] Manolo Florentino, 'Sobre minas, crioulos e a liberdade costumeira no Rio de Janeiro, 1789–1871', in Manolo Florentino (ed.), *Tráfico, cativeiro e liberdade Rio de Janeiro, séculos XVII–XIX* (Rio de

cont.

of *alforrias* shows that males being freed had a far higher ratio of skilled occupations than did the slave population in general, and that women being freed were far more likely to be in domestic service than the general female slave population.[19]

Finally it is worth noting a sub-set of contracts that historians have found among the self-purchasing slave manumissions. A minority of these sales involved purchases by third parties. In the region of São Paulo, for example, samples from the nineteenth century show that 31 per cent of 1,338 slaves manumitted were self-purchased, of whom a minority were purchased by a relative of the slave (called *pagantes na família*),[20] while in the district of Porto Alegre and its hinterland, some 44 per cent of the *cartas de alforria* registered between 1800 and 1834 involved self-purchase, of which 16 per cent involved purchases by third parties. Of the total of self-purchase contracts available from Rio de Janeiro in the mid-nineteenth century, only 22 per cent were paid for by third parties.[21] In the Minas town of Juiz de Fora between 1844 and 1888 there were some 992 manumissions, only 12 per cent of which were self-purchased. Of these purchased freedoms, 60 per cent were paid for by the slave being freed, 10 per cent by family members, and 30 per cent by third parties.[22] In the southern town of Porto Alegre, of some 3,101 slaves whose manner of liberation was known between 1858 and 1887, 45 per cent purchased their freedom, and of these self-purchases, third parties paid for 25 per cent of sales, a figure quite similar to that found in the Rio de Janeiro sample. Of these third parties, two-thirds were parents, 14 per cent were free union spouses (*amasios*), and 10 per cent were godparents.[23] It is interesting to note that when

Janeiro: Civilização Brasileira, 2005), pp. 331–66, tabela 2, p. 349. Using the Florentino dataset, which now includes 17,201 manumissions from Rio de Janeiro from 1840 to 1871, one recent study has concluded that the volume and timing of self-purchased slaves was exclusively based on the ability of slave families, and especially women, to accumulate funds, and is in no way related to external developments such as the end of the slave trade; see Carlos Eduardo Valencia Villa, 'Produzindo alforrias no Rio de Janeiro no século xix', unpublished Masters dissertation, Universidade Federal do Rio de Janeiro, 2008. Villa also shows that slaves consistently paid higher real prices for their freedom than masters paid for such slaves on the open market, and that the rising real prices paid for manumission over time (which correlated with the rise in slave prices in general) had no impact on reducing the volume of self-purchases: 'Produzindo alforrias no Rio de Janeiro', pp. 58–62.

[19] Eisenberg, 'Ficando livre: As alforrias em Campinas', tabela 7, p. 195.

[20] Enidelce Bertin, *Alforrias na São Paulo do século XIX: Liberdade e dominação* (São Paulo: Humanitas FFFCH(USP, 2004), tabelas 1, 11, 18, pp. 69, 97, 116. According to Bertin some 23 per cent of all manumissions were paid for by family members.

[21] Florentino and Góes, 'Do que Nabuco já sabia', tabela 1.

[22] Antônio Henrique Duarte Lacerda, 'Economia cafeeira, crescimento populacional, manumissões onerosas e gratuitas condicionais em Juiz de Fora na segunda metade do século XIX', *X Seminário sobre a Economia Mineira 2002*, tabelas 2 and 4, pp. 11, 16. Please note that this and all other papers cited in this chapter that were presented at the annual meetings in Diamantina, Minas Gerais, will be found at www.cedeplar.ufmg.br/seminarios/economia-mineira/sobre-a-economia-mineira.php

[23] Paulo Roberto Staudt Moreira, *Os cativos e os homens de bem: Experiências negras no espaço urbano, Porto Alegre 1858–1888* (Porto Alegre: EST Edições, 2003), pp. 187, 259, 272. In these calculations

cont.

the number self-purchased by third parties is broken down by origin, there is an important shift in importance from Africans to native-born. While 54 per cent of the Africans who were freed did it through self-purchase, this compared to only a quarter of the creole slaves who did so. But when adding in third-party purchases of freedom, creoles predominated and accounted for 92 per cent of the fifty-three third-party purchases. Thus 30 per cent of the 164 creole purchase agreements involved third parties paying the price, whereas just 3 per cent of the 124 African purchase agreements involved third parties.[24]

Studies of slavery in the classical and modern period suggest that it made economic sense for masters to give skilled slaves the incentives of income and promises of manumission to obtain their cooperation.[25] Thus masters were willing to negotiate self-purchase arrangements with slaves who were working in skilled occupations where force alone could not produce any viable economic returns. Moreover, the self-purchase process was not an uneconomic one as far as the masters were concerned. For the manumitted who paid for their own freedom or had someone buy their freedom, the price paid was usually the current market price, not the original price of purchase. The freedmen and slaves constantly fought in the courts to have the price set at what was declared a 'just price', which for them meant the original purchase price, or, if raised in slavery, the average adult slave price. At some periods of time the courts ruled in their favour, but in most cases the current evaluation was the price used. Thus masters were receiving the full funds for replacement and could re-enter the market for new slaves with the funds they received.

The self-purchase schemes often were done in instalments, with usually one-third to one-half down, and a stipulated number of years then set for complete payment. During this period of *coartação*, a *coartado* slave could not be sold to another master without his or her permission, and other restrictions applied that protected their rights. The *coartado* slave also received an official document, called a *Carta de Corte*, which legally allowed some physical mobility away from the master and the right of the *coartado* slave to make contracts in order to obtain funds for their self-purchase. The master in turn continued to receive the earnings of the *coartado* slave and paid for their maintenance until such time as the final instalment was paid. A not unusual case of this process was that of the slave tailor Gonçalo who was brought to Rio de Janeiro in the 1750s. His price as an adult was estimated at 142$500 réis, and he was allowed to purchase his freedom at 134$400 réis. The

we have assumed that if self-purchases did not list a source (*não consta*), it was the individual slave who made the purchase – thus reaching the individual self-purchase figure of 1,060.

[24] Gabriel Aladrén 'Liberdades negras nas paragens do Sul: Alforria e inserção social de libertos em Porto Alegre, 1800–1835', unpublished Masters dissertation, Universidade Federal Fluminense, 2008, tabelas 1.2 to 1.4, pp. 43, 48, 55.

[25] Stefano Fenoaltea, 'Slavery and Supervision in Comparative Perspective: A Model', *Journal of Economic History* 44:3 (1984), pp. 635–68, see p. 636.

discounted sale price was due to the shift of daily maintenance costs to the slave. He was to pay this price in daily amounts for 840 days, but he was now to pay for his own sustenance, a cost which his owner had previously borne.[26]

Aside from freeing their slaves in public acts notarised by officials, the master class in Brazil also manumitted slaves at baptism. This was the usual route for fathers recognising their bastard offspring and it required just the declaration of the parents and godparents to set a child free. Also all foundling children were declared free, no matter what their colour. An analysis of the parish registers of Parati, a sugar – and *aguardente* – producing coastal region of Rio de Janeiro in the early nineteenth century, revealed that 1 per cent of the total local births were slave children being freed. These children were not later registered with formal *cartas de alforria* (certificates of manumission), which were the usual records used for all other manumissions. These seemingly few births out of all births added 16 per cent to the total number of manumitted in the five-year period under consideration.[27] Interestingly in another recent study of the 14,949 slave births registered in the Minas town of São João del Rei between 1770 and 1850, some 318 (or 2.1 per cent) of newborn slaves were manumitted at the baptismal font,[28] and none indicated that the father was freeing his children, even though subsequent wills and testaments showed that several of these children were fathered by their masters.[29] These children were also about 55 per cent female, further strengthening the female predominance among the freed slaves.[30] Of some 2,471 slave baptisms in the *mineira* districts of Muriaé and Juiz de Fora from 1851 to 1888, 2 per cent of these births involved the freeing of the newborn slave,[31] while in the parish of Nossa Senhora de Pilar in Ouro Preto between 1801 and 1840, some 34 (or 3 per cent) of 1,236 slave children baptised were freed on birth.[32] Finally between 1753 and 1831, in the freguesia de São Salvador in the sugar plantation zone of Campos dos Goitacases, Rio de Janeiro, some 348 children were freed at the baptismal

[26] Sílvia Hunold Lara, *Campos da violência: Escravos e senhores na Capitania do Rio de Janeiro, 1750–1808* (Rio de Janeiro: Paz e Terra, 1988), pp. 252–4.

[27] Kiernan, 'Baptism and Manumission in Brazil', pp. 61–5.

[28] See Cristiano Lima da Silva, 'As alforrias nos registros de batismos da matriz de Nossa Senhora do Pilar de São João del-Rei: Uma análise demográfica (1751–1850)', *Anais do 2° seminário regional do CEO – Centro de Estudos do Oitocentos* (Juiz de Fora: Clio Edições Eletrônicas, 2005), tabela 1.

[29] Cristiano Lima da Silva, 'Senhores e pais: Reconhecimento de paternidade dos alforriados na pia batismal na Freguesia de Nossa Senhora do Pilar de São João del-Rei (1770–1850)', *Anais do I Colóquio dos LAHES (Laboratório de Historia Econômica e Social)* (Juiz de Fora: Laboratório de Historia Econômica e Social, 2005), n.p.

[30] The sex ratio for the 315 births whose sex was known was 82 males per 100 females. Silva, 'As alforrias nos registros de batismos', tabela 3.

[31] Rômulo Andrade, 'Ampliando estudos sobre famílias escravos no século XIX (crianças cativas em Minas Gerias: Legitimidade, alforria e establidade familial)', *Revista Universidade Rural, Série Ciências Humanas* 24:1–2 (2002), pp. 101–13, tabela 7, p. 107.

[32] Márcio de Sousa Soares, *A remissão do cativeiro: A dádiva da aforría e o governo dos escravos nos Campos dos Goitacases, c. 1750–1830* (Rio de Janeiro: Apicuri, 2009), p. 68, tabela II.1.

font, or 1.9 per cent of all the slaves born in the period.[33] If these ratios are typical for the rest of Brazil, it would have the effect of further reducing the age of the new entrants into the free coloured class and further encouraging positive rates of growth.

There is little question that manumission more frequently occurred in the urban than the rural setting and that skilled slaves more readily purchased their freedom than unskilled ones. Urban slaves had more opportunity to gain income than rural slaves and were more cognisant of their rights than the more isolated plantation slaves. But even in rural areas, manumission was possible and it was practised with some frequency. Even self-purchased freedom was possible for rural slaves through the funds accumulated from the sales of foodstuffs produced on their individual slave *roças*, or provisioning grounds, and there are even occasional references to rural slaves being paid for extraordinary work done on Sundays or rest days. One study has tried to calculate the chances of essentially rural slaves throughout Brazil being freed in the second half of the nineteenth century. Using data from the 1870s, an overall crude manumission rate of 6 per cent of all slaves were freed each year. It was then estimated that of a cohort of 10-year-old slave children who survived to the age of 40, some 16 per cent would be manumitted by that age, and that 26 per cent would be manumitted for those who survived to 60 years of age. This model assumed a high death rate and a constant manumission rate across all age groups.[34]

Finally, slaves could petition the courts for their freedom, usually arguing that masters had promised them their freedom and heirs were rejecting their claims, or that the processes of self-purchase were not being carried out. This voluntary act of slaves often resulted in positive results. Thus in Rio de Janeiro, the *Corte de Apelação*, the highest court in the empire, heard some 381 such cases demanding freedom in the nineteenth century. In the 351 cases in which a decision was rendered, slaves gained unconditional freedom in 158 cases, and conditional freedom (with self-purchases and work obligations for limited times) for another 28, which meant that 53 per cent of the cases decided supported the claim of liberation of the slaves.[35] It should also be noted that when slaves did win their court cases, they were usually charged for the judicial fees and costs involved.[36]

[33] Miriam Moura Lott, 'A lista nominativa de 1838, características demográficas, econômicas e sociais de Ouro Preto', *Anais do XIII Seminário sobre a Economia Mineira* (2008), quadro 1, available at http://ideas.repec.org/s/cdp/diam08.html. In the same parish in this period, there were 429 baptisms of adult slaves, which represented 26 per cent of the total of 1,665 slave baptisms.

[34] Robert W. Slenes, 'The Demography and Economics of Brazilian Slavery, 1850–1888', unpublished PhD thesis, Stanford University, 1976, pp. 489–93, and especially table 10.2, p. 491, which summarises his complex discussion.

[35] Keila Grinberg, *Liberata, a lei da ambigüidade: As ações de liberdade da Corte de Apelação do Rio de Janeiro no século XIX* (Rio de Janeiro: Relume Dumará, 1994), p. 27. The period covered seems to be 1806–88 (see gráfico 1, p. 109).

[36] Hunold Lara, *Campos da violência*, pp. 256–7.

Given the growing size of the free coloured population, the youth of those entering, and the high number of young women manumitted, then, natural growth rates of the free coloured class were quite high, as we will see in a later analysis. This means that it is often difficult to estimate the relative importance of recently manumitted slaves within the free coloured population. The few data available suggest quite wide variations by time and place. Clearly in the early colonial period, most of the free coloured class were *forros* or *libertos,* that is, persons manumitted in their own lifetimes. But over time the ratio of *forros* or *libertos* declined and the number of persons of colour born free (*livres*) increased.

In the *mineiro* town of São João del Rei in 1795, *forros* represented an extraordinarily high 57 per cent of the free coloured class, thus still reflecting the earlier colonial patterns. The sex ratio of the *pardos* and *pretos livres* (blacks and *mulattos* born free) was almost equal at 97 men per 100 women, but among the *forro* population, as expected, it was just 87 men per 100 women.[37] It is probable, given the dramatic population growth of the free coloured class in the nineteenth century, that the ratio of *forros* to total resident free coloured was much lower after 1800 than the rate found in this *mineiro* town. But that *forros* remained an important part of the free coloured population and were a major element in its growth can be seen from the estimates of annual population growth of the free coloured class in the nineteenth century.

Since the free population of colour were often the poorest free persons in their respective regions they tended to have a high mortality rate which probably differed only moderately from that of the slave population.[38] It would thus be surprising if the natural growth rate of the free coloured population was above the nineteenth-century West European norm of 1 to 1.5 per cent growth per annum.[39] The 2 per cent to over 3 per cent annual growth rates experienced by the free coloured in the various provinces in Brazil in the nineteenth century had to have been greatly influenced by the steady migration into this class of newly freed ex-slaves. An estimate for the entire empire suggests an overall imperial rate of natural growth of the free coloured class at an extraordinary 3.7 per cent per annum for the period 1817–18 to 1872.[40]

The impact of these former slaves can be seen by examining the age cohorts of the free population by colour and sex for sixteen *municípios* in Minas Gerais in

[37] Libby and Paiva, 'Alforrias e forros em uma freguesia mineira', tabelas 1 and 2, pp. 22, 24.

[38] Eduardo E. Arriaga, *New Life Tables for Latin American Populations in the Nineteenth and Twentieth Centuries* (Berkeley, 1968), table 3, pp. 29–30.

[39] Angus Maddison, *The World Economy: A Millennial Perspective* (Paris: OECD, 2001), table A-1d, p. 186. Portugal did not grow more than 1 per cent per annum until the twentieth century, and the twelve major West European countries grew by 1 per cent in 1820–70 and 1.3 per cent per annum in 1870–1913.

[40] Thomas W. Merrick and Douglas H. Graham, *Population and Economic Development in Brazil, 1800 to the Present* (Baltimore: Johns Hopkins University Press, 1979), p. 65, table VI.5.

the census years of 1831–2. It is evident that free coloureds had a steady over-representation of women compared to whites in all ages 10 years and above, and that this is reflected in the overall sex ratio of the free coloureds being 91 males per 100 females, compared to a balanced ratio of 100 males to 100 females among the whites. Assuming that the white population had relatively low immigration or emigration, it can be assumed that the free coloureds would have had this same pattern of male and female distribution were it not for a fairly steady in-migration of women who were born slaves into the free coloured class.

These age and sex biases suggest that the free coloured class was receiving a dynamic element into their midst that was more heavily female and relatively young. The reproductive rates among the free coloured population were thus consistently higher than among the slaves. Not only were the creole freedmen reproducing themselves at a positive rate of growth, but they were receiving from the slave class a steady stream of entrants who were also prone to high reproductive rates – that is, younger and fertile women – which helps to explain their unusually high annual growth rates. In Minas Gerais, which had the second largest of Brazil's free coloured population, the crude birth rate of the free coloureds in 1814 was 42 per 1,000, and the death rate was 34 per 1,000. In contrast, the white population had a crude birth rate of 37 per 1,000, and a death rate of 27 per 1,000.[41] Several other estimates support the idea that the free coloureds had intrinsically higher fertility than any other population group in their respective societies.

Because of their high fertility and the constant flow of more women than men into their ranks through manumission, the free coloureds of Brazil had the highest ratio of women, and were, on average, the youngest of the three major population groups, of whites, slaves and freedmen. In terms of marriage, family, and kinship, however, they differed little from the free society around them. In a census of the captaincy of São Paulo in 1800, for example, married persons made up 30 per cent of the whites, around 25 per cent of free coloureds, and 18 per cent among the slaves. In a census of the São Paulo plantation region of Campinas in 1829, there was little difference in the ratio of female-headed households, married-couple households, and widows with children, between whites and free coloureds;[42] and for the entire population of Brazil in the census of 1872, married whites were 30 per cent of their respective population group, 26 per cent of all free coloureds were married, and only 8 per cent of slaves were married.

But given that the free coloureds were predominantly working-class and poor, it is not surprising that they had the highest rates of female-headed households, and relatively low rates of household heads who were married compared to the

[41] Herbert S. Klein, 'Os homens livres de côr na sociedade escravista brasileria', *Dados* (Rio de Janeiro) 17 (1978), pp. 3–27, tabela 2.

[42] Data generated from the Listas Nominativas (*or mapas*) in Arquivo Público do Estado de São Paulo, Maços de População, lata 27a.

free white population. In the *minas* census of the early 1830s, female-headed households made up 19 per cent of the 37,000 or so free coloured households, compared to only 7 per cent of the 25,000 white households. Moreover, the free coloureds had much lower marriage rates, with the hierarchy of colour being correlated with these rates. Thus, *pardos* did far better than *pretos*, with the only surprise being the Africans, who ranked higher than the *pretos*. Not only were more free coloured heads of household unmarried and probably living in consensual unions, but they also had higher births outside of marriage than the whites. This in itself did not mean a greater degree of instability in family life, but indicated a level of poverty in which church weddings were too costly an item to be worth their performance. On the other hand, all free coloureds baptised their children and, unlike the slaves, usually had both a godfather and a godmother at the christening.

Although the free coloured class tended to have very high rates of marriage endogamy, they did sometimes cross lines of status and even of colour. Thus, free coloureds sometimes married slaves, and occasionally even married whites. In the Bahia district of Cachoeira in the eighteenth century, of the 100 marriages recorded to *forros* between 1765 and 1785, some twenty-four involved *forros* marrying slaves.[43] In the mining town of Vila Rica in Minas Gerais in the period 1727 to 1826, some 832 marriages were listed where at least one partner was a *forro*. Fifty of these *forros* married slaves, representing 6 per cent of these marriages. In this case, liberated males married slave women in just 3 per cent of all marriages listing male *forros*, while liberated females had a higher tendency to marry slaves; in this case 9 per cent of their marriages were to male slaves.[44] But there are instances of even higher rates, even in the eighteenth century. In the prime sugar region of Campos dos Goitacases in Rio de Janeiro in the second half of the eighteenth century, 35 per cent of some 300 *forro* marriages involved marrying a slave. Among the 3,171 *livre* marriages, however, slave partners represented only 2 per cent of marriages.[45] Although one would expect this pattern of *forros* being more willing to marry slaves than the coloured born in freedom, this was not the case for the 2,916 marriages taking place in the *paulista* town of São José dos Pinhais between 1759 and 1888 in which at least one partner was free. Only eighty involved a slave partner, but sixty-six involved *livres* and only fourteen involved *forros*. Interestingly, the tendency seems to be for slave women to marry into the two free coloured groups more often than slave men. In São José dos Pinhais, thirty-seven slave women married *livre* men compared to only twenty-nine *livre* men who

[43] Luis Nicolau Parés, 'O processo de crioulização no Recôncavo Baiano, (1750–1800)', *Afro-Ásia* 33 (2005), pp. 87–132, tabela 5.

[44] Iraci del Nero da Costa, 'Ocupação, povoamento e dinâmica populacional', in Iraci del Nero da Costa and Francisco Vidal Luna, *Minas colonial: Economia e sociedade* (São Paulo: Pioneira, 1982), tabelas 1 and 2.

[45] Sheila de Castro Faria, *A Colônia em movimento: Fortuna e família no cotidiano colonial* (Rio de Janeiro: Nova Fronteira, 1988), quadro II.9 and II.10, pp. 143, 144.

married slave women. The same balance occurred with slave women marrying *forro* men in eight out of fourteen such marriages.[46] Of the 1,501 marriages recorded in the Minas Gerais town of Barbarcena between 1721 and 1821, slaves appeared as spouses of free persons in only eleven instances.[47] Of the 184 marriages involving slaves that occurred in the two *mineiro* districts of Muriaé and Juiz de Fora in 1872, 10 per cent involved slaves marrying free persons.[48] These scattered nineteenth-century marriage data would seem to suggest that marriage between the free coloured class and the slave population was not as common an event as the experience of the eighteenth-century samples would seem to suggest. When free persons married slaves, they were often *jornaleiros* or *agregados* (day labourers or servants) and worked on the same estate as their slave spouses, and they often agreed to remain on the estate as long as they were married and their spouses were slaves.

Crossing the colour line for marriage among free persons seems to have occurred, but with even less frequency than across the legal boundaries. In the interior Minas town of Catas Altas do Mato Dentro, in the 115 marriages that took place between 1816 and 1850, the intermarriage rate was modest, with only eight marriages involving whites and free coloureds. White men tended to marry *parda* women more than white women married *pardos*.[49]

But in one area there was very close contact between the free coloureds and the slaves, and that was in the whole process of godparenthood relations or *compadrio*. Free coloured *livres* and *forros* appeared with great frequency as godfathers (*padrinhos*) and godmothers (*madrinhas*) at slave births. In a study of the town of Livramento in Paraíba in the nineteenth century, of the 447 slave births which occurred between 1814 and 1884, *livres* were *padrinhos* in 95 per cent of the slave births, and *livres* were *madrinhas* in 54 per cent of these births. Surprisingly, there were only 2 per cent of such births where a *padrinho* did not appear, but an extraordinary 43 per cent in which a *madrinha* was absent from the baptismal records.[50] This same involvement with slave births could also be discerned in the nineteenth-century *mineira* town of Senhor Bom Jesus do Rio Pardo between 1838 and 1888. Of the 715 slave births, some 76 per cent of the *padrinhos* were free

[46] Cacilda Machado, 'Casamento & desigualdade jurídica: Primeiras notas de um estudo em uma área da região paulista no período colonial', *XIII Encontro da Associação Brasileira de Estudos Populacionais, 2002*, tabela 5, p. 10.

[47] Ana Paula dos Santos Rangel, 'Nos limites da escolha: Matrimônio e família entre escravos e forros termo de Barbacena – 1781–1821', *Revista Eletrônica de História do Brasil* 8:1–2 (2006), tabela 6.

[48] Rômulo Andrade, 'Casamentos entre escravos na região cafeeira de Minas Gerais', *Revista da Universidade Federal Rural, Série Ciências Humanas* 22:2 (2000), pp. 177–97, tabela 9.

[49] Tarcísio R. Botelho, 'Estratégias matrimoniais entre a população livre de Minas Gerais: Catas Altas do Mato Dentro, 1815–1850', *XIV Encontro Nacional de Estudos Populacionais, ABEP* (2004), tabela 3, p. 6.

[50] Solange Pereira da Rocha, 'Gente negra na Paraíba oitocentista: População, família e parentesco espiritual', unpublished PhD thesis, Universidade Federal de Pernambuco, 2007, tabela 4.2.

persons, and 72 per cent of the *madrinhas*.[51] In one of the largest of such studies of godparenthood and slave births, that of the *minas* town of São João do Rei in the period 1736 to 1850, in some 13,473 births to slave mothers, 72 per cent of *padrinhos* were *livres* and 5 per cent were *forros*.[52] Of *madrinhas* in these births, 60 per cent were *livres* and 5 per cent were *forros*.[53] Equally we often find godparents purchasing the freedom of their slave godchildren, or free coloured relatives doing the same. When third parties were involved in purchases of slaves, it was often the free coloureds who provided the funds. Of the seventy-four parents and family members who purchased the freedom of slaves in eighteenth-century Bahia, 57 per cent were free persons of colour.[54]

How colour influenced the integration of ex-slaves into both the working class as well as into the society in general is still an unstudied area. In an analysis of plebeian interactions in Mexico City, for example, it is evident that there was a great confusion about colour, and that coloured persons in court cases and in various commercial transactions would be given different colour definitions each time they were referred to by witnesses or officials.[55] This may have been the pattern in Brazil as well, given the tripartite colour scheme and the traditional Brazilian overlap of class and colour definitions for marking an individual's position as *pardo* or *preto* in the society, which often resulted in a lack of agreement on the colour designation of individuals. Another area that has yet to be explored in any detail is the housing of free coloureds. It has been noted that in nineteenth-century Puerto Rico blacks and whites lived in the same buildings and often rented rooms to each other.[56] The lack of racial ghettos, and the intense and complex economic and social relationships between free persons of colour and even poor whites and slaves, has suggested to some scholars that the lower classes themselves infrequently and often indifferently used colour terminology, and defined individuals more by their residence, sex, age, legal status and occupation than by their colour. Such fluidity, of course, may not have existed in all regions and at all times, and may be more of an urban than a rural phenomenon. While colour prejudice was clearly evident at all levels of society, for the free coloured class, colour discrimination was probably inversely

[51] Jonis Freire, 'Compadrio em uma freguesia escravista: Senhor Bom Jesus do Rio Pardo (MG) (1838–1888)', *XIV Encontro Nacional de Estudos Populacionais, ABEP* (2004), tabelas 8 and 9.

[52] Silvia Maria Jardim Brügger, *Minas patriarcal, família e sociedade (São João del Rei – séculos XVIII e XIX* (São Paulo: Annablume, 2007), p. 286, and table 5.1, p. 287.

[53] Silvia Maria Jardim Brügger, 'Compadrio e escravidão: Uma análise do apadrinhamento de cativos em São João del Rei, 1730–1850', *XIV Encontro Nacional de Estudos Populacionais, ABEP* (2004), tabelas 1 and 2. The data in her tables in this essay are more complete than those in her book since they include absent and *cortado padrinhos* and *madrinhos*.

[54] Schwartz, 'The Manumission of Slaves in Colonial Brazil', table IX.

[55] See R. Douglas Cope, *The Limits of Racial Domination: Plebeian Society in Colonial Mexico City, 1660–1720* (Madison: University of Wisconsin Press, 1994).

[56] Jay Kinsbruner, *Not of Pure Blood: The Free People of Color and Racial Prejudice in Nineteenth-Century Puerto Rico* (Durham, NC: Duke University Press, 1996).

related to mobility, with increasing racial hostility shown as they moved up the social ladder, but with racial prejudice having less impact in dealings with their poorer compatriots.

It is also clear that while voluntary associations, so important in colonial and early imperial Brazil, were prejudiced in their makeup, dividing the population by colour and status, they nevertheless performed an important function in creating a well developed sense of community among some of the free coloureds. This development of a community identity was of course aided by a continuing prejudice against blacks and *mulattos* on the part of whites, legal impediments which constantly reminded them of their partial rights, and by a government and Church which often insisted that they organise themselves strictly into colour-based voluntary associations.

The most important of such political associations was the militia. Neither Spain nor Portugal maintained a standing royal army in America. All defence was essentially in the hands of a small group of professional officers and a mass of civilian militiamen. Military service was required of all able-bodied freedmen, and the more numerous the free coloureds, the greater the number of militia companies of blacks and *mulattos* organised in their communities. It is probably no exaggeration to say that the vast majority of able-bodied freedmen did service at some time in their lives in the colonial military establishment. In times of peace, or in isolated regions with few settlers, such militias rarely intruded on the daily life of the population. They were mostly ceremonial and had few obligations. But often these military units required enormous amounts of time and costly effort. For the free coloureds in the ranks, there were only modest rewards for militia duty. But for their black and *mulatto* officers, there was access to military courts of law and other privileges. Thus, the wealthiest artisans were usually quite anxious to obtain these ranks, because they could often be protected even in their commercial activities by appeal to military justice. But there was always conflict with whites over these officer positions, and this continued after the replacement of the coloured militias by the non-colour-based national guard in the mid-nineteenth century. Though the free coloureds served in the police, the army and the navy, they rarely ascended to the ranks of the officer class.[57]

Typical was the militia experience of Francisco Joaquim de Santana, resident of the western *paulista* sugar district of Itu, who in 1820 asked to be exempted from militia service. He had already served in the auxiliary forces (called *Ordenanças*) and in his petition he noted that he had obtained his freedom only recently and was still in debt for his self-purchase. He worked as a master tailor and sustained his family with his work, and finally he thought his age too advanced to serve in

[57] Luiz Carlos Soares, *O 'Povo de Cam' na capital do Brasil: A escravidão urbana no Rio de Janeiro do século XIX* (Rio de Janeiro: Faperj/7 Letras, 2007), p. 301.

the militia.[58] In another set of cases, the head of the regional militia, the Capitão Mor of the vila of Porto Feliz, wrote to the governor of São Paulo asking for exemptions from military service for three other *forros*. One was Antonio Pedroso de Campos, a soldier of the militia regiment of Sorocaba, quartered in the vila of Porto Feliz. Pedroso was a skilled carpenter and a master of *engenhos* and was needed to repair most of the local *engenho* machines. Mor also asked for exemptions for two musicians, Inácio Máximo de Faria and Jesuíno Francisco de Paula, who were also tailors and who worked in a local shop. All had served long and well, with the musicians being particularly active in all church and festive occasions, all were still burdened with debts from obtaining their freedom, and all were needed for both familial and general societal obligations.[59] Apparently Jesuíno Francisco de Paula, the tailor musician, had been in the militia since 1815 and was still listed in the local town census (*listas nominativas*) as '*miliciano soldado*' and tailor in 1824, when he was 30 years old.[60]

The Church for its part also encouraged the free coloureds to form their own separate *irmandades*, especially as many of the white *irmandades* refused to admit them into co-equal membership. These fraternal and religious societies then became a major source for maintaining Afro-American religious cults, acted as mutual-aid societies, and cemented class and colour friendships through ritual ceremonial activity. Though created for racist reasons and supported by a white society bent on maintaining a social order that was more separate than equal, these voluntary religious organisations became pillars of the community, and gave the free coloureds a sense of worth and identity, which, like their militia units, provided them with crucial support in a racist society. Although these brotherhoods were important for slaves, they appear to have been far more important for the free persons of colour. Black brotherhoods existed in every city and town that had a substantial population of blacks and *mulattos*. Since most such confraternities did admit slaves, these organisations tended to maintain important ties between the two classes and counterbalanced the antagonism that inevitably developed between those who had a firm stake in the status quo and those who inherently opposed it. But everywhere it was the free persons who dominated. They elected the majority of officials and, given the membership fees, it was they who were the primary support for the brotherhoods.

Such brotherhoods collected their own funds, and acted as burial societies, as well as serving as organisations for sponsoring parades and festivals.[61] They were

[58] Roberto Guedes Ferreira, 'Trabalho, família, aliança e mobilidade social: Estratégias de forros e seus descendentes – Vila de Porto Feliz, São Paulo, século XIX', *V Congresso Brasileiro de História Econômica, 2003*, p. 4, available at http://ideas.repec.org/s/abp/he2003.html

[59] Ferreira, 'Trabalho, família, aliança e mobilidade social', p. 5.

[60] Ferreira, 'Trabalho, família, aliança e mobilidade social', p. 6.

[61] On the role of the black brotherhoods in burials of members, see João José Reis, *Death Is a Festival: Funeral Rites and Rebellion in Nineteenth-Century Brazil* (Chapel Hill: University of North Carolina Press, 2003), pp. 127–8.

even a source of funds for slaves purchasing their freedom.[62] While most research on these brotherhoods has been concentrated on the colonial period, there is no question that they remained a vital part of the social life of freedmen throughout the nineteenth century. Put under provincial control with the creation of the independent nation, and still required to use local priests, they continued to carry out festivals, name annual 'Congo Kings', and elect *mesas administrativas* (or governing boards), despite constant periods of government repression alternating with periods of liberalisation.[63] Finally, after 1850 the official government repression eased considerably, as they became an accepted part of the social scene, but membership seems to have declined as the Church itself became less receptive to these organisations in the late nineteenth century, at least in Salvador.[64] But at the same time in other regions such confraternities remained quite powerful. In 1871, for example, the local coloured *irmandades* of Nossa Senhora do Rosário of Porto Alegre organised and sponsored the first annual '*festa dos Navegantes*', which became a major local event tied to carnival in the following years. This popular festival remains celebrated today and has even outlasted the Rosário *irmandade*.[65]

[62] Patricia A. Mulvey, 'Slave Confraternities in Brazil: Their Role in Colonial Society', *The Americas* 39:1 (1982), pp. 39–68, see p. 51. The role of these organisations in holding slave funds is also noted by Roger Bastide, *The African Religions of Brazil: Towards a Sociology of the Interpenetration of Civilizations* (Baltimore: Johns Hopkins University Press, 1978), p. 116. Among the few studies giving membership and status for these brotherhoods was one for the Rosario of Alta Cruz brotherhood in Vila Rica of Minas Gerais in the late eighteenth century, which found that of the 4,097 members of the confraternity, 42 per cent were slaves, and the overall sex ratio was 65 men per 100 women; Célia Maia Borges, *Escravos e libertos nas irmandades do Rosário: Devoção e solidariedade em Minas Gerais – séculos XVIII e XIX* (Juiz de Fora: Universidade Federal de Juiz de Fora, 2005), p. 231, tabela 8. The *irmandade* Nossa Senhora do Rosário in Mariana (MG) between 1750 and 1819 had 850 *pretos* enrolled whose status was known. Of this number, slaves represented 62 per cent of the total membership. Interestingly, the sex ratio among the slaves was heavily biased toward males, on the order of two and a half men for every woman. Among the *forros*, the ratio was 63 males per 100 females, and the overall ratio was 166 males per 100 females; Fernanda Aparecida Domingos Pinheiro, 'Confradesdo Rosário: Sociabilidade e identidade étnica em Mariana – Minas Gerais (1745–1820)', unpublished Masters dissertation, Universidade Federal Fluminense, 2006, tabelas II and III.

[63] For an earlier period, a detailed analysis of these executive committees and their budgets is found in Antonia Aparecida Quintão, *Lá vem o meu parente, as irmandades de pretos e pardos no Rio de Janeiro em Pernambuco (século XVIII)* (São Paulo: Annablume, 2002).

[64] Elizabeth W. Kiddy, *Blacks of the Rosary: Memory and History in Minas Gerais, Brazil* (University Park: Pennsylvania State University Press, 2005), ch. 5. A study of the wills of free coloured persons in Bahia in the nineteenth century found that these persons belonged to some thirty-eight different coloured-based confraternities in Salvador. There appears to be a progressive decline over time, with almost everyone belonging to an *irmandade* in the early part of the century, and only a fifth or fewer registering membership in the post-1850 period. This was due to the attack on these types of organisations by the more romanised clergy who gained control over the Church in the second half of the century and who progressively attacked the social aspects of these organisations and tried to replace them with more orthodox-based organisations; Maria Inês Côrtes de Oliveira, *O liberto: O seu mundo e os outros, Salvador, 1790–1890* (São Paulo: Corrupio, 1988), pp. 84–5.

[65] Liane Susan Müller, 'O negro e suas devoções: A importância da Irmandade do Rosário e da Festa dos Navegantes para a formação de uma classe média negra porto-alegrense', *II Encontro 'Escravidão*

cont.

It has been claimed that most free coloured persons in Brazil belonged to such brotherhoods. One of the few estimates of membership in relation to total population is taken from a study of burials that occurred in one parish in the town of Vila Rica, Minas Gerais, in the eighteenth and early nineteenth centuries. Of the roughly 2,200 free persons (white and coloured) who were buried, just under half were members of a brotherhood (some 48 per cent for both sexes were buried by brotherhoods), but some 35 per cent of the 2,000 *forros* who died were also given their burial by a brotherhood to which they belonged. By contrast, only 6 per cent of the 8,200 slave burials were of *irmandade* members. Interestingly, slave and *forro* women were more likely to be members than their male counterparts, but the opposite occurred for *livres*. If anything, these rates for free coloureds were probably under-representative for the rest of Brazil, since of the two local parishes in Vila Rica, Pilar and Antônio Dias, this was the poorer one.[66] Thus of 155 wills of *libertos* registered in the city of Salvador de Bahia between 1790 and 1830, 80 per cent of the persons making such wills were members of an *irmandade*, with women having a somewhat higher participation rate than men (82 per cent to 78 per cent).[67] In another sample, of 416 wills from the parish of Sé in Rio de Janeiro in the period 1776–97, some three-quarters of the *testators* were *irmandade* members.[68] But these were clearly the wealthiest free coloureds, since the landless and those without income did not leave wills, and it is difficult to know how many of the poorest belonged. The burial data do suggest that class influenced *forro* participation rates.

Such confraternities also saw to the spiritual and physical needs of their members. In most of Spanish and Portuguese America, these brotherhoods were relatively poor and usually shared an altar in a church. But in a minority of cases, they accumulated large amounts of real estate and had their own separate chapels and cemeteries. Some of these brotherhoods were open to all persons, no matter what their colour or status. In other cases they were divided by both. There were also cases in which brotherhoods were based on unique ethnic origins.[69] In

e Liberdade no Brasil Meridional' (2005). Note that this and all other papers presented at this meeting will be found at www.labhstc.ufsc.br/programa.htm

[66] Among the free coloureds, 39 per cent of the women and 29 per cent of the men were buried by the *irmandade*. The data on these burials is presented in Iraci del Nero da Costa, *Vila Rica: População (1719–1826)* (São Paulo: IPE-USP, 1979), p. 235, tabela 6.

[67] Oliveira, *O liberto*, pp. 83–4. It should be noted that this ratio progressively declined over the course of the nineteenth century as all groups reduced their participation in such organisations.

[68] There were thirty-eight *forros* in this sample and among them were twenty-seven persons born in Africa, with those from the Costa da Mina predominating; Larissa Viana, *O idioma da mestiçagem: As irmandades de pardos na América Portuguesa* (Campinas: UNICAMP, 2007), quadros 1, 2, 3, pp. 184, 186, 187.

[69] On the varying patterns of inclusion or exclusion by the numerous brotherhoods, see A. J. R. Russell-Wood, 'Black and Mulatto Brotherhoods in Colonial Brazil: A Study in Collective Behavior', *Hispanic American Historical Review* 54:4 (1974), pp. 567–602, see pp. 579–81.

eighteenth-century Salvador, one brotherhood was based on African birth in Dahomey, and another was exclusively maintained for Nago-Yoruba peoples of the Ketu nation. Angolans were the first in Bahia to create the brotherhood of Nossa Senhora do Rosário. Eventually, many of these confraternities allowed native-born and others to enter their ranks, but usually reserved offices to the original African founding groups.[70]

Similar African-based *irmandades* were established in eighteenth- and nineteenth-century Rio de Janeiro.[71] Black brotherhoods devoted to Nossa Senhora do Rosário were established in all the towns in Minas Gerais, and it was the single largest such confraternal organisation in the province, accounting for some 62 out of 322 *irmandades* scattered throughout colonial Minas.[72] In Bahia in the colonial period, 86 out of 165 confraternities were black organisations dedicated to the Rosary.[73] There was even a brotherhood of the 'Good Death' which was founded in 1820 by sexagenarian black women who were Catholic and also initiated in *Candomble*.[74] The city of Salvador at this time had some sixteen primarily black or *mulatto* brotherhoods, with many more mixed ones open to them. The great period of development of these brotherhoods was the eighteenth and early nineteenth centuries, but many survived into the twentieth century as expressions of the black community. After abolition, some of these traditional *irmandades* became the source of the Afro-Brazilian cults that came to prominence in the contemporary period.[75]

These brotherhoods were not of course completely autonomous. Though allowed to elect their own officers, there were the usual provisos that slaves or illiterates could not become secretaries, presidents, or treasurers. The Church also went out of its way to control these associations. All were given white clergymen as guardians, and sometimes the government even forced these associations to accept whites to control their finances. In most cases they played a subordinate role in

[70] In the wills of well-to-do African born-free persons in Bahia in the nineteenth century, it is evident that the ethnic purity of individual confraternities had broken down and Africans of quite different origin were found in the same *irmandades*, even those that accepted only *mulatos*; Oliveira, *O liberto*, p. 81.

[71] João José Reis, 'Identidade e diversidade étnicas nas Irmandades negras no tempo da escravidão', *Tempo* (Rio de Janeiro) 2:3 (1996), pp. 7–33. See also Mariza de Carvalho Soares, *Devotos da cor: Identidade étnica, religiosidade e escravidão no Rio de Janeiro, século XVIII* (Rio de Janeiro: Civilização Brasileira, 2000).

[72] Caio Boschi, *Os Leigos e o Poder* (São Paulo: Atica, 1986), pp. 187–8; see also Kiddy, *Blacks of the Rosary*; Borges, *Escravos e libertos*; and Julita Scarano, *Devoção e escravidão – A Irmandade de Nossa Senhora do Rosário dos Pretos no Distrito Diamantino no século XVIII* (São Paulo: Editora Nacional, 1976).

[73] Patricia A. Mulvey, 'Black Brothers and Sisters: Membership in the Black Lay Brotherhoods of Colonial Brazil', *Luso-Brazilian Review* 17:2 (1980), pp. 253–79, p. 256.

[74] 'A Irmandade da Boa Morte é formada por senhoras sexagenárias, negras e que têm fé católica e iniciação no candomblé'; Carolina L. G. Braga, 'Tenha uma Boa Morte', *Científico* 4:2 (2004), n.p.

[75] On the rise of the Afro-Brazilian cults and their association with the *irmandades*, see Bastide, *The African Religions of Brazil*, chs 5 and 6.

local religious activity, but in some regions they became major economic and political powers. Outstanding in this respect were the *irmandades* in the city of Bahia in the eighteenth and early nineteenth centuries and those scattered throughout the major mining communities of Minas Gerais in the same period. It was these black brotherhoods as well as many white ones that funded major artistic activity of *mulattos* and blacks. This was especially the case in Minas Gerais which produced such extraordinary free coloured artists and architects as Antônio Francisco Lisboa, known as Aleijadinho, the son of a slave woman and a white Portuguese-born architect father. His sculptures and decorations of eighteenth-century churches of Minas earned him a reputation as Brazil's leading artist of the Rococo period, and, like his father, he also worked as an architect.[76] Another was the slave-born Manuel da Cunha, who was the leading portraitist of the age and also painted many walls and altars of Brazil's leading churches. He was trained in both Brazil and Portugal and had already achieved an outstanding career before his manumission. In music, the composers of Minas were almost all *mulattos*. The most outstanding was Emerico Lobo de Mesquita, who was organist to a major white brotherhood, a member of the *mulatto* brotherhood, and a composer totally current with the latest in European Baroque composition. A more prominent if less skilled composer was the Jesuit Padre José Mauricio Nunes Garcia, whose mother was a *forra* (a slave woman freed in her lifetime) and whose father was a *mestiço*, and who himself was appointed court composer when the imperial family moved to Brazil in 1808.[77] These exceptional artists of regional, and even international, stature were just the peak of a mass of free coloured musicians, writers, and artists who produced for both the popular masses and the elite.

Free coloureds were also to be found in all the other professions of Brazilian society. Sometimes they were forced to form their own separate craft corporations, but often they were members of the regular guilds. More common as apprentices and journeymen than as master craftsmen, they nevertheless could be found in every skilled occupation in these societies. Sometimes they were even masters of occupations legally denied to them. There were also entire occupations traditionally dominated by both free coloureds and slave artisans. The most important of such occupations was that of the barber surgeon, who often performed most of the major medical functions in the community.[78] That the free coloureds served an important

[76] For a recent review of his life and times, see Ana Helena Curti (ed.), *Aleijadinho e seu tempo: Fé, engenho e arte* (Rio de Janeiro: Banco Central do Brasil, 2006); and for the latest catalogue of his religious sculptures, Myriam Andrade Robeiro de Oliveira *et al.*, *O Aleijadinho e sua oficina: Catálogo das esculturas devocionais* (São Paulo: Capivara, 2002).

[77] On the musicians, see Daniela Miranda, 'Músicos de Sabará: A prática musical religiosa a serviço da Câmara (1749–1822)', unpublished PhD thesis, Universidade Federal de Minas Gerais, 2002; and Francisco Kurt Lang, 'A musica barroca', in Sérgio Buarque de Holanda (ed.), *História geral da civilização brasileira* (São Paulo: Difusão Européia do Livro, 1960), vol. 2, pp. 121–44.

[78] Zephyr L. Frank, *Dutra's World: Wealth and Family in Nineteenth-Century Rio de Janeiro* (Albuquerque: University of New Mexico Press, 2004).

role in all skilled crafts, and even dominated a few crucial ones, does not mean that their colour did not always affect their economic lives. The colonial and nineteenth-century records are filled with complaints by white artisans against their free coloured compatriots. For every free coloured who made it to the top of his profession, there were always others who were prevented from the free exercise of their profession by whites who used colour barriers to keep them from competing. Constant attempts were made by whites to force blacks and *mulattos* to form their own craft corporations, or make them take more extensive examinations for master's certification, or even deny them their right to carry out their craft on any level. But the government usually accepted their right to existence on the most pragmatic grounds of need and proof of success. Thus prejudice was current everywhere, but so was some social mobility and economic integration.

One of the few studies on free coloured artisans comes from the Minas Gerais town of Vila Rica in the eighteenth century. There, traditional examinations before craft judges were presented to, and officially endorsed and registered by, the town council. Of some 529 such successful examinations in skilled occupations carried out in this community in the eighteenth century, sixty-four of the successful candidates were free coloureds (twenty *forros* and forty-four *negros livres*) and twenty-three more were slaves. Together these skilled coloured craftsmen represented 16 per cent of the total.[79] For the slaves who were officially examined and registered, it meant that they could carry their official status across legal boundaries should they become free, thus guaranteeing their maintenance within the ranks of the working-class elite. Moreover, from the constant complaints of white artisans, it would appear that even unexamined and unregistered artisans were able to effectively practise their craft.

In less skilled occupations there was little opposition because whites were less numerous and less interested in competing. In domestic service, itinerant vending, stevedoring, and as draymen, sedan workers and unskilled carriers in transport, and in fishing and seafaring, for example, the free coloureds and slaves were dominant.[80] These were the types of work, however, that offered less income and less mobility for the ex-slaves and their offspring. Moreover, some free coloureds may have been engaged in labour at the margin of legality. This may have been true in the extraordinary case of the Bahia-born Bárbara de Oliveira, a *parda crioula* and *forra* of Sabará in the 1760s who was unmarried but had children and grandchildren,

[79] Geraldo Silva Filho, 'O oficialato mecânico em Vila Rica no século dezoito e a participação do escravo e do negro', unpublished Masters dissertation, Universidade de São Paulo, 1996, p. 81.

[80] On the role of the coloured workforce in fishing and seafaring, see Fábio W. A. Pinheiro, 'Tráfico atlântico de escravos na formação dos plantéis mineiros, Zona da Mata, c.1809–c.1830', unpublished Masters dissertation, Universidade Federal do Rio de Janeiro, 2007, tabela 6, p. 75; Vinicius Pereira de Oliveira, 'Sobre o convés: Marinheiros, marítimos e pescadores negros no mundo atlântico do Porto de Rio Grande, RS (século XIX)', *IX Encontro Estadual de História – ANPUH-RS* (Porto Alegre, 2008), pp. 3–5; and Staudt Moreira, *Os cativos e os homens de bem*, pp. 74–5.

and who owned lots of expensive clothing and jewellery, as well as some twenty-two slaves. More of these slaves were women than men, and when she died she noted that eighteen were *coartados* and the rest should be sold. She even left several of the women expensive clothing and other gifts. Given her lack of lands, stores, or occupational designation, and the large number of women who worked for her, it is assumed she ran a house of prostitution.[81] Such houses of prostitution run by free coloured women seem to have been relatively common throughout eighteenth-century Minas.[82] While several free coloured women were accused of being witches, in Minas it was more common to have African or creole *forros* attacked for practising this craft. Most were poor African-born *forros* and sometimes slaves, although there is the case of the *mulato forro* Antonio Julião, a master shoemaker (*mestre sapateiro*) separated from his wife who was accused of using witchcraft to make the *mulata* prostitutes of Sabará love him, and then becoming their pimp and using them to add to his income.[83]

Free coloureds were also petty merchants. In late eighteenth-century Sabará, two *forros* owned small stores (*vendas*). Bernard Correa, a *forro* from the Costa de Mina, owned three slaves – two from Angola and the other from the Mina area. These were two small boys and an adult male slave named Luis when he died. Another such free person was the creole Ignacía Ribeira, who had purchased her own freedom for 300$000 réis. She owned a dry goods store (*vendas de secos e molhados*) and at the time of her death owned a Mina slave named Ventura, who was already involved in a self-purchase arrangement with her master.[84] In the Rio de Janeiro parish of Santa Rita, a commercial census of 1841 found that forty out of 603 establishments were owned by coloured *livres* – of which thirty-three were small grocery stores selling food and vegetables (*quitandas de verdura e comida*) and seven were barber shops. More common an occupation for newly freed slaves was that of itinerant pedlars who worked throughout the city. In 1855, the African (Mina) Ignácio José Antonio petitioned the *municipal* government of the city of Rio de Janeiro (*Camara Municipal da Corte*) to allow his slave, of the same nation, to sell fish in the city. In another case the African (Nagô) Antonio Delfino de Miranda wanted permission for his two slaves, Augusto and Andre, also Nagôs, to work as *escravos de ganho* in the streets of the city.[85]

Finally, in a very few cases, even *forros* were able to make it to the top ranks of society. Some got there through inheritance. Thus the 2-year-old *forro* João Batista, born of a slave mother in 1814, inherited a 200-slave plantation from his father

[81] Paiva, *Escravidão e universo cultural*, pp. 151–3.

[82] See Laura de Mello e Souza, *Desclassificados do ouro: A pobreza mineira no século XVIII*, 4th edn (Rio de Janeiro: Edições Graal, 2004), pp. 257–8.

[83] Souza, *Desclassificados do ouro*, pp. 261–2.

[84] Paiva, *Escravidão e universo cultural*, pp. 128–9.

[85] Soares, *O 'Povo de Cam' na capital do Brasil*, p. 301.

Coronel João Antônio de Barcelos Coutinho. His several older *parda* half-sisters, also born of (different) slave women who had illicit relations with his father, were also freed and given legal recognition. Two of these sisters, Carolina Leopoldina and Joana Batista, were formally recognised with the title of Dona in documents of the 1820s, and on the marriage of one of these sisters in this decade, her birth was listed as legitimate and no reference was made in her formal marriage declarations as to her colour (*parda*) or the fact that her mother was a slave and her birth was outside of wedlock. Moreover, despite constant attacks by the colonel's other relatives, João Batista de Barcelos Coutinho was able to retain his father's impressive sugar estate, one of the largest in the Campos region of Rio de Janeiro.[86]

The case of Joaquim Barbosa, too, shows that mobility could occur through individual skill and luck. Probably born of a slave mother in the late 1770s in Itu in the province of São Paulo and freed in his early childhood, by 1813 this illegitimate *pardo forro* owned two slaves, was married, a militia soldier and a peddler of dry goods (*mascote de fazendas seca*). By 1815, he had obtained a licence from the municipal council of Porto Feliz (São Paulo) to open a dry goods store and had been elevated to the position of a junior officer or *alferes* in the militia. By then he had three adult slaves and two *pardo agregados* working for him. He continued working in his store, but slowly accumulated more slaves and began purchasing land; and though never giving up his commercial activities, he ended his life as a landowner and sugar producer with some forty-one slaves. He also loaned capital to numerous local planters, and had active commercial ties with traders in Santos and Rio de Janeiro. While he served as godparent to several free persons of both colour and white status, he did not do so for any of his slaves at their marriage or the birth of their children, though all his children had important white government and church leaders as godparents.[87]

There are also cases of *forros* who even obtained occupations officially denied them. Thus the *mulato forro* Bernardo Gonçalves Bahia, who was the illegitimate son of Bartolomeu and his slave Maria Gonçalves Bahia, and who was freed by his unmarried father shortly after his birth in Sabará in Minas Gerais, was listed in his father's will in 1752 as a priest (*padre*), a condition which should have been denied him as both a natural child and a *mulatto*.[88]

[86] Márcio de Sousa Soares, 'De pai para filho: Legitimação de escravos, herança e ascensão social de forros nos Campos dos Goitacases, c.1750 – c.1830', *V Congresso Brasileiro de História Econômica, 2003*, pp. 10–15, available at http://ideas.repec.org/s/abp/he2003.html

[87] Roberto Guedes Ferreira, 'De ex-escravo a elite escravista: A trajetória de ascensão social do pardo alferes Joaquim Barbosa Neves (Porto Feliz, São Pulo, século XIX)', in João Luis Ribeiro Fragoso *et al.* (eds), *Conquistadores e negociantes: Historias de elites no Antigo Regime nos trópicas, América lusa, séculos XVI a XVIII* (Rio de Janeiro: Civilização Brasileira, 2007), pp. 337–76, see pp. 355–73.

[88] Ana Luiza de Castro Pereira, 'O Sangue, a palavra e a lei: Ilegitimidade e transmissão da herança no Mundo Atlântico Português no século XVIII', *Nuevomundo*, 28 April 2008, p. 5, available at http:((nuevomundo.revues.org(index30893.html

But these cases of unusual success were few, at least for the *forros*, and even for persons of colour born free they were rare and such socio-economic mobility usually occurred only after two or three generations of freedom. More normal was for the recent *forros* and the first generation of persons of colour born free to be found in the lower classes. Free coloureds could be found among *agregados* in Brazil, in the households of many middling and upper-class persons. In the sugar district of Itu in the province of São Paulo in 1829, there were some 343 *agregados*, of whom just under half were free persons of colour, mostly women.[89] This ratio of free coloureds was probably lower than normal given the high concentration of slaves in this region. In the same district in 1854, *agregados* made up 11 per cent of the combined slave and *agregado* labour force, and accounted for 29 per cent of workers on the 532 cattle ranches, but only 4 per cent of workers on the 664 sugar estates. In fact, *agregados* in Itu in 1829 tended to be found more in urban than in rural households.[90] As household retainers, there are even cases of free coloured *agregados* who moved long distances among the various households of their patron. This was the case of the *mulata forra* Cândida Izabel da Conceição, 18 years of age, who was born in Campina Grande, Paraíba do Norte, in the northeast of Brazil. She was freed by her master, Joaquim José Henriques, in 1856 and two years later gave birth to a daughter, also a free coloured. In 1861, she and her daughter were residing in the house of her former owner in the southern Brazilian city of Lages in Santa Catarina, and both registered themselves as free persons in the local Santa Catarina registers. Clearly she was employed as a servant to her former master.[91] Equally landless *agregados* worked on the usufruct lands of their patrons and otherwise formed part of the agricultural labour force, which was often an extension of household labour.

Aside from working as domestics and farm and ranch hands on the estates of others, the free coloureds were also an important part of the independent small farmer population. On the frontiers, in the mountains, on the lands surrounding the towns and cities, and in the lands abandoned by the plantations, the majority of ex-slaves built their lives as free farmers. In most cases they remained squatters or were *agregados* on the lands of the *fazendeiros*, with few possessing full title to their lands.[92] They were a major element of the truck farming industry near all

[89] Eni de Mesquita Samara, *Lavoura Canavieira, trabalho livre e cotidiano, Itu 1780–1830* (São Paulo: EDUSP, 2005), tabela 6, p. 121.

[90] Eni de Mesquita Samara, 'O papel do agregado na região de Itu, 1780–1830', *Anais do Museu Paulista*, série histórica 6 (1977), pp. 11–121, see pp. 43–4.

[91] Nilsen C. Oliveira Borges, 'Meio livre, meio liberto', *II Encontro 'Escravidão e Liberdade no Brasil Meridional'* (2005), p. 7.

[92] Though the term *agregados* could include everything from free household servants to artisans or even professional full-time bandits, the majority were poor farmers who worked on the lands of the large *fazendeiros*. On their role in the Goiás frontier, see David McCrey, *Frontier Goiás, 1822–1889* (Stanford, CA: Stanford University Press, 2006), pp. 198–201.

the major urban centres and formed the bulk of the subsistence farming population even in areas where slavery was the dominant institution.

Nor is it surprising that these poor workers were to be found among the criminal elements of society. Thus, 893 *livres de côr* were imprisoned in Rio de Janeiro between 1810 and 1821. While thirty-four were imprisoned for showing solidarity with groups of slaves (*solidariedade a grupos de escravos*), 267 were involved in thefts and 263 in acts of violence. As might be expected from their class position, many of these crimes of violence and robbery were against other poor persons, many of whom were either slaves or fellow free coloureds.[93] There were also the usual conflicts over work and women, and even theft of slaves. While stealing slaves was not uncommon for whites and *livres de côr*, sometimes these incidents involved friends or lovers. Thus the *livre* José Ferreira was imprisoned in the coastal town of Parati in 1813 for having run away with a slave from Rio de Janeiro who was his lover and who gave birth to their child on her return to her owner.[94]

Given their entrance into the lowest classes of society and their lack of education and even of capital, the climb up the social ladder was slow and painful for the manumitted slaves and freedmen, but it did progress. Fundamental to all free coloureds was the right to physical mobility. In only a few regions and during only limited periods did the colonial or imperial governments restrict the movement of the free coloured population. This was in contrast to North America, where passports and other restrictions tried to tie the freedmen to their original communities. The right of internal migration was crucial for the ability of free coloured persons to respond to market incentives and to negotiate better work conditions. Physical mobility was not an automatic guarantee of economic mobility, as the experience of Brazilian frontier squatters who were forced off their lands and became urban poor suggests;[95] but it was a fundamental right that allowed freedmen to escape more oppressive exploitation by the elite.

In a detailed study of forty-one *municipios* in the province of São Paulo in the 1829–31 period, there were 9,288 free coloured households listed. Over half of these households were dedicated to farming (some 52 per cent of the total). Next in importance were artisans. But a quarter of these households listed the head as either a *jornaleiro* (day labourer) or a poor person, or even as a beggar. This was to be expected given their slave origins and ultimately poorer background, more limited education, and lack of capital. But these free coloureds, however poor, were not alone at the bottom of the social system, as the very significant participation

[93] Leila Mezan Algranti, *O feitor ausente: Estudos sobre a escravidão urbana no Rio de Janeiro, 1808–1822* (Petrópolis: Vozes, 1988), pp. 126–9.

[94] Algranti, *O feitor ausente*, pp. 135–6.

[95] For this process of expulsion of squatters and their subsequent reduction in income and status as urban poor, see Alida C. Metcalf, *Family and Frontier in Colonial Brazil, Santana de Parnaíba, 1580–1822* (Berkeley: University of California Press, 1992).

of whites in the poor and day labouring categories indicated (some 10 per cent of the 28,099 white heads of households surveyed in the province). Finally, there was no exclusive concentration of these free coloured families in ghettos or black zones, as they could be found everywhere in the province.

Moreover, their relative importance was significant in all zones and all occupations, despite the relatively recent development of an African-originated slave class in this province. They made up a quarter of all the *paulista* households and 20 per cent of all farming households. They represented 36 per cent of all the province's artisans and 37 per cent of all heads of households who worked at sea. They were, of course, over-represented among the day labourers (48 per cent of *jornaleiros*) and represented 42 per cent of the poor and beggars. Though a quarter of all households, they accounted for only 15 per cent of the liberal professions, only 12 per cent of the merchant households, and just 14 per cent of all soldiers.[96]

That some free coloureds succeeded in the market economy can be seen from their role as slave holders. In numerous studies it has been found that the free coloureds owned slaves.[97] Their slave holdings were usually much smaller than those of the white elite, and women tended to be better represented among free coloured slave owners than they were among whites. In the Minas census of 1831–2, some 49 per cent of the 25,286 white households held slaves, whereas just 11 per cent of the 37,501 free coloured households were slave-owning. In turn these white slave owners accounted for 71 per cent of all slave-owning households. White female slave owners made up just 19 per cent of all white masters, but free coloured women made up 30 per cent of all free coloured owners. Of the slave owners, whites in general had almost eight slaves per owner, whereas the free coloured had less than half that rate, at just over three slaves per owner. Though less important as a group in the newer regions of São Paulo province, here too in the late 1820s some

[96] Francisco Vidal Luna and Herbert S. Klein, *Slavery and the Economy of São Paulo, 1750–1850* (Stanford, CA: Stanford University Press, 2003), table 7.5, pp. 171–2.

[97] For recent studies showing the relative importance of free coloured persons as slave owners in various *municípios* of Brazil, see for the province of São Paulo the two studies by Francisco Vidal Luna, *Minas Gerais: Escravos e senhores* (São Paulo: IPE(USP, 1981) and 'São Paulo: População, atividades e posse de escravos em vinte e cinco localidades (1777–1829)', *Estudos Econômicos* 28:1 (1998), pp. 99–169; and Francisco Vidal Luna and Herbert S. Klein, 'Slaves and Masters in Early Nineteenth-Century Brazil: São Paulo', *Journal of Interdisciplinary History* 21:4 (1991), pp. 549–73; and most recently Vidal Luna and Klein, *Slavery and the Economy of São Paulo*. For Minas Gerais, see Herbert S. Klein and Clotilde Andrade Paiva, 'Free Persons in a Slave Economy, Minas Gerais in 1831', *Journal of Social History* 29:4 (1996), pp. 933–62; Clotilde Andrade Paiva and Herbert S. Klein, 'Slave and Free in Nineteenth-Century Minas Gerais: Campanha in 1831', *Slavery and Abolition* 15:1 (1994), pp. 1–21; and a comparison of both provinces in Klein and Luna, 'Free Coloured in a Slave Society'. For studies on two *municípios* in Bahia, see B. J. Barickman, 'As cores do escravismo: Escravistas "pretos", "pardos" e "cabras" no Recôncavo Baiano, 1835', *População e Família* 2:2 (1999), pp. 7–62. A detailed study of free coloured testaments for nineteenth-century Bahia shows that there is a high correlation between wealth and slave ownership – with virtually all the wealthier *libertos* owning slaves and the greater number of slaves the wealthier they were; Oliveira, *O liberto*, p. 38.

free coloureds owned slaves. The *paulista* free coloured slave owners made up just 6 per cent of all slave-owning households, compared to the 29 per cent of such households in Minas Gerais in the same period; but as in Minas the free coloured women were more important than white women as slave owners, making up a third of all free coloured households owning slaves, while white women slave owners accounted for only 20 per cent of white slave owners. The free coloureds in São Paulo on average held roughly the same number of slaves as they did in Minas. Finally, it is worth noting that the mean number of slaves held by the free coloureds for both provinces had a far lower standard deviation than the mean for white owners, which suggests that two-thirds of the free coloured owners held close to the three-slave average.[98]

In terms of occupations, the free coloured slave owners tended to be far less active in farming than the white slave owners and much more devoted to crafts and trades. Usually the pattern was for free coloured artisans of one kind or another to hold or rent slaves who worked in their workshops. Moreover there was a sharp difference by sex. Thus, free coloured female-headed slave-owning households were only modestly engaged in farming (29 per cent), especially compared to their free coloured male slave-owning peers (of whom 59 per cent were farmers). By contrast, some 31 per cent of these female householders were listed as artisans (compared to just 10 per cent of the free coloured males who owned slaves). But even including the slave-owning households, it was evident that in both slave- and non-slave-owning households in São Paulo, the free coloureds were over-represented among the poor and day labourers. Even in Minas Gerais, being a *jornaleiro* was a very common occupation for the free coloureds in non-slave-owning households, and was not even unknown among the slave owners.[99]

That exceptional individuals emerged out of this essentially poor class is evident when we look at the Brazilian elite. Despite being overwhelmingly white, free *pardos* and *pretos* did make it into high-status positions. In Brazil individual leaders among the free coloureds even played major political roles, both identifying with their fellow freedmen and slaves and as often as not playing independent or even hostile roles. This more complex relationship, especially in nineteenth-century Brazilian society, had more to do with their greater acceptance and the less effective racist oppositions in their own societies. Their political activities involved everything from being part of elected officialdom and holding appointive administrative

[98] Based on calculations of the Minas Gerais 1831–2 census, with data provided by Clotilde Paiva from the Arquivo Público Mineiro, Seção Provincial, Mapas de População. The mean slave holdings were 7.6 for whites and 3.4 for free coloureds. In São Paulo the means were almost the same, with 6.8 slaves for whites who owned slaves and 3.5 slaves for free coloureds who owned slaves – based on unpublished *mapas* found in Arquivo do Estado de São Paulo.

[99] Francisco Vidal Luna and Herbert S. Klein, 'Slave Economy and Society in Minas Gerais and São Paulo, Brazil in 1830', *Journal of Latin American Studies* 36:1 (2004), pp. 1–28, table 8, p. 20; and Luna and Klein, *Slavery and the Economy of São Paulo*, pp. 172–3.

and military posts, to the leadership of illegal revolutionary armies. Thus, the Rebouças family in Brazil, whose black founding father was a lawyer and elected representative in the Bahian provincial legislature, and whose sons were engineers and administrators at the imperial court, represents one type of behaviour. In the Brazilian abolitionist movement, Luis Gama and José de Patrocínio were of the free coloured class, while the *mulatto* viscount Francisco de Soles Torres, a former minister and head of the Bank of Brazil, was a supporter of slavery.

Though attacked, despised, rejected, and feared as a class of potential competitors, the free coloured class in Brazil grew rapidly under the slave regime that created them. They proved able to forge a community of freedmen capable of integrating themselves into the free market economy. They fought bitterly and sometimes successfully for the right to social and economic mobility and for the legal rights of full citizenship. This was the most difficult struggle of all, and one that would go on long after the death of slavery. But it was this never-ending struggle of the freedmen for acceptance which ultimately prepared the way for slaves to enter more successfully into free society after abolition was granted to all Africans and Afro-Americans.

12

The 'General Language' and the Social Status of the Indian in Brazil, Sixteenth to Nineteenth Centuries

ANDREA DAHER

MUCH HAS BEEN WRITTEN on the linguistic policies applied to the Indians of Brazil from the sixteenth century to the present day. But almost nothing has been stated about the strategic uses of the 'general language'[1] in the catechising of the Jesuits, nor of the importance of the imposition, in the eighteenth century, of Portuguese as the sole official language for definition of the social status of the indigenous peoples within the Portuguese, and subsequently Brazilian, social body. In this sense, and as we shall see, the centrality of the question of the Tupi language in historically successive strategies of the constitution of the social status of the Indian in Brazil, from the sixteenth to the nineteenth century, is clear. At each point in time, different figures of Indian *otherness* were traced, which ran from the Jesuits' *other* as 'the same' or 'fellow man', to the *other* as 'cultural difference' in the civilising projects of the Brazilian empire; when the Indians were apt to become, completely and definitively, the representatives of an 'American race', to be preserved alongside the *mestiço* races that attest (provide evidence for) their contemporary condition.

The Tupi language in the conduction of the Indian to the mystical body of the Portuguese empire

The *topos* '*la lengua, compañera del Imperio*' ('language, the companion of Empire'), introduced in the *Gramática de la lengua castellana* (*Grammar of the*

[1] The 'general language' was a kind of unified matrix of Tupi languages used in the colony, and gramaticalised by missionaries, notably by Anchieta in the *Arte de Gramática da língua mais usada na Costa do Brasil* (*Art of grammar of the language most used on the coast of Brazil*), published in 1595. The 'general language' is a '*língua franca*' ('open language') term which opposes the '*língua travada*' ('serried language') which means languages that interpreters often could not understand.
[2] Antonio de Nebrija, *Gramática de la lengua castellana* (Salamanca: Juan de Porras, 1492).

Proceedings of the British Academy **179**, *255–268*.

Castilian language) of Antonio de Nebrija in 1492, remained a subject of debate among scholars up to the Golden Age.[2] It extolled the expressive virtues of Castilian and its prestige compared to Latin, as well as legitimising its imposition on conquered peoples.[3] Eugenio Ascencio showed that this *topos* was, in fact, derived from Lorenzo Valla, and had been appropriated by the Aragonese lawyer, Gonzalo Garcia de Santa Maria: from being a commonplace in Valla's collection of *Elegantiae*, the *topos* came to be used for the purpose of unification of the court of Aragon in Micer Gonzalo, before assuming functions of national integration from the viewpoint of the Andalusia of Nebrija.

Less than half a century later, the *topos* was again appropriated in Portugal, in the same discursive register of Nebrija – that of grammar – by Fernão de Oliveira and Joao de Barros.[4] In the *Gramática da linguagem portuguesa* (*Grammar of the Portuguese language*) published by De Oliveira in 1536, the language appears as a type of 'natural product with a national character' which must 'cast off the traces of the foreign characteristics of the culture' and be transformed into an instrument of political cohesion for the empire.[5] In the same vein, the *Gramática* and *Cartinha* of De Barros, published in 1540, accorded the Portuguese language the opportune task of spreading Christianity throughout the world.

This maxim has since been accepted as a key to understanding linguistic theories on the Iberian peninsula in the modern era. In fact, the introduction of Castilian into Spanish America as a compulsory language occurred only in the last decades of the seventeenth century, long after the publication of Nebrija's *Gramática*, in the same way as the introduction of Portuguese into Brazil was enacted only in 1758, in the *Diretório que se deve observar nas povoações dos índios do Pará e Maranhão* (*Guide to be observed in the Indian settlements of Pará and Maranhão*). The resolutions of the Provincial Councils throughout America relating to the use of general languages for catechetic practice clashed head-on with the very linguistic imperialism expressed at that time in the monarchy's legislation. From 1515 to the end of the seventeenth century, a series of Spanish royal charters determined the imposition of Castilian on the colonies, out of concerns that the indigenous languages were not the best vehicles for the eradication of idolatry and for expressing the truths of faith.[6] In summary, it is clear that there was dissonance between,

[3] The discussions were mainly conducted by Bernardo José Aldrete, *Del origen de la lengua castellana o romance que oi se usa en España* (Rome: Carlo Vulliet, 1606); and Juan de Solórzano y Pereira, *Política Indiana* (1639; Madrid: Ediciones Atlas, 1972).

[4] Eugenio Ascencio, '"La lengua compañera del Império". Historia de una idea de Nebrija en España y Portugal', *Revista de Filologia Española* 63 (1960), pp. 399–413; Fernão de Oliveira, *Gramática da linguagem portuguesa . . .* (Lisbon: Germão Galhardo, 1536); João de Barros, *Gramática da língua portuguesa . . .* (Lisbon: Luis Rodrigues, 1540).

[5] Ascencio, '"La lengua compañera del Império"'.

[6] See Richard Konetzke, *Colección de documentos para la historia de la formación social de Hispanoamerica (1493–1810)* (Madrid: Consejo Superior de Investigaciones Cientificas, 1953).

on the one hand, the American linguistic practices implemented by the missionary orders, and, on the other, the monarchy's policies and the theories of the Iberian scholars who defended so-called 'linguistic imperialism', both in Spain and in Portugal.

The Jesuit preacher in Peru, José de Acosta, in his *De procuranda indorum salute* of 1576 – just over ten years after the conclusion of the Council of Trent (1545–63), and a few years before the Third Provincial Council of Lima began its work in 1582 – stated that those who were not 'able to hear directly' could not be priests. He argued further that if they performed their duties in 'good faith', however poorly they understood what the penitent was saying, and were 'moderately able to give suitable advice', they should not be removed from their ministry.[7] Thus, mastery of the language was based on the assumption of good faith, which the missionaries doubted of the infidels. If the widespread use of Castilian in Peru could ensure the best expression of doctrine, as the officials of the Spanish monarchy tended to believe, it could not in any way guarantee the good faith of all its speakers. More broadly, the language policies of missionary orders in America could only foresee the acquisition of general languages by the missionaries, who were endowed with good faith rather than any 'vocation for languages'.

In Brazil, the learning of Tupi was only formalised in 1560 when the first course in Tupi was established at the *Jesuit College* in Bahia. The Provincial Councils of 1568 and 1575 evidently reasserted the use of Tupi in catechetic practice; however, they also revealed the problem of a shortage of priests who were familiar with the language. It was only in the 1580s that the Roman stance on this issue was formulated. In 1583, the visiting father Cristóvão Gouveia arrived in Brazil with an order issued by the Superior General, Claudio Acquaviva, to make the learning of indigenous languages compulsory; however, according to Serafim Leite, this order may actually have been directed at Mexico.[8] The obligation to learn Tupi is contained in the Jesuit rules and was endorsed by General Council decree in 1594. In the following year, 1595, permission was granted for the publication of a grammar and the catechisms written by Anchieta which had been in wide circulation in manuscript form across Brazil since the 1550s.

Therefore, in the course of the negotiations between the positions of the monarchical administration and the religious orders, and amid the arrival of information in Rome and the reports by missionaries on the colonial environment in general, the immense 'linguistic labour' carried out by the missionaries in America should be associated, both as a whole and in each circumstance, with the logic of manuscript circulation, editorial production and the reception of the works: catechisms,

[7] José de Acosta, *De procuranda indorum salute* (Madrid: Consejo Superior de Investigaciones Cientificas, 1984), p. 431.

[8] Serafim Leite, *Suma histórica da Companhia de Jesus no Brasil (1549–1760)* (Lisbon: Junta de Investigações Ultramar, 1965), p. 563.

grammars, vocabularies, textbooks, and a wide range of genres and textual forms, which were written in indigenous languages. The co-extensive nature of grammars and catechisms is clear in those produced up to the eighteenth century, as they were usually published together in a single volume. However, the analogy between religious conversion and language translation that follows from this is not exclusive to American production. João de Barros' Portuguese grammar, published in 1540, is an irrefutable example: in the same volume as his grammar there is a dialogue, entitled *Diálogo da viciosa vergonha* ('Dialogue of vicious shame'), based on the Christian interpretation of Aristotelian ethics. It was dedicated to 'boys who have finished their letters', and therefore aimed at the discreet Portuguese public and not the brutish heathens of Brazil. Nevertheless, the condition for salvation of all souls is still the substance of letters.

In explaining the use of indigenous languages in the evangelisation of America, the historiography often emphasises the small number of missionaries faced with the huge number of souls to be saved through conversion.[9] As much as circumstances might differ in Hispanic and Portuguese America, the widespread contrast between the missionary practices that led to the massive grammaticalisation of American languages on one hand, and the Iberian theories of linguistic imperialism on the other, cannot be explained (as Lucia Binotti suggests) by 'apathy' or 'tolerance' on the part of the conquerors, which 'allowed the indigenous languages to survive with impunity'.[10] The choice to pray in indigenous languages was not fundamentally imposed by the dictates of communication. Even though there is a recurring *topos* of 'a shortage of workers' in missionary texts, on the whole, no arguments for the need to preach in indigenous languages were ever put forward. Therefore this was not merely a pragmatic issue on the part of the missionary orders, as is currently maintained, but rather an issue of the fundamental theological-political basis of these practices.

In general, the missionaries regarded Tupi as a defective language which lacked certain categories and which was distanced from the virtuous form of the Divine Word by the long years of captivity of the Indians under the enterprise of the devil. It was a forgotten language, in need of grammaticalisation in order for it to become equivalent to the vernacular languages, and in turn to share in the Divine Word. The lack of categories would, for instance, explain in theological terms why the writings of the Portuguese Jesuits never presented the Indian as endowed with speech. Consequently grammaticalising was a catechetical practice *par excellence*.

[9] Alain Milhou, 'Les politiques de la langue à l'époque moderne', in M.-C. Benassy-Berling *et al.* (eds), *Langues et cultures en Amérique Espagnole coloniale* (Paris: Presses de la Sorbonne Nouvelle, 1993), p. 24.

[10] Lucia Binotti, '"La lengua compañera del imperio". Observaciones sobre el desarrollo de un discurso de colonialismo lingüístico en el Renacimiento español', in Otto Zwartjes (ed.), *Las gramáticas misioneras de tradición hispánica (siglos XVI–XVII)* (Amsterdam: Rodopi, 2000), p. 280.

It was at the request of Manoel da Nóbrega, the Superior General of the Company of Jesus in Brazil, that José de Anchieta wrote the *Arte de gramática da língua mais usada na costa do Brasil* (*Art of the grammar of the language most used on the coast of Brazil*). A copy of the manuscript was supposedly delivered to Nóbrega in 1555, which he took with him to Bahia so that missionaries who had recently arrived could be instructed in the indigenous language. From 1556, thirty-nine years prior to its publication, the grammar was already being used for teaching Tupi at the Jesuit College in Bahia, and in 1560 Father Luís da Grã made the study of the grammar compulsory. A licence for publication of Anchieta's *Arte de gramática* was provided, for printing together with a catechism written in Tupi. But these dialogues would only be published in 1618, in the *Catecismo da língua brasílica* (*Catechism of the Brazilian language*) by Padre Antonio de Araújo, in turn 'paid for by the priests of Brazil'.[11]

The production of grammars and doctrines in indigenous languages is evidence that both offered a means for the transition from the oral native language to the written and, therefore, the fixing of syntactic forms as a guarantee that religious tradition could be perpetuated. 'This Art', said the Jesuit Quirício Caxa, Anchieta's biographer, 'is the main instrument to help our priests and brothers engaged in the conversion of Gentiles.'[12] And these materials illustrate the more general theological-political issue of the universality of conversion work through the written language, by the way in which the Indian was considered as a universal listener (or reader), as can be seen in the aims expressed in the prologues to *Arte de gramática* and *Catecismo da língua brasílica*, or through the actual rhetorical structure of the dialogues between Master and Disciple in the doctrinal works of Anchieta. In this sense, the universalisation of the reception of letters by the Indian necessarily corresponds to the projection by priests of Western cultural criteria of coherence, consistency and non-contradiction as definitions of the person.

Together with daily instruction, the grammaticalisation of the Tupi language (alongside the work of translation and versification) enabled the production of a memory and a consciousness of the Indian; or rather, the invention of his soul as a memory of a sinful past, relinquished to paganism and cannibalism, as is repeatedly affirmed through the catechisms.[13] But these acts were not merely the basis for strategies of catechesis, they were themselves theologically determined, and are a clear confirmation of the Unitarian principle of the profound divine truth

[11] Antonio de Araújo, *Catecismo da lingua brasílica, no qual se contem a summa da doctrina christã* . . . (1618; Rio de Janeiro: PUC, 1952).

[12] Quirício Caxa and Pero Rodrigues, *Primeiras biografias de José de Anchieta* (São Paulo: Edições Loyola, 1988), p. 50.

[13] The Indian in Anchieta's 'Christian Doctrine' confesses thus: '*Aimombeú / mbaé aíba xe maenduáraguéra/ xe ñeéngaíbaguéra, / xe rekó angaipábaguéra* . . . ' ('I confess / my memories of bad things / my bad words, / my sinful works . . . '); José de Anchieta, *Doutrina cristã* (São Paulo: Edições Loyola, 1993).

faced with the superficial multiplicity of human languages, ever since the dispersal of the language of Adam in the story of Babel. More than just a vehicle for strategies of catechesis, the Tupi grammar was the requirement that allowed for the exercise of the 'spiritual good of the Indians, who intend to enter into the Holy Union of the Immaculate Roman church', as Antonio de Araújo said in the prologue to the *Catecismo brasílico*.[14] By the means of Grace, accessible to man in the form of salvation, entrance to the union of the Church (through knowledge of the doctrine, reception of the mysteries of the sacraments, and Christian practice) was the sole condition offered to the Indians for blessing.

In sermons and letters written between approximately 1652 and 1662, dedicated in particular to the issue of the Indians, the Jesuit Antonio Vieira recognised (as did many of his religious cohort) the need for knowledge of the indigenous languages to make evangelical work effective. More than this, Vieira attributed a high level of difficulty to the enterprise associated with the Indians of Brazil, contrasting the simple task of preaching to people from his own nation and in his own language with the difficulty of preaching to people from a different nation and in a different language.[15] The *topos* of the '*língua escura*' (obscure language), found in texts written by chroniclers and missionaries since the sixteenth century, is also echoed in Vieira's writings, in that the indigenous languages are represented as inextricably confused due to the absence of the light of reason and Grace. To compile a grammar and provide the sounds (and the categories) to speakers of these obscure, lacking or deficient languages was – as has already been said – 'the analogy that symbolises and prepares the basis for healthy customs, practices of best policing and the salvation of the soul'.[16]

Generally speaking, the Jesuits followed the propositions defended by theologians such as Francisco de Vitoria, which were ratified at the Council of Trent, and Francisco Suárez, according to which 'the Indian does not know the Revelation, but is not excluded from natural law; therefore he is human, though at an extreme distance from good Catholic humanity'.[17] On the basis of the principles of this Iberian Second Scholasticism it can be similarly understood that otherness was not recognised as cultural difference as this is understood today. The analogy causes the 'other' to take on a degree of similarity, more or less distant from the true Good. It was the *fellow man* and not the *other* in which one could reflect or that we could negate by difference, as postulated anachronistically by studies inspired by semiotics for the sixteenth century. The conversion of the Indian

[14] Araújo, *Catecismo na lingoa brasilica*, p. 3.

[15] Alcir Pécora, 'Vieira, o índio e o corpo místico', in Adauto Novaes (ed.), *Tempo e história* (São Paulo: Companhia das Letras, 1992), p. 448.

[16] Pécora, 'Vieira, o índio e o corpo místico', p. 449.

[17] João Adolfo Hansen, 'Sem F, sem L, sem R: Cronistas, jesuítas & índio no século XVI', in E. A. Kossovitch (ed.), *A conquista da América* (Campinas: CEDES/Papirus, 1993), pp. 45–55, see p. 53.

therefore consisted in converting the same into the same: from the Indian corrupted by the long enterprise of the devil to his own original nature, closer to God.[18]

The literate devices of 'reduction' of the American languages therefore caused the general languages to function as efficient vehicles for conducting the Indians to the state of subjects of this mystical empire, according to the 'pact of subjugation', defined by Francisco Suárez in his *Defensio fidei* in 1613, where society as a 'mystical body' (or as unified will) alienates power in the mystical, fictional and idealised person of the king, declaring itself a subject.[19] Conversion – particularly by means of language – involved conducting the Indian as a *fellow man* and not his integration as the *other* – as one would think from the eighteenth century – into the different forms of imposition of the Portuguese and Castilian languages onto all of the vassals of their Catholic sovereigns.

The Tupi language in the integration of the Indian as a vassal of the Portuguese monarchy

The changes to the political, economic and cultural guidelines which were notably introduced to Brazil by Sebastião José de Carvalho e Melo, the Marquis of Pombal, the main secretary of state under D. Joseph I, continued to be predominately motivated by the cultural issues of language. In Article 6 of the *Diretório* approved in 1758, Portuguese was imposed as the sole language and not merely as the official spoken language. The correspondence between the Marquis and his brother Francisco Xavier de Mendonça Furtado, Governor of the State of Maranhão and Grão Pará in 1751, is the source of the statements conveyed in the *Diretório* which supported the measures proposed in subsequent years, and which culminated in the expulsion of the Jesuits. In addition, the correspondence clearly states the problem of language.

In the letter written by Mendonça Furtado on 21 November 1751 addressed to the 'Ilustríssimo e Excelentíssimo Senhor Meu Irmão do meu coração' ('Eminent and Most Excellent Lord My Brother of my heart'), he directed firm criticism at the *Regimento das Missões* (Rules of the Missions) which had been used in the Amazon region since 1686 to provide for the spiritual and secular administration of the Indians by the missionaries. Furtado deemed unacceptable the fact that in the *aldeias*, '[men of religion] teach them [the Gentiles] a slang they call general language', and compared this to the state of generalised barbarism. 'By stubbornly persisting in making the Indians learn the aforesaid slang, they have reached the precipice, at least seemingly, of acknowledging the plurality of gods due to the lack

[18] Alcir Pécora, *Máquina de gêneros* (São Paulo: EDUSP, 2001), p. 47.

[19] João Adolfo Hansen, 'Introduction', in Antonio Vieira, *Cartas do Brasil* (São Paulo: Hedra, 2003), p. 17.

of words to be found in it.'[20] In the same letter, Mendonça Furtado continued by explaining that the system applied to the *aldeias* in Maranhão, where everyone communicated 'in an invented slang for the confusion and complete separation of men and causing overt damage to human society'. However, according to the Governor, the use of 'slang' amongst the inhabitants had become customary for essential communication, 'to the extent that today in this city very few people speak Portuguese, especially the women, and it is even possible, as I have been told by the same priests, that they only confess in the so-called general language'.[21]

In the *Diretório*, the intended integration of the Indians remained guided by this perception that the general languages were intrinsically related to tribal customs, as Mendonça Furtado had pointed out in his letters several years earlier. The imposition of Portuguese provided for in the *Diretório*, however, once again took up the essence of 'linguistic imperialism', in the exact terms formulated on the basis of the *topos* of Nebrija and of its success in the writings of João de Barros and Fernão de Oliveira during the sixteenth century. In short, despite the linguistic practices carried out by missionaries for two centuries in Brazil, and considered to be detrimental at the time, the *Diretório* determined the exclusive use of the 'language of the prince', so that a civilisation would arise in the colony, and where as a result, the custom would enable the Indians to be integrated as legitimate vassals. According to the *Diretório*:

> The immediate introduction of a nation's own language amongst conquered peoples was always an invariable maxim practised by every nation that conquered new domains, as indisputably this is one of the most efficient ways to expel the barbarity of past customs from rustic peoples. Experience has shown that at the same time as the language of the prince who has conquered the peoples is introduced amongst these peoples, affection, veneration and obedience to the same prince also take root.

With regard to the integration of subjects, the *Diretório* also encouraged marriage between Indians and white people, and reorganised social relations in the former *aldeias*, which were transformed into village settlements where everybody would be subject to the same civil laws as those governing urban populations in Portugal. The *Diretório* served as a legal and political instrument that gave these colonial populations, both Indians and white people, the entitlement to hold positions in bodies representing Justice and Finance in the local administrations.

Although originally aimed at inhabitants of the north, the *Diretório* spread to all regions of Brazil where there were missions. In this sense, the imposition of the Portuguese language was strategically suitable both for subjugating the Indians and the white settlers as vassals of the king of Portugal, and also as a political motive

[20] Marcos Carneiro de Mendonça, *A Amazônia na era Pombalina* (Brasília: Edições do Senado Federal, 2005), vol. 1, p. 113.

[21] Mendonça, *A Amazônia na era Pombalina*, pp. 113–14.

for the demarcation of colonial territories between Portugal and Spain. From this point onwards, the linguistic difference would ultimately shift to the Portuguese and Castilian languages, and this would strengthen the ties of vassalage of speakers to their respective monarchies. Beozzo affirms that the results of the policy of forced integration contained in the *Diretório* had little effect on the enslavement of Indians, and led to their dispersion, particularly in the Amazon region where the labour force was largely indigenous.[22] This complete 'detribalisation' opened the pathway to the destruction of the Indians. The period following the abolition of the *Diretório*, which historiography has titled 'the war against the barbarians', lasted until 1845. From this point onwards, new instruments were created for civilising the Indians which put an end to armed clashes and favoured a land allocation policy.[23]

Language in the civilisational project of Couto de Magalhães

One of the most eloquent programmes of this period was presented by General Couto de Magalhães, in a book written in 1876. His main goal was evident in the title alone: *O Selvagem. Trabalho preparatório para aproveitamento do selvagem e do solo por ele ocupado no Brasil* (*The Savage. Preparatory Work for the Utilisation of the Savage and the Land He Occupies in Brazil*). In this work, the issue of language assumed the central role that it always held in historically successive strategies, now turned to the pacification and the politico-military framing of the Indian, in the mid-nineteenth century. According to Couto de Magalhães,

> to succeed in making the savage understand the Portuguese language [. . .] is equivalent to incorporating him into civilisation [. . .] which is possible with a corps of trained interpreters formed from army and navy personnel who speak both languages [. . .] For savages who cannot read, who do not know how to read, who do not possess the accumulated means to learn Portuguese, it is necessary that we who do know how to read make them capable of doing so, through interpreters who by understanding their language can teach them ours.[24]

Couto de Magalhães, successively President of the provinces of Goiás, Mato Grosso and Pará from 1863 to 1868, and of São Paulo in 1889, thus considered the

[22] J. O. Beozzo, *Leis e regimentos das missões: Política indigenista no Brasil* (São Paulo: Edições Loyola, 1983), p. 79.

[23] Beozzo, *Leis e regimentos das missões*, p. 79. The disastrous aspects of the consequences of the *Diretório*, however, are nuanced by Décio de Alencar Guzmán: 'Construtores de ciudades: Mamelucos, índios y europeos en las ciudades pombalinas de La Amazonia', in Clara García and Manuel Ramos Median (eds), *Ciudades mestizas: Intercâmbios y continuidades en la expansión occidental, siglos XVI–XIX* (Mexico: Condumex, 2011).

[24] José Vieira Couto de Magalhães, Preface to *O Selvagem* (1876; São Paulo and Rio de Janeiro: Livraria Magalhães Editora, n.d.), p. 3.

figure of the interpreter a pillar in the work of 'taming' the 'savages', together with two other figures, the soldier and the missionary, based on 'the idea of using our military colonies as auxiliaries in the settling of the *sertões* [hinterlands], where interpreters should be placed, speaking the languages of the savage populations surrounding them in order to facilitate the relationship with those savages'. Thus he shifts the linguistic work from the hands of missionaries to the hands of interpreters, on the pretext of practicality and economy: 'How is the poor missionary, the poor foreigner who does not know Portuguese, who came here in old age, supposed to learn savage languages? Is it not much easier and economical to give him an interpreter?'[25]

The interpreters would be recruited, according to Couto de Magalhães, from the soldiers in the military colonies derived from the indigenous population, and would serve both the priests for catechesis and the military for civilising purposes. This second task was now seen as separate from the first and definitively related to pacification, although both were to be mediated by the imposition of Portuguese, as can be seen in the opening pages of *O Selvagem*: 'There is no middle term. Either exterminate the savage, or teach him our language through the indispensable medium of his own, after which he is incorporated into our society, although he should later be civilised.'[26] In his project, Couto de Magalhães takes for granted the 'situation of a conquering race', endowed with the Christian duty 'to pull them [the Indians] out of the bloody barbarism in which they live, to bring them to the community of work and society in which we live', in the very terms of the letter he wrote to Joaquim Serra.[27]

Considering the central importance of language in his project, Couto de Magalhães intended to publish a second edition of *O Selvagem* together with the grammar by Anchieta. However, as he died before completing the project, the second edition was accompanied by one of his lectures entitled 'Anchieta, as raças e as línguas indígenas' ('Anchieta, the races and the indigenous languages'). He proposed a supposed continuity between the 'method of the early Jesuits' and his own, which consisted of 'learning the savage languages in order to teach the Indian boys Portuguese. Without knowledge of two languages, it is impossible to teach one.'[28] The aim of the conference held to mark the tercentenary celebrations of Anchieta, organised by Eduardo Prado in São Paulo in 1896, was undoubtedly to draw a profile of the 'current race of Brazil' in general, and of São Paulo in particular, which descended from three branches: 'two of the Old World and the Red from América'.[29] Couto de Magalhães concluded that Brazilians were neither

[25] Magalhães, Preface to *O Selvagem*, p. 3.

[26] Magalhães, Preface to *O Selvagem*, p. 3.

[27] Published at the end of the second edition of *O Selvagem*: 'Carta a Joaquim Serra, mostrando qual é a posição do índio em presença da raça conquistadora'; Magalhães, *O Selvagem*, p. 259.

[28] Magalhães, *O Selvagem*, p. 265.

[29] Magalhães, *O Selvagem*, p. 290.

European nor African, but American. In the topic dedicated to 'Guarani and Tupi Languages', in which he listed what he considered 'the best books on Tupi', beginning with Anchieta's grammar, the American feature of the 'Brazilian nation' was above all linguistic.

Couto de Magalhães used the knowledge of his time in order to fill some of the supposed gaps in the work of the Jesuits and to correct the 'inaccuracies' of early reports on the so-called Tupi-Guarani.[30] He undertook to develop a definitive Tupi vocabulary, 'so we can interpret an infinity of names of places, animals, flowers and fruits of our land'.[31] In doing so, he allotted himself a task that he judged supposedly comparable to that of Anchieta, to whom we owe the 'preservation of the indigenous races' and 'of the mixed race or *mameluco*, *cariboco* or caboclo': the true American races.[32]

Race and cultural difference

Undoubtedly, Couto de Magalhães' plan differed markedly from what he called 'the method' of Anchieta and the Jesuits in general, not only in the final imposition of Portuguese and the introduction of the key figure of the interpreter, who worked alongside the missionaries and soldiers in charge of imposing the language of the dominating authority. What actually changed was the very notion of the 'Savage'. For the Scholastics, the Indian was illuminated by the light of natural Grace, and capable of receiving the Revelation through his own language. During the Enlightenment, by contrast, the Savage was not considered able to read the true language (Portuguese). And a century later, he was seen as an obstacle to civilisation.

Alcir Pécora showed that the Jesuit Antonio Vieira had accepted the *topoi* of the theological treatises of the Iberian Scholasticism of the sixteenth century, such as the assertion that the Indians possessed the powers of the soul (especially memory and intelligence, but also will), and defended with this their capacity to receive the doctrine 'for their "natural good", that makes them predisposed to piety and catechism'. Vieira also acknowledged the existence of 'policy' as 'a system of government regulated by laws recognised as being just by the group of its members as a whole', which could even allow, by the law of the peoples, for the autonomous jurisdiction of the *aldeias* or Indian settlements.[33] Since the Indians were creatures created in the image of God, it was therefore unjust to submit them to imprisonment, as Vieira admonished King John IV in a letter of May 1653:

[30] Magalhães, *O Selvagem*, p. 290.
[31] Magalhães, *O Selvagem*, p. 297.
[32] Magalhães, *O Selvagem*, p. 270.
[33] Magalhães, *O Selvagem*, p. 427.

> If the captured Indians were freed; if those of the *aldeias* truly lived freely, working on their lands and serving only by their own free will and for pay; if the expeditions into the backlands were made truly and not simply under the pretence of peace, if the faith of Jesus Christ was preached to the Indians without any interest beyond what He came to seek in the world, which is souls; and there were many priests who learnt the languages, and applied themselves in this mystery with true zeal; there is no doubt that, through the joint action of Divine Grace and this disposition of the human instruments, the Indians will easily be brought to friendship with us, embrace the faith, and live as Christians, and with the news of the good treatment of the first, these will bring many others after them; with which, apart from their own spiritual good, and that of all their descendants, the country will also have many Indians to serve and defend it, just as they were the ones who in large part helped to restore it.[34]

In the sixteenth and seventeenth centuries, the notion of *corpus mysticum* as a unified whole of the collective will became associated with that of *respublica*, meaning the unified popular will as political body which alienates itself from power through the 'pact of subjection'. In this pact, the ways in which the three powers of the human soul must act – memory, intellect, and will, all of them identified among the Indians of Brazil since the first Jesuits – are prescribed, as subordinate faculties.[35] Following the doctrine of Francisco Suárez, the individual body of the subject is only visible (and speakable of) if it has representation, that is to say, when the faculties of its soul are incorporated into the corporative hierarchy of the 'common good' of the State. In the *corpus mysticum*, to which the Indian is led by conversion – and not the African – all the members of the Portuguese empire were eligible to be considered as a 'unique unified whole' in moral terms.[36] This concept prevailed until the middle of the eighteenth century, when – following the expulsion of the Jesuits from Brazil, and once their practices (including those that permitted the widespread use of the general language) were regarded as pernicious – the impossibility of the Indians reading the true language, Portuguese, became (as we have seen) one of the principal causes for the changes imposed by Pombal in the *Diretório dos índios*.

In any case, as has already been stated, the text of the *Diretório* did not contain any 'elimination of differences', nor did it project a future free of any racial distinction for Indians and white people.[37] In a highly hierarchical society such as the

[34] Antonio Vieira, *Cartas do Brasil* (São Paulo: Hedra, 2003), p. 436.

[35] See M. da Nóbrega, 'Diálogo sobre a conversão do gentio', in Serafim Leite (ed.), *Cartas dos primeiros Jesuítas do Brasil* (São Paulo: Comissão do IV Centenário da Cidade de São Paulo, 1954), vol. 2.

[36] For a study of the 'pact of subjection', see João Adolfo Hansen's excellent book, *A sátira e o engenho: Gregório de Matos e a Bahia do século XVII* (São Paulo: Ateliê Editorial, 2004).

[37] Garcia's affirmation is, in this sense, marked by the use of anachronistic categories that were not in play in the propositions of the *Diretório* in the mid-eighteenth century: 'Thus, [the *Diretório*] projected a future in which it would not be possible to distinguish one group from the other, either physically, due to biological mixing, or in terms of behaviour, due to a series of measures of cultural homogenisation'; Elisa Frühauf García, 'O projeto pombalino de imposição da língua portuguesa aos índios e a sua aplicação na América meridional', *Tempo* 12:23 (2007), pp. 23–38, p. 35.

Portuguese empire of the eighteenth century, the perspectives brought by Pombal advanced the concept of *otherness* based on the notion of difference (particularly recognised in the general languages). This made it possible to conceive of the integration of Indians as subjects, once they had become speakers of Portuguese and in this way civilised. It did not involve eradicating the differences between Indians and white people, but rather recognising difference as *otherness* in order to integrate the civilised into the body of society.

A century later, the Indian was apt to be considered a real obstacle to civilisation.[38] It is in this light that the proposal by Couto de Magalhães for a programme to 'tame' the savage must be read. His book is, in effect, a '*Mémoire*' written on the orders of Emperor Pedro II and addressed to the Commission for the Philadelphia World Fair, as 'testimony' that in Brazil, 'we too exert ourselves to assimilate the indigenous races of the New World'.[39] The programme created by General Couto aimed, in this sense, to institute the 'savage as an economic element'.[40] Taking his authority from the French bibliophile Ferdinand Denis, Couto de Magalhães thus expressed the task facing the Brazilian state:

> One of the scholars who has most studied and loved Brazil, Mr Ferdinand Denis, who always defends us in Europe, making more valuable our virtues and softening our defects [. . .] wrote to me from Paris last year the following words regarding my work, *Região e raças selvagens* [Region and savage races]: 'I am convinced that the future greatness of your country depends on the racial spirit, properly understood'.[41]

He then went on to maintain – again supported by a French intellectual, Jean Louis Armand de Quatrefages de Bréau – that as a workforce, 'no race serves us so well as that of the whites acclimatised by the blood of the Indians' – comparable to what happened in North America with the *yankee*.[42] And his arguments based on the authority of French intellectuals were followed by a warm elegy to the Tupi language (and 'its dialects'), considered on the one hand 'among the greatest languages on earth, if not the greatest' (by its geographical extent at the time), and on the other, in the light of the 'perfection of its grammatical forms, albeit embryonic

[38] See, in particular, Magalhães, *O Selvagem*, p. 40.

[39] Magalhães, *O Selvagem*, p. 21.

[40] Magalhães, *O Selvagem*, pp. 22–3: 'In the future, no matter, perhaps, will be so generally concerned with the development of the riches and greatness of Brazil as the taming [*amansamento*] of our savages.'

[41] Magalhães, *O Selvagem*, pp. 22–3.

[42] Magalhães, *O Selvagem*, p. 24. It is hardly surprising that Couto de Magalhães should look to Denis and Quatrefages de Bréau for support: the former was credited with the autonomy of Brazilian literature *vis-à-vis* the Portuguese; the latter, a naturalist, was the author of an *Histoire générale des races humaines*. In the same sense, both the Indian and the Tupi language were becoming legitimate and privileged objects of romantic literature and the sciences, such as a nascent Ethnology, throughout the nineteenth century. All this did not occur, as is well known, to the detriment of the important debates in the eighteenth-century academies (above all the Instituto Histórico e Geográfico Brasileiro) regarding their social status in the Brazilian empire.

in more than one respect'.[43] 'The racial spirit, properly understood' was expressed *par excellence* in the valorisation of the language.

Historically, the uses and functions of the Tupi language are clear from the sixteenth century, as it maintained its position at the heart of successive strategies to define the social status of the Indian, that is to say, during the three critical moments. Until the mid-eighteenth century, as for Anchieta, Tupi, endowed with grammars and dictionaries, became the vehicle for conducting the Indian (as *same* or *fellow man*) to the mystical body of the Empire, in such a way as to occupy the lowest place on the hierarchical scale. In 1758, in Pombal's *Diretório*, the imposition of Portuguese was the precondition for the integration of the Indian – whose representation had already begun to be sketched as *other* – into civil society, as a subject of the monarchy. Lastly, in political programmes of the nineteenth century (such as that of Couto de Magalhães), it was the language of an alterity now definitively installed as cultural difference, and an instrument of pacification and the political and military fencing-in of the Indians for the final imposition of Portuguese as the legitimate national language. As alterity, defined notably by language, the Indian came to be taken for 'a conquered race', alongside the '*mestiço* races' resulting from the conquest, and now susceptible to preservation and study, among the mass of civilising projects of the nineteenth century.[44] It was as *other*, then, that the way was opened for the legitimation of the science of its lasting cultural difference.

[43] Magalhães, *O Selvagem*, p. 35.

[44] On the different comments and projects sent by provincial authorities to the Ministry of the Empire in 1826 in response to the organisation of a 'General Plan for the Civilisation of the Indians', see John Monteiro, 'Tupis, tapuias e historiadores: Estudos de história indígena e do indigenismo', unpublished thesis, presented to obtain the title of Livre Docente, Universidade Estadual de Campinas, 2001.

13

The New Christian Divide in the Portuguese-Speaking World (Sixteenth to Eighteenth Centuries)

JOSÉ PEDRO PAIVA

HISTORIANS HAVE NOT YET ATTEMPTED to place the New Christian divide in the Portuguese-speaking world in global perspective and for the whole of the early modern era. The topic has been studied numerous times, but for specific areas of the Portuguese overseas empire (Africa, India and Brazil) and usually for shorter or medium-scale periods of time. This chapter, then, intends to offer a general, synthetic, and long-term survey of the impact of New Christian segregation throughout the Portuguese empire, between the late fifteenth and the eighteenth centuries (more precisely, up until 1773).[1]

On 5 December 1496, a royal edict ordered the expulsion of all Jews and Moors living in Portugal. Numerous barriers were simultaneously created against those who wished to leave, and some months later, in May 1497, the monarch, Manuel I, forced all those who remained in Portugal to be baptised. The Jews thus immediately became New Christians; and even if the king tried to undertake some ambiguous policies for the social integration of this community, a radical difference and social segregation separated New from Old Christians.[2] After 1497 some New

This research was undertaken in the context of the project on *Sociedades, Poderes e Culturas: Portugal e os 'Outros'*, of the Centro de História da Sociedade e da Cultura da Universidade de Coimbra (FCT).

[1] On 25 May 1773, a royal edict was published suppressing all distinction between Old and New Christians. A. J. R. Russell-Wood addressed the New Christian divide in the most recent history of Portuguese expansion. Though his proposals concerning Portuguese society are very interesting, namely that the Portuguese tried to apply their social organisation in their new territories (with certain local adaptations of course), he makes very few references to the role and legal status of the New Christian communities; A. J. R. Russell-Wood, 'A sociedade portuguesa no Ultramar', in Francisco Bethencourt and Kirti Chaudhuri (eds), *História da expansão portuguesa* (Lisbon: Círculo de Leitores, 1998), vol. 1, pp. 266–79; A. J. R. Russell-Wood, 'Comunidades étnicas' and 'Grupos sociais', in Bethencourt and Chaudhuri (eds), *História da expansão portuguesa*, vol. 2, pp. 151–88; A. J. R. Russell-Wood, 'Comunidades étnicas', in Bethencourt and Chaudhuri (eds), *História da expansão portuguesa*, vol. 3, pp. 210–22.

[2] There is a huge literature on the topic. The most recent book on the subject in English, with some new perspectives, is François Soyer, *The Persecution of the Jews and Muslims of Portugal: King Manuel*

cont.

Christians emigrated to form a diaspora, initially mainly to the north coast of Africa, Italy, Flanders, and Turkey. Between 1507 and 1520 their exit was drastically reduced, due to new restrictions imposed on their departure and also because of the policies of integration introduced by the Crown. In 1519, for instance, the king wrote to Portuguese secular authorities in Goa making clear that only New Christians holding a special permit issued by the monarch could be members of the local government.[3] Yet during the 1530s the exodus intensified drastically, especially after the creation of the Portuguese Inquisition at the end of 1536. Many New Christians escaped to some of the areas previously mentioned, but also to the Portuguese Atlantic islands, Brazil, and especially India. Some even reached China and Japan after the 1540s.[4]

This diaspora from mainland Portugal, which naturally involved the wealthier New Christians, was maintained during the seventeenth and eighteenth centuries, though with different intensities and directions. These differences depended on four basic factors:

1. The legal restrictions imposed by the Crown on New Christians trying to leave the realm.[5]
2. The presence of the Inquisition (and other ecclesiastical structures) and the patterns of its repression in the different areas of the Portuguese empire.
3. Economic trends in world trade, together with the strategic relevance of different areas of Portugal's overseas empire.
4. The configuration of family networks established by New Christians in the different areas of this empire.

This general framework explains, for example, the attraction of North Africa at the beginning of the sixteenth century. In 1509, the Portuguese king even allowed

and the End of Religious Tolerance (1496–7) (Leiden: Brill, 2007). Very useful also is Giuseppe Marocci, '"... per capillos adductos ad pillam": Il dibattito cinquecentesco sulla validitá del battesimo forzato degli ebrei in Portogallo (1496–1497)', in Adriano Prosperi (ed.), *Salvezza delle anime disciplina dei corpi: Un seminario sulla storia del battesimo* (Pisa: Edizione della Normale, 2006), pp. 339–423.

[3] The letter is published by António Baião, *A Inquisição de Goa: Correspondência dos inquisidores da Índia (1569–1630)* (Coimbra: Imprensa da Universidade, 1930), pp. 17–18.

[4] A description and analysis of these trends can be found in Anna Cannas da Cunha, *A Inquisição no Estado da Índia: Origens (1539–1560)* (Lisboa: Arquivos Nacionais/Torre do Tombo, 1995), pp. 17–26.

[5] These restrictions started soon after 1497. Some examples: in April 1499, the king forbade New Christians from exiting the realm; in April 1524, John III decreed the freedom of all New Christians to sell their properties and goods and leave the kingdom; in June 1532, John III again forbade New Christians from leaving Portugal. See Israel S. Révah, *Études portugaises* (Paris: Fundação Calouste Gulbenkian, 1975), pp. 74, 192; Direcção Geral de Arquivos/Torre do Tombo (Lisbon), Chancelaria de D. João III, livro 60, fols 26–7. Later, similar measures prohibiting New Christians from departing were decreed in 1567, 1580, 1587 and 1610; see Francisco Bethencourt, 'Campo religioso e Inquisição em Portugal no século XVI', *Estudos Contemporâneos* 6 (1984), pp. 43–60, see pp. 59–60; and Direcção Geral de Arquivos/Torre do Tombo (Lisbon), Conselho Geral do Santo Oficio, livro 99, fols 107v–108v.

the presence of a Jewish community and their total freedom of trading and religion in Safim, and some years later (in 1512) another community in Azamor, conditions that made these places particularly attractive to New Christians.[6] The New Christian exodus to India intensified until the 1560s because of the importance of the spice trade combined with the scarcity of ecclesiastical structures of repression. It was then followed by a decline, basically caused by the establishment of a tribunal of the Inquisition in Goa in 1560, exacerbated by a series of troubles in the region that provoked a crisis in Portuguese trading networks.[7] This framework also permits a better explanation of the continuously increasing New Christian diaspora spreading to Cape Verde and Guinea since the 1540s,[8] and especially to Brazil from the 1560s until the early eighteenth century, particularly because the Portuguese Inquisition (unlike that of Spain) never created a tribunal in America. Only in 1591 did the Holy Office start its first inspection of the area, and only in the eighteenth century was it able to create a consolidated network of agents (familiars and commissioners) in Brazil.[9] At the same time, Brazil grew in economic importance throughout the seventeenth century because of its sugar and slave trades.[10]

It should be noted that this persecution by secular and ecclesiastical authorities of first Jews and then (after 1497) New Christians was neither original nor specific to Portugal.[11] As Jonathan Israel has argued, between 1470 and 1570, Jewish communal life collapsed throughout western and central Europe, provoking a general exodus of Jews from very different regions.[12] Yet, according to the same scholar, after 1570 Jews started to be integrated in various western European regions

[6] For some interesting references concerning the situation in Azamor, see José Alberto Rodrigues da Silva Tavim, *Os judeus na expansão portuguesa em Marrocos durante o século XVI: Origens e actividades de uma comunidade* (Braga: Edições APPACDM Distrital de Braga, 1997), pp. 213–43.

[7] On the negative impact of the Inquisition and the disruption of Portuguese trade networks, see James C. Boyajian, *Portuguese Trade in Asia under the Habsburgs (1580–1640)* (Baltimore: Johns Hopkins University Press, 1993).

[8] See António de Almeida Mendes, 'Le rôle de l'inquisition en Guinée: Viscissitudes des présences juives sur la Petite Côte (XVe–XVIIe siècles)', *Revista Lusófona de Ciência das Religiões* 3:5–6 (2004), pp. 137–55.

[9] See Bruno Guilherme Feitler, 'Usos políticos del Santo Oficio portugués en el Atlántico (Brasil y África Occidental): El periodo filipino', *Hispania Sacra* 59:119 (2007), pp. 272–82; and Bruno Guilherme Feitler, *Inquisition, juifs et nouveaux-chrétiens au Brésil: Le Nordeste, XVIIe et XVIIIe siècles* (Leuven: Leuven University Press, 2003), pp. 67–70, 108.

[10] See Stuart B. Schwartz, *Sugar Plantations in the Formation of Brazilian Society: Bahia 1550–1835* (Cambridge: Cambridge University Press, 1985).

[11] However, the transformation of all Jews into New Christians (*conversos*) was a Portuguese peculiarity; see Francisco Bethencourt, 'A expulsão dos Judeus', in Diogo Ramada Curto (ed.), *O tempo de Vasco da Gama* (Lisboa: Comissão Nacional para as Comemorações dos Descobrimentos Portugueses/Difel, 1998), pp. 271–80.

[12] See Jonathan I. Israel, *European Jewry in the Age of Mercantilism: 1550–1750* (London: Littman Library of Jewish Civilization, 1998), pp. 8–17. Of course, there were local exceptions: see Mark D. Meyerson, *A Jewish Renaissance in Fifteenth-Century Spain* (Princeton: Princeton University Press, 2004).

(the Netherlands, Germany, France and Italy), making the Iberian peninsula and particularly Portugal isolated in a context of more tolerant policies towards Jews. This wider context allows a better understanding of the increasing exodus of Portuguese New Christians to certain European towns, particularly towns in France and Amsterdam.[13]

Portuguese New Christians also faced a set of social and political difficulties following Portugal's implementation of statutes of 'purity of blood',[14] and during the sixteenth century they were not successful in Guinea, according to António Mendes.[15] Their exclusion was probably even more dramatic in areas of the empire such as India, which had a pre-existing social and religious discriminatory system (the castes).

Concerning Portugal, one cannot talk about a single statute of 'purity of blood'. From the second half of the sixteenth century, many different institutions started to create special mechanisms to restrict or even erase the presence of New Christians among their members.[16] The regular clergy began these procedures with the Franciscans in 1558; others followed, like the Jesuits in 1593. Access to the military orders of *Avis*, *Cristo* and *Santiago* was restricted to 'Old Christians' after 1570; the 1577 regulations of the Lisbon *Misericórdia* (the most important of a widespread network of specifically Portuguese confraternities) stipulated that all its members or 'brothers' should be of 'pure blood'. After 1588, access to the secular clergy was also prohibited to New Christians. At the University of Coimbra and in some of its colleges, segregation started from 1591, while the prohibition on serving as judges or lesser local officials (*vereadores*) started in 1611 – just to name a few 'pure' institutions. Fernanda Olival argues that 'purity of blood' became increasingly important over time, especially from the seventeenth century onwards, reaching its peak by the end of the seventeenth and the first half of the eighteenth century.[17] All these measures contributed to a deeper divide within Portuguese

[13] Meyerson, *A Jewish Renaissance*, ch. 2. Escapes to France started after 1550; see José António Gonsalves de Mello, *Gente da nação: Cristãos-novos e judeus em Pernambuco, 1542–1654* (Recife: Fundação Joaquim Nabuco; Editora Massangana, 1989), p. 7. Amsterdam became attractive only after 1580; see Yosef Kaplan, *Les nouveaux-juifs d'Amsterdam: Essais sur l'histoire sociale et intellectuelle du judaisme séfarde au XVIIe siècle* (Paris: Éditions Chandeigne, 1999).

[14] The ideological roots of the system were religious and social, according to Kaplan, and in the Iberian peninsula they were the result of a general conviction that the conversion of the Jews was not, in most cases, authentic and genuine; Kaplan, *Les nouveaux-juifs*, p. 73. Israel argues that they also had economic motives (*European Jewry*, pp. 221–2), while J. Lúcio de Azevedo supports the importance of racial motivations in his *História dos Cristãos-Novos portugueses* (1921; Lisbon: Clássica Editora, 1975), p. 339. It is useful to emphasise that the status of purity of blood followed the same pattern in Portugal as in Spain, although with much delay and in a less pervasive mode.

[15] See Mendes, 'Le rôle de l'inquisition', pp. 137–55.

[16] For a good synthesis, see Fernanda Olival, 'Rigor e interesses: Os estatutos de limpeza de sangue em Portugal', *Cadernos de Estudos Sefarditas* 4 (2004), pp. 151–82.

[17] See Fernanda Olival, *As ordens militares e o Estado Moderno: Honra, mercê e venalidade em Portugal (1641–1789)* (Lisbon: Estar, 2002), pp. 284–5.

society, which also extended to its colonies, sometimes through specific decrees; for example, a royal order of February 1604 stated that only Old Christians could be appointed to church benefices in Brazil.[18] It could be argued that this general institutionalisation of 'purity of blood' statutes in Portuguese society continued and extended policies and practices of segregation towards Jews dating from the beginning of the fifteenth century, albeit of a different type. At a synod of the archbishopric of Lisbon held in 1403, for example, Jews and Christians were forbidden to live in the same neighbourhood, and Christian couples to feed Jewish children.[19] Yet it is possible that these rules were not generally observed by the population.

It is true that Manuel I adopted measures seeking the social integration of all the Jews mass-baptised in 1497. Profiting from these measures, some were admitted to the military orders, and New Christians also held positions in the churches, cathedral chapters and at the University. Still others served at the monarch's court, in the army, or in local governments as 'vereadores'. The king even gave some of them titles and patents of nobility ('escudeiros' and 'cavaleiros').[20] In 1513 Manuel I also declared fines for anyone who offended New Christians by calling them 'marranos'.[21] During the 1520s, his successor John III promoted similar measures of integration.[22] Some scholars have suggested that between 1497 and 1531, the Crown tried to promote the peaceful integration of New Christians into Portuguese society.[23] But even with such policies, after the forced conversion of 1497 the

[18] See José Justino de Andrade e Silva, *Colecção chronologica da legislação portugueza compilada e anotada* (Lisbon: Imprensa de F. X. de Souza, 1854–9), vol. 1, pp. 4–5.

[19] See Antonio García y García, *Synodicon Hispanum* (Madrid: Biblioteca de Autores Cristianos, 1982), pp. 328–9. For a recent synthesis of Jewish segregation in an important Portuguese city (Coimbra) during the thirteenth, fourteenth and fifteenth centuries, see Saul António Gomes, 'Coimbra judaica: A história e o esquecimento', in *Coimbra Judaica: Actas* (Coimbra: Câmara Municipal de Coimbra, 2009), pp. 27–42, see pp. 30–5.

[20] The best studies on this topic are those of Maria José Pimenta Ferro Tavares: see, for example, *Judaismo e Inquisição: Estudos* (Lisbon: Editorial Presença, 1987), esp. pp. 48–51, 192–3. Other interesting examples of privileges offered by the king to some members of the famous Reinel family, who traded in North Africa and established a commercial network with branches in Flanders and Rouen, can be found in António Manuel Lopes Andrade, 'De Ferrara a Lisboa: Tribulações do cristão-novo Alexandre Reinel, preso no cárcere do Santo Ofício', *Cadernos de Estudos Sefarditas* 7 (2007), pp. 83–131, see pp. 89–91.

[21] Valentim Fernandes (João José Alves Dias, ed.), *Ordenações Manuelinas. Livros I a V. Reprodução em fac-símile da edição de Valentim Fernandes (Lisboa, 1512–1513)* (Lisbon: Universidade Nova de Lisboa, 2002), vol. 2, fol. 65.

[22] A good example was the privileges offered to Álvaro Mendes, a New Christian from Tavira, who had served the king in India and was made a knight of the military Order of Christ after returning to Portugal; see Cunha, *A Inquisição*, p. 44. Also very interesting is the case of the Crasto do Rio family, who became Viscounts of Barbacena, and many other examples given by Francisco Bethencourt, in *The Inquisition: A Global History, 1478–1834* (Cambridge: Cambridge University Press, 2009), pp. 327–9.

[23] See Révah, *Études portugaises*, pp. 191–202.

difficulties of integration for New Christians did not disappear. Most of them still lived in the former ghettos, and their freedom to travel and sell goods was restricted. The populace generally hated and envied them. The best example of this climate was the massacre perpetrated against Lisbon's New Christians in 1506, when hundreds were killed by rioters egged on by Dominican friars.[24]

In some ways the divide also resulted from behaviour displayed by members of the New Christian communities themselves. In order to preserve their identity, at least during the first two or three decades after their forced conversion, a great number of them still spoke Hebrew, possessed Jewish books, preferred endogamous marriages, and secretly maintained Jewish religious practices.[25] Later, after the foundation of the Inquisition, the conditions of segregation worsened. The use of specific garments ('sambenitos') by those condemned by the Holy Office, their exhibition by hanging the 'sambenitos' on the walls of churches, the public infamy and injuries New Christians suffered during *autos da fé*, and the violent sermons preached at these rituals are good examples of this.[26] After 1672, those sentenced by the Inquisition were prohibited from wearing silk clothing or jewels and riding horses.[27] The production of anti-*converso* literature must also be considered an important tool of segregation.[28] This ambience of segregation soon reached into all areas of the Portuguese-speaking world. During the 1530s we hear echoes coming from the eastern parts of the Portuguese empire. In 1534, for example, a local secular authority in Ormuz criticised the privileges offered to New Christians by the Crown, claiming that they were still Jews and practised Judaism. Similarly, in 1541 royal officials in Arzila pressured the king to expel the New Christians from the town.[29] The level of mistrust against New Christians could reach extraordinary levels. In Brazil, in 1742, after the discovery that a certain priest was a New Christian, a debate erupted about whether or not the baptisms he celebrated were valid.[30]

With these barriers all over the empire, Portuguese New Christians tried to profit from any available opportunities in order to reach or approximate a state of complete integration, or at least to conceal their New Christian roots as far as possible. Many followed strategies of integration and, even despite all these obstacles, some

[24] One of the best reconstructions of this pogrom is Yosef Hayim Yerushalmi, *The Lisbon Massacre of 1506 and the Royal Image in the Shebet Yehudah* (Cincinnati: Hebrew Union College, 1976).

[25] See Tavares, *Judaismo e Inquisição*, p. 54; and Maria José Pimenta Ferro Tavares, 'Para o estudo dos judeus de Trás-os-Montes, no século XVI', *Cultura História e Filosofia* 4 (1985), pp. 371–401.

[26] See Bethencourt, *The Inquisition*, esp. pp. 286–91.

[27] See Azevedo, *História dos Cristãos-Novos*, p. 293.

[28] A good example is Fernão Ximenes de Aragão, *Doutrina catholica para instrucção e confirmação dos fieis e extincção das seitas supersticiosas e em particular do judaismo* (Lisbon: Pedro Craesbeck, 1625).

[29] Cunha, *A Inquisição*, pp. 19, 29.

[30] The episode was mentioned by the bishop of Maranhão: see Manuel da Cruz (Aldo Luiz Leoni, ed.), *Copiador de cartas particulares do Senhor Dom Frei Manuel da Cruz, bispo do Maranhão e de Mariana (1739–1762)* (Brasília: Edições do Senado Federal, 2008), p. 66.

succeeded. José de Mello has shown that among the most powerful and rich Portuguese living in Pernambuco, Brazil, at the end of the sixteenth century were three New Christians.[31] He also demonstrated how New Christians held important positions in the sugar and slave trade, farmed royal taxes, or played crucial roles in financing local economic activities.[32] Arnold Wiznitzer remarked that when the first Inquisitorial delegation reached Brazil, Bahia contained a very prosperous and rich community of New Christians, some of them established since the beginning of Portuguese settlement in the region.[33]

In India, until 1530, they managed to serve in the army (*milícia*) and local government while trying to profit from trading opportunities and money lending, as did Old Christians. Some created deeper local roots than Old Christians because they never returned to Portugal, whereas most other Portuguese went back after some years of residence in the East.[34] Some Portuguese *fidalgos* in Asia even protected New Christians from the Inquisition because they were their associates in profitable trading ventures.[35] By the mid-sixteenth century, some New Christians in Pernambuco succeeded in marrying their daughters to Old Christians holding good positions in the army or local government.[36] Feitler, who studied the New Christian community of Paraiba during the seventeenth century, provided good evidence that they still practised hidden forms of crypto-judaism, yet stressed that socially and outside the home they adopted lifestyles very similar to those of their Old Christian neighbours: baptising their children, attending Sunday mass, confessing during Easter, parading during processions, enrolling in local confraternities, and so forth.[37] Similar situations can be found in Cape Verde or Cochim in India.[38] Some New Christians even became priests and obtained benefices in churches and even cathedrals, as was the case of the half-canon Manuel Afonso in Bahia around 1560.[39] We know of bishops who favoured them, like the prelate of

[31] Mello, *Gente da nação*, p. 51.

[32] Mello, *Gente da nação*, pp. 9–11.

[33] See Arnold Wiznitzer, *Os judeus no Brasil colonial* (São Paulo: Livraria Pioneira Editora, 1966), pp. 5–24.

[34] See Cunha, *A Inquisição*, pp. 24–5, 39. Other very good examples for Cochim, by the middle of the sixteenth century, are given by José Alberto Rodrigues da Silva Tavim, *Judeus e cristãos-novos de Cochim: História e memória (1500–1662)* (Lisbon: Universidade Nova de Lisboa, 2001), pp. 223–6.

[35] Boyajian, *Portuguese Trade*, pp. 174–5, and Francisco Bethencourt, 'A Igreja', in Bethencourt and Chaudhuri (eds), *História da expansão portuguesa*, vol. 1, pp. 369–86, see p. 385.

[36] As was the case of a certain Branca Dias; tried by the Lisbon Inquisition in 1545, she travelled afterwards to Pernambuco with her husband, where they became rich sugar producers and some of their daughters married prominent Old Christians; see Mello, *Gente da nação*, pp. 129–30.

[37] Guilherme Feitler, *Inquisition, juifs et nouveaux-chrétiens*, pp. 283–358.

[38] See Filipa I. Ribeiro da Silva, *A Inquisição em Cabo Verde, Guiné e São Tomé e Príncipe (1536–1821): Contributo para o estudo da política do Santo Ofício nos territórios africanos* (Lisbon: Universidade Nova de Lisboa, 2002); and Tavim, *Judeus e cristãos-novos de Cochim*, pp. 286–330.

[39] This example is given by José Gonçalves Salvador, *Cristãos-novos, jesuítas e Inquisição (aspectos da sua atuação nas capitanias do Sul, 1530–1680)* (São Paulo: Livraria Pioneira/Universidade de São

cont.

Rio de Janeiro, José de Barros Alarcão (1680–1700). It was common knowledge that Barros Alarcão baptised some New Christian children personally; when travelling on pastoral visitations, he lodged with members of this group, and he found ways for some to obtain papal permission to become clerics – which, as we saw, had been forbidden since 1588.[40] It is not surprising, then, that when the Inquisition began a more severe persecution of New Christians in the area of Rio de Janeiro at the beginning of the eighteenth century, arresting and condemning hundreds, some were rich farmers, others held commands in the army or even in the local administration, and many were clerics.[41]

In this context, each family combined different strategies in order to better conceal their origin. In 1609 the Coimbra Inquisition sentenced a certain André de Barros Beça. This New Christian, a canon at Oporto, told the inquisitors that he had six brothers and three sisters. All his sisters were nuns, while his elder brother was a priest in one of Oporto's most prestigious parishes. Another was in service to the Duke of Bragança, the head of Portugal's most prestigious noble family; a third brother was married to an Old Christian woman; a fourth was a Franciscan friar; a fifth had enrolled as a soldier in India; and the youngest lived with him, preparing to became a priest too.[42]

During the seventeenth and eighteenth centuries it became more difficult for a New Christian to dissimulate his origins. But some still succeeded even in passing the scrutiny of Portugal's two institutions with the strictest means for controlling the genealogy of candidates: the military orders and the Inquisition. Fernanda Olival has shown that after the Portuguese Restoration in 1640, many New Christians who served the new Portuguese king, John IV – as ambassadors in France and the Netherlands, in the wars against the Dutch in Brazil and Africa, or as important traders and bankers who loaned money to the monarch – were favoured with the most prestigious social distinction of becoming members of the Military Order of Christ.[43] In some extraordinary cases, even New Christians condemned by the Inquisition later received this distinction.[44] Moreover, a few New Christians even managed to pass the Inquisition's control to become familiars of the Tribunal.[45]

Paulo, 1969), pp. 12–13. The same scholar also provides many other examples, from Maranhão in the north to the far south, insisting that some New Christians acted this way with the permission of local bishops or by bribing ecclesiastical authorities; see pp. 30–63.

[40] Alberto Dines, *Vínculos do fogo: António José da Silva, o Judeu e outras histórias da Inquisição em Portugal e no Brasil* (Saõ Paulo: Companhia das Letras, 1999), p. 363.

[41] Wiznitzer, *Os judeus no Brasil*, p. 130.

[42] See Direcção Geral de Arquivos/Torre do Tombo (Lisbon), Inquisição de Coimbra, proc. 2349, fols 28v–29v.

[43] Olival, *As ordens militares*, p. 289; Israel stresses that this policy of favouring powerful Jews was usual everywhere in Europe; *European Jewry*, p. 89.

[44] Olival, *As ordens militares*, p. 291.

[45] A very interesting case from 1735 concerns António Soares, from Viseu, who had falsified parish registers and bribed witnesses to hide his New Christian origins; see Direcção Geral de Arquivos/Torre do Tombo (Lisbon), Conselho Geral do Santo Ofício, Maço 17, doc. 28.

This mixture forged by Inquisitorial repression, the statutes of 'purity of blood', and other mechanisms of social segregation, together with the characteristics of Portugal's seaborne empire (particularly the fact that it was dispersed through three different continents and was not continuous), had five major consequences:

1. First, and obviously, the suffering and violence that it caused in thousands of individual lives and families, some of them split apart for ever.
2. The disruption of Portugal's production and trading networks at both local and global levels.
3. The economic and spiritual enrichment of areas that benefited from the diaspora of the 'Portuguese Nation'.
4. The debilitation of Portuguese power in certain areas.
5. Finally, the contribution to the continuous rebuilding of a specific identity of the Portuguese New Christians, or the 'Portuguese Nation' as they were usually recognised and defined.

I will not comment on the first aspect, though it must not be forgotten or dismissed.[46] By contrast, I would like to expand on the others. We possess numerous examples of the negative economic impact of the segregation of New Christians. In India, by the late 1550s, when the Tribunal of Goa was about to begin operating, many New Christians, some of whom played important roles in spice trading, fled to Ormuz, Turkey, and other places, provoking difficulties in the spice trade.[47] In Brazil, the massive attack of the Inquisition during the first half of the eighteenth century quite destroyed the capacity of sugar plantations in the region of Rio de Janeiro, where New Christians were major farmers.[48] On the western coast of Africa, particularly in Senegambia, there was a prosperous community of New Christians, established during the sixteenth century, of whom some were involved in local trade and others in the global networks of the slave trade. This community was strongly persecuted by an Inquisitorial inspection held between 1596 and 1598, during which around 20 per cent of the accused were New Christian traders.[49] Following this and other repressive measures, the New Christian presence in the region was drastically reduced after 1625.[50] Some scholars have even argued that

[46] See the touching end of a letter written in the second half of the sixteenth century by a New Christian woman: 'Feita de noite, as doze horas, com muitas lagrimas de vontade e saudades grandes que cheguam ao coraçam', quoted in Andrade, 'De Ferrara a Lisboa', p. 126.

[47] See Cunha, *A Inquisição*, pp. 32–3.

[48] Though not very systematic, there is good data available to demonstrate this in Dines, *Vínculos do fogo*.

[49] See José Augusto Nunes da Silva Horta, 'A Inquisição em Angola e Congo: O inquérito de 1596–98 e o papel mediador das justiças locais', *Arqueologia do Estado: Primeiras Jornadas sobre formas de organização e exercício dos poderes na Europa do Sul, Séculos XIII–XVIII*, 2 vols (Lisbon: História & Crítica, 1988), vol. 1, pp. 387–415, see p. 391.

[50] See Peter Mark, *'Portuguese Style' and Luso-African Identity: Precolonial Senegambia, Sixteenth–Nineteenth Centuries* (Bloomington: Indiana University Press, 2002), p. 16.

economic rivals of New Christians used the Inquisition as a tool to remove them from the market.[51]

Another consequence of the New Christians' persecution and segregation was their escape in search of safety and more freedom, both of trading and religion. This, of course, promoted economic growth in those areas that received them. This was the case in certain towns on the north coast of Africa, including Marrakech and Fez, and certain areas of Turkey and Beirut, which benefited from the exodus of those fleeing India.[52] The same phenomenon recurred in Brazil. After the first visit of the Inquisition to the region of Bahia (in 1591–5), some rich sugar producers, bankers and slave traders escaped to Amsterdam; one of them, Jacob Tirado, founded the first synagogue of the Portuguese Nation in the Low Countries.[53] The exodus intensified after the second visit of the Inquisition to Brazil in 1618, with others seeking security in other parts of the Americas such as Buenos Aires or Chile,[54] or even in other Brazilian regions, such as Espírito Santo, which were less well controlled by the Inquisition.[55]

The erosion of Portuguese power in some of its overseas possessions could also be considered. According to Anita Novinsky, the conquest of Bahia by the Dutch in 1624, and later Paraíba and Pernambuco (1634–5), was directly linked to the previous repression of New Christians by the Inquisition. Novinsky suggests that the exodus of some Portuguese to the Netherlands, and the lack of financial support to sustain an army capable of facing the Dutch invasion, were direct consequences of the repression of New Christians.[56] The same logic could also be applicable to the case of Luanda and the island of São Tomé, also invaded and conquered by Dutch troops in 1642. Similarly, Boyajian argued that the Inquisitorial repression in India, which intensified after the 1630s, anticipated the collapse of the Portuguese empire confronted with a major Dutch and English presence in the region.[57]

Finally, social segregation was largely responsible for the continuous reconstruction of a specific identity of the Portuguese New Christians. Their 'identity is the product of a continuous process, or more precisely, a continuously dynamic process'.[58] Nathan Wachtel is one of the authors who have linked the strongest marks of New Christian identity to the repression and segregation they suffered in

[51] For Cochim, see examples given by Tavim, *Judeus e cristãos-novos de Cochim*, p. 225; or for Goa, Boyajian, *Portuguese Trade*, p. 184.

[52] Some good examples in Tavim, *Os judeus na expansão portuguesa*; and Tavim, *Judeus e cristãos-novos de Cochim*; also in Cunha, *A Inquisição*, pp. 58–9.

[53] Mello, *Gente da nação*, pp. 17–19.

[54] Wiznitzer, *Os judeus no Brasil*, pp. 34–5.

[55] Good examples in Dines, *Vínculos do fogo*, pp. 376–7.

[56] See Anita Novinsky, *Cristãos novos na Bahia* (São Paulo: Perspectiva, 1972).

[57] Boyajian, *Portuguese Trade*.

[58] Mark, *'Portuguese Style'*, p. 5.

Portugal and its empire.[59] In fact, some aspects of the Portuguese Nation's identity were the outcome of that 'continuous process': the permanent geographical, social and even religious mobility of these communities, as remarked upon by Yosef Kaplan;[60] their economic dynamism, which transformed them into a powerful economic nation, but one without a territory (a 'nonterritorial nation' according to Studnicky-Gizbert);[61] and their huge heterogeneity and hybridism, even from the point of view of their religious practices and beliefs, as Wachtel has underlined. Wachtel argues that the specific religious field of the New Christians was neither Judaic nor Christian, but resulted from a permanent tension between the two religions, with all the hesitations, doubts of conscience, and processes of double sincerity this provoked, but also sceptical and radical ruptures.[62] Accordingly, what unified them was not religion, but the 'faith of remembrance' and pride in the blood of common ancestors who had shared suffering, segregation and even death for being Jews. In essence, it was awareness of a distinctive collective history that united them.[63] In this sense they provide a good example of deep 'cultural *métissage*', that is, the result of 'the interaction and assimilation between two or more discrete cultures, the product of which is a new mixed culture'.[64] The crypto-judaism some performed, with diverse characteristics according to specific time and space, is a good example of this.

Despite all this apparatus of policies of segregation, undertaken by the Crown and the Church and reflected in the attitudes and behaviours of much of the population, Portuguese New Christians – or rather, a few of them – managed to create powerful economic and trading networks all over the world. James Boyajian put it very explicitly:

> The Portuguese overseas trade placed Europeans for the first time on virtually every continent and in every ocean, exchanging Chinese silks, Sumatran pepper, and Indian cottons for Mexican and Peruvian silver, and Indonesian spices and Indian diamonds for Portuguese wines, Baltic grains and naval stores, and German and English hardware. And Portuguese merchants created a wholly new South Atlantic trade, based on the unprecedented expansion of sugar cultivation in Brazil and the supply of African slave labour, and linked it to Asia via the Cape. The leading New Christian

[59] Nathan Wachtel, *A fé da lembrança: Labirintos marranos* (2001; Lisboa: Caminho, 2002), esp. pp. 353–4.

[60] Kaplan, *Les nouveaux-juifs*, pp. 34–41.

[61] See Daviken Studnicky-Gizbert, 'La "nation portugaise": Réseaux marchands dans l'espace atlantique à l'époque moderne', *Annales. Histoire, Sciences Sociales* 58:3 (2003), pp. 627–48, see pp. 627–8, 632.

[62] Nathan Wachtel, 'Frontières intérieures: La religiosité marrane en Amérique hispanique (XVII siècle)', in Rui Manuel Loureiro and Serge Gruzinski (eds), *Passar as fronteiras. Actas do II Colóquio Internacional sobre mediadores culturais. Séculos XV a XVIII* (Lagos: Centro de Estudos Gila Eanes, 1999), pp. 111–32, see p. 111.

[63] Wachtel, *A fé da lembrança*, esp. pp. 28–32 and the Conclusion.

[64] Mark, *'Portuguese Style'*, p. 5.

> merchants were major players in all of the overseas endeavours, and they probably were the only Portuguese merchant families represented in all of these regions at once.[65]

Thus, I must agree with Fernanda Olival that the policies of 'blood purity' in Portugal, though restrictive for New Christians and tending to prevent social integration and social mobility, existed for 'disciplining society' but were not 'an insurmountable barrier'.[66] Yet, as I have tried to show, they traced a deep divide that marked New Christians throughout the Portuguese-speaking world.

[65] Boyajian, *Portuguese Trade*, preface, p. xiii. Wachtel also stressed that even though New Christians were subjected to policies of 'purity of blood' which created situations of severe segregation, they were able to create 'des vastes réseaux de solidarité, renforcés par des liens de parentés'; Wachtel, 'Frontières intérieures', p. 111.
[66] Olival, *As ordens militares*, p. 393.

14

From Marco Polo to Manuel I of Portugal: The Image of the East African Coast in the Early Sixteenth Century

JEAN MICHEL MASSING

FOR THE LATE FIFTEENTH and early sixteenth century, information, especially visual information, concerning East Africa is so rare that it has never been studied before, while ethnic relations cannot be easily assessed either as the sources are so sparse. Globally, in the sixteenth century (and this is certainly true for the accounts of both Africa and America), race and skin colour were not seen as the most fundamental division between peoples. First came the basic, definitive split between Christians and Muslims – who were seen as having rejected Christ's message – while people from other religions or 'without religion' were seen as potential Christians. Lineage too was fundamental. Kings were respected for their social status, especially when they became Christians, while slaves (and there were certainly many more black slaves) were treated as such. Another important aspect was European notions of civility dividing the world between 'civilised' and 'savage' peoples.[1] Race and colour were obviously divisive, but were more often seen as reflecting the diversity of the world than in the eighteenth and nineteenth centuries, when prejudice underpinned complex racial theories ordering the world; these theories were later reinforced by Darwinism and social Darwinism, which saw human evolution as a step from the primitive to the civilised.[2] These basic distinctions often overlapped or were given more or less prominence by authors who had specific agendas and saw Africa either as an economic partner or as a foe, as a land of infidels or of souls to conquer – or of people to enslave.

[1] See, for example, Jean Michel Massing, 'From the "Age of Discovery" to the Age of Abolition: Europe and the World Beyond' in David Bindman and Henry Louis Gates (eds), *The Image of the Black in Western Art*, vol. 3.2 (Cambridge, MA: Harvard University Press, 2011), p. 2; see also pp. 395–9 for anthropological accounts.

[2] See, for example, David Bindman, *Ape to Apollo: Aesthetics and the Idea of Race in the 18th Century* (London: Reaktion Books, 2002).

Proceedings of the British Academy **179**, *281–311.*

Black Africans, as with peoples of all nations of the world, were stereotyped, sometimes in a dichotomic manner between those who looked like Europeans in all but colour, and those who were considered to have more marked African characteristics, especially wide white eyes, snub and flat noses, thick lips and white teeth. Stereotypes characterised peoples and nations: Africans were often considered carefree, while Portuguese people, in the sixteenth century, were seen as being gloomy and melancholic.[3] The importance given to rank, as we know from the chronicles of Rui de Pina and João de Barros, explains the fact that the African prince 'Bemoim' was received in great pomp by King João II in Lisbon in 1488 – he and his retinue were issued with European clothing suitable to their rank and even servants.[4] This is also why Dom Enrique, a son of Dom Afonso I, king of Kongo, became bishop of Utica in 1518.[5] The situation on the east coast of Africa also reflected contradictory elements in the assessment of the local populations, as it included a whole range of black African groups, Swahili people, as well as the rich human diversity of the people found around the Indian Ocean, including Arab and Gujarati merchants. There were many different ethnicities, degrees of civility, religions, and of course skin colours, and this is reflected in the interest of Portuguese chronicles and in the imagery.[6]

When Vasco da Gama reached the Indian Ocean, he connected for the first time two major trade areas, the Mediterranean and the Indian Ocean.[7] The European vision of the world then changed radically in economic and political terms, through trade, cultural exchange and political alliances. The famous Catalan Atlas of 1375, the finest surviving medieval world map, stressed trade and navigation on its left half, as the Mediterranean area is based on a sea chart (portolan), while the oriental

[3] Carmen Radulet, 'An Outsider's Inside View of Sixteenth-Century Portugal', *Portuguese Studies* 13 (1997), pp. 152–8, see p. 153; see also Kate Lowe, 'The Stereotyping of Black Africans in Renaissance Europe', in Thomas Foster Earle and Kate J. P. Lowe (eds), *Black Africans in Renaissance Europe* (Cambridge: Cambridge University Press, 2005), pp. 17–47, see pp. 26–7.

[4] The two chronicles have been studied by Peter Edward Russell, 'White Kings on Black Kings: Rui de Pina and the Problem of Black African Sovereignty', in *Portugal, Spain and the Atlantic, 1340–1490: Chivalry and Crusade from John of Gaunt to Henry the Navigator* (Aldershot: Variorum, 1995), pp. 151–63; see also Lowe, 'The Stereotyping of Black Africans', pp. 43–4.

[5] Charles-Martial de Witte, 'Henri de Congo, évêque titulaire d'Utique († c.1531), d'après les documents romains', *Euntes docete* 21 (1968), pp. 587–99; François Bontinck, 'Ndoadidiki Ne-Kinu a Mubemba, premier évêque Kongo (c. 1495–c. 1531)', *Revue africaine de théologie* 3:6 (1979), pp. 149–69.

[6] In Burgkmair's People of Africa and India woodcut, it is the king of Cochin carried by his subjects who testifies for great kingdoms (for the woodcut see below, esp. note 60). For a painting recently discovered representing this scene, see Jean Michel Massing, in Jay A. Levenson (ed.), *Encompassing the Globe: Portugal and the World in the 16th and 17th Centuries: Reference Catalogue* (Washington, DC: Arthur M. Sackler Gallery, Smithsonian Institution, 2007), p. 35, no. and fig. P-31.

[7] For Vasco da Gama's travels, see Alvaro Velho (Damião Peres, António Baião and Artur de Magalhães Basto, eds), *Diário da viagem de Vasco da Gama*, 2 vols (Porto: Livraria Civilização, 1945); I have used the English translation and edition by Ernest Ravenstein: Alvaro Velho, *A Journal of the First Voyage of Vasco de Gama, 1497–1499* (London: Hakluyt Society, 1898).

half was constructed not only with the help of biblical information, apocalyptic writings, and ancient and medieval sources, but also travellers' accounts, especially information from Marco Polo.[8] The cartographer, who has been identified as Abraham Cresque, took as his main source the account of the voyage to China. Marco's father and uncle, Nicolo and Maffeo Polo, had been there before, returning to Europe in 1269.[9] They revisited China two years later, travelling overland with the young Marco, who stayed at the court, and made expeditions in the service of Kublai Khan, the emperor who founded the Yuan Dynasty. Marco Polo stayed in China until 1292, when he returned by sea from Zhangzhou to Sumatra, Ceylon and India, providing a firsthand account of these countries in his *Description of the World* (*Il Milione*). He arrived back in Venice in 1295. The Catalan Atlas describes the eastern part of the world as he recorded it, but without precise geographical knowledge. In cartographic terms, Asia is based on the medieval *mappae mundi* mixture of written sources with a very approximate definition of an enormous region whose importance is clearly understood, but not its form. Cities are often located in the order they appear in lists and travel accounts, in lands in which sophisticated old cultures are shown side-by-side with fabulous and monstrous 'races' from the edges of the world.[10]

But Asia was also the land of spices. The map divides the world roughly at the level of the tropic of Cancer, creating a seaway from the Persian Gulf to the Indian Ocean and from there towards China, through the lands of spices, of precious wares, of silver and of gold – Marco Polo's tantalising East. For European trade, the problem came from the fact that the Arabs controlled the Near East, and goods had to go overland to reach the Mediterranean (Figure 14.1). Abraham Cresque, if

[8] Abraham Cresque (?), *El Atlas catalán. Primera edición completa en el sexcentésimo aniversario de su realización 1375–1975* (Barcelona: Diáfora, 1975); Hans-Christian Freiesleben, *Der katalanische Weltatlas vom Jahre 1375* (Stuttgart: Brockhaus, Abt. Antiquarium, 1977); for my quote I have used the edition by Georges Grosjean of Cresque Abraham (?), *Mappa Mundi: The Catalan Atlas of the Year 1375* (Zurich: Urs Graf, 1978). For serious doubts about the identification of Abraham Cresque as the author, see Tony Campbell, *Early Maps* (New York: Abbeville Press, 1981), p. 116. For a study, see Jean Michel Massing, 'Observations and Beliefs: The World of the Catalan Atlas', in Jay A. Levenson (ed.), *Circa 1492: Art in the Age of Exploration* (New Haven: Yale University Press, 1991), pp. 27–33, see also pp. 120–1, no. and fig. 1; the article is reproduced in Jean Michel Massing, *Studies in Imagery*, vol. 2, *The World Discovered* (London: Pindar, 2007), pp. 1–22.

[9] For the *Description of the World* (*Il Milione*) see Marco Polo (Arthur Christopher Moule and Paul Pelliot, eds), *The Description of the World*, 2 vols (London: G. Routledge, 1938). For an Aragonese version, see Juan Fernández de Heredia (John J. Nitti, ed.), *Juan Fernández de Heredia's Aragonese Version of the Libro de Marco Polo* (Madison, WI: Hispanic Seminary of Medieval Studies, 1980). For studies, see Leonard Olschki, *L'Asia di Marco Polo: Introduzione alla lettura e allo studio del Milione* (Venice and Rome: Istituto per la collaborazione culturale, 1957); Paul Pelliot, *Notes on Marco Polo*, 3 vols (Paris: Imprimerie Nationale, 1959–73); and the various studies in E. Balazs *et al.*, *Oriente Poliano: Studi e conferenze . . . in occasione del VII centenario della nascita di Marco Polo (1254–1954)* (Roma: Istituto italiano per il Medio e Estremo Oriente, 1957).

[10] For an overall view of the map in geo-political and cultural terms, see Massing, 'Observations and Beliefs', pp. 27–33, 120–1.

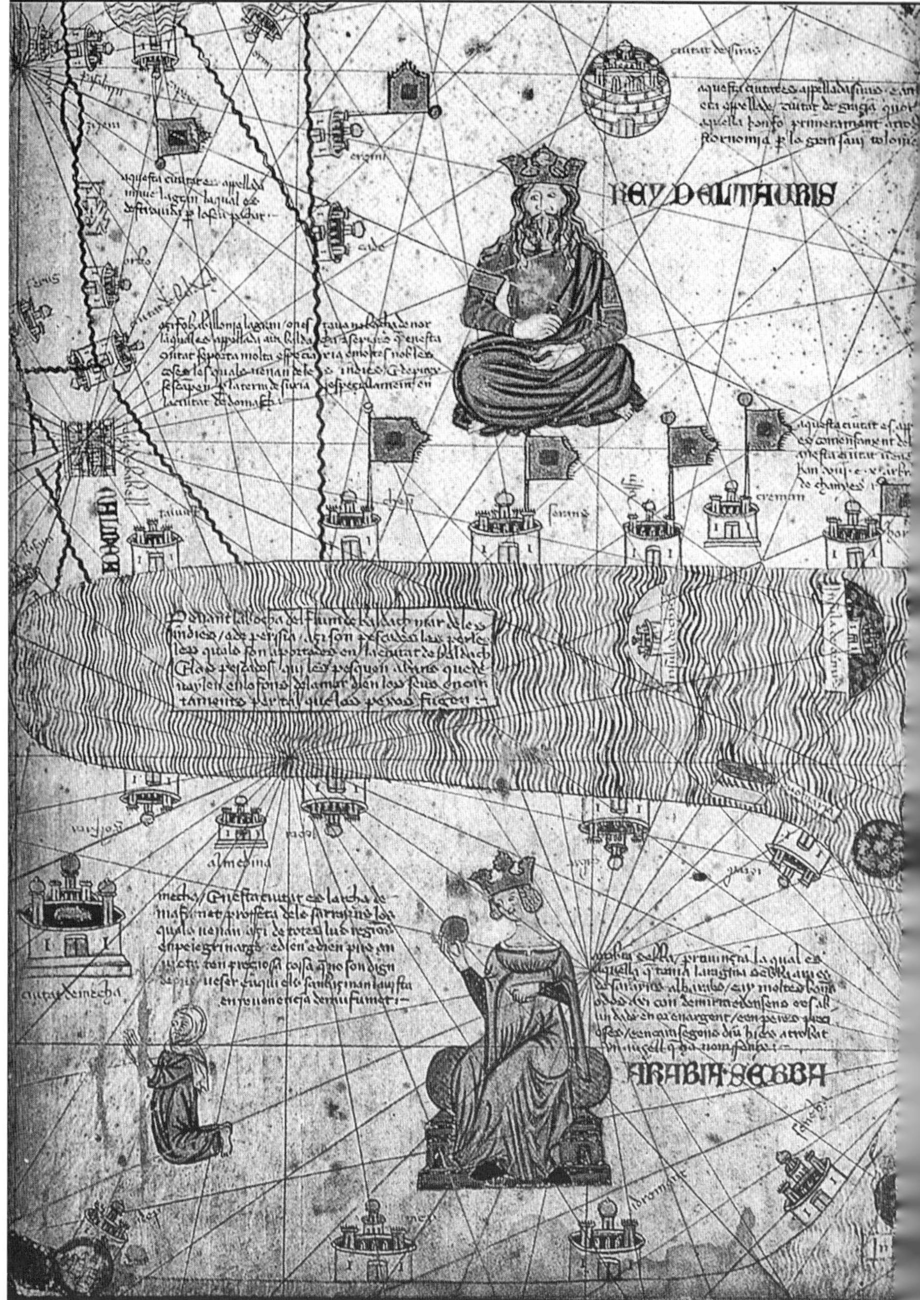

Figure 14.1. *Catalan Atlas*, 1375, Paris, Bibliothèque nationale de France

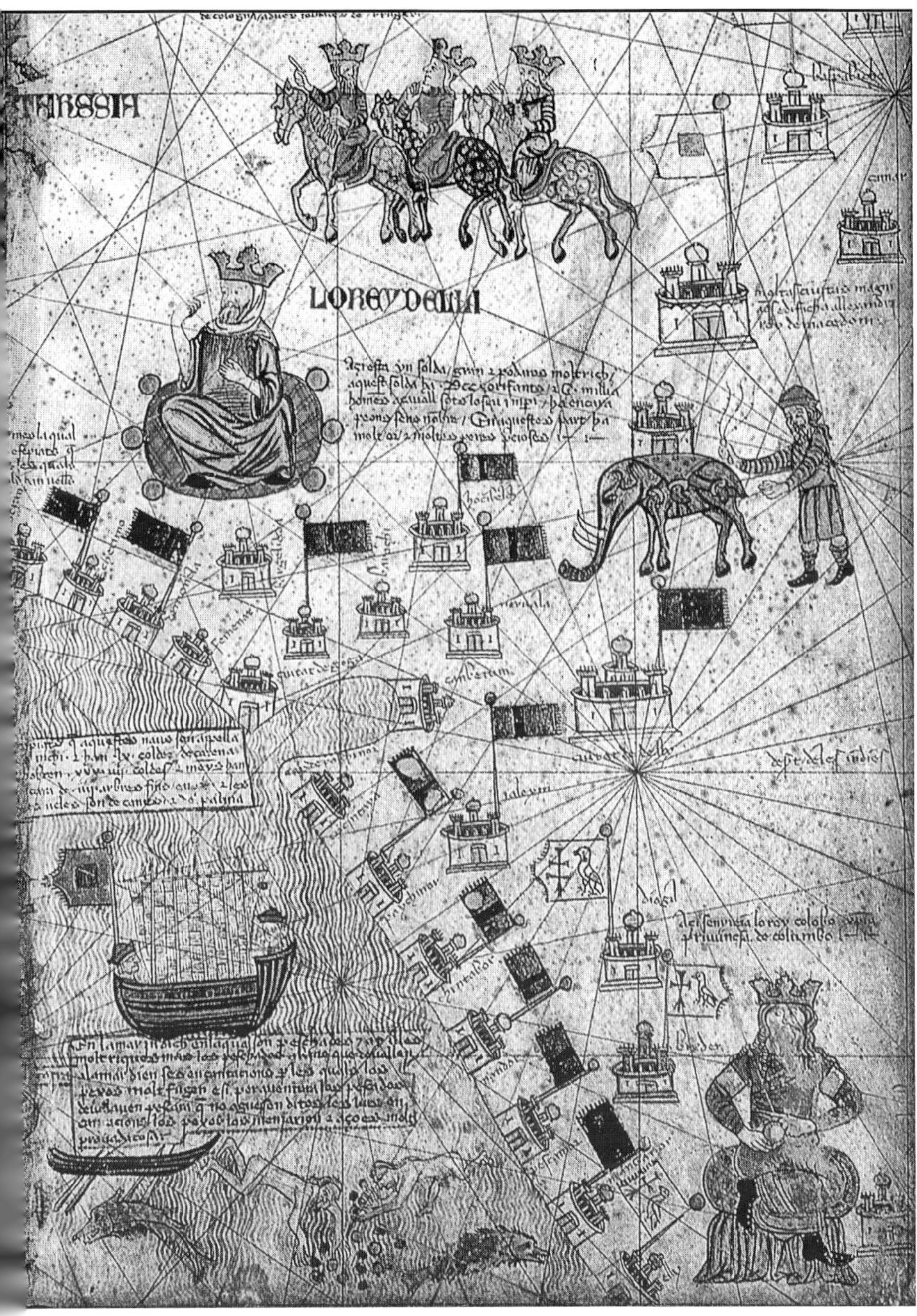

he was indeed the cartographer, was evidently aware of this: 'Through this [Red] sea pass most of the spices that come from India to Alexandria';[11] and 'In the town of Chos [Quseir] the spices that have come from India are taken on land. From here they are taken to Babylon and Alexandria'[12] – and from there, of course, to Europe. Trade also passed through the Persian Gulf and Baghdad: 'Know that in this town many spices and precious wares which come from India arrive and from here are transported and sold throughout the Syrian land, especially in Damascus.'[13] Eastwards, trading stations are indicated on the shore of the Indian Ocean from Hormuz, 'where India begins', to Quillon.[14] In the sea, a boat is represented that is similar to another one east of India: 'Know', informs a cartouche, 'that these ships are called "nichi", and the length of the keel is 60 ells, with a draught of 34 ells, at least four but sometimes as many as ten masts, and sails made of bamboo and palm leaves' – perhaps a reference to Chinese junks.[15] In India, rich in gold and precious stones, are found two rulers: the great, powerful and very wealthy Sultan of Delhi, who commands a cavalry of 700 elephants, 100,000 horsemen, and innumerable foot soldiers;[16] and the Kingdom of Vijayanagar, where the king of Colombo rules 'over the Christian Province of Colombo'.[17] The East African coast, however, except for the areas bordering the Red Sea, is not even mentioned.

This would change with the voyage of Bartolomeu Dias, who rounded the Cape of Good Hope in 1487–8 – an event documented in Henricus Martellus's world map of *circa* 1489, which has Africa seriously disproportioned along the latitudinal axis but shows a few places on the southeastern coast of the continent. Although some place names are of Ptolemaic origin – while Zanzibar and Madagascar owe

[11] Cresque (?), *Mappa Mundi*, p. 76.

[12] Cresque (?), *Mappa Mundi*, p. 77. For the importance of Quseir, see Albert Kammerer, *La Mer Rouge, l'Abyssinie et l'Arabie depuis l'antiquité: Essai d'histoire et de géographie historique*, vols 1.1–3.3 (Cairo: Société royale de géographie d'Égypte, 1929–52), vol. 1.1, pp. 81–2; see also Marino Sanudo, *Liber secretorum fidelium crucis super Terrae Sanctae recuperatione et conservatione*, in Jacques Bongars (ed.), *Gesta Dei per Francos, sive, Orientalium expeditionum, et Regni Francorum Hierosolimitani historia* (Hanover: Wechelianis apud haeredes Ioan Aubrii, 1611), vol. 2, pp. 22–3.

[13] Cresque (?), *Mappa Mundi*, p. 81.

[14] Cresque (?), *Mappa Mundi*, p. 81. For Hormus in the Persian Gulf, see Pelliot, *Notes on Marco Polo*, vol. 1, pp. 576–82; and Alfons Gabriel, *Marco Polo in Persien* (Vienna: Verlag Typographische Anstalt, 1963), pp. 147–51; for Quilon, see pp. 399–402. *The Periplus of the Erythrean Sea*, a Roman text written in Greek *c.* AD 50, lists the towns on the coast of India from the Indus to the Ganges; see Wilfred Harvey Schoff (ed.), *The Periplus of the Erythraean Sea: Travel and Trade in the Indian Ocean by a Merchant of the First Century* (New York: Longmans, Green, and Co., 1912).

[15] Cresque (?), *Mappa Mundi*, p. 84. For Marco Polo's description of Chinese ships, see Polo, *The Description of the World*, vol. 1, pp. 354–7; see also Marco Polo, *The Travels of Marco Polo: The Complete Yule-Cordier Edition*, 2 vols (New York: Dover, 1993), vol. 2, pp. 249–53, with interesting notes. For the boat, see Joseph Needham, with Wang Ling and Lu Gwei-Djen, *Science and Civilisation in China: Civil Engineering and Nautics* (Cambridge: Cambridge University Press, 1971), pp. 471–3, fig. 977b.

[16] Cresque (?), *Mappa Mundi*, p. 84.

[17] Cresque (?), *Mappa Mundi*, p. 84.

their location to a misunderstanding of Marco Polo's text – the furthest point reached by Dias, the great Fish River, is duly indicated: 'Up to here, next to *ilha de fonti*, arrived the last Portuguese expedition in the year of the Lord 1489.'[18] Vasco de Gama left Lisbon in July 1497, stopped at Cape Verde, and then after a long voyage of 3,800 miles, reached the Swahili ports of Quelimane, Mozambique, Mombassa and Malindi, on the east coast of Africa, connected to the Indian trade. From Malindi, an Omani pilot took him straight to Calicut on the west coast of India, which he reached in May 1498.[19] After this voyage, the eastern half of the globe, on world maps, progressively became a sea chart. The world of gold, pearls, porcelain, incense and spices, the world of Marco Polo, could now be reached directly by the Portuguese carracks.[20]

Of the images of this newly explored world, the Cantino map of *circa* 1502 is one of the most elaborate (Figure 14.2).[21] The contrast with the Catalan Atlas is striking. The latter presents a narrow trade corridor from the Persian Gulf to the Indian Ocean and from the Gulf of Bengal to the Chinese Sea, with boats and islands covering the immensity of the sea. The Cantino planisphere, however, shows a new trade world, with the West Indies and part of the east coast of America now recorded, with Africa circumscribed and the west coast of India delineated (although the eastern half still only has a rather formulaic shape). Commissioned by Alberto Cantino for Ercole d'Este, Duke of Ferrara, the map shows familiarity with the

[18] Robert Almagià, 'Il Mappamondi di Enrico Martello e alcuni concetti geografici di Cristoforo Colombo', *La Bibliofilia* 42–3 (1940), pp. 288–311; Tony Campbell, *The Earliest Printed Maps, 1472–1500* (Berkeley: University of California Press, 1987), pp. 72–4, 77–8; Francesc Relaño, *The Shaping of Africa: Cosmographic Discourse and Cartographic Science in Late Medieval and Early Modern Europe* (Aldershot: Ashgate, 2002), pp. 165–7. See also Jean Michel Massing, in Levenson (ed.), *Circa 1492*, p. 230, no. and fig. 129; Angelo Cattaneo, in Levenson (ed.), *Encompassing the Globe*, pp. 12–13, no. and fig. P-2.

[19] For a short but useful survey of the Portuguese voyages to the east, see British Museum, *Prince Henry the Navigator and Portuguese Maritime Enterprise* (London: British Museum, 1960), esp. pp. 16–17, 21.

[20] Philip D. Curtin, *Cross-Cultural Trade in World History* (Cambridge: Cambridge University Press, 1984), pp. 109–35, for example. In the *Catalan Atlas*, pearl fishing is associated with the Gulf and the Indian Ocean; Cresque (?), *Mappa Mundi*, pp. 81, 84–5. Polo, *The Description of the World*, vol. 1, pp. 383–4, associated pearl fishing with Ceylon (Sri Lanka). For the Portuguese involvement, see Chandra Richard de Silva, 'The Portuguese and Pearl Fishing off South India and Sri Lanka', *South Asia*, new series 1:1 (1978), pp. 14–28.

[21] Duarte Leite, 'O mais antigo mapa do Brasil', in Carlos Malheiro Dias (ed.), *História da colonização portuguesa do Brasil* (Oporto: Litografía Nacional, 1921–6), vol. 3, pp. 227–30; Armando Cortesão and Avelino Teixeira de Mota, *Portugaliae Monumenta Cartographica*, 6 vols (Lisbon: Comissão Executiva do V Centenário da morte do Infante D. Henrique, 1960), vol. 1, pp. 7–13; Luis de Albuquerque, 'Algumas observações sobre o Planisfério Cantino (1502)', *Boletim do Centro de Estudos Geográficos* 3:22–3 (1966–7), pp. 57–84; Avelino Teixeira da Mota, 'A África no planisfério português anónimo "Cantino" (1502)', *Revista da Universidade de Coimbra* 26 (1978), pp. 1–13; Ernesto Milano, *La Carta del Cantino, e la rappresentazione della terra nei codici e nei libri a stampa della Biblioteca Estense* (Modena: Il Bulino, 1991), pp. 87–156; Relaño, *The Shaping of Africa*, pp. 179–81. More recently, João Carlos Garcia, in Levenson (ed.), *Encompassing the Globe*, pp. 60–2, no. and fig. 3.

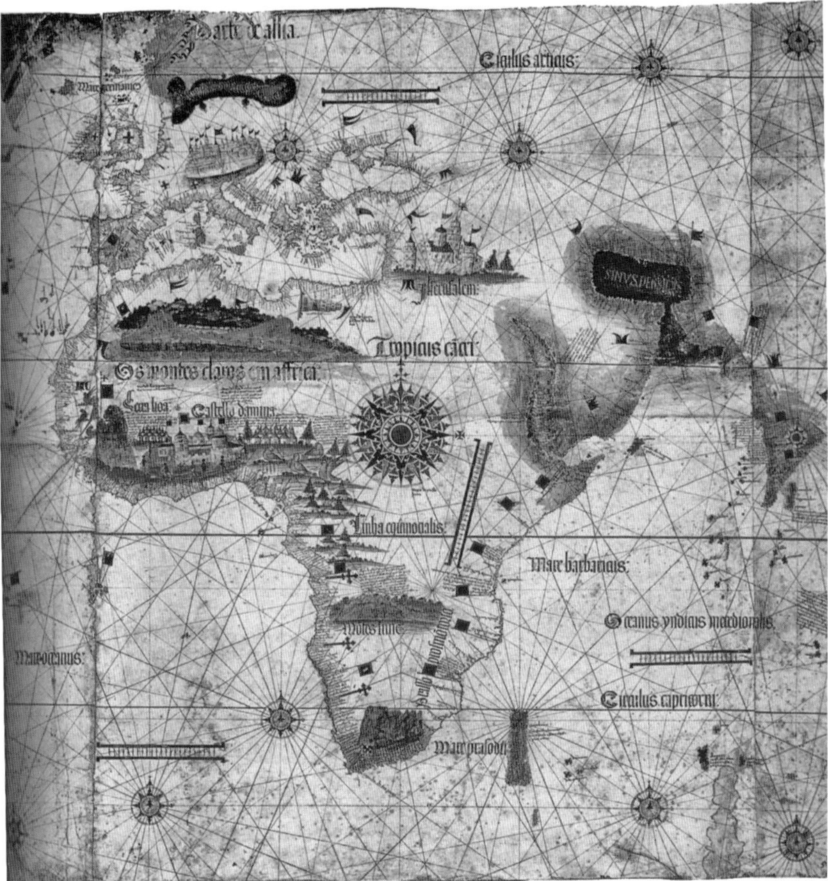

Figure 14.2. *Cantino Map*, 1502, Modena, Biblioteca Estense Universitaria

official Lusitanian charts and maps kept at the *Armazém da Guiné e das Indias* in Lisbon, and presents a world open to Portuguese trade. The seas have become the main focus of the maps, allowing ships to pass from the Mediterranean to the Indian Ocean and thus opening new lands to Portuguese trade. The medieval *mappa mundi* has given place to a sea chart encouraging trade and exploration of the still unrecorded Southeast Asia and China Sea. The coastline, the trading posts and the coastal indications now define the route to India and its riches. The earth masses are coloured – as is the Persian Gulf, and the Red Sea – emphasising how the oceans are open to Portuguese navigation and trade following the monopoly accorded by the Treaty of Tordesillas, signed on 7 June 1494, when the newly discovered world was divided between Spain and Portugal along a meridian 370 leagues west of the Cape Verde islands, Portugal gaining control over the eastern routes.[22] On the southwest coast of Africa can be seen four *padrões*, the stone monuments brought from Portugal to mark for Portugal the newly discovered countries: the *padrão* de São Jorge, erected by Diogo Cão at the mouth of the Congo River in 1483; the *padrão* of Cabo Negro which Cão raised during a second voyage in 1485; a *padrão* misplaced near the Golfo da Conçepcam; and finally, that also raised by Diogo Cão near the Cape of Good Hope in 1486.[23] No *padrão*, but six Portuguese flags, appear on the east coast of Africa, recorded here with its correct north-south orientation and a relatively accurate definition of the coastline. Among the sixty-three place names are Çaffalla (Sofala), Mozunbique (Mozambique island), Kilwa, Mõbaça (Mombassa), Melinde (Melinda), Pate, and Mogodoxo (Mogadishu).[24] Next to Melinda, Vasco de Gama's welcome by the local ruler is duly remembered: 'Here is the King of Melinde, a great nobleman and friend of the King of Portugal.'[25]

On the east coast of Africa, the Portuguese came across gold brought from Zimbabwe. Already in the fourteenth century, the Arab traveller Ibn Battüta was aware of the gold trade there. He describes the town of Kilwa as a large city on the sea-coast, most of whose inhabitants are Zinj, jet black in colour and 'with tattoo marks on their faces'. The city itself 'is one of the finest and most substantially built towns; all the buildings are of wood, and the houses are roofed with *dīs* reeds' (*ampelodesmos tenax*). The gold trade is also mentioned, specifically that between southern Zimbabwe and Sofala; also the Sultan's treasury, where he kept a portion of the booties captured for the relatives of the Prophet.[26] When the Portuguese arrived, Kilwa had 'storied houses very stoutly built of masonry and covered with plaster, numerous domed mosques, while the sultan was living in a fortress'. We also read that 'they sail from here 255 leagues to Sofala whence they bring the gold to other places'.[27] The first contacts with Kilwa were not very successful,

[22] For the treaty, see Antonio Rumeu de Armas, *El Tratado de Tordesillas* (Madrid: Mapfre, 1992); Agustín Remesal, *1494, La Raya de Tordesillas* (Valladolid: Junta de Castilla y León, 1994); see also Paulo Pereira and Zoltán Biedermann, in Michael Kraus and Hans Ottomeyer (eds), *Novos Mundos – Neue Welten: Portugal und das Zeitalter der Entdeckungen* (Dresden: Sandstein, 2007), pp. 348–9, no. IV.5, and 194–5, fig. 3.

[23] For the *padrões* on the map, see Wilhelm Kalthammer, *Portugiesenkreuze in Africa und Indien . . .* (Basel: Basler Afrika Bibliographien, 1984), pp. 73–5, fig. 18; for the crosses, see, respectively, pp. 26–7, 27–30, 30–42.

[24] For the name lists on early maps of southeast Africa, see Kammerer, *La Mer Rouge*, vol. 2.2, App. 1.

[25] Relaño, *The Shaping of Africa*, pp. 180, 183, n. 15.

[26] Ibn Battūta (H. A. R. Gibb, ed.), *The Travels of Ibn Battūta, A.D. 1325–1354*) (Cambridge: Hakluyt Society, 1962), pp. 379–80. For Kilwa, see Neville Chittick, *Kilwa: An Islamic Trading City on the East African Coast*, 2 vols (Nairobi: British Institute in Eastern Africa, 1974); for Ibn Battūta's description, see *The Travels of Ibn Battūta*, vol. 1, p. 248.

[27] For Kilwa, see National Archives of Rhodesia/Centro de Estudos Históricos Ultramarinos, *Documentos sobre os portugueses em Moçambique e na África central, 1497–1840 – Documents on the Portuguese in Mozambique and Central Africa, 1497–1840*, 9 vols (Lisbon: National Archives of Rhodesia/Centro de Estudos Históricos Ultramarinos, 1962), vol. 1, pp. 327–9; Chittick, *Kilwa*, pp. 249–51 (p. 250, for the quote).

however, so King Manuel sent Vasco da Gama back during his second voyage to India. Vasco's main aim was to investigate the gold trade and perhaps discover the mine from which King Salomon had obtained his gold. Manuel also advised him to sign a peace treaty with the Sultan, who was handed an ultimatum to trade 2,000 *mithquals* of gold with the Portuguese, accept allegiance to their king, and pay a yearly tribute of pearls. After protests the Sultan eventually agreed to pay an annual tribute of 1,500 *mithquals* of gold, and handed over the first year's commitment, which was taken to Lisbon.[28]

The Portuguese chronicler João de Barros records Vasco da Gama's triumphal return in 1503:

> And as, at this time, the king was in Lisbon, when he went to him, he [Vasco da Gama] took with him the tribute that he had received from the king of Kilwa; with trumpets and kettledrums, accompanied by all the men that there were in the court. From which tributes, the king ordered a monstrance to be made that would be as rich in its work as in its weight.[29]

In Manuel's will, made in 1517, there is a clear reference to this work, with the identification of the goldsmith responsible ('Item I order that the Monastery of Our Lady of Belém be given the monstrance made by Gil Vicente for the same institution'). The origin of the monstrance of Belém in the gold of Kilwa is acknowledged in an inscription around the base ('O MUITO. ALTO PRICIPE. E. PODEROSO. SEHOR. REI. DO. MANUELI. A.MDOU. FAZER. DO. OURO. I. DAS. PARIAS. DE. QILUA. AQUABOV.E CCCCVI.' [The most powerful Lord and King Dom Manuel I ordered this monstrance to be made from the gold of the tributes from Kilwa. Completed in 1506]).

The monstrance is decorated with glass, and opaque and translucent enamels (Figure 14.3). The base is divided into six compartments filled with three-dimensional enamelled motifs of peacocks, parrots and exotic birds of various forms, as well as shells and molluscs set against a background of freely arranged arabesques. The stem, covered with Gothic fenestrations, has two rings and, between, a larger knot composed of six armillary spheres, the well-known device of Manuel. From the stem spreads luxuriant vegetation under the platform supporting the twelve Apostles kneeling in a circle, around the cylindrical glass case for the host. On either side is an architecture structure with two musician angels on the exterior, and with the Virgin and the Archangel Gabriel facing each other. The intention evidently was not just to allude to the angelic salutation but to link the words of Isaiah 7:14 ('Behold a Virgin shall conceive, and bear a son, and his name shall be called Emmanuel') and the text of Matthew 1:23 ('Behold a Virgin shall be with child,

[28] For the Kilwa negotiations, see Eric Axelson, *Portuguese in South-East Africa, 1488–1600* (Johannesburg: C. Struik, 1973), p. 33.

[29] João de Barros, *Asia* (Lisbon: G. Galharde, 1552), fol. 77. For the monstrance, see Leonor d'Orey, in Levenson (ed.), *Encompassing the Globe*, pp. 77–8, no. and fig. 19.

Figure 14.3.
Belém Monstrance, 1506, Lisbon, Museu Nacional de Arte Antiga

and bring forth a son, and they shall call his name Emmanuel, which being interpreted is, God with us') to King Manuel himself. The Annunciation, in fact, is completed by the dove of the Holy Ghost above the scene, in the two-tiered, dome-shaped structure which is linked by flying buttresses to the side pillars on which can be seen another ten music-making angels, while the central structure retains three of the six prophets that originally decorated it. In the opening above the dove is the figure of God the Father, while the host, of course, embodied the third person of the Trinity, Christ. In this elaborate theological programme, Gil Vicente, or some adviser, included the twelve Apostles around the Eucharist, recalling the Last Supper, in addition to the Annunciation, while the overall theme suggests an Adoration of the Trinity. The goldsmith ingeniously designed his enamelled masterpiece in two parts; the top half can be removed to introduce the host into the monstrance. The division is also iconographical as the base stands for the earthly sphere, stressing Manuel's achievements, while the upper half represents the City of God, with angels, prophets and, of course, the Trinity. The gold of the Swahili is now dedicated to the God of the Christians.

By the early sixteenth century, gold came to Portugal from Mauretania, Senegal, Gambia, Sierra Leone, Ghana and East Africa, boosting the Portuguese economy. East African gold came mainly from the interior, and was of course traded through Sofala and Kilwa. In Sofala, Vasco da Gama was told that the region produced, in time of peace, two million *mithquals* a year. Originally, the word *mithqual* meant the weight of something, before the name was given to the Syrian gold dinar and those minted in a number of Islamic states. In 1505, a *mithqual* of Kilwa was approximately 4,223 grams of gold and worth 460 reis, which means that the tribute used for the monstrance was more than 6.3 kilograms of pure gold.[30] In Manuel's Portugal, and after 1510 in Goa and in Malacca, the gold of Africa was minted as coins, respectively the *português*, the *cruzado* and, after 1517, the *quarto de cruzado*.[31] Most splendid and largest of these coins is the *português*, stamped after 1499–1502, and weighing 35.6 grams (Figure 14.4). Its size allowed on the obverse a two-line Latin legend, such as:

> MANUEL I KING OF PORTUGAL, OF THE ALGARVES, FROM THE LANDS ON THIS SIDE AND OVERSEAS IN AFRICA, LORD OF GUINEA, OF CONQUEST, NAVIGATION AND TRADE IN ETHIOPIA, ARABIA, PERSIA

[30] Vitorino de Magalhães Godinho, *Os descobrimentos e a economia mundial*, 2 vols (Lisbon: Arcádia, 1963), vol. 1, p. 228; Axelson, *Portuguese in South-East Africa*, pp. 32–3, esp. n. 63. According to Chittick, *Kilwa*, p. 250, 'gold is not used for coin but by the weight of the *mitical* worth 460 rs. in Portugal'.

[31] Alberto Gomes, *Moedas portuguesas e do território português antes da fundação da nacionalidade* (Lisbon: A. Gomes, 1996), p. 167, nos. 51.01–51.08; see also pp. 156–67. For a survey of Manuel's coinage, with fine illustrations, see Vilma Faria Rodrigues d'Almeida, 'D. Manuel 1', in Rejane Maria Lobo Vieira (ed.), *Moedas portuguesas da época dos descobrimentos na coleção do Museu Histórico Nacional 1383–1583* (Rio de Janeiro: Museu Histórico Nacional, 2000), pp. 126–57.

AND INDIA (+ I: EMANUEL: R: PORTUGALIE: AL: C. VL. IN: A.D: G//C. N: C. ETHIOPIE: ARABIE: PERSIE: I:).

On the reverse, the inscription 'IN HOC SIGNO VINCES' [With this sign you shall conquer] is the Latin version of the Greek message which appeared to Emperor Constantine I before the battle of the Milvian Bridge against the pagan Maxentius, together with the Christian *chi-ro*, the first letters of the name, and an early Christian symbol, of Christ. The cross on the crown, however, refers to the military Order of Christ founded by King Dinis and approved by a papal bill on 14 March 1319, which was closely associated with the Portuguese monarchy and the overseas expansion.[32] On the gold *cruzado* weighing 3.62 grams, Manuel, who was Grand Master of the Order, is simply called King of Portugal and the Algarve, Lord of Guinea (+1: 'EMANUEL: R:P:ET:A:D:GUINEE', for example).[33] In 1499, Manuel I ordered the issue of a new coin, the *indio* (Indian), probably as a commemoration of the maritime route to the Indian Ocean; this one, however, was minted in an alloy of silver.[34]

If the perception of the East Indies in Portugal was linked to overseas expansion, gold, spices and exotic goods, early sixteenth-century Netherlandish tapestry workshops visualised the East Indies in a conventional manner which combined information from the newly discovered lands with fanciful renderings. The twenty-six surviving works known as the tapestries of the Indies clearly belong to different sets from the workshops of Jean Grenier and Arnould Poissonnier in Tournai. They

Figure 14.4. *Português*, Rio de Janeiro, Museu Histórico Nacional

[32] Gomes, *Moedas portuguesas*, p. 167, no. and fig. 51.7; see d'Almeida, 'D. Manuel 1', pp. 130, 137, no. and fig. 095, for example.

[33] See, for example, d'Almeida, 'D. Manuel 1', pp. 138–9, nos. and figs 096–099; for the gold *cruzados*, see Gomes, *Moedas portuguesas*, pp. 166–7.

[34] For example, d'Almeida, 'D. Manuel 1', pp. 132, 144, no. and fig. 106; for Manuel's *indio*, see Gomes, *Moedas portuguesas*, p. 162, no. and fig. 31.01.

represent caravans of dromedaries, giraffes and elephants surrounded by European-looking, as well as native people (Figures 14.5–14.7), a lion hunt (Figure 14.8) and a harbour scene which includes the shipping of wild animals in an African or Indian harbour (Figure 14.9).[35] The earliest document related to any of the tapestries records that Philip the Fair acquired from Grenier in 1504 a '*riche tapisserie bien richement faite, [à] la manière de Portugal et de Indye*' for an unnamed French prince.[36] One year later, King Manuel I had in his possession a tapestry with 'a

Figure 14.5. Netherlandish tapestry, *Triumphal Procession with Elephants*, from the *Discovery of the Indies* series, Paris, Musée du Louvre

[35] The best syntheses are found in Jean-Paul Asselberghs, *La tapisserie tournaisienne au XVIe siècle* (Tournai: n.p., 1968), pp. 12–16, plates 3–8; Paul Vandenbroeck, in Anon. (ed.), *America, Bride of the Sun: 500 Years of Latin America and the Low Countries* (Ghent: Imschoot Books, 1992), pp. 384–5; Maria Antónia Gentil Quina, *À maneira de Portugal e da India: Uma série de tapeçaria quinhentista* (Lisbon: Fundação Abel de Lacerda, Museu do Caramulo, 1998); Pedro Dias, *À maneira de Portugal e da Índia: Uma tapeçaria inédita* (Porto: Pedro Aguiar Branco, 2007); Jessica Hallett (ed.), *Cortejo triunfal com girafas: Animais exóticos ao serviço do poder/Trimphal Procession with Giraffes: Exotic Animals in the Service of Power* (Lisbon: Fundação Ricardo do Espírito Santo Silva, 2009); all with numerous archival references and lists of tapestries. The tapestries representing orientalised gypsies (perhaps the *Carrabarra* tapestries) were studied by Paul Vandenbroeck, *Over wilden en narren, boeren en bedelaars: Beeld van de andere, vertoog over het zelf* (Antwerp: Koninklijk Museum voor schone Kunsten, 1987), pp. 20–32, with illustrations. Gerardina Tjaberta van Ysselsteyn, *Tapestry, the Most Expensive Industry of the XVth and XVIth Centuries* (The Hague and Brussels: Van Goor, 1969), p. 140, figs 133–4, proposes adding two more pieces to the series.

[36] Eugène Soil, *Les tapisseries de Tournai: Les tapissiers et les hautelisseurs de cette ville* (Tournai-Lille: Société Historique, 1891), p. 248, no. 84; see also Jules Houdoy, *Les tapisseries de hautes-lisses: Histoire de la fabrication lilloise du XIVe au XVIIIe siècle . . .* (Paris, 1871), pp. 141–2.

city in the centre, with elephants and many other beasts' below; a port running along the bottom could suggest that the Portuguese king was behind the original commission.[37]

Other records of royal ownership include sets of five tapestries, one of an '*ystoire de gens et de bestes sauvaiges à la manière de calcut* [Calicut]'[38] and another of a '*voyage de caluce*';[39] the first was purchased by Maximilian I in 1510, the second, 155 aulnes long, was given by the *Consaux* of Bruges to Robert de Wyctfel in 1513, both from Arnould Poissonier, a well-known tapestry maker and dealer of Tournai. A seven-piece set of an '*histoire indienne à oliffans et jeraffes*' was sold by the

Figure 14.6. Netherlandish tapestry, *Triumphal Procession with Giraffes and a Camel*, from the *Discovery of the Indies* series, Paris, Musée du Louvre

[37] M. Silva Marquês, 'Armas e tapeçarias reais num inventário de 1505', *Publicações do Congresso do Mundo Português. Congresso da História dos Descobrimentos*, 19 vols (Lisbon: Comissão Executiva dos Centenários, 1940), vol. 3, p. 596; Quina, *À maneira de Portugal e da India*, p. 224, no. 35-c; see also Hallett (ed.), *Cortejo triunfal com girafas*, p. 13.

[38] Houdoy, *Les tapisseries de hautes-lisses*, p. 143; Soil, *Les tapisseries de Tournai*, pp. 256, no. 96, and 322.

[39] Soil, *Les tapisseries de Tournai*, p. 258, no. 104; see Thomas P. Campbell, *Henry VIII and the Art of Majesty: Tapestries at the Tudor Court* (New Haven: Yale University Press, 2007), p. 112.

Figure 14.7. Netherlandish tapestry, *Triumphal Procession with Giraffes and a Zebra*, from the *Discovery of the Indies* series, Paris, Musée du Louvre

dealer Pieter van Aelst to Emperor Charles V in 1522,[40] while King François I owned five '*tappiz de la calavane* [*caravane*]' in 1532.[41] A '*carvanne*' was also recorded in the inventory of Cardinal Georges d'Amboise in Gaillon (1550).[42] Arnould Poissonier's posthumous inventory (1539) mentions two nine-piece sets, the first representing an '*histoire de la caravane*', 480 aulnes long,[43] the second an

[40] Houdoy, *Les tapisseries de hautes-lisses*, p. 144.

[41] Sophie Schneebalg-Perelman, 'Richesse du garde-meuble parisien de François Ier, inventaires inédits de 1542 et 1551', *Gazette des Beaux-Arts*, 6th series, 78 (1971), p. 276, no. 61 (*Cinq tappiz de la Calavanne*). For François I's collection, see also Janet Cox-Rearick, *The Collection of François Ier: Royal Treasures* (Antwerp: Mercator Paribas, 1995).

[42] Jean Achille Deville, *Compte de dépenses de la construction du château de Gaillon* . . . (Paris, 1850), p. 544 ('Six pieces de laine nommée la carvanne').

[43] Soil, *Les tapisseries de Tournai*, pp. 281, no. 143, and 414.

Figure 14.8. Netherlandish tapestry, *Lion Hunt*, from the *Discovery of the Indies* series, Paris, Musée du Louvre

'*Histoire de Calcou*', 265 aulnes long,[44] sold respectively to the Antwerp merchant Jehan Ballincq and to a seigneur de Halluy. The cardinal-bishop of Liège, Erard de la Marck, also owned a six-piece set described as a '*caravanne*' and, in a later (1532) inventory, as representing '*sauvaiges*'.[45] Larger sets were also known: at his death in 1522, Poissonier owned a nine-piece set, '*histoire de Carvenc*', 480 aulnes long,[46] and another nine-piece set, '*histoire de Calcou*', 265 aulnes long.[47] In 1539, his estate still included a seventeen-piece series of an '*aultre histoire de*

[44] Soil, *Les tapisseries de Tournai*, pp. 282, no. 146, and 412.

[45] Jan-Karel Steppe and Guy Delmarcel, 'Les tapisseries du Cardinal Érard de la Marck, prince-évêque de Liège', *Revue de l'Art* 25 (1974), pp. 35–51, p. 48, no. 18 ('six pieches de sauvaiges').

[46] Soil, *Les tapisseries de Tournai*, pp. 47 and 176 ('Aultre histoire de Carvenc. 9 pieches 480 aulnes').

[47] Soil, *Les tapisseries de Tournai*, pp. 47, 175 and 323 ('Aultre histoire de Calcou. 9 pieches 265 aulnes').

Figure 14.9. Netherlandish tapestry, *Arrival in the Indies*, from the *Discovery of the Indies* series, Lisbon, Caixa Geral de Depósitos, on loan to Museu Nacional de Arte Antiga

Carrabara dite des Egyptians', 445 aulnes long, which probably reflects a further development of the '*Maneira de Portugal e da India*' tapestries: tapestries from this series were also listed as a fourteen-piece set (265 aulnes long), as a single tapestry and as a two-piece set.[48]

The earliest commissions by Philip the Fair in 1504 and by King Manuel himself in 1505 may have been single tapestries, of the type known as 'The Discovery of India' and traditionally said to show the arrival of a Portuguese traveller, presumably Vasco da Gama, who delivers a letter from Manuel I to an Indian ruler; the gate on the left in Figure 14.9 identifies the city as being in the 'New' Indies ('INDAS NOVAE'), a designation which presumably includes the countries surrounding the Indian Ocean and may even specifically refer to the African coast. Rather than illustrating the arrival in Calicut or Cochin, the Portuguese voyager might be approaching rulers of the East African coast: potential candidates are those of Kilwa, Malindi or Zanzibar, for example.[49] Ships – perhaps suggesting Gama's *São Gabriel*, *São Rafael* and the *Bérrio* – fill the harbours, loaded with exotic animals and birds.[50] The evidence of both documents and surviving sets of tapestries confirms that by 1510 five-piece sets were available, such as those owned by Maximilian I, François I, Henry VIII and Georges d'Amboise. It is only in 1522 that larger sets are recorded, of six, nine and seventeen pieces.

The two surviving sets in Caramulo and in the Louvre (Figures 14.5–14.8),[51] however, only include four tapestries: one with a lion hunt, the others with caravans of wild animals including camels, giraffes, elephants and even zebras. The 'Indies' tapestries show mainly African animals, including sheep and goats with long, hanging ears, camels, elephants, giraffes, lions, monkeys and zebras, in what is – except for the Discovery of India and the Lion Hunt tapestries – a continuous narrative, reminding the viewer of a caravan or rather a triumphal procession. Standing and walking figures occupy the foreground, while the much larger animals behind – including the giraffes and the zebras – are ridden by adults, though naked

[48] Soil, *Les tapisseries de Tournai*, p. 47 ('Aultre histoire de Carrabara dit des Egiptiens, dix sept pieches. 445 aulnes'); see also pp. 281, under no. 144, 323 and 412.

[49] Respectively Dias, *À maneira de Portugal e da Índia*, p. 34; and Hallett (ed.), *Cortejo triunfal com girafas*, p. 54.

[50] For this tapestry, see Quina, *À maneira de Portugal e da India*, pp. 57–77, with illus.; Pedro Dias, in Levenson (ed.), *Encompassing the Globe*, pp. 34–5, no. and fig. P-30; see also Pedro Dias, 'La tapisserie flamande au Portugal', in John Everaert and Eddy Stols (eds), *Flandre et Portugal: Au confluent de deux cultures* (Antwerp: Mercator, 1991), pp. 178–82. The notion of 'INDAS NOVAE' has a rich semantic implication, referring to the Indies, and probably not specifically India: see, for example, Polo, *The Travels of Marco Polo*, vol. 2, pp. 425–7.

[51] Madeleine Jarry, 'L'homme sauvage', *L'Oeil* 183 (1970), pp. 14–21; p. 18, ill. p. 15, for a detail from a tapestry then at the Musée de Saint-Malo; as such in Quina, *À maneira de Portugal e da India*, pp. 24, no. B.5, and 95–6, fig. 44. This tapestry is part of an unpublished set of four belonging to the Musée du Louvre (OAR 62, OAR 66, OAR 74 and OAR 99); see Fabienne Joubert, *La tapisserie médiévale au musée de Cluny* (Paris: Réunion des Musées Nationaux, 1987), p. 185.

children sometimes sit on giraffes' heads. Here, however, it seems we are still in the world of Marco Polo rather than that of Manuel, for example, when the former writes about the island of Zanzibar:

> Very great trade is done there for many merchants come there with many ships which bring there many goods, all which they sell in these islands, and they carry away again plenty of the wares of the island and especially they carry away great quantity of elephants' tusks which are there in plenty.

He also mentions the inhabitants:

> And again you may know that the lords of this island sometimes go to war among themselves, and these men of this island are very good fighters and fight very hard in battle, for they are strong and are not at all afraid of death. They are not however brave, as I have said, in proportion to their size: And they have no horses but they fight on camels and on elephants. For I tell you that they make castles of wood on the elephants and cover them very well with skins of wild beasts & with boards and then they mount up there in each of those castles from sixteen men to twenty with lances and with swords and with stones, and it is a very mighty battle, that which is made upon the elephants. And they have no arms but shields of leather and lances and swords and they kill one another well all together.[52]

To the north, in Middle India, are Christians (the Ethiopians) and *Saracens* surrounded by outlandish animals also found in the tapestries:

> They have many elephants, but not that they are much bred there, but they have them from many parts of the islands of the other Indie. But the giraffes are indeed bred there and they have them in great abundance. They have bears & lions and leopards and lynxes enough; and they have many other beasts also in multitudes very different from those of our countries. And wild asses enough are also bred there. They have likewise birds of many kinds totally distinct from all the others. They have hens the most beautiful in the world to see. And they have great ostriches not at all smaller than an ass.[53]

Almost all these animals are found in the tapestries. It is more difficult to identify the people in the tapestries – Marco Polo does not say much about their aspect, except in the case of the inhabitants of Zanzibar, who are seen through medieval stereotypes:

> And they are all black and go quite naked except that they are covered in their natural parts. And they do very wisely to cover them for they have them very large and ugly and horrible to see. And they all have the hair so curly and black like pepper that it could hardly be made to stretch out with water. And they have so great a mouth also and the great and red nose so flat and turned upwards, towards the forehead, like an ape, and beards, and nostrils so thick that it is wonderful. They have the ears large, and the lips thick, turned outwards, and the eyes so large and so bloodshot and so red that they are a very horrible thing to see. They are great merchants and do great trade.

[52] Polo, *The Description of the World*, pp. 432, 433.
[53] Polo, *The Description of the World*, p. 439.

But the tapestries include Europeans, Orientals and black Africans, and feature a whole range of figures recalling the traditional late medieval definition of Arabs, Mamluks and their allies – with the categorisation of Africans as either black or white Moors – and even gypsies, all reflecting a Netherlandish view of a geographic area and its human diversity known mainly through literary sources.[54] All of which suggests that the tapestry traditionally identified as the arrival of Vasco da Gama in Calicut could simply show Marco Polo handing over a letter from the Chinese Emperor to an East African ruler involved – as was the ruler of Zanzibar for example – in the Indian Ocean trade.

One of the most interesting tapestries from the unpublished cycle in the Louvre shows a procession of four large elephants, with another two baby animals ridden by children in the foreground (Figure 14.5). In the middle of the composition stand a man and a woman, the latter based on a woodcut by Hans Burgkmair showing people from the Swahili coast of Africa ('IN ARABIA') (Figure 14.11). That print, like those showing people from Guinea and Algoa Bay, illustrates the travel accounts of Balthasar Springer and Hans Mayr. Springer, an agent of the Welsers, the famous merchant family from Augsburg, joined the ships furnished by German merchants on Don Francisco d'Almeida's famous expedition to India.[55] In the 1505–6 fleet of more than twenty ships, and some 1,500 soldiers, three vessels were chartered by Nuremberg and Augsburg merchants. Springer's *Indienfahrt*, published in Oppenheim in 1509 with woodcuts by Wolf Traut, was best known, and was translated into Latin, Dutch and English.[56]

The fleet left Lisbon on 23 March 1505, stopped at the Bijagós Islands, and passed the Cape of Good Hope before landing at Kilwa on 19 July, without having

[54] These characteristics have been analysed by Hallett (ed.), *Cortejo triunfal com girafas*, pp. 43–55; Polo, *The Description of the World*, p. 432.

[55] For the various publications of Springer's account, most of which are illustrated, see Henry Harrisse, *Americus Vespuccius: A Critical and Documentary Review of Two Recent English Books Concerning the Navigator* (London: B. F. Stevens, 1895), pp. 36–67, nos. L–0; Franz Schulze, *Balthasar Springers Indienfahrt, 1505/06* . . . (Strasbourg: Heitz, 1902), esp. pp. 8–20, to be completed by Walther Ruge's review in *Deutsche Litteraturzeitung* 24 (1903), pp. 359–60; W. Ruge, 'Aelteres kartographisches Material in deutschen Bibliotheken', *Nachrichten von der Königlichen Gesellschaft der Wissenschaften zu Göttingen, Philologisch-historische Klasse, Beiheft* (1916), pp. 87–92, nos. 62a–63; Franz Hümmerich, 'Quellen und Untersuchungen zur Fahrt der ersten deutschen nach dem portugiesischen Indien, 1505/6', *Abhandlungen der Königlich Bayerischen Akademie der Wissenschaften, Philosophisch-philologische und historische Klasse* 30:3 (1918), esp. pp. 7–35; Renate Kleinschmid, 'Balthasar Springer (Eine quellenkritische Untersuchung)', *Mitteilungen der Anthropologischen Gesellschaft in Wien* 96–7 (1967), pp. 150–2, gives an account of their chronology.

[56] For this very rare little booklet, see Schulze, *Balthasar Springers Indienfahrt*, with facsimile; the woodcuts were first attributed to Wolf Traut by Campbell Dodgson, *Catalogue of Early German and Flemish Woodcuts Preserved in the Department of Prints and Drawings in the British Museum*, 2 vols (London: British Museum, 1911), vol. 2, p. 72. For the identification of the printer, see Josef Benzing, *Jakob Köbel zu Oppenheim, 1494–1533: Bibliographie seiner Drucke und Schriften* (Wiesbaden: G. Pressler, 1962), pp. 17–18, no. 14.

sighted the southern tip of the African continent. They took Kilwa and Mombasa by assault, then put into Malindi before crossing the Indian Ocean and arriving on the east coast of India, where they stayed until 21 January 1506. On the return journey, they stopped on the southeast coast of Africa, reaching Algoa Bay (*Labay de Allogow*) on 18 June 1506, and then putting into San Francisco Bay and then Mossel Bay, before passing the Cape of Good Hope between 6 and 8 July 1506, reaching Lisbon four weeks later.[57] The travel account of Balthasar Springer was the source of Hans Burgkmair's multipart woodcut representing people from Africa and India,[58] but for the triumph of the king of Cochin Burgkmair followed Hans Mayr's text more closely.[59]

Hans Burgkmair's *Riesenholzschnitt* of 1508, a frieze almost two metres long, was printed from eight woodcuts showing *People of Africa and India*. It included representatives of West Africa ('IN GENNEA'), South Africa ('IN ALLAGO'), East Africa ('IN ARABIA') and Greater India ('GROS INDIA'), culminating with the triumph of the king of Cochin ('DER KUNIG VON GUTZIN') led by a group on camels.[60] The series was republished in 1511. It was also copied, with a number

[57] See above, note 50. For a summary in English, see Walter Hirschberg, *Schwarzafrika* (Graz: Akademische Druckund Verlagsanstalt, 1967), pp. 3–6.

[58] Jean Michel Massing, 'Hans Burgkmair's Depiction of Native Africans', *RES: Anthropology and Aesthetics* 27 (1995), pp. 39–51, see pp. 39–40.

[59] Beate Borowka-Clausberg, *Balthasar Sprenger und der frühneuzeitliche Reisebericht* (Munich: Ludicium, 1999), p. 53; see also Jean Michel Massing, *Encompassing the Globe, Reference Catalogue* (Washington, DC: Arthur M. Sackler Gallery, Smithsonian Institution, 2007), p. 35, no. and fig. P-31.

[60] Friedrich Wilhelm Heinrich Hollstein, *German Engravings, Etchings and Woodcuts, c. 1400–1700* (Amsterdam: M. Hertzberger, 1954), pp. 132–3, nos. 731–6, with illustrations of first state; Max Geisberg (rev. Walter L. Strauss), *The German Single-Leaf Woodcut: 1500–1550* (New York: Hacker Art Books, 1974), pp. 478–81, nos. G 509–14; see also Jean Devisse and Michel Mollat, 'Les Africains dans l'ordonnance chrétienne du monde (XIVe–XVIe siècle)', in Ladislas Bugner (ed.), *L'image du noir dans l'art occidental* (Paris: Bibliothèque des Arts, 1979), pp. 242–9, 292–3, ns 209–12. For an art historical account, see also *Hans Burgkmair: Das graphische Werk* (Stuttgart: Staatsgalerie, Graphische Sammlung, 1973), nos. 23–7, figs 30–4; *Hans Burgkmair, 1473–1531: Holzschnitte, Zeichnungen, Holzstöcke* (Berlin: Staatliche Museen zu Berlin, 1974), pp. 14, 39–44. The prints described by Dodgson, *Catalogue of Early German and Flemish Woodcuts*, vol. 2, pp. 71–2, no. 11.2, seem to be copies of Burgkmair's woodcuts not otherwise recorded. For an analysis of the woodcut 'IN GENOA', see Kleinschmid, 'Balthasar Springer', pp. 152–7. Quotes from Springer's text are based on the German version published in 1509, reproduced in facsimile in Schulze, *Balthasar Springers Indienfahrt*. Burgkmair's *People of Africa and India* is found twice in the collection of prints of Ferdinand Columbus (1488–1539), once in eleven-sheet with a French text below, and once in the more traditional form (both dated 1508 and with monogram); see Mark P. McDonald, *The Print Collection of Ferdinand Columbus (1488–1539): A Renaissance Collector in Seville* (London: British Museum, 2004), vol. 2, respectively pp. 503–4, no. 2752, and 515, no. 2795 (see also vol. 1, pp. 80, 87, 111, 161–2, 179, 237 and fig. 413); see also Mark P. McDonald, 'Burgkmair's Woodcut Frieze of Natives of Africa and India', *Print Quarterly* 20 (2003), pp. 227–44. I have focused at length on the ethnographic information in Massing, 'Hans Burgkmair's Depiction of Native Africans', pp. 39–51, which seems to have influenced Stephanie Leitsch, 'Burgkmair's *People of Africa and India* (1508) and the Origins of Ethnography in Print', *Art Bulletin* 41 (2009), pp. 134–59.

of modifications, by Georg Glockendon in 1509, in a set of woodcuts republished in 1511,[61] and, apparently, with verses of *Albrecht Glockendon Illuminist*, in 1541.[62] The woodcuts influenced those by Wolf Traut illustrating Springer's *Indienfahrt* published in Oppenheim in 1509.[63] They became the source of illustrations to various early sixteenth-century accounts of Springer's travels, which were published as broadsheets and books.[64] Burgkmair's woodcuts were still being recycled in the seventeenth century; they are partially reproduced at the end of an edition of Giovanni Botero's *Delle Relationi universali* published in Venice in 1618.[65]

Algoa Bay, for Springer, is a generic name for an area that stretches 550 miles south along the coast of East Africa. The text on the woodcut, inscribed 'IN ALLAGO' (Figure 14.10) and based on Springer's account, claims that:

> In the country which is called the kingdom of Sofala, the people clothe themselves with skins and animal furs. The men wear quivers or scabbards in wood or leather over their genitals. But the women cover themselves with a fur and wear a sheep skin on their heads as a veil, or the fur of some other animal.

Then the text provides more factual information: 'The little boy's penis is bound upwards. Some of the men daub their hair with pitch. They carry little white sticks.

[61] Christiane Andersson and Charles Talbot, *From a Mighty Fortress: Prints, Drawings, and Books in the Age of Luther, 1483–1546* (Detroit: Detroit Institute of Arts, 1983), pp. 210–11, no. 113, with illustration and a short account of the differences from Burgkmair's original (for a longer account, see Hümmerich, 'Quellen und Untersuchungen', pp. 56–8). Georg Glockendon could not resist adding references to cannibalism, which has nothing to do with Springer's text; here he relied on an early German woodcut from Augsburg (*circa* 1505) showing native Americans with a short explanatory text based on Vespucci's *Mundus novus*, a work first published in 1503; Susi Colin, *Das Bild des Indianers im 16. Jahrhundert* (Idstein: Schulz-Kirchner, 1988), pp. 186–7, no. B10, fig. 5). Susi Colin is the first to link the Indians with those in the *De novo mondo* broadsheet (pp. 191–2, no. B19, and 392, fig. 6) published in facsimile by Maria Elizabeth Kronenberg, *De novo mondo, Antwerp, Jan van Doesborch [about 1520]: A Facsimile of an Unique Broadsheet* (The Hague: Martinus Nijhoff, 1927), containing an early account of the inhabitants of South America together with a short version of Springer's text.

[62] Ruge, 'Aelteres kartographisches Material in deutschen Bibliotheken', p. 90, no. 62d, mentioned an impression in Gotha dated 1541 (Museum des Herzogl. Hauses), which had five verses printed on an extra piece of paper below each scene. For the text, from an impression in Augsburg, Fürstliche und Gräfliche Fuggerische Stiftungen, see Borowka-Clausberg, *Balthasar Sprenger*, pp. 217–19 and 216, figs. 27a–27b.

[63] See above, note 51.

[64] Albericus Vespuccius (Charles Henry Coote, ed.), *The Voyage from Lisbon to India, 1505–06. Being an Account and Journal of Albericus Vespuccius* (London: B. F. Stevens, 1894); Kronenberg, *De novo mondo*. For the English edition, see *Of the newe landes and of ye people found by the messengers of the kynge of Portyngale named Emanuel* (Antwerp, n.d.). They were all published by Jan van Doesborch of Antwerp and illustrated with woodcuts from the same blocks.

[65] Walter Oakeshott, *Some Woodcuts by Hans Burgkmair Printed as an Appendix to the Fourth Part of 'Le relationi universali di Giovanni Botero, 1618'* (Oxford: for the Roxburghe Club, 1960), studies this book in detail. For another copy of this extremely rare edition, see London, Hünersdorff, catalogue 17, *Travel and Exploration, Maritime Trade, Earth Sciences, Topography, Ethnology* (1994), pp. 14–17, no. 13, illustrations.

Figure 14.10. Hans Burgkmair, *People of Africa and India* (IN ALLAGO), 1508, Neunhof bei Lauf an der Pegnitz, Freiherrlich von Welsersche Familienstiftung

Their weapons are long spears which they throw. They wear leather shoes on their feet, as shown here.'[66] While the wording recalls Springer, Burgkmair seems to have had further visual information that allowed him to render the so-called Hottentots' costume with precision, down to the leather shoes, the man's penis pouch, and the animal entrails around the necks of the man and child in the woodcut.

These details are all known from later sources but are not found in Springer's – or any other contemporary – text. Burgkmair could not have seen any African from the area, but he must have known sketches made by Springer or some other navigator during the voyage to India, for only thus could he have been able to characterise the inhabitants of Algoa Bay the way he did.[67]

The text above the next woodcut ('IN ARABIA'), which in fact concerns the Swahili coast, informs us that 'In Arabia we saw people dressed as shown in the picture', a reference to Springer's 'In Arabia we saw people as dressed here and from the kingdom came one of the three kings' (Figure 14.11); it also confirms that there were drawings brought back from the voyage. Furthermore, we are told that there are four islands there: [Isle de] Mozambique, Kilwa, Mombassa and Malindi.[68] The dress of the inhabitants refers to the full text of Balthasar Springer's *Merfart*, then only available in manuscript: 'The people here [. . .] go about in cloaks made of linen or silk which they weave over their bare bodies. With gold they buy linen or silk, which they use in the way shown in the pictures.'[69]

The woodcut, again illustrating a man, a woman, and a child, includes details, such as the hat of the man, not mentioned by any written source. Except for the fact that the woman is shown bare-breasted, there is certainly less interest demonstrated by Springer and Burgkmair in the Swahili coast inhabitants than in the Hottentots. Explorers from all cultures, after all, are generally more interested in differences than in similarities. The allure of familiarity, too, may explain why ethnographic interest in East Africa after 1510 is relatively poor compared with earlier accounts, such as those of Vasco da Gama's voyages. Alvaro Coelho, for example, wrote that near the Kiliman river,

> The people are black and well made. They go naked, merely wearing a piece of cotton stuff around their loins, that worn by the women being larger than that worn by the men [. . .] Their lips are pierced in three places, and they wear in them bits of twisted tin.[70]

Swahili influence could be seen here as two merchants, described by Coelho, wore a cap (*touca*), in one case with a fringe embroidered in silk, and in the other of green satin, while the man who accompanied them 'had come from a distant country and

[66] For the ethnographic interest of Springer's writings and Burgkmair's woodcuts, see Hümmerich, 'Quellen und Untersuchungen', pp. 110–12; Hirschberg, *Schwarzafrika*, pp. xviii–xxi, 3–6; Kleinschmid, 'Balthasar Springer', pp. 147–90; more recently, Massing, 'Hans Burgkmair's Depiction of Native Africans', pp. 39–51; and Leitsch, 'Burgkmair's *People of Africa and India*', pp. 134–59. On the iconography of Hottentots, see also Ezio Bassani and Letizia Tedeschi, 'The Image of the Hottentot in the Seventeenth and Eighteenth Centuries: An Iconographic Investigation', *Journal of the History of Collections* 2 (1990), pp. 157–86.

[67] Massing, 'Hans Burgkmair's Depiction of Native Africans', p. 43, see also pp. 44–8.

[68] Hümmerich, 'Quellen und Untersuchungen', p. 16; Kleinschmid, 'Balthasar Springer', pp. 183–9.

[69] Hümmerich, 'Quellen und Untersuchungen', p. 16; Kleinschmid, 'Balthasar Springer', pp. 188–9.

[70] Velho, *A Journal of the First Voyage of Vasco de Gama*, p. 20.

Figure 14.11. Hans Burgkmair, *People of Africa and India* (IN ARABIA), 1508, Neunhof bei Lauf an der Pegnitz, Freiherrlich von Welsersche Familienstiftung

had already seen big ships like ours'. Further along the coast, on Mozambique island,

> The people [. . .] are of a ruddy complexion and well made. They are Mohammedans and their language is the same as that of the Moors. Their dresses are of fine linen or cotton stuffs, with rich and elaborate workmanship. They all wear *toucas* with borders of silk embroidered in gold. They are merchants and have transactions with white Moors.[71]

This indicates that they were connected to the Indian Ocean trade networks. This meant that their culture and their costume were less novel, and therefore less interesting, to the Portuguese, falling into the broad category of either black or white Moors, and explains why the Portuguese were more interested in the customs and the costumes of the so-called Hottentots than in Swahili culture.

In terms of historical evidence, the most extensive cycle of the first decade of the sixteenth century must have been – or would have been, if it had been completed – the set of twenty-five pieces of tapestry commissioned by King Manuel I before 1510 to commemorate the establishment of the Portuguese presence in the Indian Ocean. A description of them was written by António Carneiro, the royal secretary, and records Vasco da Gama's famous voyage and the presence of the Portuguese in Africa and India.[72] It is an 'order book' for tapestries (the inscription on the spine runs '*Pera os pannos que El Rey nosso senhor quer hordenar*' [For the tapestries the King our Lord wishes to commission]), sent to unnamed Antwerp craftsmen (see Appendix). The text insists that images and events should be represented in a lifelike manner, from Vasco da Gama's preliminary audience before the king, to his departure, his arrival in India, and the successful return of the armada to Lisbon. The first tapestry was to show Vasco da Gama, Paulo da Gama and Nicolau Coelho before Manuel I, who hands them the instructions for Vasco's voyage; this is followed by the procession from the Chapel of Our Lady of Belém to the Praia do Restello, from which the ships set off and to which they later returned. The fall of Kilwa (1505) was to be shown, with the Portuguese flags on the walls, as well as Dom Francisco de Almeida crowning the king who accepts allegiance and homage to the king of Portugal. A similar scene is portrayed as the 'Act of Homage rendered

[71] Velho, *A Journal of the First Voyage of Vasco de Gama*, p. 23.

[72] This text was published by Joannes A. da Graça Barreto, *A descoberta da India ordenada em tapeçaria por mandado de El-Rey D. Manuel* . . . (Coimbra, 1880); see also José Teixeira, in Levenson (ed.), *Circa 1492*, pp. 151–2. For evidence suggesting that the tapestries were woven, see Reynaldo Dos Santos, *As tapeçarias de Tomada de Arzila* (Lisbon: Biblioteca Nacional, 1925), p. 73; and Luis Keil, 'Tapisseries de Flandre au Portugal pendant les XVe et XVIe siècles', in Leo van Puyvelde (ed.), *Miscellanea Leo van Puyvelde* (Brussels: Editions de la Connaissance, 1949), p. 310. For oriental themes in Portuguese tapestries, see Francisco Marques Sousa Viterbo, *Artes et artistas em Portugal: Contribuições para a historia das artes e industrias Portuguezas* (Lisbon, 1920), pp. 91–101; for a much later set of tapestries, see *Tapeçarias de D. João de Castro*, Francisco Faria Paulino coord., Exhibition catalogue, Museu Nacional de Arte Antiga, 1995.

by the king of Cochin', who receives a gold cup as a present from Manuel I. To be included too was the foundation of forts in Mozambique (1507), Cochin (1503) and Cananor (1505). The scenes were to be carefully depicted: for example the twenty-third tapestry, relating to Cochin and including the local prince, was to show 'the make-up of the people, their colour and dress and arms, true to nature with their litters, elephants, and parasols'; elsewhere were indigenous women wearing 'jewels on their toes' – a detail straight out of the *Roteiro da Primeira Viagem de Vasco da Gama*. Another tapestry was to depict 'the Cape of Good Hope [. . .] with some animals, including elephants and blacks and cattle and houses in the style of the place and shepherds with flocks'. In the next, representing the city of Sofala, were to be shown 'the Moors and the Kaffirs in their typical colours and cloth [. . .] the Moors on one headland and the Kaffirs on another [. . .] On the land the trees and elephants and lions and buffaloes, all depicted lifelike.'[73]

Although no tapestry from this set has been identified, it must (or would) have been the most formidable record of Portuguese discoveries, insisting on their historical importance. Some of the tapestries at least seem to have been woven, as we know from the great Portuguese historian João de Barros, who mentions that on official occasions, the king's palace was decorated with tapestries which were commissioned to celebrate the discovery of the Indies and the conquest of Kilwa.[74] And for the engagement of the Infanta D. Maria, daughter of João III, in 1543, the great hall of the royal Ribeira palace in Lisbon was decorated with tapestries representing the conquest of the Indies.[75] Finally, in 1571 the papal legate Cardinal Alexandrino (1541–98) recorded, in the St Miguel chapel of the royal Alcáçova palace, also in Lisbon, a tapestry representing, 'in a lifelike way, the king, Dom Manuel I, surrounded by the Council of Nobles when he decided to order the conquest of the Portuguese Indies'.[76]

Less than fifteen years after the circumnavigation of the southern tip of Africa, European artists had developed a view of the newly discovered land ranging from highly exotic and sometimes quite fanciful renderings based on medieval sources to careful ethnographic illustrations, then producing a historically based set of tapestries suited to the maritime dominance of Portugal. These few years – and the three projects discussed – record a moment of European fascination with the east

[73] For all these passages, see Barreto, *A descoberta da India*, pp. 11–15.

[74] Barros, *Asia*, fol. 99r.

[75] Antonio Caetano Sousa, *História Genealógica da Casa Real Portuguesa*, 12 vols (Coimbra: Atlântida, 1948), vol. 3, p. 140; see also Viterbo, *Artes et artistas em Portugal*, p. 98.

[76] Viterbo, *Artes et artistas em Portugal*, p. 98, for the detail of this document; see also Santos, *As tapeçarias de Tomada de Arzila*, p. 73. Joseph Pereira de Santa Anna, *Chronica dos Carmelitas da Antiga*, 2 vols (Lisbon: Herdeiros de A. Pedrozo Galram, 1745–51), vol. 2, p. 337, mentions a tapestry left by P. André Coutinho in his will to his friend D. Miguel da Gama, in which the exploits of the Gamas were depicted ('panos de Raz aonde as proezas dos Gamas estavaõ bem debuxadas'); see Viterbo, *Artes et artistas em Portugal*, p. 99.

coast of Africa and its multicultural inhabitants. However, due to the newly developed contacts with China and Japan, the weight of trade quickly switched eastwards, and remained focused on that area for a very long time. In the early sixteenth century, Europe's image of East Africa was coastal and focused, as a sea chart, on harbours, trade posts and a few islands for the Portuguese intercontinental trade. Gold and ivory were the most valuable goods found there, until the slave trade gave the area a new importance.[77]

Appendix: Documento da Encomenda Manuelina de 26 'Encasamentos' de Tapeçaria (*c.* 1510).

A descoberta da Índia ordenada em tapeçaria por mandado de El-Rei D. Manuel. Documento inedito del seculo XVI publicado por Joannes A. da Graça Barreto em commemoração do terceiro centenario de Camões (Coimbra: Imp. Académica, 1880), pp. 11–15.

it. primeiramente em como ho almirante e seu irmão e nicolao coelho todos tres se estando espedimdo de mym e tomamdo seu Regimento no tempo do primeiro descobrimento. e ysto em huũ encasamento.

it. Em outro encasamento nosa senhora de belem pello natural. e os frades em precisam ate agoa com suas capas e cirios e as naaos quatro que vaao a veella com as cruzes de xpos nas veellas e os amjos diante que leuauam. E o nome de cada nao no costado ou omde lhe mylhor parecer. e a capitayna com ha bamdeira de xpos e a das armas na quadra o outras de devisa. e huũa das armas dos capitaes em cada nao. e la no despidimento os nomes.

it. Em outro o cabo da boõa esperamça e com ho nome sprito que diga praso presmomtoryo com alguũas alymarias dalifamtes e negros e gaado vacuã e casas a maneira de la e pastores com manadas e as tres naos asy como partiram de lixboa que vaão em Rostro de cabo. E no cabo posto huu padram com as armas e + de xpos em cyma. e a era em que foram postos e alguua letra que bem parecer. as armas e o pelicano em baixo e a + de + dos em çyma.

Em outro çufalla pello naturall e as naaos ancoradas com suas bamdeiras e como saem em terra nos bates e pohem o padram. e os mouros e caferes no natural e nas cores e vestidos. como Resgatam o óuro. com elles vem e cada huũ resgata e parte em seu batel das naos .s. os mouros em huũ cabo apartadamente e os caferes em

[77] For Portugal and the slave trade in this period, see A. C. de M. Saunders, *A Social History of Black Slaves and Freedmen in Portugal, 1441–1555* (Cambridge: Cambridge University Press, 1982). More recently, for example, Didier Lahon, 'Black African Slaves and Freedmen in Portugal during the Renaissance: Creating a New Pattern of Reality', in Earle and Lowe (eds), *Black Africans in Renaissance Europe*, pp. 261–79.

outro stando huũs e outros em terra. e o Rey de cufala como vem fallar ao capitam e asentar paz e tomar bandeira das armas. e a maneira em que se lhe daa. E na terra seja pello natural. as aruores e alyfamtes e lyoes e bufaros.

it. Em outro moçanbique [ilha, *in the margin*] huũa forteleza e porto de mar e naaos nelle que emtram e saem de huũ cabo e do outro em maneira de duas frotas e com duas naos capitaynas cada huua de sua parte com bambeira na gauea da + de xpos. e as outras como as outras.

it. Em outro quyloa [ilha, *in the margin*] tambem no naturall forteleza apartada ilha com bandeiras das armas e cidade. e com ha frota diante e como a gente entra pela cidade e se toma e como se faz o Rey pelo capitam moor e lhe toma menajem e juramento de sogeyto.

it. Em outro mambaça [ilha, *in the margin*]. como se toma e a gente entra por ilha duas partes e o modo do desembarcar. e asy o fogo da cidade e como se pohem as bamdeiras nas torres e modo da sayda da gente fora da cidade e mortos tudo pello naturall e asy nos trajos dos homens de la da terra e suas bandeiras e modo de suas armas e recolhimento dos despojos as naaos que aqui ouue.

it. a tomada de braua como foy.

it. Em outro o fecto de çoçotora tambem pello naturall como foy.

it. o fecto de ormuz com os lugares que forem pera poher.

it. o fazimento da forteleza de cochy e os capitães como ha amdam fazemdo. e as naaos como estam no mar e as duas armadas e capitães delas e huua Igreja e como se bautizam os da terra. e que venhao [sic].

it. o fazimento de cananor asy como se fez e as bandeiras com suas armas.

it. o desbarato da armada dos Rumes pelo natural e com toda fremosura que se lhe poder fazer e as naaos todas leuaram aquelas que teuerem capitães conhecidos huũa bamdeira em cada huua das suas armas.

it. o desbarato da armada dos mouros que fez dom Lourenço tanbem na maneira em que estaa. e com toda outra fremosura que se lhe posa fazer.

it. Mostra do asemto que fez o capitam delRey nosso Senhor com elRey de cochy e como se viram e fallaram a borla dagoa .s. o capitam delRey em seus batees e com os capitaes em seus bates e trombetas e toda booa pymtura e elRey de cochy como chega em seu amdor e acompanhado de seus nayres e entra no batel do capitam moor e como aly Recebe a paz e amizade delRey e mostra de como se faz seu seruidor e vasallo.

it. o desbarato e destroiçam que fez lopo soares a maneira em que foy e a maneira em que estauam as naaos dos miguos e como armadas e aparelhadas e como as naaos estauam e asy as nosas e como foram as gentes delRey nos bates das suas naaos a pellejar com elles e com a deferenca dos imigos .s. de gemtes e trajos e armas e asy bamdeiras delRey e dos capitães e dos imigos e fogo das naos e asento das artelharyas em terras pera as defenderem.

it. o descobrimento da taprobana e como chegam as naos e pohem o padram e o Rey da tore como Recebe os embaixadores e na maneira em dizem que elle estaua. e como caregam de canella os da terra a meter nas naaos.

it. a tomada de chaul na maneira em que foy e que ho viso Rey tomou neste caminho.

it. A tomada de calecut e no modo em que foy.s. queymar das naaos e do seu serame entrada da cidade e queymamento da sua mezquita e entrada dos pacos delRey de calecut e despojo da cidade. e o modo da sayda da gente e as bamdeiras dos capitaães.

it. a chegada do almyrante a callecut tres naaos e o modo em que hiam e como poseram os padrões e como foy Reçebido pella gente da terra.

it. A tornada do almirante e chegada a lixboa. com suas naaos. e como foy Recebido e chegou a elRey com o tributo e parias que trouxe. de quiloa.

it. em cochy a casa da feituria e modo que se tem na compra e vemda das especiarias com os mercadores e joyas. e como descaregam.

E como se daa a copa a elRey de cochy e a cerimonya com que se lhe daa.

E a pyntura. das geentes cor e vistido e armas o natural e seus amdores e alifantes e sombreiros.

it. as molheres como se queymam com o modo todo em que se faz.

it. o Rey que se espedaça e o modo em que ho faz.

it. as molheres que se metem nos cambos.

it. o modo de trazer as joyas nos dedos dos pes e o modo em que as trazem.

it. os amdores como sam garneçidos de pedraria.

Bibliography

Primary sources and early printed material (to 1900)

Acosta, José de, *De procuranda indorum salute* (Madrid: Consejo Superior de Investigaciones Cientificas, 1984).

Aldrete, Bernardo José, *Del origen de la lengua castellana o romance que oi se usa en España* (Rome: Carlo Vulliet, 1606).

Anchieta, José de, *Doutrina cristã* (São Paulo: Edições Loyola, 1993).

Anon., *Catalogo dos Governadores de Angola* (1825).

Anon., *Colleçao de noticias para a historia das nações ultramarinas* (Lisbon: Academia Real das Sciencias, 1826).

Antonil, A. J., *Cultura e opulência do Brasil*, 3rd edn (1711; São Paulo: Editora Itatiaia, 1982).

Aragão, Fernão Ximenes de, *Doutrina catholica para instrucção e confirmação dos fieis e extincção das seitas supersticiosas e em particular do judaismo* (Lisbon: Pedro Craesbeck, 1625).

Araújo, Antonio de, *Catecismo na lingoa brasilica, no qual se contem a summa da doctrina christã* . . . (1618; Rio de Janeiro: PUC, 1952).

Bandeira, Sá da, 'Relatório do Secretário de Estado dos Negócios da Marinha e Ultramar', *Arquivo das Colónias*, vol. 1 (1836), pp. 13–18.

— *O Trabalho Rural Africano e a Administração Colonial* (Lisbon: Imprensa Nacional, 1873).

Barreto, Joannes A. da Graça, *A descoberta da India ordenada em tapeçaria por mandado de El-Rey D. Manuel* . . . (Coimbra, 1880).

Barros, João de, *Gramática da língua portuguesa* . . . (Lisbon: Luis Rodrigues, 1540).

— *Asia* (Lisbon: G. Galharde, 1552).

Battūta, Ibn (H. A. R. Gibb, ed.), *The Travels of Ibn Battūta, A.D. 1325–1354*) (Cambridge: Hakluyt Society, 1962).

Beaulieu, Leroy, *De la colonisation chez les peuples modernes* (1874; Paris: Guillaumin et Cie, 1882).

Botelho, Sebastião Xavier, *Escravatura: Benefícios que podem provir às nossas possessões d'África da prohibição daquelle tráfico* (Lisbon: Typographia de José B. Morando, 1840).

Brandão, Ambrosio Fernandes, *Diálogos das grandezas do Brasil* (1618; Rio de Janeiro: Dois Mundos, 1943).

Cadornega, Antônio de Oliveira de, *História geral das guerras angolanas*, 3 vols (1681; Lisbon: Agência Geral do Ultramar, 1972).

Castilho, Augusto de, *Memoria Ácerca da Extincção da Escravidão e do Trafico de Escravatura no Territorio Portuguez* (Lisbon: Publicação do Ministério da Marinha, 1889).

Castro, Afonso de, 'Résumé historique de l'établissement portugais à Timor, des us et coutumes de ses habitants', *Tijdschrift voor Indische Taal-, Land- en Volkenkunde* 11 (1862), pp. 465–506.

Caxa, Quirício, and Pero Rodrigues, *Primeiras biografias de José de Anchieta* (São Paulo: Edições Loyola, 1988).

Corvo, João de Andrade, *Estudos sobre as Províncias Ultramarinas* (Lisbon: Academia Real das Sciencias, 1883–7).

Coutinho, José Azeredo, *Ensaio economico sobre o commercio de Portugal e suas colonias* (Lisbon: Typografia da Academia Real das Sciencias, 1794).

— *Analyse sobre a justiça do Commercio do Resgate dos Escravos da Costa de Africa, novamente revista e acrescentada por seu author* (Lisbon: Nova Officina de João Rodrigues Neves, 1808).

— *Concordância das leis de Portugal e das Bullas Pontifícias, das quaes humas permittem a escravidão dos pretos d'Africa, e outras prohibem a escravidão dos Indios do Brazil* (Lisbon: Nova Officina de João Rodrigues Neves, 1808).

Cresque, Abraham (?), *El Atlas catalán. Primera edición completa en el sexcentésimo aniversario de su realización 1375–1975* (Barcelona: Diáfora, 1975).

— (Georges Grosjean, ed.), *Mappa Mundi: The Catalan Atlas of the Year 1375* (Zurich: Urs Graf, 1978).

Cruz, Manuel da (Aldo Luiz Leoni, ed.), *Copiador de cartas particulares do Senhor Dom Frei Manuel da Cruz, bispo do Maranhão e de Mariana (1739–1762)* (Brasília: Edições do Senado Federal, 2008).

Delany, Martin, *The Condition, Elevation, Emigration, and Destiny of the Colored People of the United States* (1852; Project Gutenberg Ebook, www.pgdp.net).

Denis, Ferdinand, *Histoire et description du Brésil* (Paris: Didot Frères, 1839).

Deville, Jean Achille, *Compte de dépenses de la construction du château de Gaillon . . .* (Paris, 1850).

Enes, António, *Moçambique: Relatório apresentado ao governo* (1893; Lisbon: Imprensa Nacional, 1971).

Fernandes, Valentim (João José Alves Dias, ed.), *Ordenações Manuelinas. Livros I a V. Reprodução em fac-símile da edição de Valentim Fernandes (Lisboa, 1512–1513)* (Lisbon: Universidade Nova de Lisboa, 2002).

Fernández de Heredia, Juan (John J. Nitti, ed.), *Juan Fernández de Heredia's Aragonese Version of the Libro de Marco Polo* (Madison, WI: Hispanic Seminary of Medieval Studies, 1980).

França, Bento da, *Macao e os seus habitantes. Relações com Timor* (Lisboa: Imprensa Nacional, 1897).

Girault, Arthur, *Principes de colonisation et de législation coloniale* (1895; Paris: Librairie de la Sociètè du Recueil J.-B. Sirey, 1907).

— 'La main d'oeuvre aux colonies', *Revue d'Économie Politique* 10 (1896), p. 147 ff.

Harrisse, Henry, *Americus Vespuccius: A Critical and Documentary Review of Two Recent English Books Concerning the Navigator* (London: B. F. Stevens, 1895).

Hegel, Georg Wilhelm Friedrich, *Lectures on the Philosophy of World History. Introduction: Reason in History* (Cambridge: Cambridge University Press, 1975).

Houdoy, Jules, *Les tapisseries de hautes-lisses. Histoire de la fabrication lilloise du XIVe au XVIIIe siècle . . .* (Paris, 1871).

Humboldt, Alexander von (Thomasina Ross, ed.), *Personal Narrative and Travels to the Equinoctial Regions of America during the Years 1799–1804* (London: George Routledge and Sons, 1895).

Hume, David, 'On National Characters' (1741), in Stephen Copley and Andrew Edgar (eds), *Selected Essays* (Oxford: Oxford University Press, 1993), pp. 113–25.

Hurd, John Codman, *The Law of Freedom and Bondage in the United States*, 2 vols (Boston: Little Brown & Co., 1858–62).

Konetzke, Richard, *Colección de documentos para la historia de la formación social de Hispanoamerica (1493–1810)* (Madrid: Consejo Superior de Investigaciones Cientificas, 1953).

Koster, Henry, *Travels in Brazil*, 2 vols (London, 1817).

Kronenberg, Maria Elizabeth, *De novo mondo, Antwerp, Jan van Doesborch [about 1520]: A Facsimile of an Unique Broadsheet* (The Hague: Martinus Nijhoff, 1927).

Leroy-Beaulieu, Paul, *De la colonisation chez les peuples modernes* (Paris: Guillaumin et Cie, 1874).

Lima, José Joaquim Lopes de, *Ensaios sobre a statistica das possessões portuguezas na Africa Occidental e Oriental; na Asia Occidental; na China, e na Oceania* (Lisbon: Imprensa Nacional, 1844–62).

Magalhães, José Vieira Couto de, *O Selvagem* (1876; São Paulo and Rio de Janeiro: Livraria Magalhães Editora, n.d.).

Malheiro, Perdigão, *A escravidão no Brasil – Ensaio jurídico, histórico, social*, 2 vols (1866; Petrópolis: Vozes, 1976).

Martins, Joaquim Pedro Oliveira, *Elementos de antropologia* (1880; Lisbon: Guimarães, 1954).

— *O Brasil e as colónias portuguesas*, 3rd edn (1880; Lisbon: Livraria Antonio Maria Pereira, 1888; also Lisboa: Guimarães, 1978).

— *As raças humanas e a civilização primitiva* (1881–3; Lisbon: Guimarães Editores, 1955).

Menezes, Sebastião Lopes de Calheiros e, *Relatório do Governador Geral da Província de Angola* (Lisbon: Imprensa Nacional, 1867).

Nabuco, Joaquim, *O Abolicionismo* (1883; São Paulo: Publifolha, 2000).

National Archives of Rhodesia/Centro de Estudos Históricos Ultramarinos, *Documentos sobre os portugueses em Moçambique e na África central, 1497–1840/Documents on the Portuguese in Mozambique and Central Africa, 1497–1840*, 9 vols (Lisbon: National Archives of Rhodesia/Centro de Estudos Históricos Ultramarinos, 1962).

Nebrija, Antonio de, *Gramática de la lengua castellana* (Salamanca: Juan de Porras, 1492).

Neves, José Acúrsio das, *Considerações politicas, e commerciaes sobre os descobrimentos, e possessões dos Portuguezes na Africa, e na Asia* (Lisbon: Impressão Régia, 1830).

Nóbrega, M. da, 'Diálogo sobre a conversão do gentio', in Serafim Leite (ed.), *Cartas dos primeiros Jesuítas do Brasil* (São Paulo: Comissão do IV Centenário da Cidade de São Paulo, 1954).

Nogueira, A. F., *A raça negra sob o ponto de vista da civilisação da África* (Lisbon: Nova Minerva, 1880).

Oliveira, Fernão de, *Grammatica da lingoagem portuguesa* . . . (Lisbon: Germão Galhardo, 1536).

Polo, Marco (Arthur Christopher Moule and Paul Pelliot, eds), *The Description of the World*, 2 vols (London: G. Routledge, 1938).

— *The Travels of Marco Polo. The Complete Yule-Cordier Edition*, 2 vols (New York: Dover, 1993).

Sá, C. and P. Castro (eds), *Memórias do descobrimento do Brasil* (Rio de Janeiro: Museu da República, 2005).

Salvador, Fray Vicente do, *História do Brasil, 1500–1627*, 7th edn (*c*. 1627; São Paulo: Ed. Itatiaia, 1982).

Santa Anna, Joseph Pereira de, *Chronica dos Carmelitas da Antiga*, 2 vols (Lisbon: Herdeiros de A. Pedrozo Galram, 1745–51).

Sanudo, Marino, *Liber secretorum fidelium crucis super Terrae Sanctae recuperatione et conservatione*, in Jacques Bongars (ed.), *Gesta Dei per Francos, sive, Orientalium expeditionum, et Regni Francorum Hierosolimitani historia* (Hanover: Wechelianis apud haeredes Ioan Aubrii, 1611).

Schoff, Wilfred Harvey (ed.), *The Periplus of the Erythraean Sea: Travel and Trade in the Indian Ocean by a Merchant of the First Century* (New York: Longmans, Green, and Co., 1912).

Silva, António de Moraes and Rafael Bluteau, *Diccionario da lingua portugueza composto pelo padre D. Rafael Bluteau; Reformado, e accrescentado por António de Moraes Silva natural do Rio de Janeiro* (Lisbon: Officina de Simão Thaddeo Ferreira, 1789).

Silva, Celestino da, *Instruções para os comandantes militares* (Macau: n.p., 1896).

Silva, Joaquim Norberto de Souza e, *Investigações sobre os recenseamentos da população geral do império* . . . (1870; São Paulo: IPE-USP, 1986).

Silva, José Justino de Andrade e, *Collecção chronologica da legislação portugueza compilada e anotada* (Lisbon: Imprensa de F. X. de Souza, 1854–9).

Soil, Eugène, *Les tapisseries de Tournai: Les tapissiers et les hautelisseurs de cette ville* (Tournai-Lille: Société Historique, 1871).

Solórzano y Pereira, Juan de, *Política Indiana* (1639; Madrid: Ediciones Atlas, 1972).

Sousa, José de Albuquerque, *Código do trabalho rural do Ultramar. Edição revista, com indices alfabético e sistemático* (Coimbra: Coimbra Editora, 1962).

Spix, Johann Baptist Von and Carl Friedrich Philipp Von Martius, *Travels in Brazil in the Years 1817–1820* . . . (London: Longman, 1824).

Vaquinhas, J. S., 'Timor. Usos – Superstições de guerra', *Boletim da Sociedade de Geografia de Lisboa* 4 (1884), pp. 484–91.

Vasconcellos, Simão de, *Crônica da Companhia de Jesus*, 2 vols (1663; Petrópolis: Vozes, 1977).

Velho, Alvaro (Ernest Ravenstein, ed.), *A Journal of the First Voyage of Vasco de Gama, 1497–1499* (London: Hakluyt Society, 1898).

— (Damião Peres, António Baião and Artur de Magalhães Basto, eds), *Diário da viagem de Vasco da Gama*, 2 vols (Porto: Livraria Civilização, 1945).

Vespuccius, Albericus (Charles Henry Coote, ed.), *The Voyage from Lisbon to India, 1505–06. Being an Account and Journal of Albericus Vespuccius* (London: B. F. Stevens, 1894).

Vieira, Antonio, *Cartas do Brasil* (São Paulo: Hedra, 2003).

Secondary sources

Adorno, T. W., E. Frenkel-Brunswik, D. J. Levinson and R. N. Sanford, *The Authoritarian Personality* (New York: Harper and Row, 1950).

Afolabi, Niyi, Esmeralda Ribeiro and Márcio Barbosa, *The Afro-Brazilian Mind: Contemporary Afro-Brazilian Literary and Cultural Criticism* (Trenton, NJ: Africa World Press, 2007).

— *Cadernos Negros – Black Notebooks: Contemporary Afro-Brazilian Literature* (Trenton, NJ: Africa World Press, 2008).

Agier, Michel, Manuela Alvarez, Odile Hoffmann and Eduardo Restrepo, *Tumaco: Haciendo ciudad* (Bogotá: Universidad del Valle, 1999).

Aladrén, Gabriel, 'Liberdades negras nas paragens do Sul: Alforria e inserção social de libertos em Porto Alegre, 1800–1835', unpublished Masters dissertation, Universidade Federal Fluminense, 2008.

Albuquerque, Luis de, 'Algumas observações sobre o Planisfério Cantino (1502)', *Boletim do Centro de Estudos Geográficos* 3:22–3 (1966–7), pp. 57–84.

Alden, Dauril, 'The Population of Brazil in the Late Eighteenth Century: A Preliminary Study', *Hispanic American Historical Review* 43:2 (1963), pp. 173–205.

— 'Late Colonial Brazil, 1750–1808', in Leslie Bethell (ed.), *Colonial Brazil* (Cambridge: Cambridge University Press, 1987), pp. 284–343.

— *Charles R. Boxer: An Uncommon Life: Soldier, Historian, Teacher, Collector, Traveller* (Lisbon: Fundação Oriente, 2001).

Alencastro, Luiz Felipe de, 'Prolétaires et esclaves: Immigrés portugais et captifs africains à Rio de Janeiro 1850–1872', *Cahiers du CRIAR* (Rouen) 4 (1984), pp. 119–56.

— *O trato dos viventes: Formação do Brasil no Atlântico Sul, séculos XVI e XVII* (São Paulo: Companhia das Letras, 2000).

Alexandre, Valentim, 'Questão nacional e questão colonial em Oliveira Martins', *Análise Social* 31:1 (1996), pp. 183–201.

— 'A questão colonial no Portugal oitocentista', in Joel Serrão and A. H. de Oliveira Marques (eds), *Nova História da Expansão Portuguesa* (Lisbon: Estampa, 1998), vol. 10, pp. 101–8.

— 'Nação e império', in Francisco Bethencourt and Kirti Chaudhuri (eds), *História da expansão portuguesa*, vol. 4 (Lisbon: Círculo de Leitores, 1998), pp. 90–142.

— 'O império e a ideia de raça, séculos XIX e XX', in Jorge Vala (ed.), *Novos Racismos* (Oeiras: Celta, 1999), pp. 133–44.

— *A questão colonial no Parlamento (1821–1910)* (Lisbon: Dom Quixote, 2008).

Alexandre, Valentim and Jill Dias (eds), *O império africano, 1825–1890* (Lisbon: Estampa, 1988).

Algranti, Leila Mezan, *O feitor ausente: Estudos sobre a escravidão urbana no Rio de Janeiro, 1808–1822* (Petrópolis: Vozes, 1988).

Almagià, Robert, 'Il Mappamondi di Enrico Martello e alcuni concetti geografici di Cristoforo Colombo', *La Bibliofilia* 42–3 (1940), pp. 288–311.

Almario, Oscar, 'Dinámica y consecuencias del conflicto armado colombiano en el Pacífico: Limpieza étnica y desterritorialización de afrocolombianos e indígenas y "multiculturalismo" de Estado e indolencia nacional', in Eduardo Restrepo and Axel Rojas (eds), *Conflicto e (in)visibilidad: Retos en los estudios de la gente negra en Colombia* (Popayán: Universidad del Cauca, 2004).

Almeida, A., *Impacto da imigração em Portugal nas contas do Estado* (Lisbon: ACIDI, 2003).

Amado, Jorge, *Tenda dos milagres*, 45th edn (Rio de Janeiro: Record, 2006).

Anderson, Benedict, *Imagined Communities* (1983; New York: Verso, 1991).

Anderson, Mark, *Black and Indigenous: Garifuna Activism and Consumer Culture in Honduras* (Minneapolis: University of Minnesota Press, 2009).

Andersson, Christiane and Charles Talbot, *From a Mighty Fortress: Prints, Drawings, and Books in the Age of Luther, 1483–1546* (Detroit: Detroit Institute of Arts, 1983).

Andrade, António Manuel Lopes, 'De Ferrara a Lisboa: Tribulações do cristão-novo Alexandre Reinel, preso no cárcere do Santo Ofício', *Cadernos de Estudos Sefarditas* 7 (2007), pp. 83–131.

Andrade, Augusto Freire de, *Relatórios sobre Moçambique*, 6 vols (Lourenço Marques: Imprensa Nacional, 1909–10).

— *A questão dos serviçaes de S. Thomé. Carta de A. Freire D'Andrade* (Lisbon: Agência Colonial, 1913).

— *Relatório feito pelo Director-Geral das colónias acêrca do livro Portuguese Slavery escrito pelo Sr. John H. Harris* (Lisbon: Imprensa Nacional, 1913).

Andrade, Rômulo, 'Casamentos entre escravos na região cafeeira de Minas Gerais', *Revista da Universidade Federal Rural, Série Ciências Humanas* 22:2 (2000), pp. 177–97.

— 'Ampliando estudos sobre famílias escravos no século XIX (crianças cativas em Minas Gerias: Legitimidade, alforria e establidade familial)', *Revista Universidade Rural, Série Ciências Humanas* 24:1–2 (2002), pp. 101–13.

Andrews, George Reid, 'Brazilian Racial Democracy, 1900–90: An American Counterpoint', *Journal of Contemporary History* 31:3 (1996), pp. 483–507.

— 'Afro-Latin America: Five Questions', *Latin American and Caribbean Ethnic Studies* 4:2 (2009), pp. 191–210.

Anghie, Antony, *Imperialism, Sovereignty and the Making of International Law* (Cambridge: Cambridge University Press, 2007).

Anon. (ed.), *America, Bride of the Sun: 500 Years of Latin America and the Low Countries* (Ghent: Imschoot Books, 1992).

Anon., *Hans Burgkmair: Das graphische Werk* (Stuttgart: Staatsgalerie, Graphische Sammlung, 1973).

Anon., *Hans Burgkmair, 1473–1531: Holzschnitte, Zeichnungen, Holzstöcke* (Berlin: Staatliche Museen zu Berlin, 1974).

Anon., *Le règime et l'organisation du travail des indigènes dans les colonies tropicales* (Bruxelles: Etablissements Généraux d'Imprimerie, 1929).

Anstey, Roger, *Britain and the Congo in the Nineteenth Century* (Oxford: Clarendon Press, 1962).

António, J. and V. Policarpo, *A imigração em Portugal aos olhos dos portugueses* (Lisbon: Universidade Católica Portuguesa, 2011).

Armas, Antonio Rumeu de, *El Tratado de Tordesillas* (Madrid: Mapfre, 1992).

Arocha, Jaime, *Ombligados de Ananse: Hilos ancestrales y modernos en el Pacífico colombiano* (Bogotá: Universidad Nacional de Colombia, 1999).

Arriaga, Eduardo E., *New Life Tables for Latin American Populations in the Nineteenth and Twentieth Centuries* (Berkeley: University of California Press, 1968).

Arruti, José Mauricio Andion, 'A emergência dos "remanescentes": Notas para o diálogo entre indígenas e quilombolas', *Mana. Estudos de Antropología Social* 3:2 (1997), pp. 7–38.

— 'Comunidades negras rurais: Entre a memória e o desejo', *Tempo e Presença* 298 (1998), pp. 15–18.

Ascencio, Eugenio, '"La lengua compañera del Império". Historia de una idea de Nebrija en España y Portugal', *Revista de Filologia Española* 63 (1960), pp. 399–413.

Aspe-Fleurimont, Lucien, *La colonisation française avec des observations spéciales sur l'Afrique Occidentale* (Paris: V. Giard and E. Brière, 1902).

Asselberghs, Jean-Paul, *La tapisserie tournaisienne au XVIe siècle* (Tournai: n.p., 1968).

Assembleia Nacional, *Constituição política da República portuguesa, actualizada de harmonia com a Lei n° 2.048 de 11 de Junho de 1951* (Lisbon: Assembleia Nacional, 1952).

Axelson, Eric, *Portugal and the Scramble for Africa* (Johannesburg: Witwatersrand University Press, 1967).

— *Portuguese in South-East Africa, 1488–1600* (Johannesburg: C. Struik, 1973).

Azevedo, Celia M. Marinho de, 'O abolicionismo transatlântico e a memória do paraiso racial brasileiro', *Estudos Afro-Asiáticos* 30 (1996), pp. 7–40.

— *Abolicionismo: Estados Unidos e Brasil, uma história comparada (século XIX)* (São Paulo: Annablume, 2003).

Azevedo, J. Lúcio de, *História dos Cristãos-Novos portugueses* (1921; Lisbon: Clássica, 1975).

Azevedo, Thales, *As elites de cor numa cidade brasileira: Um estudo de ascensão social & classes sociais e grupos de prestígio* (1953; Salvador: EDUFBA, 1996).

Baião, António, *A Inquisição de Goa: Correspondência dos inquisidores da Índia (1569–1630)* (Coimbra: Imprensa da Universidade, 1930).

Balazs, E. *et al.*, *Oriente Poliano: Studi e conferenze . . . in occasione del VII centenario della nascita di Marco Polo (1254–1954)* (Roma: Istituto italiano per il Medio e Estremo Oriente, 1957).

Bannister, Jr., Robert C., 'William Graham Sumner's Social Darwinism: A Reconsideration', *History of Political Economy* 5:1 (1973), pp. 89–109.

Banton, Michael, *The Idea of Race* (London: Tavistock, 1977).

— 'Historical and Contemporary Modes of Racialization', in Karim Murji and John Solomos (eds), *Racialization: Studies in Theory and Practice* (Oxford: Oxford University Press, 2005), pp. 51–68.

Barbary, Olivier and Fernando Urrea (eds), *Gente negra en Colombia, dinámicas sociopolíticas en Cali y el Pacífico* (Cali and Paris: CIDSE/Univalle, IRD, Colciencias, 2004).

Barbary, Olivier, Héctor F. Ramírez and Fernando Urrea, 'Identidad y ciudadanía afrocolombiana en el Pacífico y Cali', in Olivier Barbary and Fernando Urrea (eds), *Gente negra en Colombia: dinámicas sociopolíticas en Cali y el Pacífico* (Cali and Paris: CIDSE/Univalle, IRD, Colciencias, 2004), pp. 245–82.

Barbosa, Márcio (ed.), *Frente negra brasileira: Depoimentos* (São Paulo: Quilombhoje, 1998).

Barickman, B. J., 'As cores do escravismo: Escravistas "pretos", "pardos" e "cabras" no Recôncavo Baiano, 1835', *População e Família* 2:2 (1999), pp. 7–62.

Barker, M., *The New Racism* (London: Junction Books, 1981).

Barot, Rohit and John Bird, 'Racialization: The Genealogy and Critique of a Concept', *Ethnic and Racial Studies* 24:4 (2001), pp. 601–18.

Barth, Boris and Jürgen Osterhammel (eds), *Zivilisierungsmissionen: Imperiale Weltverbesserung seit dem 18. Jahrhundert* (Konstanz: UVK, 2005).

Bassani, Ezio and Letizia Tedeschi, 'The Image of the Hottentot in the Seventeenth and Eighteenth Centuries: An Iconographic Investigation', *Journal of the History of Collections* 2 (1990), pp. 157–86.

Bastide, Roger, 'A imprensa negra do Estado de São Paulo', in *Estudos Afro-Brasileiros* (São Paulo: Perspectiva, 1973).

— *The African Religions of Brazil: Towards a Sociology of the Interpenetration of Civilizations* (Baltimore: Johns Hopkins University Press, 1978).

Bastide, Roger and Florestan Fernandes, *Relações raciais entre negros e brancos em São Paulo* (São Paulo: Anhembi, 1955).

Bastos, Cristiana, 'Um luso-tropicalismo às avessas: Colonialismo científico, aclimação e pureza racial em Germano Correia', in M. C. Ribeiro and A. P. Ferreira (eds), *Fantasmas e fantasias imperiais no imaginário português contemporâneo* (Porto: Campo das Letras, 2003), pp. 227–53.

Bayle, Stanley R., 'Unmixing for Race Making in Brazil', *American Journal of Sociology* 114:3 (2008), pp. 577–614.

Bender, Gerald J., *Angola under the Portuguese: The Myth and the Reality* (London: Heinemann, 1978; also Berkeley: University of California Press, 1992).

Benzing, Josef, *Jakob Köbel zu Oppenheim, 1494–1533: Bibliographie seiner Drucke und Schriften* (Wiesbaden: G. Pressler, 1962).

Beozzo, J. O., *Leis e regimentos das missões: Política indigenista no Brasil* (São Paulo: Edições Loyola, 1983).

Berlin, Ira, *Slaves without Masters: The Free Negro in the Antebellum South* (New York: W. W. Norton, 1974).

Berman, Bruce and John Lonsdale, *Unhappy Valley: Conflict in Kenya and Africa. 1. State and Class* (London, Nairobi and Athens, OH: James Currey/Heinemann/Ohio University Press, 1992).

Berquó, Elza, 'Demografia da desigualdade. Algumas considerações sobre os negros no Brasil', *Novos Estudos – CEBRAP* 21 (1988), pp. 74–84.

Berthe, Louis, 'Le mariage par achat et la captation des gendres dans une société semi-féodale: Les Buna' de Timor central', *L'Homme* 1:3 (1961), pp. 5–31.

Bertin, Enidelce, *Alforrias na São Paulo do século XIX: Liberdade e dominação* (São Paulo: Humanitas FFFCH(USP, 2004).

Bethell, Leslie, *The Abolition of the Brazilian Slave Trade. Britain, Brazil and the Slave Trade Question, 1807–1869* (Cambridge: Cambridge University Press, 1970).

Bethencourt, Francisco, 'Campo religioso e Inquisição em Portugal no século XVI', in *Estudos Contemporâneos* 6 (1984), pp. 43–60.

— 'A expulsão dos Judeus', in Diogo Ramada Curto (ed.), *O tempo de Vasco da Gama* (Lisboa: Comissão Nacional para as Comemorações dos Descobrimentos Portugueses/ Difel, 1998), pp. 271–80.

— 'A Igreja', in Francisco Bethencourt and Kirti Chaudhuri (eds), *História da expansão portuguesa*, 5 vols (Lisbon: Círculo de Leitores, 1998–9), vol. 1, pp. 369–86.

— 'Low Cost Empire: Interaction between the Portuguese and Local Societies in Asia', in Ernst van Veen and Leonard Blusse (eds), *Rivalry and Conflict: European Traders and Asian Trading Networks in the 16th and 17th Centuries* (Leiden: CNWS, 2005), pp. 108–30.

— 'The Political Correspondence of Alburquerque and Cortés', in Francisco Bethencourt and Florike Egmond (eds), *Correspondence and Cultural Exchange in Europe, 1400–1700* (Cambridge: Cambridge University Press, 2007), pp. 219–73.

— 'Race Relations in the Portuguese Empire', in Jay A. Levenson (ed.), *Encompassing the Globe: Portugal and the World in the 16th and 17th Centuries* (Washington, DC: Smithsonian Institution, 2007), pp. 45–53.

— *The Inquisition: A Global History, 1478–1834* (Cambridge: Cambridge University Press, 2009).

Bethencourt, Francisco and Kirti Chaudhuri (eds), *História da expansão portuguesa*, 5 vols (Lisbon: Círculo de Leitores, 1998–9).

Bindman, David, *Ape to Apollo: Aesthetics and the Idea of Race in the 18th Century* (London: Reaktion Books, 2002).

Binotti, Lucia, '"La lengua compañera del imperio". Observaciones sobre el desarrollo de un discurso de colonialismo lingüístico en el Renacimiento español', in Otto Zwartjes (ed.), *Las gramáticas misioneras de tradición hispánica (siglos XVI–XVII)* (Amsterdam: Rodopi, 2000).

Bittencourt, Marcelo, *Dos jornais às armas: Trajectórias da contestação angolana* (Lisbon: Vega, 1999).

— 'A resposta dos "Crioulos Luandenses" ao intensificar do processo colonial nos finais do século XIX', in *A África e a instalação do sistema colonial (c.1885 – c.1930)*, Actas da III Reunião Internacional de História da África, 1999 (Lisbon: IICT, 2000), pp. 655–71.

Blévis, Laure, 'Les avatars de la citoyenneté en Algérie coloniale ou les paradoxes d'une catégorisation', *Droit et Société* 48 (2001), pp. 557–80.

Bloch, Marc, *La société féodale* (1939; Paris: Albin Michel, 1982).

Bluteau, Rafael, *Vocabulario Portuguez e Latino*, 10 vols (Coimbra and Lisbon: Colégio das Artes, 1712–28).

Bontinck, François, 'Ndoadidiki Ne-Kinu a Mubemba, premier évêque Kongo (c. 1495 – c. 1531)', *Revue africaine de théologie* 3:6 (1979), pp. 149–69.

Borges, Célia Maia, *Escravos e libertos nas irmandades do Rosário: Devoção e solidariedade em Minas Gerais – séculos XVIII e XIX* (Juiz de Fora: Universidade Federal de Juiz de Fora, 2005).

Borges, Nilsen C. Oliveira, 'Meio livre, meio liberto', *II Encontro 'Escravidão e Liberdade no Brasil Meridional'* (2005).

Borowska-Clausberg, Beate, *Balthasar Sprenger und der frühneuzeitliche Reisebericht* (Munich: Ludicium, 1999).

Boschi, Caio, *Os Leigos e o Poder* (São Paulo: Atica, 1986).

Bowden, Brett and Leonard Seabrooke, 'Global Standards of Market Civilization', in Martin Hall and Patrick Thaddeus Jackson (eds), *Civilizational Identity: The Production and Reproduction of 'Civilizations' in International Relations* (New York: Palgrave Macmillan, 2007), pp. 119–33.

Boxer, Charles R., *Race Relations in the Portuguese Colonial Empire, 1415–1825* (Oxford: Clarendon Press, 1963).

— *The Portuguese Seaborne Empire, 1415–1825* (London: Hutchinson, 1969).

Boyajian, James C., *Portuguese Trade in Asia under the Habsburgs (1580–1640)* (Baltimore: Johns Hopkins University Press, 1993).

Braga, Carolina L. G., 'Tenha uma Boa Morte', *Científico* 4:2 (2004), n.p.

Bravo, Nelson Saraiva, *A cultura algodoeira na economia do Norte de Moçambique* (Lisbon: Junta de Investigações do Ultramar, 1963).

British Museum, *Prince Henry the Navigator and Portuguese Maritime Enterprise* (London: British Museum, 1960).

Brookshaw, David, *Race and Color in Brazilian Literature* (Metuchen, NJ and London: Scarecrow Press, 1986).

Brown, R., *Prejudice* (Oxford: Blackwell, 1995).

Burke, Peter and Maria Lúcia G. Pallares-Burke, *Gilberto Freyre: Social Theory in the Tropics* (Oxford: Peter Lang, 2008).

Cabecinhas, R., *Preto e Branco: A naturalização da discriminação racial* (Porto: Campo das Letras, 2007).

Cahen, Michel, 'Corporatisme et colonialisme: Approche du cas mozambicain (1933–1979)', *Cahiers d'études africaines* (Paris) 92 (1983), pp. 383–417, and 93 (1984), pp. 5–24.

— *Les bandits: Un historien au Mozambique, 1994* (Paris: Centre Culturel Calouste Gulbenkian, 2002).

Camargo, Oswaldo de, *O carro do êxito* (São Paulo: Livraria Martins Editora, 1972).

— *A descoberta do frio* (São Paulo: Edições Populares, 1979).

Campbell, Thomas P., *Henry VIII and the Art of Majesty: Tapestries at the Tudor Court* (New Haven: Yale University Press, 2007).

Campbell, Tony, *Early Maps* (New York: Abbeville Press, 1981).

— *The Earliest Printed Maps, 1472–1500* (Berkeley: University of California Press, 1987).

Cardoso, Fernando Henrique, *Capitalismo e escravidão no Brasil meridional: O negro na sociedade escravocrata do Rio Grande do Sul* (São Paulo: Difusão Européia do Livro, 1962).

— 'Livros que inventaram o Brasil', *Novos Estudos* 37 (1993), pp. 21–36.

Cardoso, Fernando Henrique and Octávio Ianni, *Côr e mobilidade social em Florianópolis: Aspectos das relações entre negros e brancos numa comunidade do Brasil Meridional* (São Paulo: Editora Nacional, 1960).

Carpenter, Stanford, 'What We Bring to the Table: The Means of Imagination in an African American Family', in James Faubion (ed.), *The Ethics of Kinship: Ethnographic Inquiries* (Oxford: Rowman and Littlefield, 2001).

Carril, Lourdes de Fátima Bezerra, 'Quilombo, território e geografia', *Agrária* 3 (2006), pp. 156–71.

Castelo, Claudia, *'O modo português de estar no mundo': O Luso-tropicalismo e a ideologia colonial portuguesa, 1933–1961* (Porto: Afrontamento, 1998).

— 'A migração de metropolitanos para Angola e Moçambique 1945–1974', paper presented at the VIII Congresso Luso-Afro-Brasileiro de Ciências Sociais, Coimbra, September 2004.

— *Passagens para Africa: O povoamento de Angola e Moçambique com naturais de metrópole 1920–1974* (Porto: Afrontamento, 2007).

Castro, Alberto Osório de, *Flores de Coral*, in *Obra Poética* (António Osório, ed.) (Lisbon: INCM, 2004), vol. 1, p. 494.

Castro, Armando, *O sistema colonial português em África (meados do século XX)* (Lisbon: Editorial Caminho, 1978).

Castro, Yeda Pessoa de, *Falares africanos na Bahia* (Rio de Janeiro: Academia Brasileira de Letras/Topbooks, 2005).

Catarino, Petra Kátia Amaral, 'Sociedade civil angolana. Contributos para a democracia, paz e desenvolvimento', unpublished Masters dissertation, Universidade Técnica de Lisboa, 2006.

Catroga, Fernando, 'A importância do positivismo na consolidação da ideologia republicana em Portugal', *Biblos* 53 (1977), pp. 283–327.

Caudill, Edward, *Darwinian Myths: The Legends and Misuses of a Theory* (Knoxville, TN: University of Tennessee Press, 1997).

Central Intelligence Agency, *World Factbook*, 2010, available at www.cia.gov/library/publications/the-world-factbook/geos/ao.html

Cèsaire, Aimé, *Cahier d'un retour au pays* (Paris: Présence Africaine, 1956).

Chichava, Sérgio, 'Le "Vieux Mozambique": L'identité politique de la Zambézie', unpublished PhD thesis, Université de Bordeaux, 2007.

Chittick, Neville, *Kilwa: An Islamic Trading City on the East African Coast*, 2 vols (Nairobi: British Institute in Eastern Africa, 1974).

Clarence-Smith, William G., 'The Myth of Uneconomic Imperialism: The Portuguese in Angola, 1836–1926', *Journal of Southern African Studies* 5:2 (1979), pp. 165–80.

— 'Class Structure and Class Struggles in Angola in the 1970s', *Journal of Southern African Studies* 7:1 (1980), pp. 109–26.

— *The Third Portuguese Empire, 1825–1975: A Study in Economic Imperialism* (Manchester: Manchester University Press, 1985).

— 'Labour Conditions in the Plantations of São Tomé and Príncipe, 1875–1914', in Michael Twaddle (ed.), *The Wages of Slavery: From Chattel Slavery to Wage Labour in Africa, the Caribbean, and England* (London: Frank Cass, 1993), pp. 149–67.

Clark, Christopher and Wolfram Kaiser (eds), *Culture Wars: Secular-Catholic Conflict in Nineteenth-Century Europe* (Cambridge: Cambridge University Press, 2003).

Cleary, David, 'Race, Nationalism and Social Theory in Brazil: Rethinking Gilberto Freyre', David Rockefeller Center for Latin American Studies, Harvard University, working paper WPTC-99-09.

Colin, Susi, *Das Bild des Indianers im 16. Jahrhundert* (Idstein: Schulz-Kirchner, 1988).

Comaroff, John L., 'Reflections on the Colonial State, in South Africa and Elsewhere: Fragments, Factions, Facts and Fictions', *Social Identities* 4:3 (1998), pp. 321–61.

Conklin, Alice K., *A Mission to Civilize: The Republican Idea of Empire in France and West Africa, 1895–1930* (Stanford, CA: Stanford University Press, 1997).

Coombes, Annie and Avtar Brah (eds), *Hybridity and Its Discontents: Politics, Science, Culture* (London: Routledge, 2000).

Cooper, Frederick, *Plantation Slavery on the East Coast of Africa* (1977; Portsmouth, NH: Heinemann, 1997).

— 'The Problem of Slavery in African Studies', *Journal of African History* 20:1 (1979), pp. 103–25.

— 'States, Empires, and Political Imagination', in *Colonialism in Question: Theory, Knowledge, History* (Berkeley: University of California Press, 2005), pp. 153–203.

Cooper, Frederick and Ann Stoler, *Tensions of Empire: Colonial Cultures in a Bourgeois World* (Berkeley: University of California Press, 1997).

Cope, R. Douglas, *The Limits of Racial Domination: Plebeian Society in Colonial Mexico City, 1660–1720* (Madison: University of Wisconsin Press, 1994).

Cordeiro, Luciano, 'Portugal e o movimento geográfico moderno' (1877), in *Questões coloniais* (Coimbra: Imprensa da Universidade, 1934), pp. 1–29.

— *Questões coloniais* (Coimbra: Imprensa da Universidade, 1934).

Corominas, Joan, *Diccionario crítico etimológico castellano e hispánico*, 7 vols (Madrid: Gredos, 1981).

Cortesão, Armando and Avelino Teixeira de Mota, *Portugaliae Monumenta Cartographica*, 6 vols (Lisbon: Comissão Executiva do V Centenário da morte do Infante D. Henrique, 1960).

Cortesão, Jaime, *O Ultramar português depois da Restauração* (Lisbon: Portugalia, 1971).

Costa, Eduardo da, *Estudo sobre a Administração Civil das nossas Possessões Africanas. Memória Apresentada ao Congresso Colonial* (Lisbon: Imprensa Nacional, 1903).

Costa, Emilia Viotti da, 'The Myth of Racial Democracy', in *The Brazilian Empire: Myths and Histories*, rev. edn (Chapel Hill: University of North Carolina, 2000), pp. 234–46.

Costa, Iraci del Nero da, *Vila Rica: População (1719–1826)* (São Paulo: IPE-USP, 1979).

— 'Ocupação, povoamento e dinâmica populacional', in Iraci del Nero da Costa and Francisco Vidal Luna, *Minas colonial: Economia e sociedade* (São Paulo: Pioneira, 1982).

Costa, Luís, *Dicionário de Tetum-Português* (Lisbon: Colibri, 2001).

Costa, Sérgio, 'A construção sociológica da raça no Brasil', *Estudos Afro-Asiáticos* 24:1 (2002), pp. 35–61.

Costa, Tereza C. N. Araújo, 'O princípio classificatório "cor", sua complexidade e implicações para o uso censitário', *Revista Brasileira de Geografia* 36:3 (1974), pp. 91–103.

— 'A classificação de "cor" do IBGE: notas para uma discussão', *Cadernos de Pesquisa* (Fundação Carlos Chagas) 63 (1987), pp. 14–16.

Costantini, Dino, *Mission civilisatrice: Le rôle de l'histoire coloniale dans la construction de l'identité politique française* (Paris: La Découverte, 2008).

Couceiro, Henrique de Paiva, *Angola. Dois anos de governo (Junho 1907–Junho 1909): história e comentários* (Lisbon: Tipografia Portuguesa, 1948).

Cox-Rearick, Janet, *The Collection of François Ier: Royal Treasures* (Antwerp: Mercator Paribas, 1995).

Crusoé, Romeu, *A maldição de Canaan*, 2nd edn (Rio de Janeiro: Irmãos di Giorgio, 1955).

Cruz, Elisabeth Ceita Vera, *O estatudo do indigenato e a legislação da discriminação na colonização portuguesa: O caso de Angola* (Coimbra: Novo Imbondeiro, 2005).

Cunha, Anna Cannas da, *A Inquisição no Estado da Índia: Origens (1539–1560)* (Lisboa: Arquivos Nacionais/Torre do Tombo, 1995).

Cunha, J. M. Silva, *O trabalho indígena. Estudo de direito colonial* (Lisbon: Agência Geral do Ultramar, 1954).

Cunha, Manuela Carneiro da, *Negros, estrangeiros: Os escravos libertos e sua volta à África* (São Paulo: Brasiliense, 1985).

Curti, Ana Helena (ed.), *Aleijadinho e seu tempo: Fé, engenho e arte* (Rio de Janeiro: Banco Central do Brasil, 2006).

Curtin, Philip D., *The Image of Africa: British Ideas and Action, 1780–1850* (Madison: University of Wisconsin Press, 1964).

— *The Atlantic Slave Trade: A Census* (Madison: University of Wisconsin Press, 1969).

— *Cross-Cultural Trade in World History* (Cambridge: Cambridge University Press, 1984).

— *The Rise and Fall of the Plantation Complex: Essays in Atlantic History* (Cambridge: Cambridge University Press, 1990).

Curto, José C., 'The Anatomy of a Demographic Explosion: Luanda, 1844–1850', *International Journal of African Historical Studies* 32:2–3 (1999), pp. 381–405.

— 'Americanos', in 'Angola: The Brazilian Community in Benguela, c. 1722–1832', unpublished paper, 2003.

Curto, José C. and Raymond R. Gervais, 'The Population History of Luanda during the Late Atlantic Slave Trade, 1781–1844', *African Economic History* 29 (2001), pp. 1–59.

Cuti, *Quizila* (São Paulo: Edições Quilombhoje, 1987).

Cuti, *Negros em contos* (Belo Horizonte: Mazza Edições, 1996).

Dantas, Carolina Vianna, 'O Brasil cafe com leite. Debates intelectuais sobre mesticagem e preconceito de cor na primeira republica', *Tempo – Revista do Departamento de Historia da UFF* 1 (2009).

DataFolha, 1995, 300 anos de Zumbi.

DataFolha, Pesquisa sobre racismo, 2008.

Daughton, James P., *An Empire Divided: Religion, Republicanism, and the Making of French Colonialism, 1880–1914* (Oxford: Oxford University Press, 2007).

Davis, David Brion, *The Problem of Slavery in the Western World* (Ithaca, NY: Cornell University Press, 1966).

— *The Problem of Slavery in the Age of Revolution, 1770–1823* (Ithaca, NY: Cornell University Press, 1975).

— *Slavery and Human Progress* (Oxford: Oxford University Press, 1984).

Daynes, Sarah and Orville Lee, *Desire for Race* (Cambridge: Cambridge University Press, 2008).

Degler, Carl N., *Neither Black nor White: Slavery and Race Relations in Brazil and the United States* (New York: Macmillan, 1971).

Departamento Administrativo Nacional de Estadística (DANE), *Colombia una nación multicultural: Su diversidad étnica* (Bogotá: Departamento Administrativo Nacional de Estadística, 2006).

Departamento Intersindical de Estatísticas e Estudos Socio-Econômicos/Instituto Sindical Interamericano pela Igualdade Racial, *Mapa da população negra no mercado de trabalho – regiões metropolitanas de São Paulo, Salvador, Recife, Belo Horizonte, Porto Alegre e Distrito Federal* (São Paulo: INSPIR/Centro de Solidariedade AFLCIO/DIEESE, 1999).

Depestre, René, *Bonjour et adieu à la negritude* (Paris: R. Laffont, 1980).

Deutsch, Jan-Georg, *Emancipation without Abolition in German East Africa c. 1884–1914* (Oxford: James Currey, 2006).

Devisse, Jean and Michel Mollat, 'Les Africains dans l'ordonnance chrétienne du monde (XIVe–XVIe siècle)', in Ladislas Bugner (ed.), *L'image du noir dans l'art occidental* (Paris: Bibliothèque des Arts, 1979).

Dias, Jill, 'Famine and Disease in the History of Angola, c. 1830–1930', *Journal of African History* 22:3 (1981), pp. 349–78.

— 'Uma questão de identidade: Respostas intelectuais às transformações económicas no seio da elite crioula da Angola portuguesa entre 1870 e 1930', *Revista Internacional de Estudos Africanos* (Lisbon) 1 (1984), pp. 61–94.

— 'Mudanças nos padrões de poder do "Hinterland" de Luanda: O impacto da colonização sobre os Mbundu (c.1845–1920)', *Penélope. Fazer e desfazer a história* 14 (1994), pp. 43–91.

— 'Angola', in Valentim Alexandre and Jill Dias (eds), *O império africano, 1825–1890*, vol. 10 of *Nova História da Expansão Portuguesa* (Lisbon: Estampa, 1998).

Dias, Jorge, *Portuguese Contributions to Cultural Anthropology* (Johannesburg: Witwatersrand University Press, 1961).

Dias, Pedro, 'La tapisserie flamande au Portugal', in John Everaert and Eddy Stols (eds), *Flandre et Portugal: Au confluent de deux cultures* (Antwerp: Mercator, 1991), pp. 178–82.

— *À maneira de Portugal e da Índia: Uma tapeçaria inédita* (Porto: Pedro Aguiar Branco, 2007).

Dines, Alberto, *Vínculos do fogo: António José da Silva, o Judeu e outras histórias da Inquisição em Portugal e no Brasil* (Saõ Paulo: Companhia das Letras, 1999).

Diretoria Geral de Estatística, 'Imperio do Brazil: Quadro geral da população escravo . . .', in *Recenseamento Geral do Brazil de 1872* (n.p., n.d.).

Dodgson, Campbell, *Catalogue of Early German and Flemish Woodcuts Preserved in the Department of Prints and Drawings in the British Museum*, 2 vols (London: British Museum, 1911).

Doise, W., 'Préface', in M. Sanchez-Mazas and L. Licata (eds), *L'autre – Regards psychosociaux* (Grenoble: PUG, 2005).

Douglas, R. M., Michael D. Callahan and Elizabeth Bishop (eds), *Imperialism on Trial: International Oversight of Colonial Rule in Historical Perspective* (Lanham, MD: Lexington Books, 2006).

Dovidio, J. F. and S. L. Gaertner, 'Aversive Racism', in M. P. Zanna (ed.), *Advances in Experimental Social Psychology* (San Diego: Academic, 2004), vol. 36, pp. 1–51.

Drescher, Seymour, 'Brazilian Abolition in Comparative Perspective', in Rebecca J. Scott *et al.* (eds), *The Abolition of Slavery and the Aftermath of Emancipation in Brazil* (Durham, NC: Duke University Press, 1988), pp. 23–54.

— *Abolition: A History of Slavery and Antislavery* (Cambridge: Cambridge University Press, 2009).

Driver, Felix, *Geography Militant: Cultures of Exploration and Empire* (Oxford: Blackwell, 2001).

Duarte, Teophilo, *Timor (Antecâmara do Inferno?!)* (Famalicão: Minerva, 1930).

— *O Rei de Timor* (Lisbon: A. M. Pereira, 1931).

DuBois, W. E. B., 'The Conservation of Races', in *Writings* (New York: Library of America, 1986).

Duffy, James, *Portuguese Africa* (Cambridge, MA: Harvard University Press, 1959).

— *A Question of Slavery: Labour Policies in Portuguese Africa and the British Protest, 1850–1920* (Oxford: Oxford University Press, 1967).

Durkheim, Emile and M. Mauss, 'De quelques formes de classification – contribution à l'étude des représentations collectives', *Année Sociologique* (Paris) 6 (1903); published in Brazil as 'Algumas formas primitivas de classificação', in *Ensaios de Sociologia* (São Paulo: Perspectiva, 1981).

Eisenberg, Peter L., 'Ficando livre: As alforrias em Campinas no século XIX', *Estudos Econômicos* 17:2 (1987), pp. 175–216.

Elliott, J. H., *Empires of the Atlantic World: Britain and Spain in America, 1492–1830* (New Haven: Yale University Press, 2006).

Eltis, David (ed.), *Coerced and Free Migration: Global Perspectives* (Stanford, CA: Stanford University Press, 2002).

Emmer, P. C. (ed.), *Colonialism and Migration: Indentured Labour Before and After Slavery* (Dordrecht: Martinus Nijhoff Publishers, 1986).

Engerman, Stanley L., 'Contract Labor, Sugar, and Technology in the Nineteenth Century', *Journal of Economic History* 43:3 (1983), pp. 635–59.

— 'Slavery, Serfdom and Other Forms of Coerced Labour: Similarities and Differences', in M. L. Bush (ed.), *Serfdom and Slavery: Studies in Legal Bondage* (London: Longman, 1996), pp. 18–41.

— (ed.), *Terms of Labor: Slavery, Serfdom, and Free Labor* (Stanford, CA: Stanford University Press, 1999).

Engerman, Stanley L. and Kenneth L. Sokoloff, 'The Evolution of Suffrage Institutions in the New World', *Journal of Economic History* 65:4 (2005), pp. 891–921.

Eriksen, Thomas Hylland, *Ethnicity and Nationalism: Anthropological Perspectives* (London: Pluto Press, 1993).

Escobar, Arturo, *Territories of Difference: Place, Movements, Life, Redes* (Durham, NC: Duke University Press, 2008).

Esses, V. M., J. F. Dovidio, L. M. Jackson and T. L. Armstrong, 'The Immigration Dilemma: The Role of Perceived Group Competition, Ethnic Prejudice, and National Identity', *Journal of Social Issues* 57 (2001), pp. 389–412.

Evaristo, Conceição, *Ponciá Vicêncio* (Belo Horizonte: Mazza Edições, 2003).

Falcão, J. and R. M. Barboza de Araújo (eds), *O Imperador das idéias* (Rio de Janeiro: Topbooks, 2001).

Fanon, Frantz, *Black Skin, White Masks* (New York: Grove Press, 1967).

— *The Wretched of the Earth* (Harmondsworth: Penguin, 1967).

Faria, Sheila de Castro, *A Colônia em movimento: Fortuna e familía no cotidiano colonial* (Rio de Janeiro: Nova Fronteira, 1988).

Felinto, Marilene, *As mulheres de Tijucopapo*, 2nd edn (Rio de Janeiro: Editora 34, 1992).

Felner, A. de Albuquerque, *Angola – Apontamentos sôbre a colonização dos planaltos e litoral do Sul de Angola* (Lisbon: Agência Geral das Colônias, 1940).

Fenoaltea, Stefano, 'Slavery and Supervision in Comparative Perspective: A Model', *Journal of Economic History* 44:3 (1984), pp. 635–68.

Ferguson, Niall, *Empire: How Britain Made the Modern World* (London: Penguin, 2003).

Fernandes, Abílio José, *Esboço histórico e do estado actual das missões de Timor . . .* (Macau: Mercantil, 1931).

Fernandes, Florestan, *A integração do negro na sociedade de classes* (São Paulo: Dominus, 1965); 3rd edn, 2 vols (São Paulo: EDUSP, 1978).

Ferrara, Miriam Nicolau, *A imprensa negra paulista (1915–1963)* (São Paulo: FFLCH/USP, 1986).

Ferreira, E. S., H. Rato and M. J. Mortágua, *Viagens de Ulisses: Efeitos da imigração na economia portuguesa* (Lisbon: Alto Comissariado para a Imigração e Minorias Étnicas, 2004).

Ferreira, Roberto Guedes, 'Trabalho, família, aliança e mobilidade social: Estratégias de forros e seus descendentes – Vila de Porto Feliz, São Paulo, século XIX', *V Congresso Brasileiro de História Econômica, 2003*, available at http://ideas.repec.org/s/abp/he2003.html

—'Pardos: Trabalho, família, aliança e mobilidade social, Porto Feliz, São Paulo, c. 1798–c. 1850', unpublished PhD thesis, Universidade Federal do Rio de Janeiro, 2005.

—'De ex-escravo a elite escravista: A trajetória de ascensão social do pardo alferes Joaquim Barbosa Neves (Porto Feliz, São Pulo, século XIX)', in João Luis Ribeiro Fragoso, Carla Maria Carvalho de Almeida and Antonio Carlos Juca de Sampaio (eds), *Conquistadores e negociantes: Historias de elites no Antigo Regime nos trópicas, América lusa, séculos XVI a XVIII* (Rio de Janeiro: Civilização Brasileira, 2007), pp. 337–76.

Ferreira, Roquinaldo, 'Transforming Atlantic Slaving: Trade, Warfare and Territorial Control in Angola, 1650–1800', unpublished PhD thesis, University of California, Los Angeles, 2003.

Filho, Geraldo Silva, 'O oficialato mecânico em Vila Rica no século dezoito e a participação do escravo e do negro', unpublished Masters dissertation, Universidade de São Paulo, 1996.

Filho, Mário, *O Negro no futebol brasileiro*, 5th edn (1947; Rio de Janeiro: Faperj, 2003).

Finley, M. I., 'Slavery', in *International Encyclopedia of the Social Sciences*, vol. 14 (New York: Macmillan, 1968), pp. 307–13.

Fischer-Tiné, Harald and Michael Mann (eds), *Colonialism as Civilizing Mission: Cultural Ideology in British India* (London: Anthem Press, 2004).

Florentino, Manolo, 'Sobre minas, crioulos e a liberdade costumeira no Rio de Janeiro, 1789–1871', in Manolo Florentino (ed.), *Tráfico, cativeiro e liberdade Rio de Janeiro, séculos XVII–XIX* (Rio de Janeiro: Civilização Brasileira, 2005), pp. 331–66.

—'Da atualidade de Gilberto Freyre', in Peter Fry *et al.* (eds), *Divisões perigosas: Políticas raciais no Brasil contemporâneo* (Rio de Janeiro: Civilização Brasileira, 2007).

Florentino, Manolo and José Roberto Pinto de Góes, 'Do que Nabuco já sabia: Mobilidade e miscigenação racial no Brasil escravista', unpublished MS presented at the Congresso Internacional Brasil – Portugal Ano 2000 – Sessão de História.

Forman, Sheppard, 'East Timor: Exchange and Political Hierarchy at the Time of the European Discoveries', in Karl L. Hutterer (ed.), *Economic Exchange and Social Interaction in Southeast Asia: Perspectives from Prehistory, History, and Ethnography* (Ann Arbor: CSSAS/University of Michigan, 1977), pp. 97–111.

Förster, S., W. J. Mommsen and R. Robinson (eds), *Bismarck, Europe, and Africa: The Berlin Africa Conference, 1884–1885, and the Onset of Partition* (Oxford: Oxford University Press/German Historical Institute of London, 1988).

Fox, James (ed.), *The Flow of Life: Essays in Eastern Indonesia* (Cambridge, MA: Harvard University Press, 1980).

França, Edson, 'Uma breve reflexão sobre o Congresso Nacional de Negras e Negros do Brasil', *Vermelho* Online, 15 April 2008.

Frank, Zephyr L., *Dutra's World: Wealth and Family in Nineteenth-Century Rio de Janeiro* (Albuquerque: University of New Mexico Press, 2004).

Fredrickson, George M., *White Supremacy: A Comparative Study in American and South African History* (Oxford: Oxford University Press, 1981).

— *Racism: A Short History* (Princeton: Princeton University Press, 2002).

Freiesleben, Hans-Christian, *Der katalanische Weltatlas vom Jahre 1375* (Stuttgart: Brockhaus, Abt. Antiquarium, 1977).

French, Jan Hoffman, *Legalizing Identities: Becoming Black or Indian in Brazil's Northeast* (Chapel Hill: University of North Carolina Press, 2009).

Freudenthal, Aida, 'Voz de Angola em tempo de ultimato', *Estudos Afro-Asiáticos* 23:1 (2001), pp. 139–69.

Freyre, Gilberto, *Casa-grande & senzala; Formação da família brasileira sob o regimen de economia patriarchal* (1933; Rio de Janeiro: Editora Record, 1998); published in English as *The Masters and the Slaves: A Study in the Development of Brazilian Civilization* (New York: Alfred A. Knopf, 1946; also Berkeley: University of California Press, 1986).

— *Sobrados e Mucambos* (1936; São Paulo: Global, 2006).

— 'O Brasil em face das Áfricas Negras e Mestiças', paper presented at a conference held at the Gabinete Português de Leitura, 10 June 1962, in *Edição de um grupo de amigos e admiradores portugueses para distribuir gratuitamente às escolas* (Lisbon, 1963).

— 'Interação eurotropical: Aspectos de alguns dos seus varios processos, inclusive o lusotropical', *Journal of Inter-American Studies* 8:1 (1966), pp. 1–10.

— 'O homem situado no trópico, metarraça e morenidade', in *Gilberto Freyre: Seleta para jovens* (Rio de Janeiro: José Olympio, 1971).

— 'Brasileiro – sua cor?', *Folha de São Paulo*, 5 Dec. 1979, p. 3.

Friedemann, Nina de, 'Contextos religiosos en una área negra de Barbacoas, Nariño', *Revista Colombiana de Folclor* 4:10 (1966–9), pp. 63–83.

— *Ma Ngombe: Guerreros y ganaderos en Palenque* (Bogotá: Carlos Valencia, 1980).

— '"Troncos" among Black Miners in Colombia', in T. Greaves and W. Culver (eds), *Miners and Mining in the Americas* (Manchester: Manchester University Press, 1985).

Friedemann, Nina de and Jaime Arocha, *De sol a sol: Génesis, transformación y presencia de los negros en Colombia* (Bogotá: Planeta, 1986).

Fry, Peter, 'O que a Cinderela Negra tem a dizer sobre a "política racial" no Brasil', *Revista da USP* (São Paulo) 28 (1995–6), pp. 122–36.

— 'Brazil: The Burden of the Past; the Promise of the Future', *Daedalus* 129:2 (2000), pp. 83–118.

— 'Estética e política: Relações entre "raça", publicidade e produção da beleza no Brasil', in Mirian Goldenberg (ed.), *Nu e vestido: Dez antropólogos revelam a cultura do corpo carioca* (Rio de Janeiro: Record, 2002).

— *A persistência da raça: Ensaios antropológicos sobre o Brasil e a África Austral* (Rio de Janeiro: Civilização Brasileira, 2005).

Fry, Peter, Yvonne Maggie, Marcos Chor Maio, Simone Monteiro and Ricardo Ventura Santos (eds), *Divisões perigosas: Políticas raciais no Brasil contemporâneo* (Rio de Janeiro: Civilização Brasileira, 2007).

Gabriel, Alfons, *Marco Polo in Persien* (Vienna: Verlag, 1963).

Galvão, Henrique, *Huíla: Relatório de governo* (Vila Nova de Famalicão: Minerva, 1929).

— *Santa Maria: My Crusade for Portugal* (Cleveland, OH: World Publishing Co., 1961).

Gann, L. H., 'The Berlin Conference and the Humanitarian Conscience', in S. Förster, W. J. Mommsen and R. Robinson (eds), *Bismarck, Europe, and Africa: The Berlin Africa Conference, 1884–1885, and the Onset of Partition* (Oxford: Oxford University Press/German Historical Institute of London, 1988), pp. 321–31.

García, Elisa Frühauf, 'O projeto pombalino de imposição da língua portuguesa aos índios e a sua aplicação na América meridional', *Tempo* 12:23 (2007), pp. 23–38.

García, Fernando Emygdio, *Colonização e colónias portuguesas, 1864–1914* (Coimbra: F. França Amado, 1915).

García y García, Antonio, *Synodicon Hispanum* (Madrid: Biblioteca de Autores Cristianos, 1982).

Geffray, Christian, 'Le Lusotropicalisme comme discours de l'amour dans la servitude', *Lusotopie* (1997), pp. 361–72.

Geisberg, Max (rev. Walter L. Strauss), *The German Single-Leaf Woodcut: 1500–1550* (New York: Hacker Art Books, 1974).

Geraldo, Endrica, 'O "perigo alienígena": Política imigratória e pensamento racial no governo Vargas (1930–1945)', unpublished PhD thesis, UNICAMP, 2007.

Ghioldi, R., 'Freyre, sociologo reaccionario', in *Escritos*, 4 vols (Buenos Aires: Anteo, 1975–7), vol. 4, pp. 16–44.

Gilroy, Paul, *The Black Atlantic: Modernity and Double Consciousness* (London: Verso, 1993).

Godinho, Vitorino de Magalhães, *Os descobrimentos e a economia mundial*, 2 vols (Lisbon: Arcádia, 1963).

Goldberg, David Theo, *Racist Culture: Philosophy and the Politics of Meaning* (Oxford: Blackwell, 1993).

— *The Racial State* (Oxford: Blackwell, 2002).

— 'Racial States', in David Theo Goldberg and John Solomos (eds), *A Companion to Racial and Ethnic Studies* (Oxford: Blackwell, 2002), pp. 233–58.

Golebiowska, Ewa A., 'The Contours and Etiology of Whites' Attitudes toward Black-White Interracial Marriage', *Journal of Black Studies* 38:2 (2007), pp. 268–87.

Gomes, Alberto, *Moedas portuguesas e do território português antes da fundação da nacionalidade* (Lisbon: A. Gomes, 1996).

Gomes, Flávio and Roquinaldo Ferreira, 'A miragem da miscigenação', *Novos estudos – CEBRAP* 80 (2008), pp. 141–60.

Gomes, Mércio Pereira, 'Por que sou rondoniano', *Estudos Avançados* 23:65 (2009), pp. 173–91.

Gomes, Saul António, 'Coimbra judaica: A história e o esquecimento', in *Coimbra Judaica: Actas* (Coimbra: Câmara Municipal de Coimbra, 2009), pp. 27–42.

Gonçalves, Rita, Helder Spinola and António Brehm, 'Y-Chromosome Lineages in São Tomé e Principe and Cabo Verde Islands: Different Input of European Influence', *Forensic Science International: Genetics Supplement Series* 1:1 (2008), pp. 210–11.

Gong, Gerrit W., *The Standard of 'Civilization' in International Society* (Oxford: Clarendon Press, 1984).

Gorender, Jacob, *O escravismo colonial*, 4th edn (São Paulo: Editora Ática, 1985).

Graham, Richard, 'Free African Brazilians and the State in Slavery Times', in Michael Hanchard (ed.), *Racial Politics in Contemporary Brazil* (Durham, NC: Duke University Press, 1999), pp. 30–58.

Grande Dizionario della Lingua Italiana (Turin: Unione Tipografico Editrice Torinese, 1990).

Grant, Kevin, *A Civilized Savagery: Britain and the New Slaveries in Africa, 1884–1926* (New York: Routledge, 2005).

Grinberg, Keila, *Liberata, a lei da ambigüidade: As ações de liberdade da Corte de Apelação do Rio de Janeiro no século XIX* (Rio de Janeiro: Relume Dumará, 1994).

Grueso, Libia, Carlos Rosero and Arturo Escobar, 'The Process of Black Community Organizing in the Southern Pacific Coast of Colombia', in Sonia Alvarez, Evelina Dagnino and Arturo Escobar (eds), *Cultures of Politics, Politics of Cultures: Re-Visioning Latin American Social Movements* (Boulder, CO: Westview, 1998), pp. 196–219.

Guilherme Feitler, Bruno, *Inquisition, juifs et nouveaux-chrétiens au Brésil: Le Nordeste, XVIIe et XVIIIe siècles* (Leuven: Leuven University Press, 2003).

— 'Usos políticos del Santo Oficio portugués en el Atlántico (Brasil y África Occidental): El periodo filipino', *Hispania Sacra* 59:119 (2007), pp. 272–82.

Guimarães, Antonio Sérgio, *Racismo e anti-racismo no Brasil* (São Paulo: Editora 34, 1999).

— 'Racial Democracy', in J. Souza and W. Sinder (eds), *Imagining Brazil* (Lanham, MD: Lexington Books, 2005), pp. 119–40.

Guimarães, Geni, *A cor da ternura*, 12th edn (São Paulo: FTD, 1998).

Gullickson, Aaron, 'Racial Boundary Formation at the Dawn of Jim Crow: The Determinants and Effects of Black/Mulatto Occupational Differences in the United States, 1880', *American Journal of Sociology* 116:1 (2010), pp. 187–231.

Gunter, Janet, '*Kabita-Kaburai, de cada dia*: Indigenous Hierarchies and the Portuguese in Timor', *Portuguese Literary and Cultural Studies* 17–18 (2010), pp. 281–301.

Guzmán, Décio de Alencar, 'Construtores de ciudades: Mamelucos, índios y europeos en las ciudades pombalinas de La Amazonia', in Clara García and Manuel Ramos Median (eds), *Ciudades mestizas: Intercâmbios y continuidades en la expansión occidental, siglos XVI–XIX* (Mexico: Condumex, 2011).

Haberly, David T., *Three Sad Races: Racial Identity and National Consciousness in Brazilian Literature* (Cambridge: Cambridge University Press, 1983).

Hall, Catherine, *Civilising Subjects: Metropole and Colony in the English Imagination, 1830–1867* (Chicago: University of Chicago Press, 2002).

Hallett, Jessica (ed.), *Cortejo triunfal com girafas: Animais exóticos ao serviço do poder/Trimphal Procession with Giraffes: Exotic Animals in the Service of Power* (Lisbon: Fundação Ricardo do Espírito Santo Silva, 2009).

Hammond, Richard J., *Portugal and Africa, 1815–1910: A Study in Uneconomic Imperialism* (Stanford, CA: Stanford University Press, 1966).

— 'Uneconomic Imperialism: Portugal in Africa before 1910', in L. H. Gann and Peter Duignan (eds), *Colonialism in Africa, 1870–1960* (Cambridge: Cambridge University Press, 1969), pp. 352–82.

Hanchard, Michael G., *Orpheus and Power: The* Movimento Negro *of Rio de Janeiro and São Paulo, Brazil, 1945–1988* (Princeton: Princeton University Press, 1994).

— *Racial Politics in Contemporary Brazil* (Durham, NC: Duke University Press, 1999).

Hansen, João Adolfo, 'Sem F, sem L, sem R: Cronistas, jesuítas & índio no século XVI', in E. A. Kossovitch (ed.), *A conquista da América* (Campinas: CEDES/Papirus, 1993), pp. 45–55.

— *A sátira e o engenho, Gregório de Matos e a Bahia do século XVII* (São Paulo: Ateliê Editorial, 2004); 2nd edn (Campinas: Unicamp, 2004).

Harris, Marvin, 'Les relations raciales à Minas Velha communauté rurale de la région montagneuse du Brésil Central', in Charles Wagley (ed.), *Races et classes dans le Brésil rural* (Paris: UNESCO, 1952).

— *Town and Country in Brazil* (New York: Columbia University Press, 1956).

— 'Portugal's African "Wards": A First-Hand Report on Labor and Education in Mocambique', *Africa Today* 5:6 (1958), pp. 3–36.

— 'Racial Identity in Brazil', *Luso-Brazilian Review* 1:2 (1964), pp. 21–8.

— 'Referential Ambiguity in the Calculus of Brazilian Racial Identity', *Southwestern Journal of Anthropology* 26:1 (1970), pp. 1–14.

Harris, Marvin and Conrad Kotak, 'The Structural Significance of Brazilian Categories', *Sociologia* 25:3 (1963), pp. 203–8.

Harris, Marvin *et al.*, 'Who Are the Whites? Imposed Census Categories and the Racial Demography of Brazil', *Social Forces* 72:2 (1993), pp. 451–62.

Hawkins, Mike, *Social Darwinism in European and American Thought, 1860–1945: Nature as Model and Nature as Threat* (Cambridge: Cambridge University Press, 1997).

Heintze, Beatrix, *Pioneiros africanos: Caravanas de carregadores na África Centro-Ocidental (entre 1850–1890)* (Lisbon: Caminho, 2004).

— 'Between Two Worlds: The Bezerras, a Luso-African Family in Nineteenth Century Western Central Africa', in Ph. J. Havik and Malyn Newitt (eds), *Creole Societies in the Portuguese Colonial Empire* (Bristol: University of Bristol, 2007), pp. 127–53.

— 'Translocal "Kinship" Relations in Central African Politics of the 19th Century', *Global Studies in Global Social History* 4 (2010), pp. 179–204.

Hellwig, David J., 'Racial Paradise or Run-Around? Afro-North American Views of Race Relations in Brazil', *American Studies* 31:2 (1990), pp. 43–60.

— (ed.), *African-American Reflections on Brazil's Racial Paradise* (Philadelphia: Temple University Press, 1992).

Henriques, Isabel Castro, *Commerce et changement en Angola au XIXe siècle: Imbangala et Tshokwe face à la modernité*, 2 vols (Paris: L'Harmattan, 1995).

— *Percursos da modernidade em Angola: Dinâmicas comerciais e transformações sociais no século XIX* (Lisbon: Instituto de Investigação Científica Tropical/Instituto da Cooperação Portuguesa, 1997).

— *São Tomé e Príncipe: A invenção de uma sociedade* (Lisbon: Véga, 2000).

Heywood, Linda, 'Slavery and Forced Labor in the Changing Political Economy of Central Angola, 1850–1949', in Suzanne Miers and Richard Roberts (eds), *The End of Slavery in Africa* (Madison: University of Wisconsin Press, 1988), pp. 415–36.

— 'Portuguese into African: The Eighteenth-Century Central African Background to Atlantic Creole Cultures', in Linda Heywood (ed.), *Central Africans and Cultural Transformations in the American Diaspora* (Cambridge: Cambridge University Press, 2002), pp. 91–114.

Higgins, Kathleen J., *'Licentious Liberty' in a Brazilian Gold-Mining Region: Slavery, Gender, and Social Control in Eighteenth-Century Sabará, Minas Gerais* (University Park: Pennsylvania State University Press, 1999).

Hill, Lawrence F., 'The Confederate Exodus to Latin America', *Southern Historical Quarterly* 39:2 (1935), pp. 100–34.

Hirschberg, Walter, *Schwarzafrika* (Graz: Akademische Druckund Verlagsanstalt, 1967).

Hobsbawm, Eric and Terence Ranger (eds), *The Invention of Tradition* (Cambridge: Cambridge University Press, 1983).

Hochschild, Adam, *King Leopold's Ghost: A Study of Greed, Terror and Heroism in Colonial Africa* (Boston: Mariner Books, 1999).

Hollstein, Friedrich Wilhelm Heinrich, *German Engravings, Etchings and Woodcuts, c. 1400–1700* (Amsterdam: M. Hertzberger, 1954).

Hooker, Juliet, 'Indigenous Inclusion/Black Exclusion: Race, Ethnicity and Multicultural Citizenship in Contemporary Latin America', *Journal of Latin American Studies* 37:2 (2005), pp. 285–310.

— *Race and the Politics of Solidarity* (Oxford: Oxford University Press, 2009).

Horta, José Augusto Nunes da Silva, 'A Inquisição em Angola e Congo: O inquérito de 1596–98 e o papel mediador das justiças locais', *Arqueologia do Estado: Primeiras Jornadas sobre formas de organização e exercício dos poderes na Europa do Sul, Séculos XIII–XVIII*, 2 vols (Lisbon: História & Crítica, 1988), vol. 1, pp. 387–415.

Hoskins, Janet, 'Slaves, Brides and Other "Gifts": Resistance, Marriage and Rank', *Slavery and Abolition* 25:2 (2004), pp. 1–18.

Houaiss, Antônio, Mauro de Salles Villar and Francisco Manoel de Mello Franco (eds), *Dicionário Houaiss da lingua portuguesa* (Rio de Janeiro: Objectiva/Instituto Houaiss, 2001).

Hümmerich, Franz, 'Quellen und Untersuchungen zur Fahrt der ersten deutschen nach dem portugiesischen Indien, 1505/6', *Abhandlungen der Königlich Bayerischen Akademie der Wissenschaften, Philosophisch-philologische und historische Klasse* 30:3 (1918).

Huntington, S. P., *Who Are We? The Challenges to America's National Identity* (New York: Simon and Schuster, 2004).

Hutchinson, H. W., 'Les relations raciales dans une communauté rurale du Reconcavo (État de Bahia)', in C. Wagley (ed.), *Races et classes dans le Brésil rural* (Paris: UNESCO, 1952).

— *Village and Plantation Life in Northeastern Brazil* (Seattle: University of Washington Press, 1957).

Ianni, Octávio, *As metamorfoses do escravo: Apogeu e crise da escravatura no Brasil meridional* (São Paulo: Difusão Européia do Livro, 1962).

Instituto Brasileiro de Geografía y Estatística, 'Apêndice: Estatísticas de 500 anos de povoamento', in *Brasil: 500 anos de povoamento* (Rio de Janeiro: IBGE, 2000).

Isaacman, Allen F., *Mozambique: The Africanization of a European Institution: The Zambezi* Prazos, *1750–1902* (Madison: University of Wisconsin Press, 1972).

Isaacman, Allen F. and Barbara S. Isaacman, 'Os prazeiros como trans-raianos: Um estudo sobre transformação social e cultural', *Arquivo* (Maputo: Arquivo Histórico de Moçambique), 10 (1991), pp. 5–48.

— *Slavery and Beyond: The Making of Men and Chikunda Ethnic Identities in the Unstable World of South-Central Africa, 1750–1920* (Portsmouth, NH: Heinemann, 2004).

Isfahani-Hammond, Alexandra, *White Negritude: Race, Writing, and Brazilian Cultural Identity* (New York: Palgrave Macmillan, 2008).

Israel, Jonathan I., *European Jewry in the Age of Mercantilism: 1550–1750* (London: Littman Library of Jewish Civilization, 1998).

Jahoda, Gustav, *Images of Savages: Ancient Roots of Modern Prejudice in Western Culture* (New York: Routledge, 1998).

Jardim Brügger, Silvia Maria, *Minas patriarcal, família e sociedade (São João del Rei – séculos XVIII e XIX* (São Paulo: Annablume, 2007).

Jarry, Madeleine, 'L'homme sauvage', *L'Oeil* 183 (1970), pp. 14–21.

Jerónimo, Miguel Bandeira, 'Os missionários do alfabeto nas colónias portuguesas (1880–1930)', in Diogo Ramada Curto (ed.), *Estudos de sociologia da leitura em Portugal no século XX* (Lisbon: Fundação Calouste Gulbenkian, 2006), pp. 29–67.

— 'Religion, Empire, and the Diplomacy of Colonialism: Portugal, Europe, and the Congo Question, ca. 1820–1890', unpublished PhD thesis, University of London, 2008.

— *Livros Brancos, Almas Negras: A 'missão civilizadora' do colonialismo Português (c. 1870–1930)* (Lisbon: Imprensa de Ciências Sociais, 2009).

— 'Empire-Rebuilding, State-Remaking and Nation-Reformation: The Case of Nineteenth-Century Portugal', unpublished typescript.

Jesus, Alysson Luiz Freitas de, *No sertão das Minas: Escravidão, violência e liberdade (1830–1888)* (São Paulo: Annablume, 2007).

Johnson, Lyman L., 'Manumission in Colonial Buenos Aires, 1776–1810', *Hispanic American Historical Review* 59:2 (1979), pp. 258–79.

Jones, James M., *Prejudice and Racism*, 2nd edn (New York: McGraw Hill, 1997).

Jouana, Arlette, *L'idée de race en France au XVIe siècle et début du XVIIe*, 2nd edn, 2 vols (Montpellier: Université Paul Valéry, 1981).

Joubert, Fabienne, *La tapisserie médiévale au musée de Cluny* (Paris: Réunion des Musées Nationaux, 1987).

Kalthammer, Wilhelm, *Portugiesenkreuze in Africa und Indien* . . . (Basel: Basler Afrika Bibliographien, 1984).

Kammerer, Albert, *La Mer Rouge, l'Abyssinie et l'Arabie depuis l'antiquité: Essai d'histoire et de géographie historique*, vols 1.1–3.3 (Cairo: Société royale de géographie d'Égypte, 1929–52).

Kantor, Íris, 'Pacto festivo em Minas colonial: A entrada triunfal do primeiro bispo na Sé de Mariana, 1748', unpublished Masters dissertation, Universidade de São Paulo, 1996.

Kaplan, Yosef, *Les nouveaux-juifs d'Amsterdam: Essais sur l'histoire sociale et intellectuelle du judaisme séfarde au XVIIe siècle* (Paris: Éditions Chandeigne, 1999).

Karasch, Mary C., *Slave Life in Rio de Janeiro, 1808–1850* (Princeton: Princeton University Press, 1987).

— 'Construindo comunidades: As irmandades de Pretos e Pardos no Brasil colonial e Goiás', paper presented at conference on 'American Counterpoint: New Approaches to Slavery and Abolition in Brazil', Yale University, October 2010.

Katz, I. and R. G. Hass, 'Racial Ambivalence and American Value Conflict: Correlational and Priming Studies of Dual Cognitive Structures', *Journal of Personality and Social Psychology* 55 (1988), pp. 893–905.

Katzew, Ilona, *Casta Painting: Images of Race in Eighteenth Century Mexico* (New Haven: Yale University Press, 2004).

Keese, Alexander, *Living with Ambiguity: Portuguese and French Colonial Administrators, Mutual Influences, and the Question of Integrating an African Elite, 1930–1963* (Stuttgart: Steiner, 2007).

— 'Early Limits of Local Decolonisation: Forced Labour, Decolonisation and the "Serviçal" Population in São Tomé and Príncipe, from Colonial Abuses to Post-Colonial Disappointment, 1945–1976', *International Journal of African Historical Studies* (forthcoming).

Keil, Luis, 'Tapisseries de Flandre au Portugal pendant les XVe et XVIe siècles', in Leo van Puyvelde (ed.), *Miscellanea Leo van Puyvelde* (Brussels: Editions de la Connaissance, 1949).

Kelly, D. J. *et al.*, 'Development of the Other-Race Effect during Infancy: Evidence toward Universality?' *Journal of Experimental Child Psychology* 104 (2009), pp. 105–14.

Kelman, H. C., 'Two Phases of Behavior Change', *Journal of Social Issues* 8 (1952), pp. 81–8.

Kessler, Arnold, 'Bahian Manumission Practices in the Early Nineteenth Century', paper delivered at the American Historical Association, 29 December 1973.

Kiddy, Elizabeth W., *Blacks of the Rosary: Memory and History in Minas Gerais, Brazil* (University Park: Pennsylvania State University Press, 2005).

Kiernan, James P., 'Baptism and Manumission in Brazil: Paraty, 1789–1822', *Social Science History* 3:1 (1978), pp. 56–71.

Kinder, D. R. and D. O. Sears, 'Prejudice and Politics: Symbolic Racism versus Racial Threats to the Good Life', *Journal of Personality and Social Psychology* 40 (1981), pp. 414–31.

Kinsbruner, Jay, *Not of Pure Blood: The Free People of Color and Racial Prejudice in Nineteenth-Century Puerto Rico* (Durham, NC: Duke University Press, 1996).

Klein, Herbert S., 'Os homens livres de côr na sociedade escravista brasileria', *Dados* (Rio de Janeiro) 17 (1978), pp. 3–27.

Klein, Herbert S. and Clotilde Andrade Paiva, 'Free Persons in a Slave Economy: Minas Gerais in 1831', *Journal of Social History* 29:4 (1996), pp. 933–62.

Klein, Herbert S. and Francisco Vidal Luna, 'Free Colored in a Slave Society: São Paulo and Minas Gerais in the Early Nineteenth Century', *Hispanic American Historical Review* 80:4 (2000), pp. 913–41.

— *Slavery in Brazil* (Cambridge: Cambridge University Press, 2010).

Kleinschmid, Renate, 'Balthasar Springer (Eine quellenkritische Untersuchung)', *Mitteilungen der Anthropologischen Gesellschaft in Wien* 96–7 (1967).

Kline, R. B., *Principles and Practices of Structural Equation Modeling* (New York: Guilford, 1998).

Koskenniemi, Martti, *The Gentle Civilizer of Nations: The Rise and Fall of International Law, 1870–1960* (Cambridge: Cambridge University Press, 2002).

Kraus, Michael and Hans Ottomeyer (eds), *Novos Mundos – Neue Welten: Portugal und das Zeitalter der Entdeckungen* (Dresden: Sandstein, 2007).

Kurt Lang, Francisco, 'A musica barroca', in Sérgio Buarque de Holanda (ed.), *História geral da civilização brasileira* (São Paulo: Difusão Européia do Livro, 1960).

Lacerda, Antônio Henrique Duarte, *Os padrões das alforrias em um município cafeeiro em expansão: Juiz de Fora, Zona da Mata de Minas Gerais, 1844–88* (São Paulo: Annablume, 2006).

Lago, Enrico Dal and Constantina Katsari, 'The Study of Ancient and Modern Slave Systems: Setting an Agenda for Comparison', in Enrico Dal Lago and Constantina Katsari (eds), *Slave Systems: Ancient and Modern* (Cambridge: Cambridge University Press, 2008).

Lahon, Didier, 'Black African Slaves and Freedmen in Portugal during the Renaissance: Creating a New Pattern of Reality', in Thomas Foster Earle and Kate J. P. Lowe (eds), *Black Africans in Renaissance Europe* (Cambridge: Cambridge University Press, 2005), pp. 261–79.

Lara, Sílvia Hunold, *Campos da violência: Escravos e senhores na Capitania do Rio de Janeiro, 1750–1808* (Rio de Janeiro: Paz e Terra, 1988).

Law, Robin (ed.), *From Slave Trade to 'Legitimate' Commerce: The Commercial Transition in Nineteenth-Century West Africa* (Cambridge: Cambridge University Press, 1995).

— *Ouidah: The Social History of a West African Slaving 'Port', 1727–1892* (Athens, OH: Ohio University Press, 2004).

Leite, Duarte, 'O mais antigo mapa do Brasil', in Carlos Malheiro Dias (ed.), *História da colonização portuguesa do Brasil* (Oporto: Litografía Nacional, 1921–6), vol. 3, pp. 227–30.

Leite, José Correia, . . . *E disse o velho militante José Correia Leite* (São Paulo: Secretaria Municipal de Cultura, 1992).

Leite, Serafim, *História da Companhia de Jesus no Brasil, 1549–1760*, 10 vols (Lisbon and Rio de Janeiro: Livraria Portugália/Civilização Brasileira, 1938–50).

— *Suma histórica da Companhia de Jesus no Brasil (1549–1760)* (Lisbon: Junta de Investigações Ultramar, 1965).

Leitsch, Stephanie, 'Burgkmair's *People of Africa and India* (1508) and the Origins of Ethnography in Print', *Art Bulletin* 41 (2009), pp. 134–59.

Léonard, Yves, 'Salazarisme et lusotropicalisme, histoire d'une appropriation', *Lusotopie* (1997), pp. 211–26.

— 'O ultramar português', in Francisco Bethencourt and Kirti Chaudhuri (eds), *História da expansão portuguesa*, 5 vols (Lisbon: Círculo de Leitores, 1998–9), vol. 5, pp. 31–50.

Lesser, Jeffrey, *Negotiating National Identity: Immigrants, Minorities, and the Struggle for Ethnicity in Brazil* (Durham, NC: Duke University Press, 1999).

Levenson, Jay A. (ed.), *Circa 1492: Art in the Age of Exploration* (New Haven: Yale University Press, 1991).

— *Encompassing the Globe: Portugal and the World in the 16th and 17th Centuries: Reference Catalogue* (Washington: Arthur M. Sackler Gallery, Smithsonian Institution, 2007).

Levine, Richard M., 'The First Afro-Brazilian Congress', *Race* 15 (1973), pp. 185–93.

Lévi-Strauss, C., *Race and History* (Paris: UNESCO, 1958).

— 'Préface', in L. Frois (ed.), *Européens et Japonais* (Paris: Chandeigne, 1998).

Leyens, J.-P., B. Cortés, S. Demoulin, J. F. Dovidio, S. T. Fiske, R. Gaunt *et al.*, 'Emotional Prejudice, Essentialism, and Nationalism: The 2002 Tajfel Lecture', *European Journal of Social Psychology* 33 (2003), pp. 703–17.

Leyens, J.-P., P. M. Paladino, R. Rodriguez-Torres, J. Vaes, S. Demoulin, A. Rodriguez-Perez *et al.*, 'The Emotional Side of Prejudice: The Attribution of Secondary Emotions to In-Groups and Out-Groups', *Personality and Social Psychology Review* 4 (2000), pp. 186–97.

Libby, Douglas Cole and Clotilde Andrade Paiva, 'Alforrias e forros em uma freguesia mineira: São José d'El Rey em 1795', *Revista Brasileira de Estudos de População* 17:1–2 (2000), pp. 17–46.

Lima, Adriano Bernardo Moraes, 'Trajetórias de crioulos: Um estudo das relações comunitárias de escravos e forros no termo da Vila de Curitiba (c.1760–c.1830)', unpublished Masters dissertation, Universidade Federal do Paraná, Curitiba, 2001.

Loff, Manuel, 'As colónias portuguesas de África entre a IIª Guerra Mundial e a Guerra colonial: A visão anglo-americana', in Adriana Pereira Campos (ed.), *Trabalho forçado africano: Experiências coloniais comparadas* (Porto: Campo das Letras, 2006), pp. 395–442.

Lovejoy, Arthur O., 'The Chinese Origin of a Romanticism', in *Essays in the History of Ideas* (New York: Capricorn Books, 1960), pp. 99–135.

Lovejoy, Paul, *Transformations in Slavery: A History of Slavery in Africa* (1983; Cambridge: Cambridge University Press, 2000).

Lowe, Kate, 'The Stereotyping of Black Africans in Renaissance Europe', in Thomas Foster Earle and Kate J. P. Lowe (eds), *Black Africans in Renaissance Europe* (Cambridge: Cambridge University Press, 2005), pp. 17–47.

Lucci, Luís Schwalbach, *Emigração e colonização: Tese para o concurso de lente substituto da 2ª cadeira da escola colonial* (Lisbon: Annuario Commercial, 1914).

Luna, Francisco Vidal, *Minas Gerais: Escravos e senhores* (São Paulo: IPE(USP, 1981).

— 'São Paulo: População, atividades e posse de escravos em vinte e cinco localidades (1777–1829)', *Estudos Econômicos* 28:1 (1998), pp. 99–169.

Luna, Francisco Vidal and Herbert S. Klein, 'Slaves and Masters in Early Nineteenth-Century Brazil: São Paulo', *Journal of Interdisciplinary History* 21:4 (1991), pp. 549–73.

— *Slavery and the Economy of São Paulo, 1750–1850* (Stanford, CA: Stanford University Press, 2003).

— 'Slave Economy and Society in Minas Gerais and São Paulo, Brazil in 1830', *Journal of Latin American Studies* 36:1 (2004), pp. 1–28.

Macagno, Lorenzo, 'Um antropólogo americano no "mundo que o português criou": Relações raciais no Brasil e em Moçambique segundo Marvin Harris', *Lusotopie* (1999), pp. 143–61.

Machado, F. L., 'Contextos e percepções de racismo no quotidiano', *Sociologia Problemas e Práticas* 36 (2001), pp. 53–80.

Maddison, Angus, *The World Economy: A Millennial Perspective* (Paris: OECD, 2001).

Magalhães, José Calvet de, 'Portugal e Inglaterra: De D. Fernando ao mapa cor-de-rosa (II)', *Janus* 1999–2000, 10 Dec. 2010.

Maggie, Yvonne, 'Cor, hierarquia e sistema de classificação: A diferença fora do lugar', *Estudos Históricos* (Rio de Janeiro) 7:14 (1994), pp. 149–60.

— 'Aqueles a quem foi negada a cor do dia: As categorias de cor e raça na cultura brasileira', in Marcos C. Maio and Ricardo V. Santos (eds), *Raça, ciência e sociedade* (Rio de Janeiro: Fiocruz/Centro Cultural Banco do Brasil, 1996).

Maino, Elisabetta, 'Le kaléidoscope identitaire: Anthropologie historique de São Tomé e Príncipe', unpublished PhD thesis, École des Hautes Etudes en Sciences Sociales, Paris, 2004.

Malik, Kenan, *The Meaning of Race: Race, History and Culture in Western Society* (London: Macmillan, 1996).

Mann, Kristin, *Slavery and the Birth of an African City: Lagos, 1760–1900* (Bloomington and Indianapolis: Indiana University Press, 2007).

Mann, Michael, 'The Autonomous Power of the State: Its Origins, Mechanisms, and Results', *Archives Européennes de Sociologie* 25 (1984), pp. 185–213.

Margarido, Alfredo, 'Littérature et Nationalité', *Politique Africaine* 29 (1988), pp. 58–70.

Mark, Peter, *'Portuguese Style' and Luso-African Identity: Precolonial Senegambia, Sixteenth–Nineteenth Centuries* (Bloomington: Indiana University Press, 2002).

Marocci, Giuseppe, '"... per capillos adductos ad pillam": Il dibattito cinquecentesco sulla validitá del battesimo forzato degli ebrei in Portogallo (1496–1497)', in Adriano Prosperi (ed.), *Salvezza delle anime disciplina dei corpi: Un seminario sulla storia del battesimo* (Pisa: Edizione della Normale, 2006), pp. 339–423.

Marques, A. H. de Oliveira (ed.), *O império africano, 1890–1930* (Lisbon: Estampa, 2001).

Marques, João Pedro, 'O retorno do escravismo em meados do século XIX', *Análise Social* 180 (2006), pp. 671–92.

— *The Sounds of Silence: Nineteenth-Century Portugal and the Abolition of the Slave Trade* (Oxford: Berghahn Books, 2006).

— *Sá da Bandeira e o fim da escravidão: Vitória da moral, desforra do interesse* (Lisboa: Imprensa de Ciências Sociais, 2008).

Marquês, M. Silva, 'Armas e tapeçarias reais num inventário de 1505', *Publicações do Congresso do Mundo Português. Congresso da História dos Descobrimentos*, 19 vols (Lisbon: Comissáo Executiva dos Centenários, 1940), vol. 3.

Marquese, Rafael de Bivar, 'A dinâmica da escravidão no Brasil: Resistência, tráfico negreiro e alforrias, séculos XVII a XIX', *Novos estudos – CEBRAP* 74 (2006), pp. 107–23.

Massing, Jean Michel, 'Observations and Beliefs: The World of the *Catalan Atlas*', in Jay A. Levenson (ed.), *Circa 1492: Art in the Age of Exploration* (New Haven: Yale University Press, 1991), pp. 27–33.

— 'Hans Burgkmair's Depiction of Native Africans', *RES: Anthropology and Aesthetics* 27 (1995), pp. 39–51.

— 'Observations and Beliefs: The World of the *Catalan Atlas*', in *Studies in Imagery*, vol. 2, *The World Discovered* (London: Pindar, 2007).

— (David Bindman and Henry Louis Gates, eds), *The Image of the Black in Western Art*, vol. 3.2, *From the 'Age of Discovery' to the Age of Abolition: Europe and the World Beyond* (Cambridge, MA: Harvard University Press, 2011).

Mata, Maria Eugénia, 'Interracial Marriage in the Last Portuguese Colonial Empire', *E-Journal of Portuguese History* 5:1 (2007), pp. 1–23.

Matory, J. Lorand, *Black Atlantic Religion: Tradition, Transnationalism, and Matriarchy in the Afro-Brazilian Candomblé* (Princeton: Princeton University Press, 2005).

— 'The "New World" Surrounds an Ocean: Theorizing the Live Dialogue between African and African American Cultures', in Kevin Yelvington (ed.), *Afro-Atlantic Dialogues: Anthropology in the Diaspora* (Santa Fe, NM: School of American Research Press, 2006), pp. 151–92.

Matos, Artur Teodoro de, *Timor Português 1515–1769: Contribuição para a sua história* (Lisbon: IHIH, 1974).

Matos, Patrícia Ferraz de, *As cores do Império: Representações raciais no império colonial português* (Lisbon: Imprensa de Ciências Sociais, 2006).

Mattos, Hebe M. Castro, 'A cor inexistente: Relações raciais e trabalho rural no Rio de Janeiro pós-escravidão', *Estudos Afro-Asiáticos* 28 (1995), pp. 101–28.

Mattoso, Kátia M. de Queirós, 'A propósito de cartas de alforria: Bahia, 1779–1850', *Anais de História* 4 (1972), pp. 23–52.

Maurício, Carlos, *A invenção de Oliveira Martins: Política, historiografia e identidade nacional no Portugal contemporâneo (1867–1960)* (Lisbon: Imprensa Nacional-Casa da Moeda, 2005).

McConahay, J. B. and J. C. Hough, 'Symbolic Racism', *Journal of Social Issues* 32 (1976), pp. 23–45.

McCreery, David, *Frontier Goiás, 1822–1889* (Stanford, CA: Stanford University Press, 2006).

McDonald, Mark P., 'Burgkmair's Woodcut Frieze of Natives of Africa and India', *Print Quarterly* 20 (2003), pp. 227–44.

— *The Print Collection of Ferdinand Columbus (1488–1539): A Renaissance Collector in Seville* (London: British Museum, 2004).

Meade, Teresa and Gregory Alonso Pirio, 'In Search of the Afro-American "Eldorado": Attempts by North American Blacks to Enter Brazil in the 1920s', *Luso-Brazilian Review* 25:1 (1988), pp. 85–110.

Meillassoux, Claude, *Femmes, greniers et capitaux* (Paris: Maspéro, 1982).

Mello, Evaldo Cabral de, 'O "Ovo de Colombo" Gilbertiano', in J. Falcão and R. M. Barboza de Araújo (eds), *O Imperador das idéias* (Rio de Janeiro: Topbooks, 2001).

Mello, José António Gonsalves de, *Gente da nação: Cristãos-novos e judeus em Pernambuco, 1542–1654* (Recife: Fundação Joaquim Nabuco/Editora Massangana, 1989).

Mello, Lopo Vaz de Sampayo e, *Política indígena* (Porto: Magalhães e Moniz, 1910).

Melo, Ovídio de Andrade, *Recordações de um removedor de mofo no Itamaraty* (Rio de Janeiro: Fundação Alexandre de Gusmão, 2009).

Mendes, António de Almeida, 'Le rôle de l'inquisition en Guinée: Viscissitudes des présences juives sur la Petite Côte (XVe–XVIIe siècles)', *Revista Lusófona de Ciência das Religiões* 3:5–6 (2004), pp. 137–55.

Mendes, M. F. M., *Imigração, identidades e discriminação: Imigrantes russos e ucranianos na área metropolitana de Lisboa* (Lisbon: Imprensa de Ciências Sociais, 2010).

Mendes Júnior, João, *Os indígenas do Brazil: Seus direitos individuais e políticos* (São Paulo: Hennies Irmãos, 1912).

Mendonça, Marcos Carneiro de, *A Amazônia na era Pombalina* (Brasília: Edições do Senado Federal, 2005).

Meneses, Maria Paula G., 'O "indígena" africano e o colono "europeu": A construção da diferença por processos legais', *e-cadernos CES* (Coimbra) (2010), pp. 68–93.

Merrick, Thomas W. and Douglas H. Graham, *Population and Economic Development in Brazil, 1800 to the Present* (Baltimore: Johns Hopkins University Press, 1979).

Mesquita Samara, Eni de, 'O papel do agregado na região de Itu, 1780–1830', *Anais do Museu Paulista*, série histórica 6 (1977), pp. 11–121.

— *Lavoura Canavieira, trabalho livre e cotidiano, Itu 1780–1830* (São Paulo: EDUSP, 2005).

Messiant, Christine, 'Sur la première génération du MPLA: 1948–1960 – Mário de Andrade, entretiens avec Christine Messiant (1982)', *Lusotopie* (1999), pp. 185–221.

— *1961: L'Angola colonial, l'histoire et la société, les premises du mouvement nationaliste* (Basel: P. Schlettwein, 2006).

Metcalf, Alida C., *Family and Frontier in Colonial Brazil, Santana de Parnaíba, 1580–1822* (Berkeley: University of California Press, 1992).

Meyerson, Mark D., *A Jewish Renaissance in Fifteenth-Century Spain* (Princeton: Princeton University Press, 2004).

Miers, Suzanne, *Britain and the Ending of the Slave Trade* (London: Longman, 1975).

— 'Humanitarianism at Berlin: Myth or Reality?', in S. Förster, W. J. Mommsen and R. Robinson (eds), *Bismarck, Europe, and Africa: The Berlin Africa Conference, 1884–1885, and the Onset of Partition* (Oxford: Oxford University Press/German Historical Institute of London, 1988), pp. 333–45.

— *Slavery in the Twentieth-Century: The Evolution of a Global Problem* (Walnut Creek, CA: Altamira Press, 2003).

Miers, Suzanne and Martin Klein (eds), *Slavery and Colonial Rule in Africa* (London: Frank Cass, 1999).

Miers, Suzanne and Richard Roberts (eds), *The End of Slavery in Africa* (Madison: University of Wisconsin Press, 1988).

Milano, Ernesto, *La Carta del Cantino, e la rappresentazione della terra nei codici e nei libri a stampa della Biblioteca Estense* (Modena: Il Bulino, 1991).

Miles, Robert, *Racism* (London: Routledge, 1989).

Milhou, Alain, 'Les politiques de la langue à l'époque moderne', in M.-C. Benassy-Berling, J.-P. Clément and A. Milhou (eds), *Langues et cultures en Amérique Espagnole coloniale* (Paris: Presses de la Sorbonne Nouvelle, 1993).

Miller, Roberta B., 'Science and Society in the Early Career of H. F. Vervoerd', *Journal of Southern African Studies* 19:4 (1993), pp. 634–61.

Miranda, Daniela, 'Músicos de Sabará: A prática musical religiosa a serviço da Câmara (1749–1822)', unpublished PhD thesis, Universidade Federal de Minas Gerais, 2002.

Missão de Inquérito Agrícola, *Recenseamento agrícola de 1930–1940: Contribuição para o recenseamento agrícola mundial* (Lourenço Marques: Imprensa Nacional de Moçambique/Repartição Técnica de Estatística, 1944).

Monteiro, John M., *Negros da terra: Índios e bandeirantes nas origens de São Paulo* (São Paulo: Companhia das Letras, 1994).

— 'Tupis, tapuias e historiadores: Estudos de história indígena e do indigenismo', unpublished thesis, presented to obtain the title of Livre Docente, Universidade Estadual de Campinas, 2001.

Monteiro, M. B., D. X. França and R. Rodrigues, 'The Development of Intergroup Bias in Childhood: How Social Norms Can Shape Children's Racial Behaviours', *International Journal of Psychology* 44 (2009), pp. 29–39.

Moreira, Paulo Roberto Staudt, *Faces da liberdade, máscaras do cativeiro: Experiências de liberdade e escravidão precebidas através das cartas de alforria – Porto Alegre (1858–1888)* (Porto Alegre: EDIPUCRS, 1996).

— *Os cativos e os homens de bem: Experiências negras no espaço urbano, Porto Alegre 1858–1888* (Porto Alegre: EST Edições, 2003).

Moscovici, S. and J. A. Pérez, 'Prejudice and Social Representations', *Papers on Social Representations* 6 (1997), pp. 27–36.

Mota, Avelino Teixeira da, 'A África no planisfério português anónimo "Cantino" (1502)', *Revista da Universidade de Coimbra* 26 (1978), pp. 1–13.

Moura, Clovis, 'A quem interessam as mulatas', *Versus* 19 (1978), pp. 39–40.

Mulvey, Patricia A., 'Black Brothers and Sisters: Membership in the Black Lay Brotherhoods of Colonial Brazil', *Luso-Brazilian Review* 17:2 (1980), pp. 253–79.

— 'Slave Confraternities in Brazil: Their Role in Colonial Society', *The Americas* 39:1 (1982), pp. 39–68.

Munanga, Kabengele, *Negritude: Usos e sentidos* (São Paulo: Ática, 1986).

Murji, Karim and John Solomos (eds), *Racialization: Studies in Theory and Practice* (Oxford: Oxford University Press, 2005).

Myrdal, G., *An American Dilemma: The Negro Problem and Modern Democracy* (New York: Harper & Bros., 1944).

Nascimento, Abdias do, *O negro revoltado* (Rio de Janeiro: Nova Fronteira, 1982).

Nascimento, Augusto, 'São Tomé e Príncipe', in Valentim Alexandre and Jill Dias (eds), *O Império Africano, 1825–1890* (Lisboa: Editorial Estampa, 1988), pp. 269–318.

— 'A "crise braçal" de 1875 em São Tomé', *Revista Crítica de Ciências Sociais* 34 (1992), pp. 317–29.

— 'S. Tomé e Príncipe no século XIX: Um espaço de interpretação das mudanças sociais', in Valentim Alexandre (ed.), *O Império Africano (Séculos XIX e XX)* (Lisbon: Edições Colibri, 2000), pp. 95–116.

— *Poderes e quotidiano nas roças de S. Tomé e Príncipe, de finais de oitecentos a meados de novecentos* (Lousã, Portugal: author, 2002).

Nash, Roy, *The Conquest of Brazil* (New York: Harcourt, Brace & Co., 1926).

Needell, Jeffrey D., 'Identity, Race, Gender, and Modernity in the Origins of Gilberto Freyre's *Oeuvre*', *American Historical Review* 100:1 (1995), pp. 51–77.

Needham, Joseph, with Wang Ling and Lu Gwei-Djen, *Science and Civilisation in China: Civil Engineering and Nautics* (Cambridge: Cambridge University Press, 1971).

Neto, María da Conceição, 'Nas malhas da rede: O impacto económico e social do transporte rodoviário na região do Huambo c. 1920 – c. 1960', in Beatrix Heintze and Achim von Open (eds), *Angola on the Move: Transport, Routes, Communications and History/ Angola em movimento: Vias de transporte, comunicações e história* (Frankfurt: Otto Lambeck, 2008), pp. 117–29.

— 'Race in the Law and in Everyday Life: Living under the "Native Statute" (*Estatuto dos Indígenas*) in Central Angola, 1926–1961', paper presented at King's College London, Symposium on 'Race Relations: The Portuguese-Speaking Countries in Comparative Perspective', 10–11 December 2009.

Nevinson, Henry W., *A Modern Slavery* (London: Harper and Brothers, 1906).

Newbury, Colin, 'Labour Migration in the Imperial Phase: An Essay in Interpretation', *Journal of Imperial and Commonwealth History* 3 (1974–5), pp. 234–56.

Newitt, Malyn D. D., *Portuguese Settlement on the Zambezi* (London: Longman, 1973).

— *The History of Mozambique* (London: C. Hurst & Co., 1995).

— *A History of the Portuguese Overseas Expansion, 1540–1668* (London: Routledge, 2005).

— 'Uma viagem pelo Norte de Moçambique durante a Segunda Guerra Mundial', in P. Havik, C. Saraiva and J. A. Tavim (eds), *Caminhos cruzados em História e Antropologia: Ensaios de homenagem a Jill Dias* (Lisbon: Instituto de Ciênças Sociais, 2010), pp. 143–58.

Newitt, Malyn D. D. and Philip Havik (eds), *Creole Societies in the Portuguese Colonial Empire: Proceedings of the Charles R. Boxer Centenary Conference* (Bristol: Seagull/Faoileán, 2007).

Niermeyer, J. C. and C. van De Kieft, *Mediæ Latinitatis Lexicon Minus*, 2nd edn, 2 vols (Leiden: Brill, 2002).

Nirenberg, David, 'Was There Race Before Modernity? The Example of "Jewish" Blood in Late Medieval Spain', in Miriam Eliav-Feldon, Benjamin Isaac and Joseph Ziegler (eds), *The Origins of Racism in the West* (Cambridge: Cambridge University Press, 2009), pp. 232–64.

Nishida, Meiko, 'Manumission and Ethnicity in Urban Slavery: Salvador, Brazil 1808–1888', *Hispanic American Historical Review* 73:3 (1993), pp. 361–91.

Nobles, Melissa, *Shades of Citizenship: Race and the Census in Modern Politics* (Stanford, CA: Stanford University Press, 2000).

Northrup, David, *Indentured Labor in the Age of Imperialism, 1834–1922* (Cambridge: Cambridge University Press, 1995).

Novinsky, Anita, *Cristãos novos na Bahia* (São Paulo: Perspectiva, 1972).

Nunes, Zita, *Cannibal Democracy: Race and Representation in the Literature of the Americas* (Minneapolis: University of Minnesota Press, 2008).

Oakeshott, Walter, *Some Woodcuts by Hans Burgkmair Printed as an Appendix to the Fourth Part of 'Le relationi universali di Giovanni Botero, 1618'* (Oxford: for the Roxburghe Club, 1960).

Olival, Fernanda, *As ordens militares e o Estado Moderno: Honra, mercê e venalidade em Portugal (1641–1789)* (Lisbon: Estar, 2002).

— 'Rigor e interesses: Os estatutos de limpeza de sangue em Portugal', *Cadernos de Estudos Sefarditas* 4 (2004), pp. 151–82.

Oliveira, Maria Inês Côrtes de, *O liberto: O seu mundo e os outros, Salvador, 1790–1890* (São Paulo: Corrupio, 1988).

Oliveira, Myriam Andrade Robeiro de *et al.*, *O Aleijadinho e sua oficina: Catálogo das esculturas devocionais* (São Paulo: Capivara, 2002).

Oliveira, Vinicius Pereira de, 'Sobre o convés: Marinheiros, marítimos e pescadores negros no mundo atlântico do Porto de Rio Grande, RS (século XIX)', *IX Encontro Estadual de História – ANPUH-RS* (Porto Alegre, 2008).

Olschki, Leonard, *L'Asia di Marco Polo: Introduzione alla lettura e allo studio del Milione* (Venice and Rome: Istituto per la collaborazione culturale, 1957).

Omi, Michael and Howard Winant, *Racial Formation in the United States: From the 1960s to the 1980s* (1986; New York: Routledge, 1994).

Operario, D. and S. T. Fiske, 'Racism Equals Power plus Prejudice: A Social Psychological Equation for Racial Oppression', in J. L. Eberhardt and S. T. Fiske (eds), *Confronting Racism: The Problem and the Response* (Thousand Oaks, CA: Sage, 1998), pp. 33–53.

Osório, Rafael G., *O sistema de classificação de "cor ou raça" do IPEA*, working paper, no. 996, 2003.

Paiva, Clotilde Andrade and Herbert S. Klein, 'Slave and Free in Nineteenth-Century Minas Gerais: Campanha in 1831', *Slavery and Abolition* 15:1 (1994), pp. 1–21.

Paiva, Eduardo França, *Escravidão e universo cultural na colônia, Minas Gerais, 1716–1789* (Belo Horizonte: Universidade Federal de Minas Gerais, 2001).

Pallares-Burke, Maria Lúcia G., *Gilberto Freyre, um vitoriano dos trópicos* (São Paulo: UNESP, 2005).

Paquette, Gabriel, 'After Brazil: Portuguese Debates on Empire, c. 1820–1850', *Journal of Colonialism and Colonial History* 11:2 (2010).

Parés, Luis Nicolau, 'O processo de crioulização no Recôncavo Baiano (1750–1800)', *Afro-Ásia* 33 (2005), pp. 87–132.

Park, Robert, 'The Career of the Africans in Brazil', Introduction to Donald Pierson, *Negroes in Brazil* (Chicago: University of Chicago Press, 1942).

Parsons, Talcott, 'The Problem of Polarization on the Axis of Color', in John Hope Franklin (ed.), *Color and Race* (Boston: Beacon Press, 1969), pp. 349–73.

Patterson, Orlando, *Slavery and Social Death: A Comparative Study* (Cambridge, MA: Harvard University Press, 1985).

Paulo, João Carlos, 'Da "educação colonial portuguesa" ao ensino no Ultramar', in Francisco Bethencourt and Kirti Chaudhuri (eds), *História da expansão portuguesa*, 5 vols (Lisbon: Círculo de Leitores, 1998–9), vol. 5, pp. 304–33.

Pearson, M. N., *The Portuguese in India* (Cambridge: Cambridge University Press, 1987).

Pécora, Alcir, 'Vieira, o índio e o corpo místico', in Adauto Novaes (ed.), *Tempo e história* (São Paulo: Companhia das Letras, 1992).

— *Máquina de gêneros* (São Paulo: EDUSP, 2001).

Pedreira, Jorge, 'O Sistema de Trocas', in Francisco Bethencourt and Kirti Chaudhuri (eds), *História da expansão portuguesa*, 5 vols (Lisbon: Círculo de Leitores, 1998–9), vol. 4, pp. 214–99.

Pedrosa, Alvaro *et al.*, 'Movimiento negro, identidad y territorio: Entrevista con la Organización de Comunidades Negras', in Arturo Escobar and Alvaro Pedrosa (eds), *Pacífico: ¿desarrollo o biodiversidad? Estado, capital y movimientos sociales en el Pacífico colombiano* (Bogotá: CEREC, 1996), pp. 245–65.

Pelissier, René, *Naissance du Mozambique: Résistance et révoltes anticoloniales (1854–1918)*, 2 vols (Orgeval: Ed. Pélissier, 1984).

— *História das campanhas de Angola: Resistência e revoltas, 1845–1941* (Lisbon: Estampa, 1986).

— *História de Moçambique: Formação e oposição, 1854–1918* (Lisbon: Estampa, 1987–8).

— *Les campagnes coloniales du Portugal, 1844–1941* (Paris: Pygmalion, 2004).

Pelliot, Paul, *Notes on Marco Polo*, 3 vols (Paris: Imprimerie Nationale, 1959–73).

Pena, Sergio, 'Retrato molecular do Brasil', in J. Falcão and R. M. Barboza de Araújo (eds), *O Imperador das idéias* (Rio de Janeiro: Topbooks, 2001), pp. 283–300.

Penvenne, Jeanne-Marie, *African Workers and Colonial Racism: Mozambican Strategies and Struggles in Lourenço Marques, 1877–1962* (Portsmouth, NH, Johannesburg and London: Heinemann/Witwatersrand University Press/James Currey, 1995).

Pereira, Ana Leonor, *Darwin em Portugal. Filosofia. História. Engenharia social (1865–1914)* (Coimbra: Almedina, 2001).

Pereira, Ana Luiza de Castro, 'O Sangue, a palavra e a lei: Ilegitimidade e transmissão da herança no Mundo Atlântico Português no século XVIII', *Nuevomundo*, 28 April 2008.

Pereira, C., J. Vala and R. Costa-Lopes, 'From Prejudice to Discrimination: The Legitimizing Role of the Perceived Threat in Discrimination against Immigrants', *European Journal of Social Psychology* 40 (2010), pp. 1,231–50.

Pereira, C., J. Vala and J. P. Leyens, 'From Infra-Humanization to Discrimination: The Mediation of Symbolic Threat Needs Egalitarian Norms', *Journal of Experimental Social Psychology* 45 (2009), pp. 336–44.

Pérez, J. A., S. Moscovici and B. Chulvi, 'The Taboo Against Group Contact: Hypothesis of Gypsy Ontologization', *British Journal of Social Psychology* 46 (2007), pp. 249–72.

Pesquisa Social Brasileira, Universidade Federal Fluminense, 2002.

Pessoa, Raimundo Agnelo Soares, 'Gente sem sorte: Os Mulatos no Brasil colonial', unpublished PhD thesis, Universidade Estadual Paulista, 2007.

Petersson, Niels P., 'Markt, Zivilisierungsmission und Imperialismus', in Boris Barth and Jürgen Osterhammel (eds), *Zivilisierungsmissionen: Imperiale Weltverbesserung seit dem 18. Jahrhundert* (Konstanz: UVK, 2005), pp. 33–54.

Petruccelli, José Luís, 'Raça, etnicidade e origem nos censos de EUA, França, Canadá e Grã-Bretanha', *Estudos Afro-Asiáticos* 24:3 (2002), pp. 533–62.

Pettigrew, T. F., 'Normative Theory in Intergroup Relations: Explaining Both Harmony and Conflict', *Psychology and Developing Societies* 3 (1991), pp. 3–16.

Pettigrew, T. F. and R. W. Meertens, 'Subtle and Blatant Prejudice in Western Europe', *European Journal of Social Psychology* 25 (1995), pp. 57–75.

Pettigrew, T. F., J. S. Jackson, J. B. Brika, G. Lemaine, R. W. Meertens, U. Wagner and A. Zick, 'Outgroup Prejudice in Western Europe', *European Review of Social Psychology* 8 (1997), pp. 241–73.

Pierson, Donald, *Negroes in Brazil: A Study of Race Contact in Bahia* (Chicago: University of Chicago Press, 1942); published in Portuguese as *Brancos e pretos na Bahia* (São Paulo: Editora Nacional, 1971).

Pieterse, Jan Nederveen, *White on Black: Images of Africa and Blacks in Western Popular Culture* (New Haven: Yale University Press, 1992).

Pimenta, Fernando, 'Ideologia nacional dos brancos angolanos (1900–1975)', paper presented at the VIII Congresso Luso-Afro-Brasileiro de Ciências Sociais, Coimbra, September 2004.

Pimentel, Maria do Rosário, *Viagem ao fundo das consciências: A escravatura na época moderna* (Lisbon: Colibri, 1995).

Pina-Cabral, João de, 'Galvão among the Cannibals: The Emotional Constitution of Colonial Power', *Identities* 8:4 (2001), pp. 483–515.

— *Between China and Europe: Person, Culture and Emotion in Macao* (New York: Continuum/Berg, 2002).

Pinheiro, Fábio W. A., 'Tráfico atlântico de escravos na formação dos plantéis mineiros, Zona da Mata, c.1809–c.1830', unpublished Masters dissertation, Universidade Federal do Rio de Janeiro, 2007.

Pinheiro, Fernanda Aparecida Domingos, 'Confradesdo Rosário: Sociabilidade e identidade étnica em Mariana – Minas Gerais (1745–1820)', unpublished Masters dissertation, Universidade Federal Fluminense, 2006.

Pinto, António Costa, *O fim do império português* (Lisbon: Livros Horizonte, 2001).

Pinto, F. Latour da Veiga, *Le Portugal et le Congo au XIXe Siècle: Étude d'histoire des relations internationales* (Paris: Presses Universitaires de France, 1972).

Pinto, Luis Aguiar Costa, *O negro no Rio de Janeiro: Relações de raças numa sociedade em mudança* (1953; Rio de Janeiro: Editora Nacional, 1998).

Pinto, Regina Pahim, *O movimento negro em São Paulo: Luta e identidade* (São Paulo: FFLCH/USP, 1993).

Pogliano, Claudio, *L'ossessione della razza: Antropologia e genetica nel XX secolo* (Pisa: Scuola Normale Superiore, 2005).

Popp, Valerie, 'Where Confusion Is: Transnationalism in the Fiction of Jessie Redmon Fauset', *African American Review* 43:1 (2009), pp. 131–44.

Porter, Andrew, 'Commerce and Christianity: The Rise and Fall of a Nineteenth-Century Missionary Slogan', *Historical Journal* 28:3 (1985), pp. 597–621.

— *European Imperialism, 1860–1914* (London: Macmillan, 1994).

— *Religion vs. Empire? British Protestant Missionaries and Overseas Expansion, 1700–1914* (Manchester: Manchester University Press, 2004).

Prado, Paulo (Carlos A. Calil, ed.), *Retrato do Brasil: Ensaio sobre a tristeza brasileira* (1928; São Paulo: Companhia das Letras, 1997).

Prestage, E., *D. Francisco Manuel de Melo – esboço biographico* (Coimbra: Imprensa da Universidade, 1914).

Quina, Maria Antónia Gentil, *À maneira de Portugal e da India: Uma série de tapeçaria quinhentista* (Lisbon: Fundação Abel de Lacerda, Museu do Caramulo, 1998).

Quintão, Antonia Aparecida, *Lá vem o meu parente, as irmandades de pretos e pardos no Rio de Janeiro em Pernambuco (século XVIII)* (São Paulo: Annablume, 2002).

Radulet, Carmen, 'An Outsider's Inside View of Sixteenth-Century Portugal', *Portuguese Studies* 13 (1997), pp. 152–8.

Ramos, A. and J. Vala, 'Predicting Opposition towards Immigration: Economic Resources, Social Resources and Moral Principles', in A. Gari and K. Mylonas (eds), *Quod Erat Demonstrandum: From Herodotus' Ethnographic Journeys to Cross-Cultural Research* (Athens: Pedio Books, 2009), pp. 245–64.

Ramos, A., J. Vala and C. Pereira, 'Racial Prejudice and Opposition to Anti-Racist Policies in Europe: Individual and Contextual Predictors', paper presented at Annual Conference of the European Survey Research Association, Prague, 2009.

Ramos, Alberto Guerreiro, 'O problema do negro na sociedade brasileira', in *Cartilha brasileira do aprendiz de sociólogo* (Rio de Janeiro: Andes, 1954).

Ramos, Jair de Souza, 'Dos males que vêm com o sangue: As representações raciais e a categoria do imigrante indesejável nas concepções sobre imigração da década de 20', in Marcos Chor Maio and Ricardo Ventura Santos (eds), *Raça, ciência e sociedade no Brasil* (Rio de Janeiro: FioCruz, 1996), pp. 59–82.

— 'Afinal, o que é preciso para ser "brasileiro"? Leitura de um texto que fala sobre as lutas por esta e outras identidades', *História, ciência e saúde – Manguinhos* 7:1 (2000), pp. 197–204.

Ramos, Rui, 'Um novo Brasil de um novo Portugal: A história do Brasil e a ideia de colonização em Portugal nos séculos XIX e XX', *Penélope* 23 (2000), pp. 129–52.

Rampinelli, Waldir José, *As duas faces da moeda – as contribuições de JK e Gilberto Freyre ao colonialismo português* (Florianópolis: UFSC, 2004).

Rangel, Ana Paula dos Santos, 'Nos limites da escolha: Matrimônio e família entre escravos e forros termo de Barbacena – 1781–1821', *Revista Eletrônica de História do Brasil* 8:1–2 (2006).

Read, Ian William Olivo, 'Unequally Bound: The Conditions of Slave Life and Treatment in Santos County, Brazil, 1822–1888', unpublished PhD thesis, Stanford University, 2006.

Redkey, Edwin S., *Black Exodus: Black Nationalist and Back-to-Africa Movements, 1890–1910* (New Haven: Yale University Press, 1969).

Reeves, Frank, *British Racial Discourse: A Study of British Political Discourse about Race and Race-Related Matters* (Cambridge: Cambridge University Press, 1983).

Reichmann, Rebecca (ed.), *Race in Contemporary Brazil: From Indifference to Inequality* (University Park: Pennsylvania State University Press, 1999).

Reinsch, Paul S., 'The Negro Race and European Civilization', *American Journal of Sociology* 11:2 (1905), pp. 145–67.

— *Colonial Administration* (1905; London: Macmillan, 1912).

Reis, João José, 'Identidade e diversidade étnicas nas Irmandades negras no tempo da escravidão', *Tempo* (Rio de Janeiro) 2:3 (1996), pp. 7–33.

— 'De olho no canto: Trabalho de rua na Bahia na véspera da Abolição', *Afro-Ásia* 24 (2000), pp. 199–242.

— *Death is a Festival: Funeral Rites and Rebellion in Nineteenth-Century Brazil* (Chapel Hill: University of North Carolina Press, 2003).

Relaño, Francesc, *The Shaping of Africa: Cosmographic Discourse and Cartographic Science in Late Medieval and Early Modern Europe* (Aldershot: Ashgate, 2002).

Remesal, Agustín, *1494, La Raya de Tordesillas* (Valladolid: Junta de Castilla y León, 1994).

Renard-Clamagirand, Brigitte, *Marobo: Une société Ema de Timor* (Paris: SELAF, 1982).

Renault, François, *Lavigerie, l'esclavage africain et l'Europe, 1868–1892*, 2 vols (Paris: Boccard, 1971).

— *Libération d'esclaves et nouvelle servitude: Les rachats de captifs africains pour le compte des colonies françaises après l'abolition de l'esclavage* (Dakar and Abidjan: Nouvelles Editions Africaines, 1976).

Révah, Israel S., *Études portugaises* (Paris: Fundação Calouste Gulbenkian, 1975).

Rey, Alain (ed.), *Dictionnaire historique de la langue française*, 3 vols (Paris: Le Robert, 1998).

Rey, Pierre-Philippe, *Colonialisme, néo-colonialisme et transition au capitalisme* (Paris: Maspéro, 1971).

Ribeiro, René, *Religião e relações raciais* (Rio de Janeiro: Ministério da Educação e Cultura, 1956).

Ricupero, Bernardo (ed.), *Gilberto Freyre* (Rio de Janeiro: Beco do Azougue, 2010).

Rios, J. Arthur, 'Assimilation of Emigrants from the Old South in Brazil', *Social Forces* 26:2 (1947), pp. 145–52.

Rocha, Solange Pereira da, 'Gente negra na Paraíba oitocentista: População, família e parentesco espiritual', unpublished PhD thesis,, Universidade Federal de Pernambuco, 2007.

Rodrigues, Armando Lourenço, 'A produção no sector indígena de Moçambique', unpublished undergraduate dissertation, Instituto Superior de Estudos Ultramarinos, Lisbon, 1960.

Rodríguez Garavito, César, Tatiana Alfonso Sierra and Isabel Cavelier Adarve, *Informe sobre discriminación racial y derechos de la población afrocolombiana: Raza y derechos humanos en Colombia* (Bogotá: Universidad de los Andes, 2009).

Roeykens, Auguste, *Le dessein africain de Léopold II: Nouvelles recherches sur sa genèse et sa nature (1875–1876)* (Bruxelles: Académie Royale des Sciences Coloniales, 1956).

— *Léopold II et la Conférence Géographique de Bruxelles (1876)* (Bruxelles: Académie Royale des Sciences Coloniales, 1956).

Roland, Maria Inês, *A Revolta da Chibata* (São Paulo: Editora Saraiva, 2000).

Roque, Ricardo, *Antropologia e império: Fonseca Cardoso e a expedição à Índia em 1895* (Lisbon: Imprensa de Ciências Sociais, 2001).

— '"Portugueses da Índia": Germano Correia e a antropologia dos luso-descendentes de Goa', in *VI Congresso Luso-Afro-Brasileiro de Ciências Sociais* (Porto: Fac. Letras Porto, 2002), pp. 339–46.

— *Headhunting and Colonialism: Anthropology and the Circulation of Human Skulls in the Portuguese Empire, 1870–1930* (New York: Palgrave Macmillan, 2010).

— 'The Colonial Command of Ceremonial Language: Etiquette and Custom-Imitation in Nineteenth-Century East Timor', in Laura Pang (ed.), *Portuguese and Luso-Asian Legacies, 1511–2011: Complexities of Engagement, Culture, and Identity in Southeast Asia*, vol. 2, *The Tenacities and Plasticities of Culture and Identity*, 2 vols (Singapore: Institute of Southeast Asian Studies, 2011).

— 'Os portugueses e os *reinos* de Timor no século XIX/The Portuguese and the Kingdoms of Timor during the Nineteenth Century', *Oriente* 20 (2011), pp. 91–111.

Rosero-Labbé, Claudia Mosquera, *Acá antes no se veían negros: Estrategias de inserción de migrantes del Pacífico colombiano en Bogotá* (Bogotá: Observatorio de Cultura Urbana, 1988).

Rosero-Labbé, Claudia Mosquera and Luiz Claudio Barcelos (eds), *Afro-reparaciones: Memorias de la esclavitud y justicia reparativa para negros, afrocolombianos y raizales* (Bogotá: Universidad Nacional de Colombia, 2007).

Ross, Edward A., *Report on Employment of Native Labour in Portuguese Africa* (New York: Abbott Press, 1925).

Ruge, W., 'Aelteres kartographisches Material in deutschen Bibliotheken', *Nachrichten von der Königlichen Gesellschaft der Wissenschaften zu Göttingen, Philologisch-historische Klasse, Beiheft* (1916).

Russell, Peter Edward, 'White Kings on Black Kings: Rui de Pina and the Problem of Black African Sovereignty', in *Portugal, Spain and the Atlantic, 1340–1490: Chivalry and Crusade from John of Gaunt to Henry the Navigator* (Aldershot: Variorum, 1995), pp. 151–63.

Russell-Wood, A. J. R., 'Black and Mulatto Brotherhoods in Colonial Brazil: A Study in Collective Behavior', *Hispanic American Historical Review* 54:4 (1974), pp. 567–602.

— 'A sociedade portuguesa no Ultramar', in Francisco Bethencourt and Kirti Chaudhuri (eds), *História da expansão portuguesa*, 5 vols (Lisbon: Círculo de Leitores, 1998–9), vol. 1, pp. 266–79.

— 'Comunidades étnicas', in Francisco Bethencourt and Kirti Chaudhuri (eds), *História da expansão portuguesa*, 5 vols (Lisbon: Círculo de Leitores, 1998–9), vol. 2, pp. 151–68.

— 'Comunidades étnicas', in Francisco Bethencourt and Kirti Chaudhuri (eds), *História da expansão portuguesa*, 5 vols (Lisbon: Círculo de Leitores, 1998–9), vol. 3, pp. 210–22.

— 'Grupos sociais', in Francisco Bethencourt and Kirti Chaudhuri (eds), *História da expansão portuguesa*, 5 vols (Lisbon: Círculo de Leitores, 1998–9), vol. 2, pp. 169–88.

Salles, Fritz Teixeira, *Associações religiosas no ciclo do ouro: Introduçao ao estudo do comportamento social das irmandades de Minas no século XVIII* (Belo Horizonte: Universidade Federal de Minas Gerais, 1963).

Salvador, José Gonçalves, *Cristãos-novos, jesuítas e Inquisição (aspectos da sua atuação nas capitanias do Sul, 1530–1680)* (São Paulo: Livraria Pioneira/Universidade de São Paulo, 1969).

Sansi-Roca, Roger, 'The Fetish in the Lusophone Atlantic', in Nancy Naro, Roger Sansi-Roca and David Treece (eds), *Cultures of the Lusophone Black Atlantic* (New York: Palgrave Macmillan, 2007), pp. 19–39.

Sansone, Livio, 'Pai preto, filho negro: Trabalho, cor e diferenças de geração', *Estudos Afro-Asiáticos* 25 (1993), pp. 73–98.

— *Blackness Without Ethnicity: Constructing Race in Brazil* (Basingstoke: Palgrave Macmillan, 2003).

— *Negritude sem etnicidade: O local e o global nas relações raciais e na produção da cultura negra do Brasil* (Salvador and Rio de Janeiro: EDUFBA/Pallas, 2004).

Santil, Juliana Marçano, '"Ce métis qui nous trouble"; Les représentations du Brésil dans l'imaginaire politique angolais: L'empreinte de la colonialité sur le savoir', unpublished PhD thesis, Université de Bordeaux IV, 2006.

Santos, Catarina Madeira, 'Um governo "polido" para Angola: Reconfigurar dispositivos de domínio (1750 – ca. 1800)', unpublished PhD thesis, Universidade Nova de Lisboa, 2005.

— 'Écrire le pouvoir en Angola', *Annales. Histoire, Sciences* Sociales 64:4 (2009), pp. 767–95.

Santos, Catarina Madeira and Ana Paula Tavares, *Africae Monumenta. A apropriação da escrita pelos Africanos, t. 1, Arquivo Caculo Cacahenda* (Lisbon: Instituto de Investigaçao Científica Tropical, 2002).

Santos, Gonçalo Duro dos, *A Escola de Antropologia de Coimbra, 1885–1950* (Lisbon: Imprensa de Ciências Sociais, 2005).

Santos, Maria Emilia Madeira and Vítor Luís Gaspar Rodrigues, 'No rescaldo da escravatura: As ciências sociais chamadas à iça nos anos 30 (século XX)', *Africana Studia* (Porto) 8 (2005), pp. 259–73.

Santos, Reynaldo dos, *As tapeçarias de Tomada de Arzila* (Lisbon: Biblioteca Nacional, 1925).

Santos, Ricardo Ventura and Marcos Chor Maio, 'Qual "Retrato do Brasil?": Raça, biología, identidades e politica na era da genômica', *Mana* 10:1 (2004), pp. 61–95.

— 'Race, Genomics, Identities and Politics in Contemporary Brazil', *Critique of Anthropology* 24 (2004), pp. 347–78.

Santos, Ricardo Ventura *et al.*, 'Colour, Race and Genomic Ancestry in Brazil: Dialogues between Anthropology and Genetics', *Current Anthropology* 50:6 (2009), pp. 805–6.

Saunders, A. C. de M., *A Social History of Black Slaves and Freedmen in Portugal, 1441–1555* (Cambridge: Cambridge University Press, 1982).

Scarano, Julita, *Devoção e escravidão – A Irmandade de Nossa Senhora do Rosário dos Pretos no distrito diamantino no século XVIII* (1976; São Paulo: Companhía Editora Nacional, 1978).

Schneebalg-Perelman, Sophie, 'Richesse du garde-meuble parisien de François Ier, inventaires inédits de 1542 et 1551', *Gazette des Beaux-Arts*, sixth series, 78 (1971).

Schuler, Monica, 'The Recruitment of African Indentured Labourers for European Colonies in the Nineteenth Century', in P. C. Emmer (ed.), *Colonialism and Migration: Indentured Labour Before and After Slavery* (Dordrecht: Martinus Nijhoff Publishers, 1986), pp. 125–61.

Schulze, Franz, *Balthasar Springers Indienfahrt, 1505/06 . . .* (Strasbourg, 1902).

Schwarcz, Lilia Moritz, *Retrato em branco e negro: Jornais, escravos e cidadãos em São Paulo no final do século XIX* (São Paulo: Companhia das Letras, 1987).

— *O espetáculo das raças: Cientistas, instituições e questão racial no Brasil, 1870–1930* (São Paulo: Companhia das Letras, 1993).

— *Racismo no Brasil* (São Paulo: Folha Explica, 2001).

Schwartz, S., 'Value Priorities and Behavior: Applying a Theory of Integrated Value Systems', in C. Seligman, J. M. Olson and M. P. Zanna (eds), *The Psychology of Values: The Ontario Symposium* (Mahwah, NJ: Lawrence Erlbaum Associates, 1996), vol. 8, pp. 1–24.

Schwartz, Stuart B., 'The Manumission of Slaves in Colonial Brazil: Bahia, 1684–1745', *Hispanic American Historical Review* 54:4 (1974), pp. 603–35.

— *Sugar Plantations in the Formation of Brazilian Society: Bahia 1550–1835* (Cambridge: Cambridge University Press, 1985).

Schwegler, Armin, *Chi ma nkongo: Lengua y rito ancestrales en El Palenque de San Basilio (Colombia)*, 2 vols (Frankfurt and Madrid: Vervuert Verlag Iberoamericana, 1996).

Sears, D. O. and P. J. Henry, 'The Origins of Symbolic Racism', *Journal of Personality and Social Psychology* 85 (2003), pp. 259–75.

Seibert, Gerhard, 'Le massacre de février 1953 à São Tomé, raison d'être du nationalisme santoméen', *Lusotopie* 4 (1997), pp. 173–92.

— *Comrades, Clients and Cousins: Colonialism, Socialism and Democratization in São Tomé and Príncipe* (Leiden: University of Leiden, 1999).

Seigel, Micol, *Uneven Encounters: Making Race and Nation in Brazil and the United States* (Durham, NC: Duke University Press, 2009).

Sen, Amartya, *Identity and Violence: The Illusion of Destiny* (New York: W. W. Norton, 2006).

Senghor, Léopold Sédar, *Négritude, arabisme et francité: Réflexions sur le problème de la culture* (Beyrouth: Dar al-Kitab Allubnani, 1967).

Serres, Michel, *Le parasite* (Paris: Hachette, 1997).

Sharp, William, 'Manumission, Libres and Black Resistance: The Chocó 1680–1810', in Robert Toplin (ed.), *Slavery and Race Relations in Latin America* (Westport, CT: Greenwood Press, 1974).

Shepherd, W. R., 'Brazil as a Field for Historical Study', *Hispanic American Historical Review* 13:4 (1933), pp. 428–36.

Sheriff, Robin E., *Dreaming Equality: Color, Race, and Racism in Urban Brazil* (New Brunswick, NJ: Rutgers University Press, 2001).

Sibeud, Emmanuelle, *Une science impériale pour L'Afrique: La construction des savoirs africanistes en France, 1878–1930* (Paris: École des Hautes Études en Sciences Sociales, 2002).

Silva, Ana Cristina Nogueira da, 'A cidadania nos Trópicos: O Ultramar no constitucionalismo monárquico português (1820–1880)', unpublished PhD thesis, Universidade Nova de Lisboa, 2004.

— *Constitucionalismo e império: A cidadania no Ultramar português* (Coimbra: Almedina, 2009).

Silva, Chandra Richard de, 'The Portuguese and Pearl Fishing off South India and Sri Lanka', *South Asia*, new series 1:1 (1978), pp. 14–28.

Silva, Cristiano Lima da, 'As alforrias nos registros de batismos da matriz de Nossa Senhora do Pilar de São João del-Rei: Uma análise demográfica (1751–1850)', *Anais do 2º seminário regional do CEO – Centro de Estudos do oitocentos* (Juiz de Fora: Clio Edições Eletrônicas, 2005).

— 'Senhores e pais: Reconhecimento de paternidade dos alforriados na pia batismal na Freguesia de Nossa Senhora do Pilar de São João del-Rei (1770–1850)', *Anais do I Colóquio dos LAHES (Laboratório de Historia Econômica e Social)* (Juiz de Fora: Laboratório de Historia Econômica e Social, 2005).

Silva, Filipa I. Ribeiro da, *A Inquisição em Cabo Verde, Guiné e São Tomé e Príncipe (1536–1821): Contributo para o estudo da política do Santo Ofício nos territórios africanos* (Lisbon: Universidade Nova de Lisboa, 2002).

Silva, Josenilda, 'A União dos Homens de Cor: Aspectos do movimento negro dos anos 40 e 50', *Estudos Afro-Asiáticos* 25:2 (2003), pp. 215–36.

Silva, Nelson Valle, 'Distância social e casamento inter-racial no Brasil', *Estudos Afro-Asiáticos* 14 (1987), pp. 54–84.

— 'Uma nota sobre "raça social" no Brasil', *Estudos Afro-Asiáticos* 26 (1994), pp. 67–80.

— 'Morenidade: Modo de usar', *Estudos Afro-Asiáticos* 30 (1996), pp. 79–95.

Simmel, Georg (Donald Levine, ed.), *On Individuality and Social Forms: Selected Writings* (Chicago: University of Chicago Press, 1971).

Simpson, J. A. and E. S. C. Weiner (eds), *Oxford English Dictionary*, 20 vols (Oxford: Clarendon Press, 1989).

Skidmore, Thomas, *Black into White: Race and Nationality in Brazilian Thought* (New York: Oxford University Press, 1974).

Slenes, Robert W., 'The Demography and Economics of Brazilian Slavery, 1850–1888', unpublished PhD thesis, Stanford University, 1976.

Sniderman, P. M. and P. E. Tetlock, 'Symbolic Racism: Problems of Motive Attribution in Political Analysis', *Journal of Social Issues* 42 (1986), pp. 129–50.

Soares, Luiz Carlos, *O 'Povo de Cam' na capital do Brasil: A escravidão urbana no Rio de Janeiro do século XIX* (Rio de Janeiro: Faperj/7 Letras, 2007).

Soares, Márcio de Sousa, *A remissão do cativeiro: A dádiva da aforría e o governo dos escravos nos Campos dos Goitacases, c. 1750–1830* (Rio de Janeiro: Apicuri, 2009).

Soares, Mariza de Carvalho, *Devotos da cor: Identidade étnica, religiosidade e escravidão no Rio de Janeiro, século XVIII* (Rio de Janeiro: Civilização Brasileira, 2000).

Sodré, Muniz, *Santugri* (Rio de Janeiro: Livraria José Olympio Editora, 1988).

Sousa, Antonio Caetano, *História Genealógica da Casa Real Portuguesa*, 12 vols (Coimbra: Atlântida, 1948).

Souza, Florentina da S., *Afro-descendência em Cadernos Negros e Jornal do MNU* (São Paulo: Autêntica, 2005).

Souza, José Ferreira Marnoco e, *Administração colonial. Preleccções feitas ao curso do 4.º anno juridico do anno de 1905–1906* (Coimbra: França Amado, 1905).

Souza, Laura de Mello e, *Desclassificados do ouro: A pobreza mineira no século XVIII*, 4th edn (Rio de Janeiro: Edições Graal, 2004).

Soyer, François, *The Persecution of the Jews and Muslims of Portugal: King Manuel and the End of Religious Tolerance (1496–7)* (Leiden: Brill, 2007).

Spini, D. and W. Doise, 'Organizing Principles of Involvement in Human Rights and Their Social Anchoring in Value Priorities', *European Journal of Social Psychology* 28 (1998), pp. 603–22.

Stanley, Brian, 'Commerce and Christianity: Providence Theory, the Missionary Movement, and the Imperialism of Free Trade, 1842–1860', *Historical Journal* 26:1 (1983), pp. 71–94.

Steil, Carlos Alberto (ed.), *Cotas raciais na universidade: Um debate* (Porto Alegre: Universidade Federal do Rio Grande do Sul, 2006).

Steinfeld, Robert J., *The Invention of Free Labor: The Employment Relation in English and American Law and Culture, 1350–1879* (Chapel Hill: University of North Carolina, 1991).

— *Coercion, Contract and Free Labor in the Nineteenth Century* (New York: Cambridge University Press, 2001).

Steinfeld, Robert J. and Stanley L. Engerman, 'Labor – Free or Coerced? An Historical Reassessment of Differences and Similarities', in Tom Brass and Marcel van der Linden (eds), *Free and Unfree Labour: The Debate Continues* (Bern: Peter Lang, 1997), pp. 107–26.

Steppe, Jan-Karel and Guy Delmarcel, 'Les tapisseries du Cardinal Érard de la Marck, prince-évêque de Liège', *Revue de l'Art* 25 (1974), pp. 35–51.

Stoddard, Lothrop, *The Rising Tide of Color against White-World Supremacy* (1920; Brighton: Historical Review Press, 1981).

Stoler, Ann Laura, 'Tense and Tender Ties: The Politics of Comparison in North American History and (Post) Colonial Studies', *Journal of American History* 88:3 (2001), pp. 829–65.

Studnicky-Gizbert, Daviken, 'La "nation portugaise": Réseaux marchands dans l'espace atlantique à l'époque moderne', *Annales. Histoire, Sciences Sociales* 58:3 (2003), pp. 627–48.

Sumner, William G., *Folkways: A Study of the Sociological Importance of Usages, Manners, Customs, Mores, and Morals* (Boston: Ginn and Co., 1907).

Sweet, James H., 'Manumission in Rio de Janeiro, 1749–54: An African Perspective', *Slavery and Abolition* 24:1 (2003), pp. 54–70.

— *Recreating Africa: Culture, Kinship, and Religion in the African-Portuguese World, 1441–1770* (Chapel Hill: University of North Carolina Press, 2003).

Taguieff, P. A., *La force du préjugé: Essai sur le racism et ses doubles* (Paris: Éditions La Découverte, 1987).

Tannenbaum, Frank, *Slave and Citizen: The Negro in the Americas* (New York: Vintage Books, 1946).

Tavares, Maria José Pimenta Ferro, 'Para o estudo dos judeus de Trás-os-Montes, no século XVI', *Cultura História e Filosofia* 4 (1985), pp. 371–401.

— *Judaismo e Inquisição: Estudos* (Lisbon: Editorial Presença, 1987).

Tavim, José Alberto Rodrigues da Silva, *Os judeus na expansão portuguesa em Marrocos durante o século XVI: Origens e actividades de uma comunidade* (Braga: Edições APPACDM Distrital de Braga, 1997).

— *Judeus e cristãos-novos de Cochim: História e memória (1500–1662)* (Lisbon: Universidade Nova de Lisboa, 2001).

Teixeira, André Pinto de Sousa Dias, *A ilha de São Nicolau de Cabo Verde nos séculos XV a XVIII* (Lisbon: Universidade Nova de Lisboa, 2004).

Teixeira, Manuel, *Macau e a sua Diocese: Missões de Timor* (Macao: Missão do Padroado, 1974).

— *O comércio de escravos em Macau/The So-Called Trade in Slaves in Macao* (Macau: Imprensa Nacional, 1976).

Teixeira, Moema P., 'A questão da cor nas relações e representações de um grupo de baixa renda', *Estudos Afro-Asiáticos* 14 (1987), pp. 85–97.

Telles, Edward E., 'Racial Ambiguity among the Brazilian Population', revised version of a paper presented at a Brown University Sociology Department colloquium, September 1998.

— 'Racial Ambiguity among the Brazilian Population', *Ethnic and Racial Studies* 25:3 (2002), pp. 415–41.

— *Race in Another America: The Significance of Skin Color in Brazil* (Princeton: Princeton University Press, 2004).

Telles, Edward E. and R. Flores, 'Not Just Color: Whiteness, Nation and Status in Latin America', *Hispanic American Historical Review* (forthcoming).

Telles, Edward E. and Nelson Lim, 'Does It Matter Who Answers the Race Question? Racial Classification and Income Inequality in Brazil', *Demography* 35:4 (1998), pp. 465–74.

Terray, Emmanuel, *Une histoire du royaume abron du Gyaman: Des origines à la conquête coloniale* (Paris: Karthala, 1995).

— 'Dernière séance', *Cahiers d'études africaines* (Paris) 50:198/199/200 (2010), pp. 529–44.

Thesaurus Linguae Latinae, 8 vols (Lipsiae: E. B. Teubneri, 1931–53).

Thomas, Nicholas, *Colonialism's Culture: Anthropology, Travel and Government* (Princeton: Princeton University Press, 1994).

Thomaz, Omar Ribeiro, *Ecos do Atlântico Sul: Representações sobre o Terceiro Império Português* (Rio de Janeiro: Universidade Federal do Rio de Janeiro, 2002).

Tinker, Hugh, *A New System of Slavery: The Export of Indian Labour Overseas, 1830–1920* (London: Oxford University Press, 1974).

Tomas, Gil, Luisa Seco, Susana Seixas and Paula Faustino, 'The Peopling of Sao Tome (Gulf of Guinea): Origins of Slave Settlers and Admixture with the Portuguese', *Human Biology* 74:3 (2002), pp. 397–411.

Torres, Adelino, *O império português entre o real e o imaginário* (Lisbon: Escher, 1991).

Tragen, Irving G., 'Statutory Prohibitions against Interracial Marriage', *California Law Review* 32:3 (1944), pp. 269–80.

Tragtenberg, Marcelo H. R., 'Programa de Ações Afirmativas da UFSC: Fundamentos e resultados preliminares', available at www.stf.jus.br/portal/cms/verTexto.asp?servico=processoAudienciaPublicaAcaoAfirmativa

Traube, Elizabeth, *Cosmology and Social Life: Ritual Exchange among the Mambai of East Timor* (Chicago: University of Chicago Press, 1986).

Trovoada, Maria Jesus, Luísa Pereira, Leonor Gusmão, Augusto Abade, António Amorim and Maria João Prata, 'Insights from Patterns of mtDNA Variation into the Genetic History of São Tomé e Príncipe', *International Congress Series* 1,261 (2004), pp. 377–9.

Turra, C. and G. Venturi (eds), *Racismo cordial: A mais completa análise sobre o preconceito de cor no Brasil* (São Paulo: Ática, 1995).

Ulrich Ennes, Ruy, *Ciência e administração colonial* (Coimbra: Imprensa da Universidade, 1908).

— *Política colonial: Lições feitas ao curso do 4.º anno juridico no anno de 1908–1909* (Coimbra: Imprensa da Universidade, 1909).

Universidade Federal de Minas Gerais, Pesquisa da Região Metropolitana de Belo Horizonte, 2002.

Vail, Leroy and Landeg White, *Capitalism and Colonialism in Mozambique: A Study of Quelimane District* (London: Heinemann, 1980).

Vala, Jorge, 'Editorial: Expressions of New Racism', *International Journal of Psychology* 44 (2009), pp. 1–3.

Vala, Jorge, R. Brito and D. Lopes, *Expressões dos Racismos em Portugal* (Lisbon: Imprensa de Ciências Sociais, 1999).

Vala, Jorge, M. Lima and D. Lopes, 'Social Values, Prejudice and Solidarity in the European Union', in W. Arts and L. Halman (eds), *European Values at the End of the Millennium* (Leiden: Brill, 2004), pp. 139–63.

Vala, Jorge, D. Lopes and M. Lima, 'Black Immigrants in Portugal: Luso-Tropicalism and Prejudice', *Journal of Social Issues* 64 (2008), pp. 287–302.

Vala, Jorge, C. Pereira and R. Costa-Lopes, 'Is the Attribution of Cultural Differences to Minorities an Expression of Racial Prejudice?', *International Journal of Psychology* 44 (2009), pp. 20–8.

Vala, Jorge, C. Pereira, R. Costa-Lopes and J. C. Deschamps, 'Atitudes Face á Imigração e Identidade Nacional', in J. Sobral and J. Vala (eds), *Identidade nacional: Inclusão e exclusão* (Lisbon: Imprensa de Ciências Sociais, 2010), pp. 191–210.

Vala, Jorge, C. Pereira and A. Ramos, 'Racial Prejudice, Threat Perception and Opposition to Immigration: A Comparative Analysis', *Portuguese Journal of Social Sciences* 5 (2006), pp. 119–40.

Vale de Almeida, Miguel, 'Portugal's Colonial Complex: From Colonial Lusotropicalism to Postcolonial Lusophony', paper presented at Queen's Postcolonial Research Forum, April 2008 (available at http://site.miguelvaledealmeida.net/wp-content/uploads/portugals-colonial-complex.pdf).

Valeri, Valerio, 'Buying Women But Not Selling Them: Gift and Commodity Exchange in Huaulu Alliance', *Man*, new series 29:1 (1994), pp. 1–26.

Van Cott, Donna Lee, *The Friendly Liquidation of the Past: The Politics of Diversity in Latin America* (Pittsburgh: University of Pittsburgh Press, 2000).

— 'Constitutional Reform in the Andes', in Rachel Sieder (ed.), *Multiculturalism in Latin America: Indigenous Rights, Diversity and Democracy* (Basingstoke: Palgrave Macmillan, 2002).

Vandenbroeck, Paul, *Over wilden en narren, boeren en bedelaars: Beeld van de andere, vertoog over het zelf* (Antwerp: Koninklijk Museum voor schone Kunsten, 1987).

Vasconcelos, José, *La raza cósmica: Misión de la raza Iberoamericana* (1925; Mexico City: Espasa-Calpe, 1966).

Vellut, Jean-Luc, 'New Perspectives on the Ambaquista Network', *Journal of African History* 45:2 (2004), pp. 327–9 (review).

Venturi, G., *Discriminação racial e preconceito de cor no Brasil* (São Paulo: Fundação Perseu Abramo/Rosa Luxemburg Stiftung, 2003).

Vergara y Velasco, Francisco, *Nueva geografía de Colombia*, 3 vols (1901; Bogotá: Banco de la República, 1974).

Viana, Larissa, *O idioma da mestiçagem: As irmandades de pardos na América Portuguesa* (Campinas: UNICAMP, 2007).

Vianna, Hermano, *The Mystery of Samba: Popular Music and National Identity in Brazil* (Chapel Hill: University of North Carolina Press, 1999).

— 'A meta mitológica da democracia racial', in Joaquim Falcão and Rosa Maria Barboza de Araujo (eds), *O Imperador das idéias: Gilberto Freyre em questão* (Rio de Janeiro: Topbooks, 2001).

Vieira, Rejane Maria Lobo (ed.), *Moedas portuguesas da época dos descobrimentos na coleção do Museu Histórico Nacional 1383–1583* (Rio de Janeiro: Museu Histórico Nacional, 2000).

Villa, Carlos Eduardo Valencia, 'Produzindo alforrias no Rio de Janeiro no século xix', unpublished Masters dissertation, Universidade Federal do Rio de Janeiro, 2008.

Viterbo, Francisco Marques Sousa, *Artes et artistas em Portugal: Contribuições para a historia das artes e industrias Portuguezas* (Lisbon: Livraria Ferin Editora, 1920).

Wachtel, Nathan, 'Frontières intérieures: La religiosité marrane en Amérique hispanique (XVII siècle)', in Rui Manuel Loureiro and Serge Gruzinski (eds), *Passar as fronteiras. Actas do II Colóquio Internacional sobre mediadores culturais. Séculos XV a XVIII* (Lagos: Centro de Estudos Gila Eanes, 1999), pp. 111–32.

— *A fé da lembrança: Labirintos marranos* (2001; Lisboa: Caminho, 2002).

Wacquant, Loïc J. D., 'For an Analytic of Racial Domination', *Political Power and Social Theory* 11 (1997), pp. 221–34.

Wade, Peter, *Blackness and Race Mixture: The Dynamics of Racial Identity in Colombia* (Baltimore: Johns Hopkins University Press, 1993).

— 'The Cultural Politics of Blackness in Colombia', *American Ethnologist* 22:2 (1995), pp. 342–58.

— 'Working Culture: Making Cultural Identities in Cali, Colombia', *Current Anthropology* 40:4 (1999), pp. 449–71.

— *Music, Race and Nation:* Música Tropical *in Colombia* (Chicago: University of Chicago Press, 2000).

— 'The Colombian Pacific in Perspective', *Journal of Latin American Anthropology* 7:2 (2002), pp. 2–33.

— *Race, Nature and Culture: An Anthropological Perspective* (London: Pluto Press, 2002).

— 'Afro-Latin Studies: Reflections on the Field', *Latin American and Caribbean Ethnic Studies* 1:1 (2006), pp. 105–24.

— *Race and Sex in Latin America* (London: Pluto Press, 2009).

— *Race and Ethnicity in Latin America*, 2nd edn (London: Pluto Press, 2010).

Wagley, Charles (ed.), *Race and Class in Rural Brazil* (Paris: UNESCO, 1952); published in French as *Race et classe dans le Brésil rural* (Paris: UNESCO, 1952).

— 'The Concept of Social Race in the Americas', in *The Latin American Tradition* (New York: Columbia University Press, 1968), pp. 155–74.

Walker, I., 'The Changing Nature of Racism: From Old to New?', in M. Augoustinos and K. J. Reynolds (eds), *Understanding Prejudice, Racism, and Social Conflict* (London: Sage, 2001), pp. 24–42.

Wallerstein, Immanuel, *Le capitalisme historique* (Paris: La Découverte, 2002).

Watson, James L., 'Slavery as an Institution: Open and Closed Systems', in James L. Watson (ed.), *Asian and African Systems of Slavery* (Oxford: Basil Blackwell, 1980), pp. 1–15.

West, Cornel, *Prophesy Deliverance! An Afro-American Revolutionary Christianity* (Philadelphia: Westminster Press, 1982).

— *The Cornel West Reader* (New York: Basic Civitas Books, 1999).

Wheeler, Douglas, '"Angola Is Whose House?" Early Stirrings of Angolan Nationalism and Protest, 1822–1910', *African Historical Studies* 2:1 (1969), pp. 1–22.

— 'The Forced Labor "System" in Angola, 1903–1947: Reassessing Origins and Persistence in the Context of Colonial Consolidation, Economic Growth and Reform Failures', in Adriana Pereira Campos (ed.), *Trabalho forçado africano: Experiências coloniais comparadas* (Porto: Editora Campo das Letras, 2006).

— 'The Galvão Report on Forced Labor (1947) in Historical Context and Perspective: Trouble-Shooter Who Was "Trouble"', *Portuguese Studies Review* 16:1 (2009), pp. 115–52.

Wieviorka, M., *Le racism: Une introduction* (Paris: La Découverte, 1998).

Wimmer, Andreas and Nina Glick Schiller, 'Methodological Nationalism and Beyond: Nation-State Building, Migration and the Social Sciences', *Global Networks: A Journal of Transnational Affairs* 2 (2002), pp. 301–34.

Witte, Charles-Martial de, 'Henri de Congo, évêque titulaire d'Utique (†. c.1531), d'après les documents romains', *Euntes docete* 21 (1968), pp. 587–99.

Wiznitzer, Arnold, *Os judeus no Brasil colonial* (São Paulo: Livraria Pioneira Editora, 1966).

Wood, Charles, 'Categorias censitárias e classificações subjetivas de raça no Brasil', in Peggy A. Lovell (ed.), *Desigualdade racial no Brasil contemporâneo* (Belo Horizonte: CEDEPLAR/FACE/UFMG, 1991), pp. 93–111.

Woods, Randall B., *A Black Odyssey: John Lewis Waller and the Promise of American Life, 1878–1900* (Lawrence: Regents Press of Kansas, 1981).

Wouters, Mieke, 'Ethnic Rights under Threat: The Black Peasant Movement against Armed Groups' Pressure in the Chocó, Colombia', *Bulletin of Latin American Research* 20:4 (2001), pp. 498–519.

Xavier, Ângela Barreto, 'David contra Golias na Índia seiscentista e setecentista. Escrita identitária e colonização interna', *Ler História* 49 (2005), pp. 107–43.

— *A invenção de Goa: Poder imperial e conversões culturais nos séculos XVI e XVII* (Lisbon: ICS, 2008).

— 'Dissolver a diferença: Mestiçagem e conversão no império português', in Manuel Villaverde Cabral, Karin Wall, Sofia Aboim and Filipe Carreira da Silva (eds), *Itinerários: A investigação nos 25 anos do ICS* (Lisbon: Imprensa de Ciências Sociais, 2008), pp. 709–27.

Xavier, Ângela Barreto and Catarina Madeira Santos, 'Nobreza per geração. Os descendentes dos Portugueses na Goa seiscentista', *Cultura – História e Teoria das Ideias* 25 (2007), pp. 89–118.

Yashar, Deborah, *Contesting Citizenship in Latin America: The Rise of Indigenous Movements and the Postliberal Challenge* (Cambridge: Cambridge University Press, 2005).

Yelvington, Kevin (ed.), *Afro-Atlantic Dialogues: Anthropology in the Diaspora* (Santa Fe, NM: School of American Research Press, 2006).

Yerushalmi, Yosef Hayim, *The Lisbon Massacre of 1506 and the Royal Image in the Shebet Yehudah* (Cincinnati: Hebrew Union College, 1976).

Young, Crawford, *The African Colonial State in Comparative Perspective* (New Haven: Yale University Press, 1994).

Young, Robert J., *Colonial Desire: Hybridity in Theory, Culture and Race* (New York: Routledge, 1995).

Ysselsteyn, Gerardina Tjaberta van, *Tapestry, the Most Expensive Industry of the XVth and XVIth Centuries* (The Hague and Brussels: Van Goor, 1969).
Zimermann, B., 'Les relations raciales dans la région aride du Sertão', in Charles Wagley (ed.), *Races et classes dans le Brésil rural* (Paris: UNESCO, 1952).

Index

solving (Cha 2011; Jung 2009) in a tacit way. It is remarkable that the characters in *Pororo* demonstrate how to solve a problem or a conflict through cooperative work without any adult intervention. However, as mentioned above, the image of the independent self has been missing in such a process. Rather, *Pororo* highlights interdependence between oneself and the others which reflects the current Korean views of childhood and children.

From this perspective, this analysis of a Korean popular picture book series developed by the Korean Educational Broadcasting System harkens to what Derrida insisted: the reading of a piece of popular culture is not only a personal reaction to the text but is also a socially situated practice that is inevitably related to the "con-texts" within which the text is seen as a social production (Derrida 1976 & 1978). "There is nothing outside of the text" (Derrida 1976, 158). As a result, children's popular culture cannot be examined without considering the context into which it is produced, circulated, and consumed (Derrida 1976; Hall 1980).

Pororo, the program developed by the Korean educational broadcasting network, intersects children's interests with adults' concerns. The show utilizes popular culture for educational purposes. From this perspective, it is necessary for an edutainment program such as *Pororo* to consider that its important task has to do with how to reconcile many adults' negative perceptions of popular culture (that it is superficial, sensational, and easy) with legitimate and official knowledge that is socially accepted and valued (Apple 2004).

This task of the edutainment programs may be possible when young children's own authentic interpretations and great ability to analyze messages under adults' direction are considered. As observed earlier, some representation of childhood and children in *Pororo*, such as the problem solving process and reservation of one's feelings, could have been more evolved and developed appropriately for enhancing young children's social skills. Given that what they bring to the cultural text is what makes their interpretations vary, a teacher of young children can have a teachable moment by encouraging them to actively select and organize the elements of *Pororo* by means of their own experiences, assumptions, matters of concern, and internal desires. By adapting this perspective, then, not only early childhood educators but also young children's parents as well as edutainment producers for young children can create a place where having fun and learning simultaneously occurs by connecting media and popular culture to young children's knowledge, interests, and experience. In this way, their school learning can be fostered in a meaningful and interesting way.

Works Cited

Apple, Michael. *Ideology and Curriculum.* 3rd ed. New York: RoutledgeFalmer, 2004.

Archard, David. *Children: Rights and Childhood.* New York: Routledge, 1993.

Bauman, Zygmunt. *Liquid Love: On the Frailty of Human Bonds.* Cambridge: Polity Press, 2003.

Bazalgette, Cary, and David Buckingham. "The Invisible Audience." In *In Front of the Children: Screen Entertainment and Young Audiences*, edited by Cary Bazalgette and David Buckingham, 1–14. London: British Film Institute, 1995.

Bourdieu, Pierre. *Distinction: A Social Critique of the Judgment of Taste.* Cambridge: Harvard University Press, 1984.

Buckingham, David, and Margaret Scanlon. *Education, Edutainment, and Learning in the Home*. Cambridge: Open University, 2002.

Cannella, Gaile. *Deconstructing Early Childhood Education: Social Justice & Revolution.* New York: Peter Lang, 1997.

Cha, Hyungseuk. "The Value of the Pororo." Online Newspaper. *Sisainlive.* www.sisainlive.com/news/articleView.html?idxno=10273. 2011 (accessed April 29, 2012).

Christian-Smith, Linda K., and Jean I. Erdman. "'Mom, It's Not Real!': Children Constructing Childhood through Reading Horror Fiction." In *Kinder-Culture: The Corporate Construction of Childhood*, edited by Shirley R. Steinberg and Joe Kincheloe, 129–152. Boulder, CO: Westview Press, 1997.

Cleverly, John, and D. C. Phillips. *Visions of Childhood: Influential Models from Locke to Spock*. Revised Edition. New York: Teachers College Press. 1986.

Corsaro, William. *We're Friends, Right?: Inside Kids' Culture*. Washington: Joseph Henry Press, 2003.

Cunningham, Hugh. *Children and Childhood in Western Society since 1500.* London: Harlow, 1995.

Damon, William. *The Moral Child: Nurturing Children's Natural Moral Growth.* New York: Free Press, 1988.

Dearden, R. F. *The Philosophy of Primary Education*. London: Routledge & Kegan Paul, 1968.

Derrida, Jacques. *Of Grammatology*. London: Johns Hopkins University Press, 1976.

———. *Writing and Difference*. Chicago: University of Chicago Press, 1978.

Egenfeldt-Nielsen, Simon. "Third Generation Educational Use of Computer Games." *Journal of Educational Multimedia and Hypermedia* 16, no. 3 (2007): 263–281.

Elkind, David. *The Hurried Child: Growing Up Too Fast Too Soon*. Reading, MA: Addison-Wesley, 1981.

———. *Reinventing Childhood.* Rosemont, NJ: Modern Learning Press, 1998.

Fraenkel, Jack R., and Norman E. Wallen. *How to Design and Evaluate Research in Education*. 4th ed. New York: McGraw Hill, 2000.

Fisch, Shalom M. *Children's Learning from Educational Television: Sesame Street and Beyond.* Mahwah, NJ: Lawrence Erlbaum, 2004.

Giroux, Henry. "Animating Youth: The Disneyfication of Children's Culture." *Socialist Review* 24, no. 3 (1995): 23–55.

Green, Mary, and Mary N. McNeese. "Using Edutainment Software to Enhance Online Learning." *International Journal on Elearning* 6, no. 1 (2007): 5–16.

Greven, Philip, J. 1988. *The Protestant Temperament: Patterns of Child-Rearing, Religious Experience, and the Self in Early America.* 1977. Reprint, Chicago: University of Chicago Press.

Hall, Stuart. "Introduction to Media Studies at the Centre." In *Culture, Media, Language,* edited by Stuart Hall, Dorothy Hobson, Andy Lowe, and Paul Willis, 117–121. London: Hutchinson, 1980.

Hood-Williams, John. "Power Relations in Children's Lives." In *Childhood in Europe: Approaches, Trends, Findings,* edited by Manuela Du Bois-Reymond, Heinz Sűnker, and Heinz-Hermann Krűger, 91–116. New York: Peter Lang, 2001.

Ito, Mizuko. "Engineering Play: Children's Software and the Cultural Politics of Edutainment." *Discourse: Studies in the Cultural Politics of Education* 27, no. 2 (2006): 139–160.

James, Allison, and Chris Jenks, and Alan Prout. *Theorizing Childhood.* New York: Teachers College Press, 1998.

James, Allison, and Alan Prout. *Constructing and Reconstructing Childhood: Contemporary Issues in the Sociological Study of Childhood.* Bristol: Falmer Press, 1997.

Jenks, Chris. *The Sociology of Childhood: Essential Readings*. London: Batsford Academic, 1982.

Jung, Daehyun, Ockkyung Jung, and Haejung Lee. "An Analysis of Friendship Factors and the Process of Forming Friendship in TV Edutainment Animation: Focused on a Program 'Porongporong Pororo.'" *Children Media Research* 9, no. 1 (2011): 333–356.

Jung, Joohee. "The 'Korean Star' of Animation: The Little Penguin, Pororo." *eTV*. etv.donga.com/view.php?idxno=200905220021759&page=top. 2009 (accessed April 29, 2012).

Kenway, Jane, and Elizabeth Bullen. *Consuming Children: Education, Entertainment, Advertising*. Philadelphia: Open University Press, 2001.

Kim, Hyekyung, and Sungyeon Cho. "Family Environment Depending on Family Structures and Young Children's Socio-Emotional Development." *Korean Family Welfare Study* 7, no. 2 (2002): 3–16.

Kim, Kyungae. "Job Loss in Poverty and Familial Responses to It." *Life Science Research* 8 (2003): 219–235.

Kline, Stephen. *Out of the Garden: Toys, TV and Children's Culture in the Age of Marketing*. London: Verso, 1993.

Lemish, Dafna. *Children and television: A Global Perspective.* Malden, MA: Blackwell Publishing, 2007.

Ministry of Education, Science and Technology. *Korean Early Childhood Education Curriculum*. Seoul: Mirae and Culture Group, 2007.

Popkewitz, Thomas. "The Formation of School Subjects and the Political Context of Schooling." In *The Formation of School Subjects: The Struggle for Creating an American Institution*, edited by Thomas Popkewitz, 1–24. NewYork: Falmer Press, 1986.

Postman, Neil. *The Disappearance of Childhood*. New York: Vintage Books, 1994.

Schaffer, H. Rudolph. *Making Decisions about Children: Psychological Questions and Answers*. Oxford: Blackwell, 1990.

Sieter, Ellen. *Sold Separately: Children and Parents in Consumer Culture*. New Brunswick, NJ: Rutgers University Press, 1995.

Stainton-Rogers, Rex. "The Social Construction of Childhood." In *Child Abuse and Neglect*, edited by Wendy Stainton-Rogers, Denise Henry, and Elizabeth Ash, 23–29. London: Open University Press, 1989.

Steinberg, Shirley, and Joe Kincheloe, Eds. *Kinderculture: The Corporate Construction of Childhood*. Boulder, CO: Westview Press, 1997.

Walkerdine, Valerie. "Developmental Psychology and the Child-Centered Pedagogy." In *Changing the Subject: Psychology, Social Regulation and Subjectivity*, edited by Julian Henriques, Wendy Hollway, Cathy Urwin, Couze Venn, and Valerie Walerdine, 153–202. New York: Methuen, 1984.

Woodhead, Martin. "Psychology and the Cultural Construction of Children's Needs." In *Constructing and Reconstructing Childhood: Contemporary Issues in the Sociological Study of Childhood,* edited by Allison James and Alan Prout, 63–84. Philadelphia: Falmer Press, 1997.

Wright, John C., Aletha C. Huston, Ronda Scantlin, and Jennifer Kotler. "The Early Window Project: Sesame Street Prepares Children for School." In *"G" Is for Growing: Thirty Years of Research on Children and Sesame Street,* edited by Shalom Fisch and Rosemarie T. Truglio, 97–114. Mahwah, NJ: Lawrence Erlbaum, 2001.

Chapter Seven
Accidental Deaths: The Violence of Representing Childhood in *Law & Order: Special Victims Unit*
by Morgan Genevieve Blue

The broadcast of Casey Anthony's murder trial captivated many in recent months, and her acquittal sparked public ire, blaming a lack of evidence for the jury's inability to convict.[1] As the trial came to a close, speculation arose over whether or not Anthony would be offered her own reality TV show or be able to profit from her daughter's mysterious death by offering interviews to networks willing to pay or by selling her story. Whether or not such an agreement will be struck remains to be seen, but one public relations writer claims, "One thing you can count on is a *Law and Order* episode 'based' on this case with a nice disclaimer that the story is not real. And they won't have to pay anyone a dime."[2] And it wouldn't be the first time *Law & Order—Law & Order: Special Victims Unit* (*SVU*), in this case—would capitalize on Anthony's story.[3] Some have argued that it is unlikely that a television network would agree to pay for her story or produce a show that focuses on her life after the trial, expressly because "just talking about capitalizing on the death of a child feels dirty. Profiting in any way won't sit well with anyone. It seems wrong."[4] What makes this case and its potential reproduction in popular media forms especially compelling, then, is the specter of Caylee Anthony, the toddler whose tragic death has aired family secrets and whose lack of vindication makes her a haunting symbol for the inefficacy of U.S. systems of justice. In *SVU*'s early adaptation of Casey Anthony's story in a season 10 episode called "Selfish," Caylee (renamed Ciara) is represented in photos and video footage, her face plastered on T-shirts and screens. Though a measles outbreak causes Ciara's death and her mother's trial is dispatched two-thirds of the way through the episode as the narrative evolves into a battle over parents' rights, the image that returns throughout is that of smiling, young Ciara—"the truly innocent victim," according to the show's assistant district attorney (played by Stephanie March). Through plot twists and complications, Ciara haunts the narrative, invoked in name, in photo, and rhetorically during moments of heightened dramatic tension. This repeated use of the child's image, evidenced across a multitude of different episodes, calls into question just how childhood is constructed in relation to violence on *Law & Order: SVU* and what might be the ideological ramifications of such constructions.

SVU & TV Realism

Airing its thirteenth season in fall 2011, *Law & Order: SVU* is an award-winning police procedural and drama that attracts audiences in prime-time and late-night line-ups on NBC, as well as in cable syndication. A spin-off of America's longest-running prime-time drama, *Law & Order* (1990–2010), *SVU* is part of a narrative franchise[5] long distinguished from other crime and legal dramas by its claims to incorporate stories "ripped from the headlines." Many episodes refer to criminal cases in the news. For instance, "Starved" includes a debate between a young woman's mother and her murderous husband over whether or not she should remain on life support, which calls to mind coverage of the battle over the removal of Terri Schiavo's feeding tube.[6] "Storm" deals with the abduction from New Orleans of three children who lost their parents in Hurricane Katrina.[7] Regardless of fleeting disclaimers before or following some episodes warning of the fictional nature of the story, its characters, and events, *SVU* relies heavily on crimes depicted in the news to draw audiences for all of its story lines—whether or not they directly relate to specific headlines. Its focus on sexually based offenses frequently involving children makes *SVU* a compelling case for analyzing the ideological functions of the imagined child in relation to the state of childhood in American culture.

Set in contemporary New York City, *SVU* finds as its focus the work of two police detectives, investigating violent and sexual crimes and advocating for the rights and safety of their victims who represent a range of class and racial differences, ages, religious affiliations, and lifestyles. The pleasures offered by realist fictional television such as this are often based on the story's apparent seamlessness, usually provided by editing and cinematography. And these conventions of production also work for creating "realistic" news programming. In order to present the appearance of a coherent, unedited segment or story, televised news employs similar camera work and editing, such as the shot/reverse shot to establish point of view and the insertion of reaction shots.[8] This intersection between different representations of the "real" calls into question the ideological function of the fictional show that adapts stories from actual events reported in the news. "Ideology and realism are inseparable."[9]

Certainly, *SVU* gains a degree of credibility by claiming relevance to contemporary social issues raised in the news. And there is evidence of congruity between news reporting and the narratives concurrently in the collective awareness, including what is popular on television.[10] "The realisticness of the image directly affects its believability and thus is a vital part of the cultural form through which the ideological practice operates."[11] Disparate realist representations are connected via the ideological work of television—or rather via the work of ideology that engages those who view and interpret televisual representations.

Despite its many claims to realism, a content analysis of the show's fifth season (2003–2004) reveals that, like most popular television programming, *SVU* does not accurately represent the racial diversity of its locale. Researchers found that 44 percent of *SVU* victims during that season were under eighteen years old—legal minors—and 37 percent were female.[12] "According to the U.S. Census 2000 just over one-half (54 percent) of the individuals who lived in Manhattan, New York are white, on *SVU* almost three-quarters (72 percent) of all the characters are white."[13] In her research on girlhood in popular culture, Valerie Walkerdine asserts that it is the blonde, middle-class girl who appears to be most in need of adult protection, and that the working-class girl "threatens the safety of the discourse of the innocent and natural child. She is too precocious, too sexual."[14] While the notion of the blonde (white) female child as most vulnerable has dominated Western discourses about children, several *SVU* episodes (including "9-1-1," which is discussed in detail below) do manage to complicate this a bit by representing children of color in middle-class families and by frequently relating the work of the detectives to protect working-class and impoverished children—both boys and girls and not exclusively white. It is important to acknowledge the complicated identity politics at work in the program as it struggles to offer realistic depictions in a commercial medium like network television that often requires adherence to hegemonic, normative ideologies and representations. In order to illustrate some moments at which *SVU* both upholds and subverts such ideologies, I have selected a few episodes from a broader, purposeful sample of eight seasons of the series. Since my interest lies in representations of children and childhood, the episodes analyzed here foreground children in distinct ways. The episodes selected for this discursive and narrative textual analysis, and contextualized a bit in the following paragraphs, exemplify some of the ways in which the body of the child and the discourses of remembered or imagined childhoods function, through violence, as vessels for adult anxieties.

SVU's second season aired on U.S. broadcast television network NBC from fall 2000 through spring 2001 and marks an early turning point in the diversity of recurring characters in the series. This season sees the departure of one character of color, detective Monique Jeffries (Michelle Hurd), and the arrival of another, detective Fin Tutuola (played by Ice-T), which is significant in that the role is expanded to eventually incorporate into the ongoing narrative arc issues from Tutuola's personal life, providing a bit more racial diversity among the detective squad. In fact, this program frequently presents nonwhite characters in positions of prominence, skill, and expertise as authorities on the show, though the most prominent cast of detectives Elliot Stabler (played by Chris Meloni) and Olivia Benson (Mariska Hargitay), Captain Donald Cragen (Dann Florek), and the overwhelming majority of the show's assistant district attorneys (including Stephanie March as Alexandra Cabot, Diane Neal as Casey Novak, among many others)[15] are all coded as white and middle-class. Airing in the year following the Y2K millennial panics, during the final days of the 2000 U.S. presidential campaigns and the first election and inauguration of George W. Bush, just one year prior to the attacks on the Twin Towers and the Pentagon, episodes in this season cover issues such as Taliban "honor killings," child abuse, religiously motivated serial crime, kidnapping, rape, and murder, several of which are adapted from crime stories in the news. Having been produced during a time of historic change, nationwide political tension, and increasing international conflict, this season is rich for analysis and provides, in "Baby Killer," one of the few episodes that treats the child as both victim and criminal in the context of racially motivated urban warfare.

The seventh season of *SVU* aired from fall 2005 through spring 2006 and tackles controversial issues such as child pornography, Internet predators, teen sexuality, HIV/AIDS, hate crimes, obesity, incest, and abduction, as well as debates over the nature of pedophilia, mental illness, and psychiatric drug use, and the rights to life of fetuses and of persons in a persistent vegetative state. In multiple episodes, characters discuss whether or not sex offenders—pedophiles in particular—can be rehabilitated. Detectives Benson and Stabler consistently advocate for the rights and well-being of the children whose cases they investigate and feel strongly that sex offenders can never change, while the forensic psychiatrist, Dr. Huang (played by B. D. Wong), argues that pedophilia is not biological, but a social and cultural problem. Ultimately, their questions and concerns remain unanswered. Panic over pedophilia and child sex abuse persists in the news, focusing more and more on the ways in which children may be endangered by new technologies. Thus, this season of *SVU* offers episodes about tech-savvy criminals, dangerous online predators, and child pornography. *SVU* stays current by feeding on contemporary issues in mainstream news and may add fuel to the fires under related moral panics.[16] The seventh season offers one very compelling episode that deals with child sex trafficking and another that confronts homophobic bullying in "9-1-1" and "Alien," respectively. Along with "Baby Killer," mentioned above, these episodes allow for discussion of distinct, yet fluid, discursive constructions of the child in *SVU*.

Imagining the Child

Before embarking on analysis, it is necessary, first, to explore how I use the terms "child," "childhood," and "victim," and what those terms have come to signify for me and for other scholars. The American child is an amalgamation of imagined and lived experiences and a shifting, ideological, discursive, social construct—a way to differentiate persons who are in the most visible state(s) of physical, mental, and emotional development, but are assumed to have not yet experienced puberty and therefore lack not only certain mental and emotional capabilities, but also, and perhaps most significantly, sexuality. Though such differentiation promotes dichotomous thinking and prejudice based on age and abstractions like maturity level, it would be misguided to ignore the conventional discourses of childhood.

The terms "child" and "children" in this chapter refer to the imagined prepubescent child who is generally construed as being asexual and therefore innocent; the term "youth," then, refers to the sexual adolescent or teen.[17] As James Kincaid argues, "Faced with the growing ease of access and frequency of sexual activity among young people . . . we may well have shifted innocence more decisively backward, onto younger and yet younger people. Along with innocence, we have loaded them with all its sexual allure."[18] While the child may be generally presented as asexual in popular media, the culture of erotic innocence that creates such representations can make the child an object of desire. Constructed within popular imagination under late capitalism, this child, then, is a complex of contradictions.

The discursive child is both innocent and beguiling, at once naïve and wise, always/already vulnerable, feminized, and inevitably victimized yet asexual, resilient, capable, and forgiving. For some, "Childhood is about impotence and weakness. Acceptable victimization is part of the visual repertoire with which the concept of childhood crosses and influences the concepts of race and class."[19] If childhood is inextricable from victimhood, then victimization must also be conceptualized here in relation to the intersecting forms of marginalization, oppression, and violence that distinguish childhoods. The images of children discussed in this chapter convey not only physical violence and endangerment of children, but also the formative and destructive power of the inequalities of age, race, gender, and socioeconomic class status that each child faces to a differing degree. But the child victim is not without contradiction. Though frequently imagined as victims, children also resist. Children disrupt the discursive ideals constructed around and through them. "The image of childhood poses the problem of generations, of continuity and renewal. Children are expected to mature into the established patriarchal order, yet they stand as a threat to that order."[20] The child is not simply a tragic figure of victimhood languishing under the weight of oppression or danger. When the child expresses herself, she challenges the systems that objectify her. Victimization prevents some children from symbolizing unlimited hope for the future, but children's resistance to victimization alters notions of what childhood can be and may even be recuperated among adults as justification for such hopefulness.

Christopher Jenks argues that Western societies no longer cling to the dependent child for a vision of a promising future, but rather rely on the child to reciprocate trust, respect, and love, having recognized the unattainability of such a future. He states that "children are now seen not so much as 'promise' but as primary and unequivocal sources of love, but also as partners in the most fundamental, unchosen, unnegotiated form of relationship. The trust that was previously anticipated from marriage partnership, friendship, class solidarity and so on, is now invested more generally in the child."[21] I would argue that, in the context of *SVU*, certain tenets of the idealized modern child do hold fast in post-modernity, such as the child as a symbol of futurity, longing, hope, and potential. If the child is now brought into partnerships with adults, acquiring certain rights and/or responsibilities, it also continues to function as a receptacle for adult hopes and desires. The child is envisioned as innocent until corrupted by time, knowledge, or experience—all of which are inevitable. The child can thus simultaneously call forth nostalgia for a frozen past and represent hope for the unknowable future. The inevitabilities of life, however, still render the child a tragic and hopeless figure. It is here, within the child victim, that compelling tensions lie—tensions created by the interplay between adult nostalgia and interiority, the adult desires and hopes to be carried by the child, and the cultural representations of the child's experience generated for adult consumption.

Yet, who is this illusive or imagined child, and whose desires does that child represent? The idealized or normative childhoods frequently theorized, though they are complex and contradictory in nature, do not directly reflect the differences that work to always/already position the child as a particular body functioning within particular power relations. As Jenks explains:

> Childhood is spoken about as: a "becoming;" as a *tabula rasa*; as laying down the foundations . . . growing up; preparation; inadequacy; inexperience; immaturity; and so on. Such metaphoricity all speaks of an essential and magnetic relation to an unexplicated, but nevertheless firmly established, rational adult world. This adult world is not only assumed to be complete, recognizable and in stasis, but also, and perhaps most significantly, desirable. It is a benevolent and coherent totality which extends a welcome to the child, invites him to cast off qualities that ensure his differences, and it encourages his acquiescence.[22]

Such conceptualizations of childhood must be further explored in terms of the differences that impact power relations and subjectivities. "Power is everywhere; not because it embraces everything, but because it comes from everywhere."[23] The project at hand does employ Foucault's notions of power as diffuse, interconnected, and woven within other relationships, yet his theorizations of violence, discipline, and criminality do not allow for the specificity of the body necessary to advance discussions of representations of children and childhood in *SVU*. As Joy James points out in her critique of *Discipline and Punish*, "Foucault . . . makes no mention of sexual and racial binary oppositions to designate social inferiority and deviancy as biologically inscribed on the bodies of nonmales or nonwhites."[24] The analyses that follow aim to illuminate the ways in which representations of children and discourses of childhood rely on such oppositions, especially when they confront issues of violence and criminality.

Dr. Neil Baer,[25] one of *SVU*'s executive producers is notable for his experience in pediatrics and focus on children's and adolescent health issues. He also worked as a producer of *ER* (1994-2009), an award-winning medical drama that aired for fifteen seasons on NBC.[26] Under his direction, writers, production crew, and cast members generate compelling characters and complex plots focused on the "most heinous offenses," to quote the introductory voice-over presented at the outset of each episode. Those offenses, according to *SVU*, often involve the sexual exploitation of children. The children portrayed on the show are constructed in relation to adults—most frequently in relation to adult perpetrators of crimes against them and the police detectives who work to avenge and/or protect them. Discourses about children and childhood manifest in the detectives' references to their own childhood memories and in their need to protect children from others. Remembered experiences, and the trauma and/or motivations that stem from those memories, influence the detectives' behaviors toward these "special" victims and toward criminals who exploit children and youths.

Similarly, the constant pressure to protect the children leaves the show with a dichotomy of adulthood that attempts to plainly separate sex offenders from non sex offenders. Regardless of the debates that may play out within many episodes over the nature of pedophilia or over whether or not a rapist can be rehabilitated, the show makes quite clear the fact that the detectives and their consultants are "good" in their constant efforts to protect children from those "bad" people who are capable of actually perpetrating those "most heinous" crimes against them. In those cases in which a child is the perpetrator of a violent crime, he or she is frequently also physically victimized or viewed as the tragic product of an ill society or poor parenting. But just as there are victims, there are survivors. The figure of the resilient child rears up repeatedly to challenge and disrupt dominant discourses that position children as tragic figures at the intersections of their multiple victimhoods. The sections that follow employ episodes of *SVU* that help illuminate a few of its distinct, sometimes contradictory, often overlapping constructions of the child, including the racialized child expected to be both victim and criminal, the child that functions as adult interiority, and the child whose story can only be told by others.

Children at War

The episode titled "Baby Killer" is well suited to this project for its richness of representation and complex characterizations. In a compelling sequence before the introductory titles, kids run and scream and play on an urban public school basketball court, enclosed by stone walls and metal gates. Some of the children have audible accents and speak Spanish to each other; the children are ethnically and racially diverse—many of them are black or Latino/a. A woman monitoring the children is distracted by a group of suspicious-looking young men who linger near one of the gates, talking to a pair of small boys. The entirety of the sequence is imbued with a gray pallor—the dinginess of the cement and stone, the dimness of the lighting where only indirect sunlight makes its way into this narrow playlot. The young men wear drab colors, their faces shaded by hats, their clothes baggy and nondescript; they defy her and swear at her. As the woman confronts them and begins to call for assistance on her radio, she hears a gunshot behind her. She turns and the children scream and scatter instantly. She runs to the aid of a six-year-old girl, who lies unmoving, wounded. In a high-angle crane shot, the woman crouches over the girl in the otherwise empty, gray lot. As she cries for help, an abandoned ball rolls languidly along. This woman and girl, both black, are framed here as utterly alone and desperate. The fact of their blackness is particularly significant in this moving scene before the introduction of the show's regular stars, the detectives. Jenny Kitzinger theorizes the discursive construction of black childhood:

> The images of children (usually white) represent, not individuals, but a concept. The image of a solitary black child would represent a different concept—racism means that while a white child can represent "Childhood" the black child is only used to represent *black* childhood, or "The Third World" or "Foreign" or "Starvation."[27]

Even in a series that represents racial minorities more often than other primetime programming does, the fact of racial difference (and here, I refer to the conventional binary that positions these black characters in opposition to the white detectives who star in every episode) is an early signal to the eventual unraveling of the narrative into what appears to be an unavoidable and unending cycle of racialized violence.

In the sequence that follows, Captain Cragen looks pained as he tries to reveal who is responsible for the young girl's murder. He seems unable to speak the details—the fact that the killer is a seven-year-old boy, a classmate of the victim. Detective Stabler is resigned to meeting criminals of a particular sort. "Great, bring on the pervert," he replies. But Cragen cannot correct him; all he can do is look toward two approaching officers, each with a hand on the shoulder of the small, docile boy. While there is no discussion of race until nearly the end of the episode, the boy, Elias (Nicolas Marti Salgado), and his parents (played by Sarah Ramirez and Robert Montano) are coded as ambiguously Latino/a or Hispanic, and during an initial hearing the boy is said to pose a flight risk since "the Barreras have ties outside the country." The family is not portrayed stereotypically, which may work to provide gravitas when the episode culminates in Elias being shot by a twelve-year-old boy named TJ (played by Donovan Ian H. McKnight), who screams, "Can't kill a sister and just walk!" The young black shooter yells at the cop shoving him toward his car, "I didn't do nothing." He at once admits his guilt and defends his act as "nothing." While this violence appears to be neatly contained within the space of just a few square miles and between Latino/a and black communities, it is also shown to have the potential to spread beyond those so-called borders.

Elias's parents are sympathetic characters. They arrive, panicked, at the police station, having lost sleep at the hospital with their infant daughter and worried about the news of their son. They appear to be educated and articulate, caring and supportive of each other and their son. They might be recognized as middle-class if they weren't forced to work multiple jobs in order to pay medical bills and send their son to a cheap and somewhat unsafe child-care provider while they spend time at the hospital. This family very nearly emulates all the ideals of middle-class whiteness, suggesting the interconnectedness of racial categories with notions of class, opening up the possibility for what ultimately becomes racially motivated violence to erupt, perhaps, in predominantly white or middle-class schools and homes rather than existing only in the gang-patrolled streets of poor, urban, and particularly raced spaces. Elias, then, is easily understood as a working-class kid, worthy of sympathy—a victim of his parents' inability to afford safer child care, but sympathetic because his parents work hard to support their family.

In their efforts to investigate why Elias would murder his classmate, the detectives are continuously faced with the realities of life in a systematically oppressive society in which people of color have limited choices and opportunities. Kitzinger writes, "In sensationalizing perpetrators' grosser *abuses* of power we forget the routine use of power over children . . . children are vulnerable because they *are* children—childhood is a state of oppression (an oppression compounded by discrimination based upon sex, race, class and disability)."[28] While the program focuses much time and effort on individualizing and psychoanalyzing the criminal acts portrayed, the drama regularly allows for, indeed, requires reflection on the larger social implications for and causes of those crimes. Benson and Stabler discover that Elias's babysitter is an elderly woman whose grandson uses Elias to distribute illegal drugs. Elias is depicted as an innocent and timid child who unknowingly falls victim to circumstances beyond his control. He witnesses a drug-related murder, and then escapes with a gun, so that the culprit, Machete, will not shoot him with it. Later, at the playlot, Elias sees Machete through the fence and shoots, killing his classmate by accident. When the assistant district attorney (Stephanie March) dismisses the charges against Elias, members of the press question whether or not there will be backlash, and local black citizens protest her decision on the grounds that murderers of black children should be put to trial and punished. Seemingly propelled by the momentum of these outcries, TJ takes it upon himself to avenge the girl's death by killing Elias and making his reason known. It is not difficult to envision the limitations on TJ's future as he is ushered away and locked firmly within the criminal justice system. Elayne Rapping reveals, "We are shocked and terrified by the specter of an ever younger population of poor blacks suddenly joining the ranks of the criminally vicious."[29] And she paraphrases Franklin Zimring's work on youth violence in which he points out that "we come to the obvious conclusion that such children can no longer be considered children, but must, somehow be seen and treated as adults."[30] Afterall, TJ is depicted as being fully aware of his crime. At twelve, with access to a loaded gun, and impassioned by a need to impose justice where the legal system will not—to punish the murder of black childhood—this boy is too experienced, too mature to be called a child.

It may be argued that the black child is discursively constructed as having been born into adulthood, never a child, never innocent in the way that white childhood is often imagined, and therefore less the vulnerable victim than the resilient survivor of inevitable injustice and harm. Certainly, the black child criminal, TJ, is here imagined as the inevitable result of the community in which he lives—a poor, violent, urban community, laden with the burdens and tensions of racially charged hostilities and oppression. While this episode of *SVU* offers complex characterizations of childhood, youth, race, and violent crime, the show's claims to realism prevent subversion of the systems of oppression within which its characters and events exist. The closest it gets is in instances of reflection like in the final moments, when Detective Stabler relates the violence he sees playing out between children in the streets of New York City to the bloody conflict between nations in the Gaza Strip. He mutters, "Welcome to the Gaza Strip . . . " at the conclusion of the episode. This final analogy works to remove the children in this story even further from the innocence of idealized American childhood. While the episode's first victim is a young black girl, silenced and quickly erased, its second victim is a shy Latino boy who finds his own experience and subsequent actions made invisible—just another replication of the drug-related violence of the youths and men who surround him. Finally, the program's third-youngest victim seems almost an afterthought as he easily kills Elias and shouts at once his admission of guilt and his claim to revenge or self-defense against an unfair system and is hauled away as Stabler digests the scene and reveals his anxieties over ongoing international violence. In these depictions of childhood, children themselves are repeatedly victimized, both by a narrative that cannot allow them to survive as children as well as by a twisting plot that enacts violence against them as particularly marginalized, raced, and classed young bodies.

Ultimately, the child, whether a survivor or perpetrator, functions as a victim in *SVU*; otherwise, he is not recognizable as a child. And that victimization works, in conjunction with multiple forms of marginalization by age, race, ethnicity, class, and gender, to "other" the child, to alienate the child by implicating the child in his or her own suffering or further victimization. According to John Fiske's reading of Colin MacCabe, "an essential formal characteristic of realism is that it is always structured by a "hierarchy of discourses" and "a realistic narrative will contain a range of different and often contradictory discourses."[31] A hierarchy of discourses here allows the dominant discourses of idealized, innocent, white, middle-class American childhood to supplant racially or ethnically specific characterizations such that the child who has not been inducted directly into adulthood by the experiences associated with living in a racially diverse community functions only as a perpetual victim—in much the same way the imagined or idealized child does. But this submersion of discourses specific to nonwhite and lower-class childhoods in popular media representations echoes the marginalization of nonwhite and lower-class lives, thus perpetuating the representation of erasure and silencing of marginalized peoples on institutional and symbolic levels, to say nothing of the physical and psychological violence played out on these bodies. Such is the violence of representing childhood in these and the examples that follow—structural, symbolic, and material violences are enacted in these representations.

The Invisible, Invincible Child

This project is limited to analyses of just a few episodes from a lengthy series. Without overgeneralizing, these examples should illustrate some of the complexities of representations of childhood that are exchanged between adult network producers and audience members.[32] Such representations both perpetuate and complicate the dominant construction of early twenty-first century childhood. Chris Jenks writes of a new vision of the child as more independent than dependent, fulfilling the needs of adults by engaging in the economic, emotional, and cultural labors required by the family under late capitalism. For him the child is no longer a beacon of hope for a better tomorrow, but since that tomorrow never comes—since tomorrow the child will be nearer to adulthood—the child has become partially responsible for the functioning of the family at present and is recognized in relation only to the loss of childhood, to adult nostalgia for the inner child and for the imagined childhood of the past. But these childhoods—the childhood of nostalgia and the childhood that promises the future—coexist, tugging constantly at one another.

In the *SVU* episode titled "9-1-1," a nine-year-old Honduran girl named Maria (played by Rachel Diaz-Stand) dials 9-1-1 to report that she is being held captive against her will. Because the call is from an audibly frightened and endangered young girl, it is forwarded to Detective Benson, who must spend nearly the entire length of the show coaxing information out of the girl in order to try and locate her. The episode is primarily focused on Benson's experience, with close-ups of her talking on the phone, suppressing tears, crying, holding her head in frustration at the difficulty of locating and saving Maria. In fact, the child remains invisible—a disembodied voice—until about midway through the episode when Benson locates an old file of photos that match Maria's description. Maria reveals that she is being held captive by a man who "does bad things to [me]" and who lets his friends do them too. Benson, herself the product of her mother's rape and subsequent alcoholism (facts laid out plainly in the first episode and revisited throughout the series), clings desperately to Maria through the photos, the speakerphone, and the portable receiver. Maria and her case files reveal that she has been molested, photographed, raped—bought and sold into sexual slavery. This devastating victimization at the hands of countless men drives Benson and the other detectives on a desperate and impossible hunt.

While many episodes use still photographs to represent their young victims, this one relies also on the child's voice—her sleepy yawns, her songs, her fear and sadness, her pleas to be found and to be fed. This child is utterly dependent both on her captor to keep her alive and now on Benson to save her from him—to reconnect the body with the voice. While it may be difficult to envision this particular child as the child of modernity that Jenks speaks of, as the symbol of hope and progress, she is symbolic of Benson's passion and desire to protect. Benson is so driven that, seemingly against all odds and with a bit of luck, she eventually does find Maria. And while she appears to be too late, Maria having been shoved in a garbage bag and buried alive in a vacant lot, Benson eventually completes her mission. She digs her out of the dirt on her hands and knees, pulls her out into the open, tears at the bag and resuscitates Maria. Benson brings Maria back to life—rebirths her—at once suggesting the resilience and potential of the child to combat anything and everything she endures and also exhibiting Benson's deep need to believe in the possibility of a better life for the tortured child—and for herself. Maria gets to start anew, and Benson avoids despair over never being able to see the girl whose cries she's been trying to answer. While Maria relies wholeheartedly on Benson to save her life—even to erase the negativity of the life she's had—she also acts independently and exists to some extent in Benson's mind as any missing child might, calling forth Benson's own wish for a happy childhood. Though Maria is subjected to brutalities that she cannot control—including those perpetrated by adult men who abuse the privileges of patriarchy, whiteness, and socioeconomic class distinction—Maria's resilience and resourcefulness upset the economy of human trafficking that her captors have created. Maria is not only imagined as a tragic victim of sexualization and exoticism, but she is an agentic subject in the survival of those things, at least to the limited extent allowed her in a narrative that sustains itself on the disconnection of her voice and body. Benson's needs and desires appear to take precedence in this episode, but it is Maria's refusal to give up—her survival—that redeems Benson. In this way, Maria may simultaneously represent Jenks's idea of futurity and the nostalgia that afflicts the popular consciousness in postmodernity. But even more than this, Maria can represent the challenge to patriarchy and the disruption of accepted systems of oppression presented by agentic childhood.

In "9-1-1" Maria is rarely seen in the flesh, but a dialect expert brought in by the district attorney's office recognizes her Honduran accent and determines that she must be an immigrant. Rather than function as a threat to the ideal of "innocent and natural" (read: white, middle-class) childhood, Maria falls victim to otherness in the face of that ideal. Indeed, Maria's captor is a white middle-class man who "owns" and abuses her, keeping her locked away in a dungeon room covered in floral wallpaper and pink and white furnishings. The scene is set to accentuate Maria's youth, femininity, and innocence, and works both to exoticize her as a dark-haired, immigrant child as well as to position her within a comforting, American, middle-class dream of girlhood in attempts to mask her difference. The argument could be made that children of color are represented quite frequently in need of protection on *SVU*—often from the white middle-class ideals that threaten their well-being each day.

But what is the significance of subverting ideals of blonde, female, middle-class childhood vulnerability in this way? As the working-class girl becomes a more visible victim, she is further sexualized and further removed from the possibilities of normative childhood (whatever they may be). "A child who is known to be a victim of sexual abuse is often subject to further exploitation."[33] The "too sexual" girl, the working-class girl, the non-blonde, then, are envisioned as also already victimized and therefore more vulnerable to abuse and always, inevitably further from safety. In the context of *SVU*, the child's position in the ranks of idealized, presexual youth—her access to innocence and vulnerability and naïveté, her supposed inability to interpret her own story—excuses the child from responsibility or agency. When this "innocent" child is victimized, then, she becomes knowledgeable and is no longer a child. She becomes implicated in her own victimization and, as the next section will show, she may even become the criminal suspect and perpetrator.

The Dishonest Child

In his writing about criminal trials involving child sexual abuse, James Kincaid argues that the victimized child acts as a vessel for adult desires and is silenced in the process. The child can become "our main but stereotypical character, the empty and violated child whose story we know so well there is no need for [him] now to tell it: we hear it from within ourselves, spoken by our needs."[34] For Kincaid, the child sexual abuse victim "becomes an empty signifier, or rather, an infinitely plural one" since the child is viewed as completely honest and incapable of interpreting its own story.[35] In the *SVU* episode titled, "Alien," the plot twists its way from one suspect to the next, generating victims along the way until an eight-year-old girl, Emma (played by Raquel Castro), is revealed to be the perpetrator of the initial crime against her twelve-year-old classmate. Among the twists are substantiated accusations of physical abuse, bullying, and homophobic discrimination, and, ultimately, false accusations of child sexual abuse. After a boy is dumped from a car at the hospital, bleeding from a stab wound that leaves him paralyzed from the waist down, questioning begins. When Detective Benson and her partner, Detective Stabler, meet Emma, she is staying at her grandparents' house while her mother is in the hospital suffering from lupus. Emma, looking thin and small in pink pajamas, corroborates her older brother's story, and since he is the primary suspect in the stabbing, the detectives assume she is lying to protect him. Emma's grandmother is appalled at the suggestion that her granddaughter might not be telling the truth, but Benson knows instantly from the confidence Emma displays and the innocence she clearly knows too well how to portray that this child is lying. By the end of the episode, it's clear that the detectives believed Emma was innocent, but were not taken in by the "myth of a spotlessly honest child."[36] No matter how much Emma's family wants and needs for her to be telling the truth and no matter that Emma herself recites what she has learned in her Catholic school that "lies are vanilla sins, not mortal sins . . . but all sins are bad and that's why you should never ever do them," this child has made a choice to tell the story in such a way that protects both herself and her brother.

When Emma's biological mother dies in the hospital, Emma becomes the site of heightened tension in a custody battle between her grandmother and her other mother—"Mommy Zoey," her mother's lover and life partner. Emma's grandmother coaches her as she accuses Zoey of molesting her, but the department's psychiatrist recognizes her description as too intellectual and diagnoses Emma with parental alienation syndrome (PAS). Emma's torturous school life is at the root of her crime—the other students harass and bully her because she has two mothers. And her grandmother takes advantage of Emma's anxiety over her parents' relationship by explaining that it is against nature and against God. Thus, for Emma, anything Zoey does can now be construed as a sin because she is a lesbian, including those instances of potential evidence dug up by her grandmother—naked photos of Emma, taken by her mothers to "give her a positive body image," and massages administered to relieve stress at the direction of Emma's therapist. In her attempts to perpetuate an image of Emma as uncorrupted, innocent and honest, Emma's grandmother maps onto her certain desires and the hope that she can correct the mistake of queerness committed by her own daughter, Emma's mother. But efforts to bring the mythic child to life rely on a disavowal of the actual child, since it "empties out the child and makes it incapable of any independent action or thought."[37] In trying to preserve Emma's innocence and honesty, her grandmother forces Emma to lie and to deny her own actions. Paradoxically, Emma's grandmother's belief that her granddaughter is incapable of lying or of violence is exactly what leads her to manipulate Emma into lying about violence committed against her. Her grandmother's awareness of how Emma has been harassed and bullied at school leads her easily to believe that she also may have been victimized in other ways, elsewhere. This child then functions as a pawn in adult battles and as a sort of vehicle for adults' perceptions of what the child should be, what life should be, and for how adults relate to one another.

"Alien" is especially interesting in that it revolves less around its initial victim, the twelve-year-old boy, and more around Emma, who has stabbed him in retaliation for cutting off her ponytail and making her "ugly" and for taunting her with homophobic rants. While *SVU* episodes commonly focus on locating criminals with the help of victims and witnesses, this one finds its victim is also its primary criminal. Emma's story becomes central to the narrative precisely because she is victimized or manipulated by almost everyone in her life and is therefore continuously vulnerable to exploitation. Similar representations of children whose suffering leads to violence reverberate not only throughout popular television, but also off-screen, in the frequent displacement of blame onto seemingly uncontrollable societal ills (such as lacking legal protections for children's rights, poverty, and panics over kidnapping, sex abuse, and serial murder among other crimes) or demonized individuals (bad parents, pedophiles, murderers) and the subsequent denial of the child's ability to think, speak, and act independently. While this show enters into complex negotiations between various ways in which the child is imagined in contemporary society, it perpetuates dominant ideologies of childhood innocence, dependence, and vulnerability, which may work to erase or silence children—especially at sites of moral panic.

Conclusion

As these analyses of children in *Law & Order: Special Victims Unit* indicate, the child functions in multiple, contradictory ways. The show's claims to realism and its attention to child victims make its representations significant to discourses of childhood. If *SVU* works to represent, in some instances, the treatment of children in contemporary society, then it is in our best interest to explore the discursive construction of the child victim not simply as a representation of the experiences of a few actual children, but as always/already representative of the framework within which society *imagines*, and therefore may silence or erase, children. *SVU*'s child victims are at once inherently vulnerable to victimization and resilient enough to outlive it. While the hopeless inevitability of adulthood signified by the development or acquisition of certain forms of awareness, experience, and physicality (usually sexual) make the child of color an always/already mortal, fallible, and tragic figure, the continuous discourses of innocence, malleability, and honesty construct the idealized white, middle-class child as invincible, pure, incorruptible until she reaches a certain age. Class and/or gender distinctions may allow children of color to "pass" in some regards as "pure" or uncorrupted, yet such passing works most often in these representations to threaten the ideals of whiteness as it allows for racialized violence(s) to cross cultural boundaries. Competing discourses, then, create tensions that render any child a site for conflicting adult desires and anxieties. These tensions are by no means new, nor are they unique to popular television. They are, however, worth interrogating for instances in which they might reveal the discursive connections between childhood and victimhood and point to the ideological significance of such connections. Given opportunities for further study, it would be helpful to analyze the series' characterization of child sexual abuse and pedophilia, discussing in greater detail the hierarchy of discourses at work in these and other episodes, as well as to explore the character relationships that drive the show, and to more closely analyze the work of the child victim to call forth the child within, adult memory, nostalgia, and interiority—in what forms and to what end.

Notes

1. Multiple media outlets have referred to the "CSI effect" as a possible explanation for Anthony's acquittal, positioning jurors as disappointed in the lack of scientific evidence while naturalizing the impossible expectations raised by the effects-heavy presentation of evidence in television programs like *CSI*.

2. Glenn Selig, "Comments on Casey Anthony." *PRNews*.

3. Episode 19 of season 10, "Selfish," aired on April 28, 2009, guest starring Hilary Duff as Ashlee Walker, a character inspired by Casey Anthony, whose daughter's body was found in December 2008 after she'd been missing for several months.

4. Selig.

5. The most recent primetime incarnations of the franchise (which also includes a series of video games and a made-for-TV movie) are *Law & Order: Criminal Inten,t* which aired from 2001–2007 on NBC, then moved to the USA Network, and *Law & Order: LA* which was canceled after only one season in 2011.

6. Anon., "National Briefing," *New York Times*, August 9, 2001, http://www.nytimes.com/2001/08/09/us/national-briefing-south-florida-judge-rules-man-may-let-wife-die.html (accessed April 29, 2012).

7. Over 5,000 children went missing after Hurricane Katrina. *New York Times*, March 3, 2006, www.nytimes.com/2006/03/01/national/nationalspecial/01missing.html (accessed April 29, 2012).

8. Fiske, 29.

9. Fiske, 34.

10. While it is not my project to determine the connections between episodes and real-life events, one book by Kevin Dwyer and Jure Fiorillo does just that. *True Stories of*

Law & Order: Special Victims Unit documents some of the episodes from the first eight seasons of *SVU* that reference actual crimes in the news.

11. Fiske, 34.
12. Britto, 47.
13. Britto, 44.
14. Walkerdine, 4.
15. Other members of the alternating cast of ADAs include Michaela McManus as Kim Greylek, Melissa Sagemiller as Gillian Hardwicke, Angie Harmon as Abbie Carmichael, along with a host of others who appeared in four or fewer episodes.
16. An interesting example is the impact of false testimony about a nonexistent episode of *Law & Order* (though not *SVU*) in the Andrea Yates case. *New York Times* query.nytimes.com/gst/fullpage.html?res=9902E7DC1139F934A35752C0A9639C8B63 &sec=health (accessed April 29, 2012).
17. If the prepubescent child is defined by its lack of sexuality, then the adult is defined by its perceived knowledge and experience of sex and/or a greater degree of physical development, but also, legally, as any person aged eighteen years or over.
18. Kincaid, 54.
19. Holland, 159.
20. Holland, 20.
21. Jenks, 107.
22. Jenks, 9.
23. Foucault 1995, 93.
24. James, 26.
25. Having studied pediatrics in Los Angeles and at Harvard, Baer also taught in an elementary school and has written regularly for a teen magazine on teen health and sexuality.
26. *ER* was one of the hit series that increased ratings for the NBC network, then under the watchful eye of programming chief Warren Littlefield, who had a shaky start in 1992 after some of his predecessor Brandon Tartikoff's hit programs ended. Before hiring Tartikoff, the network had struggled to capture and maintain substantial audience attention since the 1970s.
27. Kitzinger in James & Prout, 166.
28. Kitzinger in James & Prout, 176.
29. Rapping, 225.
30. Rapping, 225.
31. Fiske, 25.
32. According to a 2006 article in the *L.A. Times*, *SVU* has a median viewer age of 49 years (James).
33. Kitzinger (1988), 80.
34. Kincaid, 193.
35. Kincaid, 211.
36. Kincaid, 211.
37. Kincaid, 211.

Works Cited

Althusser, Louis (1971). "Ideology and Ideological State Apparatuses" in *Cultural Theory & Popular Culture*. Ed. John Storey. Athens: University of Georgia Press, 1998.

Britto, Sarah, Tycy Hughes, Kurt Saltzman and Colin Stroh (2007). "Does 'Special' Mean Young, White and Female? Deconstructing the Meaning of 'Special' in Law & Order: Special Victims Unit" in *Journal of Criminal Justice and Popular Culture* 14 (1) 2007.

Crain, Patricia (1999). "Childhood as Spectacle" in *American Literary History* Vol. 11, No. 3, 545–553. Autumn, 1999.

Cuklanz, Lisa M. and Sujata Moorti (2006). "Television's 'New' Feminism: Prime-Time Representations of Women and Victimization" in *Critical Studies in Media Communication* Vol. 23, No. 4, 302–321, October, 2006.

Dwyer, Kevin and Jure Fiorillo (2007). *True Stories of Law & Order: Special Victims Unit*. New York: Berkeley Boulevard Books.

Fiske, John (1987). *Television Culture*. New York: Routledge.

Foucault, Michel (1990). *The History of Sexuality, Vol. 1, An Introduction*, second American edition. New York: Vintage Books.

———. (1995). *Discipline and Punish: The Birth of the Prison*, second American edition. New York: Vintage Books.

Holland, Patricia (2004). *Picturing Childhood: The Myth of the Child in Popular Imagery*. New York: I.B. Taurus & Co. Ltd.

James, Allison and Alan Prout, Eds. (2005). *Constructing and Reconstructing Childhood: Contemporary Issues in the Sociological Study of Childhood*, second edition. Taylor & Francis e-Library; London: Falmer Press.

James, Joy (1996). *Resisting State Violence: Radicalism, Gender, and Race in U.S. Culture*. Minneapolis: University of Minnesota Press.

James, Meg (2006). "'Law and Order' Creator Gets Fresh" *L.A. Times* January 22, 2006. Web. December 14, 2008. articles.latimes.com/2006/jan/22/business/fi-wolf22>.

Jenkins, Philip (1998). *Moral Panic: Changing Concepts of the Child Molester in Modern America*. New Haven, CT: Yale University Press.

Jenks, Chris (2002). *Childhood*. New York: Routledge.

Kincaid, James (1998). *Erotic Innocence: The Culture of Child Molesting*. Durham, NC: Duke University Press.

Kitzinger, Jenny (1988). "Defending Innocence: Ideologies of Childhood" in *Feminist Review* No. 28, *Family Secrets: Child Sexual Abuse*, Spring 1988, 77–87.

———. (2004). *Framing Abuse: Media Influence and Public Understandings of Sexual Violence against Children*. London: Pluto Press.

Lane, Philip J. (2004). "The Existential Condition of Television Crime Drama" in *Journal of Popular Culture* Vol. 34, Iss. 4, March 5, 2004, 137–151.

Law & Order: Special Victims Unit, "About the Show" Retrieved on December 14, 2008 at www.nbc.com/Law_and_Order_Special_Victims_Unit/about/index.shtml .

MacCabe, Colin (1981)."Realism and the Cinema: Notes on Some Brechtian Theses." In *Popular Television and Film*. Ed. T. Bennett et al. London: Open University Press/BFI, 216-235.

Phillips, Adam (1998). *The Beast in the Nursery*. London: Faber and Faber Limited.

Postman, Neil (1982). *The Disappearance of Childhood.* New York: Delacorte Press.
Prout, Alan (2005). *The Future of Childhood: Towards the Interdisciplinary Study of Children.* New York: RoutlegdeFalmer.
Rapping, Elayne (2003). *Law and Justice as Seen on TV.* New York: New York University Press.
Selig, Glenn (2011). "Comments on Casey Anthony Trial from Crisis Management Public Relations and Entertainment PR Expert." PRNewsChannel.com. Selig Multimedia, Inc. July 6, 2011. Web. July 12, 2011.
Sumser, John (1996). *Morality and Social Order in Television Crime Drama.* Jefferson, NC: McFarland.
Walkerdine, Valerie (1997). *Daddy's Girl: Young Girls and Popular Culture.* Cambridge, MA: Harvard University Press.
Zimring, Franklin (1998). *American Youth Violence.* New York: Oxford University Press.

Chapter Eight
"Better Multiculturalism" through Technology: *Dora the Explorer* and the Training of the Preschool Viewer(s)
by Drew Chappell

> By the late twentieth century, our time, a mythic time, we are all chimeras, theorized and fabricated hybrids of machine and organism; in short, we are cyborgs. This cyborg is our ontology; it gives us our politics.
>
> —Haraway, 149

Arizona, April 23, 2010. Governor Jan Brewer, promoted from Secretary of State when Governor Janet Napolitano left office to serve as the Secretary of Homeland Security under Barack Obama, signs Senate Bill 1070, giving state police broad power to detain and question those people they suspect of being undocumented immigrants to the United States ("Arizona Enacts Stringent Law on Immigration," "Senate Bill 1070"). This legislation has touched off a firestorm of controversy, inspiring protest on both sides of the immigration issue. Emboldened by perceived support for such draconian policies, conservative lawmakers and education officials in Arizona followed up SB 1070 with a ban on ethnic studies ("Arizona Bill Targeting Ethnic Studies Signed into Law") and a crackdown on teachers who speak English with an accent ("Arizona Grades Teachers on Fluency"). In 2011 a bill denying birth certificates to children born in the United States to undocumented individuals is expected was introduced but defeated in Arizona (Rau 2011).

Four years earlier, in the 2006 midterm election, citizens in Arizona, Colorado, and New Mexico voted on measures aimed at discouraging "illegal immigration" from Mexico and South America. Among these measures were Arizona's Propositions 103, which would establish English as the official language of the state, and 300, which would deny public program eligibility to any person who was not a lawful resident of the United States (Arizona Secretary of State's Office). Both propositions passed into law. These were not the only attempts to respond to perceived abuses of immigration policy. Bilingual education had previously been targeted; in 2000, Arizona banned bilingual programs in schools and established English as the only instructional language.

In this politically charged climate, the Nickelodeon Jr. show *Dora the Explorer*, featuring a bilingual English/Spanish speaking girl and her friends, remained a television hit, with 21.9 million viewers in November 2005 in the United States (Wingett). Preschool children (who are approximately ages 2.5–5 in the United States) watched on television what they were discouraged from encountering in their daily lives: a Spanish speaking girl who, together with her diverse group of friends, leaves her home and family and crosses multiple borders with impunity in order to pursue various objectives.

Dora the Explorer (*Dora*) constitutes a cultural phenomenon; the television show's popularity has spawned a host of commercial products including toys, games, clothing, books, music albums, and home furnishings. In fact, in the 2006 holiday season, Dora was the number one toy license (Frenck 2). The show has won numerous awards, including a Peabody (for Broadcast Media) in 2003 and two Imagens (for positive portrayal of Latino characters/culture) in 2003 and 2004 ("Awards for Dora" 1–4). It also spun off a second show featuring Dora's cousin Diego, called *Go, Diego, Go*. The show's reach and its cultural currency led me to choose *Dora* as a research site. Even before I had a preschool-age child, I could not escape the show's marketing and media coverage. I wondered what was behind its popularity. What specific narratives and performances did the show employ, and how did it construct dominant and subaltern identities that contribute to what I have elsewhere called "colonizing the imaginary": "an ideological process in which adults write their own culturally bound values, beliefs, and ideas onto narrative structures and performances intended for children's consumption (Chappell 18)?"

To interrogate this topic, I chose twelve episodes of the show that represented a cross-section of the show's storytelling strategies. I watched special double-length episodes ("Dora's Pirate Adventure," "Dora Saves the Mermaids," "Dora's World Adventure"), and standard episodes that reflected a number of tropes, ideas, and curricular goals. In watching these episodes, I paid close attention to the narratives created and the ways they called for children's embodiment—physically (speaking back to the show, moving with Dora), relationally (identifying with Dora and Boots's problems), and ideologically (grappling with the issues and values presented in the show, such as friendship). As I watched the program, with its deceptively simple formula and insistence on communicating directly to its audience, I became aware of subtle ways that the characters engage in an implicit dialog around multiculturalism (more on this term later). There is certainly more to *Dora* than there appears; the show cleverly uses surface-level representations to engage complex social and political concepts (perhaps without the viewer's awareness). Once I collected data, I used typologies and assertion development to analyze my findings. I created the typologies based on a semiotic reading of the *Dora* episodes in relation to contextual information found in the sites and spaces surrounding the show. This context included intended social use, promotional material, contemporary political discourse, and *Dora* merchandising outside the show itself. The typologies allowed for interpretation and analysis of the data (Bogdan and Biklen, Wolcott), and pointed toward a common theme put forth by the image of Dora as cultural traveler who bears the markings of a number of different subaltern identities, from a white middle-class U.S. perspective (non white, female, child, Spanish speaker), and uses networks of friends and various technologies to solve each issue she faces. I then used assertion development (Erickson) to construct a theoretical understanding of the nature of embodiment and power in the show, as follows: *Dora the Explorer suggests that technology is the road to a multicultural society, and this society will focus on similarities rather than differences.*

Television as Performance

Children's television enters the child's own space; it "invades" the private sphere of the home via a broadcast signal, cable, or other device. To watch a program, young people must gather around a television screen, often located in a common area where parents can monitor their children's viewing. Watching television is a bit like a small-scale film screening; a screen becomes the center of focus, and images tell the story. Unlike in a movie theater, however, a child can feel free to move around as much as desired, take breaks, or "multitask," playing with toys, books, and so on while watching. Also, the characters on a television screen are (typically) miniaturized, easily controlled by the viewer (wielding a remote). This use of space may lead to a familiarity, an intimacy between viewer and television character(s). There is a sense that the program is "only for me," although I know there are many others watching the same program, not being able to see them "erases" their presence. Television uses time in specific, regimented ways; programs appear according to a schedule, thus allowing the practice of viewing to become routinized. On non public broadcasting channels (such as Nick Jr.—Dora's network) programs are "interrupted" for commercial content—product and service advertising. There is a "rhythm" to watching television shows and waiting out commercials—an embodied sense of when the program will institute a twist or when a commercial is coming up. Like other media, TV trains users (starting in childhood) in its effective use.

Like film, television controls the viewer's gaze through its use of camera shots. These are typically more "claustrophobic" than in film, as many shows are filmed in studios using sets that are reused from week to week. Animated programs like *Dora* add another layer of mediation; they offer two-dimensional representations of people, places, and objects that the audience recognizes from outside experience. These referents, however, are recombined, exaggerated, and otherwise distorted through the animation process until they become more simulacra than simulations (Baudrillard). As in comic books, the tendency is for animated settings and events to transcend reality. In these worlds, extraordinary things may happen quite easily, as the animator's only limitation is what he or she can draw. Animation sets up a fantastic realm in which rules are malleable, conflict is explicitly handled, and objectives are clearly defined. Animated characters, again like their comic book counterparts, tend to be less psychologically complex and more emblematic. They bear only a passing resemblance to actual people, typically having one characteristic that defines and limits them.

As with film, television audiences are expected to sit relatively quietly and pay attention to what is happening on-screen. However, as mentioned above, television offers more opportunity for freedom of movement and "outside" actions. Typically, the viewing experience is framed as "passive," an engagement with the screen images connotes a detachment with the world at large. Much is made in the media of television's detrimental effects on children's health, as television replaces more "active" entertainment (I use quotes with active and passive to suggest that the dichotomous framing of these terms is troubling in light of the [potential] critical and semiotic activity performed while watching television). *Dora*'s creators specifically sought to get children's bodies moving when they view the program. They built in multiple opportunities for children to speak back to the characters and engage in other physical activities. The desired outcome of such a strategy is to make the viewer feel even closer to the characters, as if he or she is inhabiting and exploring Dora's world alongside her.

Most television programs have a two-pronged narrative strategy. They try to create stand-alone episode; so that viewers will have a complete experience during the half-hour or hour they spend watching. But producers also want to reward faithful viewing, and so they create larger narratives that build slowly over time. In the case of *Dora*, this larger story is not as explicitly handled; episodes are self-contained and similar, and the "rewards" for repeat viewing are a knowledge of minor characters and following Dora through multiple settings and genres and watching her persona flourish in each. The strategy of giving viewers a little at a time is part of the training process; like giving an animal a treat when it performs a desired action, a show that comes on at a specific time offers an anticipated and constant return. But children's knowledge of this predictable structure within an episode is also a form of power.

Dora, Her World, and Borders

Dora revolves around a young Latina girl and her friends traveling through various landscapes in search of missing articles or characters, or collaborating on a group objective. Each show follows a similar format, based around the narrative style and strategies of a computer game. Dora and Boots, her monkey best friend, introduce themselves, and a complication emerges. To achieve their objective, they call upon Map, a talking, rolled-up map who identifies a series of locations to which they must travel. Often during their journey, they encounter Swiper the Fox, who attempts to steal an item that Dora needs. Sometimes Swiper succeeds, and sometimes Dora and Boots foil him by chanting "Swiper, no swiping!" three times. Also on the journey, Dora utilizes her backpack (herself a character) to retrieve some necessary item from the myriad of objects she contains. Eventually, Dora and her friends achieve their objective, and sing a victory song: "We Did It." They then ask the viewer to recall his/her "favorite part" of the journey, before sharing their own. Every show follows this formula; elements such as locations, objects needed, and characters encountered may change, but the journey structure never alters.

Dora takes place in a borderland; its main character speaks two languages and Dora seems caught between Mexican and U.S. culture. Author/theorist Gloria Anzaldúa defines borders as more than physical boundaries: "Borders are set up to define the places that are safe and unsafe, to distinguish *us* from *them*. A border is a dividing line, a narrow strip along a steep edge. A borderland is a vague and undetermined space created by the emotional residue of an unnatural boundary" (3). I find this definition a useful space to begin talking about the discourse around Dora's explorations. Although Dora lives in a borderland, the only "borders" she encounters are spaces between locations, which are easily traversed. In her travels, she might be seen as a *border crosser*—someone who belongs to multiple cultures simultaneously and is able to move freely between and among them. Anzaldúa suggests that those who exist in this state are often feared, mocked, or seen as illegitimate, but Dora encounters no such prejudice. Although she holds several real-world markers of the historically subaltern or marginalized—female, nonwhite, child, Spanish speaker—she is centered in her own constructed society, and so represents the dominant identity (yet the audience has intertextual knowledge of her as a marginalized identity—at least in the U.S.).

By dominant identity, I mean that Dora represents a normative middle class U.S. childhood. She lives in a home, attends school, plays safely with her friends, and does not worry about money for meals (in fact, she sometimes gives Boots money when he doesn't have it available, as in "Ice Cream"). Her mother is an archaeologist, as we learn in "Job Day," but her father's employment (if any) is not addressed. He is mostly seen cooking and caring for Dora's younger siblings. As she is represented as a normative U.S. child, Dora also demonstrates the strategy of "selective incorporation of cultural elements from the various cultural worldviews and practices to which [she] has been exposed during . . . her life" (Chen, Benet-Martínez, and Bond 806). This reflects her positioning as bicultural within a globalized/mediatized environment.

Could Dora's border identity point to a growing knowledge and expectation of multicultural identity? Educational theorists Cameron McCarthy and Greg Dimitriades describe the current social condition: "Indeed, if this is an era of the 'post,' it is also an era of difference—and the challenge of this era of difference is the challenge of living in a world of incompleteness, discontinuity, and multiplicity" (202). This paradigm organizes Dora's world, with its border-crossing protagonist and easy acceptance of various cultural backgrounds against an external lived backdrop of controversy over immigration policy and border politics. The show may aspire to Homi Bhabha's discursive "Third Space," with narratives and environments focused not around cultural distinction, but hybridity. In *Dora*, speaking more than one language is taken for granted and imparted as useful. In her world, various cultures (and even species) collaborate and celebrate their common goals and values. In fact, the show represents a liberal humanist societal outlook in which differences are minimized and unity centered.

Yet, the ethos of the *Dora* show also reflects some of the troubling discourse around the term "multiculturalism." Rusom Bharucha writes: "There is almost an in-built expectation written into the 'multi' which assumes that 'we *have* to get along and live together.' In short, it would seem to deny the 'right to exit' a particular society or to subvert the premises of 'living together'" (10). When presented to young people, is the ideology associated with use of this term a forward-looking worldview? Or, does it seek to establish a basic and official knowledge to which all cultures should be exposed in order to mold their cultural understandings while keeping their folkloric character (Torres 198)? In other words, is Dora's border crossing transgressive, challenging accepted notions of identity as "this" or "that," or is it monolithic, attempting to homogenize multiple blended identities into a singular "human" experience? Do the characters in *Dora* have the "right to exit" their common journeys and objectives, or to question the ways in which these objectives are pursued?

Bilingualism and Border Identities

At the beginning of most *Dora* episodes, she greets the audience: "Hola! Soy Dora!" Boots joins in: "And I'm Boots." This bilingual greeting sets the tone for the show, which includes dialogue in both Spanish and English. One of the stated goals of *Dora*'s creators was to teach Spanish vocabulary ("More about Dora" 1), and so episodes introduce Spanish words for numbers, greetings, and simple phrases. Some of these are translated into English, and some are not; the viewer must make meaning of the non-translated words through context. Yet, although the program includes bilingual elements, in its U.S. form, the "default language" is English. A child who spoke no Spanish at all would have no trouble following the narrative of Dora's journey.

Media and communications scholar Richard Popp suggests that the bilingual nature of *Dora* distinguishes the show within the field of educational programming. The focus on language learning becomes a motivation for parents to encourage their children to watch the show: "Language becomes a means of advancing into the upper echelons of education, work, and even taste groups. Bilingualism can open doors and act as a symbol of one's tolerance and refinement" (17). He points out, however, that parents of children watching the show must value the cultural capital associated with being bilingual. They must also have the means to "take the next step" and provide assistance to their children in order for them to progress beyond the simple words and phrases the show teaches (12). This attention to the *kind* of bilingualism being taught by *Dora* is important; the show's educative merit is in teaching English speaking children beginning Spanish, not in assisting Spanish speakers to maintain their language. (This is also true of dual-language schools in Arizona, which can only be attended by English-proficient students—there is no provision for using Spanish to develop English-speaking skills.) Essentially, Dora is a "helpful native," a guide whose purpose is to introduce her own language to outsiders, and to translate for them when they encounter unfamiliar contexts. But where does Dora "live"? What is the terrain the show guides the audience through?

Dora's home is not specifically located in a single country, but more of a borderland, a "no-place/everyplace." This home space is a verdant landscape with tropical trees and green hills. Dora's family's house has a Spanish tile roof, and the walls around its door and windows are painted with turquoise designs. The landscape and animal clues—Dora's friends include an iguana, monkey, and bull—seem to locate the show in Mexico or South America, but even this is a computer game-style simulation, a politically charged sedimentation of U.S. fantasies of travel/exploration/colonization. Because she lives in this borderland, Dora seems to be a cultural hybrid, a combination of multiple traditions and folkloric elements. She is drawn as a Latina girl, but plays out (for example) European fairy tale and transatlantic pirate narratives. In an interview, one of the show's writers stated: "We often combine a Latino character with a fable character. But really, it's all a legacy of imagery" (Sigler 43). The "legacy of imagery" the writer speaks of suggests a view of Dora as symbolically formed from multiple imaginary strains. She is a multicultural cipher, a hybrid in the most surface-level sense of Bhabha's meaning. Without a specific racial or ethnic identity, each viewer can "download" his or her own cultural background onto Dora, molding her into whatever that child or adult needs or wants her to be. (Thus adding to her great cross-cultural appeal.)

Dora's family celebrates Christmas, with a tree in their living room and luminaria on the path outside ("A Present for Santa"). Yet the focus of the Christmas episode is on presents and their suitability for those who receive them, not on the religious or family-centered aspects of the holiday. When Swiper attempts to make off with their present for Santa, Boots hopes Christmas will bring out the fox's better nature: "Swiper wouldn't swipe on Christmas, would he, Dora?" In fact, Swiper takes the present, but returns it once he realizes it's for Santa. The present is "una guitarra" (a guitar), on which Santa serenades Boots and Dora with "Feliz Navidad." So Santa serves as a kind of universal bringer of good cheer rather than a Christian icon (this draws from his status in the culture at large, in which he has been largely stripped of religious context). Santa hails a liberal humanist/morality tale view of "Christmas" as unifying and peaceful—and yet, despite his secularization, he still represents Christian ideology; fully decontextualizing such a religious figure is not possible. In 2009, Nickelodeon premiered the episode "Dora Saves Three Kings Day," which presents a surface treatment of Latino celebrations of Epiphany and the arrival of the three kings or magi (Reyes Magos). In the episode, Dora and her friends rescue animals which are to bring them to their village for the Three Kings celebration.

One of Dora's most expansive adventures takes place in conjunction with (International) Friendship Day ("Dora's World Adventure"). On this day, Dora tells the audience that her friends dress up and have parties, and wear special friendship bracelets. The bracelets are particularly meaningful to her: "When we all wear our friendship bracelets, it means that we'll always be friends forever." Of course, Swiper steals the bracelets, and so Dora must go around the world to return them. She stops in Paris, Mount Kilimanjaro, the Winter Palace in St. Petersburg, and the Great Wall of China. In each country, she teaches the audience the local word or phrase for "hello," and provides some superficial information about the culture in each setting. She says that the French enjoy cheese in cafes, for example, and that in China, people ride bicycles and fly kites. As her friends thank her for returning the bracelets, she tells them: "Friends help friends," again privileging a liberal humanist erasure of difference and an easy characterization of the complex notion of intercultural "friendship."

When Dora travels, she does so almost instantaneously by stepping into a method of conveyance (that helpfully appears when she needs it) and then stepping off in a new location, usually after singing a brief song. These vehicles can take her across lakes, around the world, or even to another planet ("Journey to the Purple Planet"). She can also enter fairy tales by climbing into books ("Dora Saves the Prince") and breathe underwater using a magic crown to transform into a mermaid ("Dora Saves the Mermaids"). In her travels, Dora never buys a ticket or rides with other children. She has complete freedom to cross borders without documentation, and she never passes through any kind of immigration post. When she arrives at her destination, the local people and animals happily accept her. (One exception to this is when she enters Swiper's home space in "Berry Hunt" and picks berries—in this episode she is chased by a bear.) All this traveling suggests the space-bending possibilities of the Internet, a technology that allows communication and virtual travel across great distances. Because of its simulated nature, travel via the Internet does not require documentation or funds. Like Dora's transportation, it occurs instantaneously and whenever needed by the user. But, again like Dora, those who travel in this fashion are limited by the environments, people, and information available through the technology used. And these travelers must always return "home" to their physical bodies. Although Dora may cross geographic borders, she cannot escape those of the television frame; she is at the mercy of her journey narrative and when her show ends, she disappears—or transitions into a Dora controlled by the child fan, assisted by branded dolls, clothing, and so on.

Children and Technology

Dora's narrative takes the form of a computer game, and Dora herself utilizes various technologies during her adventures. Thus, the show engages questions about the relationship of young people to technology such as: How is Dora's life structured as a computerized series of binary decisions? How does Dora's use of technology engage specific forms of embodiment and identities? And how does it reflect children's experience with technology in the "outside world"?

Theorists such as Neil Postman argue that children's use of media decreases their capacity for imaginative play and exposes them to harmful stimuli. On the other side of the continuum, David Buckingham argues that new media, such as computer software, the Internet, and text messaging, provide additional venues for communication and enhance young people's ability to extend their knowledge and influence. This utopic vision positions technology as generating new forms of learning, democratic literacy, liberation from bodily identity, and creative expression (Buckingham 44). Facility with multiple media also produces the ability to adapt to change, experiment creatively with different modalities, and learn to solve problems by "doing"—without rule books or manuals (McDonnell 115–16).

Through watching *Dora*, children learn the ritualized semiotic and performative aspects of machine use (Oravec 253). As they become accustomed to technology—through representations in entertainment or use of computers at home or school—children prepare to use machines in their daily lives. But cultural theorist Jo Ann Oravec cautions that: "Technology rituals can thus displace efforts to establish or participate in more human-centered rituals, rituals that involve higher levels of human response and permit more spontaneity, playfulness, and even magic" (Oravec 254). Notice the parallel here with Postman's view. As shows like Dora engage the binary structure of computer functions (calling for one right answer), might they curb children's creative use of the technology or ability to imagine alternative solutions and narratives?

When we use technology, we participate in an exercise of control over ourselves as users. We must use the technology in the way it demands; otherwise, it will not fulfill its function. Oravec suggests that adults have explored the "strategic use of technological ritual" to reinforce structure and establish discipline over children (262–263). Teaching such processes as launching a program, starting a file, saving work, researching on the Internet, etc. constitutes an imposition of structure, a discipline of children's minds and bodies focused toward particular uses of machines. This discipline imposes a technological layer on top of other daily structures such as mealtimes, class schedules, and bedtimes. The process assists in socializing children to become technological workers in a modernist paradigm (Callahan). As Donna Haraway suggests in the quote I led with, such a process moves society into an ever closer, cyborglike relationship with its machines.

Another issue raised by Oravec is the purpose of introducing children to technology in a consumerist culture. She states: "Through these consumption rituals, children learn that technology is a consumer item, and that the purpose of human interaction with computers is to collect various devices and then follow the programmed instructions, experimenting within their affordances and constraints" (261). As children add more technological devices and media, they increase their cultural capital. Rather than calling on children to master a single program or tool, as a parent or teacher might, the consumer market suggests that diversifying one's technological portfolio provides a more direct key to success. This is reflected in the *Dora* program; Dora relies on a multitude of mechanical devices (transportation, tools, reference materials) to get where she needs to go and acquire necessary items. But she also consistently utilizes her map to access information and mark her progress. Indeed, having access to technology and exhibiting mastery in its use ensures Dora is able to complete her objectives successfully each episode. (Such consumerism/collection is also promoted through the proliferation of *Dora* merchandise, electronic and non-electronic.)

Technology in/as Dora's World

Dora makes extensive use of technology during her adventures. Some is "low tech" or magic, like the map that shows her the locations she needs to travel through to reach her objectives, or her backpack that magically holds whatever items she might need. And some is quite sophisticated—as mentioned, she has access to whatever mode of transportation she requires at any given time. In "Dora's World Adventure," she makes use of a collection of video screens that project images of her friends around the world and allow her to speak with them, as if on videophone. These screens, like Dora's instantaneous travel, suggest the possibilities of Internet communication. Dora's cousin Diego has a computerized "field journal" that he uses to collect information on animals ("Meet Diego"). The field journal seems to be linked not only to an information network about zoology, but also to a satellite feed—Diego can use it to locate any animal in seconds. The journal looks something like a Blackberry or GPS device, and its key function in the narrative gives it a "cool" factor that makes such devices attractive to the viewer.

Boots and Dora also like to "catch stars," reaching up and grabbing smiling stars that fly by them on their journey. Dora stores the stars in a special rainbow pocket on the side of her backpack. These "captive" stars, with diverse abilities and properties, prove useful as she applies them to various problems. Rocket Star, for example, can enable her to move more quickly. Glowy can light up dark places. In *Dora the Explorer: The Essential Guide*, a companion book to the television series aimed at emerging readers and their families, the author states that these small pieces of technology are "giggly star friends" (Bromberg 16), yet they seem unwilling to be caught and always fly away after being "helpful." The stars contribute to the framing of Dora's world as a video game, as they fly above the characters' heads and suggest the idea of "bonuses" when they are caught—they are objects, tools without any agency or function other than to aid Dora.

Other elements of the show suggest the mediated nature of Dora's world as well. In the original title sequence for the show, the camera zoomed in from outside a (nonanimated) child's room and focused on a desktop computer. Dora and her friends appeared on that computer. In each episode, including those currently running, a mouse pointer clicks on Dora's name to transition from the title sequence to the main part of the program. This pointer then becomes the audience's avatar in Dora's world, allowing the assumed viewer to access ("click on") objects and elements in the landscape, as he or she would if playing a computer game. Once clicked, objects activate—they fly around the screen, or appear on Dora, or perform some other useful action. Of course, this "mouse pointer" access is not personalized to each viewer; there is one master narrative it portrays. This narrative is also centered around the "correct" answer; for example, if Dora asks for a flashlight, the pointer would choose the picture of a flashlight, not (for example) a maraca that, when shaken, could attract fireflies to light her way. In this way, Dora's technology maps onto Oravec's notion of technological rituals as discipline, as it prepares the viewer to interact with machines in a specific, linear, binary fashion. Rather than imagine multiple possibilities, preschoolers are taught to choose the most obvious, straightforward answer.

Behavioral Responses

As mentioned above, another stated objective of Dora's creators was that the show's audience "be active participants—not only by answering questions, but by getting off the couch and moving their bodies" ("More about Dora" 2). Several times each episode, the show calls for audience members to engage in various types of physical embodiment. In order to issue this call, Dora and the other characters speak directly to the audience, breaking the mediated fourth wall. Dora begins each episode by telling the viewers: "I need your help," and then asking if they will help her. Regardless of the children's response, Dora assumes an affirmative, and begins her journey with the viewer compelled alongside. This participation is touted by Nickelodeon executive Brown Johnson as empowering to the preschool viewers: "It makes them feel smart, and it makes them feel strong, and it makes them feel powerful . . . No one had ever asked for that degree of audience participation before" (Ralli C2). Yet, all of the participation is carefully choreographed to overlap with Dora's success along her journey.

After gaining the viewers' support, Dora, Boots, Map, and Backpack implicate them in their activities through various physical performances. Sometimes these are in the form of compelled speech—the characters tell the children watching that they "have to say" a key word, such as "backpack" or "map." Occasionally, Dora and Boots follow this demand with "louder!" Some of these speech acts engage learning through rote: viewers learn Spanish words by repeating them after Dora, for example. Often the characters employ close-ended questioning as a teaching strategy, asking children where a certain shape or animal is that Dora somehow is having trouble seeing. Sometimes the physical performance is focused on larger movements; children are asked to jump, or reach, or point to an object. Sometimes, viewers will "earn" some reward for engaging in these performances—a friendship bracelet, for example, at the end of the World Adventure story. When this happens, the reward is "given" to the viewers by passing it under (or around) the "camera" so that it appears to have been moved out of Dora's space and into the viewer's. The show thus establishes a token economy, based on following Dora's instructions, but the token is virtual and disappears as soon as the show is over. Yet, with all these compelled actions and rewards, the fourth wall is a blurry boundary—in many ways—in *Dora.*

In all these performances, as with the computer pointer avatar, there is one "right" answer, gesture, or other response, and it is assumed that the viewer embodies this correct performance. Thus, there is essentially only one way to engage with the program's narrative, except for interpretations of animal movements or other gestures called for in a general way. The major exception occurs at the end of each episode, when viewers are asked to tell Dora and Boots their favorite part of the day's journey. The characters leave a few seconds of time for children's open responses before validating them: "I liked that part, too." After this, Dora and Boots relate their favorite parts, which may be the same as the viewers'. Only here does the viewer get to express creativity, or break out of the binary right/wrong answer structure.

The interactivity in *Dora* functions as a metanarrative of the series as a whole, since it is structured as an interactive game—perform correct action, receive reward, progress along journey. But, because it is mediated, the interactivity is false, ultimately resulting in the audience's consumption of the "correct" performance. In the "bargain" of sitting down to watch *Dora*, viewers lose the ability to express themselves creatively, but gain the comfort of knowing they can never give the "wrong" answer. This is similar to technology use; a calculator cannot give a "wrong" answer, as long as the user inputs the question correctly. Is the bargain beneficial to the viewer? What are the right answers being imparted, and what alternate solutions are left out? Ultimately, Dora leaves little room for resistant viewing or "play."

Implications: Completing the Training

As Dora explores, she transmits specific ideologies regarding childhood and society. The viewers' assumed complicity with her actions places them at the center of debates over border identity and multiculturalism, and the place of technology. Dora's journeys are carefully constructed to serve as conduits for certain values, often having to do with being a "good" person—saving a friend, finding some useful or sentimental item, working as a team. As she travels, Dora sees her world not for what it *is*, but rather as a series of locations to be passed through. Locations serve less as significant journey markers than as staging points for challenges—the no places/every places of computer games. The objective matters most—again, a linear and structural standpoint—and the show cannot end until Dora meets that objective.

The way space is used in *Dora* also serves as a marker for how the show treats other concepts. As mentioned earlier, Dora's world is a simulacrum, a decontextualized version of real landscapes, a place that never was. Sociologist Henri Lefebvre suggests that space can be *abstract*, existing in the realm of the conceptual (we will use this kitchen to cook food), or *lived*, suggesting practical, material usage (the kitchen can also be used for playing with toys, or brushing the cat, or bandaging a cut). Literary theorist Nicholas Spencer argues: "Lefebvre describes abstract space as a homogenizing and fragmenting social force that seeks to destroy the potential for oppositional cultural space that lived space represents" (142). The flattening of space creates a unilateral expectation of how it will be used, disregarding possibilities for play. As Dora moves through her own abstract space, her possibilities for use of space are limited; she cannot bring her space to the realm of the material. Like a character in a novel who is similarly confined, "she cannot integrate her various spatial experiences into a social map of her world" (144). Since Dora cannot and does not bring her experience into the material, it is up to the children viewing the show to do it for themselves. They define their own sense of Dora's space, of who she is as a pretend or aspirational peer, and how her world culturally maps onto their own. Through this relational and ideological embodiment, the show imparts its training.

Multiculturalism—that contested term—is presented in *Dora* as a sort of extended series of friendships, a liberal humanist outlook exemplified by her team's cheer: "When we work together as a team, there's nothing we can't do. 'Cause being on a team means you help me and I help you" ("We're a Team"). Dora and her friends never encounter any hardships based on difference; they don't have difficulties understanding languages, traditions, gestures, or geographies. Their challenges are skills based: they search for objects, pass through locations, outwit Swiper the Fox, and cheer up a grumpy troll by making him laugh. The characters' differences easily coalesce into a network of abilities—accentuated by technological or magic objects that conveniently appear when needed, removing any struggle connected with building assemblages—that serve a common good. The *Dora* vision of community might thus be seen as an idealistic "happy multiculturalism." The characters share a common identity, even though they are of multiple species, cultural backgrounds, and genders. (Class is not specifically represented or addressed.) Dora and her friends are brought together by common, humanistic objectives that are supposed to transcend their perceived differences.

Educational theorist Carlos Alberto Torres proposes that under such a liberal humanist vision: "Unfortunately the tension between and among these differences is rarely interrogated, presuming a 'unity of difference'—that is, that all difference is both analogous and equivalent (201). This treatment of difference tends to reject radical notions and reproduce structure in its attempts to forge a unified "personhood" (Ladson-Billings and Tate 62). In its attempts to build a liberal humanistic third space—a hybridizing, democratic borderland—*Dora* defers conversation around issues of culture and power. Children do not learn about the relationships between injustice and common cause, or misunderstanding and friendship. Both contained and enabled by the technology that frames it, the show's multicultural discourse is ultimately imaginary and temporary. Everything in *Dora* comes too easily; it is decontextualized and abstracted from cultural and linguistic tensions. In the outside world, those who look like Dora may be stopped and detained by the police if they live in Arizona. Spanish speakers contend with a state system that enforces English as a sole mode of literacy, spoken and written. Yet, *Dora's* determination to exist in a highly simulated environment, with a mysterious avatar pointer and instantaneous travel, sets it apart from the outside world and ignores complex questions around the very issues it engages. The show colonizes the imaginary around the avoidance of cultural conflict and a false sense of unity, while outside, restrictive legislation is signed, protestors gather, and children respond in English when their parents speak to them in Spanish.

Works Cited

Anzaldúa, Gloria. *Borderlands: La Frontera*. San Francisco: Aunt Lute Books, 2007.

"Arizona Bill Targeting Ethnic Studies Signed into Law." *Los Angeles Times*, May 12, 2010. articles.latimes.com/2010/may/12/nation/la-na-ethnic-studies-20100512 (accessed April 29, 2012).

"Arizona Enacts Stringent Law on Immigration." *New York Times,* June 11, 2010. (accessed May 12, 2010).www.nytimes.com/2010/04/24/us/politics/24immig.html).

"Arizona Grades Teachers on Fluency." *Wall Street Journal,* June 11, 2010.

online.wsj.com/article/SB10001424052748703572504575213883276427528.html. (accessed April 29, 2012).

Arizona Secretary of State's Office. *2006 Proposition Guide: Proposition 103*. 16 October 2007. www.azsos.gov/election/2006/Info/PubPamphlet/ Sun_Sounds/english/Prop103.htm (accessed April 29, 2012)..

——. *2006 Proposition Guide: Proposition 300*. 16 October 2007. www.azsos.gov/election/2006/Info/PubPamphlet/Sun_Sounds/english/Prop300.htm (accessed April 29, 2012)..

"Awards for *Dora the Explorer*." Internet Movie Database. www.imdb.com/title/tt0235917/awards (accessed April 29, 2012).

Baudrillard, Jean. *Simulacra and Simulation*. Ann Arbor: University of Michigan Preess, 1994.

"Berry Hunt." *Dora the Explorer*.Nick Jr. 2000.

Bhabha, Homi. *The Location of Culture*. New York: Routledge, 1994.

Bharucha, Rusom. *The Politics of Cultural Practice*. London: Athlone Press, 2000.

Bogdan, Robert, and Sari Knopp Biklen. *Qualitative Research for Education: An Introduction to Theories and Methods*, fourth ed. Boston: Allyn and Bacon, 2003.

Bromberg, Brian. *Dora the Explorer: The Essential Guide*. London, New York: DK Publishing, Inc., 2006.

Buckingham, David. *After the Death of Childhood: Growing up in the Age of Electronic Media*. Cambridge, UK: Polity Press, 2000.

Callahan, Raymond. *Education and the Cult of Efficiency*. Chicago: University of Chicago Press, 1962.

Chappell, Andrew. *Colonizing the Imaginary: Children's Embodiment of Cultural Narratives*. Diss Arizona State University, 2008.

Chen, Sylvia Xiaohua, Veronica Benet-Martínez, and Michael Harris Bond. "Bicultural Identity, Bilingualism, and Psychological Adjustment in Multicultural Societies: Immigration-Based and Globalization-Based Acculturation." *Journal of Personality* 76, no. 4, 2008.

"Dora Saves the Mermaids." *Dora the Explorer*. Nick Jr. 2007.

"Dora Saves the Prince." *Dora the Explorer*. Nick Jr. 2002.

"Dora Saves Three Kings Day." *Dora the Explorer*. Nick Jr. 2009.

"Dora's Pirate Adventure." *Dora the Explorer*. Nick Jr. 2004.

"Dora's World Adventure." *Dora the Explorer*. Nick Jr. 2006.

Erickson, Frederick. "Qualitative Methods in Research on Teaching." In *Handbook of Research on Teaching*. 3rd ed, edited by. M. C. Wittrock, 119–161. Washington, DC: American Educational Research Association, 1986.

Fernández, Idy. "Go, Diego Go." *Hispanic* 18 (2005): 68.

Frenck, Moses. "Toy Treatment." *MediaWeek* 17, no. 8 (October 19, 2007): MyM1-MyM4.

Haraway, Donna. *Simians, Cyborgs and Women: The Reinvention of Nature*. New York: Routledge, 1991.

"Job Day." *Dora the Explorer*. Nick Jr. 2004.

"Journey to the Purple Planet." *Dora the Explorer*. Nick Jr. 2006.

Ladson-Billings, Gloria and William Tate. "Toward a Critical Race Theory of Education." *Teachers College Record* 97 (1995): 47–68.

McCarthy, Cameron and Greg Dimitriades. "Globalizing Pedagogies: Power, Resentment, and the Re-Narration of Difference." In *Globalization and Education: Critical Perspectives* edited by Nicholas C Burbules and Carlos Alberto Torres,

187–204. Lanham, MD: Rowman & Littlefield Publishers, 1998.
McDonnell, Kathleen. *Honey We Lost the Kids: Rethinking Childhood in the Multimedia Age*. Toronto, Canada: Second Story Press, 2001.
"Meet Diego." *Dora the Explorer*. Nick Jr. 2003.
"More about Dora." *Dora the Explorer*. Nick Jr. 2005.October 12, 2007. nickjr.co.uk/shows/dora/more.aspx#about (accessed April 29, 2012).
Oravec, Jo Ann. "From Gigapets to Internet: Childhood Technology Rituals as Commodities." In *Rituals and Patterns in Children's Lives*, edited by. Kathy Merlock Jackson, 252-268. Madison: University of Wisconsin Press, 2005.
Popp, Richard K. "Mass Media and the Linguistic Marketplace: Media, Language, and Distinction." *Journal of Communication Inquiry* 30 (2006): 5-20.
Postman, Neil. *The Disappearance of Childhood*. New York: Vintage, 1994.
"A Present for Santa." *Dora the Explorer*. Nick Jr. 2002.
Ralli, Tania. "The Mother of 'Blue' and 'Dora' Takes a Step Up at Nickelodeon." *New York Times*, February 28, 2005. www.nytimes.com/2005/02/28/business/media/28kid.html (accessed April 29, 2012).
Rau, Alia Beard. "Arizona State Rejects 5 Major Immigration Bills." *The Arizona Republic*. February 2, 2012. http://www.azcentral.com/news/election/azelections/articles/2011/03/17/20110317arizona-birthright-citizenship-bills-rejected.html?nclick_check=1(accessed October 24, 2012).
Salaňda, Johnny. *Fundamentals of Qualitative Research*. Oxford; New York: Oxford University Press, 2011.
"Senate Bill 1070." *State Of Arizona Senate*. June 11, 2010. www.azleg.gov/legtext/49leg/2r/bills/sb1070s.pdf (accessed April 29, 2012).
Sigler, Eunice. "A Girl Named Dora." *Hispanic* 16 (2003): 42-5.
Spencer, Nicholas. *After Utopia: The Rise of Critical Space in Twentieth-Century American Fiction*. Lincoln: University of Nebraska Press, 2006.
"Sticky Tape." *Dora the Explorer*. Nick Jr. 2001.
Torres, Carlos Alberto. *Democracy, Education, and Multiculturalism: Dilemmas of Citizenship in a Global World*. Lanham, MD: Roman & Littlefield Publishers, 1998.
"We All Scream for Ice Cream." *Dora the Explorer. Nick Jr.* 2000.
"We're a Team." *Dora the Explorer*. Nick Jr. 2006.
Wingett, Yvonne. "'Dora' Unlocks Bilingual Treasure" *The Arizona Republic*. February 15, 2006. http://www.azcentral.com/arizonarepublic/news/articles/0215earlyspanish0215.html (accessed April 29, 2012).
Wolcott, Harry F. *Transforming Qualitative Data: Description, Analysis, and Interpretation*. Thousand Oaks, CA: Sage, 1994.

Part Three
Film

Chapter Nine
"Mischief of One Kind and Another": Nostalgia in *Where the Wild Things Are* as Text and Film
by Michelle Ann Abate

> A wave of nostalgia for the past has been very much in evidence for a long time now and seems to be spreading.
>
> —Mario Jacoby, *The Longing for the Past* (1985)

When Maurice Sendak first published *Where the Wild Things Are* in 1963, the now-classic picture book received a bevy of negative reviews. Everyone from parents and teachers to critics and librarians chastised the narrative for what they felt was its disturbing view of children and childhood. As Francis Spufford has written, the narrative embodied "one of the very few picture books to make an entirely deliberate, and beautiful, use of the psychoanalytic story of anger" (2002, 60). In the figure of Sendak's protagonist Max, adults encountered a young person who was frustrated, angry, and even filled with rage. As the opening lines to the book reveal: "The night Max wore his wolf suit and made mischief of one kind and another."[1] Before long, the young boy's mischievous antics cause him to be sent to bed without dinner. Once in his room, Max takes an imaginative journey to "where the wild things are." There, the young boy finds himself in a world of big, hairy and horned creatures who, not unlike Max's own behavior, "roared their terrible roars and gnashed their terrible teeth. . . and showed their terrible claws."

In this way, *Where the Wild Things Are* offered a decidedly nonromantic and even antinostalgic view of childhood. Sendak's picture book challenged longstanding notions, first established during the Enlightenment era, that youth is a time of innocence, gentleness and happiness. As Philippe Ariès, Peter Hunt and James Kincaid have written, in the eighteenth century, after generations of children being viewed as nothing more than sinful "little adults," a new concept "won acceptance: that of the innocence of childhood" (Ariès 110). To demonstrate this viewpoint, Ariès offerd the following example:

> Witness the caption to an engraving by F. Guerard showing children's toys (dolls and drums): "This is an age of innocence, to which we all must return in order to enjoy the happiness which is our hope on earth; the age when one can forgive anything, the age when hatred is unknown, when nothing can cause distress; the golden age of human life, the age which defies Hell, the age when life is easy and death holds no terrors, the age to which the heavens are open." (Ariès 110)

In the decades that followed, such attitudes only increased. By the nineteenth century, in the words of Ariès, "The comparison of angels with children was to become a common theme" (111).[2] Victorian culture in Europe and the United States was saturated with visual, print and material evidence concerning the apotheosis of childhood. From the adorable drawings of young boys and girls playing ring-around-the-rosy by popular children's book illustrator Kate Greenaway to the widespread appeal of juvenile characters who were "too perfect for this world" like Little Eva from Harriet Beecher Stowe's *Uncle Tom's Cabin* (1852), young people were viewed in an idyllic light. Even when boys and girls were not framed in ways that were so self-consciously beatific, they were still seen as the embodiment of goodness, kindness and purity. Indeed, in comments that encapsulated stereotypical societal attitudes about children through the much of the twentieth century, one mother said of her little girl: "She does a hundred and one different things: . . . she makes the sign of the cross, she begs pardon, she drops a curtsy, she blows a kiss, she shrugs her shoulders, she dances, she strokes, she holds her chin: in a word she is pretty in every particular. I watch her for hours on end" (Ariès 49).

Where the Wild Things Are did not subscribe to this view of children or childhood. As Nat Hentoff noted in an article that appeared in 1966, whereas "many contemporary picture books are still populated by children who eat everything on their plates, go dutifully to bed at the proper hour, and learn all sorts of useful facts and moral lessons by the time the book comes to an end" (39), Sendak's texts radically broke from this tradition. In the words of Jennifer Waller, *Wild Things* rejected the insipid stories about "lovable steam shovels or cute dogs or shapes" and instead dared to offer a tale that "may actually be about children" (267). As Sendak himself remarked, his 1963 picture book explored "how children master various feelings—anger, boredom, fear, frustration, jealousy—and manage to come to grips with the realities of their lives" (qtd in DeLuca 7). In so doing, it presented children in a manner that is unsentimentalized and—as Max chases his dog with a fork, scowls menacingly in his wolf suit, and vows to his mother "I'LL EAT YOU UP!"—at times even unnerving.

And unnerved many adult readers were. Ursula Nordstrom, Sendak's editor at Harper & Row Publishers who initially released *Where the Wild Things Are*, provided a sample of the critical commentary: "A reviewer for the *Journal of Nursery Education* mused, 'We would not like to have it [*Wild Things*] left about where a sensitive child might find it to pore over in the twilight.' *Publisher's Weekly*, after saying that 'the plan and technique of the illustrations are superb,' cautioned, 'But they may well prove frightening, accompanied as they are by a pointless and confusing story'" (qtd in Hentoff 66).

While Sendak's iconoclastic view of children and childhood may have alarmed teachers and parents, this quality is precisely what appealed to the book's juvenile readers, and what made *Where the Wild Things Are* such a beloved text. As Nordstrom aptly said of the book: "It is the first American picture book for children to recognize that children have *powerful* emotions" (qtd Hentoff 66). Far from being frightened by Max's outburst of anger and his romp among the "wild things," boys and girls empathized and even identified with him. As Selma G. Lanes has asserted, the three double-page "wild rumpus" scenes near the middle of Sendak's book "probably comprise the best-thumbed pages in contemporary children's literature" (93). Indeed, Sendak himself revealed in an interview: " 'One seven-year-old boy wrote me a letter . . . The boy had written, 'how much does it cost to get to where the wild things are? If it is not too expensive, my sister and I want to spend the summer there. Please answer soon'" (qtd in Hentoff 47). For some children, the appeal of Max's foray into the land of the horned, hairy and largely non-verbal wild things went even further. More than simply repeatedly looking at the book's monsters, the text inspired them to document their own. As the author-illustrator revealed in an interview, "Some [children] have sent me drawings of their own wild things, and they make mine look like cuddly fuzzballs" (qtd in Hentoff 44).

The visual composition, page layout, and aesthetic appearance that the author-illustrator chose for the book accentuates Max's experience of anger, frustration and even rage. As Sendak discussed:

> In *Where the Wild Things Are*, the device is a matching of shapes and sizes. I used it to describe Max's moods pictorially: his anger, more less normal in the beginning, expands into rage; then the explosion of fantasy serve as a release from that particular anger; and finally there is a collapse of fantasy and it's all over. (qtd in Lanes 96)

Paul G. Akarelian has documented the shifting balance between words and images throughout the text. In the the beginning of the book, the illustrations are relatively small and yield the bulk of space to the written text. Meanwhile, by the middle portion of the narrative—where Max's fury erupts in the "wild rumpus"—the images expand, filling the entire page and displacing the words altogether. Finally, in the closing segment of the story, as Max calms down, leaves the land of the wild things, and returns to his room, the illustrations shrink in size again and language reemerges (see Arakelian 122 – 3).

Where the Wild Things Are is seen as among those texts that helped usher in a new conception of childhood in the United States and a new era in the history of literature for young readers. Instead of operating via the nostalgia-fueled perception of boys and girls as perennially cute, pleasant and kind, *Where the Wild Things Are* offered a more frank and honest presentation—especially when it came to revealing some of the unsavory aspects of their personalities. Indeed, as Sendak asserted about his picture book in a 1966 *New Yorker* profile: "I am trying to draw the way children *feel*—or rather, the way I *know* I felt as a child" (Hentoff 39).

It was precisely for this reason that *Where the Wild Things Are* was awarded the Caldecott Medal—the highest accolade that can be bestowed on an illustrated narrative for children—in 1964. Sendak's acceptance speech made a candid case not simply for the aims and objectives of his book, but its importance and even necessity:

> Certainly we want to protect our children from new and painful experiences that are beyond their emotional comprehension and that intensify anxiety . . . That is obvious. But what is just as obvious—and what is too often overlooked—is that fact that from their earliest years children live on familiar terms with disturbing emotions, that fear and anxiety are an intrinsic part of their everyday lives, that they continually cope with frustration as best they can ...It is my involvement with this inescapable fact of childhood—the awful vulnerability of children and their struggle to make themselves King of all Wild Things—that gives my work whatever truth and passion it may have. (qtd in Lanes 107)

Generations of children agreed with his sentiments. As Jennifer Shaddock has written, *Where the Wild Things Are* "holds a treasured position on perhaps more bookshelves than any other American picture book in history" (155). Similarly, Selma G. Lanes credited the book with achieving "unprecedented success" (106). To be sure, Sendak himself commented that, of all his many published narratives, "The book that children have reacted to most strongly, though, is 'Where the Wild Things Are.' They wear out copies at libraries and keep rereading it at home" (qtd in Hentoff 44).

In 2009, after being adapted for a television special in the 1970s and an operatic ballet during the 1980s,[3] Sendak's picture book was made into a live-action, feature-length film. Directed by innovative auteur Spike Jonze, and adapted for the screen by Jonze and the equally pioneering writer Dave Eggers, the much-anticipated movie did not so much relocate Sendak's story into a new cultural medium as reimagine its meaning and message altogether. Whereas the rejection of nostalgia formed a signature facet of the 1963 picture book, Jonze's film embraced and even celebrated this element. In his version of *Wild Things*, the characters are at least as interested in exploring emotions, examining relationships and processing their feelings as they are in engaging in a "wild rumpus," perhaps more so. When Max first encounters the wild things, for example, they are engaged in an emotionally intense—and, at times, physically explosive—discussion about love, loss and the meaning of family. Distraught that his longtime friend K.W. has both physically and psychologically distanced herself from their group—preferring the company of her new friends Bob and Terry—Carol laments the changing nature of interpersonal relationships: "I'm the only one that cares that we don't stay together."

In this scene and many others throughout the film, Jonze's creatures as well as Max frequently cry, sentimentally emote, and engage in long, ponderous, heartfelt conversations—acts in which they never partake in Sendak's original text. When Carol asks Max about his qualifications for being king, he has one specific concern in mind: "What about loneliness?" As Douglas clarifies: "What he's saying is, will you keep out all the sadness?" Indeed, when Carol shows Max the miniature model that he has constructed—and which he and K.W. used to spend hours playing with together—he explains the loss of this friendship via the following painful comparison: "Do you know what it feels like when all your teeth are falling out really slowly and you don't realize and then you notice that, well, they're really far apart. And then one day you don't have any teeth anymore." Not surprisingly, given these experiences, when Max proposes that they build a giant fort, he offers the following rationale for the structure: "We'll take care of each other, and we'll all sleep together in a real pile." When the fort causes further strife rather than healing, K.W. takes Max to Bob and Terry for some of their sage advice. The sole question that the young boy asks the two owl creatures is telling: "How. Do. I. Make. Everyone. O. Kay."

These alterations did not go unnoticed by the film's critics. A. O. Scott, writing for *The New York Times* noted his surprise at "how 'emo' the movie turned out to be" (AR13). Meanwhile, Hugh Hart, in an article that appeared on the online media site *Underwire*, was even more blunt in his assessment. He dismissed Jonze's cinematic adaptation as merely a bunch of "middle-aged actors whining about their feelings as they walk around in furry costumes" (par 1). As a result, most critics agreed with Manohla Dargis's assertion that the bulk of the film had been "designed and directed toward a distinctly older age group than the book's original audience" (par 11). From the opening scene to the closing sequence, Jonze's *Where the Wild Things Are* was more of an adult reminiscence about being a child than a frank portrait of the feelings, thoughts and actions of actual children. Indeed, the extended tagline for the film—"Inside all of us is everything you've ever seen, everything you've ever done, everyone you've ever loved"—reveals its cognizance of at least a dual adult and child audience. In addition, the film's cinematography and visual style—with many scenes shot in brilliant golden sunlight—give it a dreamy, even wistful, look. Finally, the plot elements that Jonze and Eggers introduced to expand Sendak's picture book into a feature-length movie draw on common memories and experiences of childhood. For instance, whereas in Sendak's book, readers never learn what precisely prompts Max to "make mischief of one kind and another," in the film, the stressors are clear: first, his teenage sister ignores him while talking to her friends; then, they destroy his igloo in a snowball fight; finally, his mother is too busy first with finishing a report for work and then enjoying a dinner date with her boyfriend to spend time with him. These events vividly illustrate the difficulties of growing up, the inevitability as well as irreversibility of time passing, and the mutability of personal relationships. Indeed, when Max's mother asks him to tell one of his original stories, the narrative that he creates is revealing:

> Then there were some vampires. And one of the vampires bit the tallest building. And his fangs broke off. Then all his other teeth fell out. Then he started crying. And then all the other vampires said "Why are you crying? Aren't those just your baby teeth?' And he said, 'No, those are my grown up teeth." And the vampires knew that he couldn't be a vampire anymore. So they left him. The end. (*Where the Wild Things Are,* 2009)

Of course, all of these elements foreshadow the dynamics at play in the world of the wild things. As mentioned before, Carol compares K.W.'s waning interest in spending time together to having his teeth fall out; likewise, from the moment that Max meets Carol, he speaks of his fears that K.W. has not simply temporarily left their little family unit, but is gone for good.

Given these changes, Jonze can be seen as creating a nostalgia-fueled and backward-looking film out of Sendak's decidedly antinostalgic, forward-looking text. Whereas the original print edition of *Where the Wild Things Are* rejects romanticized, sentimentalized views of childhood, his film adaptation embraces them. Rather than spotlighting one discrete moment in a young boy's life from the perspective of that child—as Sendak's picture book does—Jonze's film reflects on the entire experience of growing up from the vantage point, in many ways, of an adult. Via comments such as Carol's assertion that "Max will bring K.W. back. He'll keep us all together. He has powers. He told us," Jonze's creatures engage in nostalgic yearning. They long to reverse the changes that have occurred with the passage of time and to return to an earlier, happier and seemingly more ideal moment in their lives.

In so doing, Jonze's cinematic version embodies another facet of what Jerry Griswold has termed the "adulteration" of children's literature—or the various adult uses and misuses of narratives intended for young people. As I have written elsewhere, Griswold points to examples ranging from "the rise of pop psychology during the 1970s predicated on nurturing your 'inner child' to the fad of businessmen wearing neckties emblazoned with cartoon characters like the Tazmanian Devil during the 1990s" to demonstrate how grown men and women, beginning in the second half of the twentieth century, "have increasingly longed to return to the seemingly carefree days of youth" (Abate *Raising*, 169).

The cinematic *Where the Wild Things Are* participates in this phenomenon. In an indication of the film's appeal to at least a dual child and adult audience, a bevy of the movie's merchandise was targeted for men and women rather than boys and girls: items ranging from throw pillows and T-shirts to collectible figurines and adult-sized wolf costumes. In so doing, the movie participates in what Zach Whalen and Laurie N. Taylor have identified as the "cultural commodification of memory through consumable media forms" (7). While they are specifically discussing the growing trend of "classic" video games—like Galaga, Pac-Man, and even PONG—that have been reissued during the past decade, the same comment could apply to the product tie-ins for *Wild Things*. The adult-aimed merchandise for Jonze's movie appeals to the current retro interest in childhood. As James Poniewozik, in an article that appeared in *Time* magazine, commented on this trend: "If you are of a certain age—somewhere between Madonna and Britney—your memories of high school or college probably include profound, intense late-night conversations that went something like this: 'Dude! Remember Lite-Brites? Remember *Webster*? Remember Frankie Goes to Hollywood?'" (2004). Evidenced in examples ranging from the aforementioned rerelease of classic video games to the enormous popularity of television programs like VH1's *I Love the '80s*, adult "rememberfests" about their childhoods, as Poniewozik has called them (par 5), have become a pervasive facet of millennial popular and material culture. *Where the Wild Things Are* is a self-conscious extension of this phenomenon, seeking to tap into this social trend, not to mention its accompanying commercial market share.

The significance of Jonze's cinematic version, however, goes far beyond merely contributing to a current cultural fad. *Wild Things* sheds new light on the millennial interest in affect, memory, and melancholy, and the important but often overlooked role that nostalgia plays in these phenomena. Wistful longing has long been as much of a revered as reviled feature of children's literature, and Jonze's film forms a powerful demonstration of its problems as well as possibilities. Ultimately, his 2009 movie posits the provocative question: What does it mean to be nostalgic for a work of antinostalgia?

Of course, Jonze's *Where the Wild Things Are* is certainly neither the first nor the only movie to participate in the cinematic treatment of this issue. Fredric Jameson, in his essay "Transformations of the Image," famously made a case for the emergence of a new cinematic genre: the nostalgia film. Citing George Lucas's *American Graffiti* (1973) as beginning this trend, Jameson noted a pronounced return to the past throughout late twentieth-century American cinema (19–21). Evidenced in everything from a powerful filmic interest in returning to bygone eras in American history—such as the 1950s in *Graffiti*—to a concern with evoking earlier cinematic styles—such as 1940s B-movie sci-fi in Lucas' later blockbuster *Star Wars* (1977)—Jameson observed a growing desire to create what he called the "look and feel" of "pastness" (19). As Vera Dika has written about this phenomenon: "The nostalgia films are not new examples of old genres in the usual sense. They are reconstructions of dead or dismantled forms, genres that are now returned after a period of absence or destruction" (11). Indeed, she continued: "In a way that is distinctive of this era of filmmaking, the lighting, the choice of colors, and the grain of the film, as well as its composition and framing, may all be manipulated to refer to past images" (10).

The 2009 cinematic version of *Where the Wild Things Are* participates in Jameson's notion of the nostalgia film while it pushes this concept in a new and different direction. With its exploration of the inevitability of the passage of time, the irreversibility of growing older, and the irrecoverablility of childhood, Jonze's film clearly traffics in the past. However, unlike in Jameson's configuration, the movie does not do so via a return to a specific historical time period or via the use of a bygone style of cinematography. Rather, Jonze does so through his movie's subject matter and, more specifically, as discussed before, through its engagement with memory, affect and psychology.

In this way, the cinematic *Where the Wild Things Are* partakes in what can be termed a "Möbius approach": Jonze's film explores what happens when the twentieth-century concept of nostalgia is looped, twisted and turned back around on itself in the twenty-first century. As Marita Sturken has written, men and women in the new millennium can be characterized as being "tourists of history." As she has documented, a bevy of "consumer culture of comfort objects such as World Trade Center snow globes, FDNY teddy bears, and Oklahoma City Memorial t-shirts and branded water, as well as reenactments of traumatic events in memorial and architectural designs" sells collective forms of sadness, markets hegemonic forms of national memory, and "offers a prepackaged set of emotions through which to respond to the tragedy" (135). In the words of Sturken, "A kitsch comfort culture contributes to a 'tourist' relationship to history: Americans can feel good about visiting and buying souvenirs at sites of national mourning without having to engage with the economic, social, and political causes of the violent events" (350; back cover).

I would argue that an analogous phenomenon is operating in the 2009 cinematic adaptation of *Where the Wild Things Are*. The film allows its adult audience an opportunity to revisit the world of childhood without requiring them to assume any of its personal problems, daily dilemmas, or psychological frustrations. From the safety, wisdom and, of course, permanence of adulthood, these individuals can be temporary tourists in the "wild rumpus" that is adolescence rather than actual residents there. Indeed, as Mario Jacoby has written on the subject of childhood nostalgia: "'How lovely it is to be a child!' can be uttered only by an adult who, looking backward, idealizes the alleged innocence and security of childhood" (5). Given this phenomenon, it is not surprising that Max's animated anger in Sendak's book is repeatedly replaced by sentimental affect in Jonze's film, or that his sustained state of being mad is replaced by one largely of being melancholy. As Jacoby reminds us, "Nostalgia has come to mean a longing for what is past, a painful yearning for a time gone by" (5).

These details offer a possible explanation for the cinematic changes to both the location of the land of the wild things, and more subtly, to the book's ending. In Sendak's text, Max may imaginatively leave the confines of his house and bedroom, but he does not do so literally. When the young boy is sent to his room without dinner, his fantasy life takes over, causing his bedroom to transform into the world "Where the Wild Things Are." As the narrative explains: "That very night in Max's room a forest grew / and grew, and grew until his ceiling hung with vines / and the walls became the world all around." The illustrations that accompany these passages chart this slow but steady transformation: first, Max's bedposts morph into trees; then, his rug grows grass; and, finally, his night table converts into a thick shrub. Even the ocean and the boat on which Max "sailed off through night and day" emerges from the confines of his room. Indeed, as Sendak says, it mysteriously "tumbled" forth. Near the end of the book, Max "returns" to his room, but this homecoming is only metaphoric. In truth, he has never actually left; his journey has only been via his imagination.

Jonze's cinematic adaptation, however, presents a far different scenario. Rather than having Max's room magically transform into the world of the wild things, the movie shows the young boy literally traveling there himself. After getting in the fight with his mother, Max runs not into his room, but physically out of the house. Viewers see him first dashing down the sidewalk, then across a street, and finally through an opening in a chain-link fence. It is in the woods behind there that Max finds a boat, climbs into it, and pushes off from an actual, tangible shore. Because Max has literally and not just figuratively left his home, when he returns from the land of the wild things, he does not arrive directly back to his room. Instead, he needs to retrace his steps. Jonze shows Max landing his small boat on the shore, sneaking back through the opening in the chain-link fence, and running back through the neighborhood and into his house. Akin to any visitor, Max enters the abode through the front door: he cautiously cracks it open and then slowly, carefully walks into the house. Interestingly, the young boy never actually makes it back to his room—he mother is sitting in the kitchen, sees him entering, and rushes over to embrace him. The final scene of the movie shows the two of them at the table together.

Together with changing the location of "Where the Wild Things Are" from a purely imaginative space to a physical if still fantastical one, Jonze's movie introduces another equally profound alteration: the amount of time that elapses while Max is with the monsters. In Sendak's text, Max's temper tantrum and thus his journey to the land of the wild things lasts mere minutes. Although the text says that the young boy "sailed back over a year, and in and out of weeks, and through a day" to return home, when he arrives back in his room, he finds that his supper—the one that he, presumably, had been previously denied—is waiting for him. Moreover, in what embodies one of the most well-known endings in all of children's literature, Sendak says: "It was still hot."

Max's travel time lasts far longer in Jonze's movie: the young boy flees before dinner and when he returns, many hours have passed. To be sure, the clock in the kitchen where he sits and eats his belated dinner with his mother indicates that it is nearly 11 p.m. In the chronology formed by Max's adventures with the wild things, these elapsed hours can translate into years, bringing the adolescent Max to adulthood—and thus to the age of the film's grown-up viewer. To be sure, the notes in Jonze's screenplay for the portrayal of the movie's final scene suggests more of a retrospective adult appreciation of one's parents than a child's realistic, in-the-moment attitude towards them. The script directions read: "Max is eating his soup. His mom is sitting at the table, too, head resting in her hand, utterly exhausted. She looks affectionately at Max. Max starts to eat his cake, and looks up at his mom. She has fallen asleep. Max tilts his head, *studying her, appreciating her, marveling at her*. END" (qtd on "Confesiones" par 10; my emphasis).

Echoing the shape of a Möbius strip, however, the twists, loops and reversals with regard to the use of nostalgia in Jonze's movie do not end here. The concept is turned back around on itself once more in the course of the movie: with the reason for Max's homecoming. In Sendak's original picture book, the young boy leaves the land of the wild things and returns to his room because he has exhausted his anger. After several pages of frolicking in the "wild rumpus," Max's mood changes: "'Now stop!' Max said and sent the wild things off to bed / without their supper. And Max the king of all wild things was lonely / and wanted to be where someone loved him best of all." The illustration that accompanies these lines shows the forlorn-looking protagonist sitting inside a circus-like tent looking glum. Whereas before, when Max was frustrated and annoyed, he enjoyed cavorting in the land of the wild things, but now that he has spent his anger, this world is unsatisfying. Indeed, in a passage that suggests that Max is not simply missing his home, but is longing for the dinner that he was denied when he was sent to his room as punishment, Sendak writes: "Then all around from far away across the world / he smelled good things to eat / so he gave up being king of where the wild things are."

Ironically, in these pages, Sendak's antinostalgic picture book evokes the original meaning as well etymological origins of the term "nostalgia": as feelings of homesickness. As Roberta Rubenstein documented, "The word nostalgia was coined by Johannes Hofer in 1688, combining the Greek *nostos*, return or the return home, with *algos*, pain or sorrow" (169 n10). For centuries, nostalgia was regarded not simply as an emotional state, but a medical condition. "In pre-twentieth century Europe, when doctors were still ignorant of infectious agents as the source of disease, they regarded nostalgia as the source of organic diseases as diverse as gastroenteritis and pleurisy" (Rubenstein 169 n10). As Sveltana Boym has written, patients suffering from nostalgia "acquired a 'lifeless and haggard countenance,' and 'indifference towards everything,' confusing past and present, real and imaginary events. One of the early symptoms of nostalgia was an ability to hear voices or see ghosts" (1). It was only in the twentieth century that the meaning of nostalgia shifted, coming to be seen "as an emotional disturbance related not to the workings of the body but to 'the workings of memory' (Starobinski, 89–90) and characterized less by the risk of literal death than by a yearning for something of emotional significance that an individual regards as absent or lost" (Rubenstein 168 no 10).

The reason for Max's decision to return in Jonze's film is markedly different. Rather than arising from a positive longing for home and the calming realization that his anger has been spent, the young boy's desire, ironically, by the need to escape continued conflict. Unlike in Sendak's printed text, Max's cinematic visit to the land of the wild things yields at least as much psychic pain, interpersonal strife and familial frustration as the precipitating incident with his mother, perhaps more so. Squabbles, arguments and even physical fights keep erupting within the group, and Max is powerless to stop them. If anything, in fact, his actions often only exacerbate the situation. For example, the "perfect fort" that the wolf-boy-king suggests that they build as a means to bring everyone literally as well as figuratively back together fails miserably. First, Judith becomes upset with Max over his special kinship with Carol: "Well let me ask you something. How does it work around here? Are we all the same, or are some of us better than others? You like to play favorites, huh, King?" When Max insists, "No. I like all you guys equally," Judith is not convinced: "Don't give me that. I can see how it is. The King has favorites, that's really cute."

Then, when K.W. intervenes, Judith turns on her. In comments that are as bitter and awful as anything that Max has encountered in the human world, Judith snarls: "You think you have power, K.W.? That's not real power. I'm talking to you! No! Not you! I'm still talking to K.W.!" Desperate to try to fix the situation, Max not only consults the advice of K.W.'s new friends Bob and Terry but even brings them back to the fort for further help. When he does so though, a jealous Carol explodes: "Why did you bring them here? This place was supposed to be for us! They're not sleeping in our pile!"

In a final desperate attempt to reunite the group, Max proposes an activity that is as fun it is cathartic: a dirt-clod war. The young boy's suggestion emerges from a powerfully idyllic impulse. As he tells his monster friends, clobbering each other with giant hunks of soil is "the best way to have a fun together." Ira agrees, and asserts in what can be seen as a nostalgic comment, "Yeah, life was simpler back then, with the dirt clods." Within minutes after the war commences, however, conflict emerges. First, The Goat complains that the other team is not playing according to the rules: "That's cheating! . . . That's not fair. Are you crazy?! That wasn't fair. Douglas hit me when I was hurt. You can't hit someone when they're hurt. I quit." Then, a few moments afterward and even more explosively, K.W. and Carol get into an argument:

> Carol: You stepped on my head!
> K.W.: What do you mean? It's a war! Douglas just did it.
> Carol.: Yeah, but he did it by accident. You did it on purpose! And he didn't step on the face part of my head!
> K.W.: It was a joke. I was just joking.
> Carol: Sure you were. Like you aren't always looking for the opportunity to step on my head. Because that's what you do.
> K.W.: Fine, fine. You know what? This is exactly why I don't ever wanna do anything with you anymore. (*Where the Wild Things Are,* 2009)

K.W. offers Carol the chance to step on her head to make things even, but he refuses. Their argument brings the dirt-clod war to an abrupt end for everyone. Later that night, Judith indicts not simply Max's idea of having the dirt-clod fight but his idea of being king: "So King. What's going on? This is how you rule a kingdom? Everyone fighting? The bad guys feel bad. Everyone feels bad." Afterward, Max confides in The Goat: "I really messed this place up." The Goat's reply forms one of the most powerful moments where idealized nostalgia is shattered by harsh reality: "You're not really a king, huh? You're just regular. I knew it. I don't even know if there's such a thing as a king who can do all the things you said."

Before long, Carol calls for the complete destruction of the fort, a symbol not only of the group's new home but also of Max's big project as king. After waking everyone up in the middle of the night, Carol announces: "We gotta tear the fort down . . . It wasn't supposed to be like this! You said we were all going to sleep together in a real pile . . . I can't trust what you say. Everything keeps changing." A few of the others try to dissuade him, but he insists. The reason that he cites sound simultaneously like a disappointed child accusing a parent who has failed to protect him and a disillusioned adult who is angry that his idyllic dreams have given way to imperfect reality. Carol says of the fort: "It was supposed to be a place where only things you wanted to have happen would happen ... You were supposed to keep us safe. You were supposed to take care of us, and you didn't." Later, when Max tries to console an emotionally shaken K.W.—assuring her about Carol, "But he loves you. You're his family"—K.W. offers the ultimate non-nostalgic view of childhood and of all phases of the human life cycle: "It's hard being a family." In the wake of this exchange, Max comes to the realization: "I'm gonna go home." In this way, the nostalgic return to childhood in Jonze's *Where the Wild Things Are* ultimately proves to be far from an enjoyable or even positive experience.

These details place Jonze's film in dialogue with what Svetlana Boym has called the difference between "restorative nostalgia" and "reflective nostalgia." Creating these two new taxonomies as a means to further "illuminate some of nostalgia's mechanisms of seduction and manipulation," she provides the following distinction between them: "Restorative nostalgia stresses *nostros* and attempts a transhistorical reconstruction of the lost home. Reflective nostalgia thrives in *algia*, the longing itself, and delays the homecoming—wistfully, ironically, desperately" (Boym xviii). To illustrate the difference that these emphases yield, Boym goes on to explain: "Restorative nostalgia protects the absolute truth while reflective nostalgia calls it into doubt" (xviii).

The nostalgia at play in Jonze's movie may initially seem like restorative—or one that indulges, feeds and perpetuates wistful longing and sentimental idealization—but it ultimately reveals itself as reflective—or as one that reveals such romanticization as flawed, faulty and even fraudulent. In this way, while Sendak's picture book helps children process the emotion of anger, Jonze's cinematic adaption can be seen as helping adults confront and conquer their feelings of nostalgia. George Wildman Ball, in what has become an oft-repeated remark, once said: "Nostalgia is a seductive liar" (qtd in Robertson 29). Whether these misconceptions occur via adult views of current children or via recollections about their own childhoods, they are just as historically faulty, personally inaccurate and—as Max's experience demonstrates—emotionally painful. Maurice Sendak once said: "'My great curiosity is about childhood as a state of being, and how children manage to get through childhood from one day to the next, how they defeat boredom, fear, pain, and anxiety, and find joy. It is a constant miracle to me that children manage to grow up" (qtd Lanes 85). For all of its appeal to adult recollections about a beloved book, Spike Jonze's feature-length film of *Where the Wild Things Are* ultimately reveals that when individuals do reach adulthood, it is best to remain in this state. In this way, if the 2009 movie is nostalgic for anything, it is for the concept of nostalgia itself—a message that, appropriately, is in keeping with the original aim and intent of Sendak's story.

Notes

1. Sendak's *Where the Wild Things Are* is not paginated. Thus, my quotations here and throughout the remainder of the essay do not contain page citations. Given the relatively short length of *Where the Wild Things Are*, readers should not have trouble locating my cited passages.

2. As figures like Henry Giroux, Lawrence Grossberg and, more recently, Robin Bernstein have written, conceptions of childhood innocence had a particular class and especially race bias. As I discuss in my book *Raising Your Kids Right*, "All too often, images of the 'innocent child' are images of white, middle-class, blue-eyed and blond-haired children. In the words of Giroux, 'When dealing with kids whose lives do not fit the Ozzie and Harriet family profile, middle-class adults invoke the antithesis of innocence'" (Abate 170).

3. The animated short was directed by Gene Deitch and debuted on American television in 1973. Meanwhile, the operatic version first opened in Brussels in 1980. For more information on this production, see George R. Bodmer's "Sendak into Opera: *Wild Things* and *Higglety Pigglety Pop!*," *The Lion and the Unicorn*, 16.2 (December 1992): 167–175.

Works Cited

Abate, Michelle Anne. *Raising Your Kids Right: Children's Literature and American Political Conservatism*. New Brunswick, NJ: Rutgers University Press, 2010.

Arakelian, Paul G. "Text and Illustration: A Stylistic Analysis of Books by Sendak and Mayer." *Children's Literature Association Quarterly*. 10.3 (Fall 1985): 122–127.

Ariès, Philippe. *Centuries of Childhood: A Social History of Family Life*. 1960. Trans. Robert Baldick. New York: Vintage, 1962.

Bernstein, Robin. *Racial Innocence: Performing American Childhood in Black and White*. New York: New York University Press, 2011.

Boym, Svetlana. *The Future of Nostalgia*. New York: Basic Books, 2001.
Dargis, Manohla. "Some of His Best Friends Are Beasts." *The New York Times*. October 16, 2009. www.nytimes.com/2009/10/16/movies/16where.html (accessed April 27, 2012).
DeLuca, Geraldine. "Exploring the Levels of Childhood: The Allegorical Sensibility of Maurice Sendak." *Children's Literature*. 12 (1984): 3–24.
Dika, Vera. *Recycled Culture in Contemporary Art and Film: The Uses of Nostalgia*. Cambridge: Cambridge University Press, 2003.
Grau, Sergi. "Where the Wild Things Are." *Confesiones de una Mente Peligrosa*. January 23, 2010. cineconfesiones.blogspot.com/2010_01_01_archive.html 14 (accessed March 11, 2011).
Hart, Hugh. "Review: *Where the Wild Things Are* Is Woolly, but Not Wild Enough." *Underwire*. October 16, 2009. www.wired.com/underwire/2009/10/review-where-the-wild-things-are-is-woolly-but-not-wild-enough/# (accessed March 11, 2010).
Hentoff, Nat. *Profiles*. "Among Wild Things." *New Yorker*, January 22, 1966: 39-73.
Hunt, Peter. *Children's Literature: An Illustrated History*. New York: Oxford, 1995.
Jacoby, Mario. *The Longing for Paradise: Psychological Perspectives on an Archetype*. Trans. Myron B. Gubitz. Boston: Sigo, 1985.
Jameson, Fredric. *Postmodernism, or the Cultural Logic of Late Capitalism*. London: Verso, 1991.
Kincaid, James. *Child-Loving: The Erotic Child and Victorian Culture*. New York: Routledge, 1994.
Lanes, Selma. *The Art of Maurice Sendak*. New York: Abrams, 1980.
McGavran, Jr. James Holt. "'The Children Sport upon the Shore': Romantic Vision in Two Twentieth-Century Picture Books." *Children's Literature Association Quarterly*. 11.4 (1986/1987): 170–175.
Poniewozik, James. "Television: Reheat & Serve." *Time Magazine*. February 2, 2004. http://www.time.com/time/magazine/article/0,9171,993231,00.html.
Robertson, Connie. *Dictionary of Quotations*, third ed. Hertfordshire, England: Wordsworth, 1998.
Rubenstein, Roberta. *Home Matters: Longing and Belonging, Nostalgia and Mourning in Women's Fiction*. New York: Palgrave, 2001.
Scott, A. O. "Unleashing Life's Wild Things." *New York Times*. November 8, 2009: AR13.
Sendak, Maurice. *Where the Wild Things Are*. 1963. New York: Harper Collins, 1991.
Shaddock, Jennifer. "*Where the Wild Things Are* Sendak's Journey into the Heart of Darkness." *Children's Literature Association Quarterly*. 22, no. 4 (Winter 1997): 155–159.
Spufford, Francis. *The Child That Books Built: A Life in Reading*. New York: Henry Holt, 2002.
Sturken, Marita *Tourists of History: Memory, Kitsch, and Consumerism from Oklahoma City to ground Zero*. Durham, NC: Duke University Press, 2007.
Taylor, Laurie N. and Zach Whalen. "Playing in the Past: An Introduction." *Playing the Past: History and Nostalgia in Video Games*. Eds. Zach Whalen and Laurie N. Taylor. Nashville, TN: Vanderbilt University Press, 2008. 1–15.
Waller, Jennifer R. "Maurice Sendak and the Blakean Vision of Childhood." *Children's Literature*. 6 (1977): 130-140.
Where the Wild Things Are. Dir. Spike Jonze. Warner Brothers, 2009.

Chapter Ten
"They Don't Really Care What Happens to Me": Divorce, Family Life, and Children's Emotional Worlds in 1950s' British Cinema

by Janet Fink

> At the limits of language, of culture, of knowledge, the child can always be used to make the familiar strange, the domestic uncanny, in a way that also draws on that attachment to the image of the child as an incitement to compassion, pity, feeling—above all the future.[1]

Introduction

In 1945 Humphrey Jennings's much-praised British documentary film *A Diary for Timothy* was released,[2] an acknowledgement of the sacrifices endured by Britain's civilian and military populations during six years of war and an indication of the hopes invested in children for a future of peace. The voice-over in this powerful film is focused upon Timothy, a newborn baby, and his family, making them the subject of a commentary in which change seems inevitable yet uncertain in its political and social outcomes. The result is a poignancy in the observations of the film as a whole but especially at its conclusion when Timothy is asked: "Are you going to make the world a different place, you and the other babies?" For children born at this particular moment in British history, the expectations and aspirations that society had for them were shaped by concern for the future together with an anxiety to exorcise a past marked for so many by fear, separation and loss. Such adult investments in the figure of the child and fears for the innocence of childhood were not new phenomena and nor was the use of documentaries and feature films to express them. However, analysis of representations of children and their emotional and psychological well-being in such sources are particularly revealing since they point both to the very pressing political and policy concerns about family life in Britain during the postwar years and to the nature of wider ideas, practices and beliefs around childhood that were being negotiated in the country's transition to peacetime.

Understanding of the social and emotional cultures that shaped such constructions of childhood in the 1950s and their intersections with policy and legal reforms has been much enriched by studies of postwar British cinema.[3] More especially, research into family melodramas and social problem films that were produced between the late 1940s and early 1960s has revealed not only the ways in which broader social concerns were displaced onto the family but also how the portrayal of familial relationships might be seen as representative of a society struggling to maintain a sense of continuity and consensus in the aftermath of the Second World War.[4]

My discussion builds upon this rich body of work through a focus on two postwar British films, *No Place for Jennifer* (1950) and *Background* (1953), which are entirely consumed by concerns about the effects of divorce upon the psychological and emotional well-being of the middle-class child. The two films are similar in terms of genre in that, using Marcia Landy's definition, they can be loosely categorised as family melodramas since both "the problematic of the home and the nuclear family haunts the narratives"[5] while the conventions of melodrama are frequently drawn upon, as in the excess of music that features so powerfully in *No Place for Jennifer*. Yet the films also employ documentary elements such as the instructional voice-over that featured in *A Diary for Timothy*. *Background* opens, for example, with a solemn commentary about the law and divorce thereby ensuring that the film's concern with children's experience of this particular postwar "social problem" is not lost or forgotten by the audience. However the significance of such a hybridization of melodrama and documentary in *No Place for Jennifer* and *Background* can best be appreciated through Lisa Cartwright's argument about hybridity in other films of the 1950s. She identifies how the juxtaposition of different genres opened up a transitional space in which social issues, generally left unspoken in postwar public culture because of stigma and shame, could be articulated and worked through.[6] Thus the transitional space that emerges out of the use of melodramatic and documentary devices and conventions in these two films about family breakdown allows for the shameful phenomenon of divorce in postwar Britain to be acknowledged and, more particularly, for children's resulting experiences of loss and distress to be portrayed and recognised.

No Place For Jennifer was produced by the Associated British Picture Corporation, having been adapted from the novel *No Difference to Me* (1949)[7] by one of the cinema company's more experienced script writers, J. Lee Thompson.[8] The film received mixed reviews but, notably, Janette Scott, the child actor who played the part of Jennifer, is praised both for "being quite remarkable" and because she "will probably earn for the film as a whole, a success it does not really deserve."[9] The second film, *Background*, was an adaptation from Warren Chetham Strode's play of the same title, first performed in the West End in 1950.[10] Its reviews noted that it was a film not "of grand emotions, although it is one of human emotions."[11] However, the performance of the child actor, Linda, played by Mandy Miller, is similarly commended with one critic declaring that she has 'an astonishing understanding which seems to have nothing to do with precocity.'[12] Indeed the moving nature of Mandy Miller's appearance in *Background* is likely to have been intensified for critics through memories of the quality and emotional intensity of her performance in the box-office success *Mandy*, a powerful account of a young deaf girl's education and struggle to acquire speech, which had been released twelve months earlier in 1952.[13] Moreover, the obvious impact that these child actors made upon the critics is of particular consequence as it reinforces Harry Hendrick's point about the power of visual imagery to portray emotion and its interpellation of the viewer to *look* and to *see* in ways which foreground children's subjective experiences of distress, vulnerability and anxiety.[14] Yet what is equally significant about these films is the way in which parents and other adults are portrayed as refusing *their* responsibilities for looking and seeing with the result that the figure of the child with divorced or divorcing parents is represented as vulnerable and potentially at risk, physically and psychologically, in both the private and public spheres of 1950s' British society.

The distressed and anxious child who features in these films about divorce indicates, then, something of the period's "structure of feeling"; an idea developed by Raymond Williams in an attempt to capture a mood, sensibility or atmosphere of a particular historical period or generation.[15] For the postwar years, when social, political and demographic change was extensive but wartime experiences had not been forgotten, Williams's argument is especially pertinent since he reminds us that culture is dynamic and is constituted both from the "residual," those elements that have been formed in the past but are still active in the present, and the "emergent," that is new meanings, values, relationships and practices.[16] And it is Williams's distinction between the residual and the emergent that suggests how the figure of the child in the cinema can be seen to stand at the heart of the often competing beliefs, values and norms about family life that were being made and remade so energetically in the structure of feeling following the end of the Second World War.

Contexts and Cultures of Childhood, Family Life and Divorce

Both *No Place for Jennifer* and *Background* are haunted by the anger, distress and uncertainty of the children's characters, following their parents' separation and divorce. The films' conceptions of the child's emotional world can be understood as embedded in a particularly specific construction of childhood which had been influenced by two major child welfare developments. First, the work of child guidance clinics in the 1930s and psychological and psychoanalytic research conducted during the war years on the emotional development of young children in residential nurseries and following wartime evacuation had had wide-ranging effects.[17] Dorothy Burlingham and Anna Freud's study, *Young Children in War-Time in a Residential Nursery*, and Susan Isaacs, *The Cambridge Evacuation Survey*,[18] had explained that it was the separation of young children from their home and primary caregivers, rather than the experiences of the actual war, which was detrimental to children's well-being; with Isaacs's evidence from essays written by evacuated children themselves providing very compelling records of the experiences of leaving "loved ones and the securities of home."[19] This is picked up, for example, in 1946 by the British Medical Association, which notes that: "The biological approach to [the young child's] physical, and more particularly mental, health is through the family."[20] And, in subsequent years, the importance of emotional well-being to children's mental health was further reinforced by influential research at the Tavistock's Separation Unit in London. This included the work on attachment and loss by the child psychoanalyst John Bowlby and his theory of maternal deprivation, disseminated in the hugely popular *Child Care and the Growth of Love*.[21] It also led to James Robertson's documentary film *A Two Year Old Goes to Hospital* (1952) which powerfully illustrated the trauma that very young children experienced when hospitalised and separated from their family.[22]

The second important influence was the postwar Labour government's determination to promote the rights and needs of individual children, as valued future citizens, to be raised within stable, secure family units. In this context the emotional well-being of children became a key element in the development of postwar social and welfare reforms, particularly in the Curtis Committee Report (1946) and Children Act (1948), establishing in turn new principles for the state in its support and protection of children within their families. Such a progressive politics of children's mental health,[23] shaped by an understanding of childhood in which the successful development of a child's personal identity and relationships depended on sustained emotional attachments, thus informed the portrayal of the figure of the child during the 1940s and 1950s. As suggested by *A Diary for Timothy* and as recounted in other short documentary films about childcare produced during the Second World War, Britain's "ultimate realisation of that brave new world of our dreams"[24] depended not only upon the future generations of its children but also their emotional well-being.

Given these aspirations for children and, relatedly, the future of Britain, it is perhaps not surprising that the question of divorce and its consequences for the children of divorcing parents was such an issue in the postwar years and was raised so insistently in popular culture and by the media. Because of the high divorce rates in this period, resulting often from both the incidence of hasty wartime marriages and the prolonged separation of some married couples as a result of their role in the armed services or the labour market, the "rights and wrongs" of divorce had become a topic of widespread and contentious debate amongst social commentators, religious leaders and politicians. The number of divorce petitions rose, for example, from 11,613 in 1942 to 18,390 in 1944, and peaked in 1946 at 41,704.[25] The establishment in 1946 of the Denning Committee, to improve the opportunities for reconciliation between separated and divorcing couples, was an attempt by the Labour government to acknowledge both the war years' legacy on personal relationships and wider fears about a future in which marriage and the nuclear family might no longer be society's bulwark. In the same year, letters to *The Times* demonstrate the extent of anxiety about the numbers of divorce petitions and contested suits, noting that "there must be hundreds of children whose home will be destroyed"[26] and arguing that attempts should be made to mitigate "the deplorable position of so many children on whom the future of the nation depends."[27]

These, then, were the policy and political contexts in which the novel, *No Difference to Me*, and the play, *Background*, had been produced and which had shaped their portrayals of troubled childhoods and family breakdown. Their screen adaptations at the beginning of the 1950s were no less embedded in public and political debates about divorce. In 1950 the Labour MP Mrs. Eirene White had introduced her Private Member's Bill, which challenged the crucial issue of matrimonial fault in divorce law and proposed that, after a period of seven years separation, a guilty party could begin divorce proceedings.[28] In response to the support for this bill, a Royal Commission on Marriage and Divorce, which sat between 1951 and 1955, was established by the government to investigate whether divorce law should be reformed, how "healthy and happy married life" could be promoted and how "the interests and well-being of children" could be safeguarded.[29] As these two films suggest, however, happy married life and children's well-being were not always mutually compatible.

The Significance of Home to Children's Emotional Well-Being

With their focus on the breakup of family homes[30] and marital relationships, both films work to portray the fluidity and fragility of children's emotional well-being as well as the child's psychological needs. *No Place for Jennifer* tells the story of a bitter court battle over the custody of Jennifer, the only child of middle-class divorced parents. The "place" which the child holds within her two family homes and in the relations between her parents is shown to be deeply problematic for she is portrayed as a liminal figure whose interests become increasingly secondary to the needs and desires of the adults around her. It is not that Jennifer is represented as being unloved; her parents are very involved in her care and treat her with great affection. However the film emphasises their lack of any psychological understanding of her needs, portraying Jennifer as a lonely, isolated child whose deep distress at her parents' separation is never recognized by them. As the film's narrative develops, this parental critique is extended with the child's emotional attachments shown to be at risk by, on the one hand, her mother's re-marriage to a musician and, on the other, the marriage of her father to Jennifer's schoolteacher who quickly becomes pregnant with his child. Jennifer herself declares: "They both make a fuss of me but they don't really care what happens to me. Nobody does."

These themes of unsettled emotional attachments and inattentive parenting run similarly through *Background*, which charts the decision to divorce by an upper middle-class barrister and his wife and the effects of this upon their three children, Jess, Adrian and Linda. Here, however, the emphasis is on how the loss of a childhood home following divorce impacts upon the child and the emotional upheaval that is provoked as a result. In line with the psychoanalytic research of the war years, *Background* suggests that home, family life and emotional stability are inextricably entwined and, as a result, children's dislocation from their homes causes deep distress. Picking up a question that the youngest child, Linda, will ask later in the film following her parents' separation, the opening voice-over of the film comments: "Children go uncomfortably to the heart of the matter: where will be our home?" One of the film's concerns, then, is to expose how the home is constituted in legal terms as the "background" to divorce while emphasising its centrality to children's sense of identity and emotional security.

Both films use such a psychoanalytically informed awareness of the child's need for a secure home life to highlight the ways in which the wartime phenomenon of childhood dislocation was being perpetuated in peacetime through the separation and divorce of married couples with children. As in other 1950s' British films such as *Mandy* (1952) and *Room at the Top* (1959), *No Place for Jennifer* uses the familiar image of the bombsite to compare the disruptions of the past with ongoing instabilities of children's family lives.[31] After she has run away from the High Court, where a decision is to be made about her custody, Jennifer is shown using an empty bombed house as a haven from the menaces of a predatory man whom she has encountered in her solitary journey across London.[32] (See illustration 10.1.)

While this derelict house provides a refuge for the child, it also serves to remind the audience that it is the actions of Jennifer's parents which have placed the child's emotional security and physical safety at risk for, through their acrimonious divorce and hasty remarriages, they have removed their daughter from the protection of her *own* home and exposed her to the dangers of the nighttime streets. It is, therefore, the private, familial space of the bombed house that preserves the innocence of Jennifer's childhood and, more especially, her gendered vulnerability in the public world.

Such evocation of the war years to critique how children continue to be damaged, emotionally and psychologically, in peacetime Britain is deployed in *Background* through the character of the children's nanny, Brownie, played by the German-born actor Lily Kann. Having also been the nanny of the children's mother, Brownie takes advantage of her long service in the household and her intimate knowledge of the family to condemn the parents' decision to divorce. As importantly, her own family background is used to remind Barbie, the mother, and the audience that the outcomes of the Second World War remain a potent and damaging feature of other lives, in other places. Brownie notes with great sadness:

> I've just come back from my sister in Berlin. She has four children; her husband is not very well so they haven't got much money. But the children are happy. You know why? Because they have got a mother and a father and so they've got a home.

Unspoken, but implicit in this comment about Berlin, is reference to the continued suffering being experienced in East and West Germany. Indeed in the original play, Brownie's description of her sister's experiences and the emphasis placed on the spatial importance of home life is much more direct: "She has four children—she used to have five. The eldest one, Fritz, the Russians took him away . . . My sister, and her husband, they live in a cellar."

Looking and Seeing the Effects of Divorce and Family Breakdown

In such ways the audience is invited to recall painful wartime experiences and to understand the distress caused by family breakdown in the present, particularly by looking and seeing children's anguish in scenes which, as the reviews by critics illustrated, were powerfully affective. *No Place for Jennifer* depicts both the psychic and physical manifestations of the child's misery with the former being portrayed through a disturbing nightmare scene. While Jennifer sleeps, her body's heavy perspiration and restless turning in the bed indicate the emotional upheaval she is experiencing, but it is through a series of kaleidoscopic images and a cacophony of noise that the degree of her mental anxiety is made explicit. As the film music increases in tempo and volume, so the noises of ringing phones and clicking metronomes are woven uncomfortably into the sound track, pointing to the chaotic disorientation of her interior world. Jennifer also dreams of a commonplace family ritual, in which she is happily framed by the figures of her parents as they celebrate her birthday, but this shifts to a nightmare when they raise a knife aggressively to destroy her birthday cake. Thus the film offers a psychoanalytic view of the child's sense of self and of the way in which her emotional well-being was being attacked by her parents' divorce and remarriages, a view reinforced through her eventual referral to a child psychology clinic because of her increasingly withdrawn behaviour and where her "wild animal feelings" are recognised by staff as the product of being "torn to pieces by conflicting loyalties." The visual tropes and discursive repertoires used to portray her tormented, frightened and anxious mind suggest also her powerless position as *victim* in the parental struggle over custody.

While such glimpses into a child's interior world might never be accessible to parents, Jennifer's mother and father are shown as failing consistently to notice the effects of their behaviour upon her even when she is in their physical presence. In scenes of conversations between them, her feelings of insecurity and anxiety are repeatedly emphasised through extended close-up shots of her face and facial expressions, which convey her emotional suffering and reinforce the sense of her isolation. During a scene in which mother and father become locked in a confrontation about custody, they lose sight, in all senses, of their daughter's distress which, as the camera pulls slowly away from the couple to focus on the child standing at the doorway, becomes increasingly evident and audible to the audience. (See illustration 10.2.)

And, through the film as a whole, Jennifer is repeatedly shown to be invisible to other adults around her. She is able to slip unnoticed from school and her teachers; after she runs away from the High Court, she successfully avoids the police who are looking for her; and she secretes herself in the home of her childhood friend, without his parents being aware of her presence. Moreover, the representation of this inability, or unwillingness, of adults to see Jennifer and her misery is reinforced by the many scenes of journeys by train and on foot that she makes alone and that situate her as a vulnerably invisible child in the public world.

This theme of children's invisibility when marital relationships break down can be similarly traced in *Background*, where the inability of the parents to appreciate the children's anger and distress at their decision to divorce is played out through strong contrasting scenes between the children and the marital couple. The two older children, Jess and Adrian, physically and verbally attack each other in an extremely violent fight over their mother's decision to marry Bill, a friend of the family, once her divorce from their father has been finalised. The fight concludes with Adrian throwing himself in tears on the floor, declaring that he'd "like to kill everyone." This is immediately followed by a scene in which the parents have dinner together to discuss arrangements for the divorce. They discuss how well Jess, Adrian and Linda had taken their news and, thereby, demonstrate no awareness of their children's emotional distress. While the parents negotiate the terms of their divorce together in a quiet and respectful manner, thus making them appreciate what they are about to lose, the older children turn their anger on each other. The relationship between the siblings breaks down and any affection between them or understanding of their respective feelings evaporates. Jess self-servingly manipulates her father and mother's prospective second husband into giving her expensive gifts and revels in the notoriety that her parents' forthcoming divorce will afford her. Adrian becomes broodingly introverted and aggressive. Manifesting a different emotional reaction, the youngest child, Linda, silently turns to the children's elderly nanny for support in her confusion and anguish.

What can be identified in *Background*, then, is a concern with the connections between family breakdown and children's maladjustment, a notion which, as Nikolas Rose has suggested, "gathered all the problems of the school age child, from temper tantrums to truancy, from nervousness to nastiness."[33] In this the film portrays how divorce and the dynamics of step-parenting might be as detrimental to a middle-class child's psychological well-being as the effects of poverty and deprivation for a working-class child, unsettling in turn dominant constructions of "problem families" in this period and their features of "low social status, low income, poor housing, poor physical and mental health, criminality and child neglect."[34] However, the film also displays a particular gendered understanding of maladjustment, with Adrian being characterised as "troubled" because of his feelings of anger and aggression towards his sister and Bill, while Jess is portrayed as dangerously shallow, acquisitive and self-absorbed. With Adrian seeking to resolve his family's problems by shooting Bill and Jess being increasingly preoccupied with how her life will improve materially once her mother remarries, these older children are illustrative of an emerging anxiety about young people's behaviour that would be drawn out much more explicitly in later 1950s' films about working-class youth, specifically in relation to issues of girls' sexuality and boys' delinquency.[35]

Yet while these differently gendered emotional responses are all shown to be cause for concern, it is the nanny, together with the audience, who is their witness not the parents. It is the nanny who sees and notes that Jess has "a bad streak" which has been aggravated by her parents' separation and which could become a permanently damaging characteristic since her parents "won't be together to help her." It is the nanny who sees the knife with which Adrian had threatened Jess and takes it into her safekeeping. And it is the nanny who comforts Linda when she is ignored by her mother, who is too absorbed in her own feelings about separating from her husband to see her young daughter's distress.

At the same time this motif of children's invisibility to their parents is contrasted with the way in which divorce also demands an equally damaging hyper-visibility of all of them, because of its powerful capacity to stigmatise individuals and families. One of Adrian's anxieties about his parents' divorce is that he will be "different" from boys at his boarding school whose parents are married and that he will become the focus of unwelcome interest. As he says about another boy with divorced parents, "He's different. There's something about him. He feels everyone's looking at him when his mother comes down to see him." This sense of being exposed to the critical scrutiny of others is shared equally by the child in *No Place for Jennifer* who is distraught at becoming a subject of gossip amongst her school friends and dreads further talk when the custody case is reported in the newspapers. For Jess, however, being the centre of attention is regarded as a welcome pleasure, and she boasts "Everyone will be looking at me. When you and daddy are divorced, I'll be jolly famous."

Resolutions to each of these films are constructed around the restoration of the children to their parents' gaze, but this is only achieved through their physical disappearance from and return to the home. Both Jennifer in *No Place for Jennifer* and Adrian in *Background* go missing and, by this action, produce intense feelings of fear and guilt in the parents and invoke in the audience the horror of losing a child. Their parents are forced to look and to see that which they have ignored prior to the child's disappearance and, moreover, to try and imagine the child's interior world too. As Adrian's father declares in an angry encounter with Bill about where the boy might be, "I'm trying to see into Adrian's mind not yours." In this respect Emma Wilson's comment about a series of films made since 1990, which have a missing child as their subject, is equally relevant for these films of the 1950s. She writes:

> The issue of the missing child enables films to mobilise questions about the protection and innocence of childhood, about parenthood and family, about the past (as childhood is constructed in retrospect as nostalgic space of safety) and about the future (as fears for children reflect anxiety about the inheritance left to future generations).[36]

These earlier films, however, firmly place responsibility for addressing these questions upon the parents of the missing child and, unlike those considered by Wilson, deny any possibilities of transforming the normative family.

In *Background*, Adrian's disappearance sparks an anxiety in the nanny that he might commit suicide as he had taken a rifle to school with him, but the boy uses the gun to shoot Bill, who suffers a minor flesh wound. Adrian's return to the family home and the shooting mean that the boy's mother finally looks and sees his feelings of anger and hatred and appreciates that her son had genuinely intended to kill Bill. As a result of this act of witnessing, Adrian's parents decide that the children's unhappiness is so great that they should not divorce. They agree their primary responsibility is to the children's well-being, irrespective of their feelings for each other: "We'll just have to do the best we can. Put a brave face on it even if it's only in front of the children." The moral and social norms of monogamous marriage and the nuclear family as the location of an ideal childhood are thus upheld and children's emotional security prioritised over the happiness and well-being of their parents.

The restoration of the marital relationship and the family home is impossible in *No Place for Jennifer* as the child's parents have divorced and remarried. Nevertheless both continue to be held out as the only possibilities for addressing the child's needs for emotional security. Like Adrian's mother, Jennifer's parents finally look and see the intensity of Jennifer's distress when she is found hiding in the home of her friend, Martin Marshall, and where she admits: "I wanted to kill myself." This realisation of the effects of their divorce and struggle for custody results in their agreement to Jennifer's request that she be allowed to stay with the Marshall family indefinitely, with her mother tearfully accepting that she must do "what's best for the child." With the Marshalls as quasi-parents, her mother acknowledges that Jennifer is sure to be "one of the family—a happy family" and the child's inclusion in this secure family unit promises her emotional needs will be met in ways in which living with either of her parents and their new spouses could not.

Concluding Remarks

Such sacrifices by the parents produce uneasy resolutions to each of these films, for while their child-centred narratives have reinforced the vulnerability of childhood and the responsibility of parents to protect and nurture their daughters and sons, there has also been a refusal to engage with the question of divorce from any point of view other than the child's. The films acknowledge the difficulties and complexities of marriage in the postwar years but the "problem" of divorce is reduced to the child's needs and relationships, with parents criticised for failing to recognise that their happiness, wishes and desires cannot be prioritised over their children's. In the case of Jennifer's parents, they are also punished by the loss of their child to another family. Audiences thus struggle to negotiate morally ambiguous narratives in which children's distress at their parents' divorce is afforded greater significance than the emotional pain of an unhappy marital relationship or losing a child. It is, however, the figure of the child which powerfully emerges as the ultimate arbiter in these negotiations for, in this historical moment, children's suffering evoked too many memories of wartime loss, separation and dislocation and too many fears about a future in which the institutions of marriage and the nuclear family might no longer provide the security understood to be needed by child and society alike.

Acknowledgements

This chapter is an extended version of an earlier article that appeared as "The Responsibilities of Looking and Seeing: Broken Homes and Troubled Childhoods in Two Postwar British Films" in *Cinemascope–Independent Film Journal*, Issue 13, Year V, July–December 2009. I am grateful for the permission from Cinemascope's Editorial Board to reprint here. The film stills that appear in this chapter are reproduced courtesy of Canal + Image UK and the BFI.

Illustrations

Illustration 10.1
The "unprotected child"
Still from the film, *No Place for Jennifer* (1950)
Reproduced courtesy of Canal + Image UK and the BFI.

Illustration 10.2
The "unseen child"
Still from the film, *No Place for Jennifer* (1950)
Reproduced courtesy of Canal + Image UK and the BFI.

Notes

1. Vicky Lebeau (2008) *Childhood and Cinema*, London: Reaktion Books, 176.

2. *A Diary for Timothy* (Humphrey Jennings, Crown Film Unit; UK, 1945). This was one of the more famous wartime documentary films made by Jennings for the Crown Film Unit. Detailed considerations of his work can be found in, for example, Anthony Aldgate and Jeffrey Richards (1994) *Britain Can Take It: The British Cinema in the Second World War*, Edinburgh: Edinburgh University Press; Geoffrey Nowell-Smith, "Humphrey Jennings: Surrealist Observer," in Charles Barr (ed.) (1986) *All Our Yesterdays: 90 Years of British Cinema*, London: BFI Publishing; and Adrian Smith (2003) "Humphrey Jennings' Heart of Britain," *Historical Journal of Film, Radio and Television*, Vol .23, No. 2, 133–151. Wendy Webster (1998) offers an insightful gendered analysis of the film in *Imagining Home: Gender, 'Race' and National Identity, 1945–64*, London: UCL Press.

3. Melanie Bell (2010) *Femininity in the Frame: Women and 1950s British Popular Cinema,* London: I. B.Tauris; Christine Geraghty (2000) *British Cinema in the Fifites: Gender, Genre and the "New Look,"* London: Routledge; Christine Gledhill and Gillian Swanson (eds.) (1996) *Nationalising Femininity: Culture, Sexuality and Briitsh Cinema in the Second World War*, Manchester: Manchester University Press; Marcia Landy (1991) *British Genres: Cinema and Society, 1930–1960,* Princeton, NJ: Princeton University Press; Lola Young (1996) *Fear of the Dark: Race, Gender and Sexuality in the Cinema*, London: Routledge.

4. Marcia Landy (1991) *British Genres: Cinema and Society 1930-1960,* Princeton, NJ: Princeton University Press.

5 Landy, *British Genres*, 285.

6. Lisa Cartwright (2008) *Moral Spectatorship. Technologies of Voice and Affect in Postwar Representations of the Child*, Durham and London: Duke University Press, 58. Christine Gledhill notes that there is a tense relationship between melodrama and realism in early postwar British cinema and such tensions are evident in these films as they shift between exaggeration and sentimentality in the depiction of family life and more sensitive attempts to portray the child's anxieties and fears. See C. Gledhill (1996) "An Abundance of Understatement: Documentary, Realism and Romance" in Christine Gledhill and Gillian Swanson (eds.), *Nationalising Femininity: Culture, Sexuality and British Cinema in the Second World War*, Manchester: Manchester University Press,. 218. The ways in which melodrama and realism might be distinguished are discussed in Julia Hallam with Margaret Marshment (2000) *Realism and Popular Cinema*, Manchester: Manchester University Press.

7. Phyllis Hambledon (1949) *No Difference to Me*, London: Sampson Low, Marston & Co., Ltd.

8. The novel was very loosely adapted by J. Lee Thompson on his return to the Associated British Picture Corporation (ABPC) after serving in the Second World War. See Sue Harper and Vincent Porter (2007) *British Cinema of the 1950s: The Decline of Deference*, Oxford: Oxford University Press. Harper and Vincent provide a full account of Thompson's work as writer and producer, noting that he was one of only two men "who managed to impose any visual style" on ABPC films (82) and that the more visual melodramatic elements of the film are likely to be the product of Thompson's reworking of the novel.

9. W. O. (1950) *Monthly Film Bulletin*, 17, 193/203, 4. On its release in the United States the film critic of *The New York Times* (July 17, 1951) was similarly less than fulsome in praise for this "tepid but touching little drama" while recognising that Janette Scott plays the part with "a fluid range between deep forlornness and beaming smiles."

10. There are very few differences between the play and the film, *Background*, perhaps because the playwright Warren Chetham Strode played a major role in the adaptation. Chetham-Strode also wrote the play *The Guinea Pig* (1946) which, in 1948, was made into a well-received film of the same title starring Richard Attenborough.

11. Anon. *Times*, October 5, 1953, 6.

12. Anon, *Times*, 6.

13. *Mandy* has been the focus of much work by film scholars. See, for example, Pam Cook (1986, 1996) '*Mandy*: Daughter of Transition' in Charles Barr (ed) *All Our Yesterdays: 90 Years of British Cinema*, London, BFI; Neil Sinyard (1992) *Children in the Movies*, London: B.T. Batsford Ltd; Annette Kuhn (1992) '*Mandy* and possibility', *Screen* Vol. 33, Issue 3, 233–243.

14. Harry Hendrick (2003) "Children's Emotional Well-Being and Mental Health in Post-War Britain," in M. Gijswit-Hofstra and H. Harland (eds.) *Cultures of Child Health in Britain and the Netherlands in the Twentieth* Century, Amsterdam: Rodopi, 221–222.

15. Raymond Williams (1961) *The Long Revolution*, London: Chatto & Windus; Raymond Williams and M. Orram (1954) *Preface to Film*, London: Film Drama.

16. Raymond Williams (1977) *Marxism and Literature*, Oxford: Oxford University Press, 122–123.

17. Denise Riley (1983) *War in the Nursery: Theories of the Child and the Mother*, London: Virago; Harry Hendrick (2003) *Child Welfare: Historical Dimensions, Contemporary Debates*, Bristol: Policy Press; Cathy Urwin and John Hood-Williams (eds) (1998) *Child Psychotherapy, War and the Normal Child: Selected Papers of Margaret Lowenfeld*, London, Free Association Books; Deborah Thom (1992) "Wishes, Anxieties, Play and Gesture: Child Guidance in Inter-War England" in Roger Cooter (ed.) *In the Name of the Child*, London, Routledge.

18. Dorothy Burlingham and Anna Freud (1942) *Young Children in War-Time: A Year's Work in a Residential Nursery*, London: Allen & Unwin; Susan Isaacs (ed.) (1941) *The Cambridge Evacuation Survey*, London: Methuen.

19. Burlingham, *Young Children*, 7.

20. Committee of the British Medical Association (1946) *A Charter for Health*, London: George Allen & Unwin.

21. John Bowlby (1953) *Child Care and the Growth of Love*, Harmondsworth: Penguin Books.

22. Harry Hendrick has very carefully and effectively explored the social and medical contexts to the production of *A Two Year Old Goes to Hospital* and the role played by Bowlby and Robertson in highlighting the emotional needs of young children in hospital to the government-appointed Committee on the Welfare of Children in Hospital. See Hendrick (2003) "Children's Emotional Well-Being and Mental Health in Post-War Britain," in M. Gijswijt-Hofstra and H. Marland (eds) *Cultures of Child Health in Britain and the Netherlands in the Twentieth Century*, Amsterdam: Rodop, 213–242.

23. Hendrick, *Cultures*, 221–222.

24. See, for example, the short documentary films *Heirs of Tomorrow* (1944), which portrays residential child care provided for the under-fives by the Red Cross and St

John's Organisation, and *The Village School* (1940), which details the work of a headmistress in a small school in the Buckinghamshire countryside.

25. For a more detailed and critical exploration of divorce statistics in this period, see O. R. McGregor (1957) *Divorce in England: A Centenary Study*, Heinemann: London, 39–57.

26. *Times*, August 28, 1946.

27. *Times*, November 18, 1946.

28. Carol Smart, "Good Wives and Moral Lives: Marriage and Divorce 1937–1951" in Christine Gledhill and Gillian Swanson (eds.) *Nationalising Feminity: Culture, Sexuality and British Cinema in the Second World War*, Manchester, Manchester University Press, 1996, 91 –105. See also discussion on divorce and everyday marital infidelity by Claire Langhammer (2006) "Adultery in Post-War England" in *History Workshop Journal*, Vol. 62, No. 1, 86–115.

29. Royal Commission on Marriage and Divorce, Report 1951-1955, London: HMSO, Cmd 9678, 7.

30. For explorations of the meanings and significance of home more generally in the postwar years, see Claire Langhammer (2005) "The Meanings of Home in Postwar Britain," in *Journal of Contemporary History*, 40, 340–362; Wendy Webster (1998) *Imagining Home: Gender "Race" and Identity, 1945–64*, London: UCL Press.

31. As Neil Sinyard notes about the film *Mandy* and its concerns with the difficulties of Mandy's family to communicate (both with her, as a deaf child and more generally), "the bomb-site is especially expressive and ironic. The rubble, on which children play, is the legacy from the previous generation and *their* tragic failure to communicate." See Sinyard (1992) *Children in the Movies*, 79. See too Christine Geraghty (2000) *British Cinema in the Fifties: Gender, Genre and New Look*, London: Routledge.

32. The stills in this chapter are used with permission of Canal + Image UK and the British Film Institute (BFI).

33. Nikolas Rose (1999) *Governing the Soul: The Shaping of the Private Self*, London: Free Association Books, 176.

34. Nikolas Rose, *Governing,* 174. There was an extensive literature in this period about "problem families" which included: Arthur T. Collis and Vera E. Poole (1950) *These Our Children*, London: Victor Gollancz; Council for Children's Welfare (1958) *Families with Problems*, London: Council for Children's Welfare; Marie Paneth (1944) *Branch Street: A Sociological Study*, London: George Allen & Unwin; Tom Stephens (ed) (1945) *Problem Families: An Experiment in Social Rehabilitation*, London: Pacifist Service Units.

35. John Hill (1995) *Sex, Class and Realism*, London: BFI.

36. Emma Wilson (2003) *Cinema's Missing Children*, London & New York: Wallflower Press, 2.

Filmography

Background. Dir. Daniel Birt. Group Three,1953.

A Diary for Timothy. Dir. Humphrey Jennings. Crown, 1945.

Mandy. Dir. Alexander MacKendrick. Ealing, 1952.

No Place for Jennifer. Dir. Henry Cass. Associated British Picture Corporation, 1950.

Room at the Top. Dir. Jack Clayton. Remus Films, 1959.

Chapter Eleven
Representations of Children in Pixar Films: 1995–2011
by Iris Shepard

Pixar, a highly successful animated film subsidiary of Disney, has produced and distributed twelve highly popular and entertaining animated films from 1995 through 2011. *Brave*, previously called *The Bear and the Bow*, was released in the summer of 2012. Even though Pixar is now owned by Disney, there seems to be a conscious attempt to distinguish Pixar films from the animated films of Disney proper. In 2006 when Disney purchased Pixar, Pixar retained its brand identity. Each Pixar film is a major cinematic event, and upon release Pixar's films have become instant children's classics. The most significant distinction between Pixar and many Disney films is that the protagonists in Pixar films are typically older than the main characters of the majority of Disney films. Pixar has dramatically reduced the number of children in their films. Russell, the boy in *Up*, is Pixar's most fully developed child character in all of Pixar's films as of this writing, but he serves primarily as a sidekick to the film's protagonist Carl who is sixty or seventy years old. Additionally, Pixar films feature very few anthropomorphized children; the main characters of Pixar films are anthropomorphized adults. The tremendous financial success of the Pixar films undoubtedly indicates that depictions of children—whether human or anthropomorphized animals or objects—are not a necessary component of successful children's films.

In Pixar films, child protagonists are replaced with primarily adult anthropomorphized characters including toys, ants, fish, cars, rats, and robots. Between the ages of three and nine, the target age for Pixar films, children's experiences involve primarily their roles in their family and school, and their relationship with their peer group. Though the anthropomorphized protagonists of Pixar's films experience situations that the young viewing audiences may be able to identify with, the solutions the protagonists develop are not transferable into the viewing child's life experience. Janet Wasko in *Understanding Disney* states that children's films allow viewers to "escape from an everyday reality that is not always pleasurable or fun, and may well pose challenging dilemmas" (224). Pixar films contain very few depictions of child protagonists navigating the world that the child viewers inhabit. Henry Giroux, in *The Mouse That Roared*, states:

> It is within the drama of animated storytelling that children are often positioned pedagogically to learn what subject positions are open to them and what positions are not. Hence, the struggle over children's culture should be considered as part of the struggle over the related discourses of citizenship, national identity, and democracy itself. (10)

The replacement of child protagonists by adult anthropomorphized animals and objects causes Pixar's films to forfeit the opportunity to offer constructive narratives about children navigating the precarious terrain of childhood. Through Pixar films, children may be learning that the best thing for them to do is to grow up as quickly as possible.

In Pixar's films, unlikely animals and machines including rats, fish, and cars are anthropomorphized to replace the children in children's films. In *Cars* and *Cars 2*, for example, the town of Radiator City is populated with adult cars instead of people—cars that sell and buy tires, cars that manufacture and drink organic fuel, even cars that care about the preservation of the town, located on historic Route 66. Each car in the film serves as a stereotyped small-town character. In a moment directly referencing films nostalgic for the 1950s such as *American Graffiti* and *Grease*, references directed towards adult viewers, the cars are shown cruising down the main strip and hanging out at the diner, but there are no humans anywhere. When traffic is diverted from Radiator City by the construction of the new interstate, the cars living in Radiator City have no revenue. The plot revolves around Lightning McQueen, a race car who is textually drawn as masculine, who accidentally finds himself in Radiator City after he gets lost on his way to the Piston Cup. McQueen ostensibly learns to value community above individuality and helps get Radiator City back on the map. In *Cars 2* the scope of the film widens, and Lightning McQueen races internationally. Instead of fighting to save the small town of Radiator City, Lightning McQueen and his sidekick Mater undertake a mission to save the world. Here are no characters that can be understood as literal or metaphorical representations of children.

Initially *The Incredibles* seems to focus on the difficult childhood of Violet and Dash, but the family struggles, sibling rivalry, and school problems, rea-l world problems that viewing children may experience, are minimized and de-emphasized by the family's actual identity as superheroes. Dash and Violet are having these problems because they are superheroes trying to fit into human society by hiding their superpowers. As superheroes with the ability to run really fast and make protective shields around themselves and their loved ones, they are separated from the viewing audience, and the strategies they use to find their place in society, like rescuing their dad and destroying Syndrome's huge machines that are threatening their parents and life on Earth, are not accessible to viewers. Dash and Violet are successful because they are not really human children.

Additionally, the lack of child protagonists in children's films may indicate a shift in American's construct of childhood. Pixar films, like all texts produced by adults for children in English, are influenced by America's understanding of the "the child." Nicholas Sammond, in *Babes in Tomorrowland*, asserts that our American definition of "the child" emerged from a specific location of class and race. The ideology that influences American viewers and filmmakers about children and childhood stems from a generic understanding of white, male, middle-class children that developed out of the 1950s. Sammond asserts that the concept of the child continues to be limiting, but "that truth may be easily swept aside in the intense affect that the figure of the child inspires" (384). Childhood in America is an externally created phenomenon that developed out of a particular period in American history. Texts created by adults for the consumption of children are directed at the concept of "the child" not actual children. Many of Pixar's films reflect a change in the idea of the imagined viewer. Children viewing Pixar's films may be expected to identify with the adult protagonists. In *The Hidden Adult*, Perry Nodelman asserts, "Children's literature is what adults want children to want . . . One of its defining characteristics may well be its imagining of a fictional child as its reader—a fictional child who it proposes as a model for the actual children who read it" (160–161). Since the "Classic" Disney films of the 1940s and 1950s there has been an aging of the protagonists in children's films while the age of the viewing audience has remained the same.

Building on the Disney Tradition

Pixar films are building on the tradition of American children's film which has been dominated by Disney for over seventy years. Begun in the 1920s by brothers Walt and Roy Disney, the Disney Company became known for its quality animation and innovative use of sound and color. By the 1930s Disney's Mickey Mouse was known globally. Through an aggressive marketing campaign, Disney secured its place as the major producer of children's film, but at the same time it has maintained its reputation as producing safe, wholesome entertainment. The Disney Corporation now dominates the entertainment business, including but not limited to children's programming. In addition to its media entertainment, Disney has created a "self-contained universe which presents consistently recognizable virtues through recurring characters and familiar, repetitive themes" (Wasko 2–3). Because of the extent of Disney's influence, it has been a major player in shaping the United States' concept of the child.

Snow White, produced in 1937 by Disney, was the first feature-length animated film. It established numerous conventions for future animated films including stereotypical gender roles in which the female character is passive and dependent on the male character. Giroux states: "Disney's negative stereotypes about women and girls gain force through the way in which similar messages are consistently circulated and reproduced, to varying degrees, in many of Disney's animated films" (100). Wasko asserts: "The Disney version presents an Americanized Snow White and might be said to have fully established the Classic Disney formula . . . Childlike behavior is featured, as cute characters abound, including Snow White herself, the animals, and dwarves" (131). *Snow White* also established a certain level of acceptable violence into children's film. Richard Schickel in *The Disney Version* asserts that the violent scenes may be "recalled with a kind of delicious shudder" (221), indicating that violence may be part of the pleasure in children's film. Including violence has become a well-established convention of children's film. The nuances of the texts for children are typically expunged, and high-contrast dualities are created. Wasko states: "Classic Disney is very emphatic in its depiction of good triumphing over evil" (132). Characters, for example, are either good or evil; there is little ambiguity in the Disney character personality, and the good characters are always victorious.

Snow White marked the beginning of Disney's "classic" period, the period of film production when Walt Disney was alive. This period includes *Pinocchio* (1940), *Fantasia* (1940), *Dumbo* (1941), *Bambi* (1942), *Cinderella* (1950), *Alice in Wonderland* (1951), *Peter Pan* (1953), *Lady and the Tramp* (1955), *Sleeping Beauty* (1959), *One Hundred and One Dalmatians* (1961), *The Sword and the Stone* (1963), and *The Jungle Book* (1967). Wasko asserts that Classic Disney, instead of being openended and imaginative as the Disney corporation asserts, is "neatly tied into a conservative vision of the world and linked directly with consumer culture" (224).

Throughout the seventies and early eighties, animated films were less popular than live-action children's film, and Disney was in financial trouble (Schweizer 3). The "New Disney" period of the eighties and nineties signaled the renewed popularity of animated films and an aggressive marketing campaign under the direction of Michael Eisner. Giroux states: "Eisner took the failing Walt Disney company in 1983 and produced record revenues for the company partly by waging aggressive advertising and licensing campaigns for merchandising children's culture" (33). The most popular "New Disney" films include *The Little Mermaid* (1989), *Beauty and the Beast* (1991), *Aladdin* (1992), *The Lion King* (1994), and *Pocahontas* (1995). These films assume, like most texts produced for children, that "children can, indeed must, change and become adults" (Nodelman 31). In "New Disney" films the protagonists grow up through the course of the film and become either powerful adult leaders (in the case of Aladdin and Simba) or marry powerful adult leaders (in the case of Ariel, Belle, and Jasmine.) Ariel in *The Little Mermaid*, for example, transitions from being a daydreaming, disobedient mermaid daughter in her father's kingdom under the sea to the wife of a powerful human prince by the end of the film.

Pixar provided a challenge to Disney's position as the lead producer of children's entertainment from its release of *Toy Story* in 1995 until 2006 when Disney bought Pixar.

Beginning in 1995 with *Toy Story*, Pixar produced the first completely computer-generated animated film. Several critics speculated that the use of computer-generated graphics instead of hand-drawn illustrations meant the end of animated children's film, but Pixar's technological inventiveness partly explains their films' huge success. Keith Booker states, "*Toy Story* (like all Pixar films) is all about the animation and about the ability of Pixar's animators to produce impressive, convincing computer generated visuals that are full of warmth and humor" (2010, 7). Many Pixar films textually emphasize technology over magic. In Pixar films, animals can talk, but their linguistic abilities are not attributed to magical intervention. In Pixar's most recent film, *Up*, the dogs' ability to talk is the result of an innovative collar that translates their barking into several different languages, a technological, instead of a magical, justification for talking animals.

In many Pixar films, the protagonists are adults from the onset of the film. The imperative to become an adult is conveyed in Pixar films by representing adult anthropomorphized characters; in Pixar films there is a tendency to expunge the child characters.

Gender Roles in Pixar Films

Pixar films rely on conventional gender stereotyping. Pixar has moved away from the passive princess motif of earlier Disney films in an attempt to offer more inclusively gendered films with more complex female characters, but just how much progress has Pixar made? The characters of Pixar films, whether they are toys, fish, ants, rats, or robots, remain highly gendered in stereotypical ways that conform to the norms of a patriarchal society. Emma Cornell asserts, "In order to be economically successful, cinema must concern itself with the subjectivity of the spectator, who, in a patriarchal culture is constructed as male . . . the conservatism of the cinema is based on its economic dependence on a male dominated culture" (35) A possible effect of the encoding of the imagined viewer as male may be the perpetuation of gender stereotypes in many Pixar films. Little Bo Peep and Mrs. Potato Head stay at home in *Toy Story 2* when Buzz heads up a rescue search party for Woody. Bo Peep give Buzz a kiss on the cheek to give to Woody; Mrs. Potato Head helps Mr. Potato Head pack, but neither female character is actually involved in the expedition. Jesse, Woody's female counterpart in the Round-Up Gang, desires to impress and please Woody by showing him fetishized images of himself, images that include episodes of a TV show starring Woody, a lunch pail sporting his face, and various other consumer products that portray his image. Her life happiness depends on Woody's decision. If he leaves her, she will return to storage, her greatest fear. She is animated only by his presence. Dory in *Finding Nemo* accompanies Marlin, Nemo's father, on his ocean quest to find his lost son. She is loyal and nurturing, but she suffers from short-term memory loss. Much of the humor in the film results from Dory's disability. The only other female character in the film besides Nemo's mother, who is dispatched minutes after the film begins, is the blue fish in the aquarium who talks to her reflection. The female characters in *Finding Nemo* behave stupidly and provide comic relief. Mike's girlfriend Celia in *Monsters, Inc.*, is possessive and abusive. In *A Bug's Life* the anthill is governed by a matriarchy, but the Princess is dominated and bullied by male grasshoppers and ultimately rescued by a male ant. The female characters of Pixar's films are "marginalized within the very narratives they dominate" (Wojcik-Andrews 173).The most surprising instances of gendering occur in *Cars*, *Cars 2*, and *WALL-E* because the protagonists are machines. The "girl cars" in *Cars* and *Cars 2* are given distinctive qualities that accent their femininity, such as long, thick eyelashes and luscious lips. *Cars* and *Cars 2* adhere to stereotypical notions of gender. The girl cars seem most interested in nurturing and serving while the "boy cars" are out enjoying tests of physical prowess.

In a limited way, Pixar's *WALL-E* seems to take steps away from gender stereotyping. WALL-E is unmistakably gendered male, and Eve is gendered female, though not in such stereotypical ways. WALL-E, gendered male, is shown pining for Eve, a robot who is gendered female. He engages in romantic fantasies in ways reminiscent of Disney's Snow White, Ariel, and Pocahontas: pining, sighing, and daydreaming. Eve seems more powerful than WALL-E; her arm is a powerful gun, and she frequently goes on shooting sprees. She seems primarily focused on her mission, while WALL-E devotes his energy to building a home. Even though the robots' behavior does not immediately identify WALL-E as male and Eve as female, young viewers easily recognized WALL-E and Eve as gendered characters. I asked my sons William (age nine) and Robin (age six) how they knew that WALL-E was a boy and Eve a girl. William said, "I could tell by their voices. Also, Eve was prettier. And cleaner." Robin added, "I could tell by her shape that Eve was a girl. It looked like she was wearing a dress." Though Pixar might be making some attempts to question dominant gender stereotyping, there are some problems with this reading because the characters do remain gendered, and film does not consistently depict Eve as self-determining. At one point, Eve is shut down, becoming totally unresponsive to external stimuli. While she is shut down, WALL-E wraps her in a string of

Christmas lights and carries her to a sunset-viewing vantage point. As the sun is setting, WALL-E forces his hand into Eve's impassive hand, acting out one of his favorite romantic fantasies after watching *I Love Lucy*. By this point in the film, Eve was fully anthropomorphized into a self-determining female character. Having WALL-E act out his romantic fantasies with her while she was unable to participate or resist undermines the earlier reversals of gender stereotypes.

Excluding the first twelve minutes of *Up*, which consists of sequences of nostalgic flashbacks about Carl, the crusty sixty-something protagonist, and his dead wife Ellie, who always dreamed of traveling to South America but was never able to, there are no female characters. Throughout the film Carl talks to Ellie; she is a haunting female presence, embodied by Carl's house. In order to effect positive changes in his life, Carl has to let his attachment to that feminine presence go. Russell's mother is shown only once, in the audience at Russell's graduation ceremony to senior wilderness scout. In addition to the exclusion of female protagonists throughout the film, *Up* is problematic as a children's film because the child Russell serves as a sidekick for Carl, who, throughout the course of the film, adopts "childlike" qualities such as enthusiasm and renewed vitality. *Up* was advertised as being about Russell's experiences, but the film primarily focuses on nostalgic images of Carl's childhood in the 1950s and his renewed love of life as an adult. Carl is Pixar's oldest protagonist to date.

Why Are There So Few Children in Pixar Films?

Pixar's decision to move away from child protagonists is motivated by numerous factors. Profit motivation behind Pixar's filmmaking partially explains anthropomorphism in the Pixar films. Cute clown fish, snuggly robot dolls, and plush Lightning McQueen pillows become an avenue for children to continue enjoying the film after the movie is over, and "Pixar is in the business of making money off of the fantasies of children" (Booker 2007, 149). The most dramatic example of creating a movie of marketable characters is *Toy Story*; the protagonists are all toys. Creating a film about the adventures and exploits of these toys conditions a young viewing audience to desire replicas of these toys creating, a "dramatization of the fascination with manufactured objects that Marx referred to as the 'commodity fetish'" (Booker 2010, 80). Interestingly, the toys in the *Toy Story* films are all adults. Their owners, the children, exist on the margins of the story. Having such a diverse array of protagonists and the worlds they inhabit from an anthill in *Bug's Life* to the racetrack in *Cars* and the toy chest of *Toy Story* creates the opportunity to manufacture and market a wide array of products and make the release of a Pixar film an event felt in a wider arena than just the movie theaters. The protagonists in many Pixar films model consumption. Many characters are actually humanized through the acquisition of consumer goods. *Ratatouille*'s Remy, a rat that is actively and viciously discriminated against by humans throughout the duration of the film, is fascinated by cookbooks, televised cooking shows, recipes, and restaurants. He becomes more endearing throughout the film as he watches TV shows and acquires cookbooks. WALL-E's home is a museum of human artifacts. He takes a lunch pail to work ever yday, and as he is compacting garbage, he keeps certain objects—lighters and Christmas lights, rubber duckies, Rubrik's cubes, and spare eyeballs. WALL-E is humanized by his acquisition of human artifacts. His association with things the audience will recognize instills in him a type of humanness. These marginalized characters display their desire for acceptance into the dominant culture despite the abuse and neglect some of these characters experience. Giroux's description of the Disney Corporation extends, in this case, to Pixar:

> Disney uses its much-touted commitment to wholesome entertainment to market toys, clothes, and gadgets to children . . . Disney's view of children as consumers has little to do with innocence and a great deal to do with corporate greed and the realization that behind the vocabulary of family fun and wholesome entertainment is the opportunity for teaching children that critical thinking and civic action in society are far less important that the role of passive consumer. (158)

The act of acquiring consumer goods humanizes Pixar's characters, but equating humanness with consumption is a highly problematic quality of children's films. Repeatedly children are shown the image of a marginalized character gaining a supportive community through the act of fetishizing consumer goods. When viewed in conjunction with Pixar's extensive co-marketing, attaching acceptance with consumption is a dangerous message to convey to viewing audiences, regardless of their age.

Children's literature and film are created by adults for consumption, ostensibly, by children, but Pixar is aware that children's films need to appeal to two distinctive audiences: children and their parents. Children's ability to view movies and interact with popular cultural texts requires the involvement of the parents. Few children have the money or the transportation at their disposal to view a movie without parental involvement. Entertaining a dual audience has become an increasingly essential quality of children's film. If Pixar's films were situated firmly in the realm of childhood, there would be fewer opportunities to appeal to adult audiences.

Pixar builds on Disney's long tradition of animating characters with appealing cuteness by extending the cuteness beyond young bunnies, bluebirds, and fawns. Pixar takes some of the most unlikely adult anthropomorphized characters and makes them endearing; in *WALL-E*, for example, even an adult robot looks cute and cuddly. When Pixar films do include anthropomorphized children, the most notable examples being Nemo, a young clown fish from *Finding Nemo*, and Dot, a girl ant from *A Bug's Life*, the adult characters, Nemo's father Marlin and Dot's friend Flik, are still at the center of the story. There is a didactical quality in the interactions between adult and children characters. The children characters are developed in accordance with traditional views about childhood. For example, Flik in *A Bug's Life* gives young Dot a lecture about how even small creatures can achieve great things. Using the metaphor of a seed growing into a mighty tree, he attempts to explain Dot's potential to effect change. The seed to tree metaphor, however, illustrates that children are widely valued not for their current state as children but for their potential greatness as adults, the very message that Pixar's exclusion of child characters is sending to viewers. *Up*'s Russell, the main child character of Pixar films, is shown having to outgrow childishness. Instead of having a mentor who directly lectures him on how to be an adult, his observation of Carl, Pixar's oldest main character, give him a negative example of how to act. The ideal human, *Up* asserts, isn't a child or an elderly adult, but rather a conglomerate of the two. Russell outgrows his childishness, and Carl outgrows his age. Carl loses stereotypical props of old age by walking upright without a walker, and the film stops referring to his "prune" smell and denture cream.

Pixar films explore the relationship between the individual and his or her community, presenting characters who are somehow different from society either because of their longings or because of a physical disability. Pixar films frequently lack a child character for the children viewers to identify with, but children respond to and identify with characters who are small and marginalized throughout the film, even though the predominant protagonists are usually adult characters voiced by adult actors. Booker writes, "American children's film sanctions acceptance of the Other and celebrates the potential achievements of the lowly and the different" (2010, 117). For example, Remy in *Ratatouille* longs to create delicious food, but his predilection for cooking is seen as a threat by his family. He leads a double life throughout much of the film, feeling torn between his ties to his family and his passion for cooking. This dichotomy is reconciled when, towards the end of the film, his entire rat clan rallies in support of him and creates, under his direction, a fantastic meal. The toys in *Toy Story* exist in marginalized spaces such as dusty bedroom shelves and toy chests. They can only assume their true nature when no humans are around, yet all of their heroic actions are performed on behalf of their owner Andy. Jesse, the cowgirl from Woody's Round-Up gang in *Toy Story 2*, illustrates the plight of toys that are abandoned by their owners. Jesse's owner "outgrew" her interest in playing cowgirls and became interested in lip gloss and boys. Jesse was forgotten under the bed for several years and finally donated to a secondhand store. Despite Jesse's negative experience with her first owner, she and Woody decide that their natural role as toys is to be constantly available to their owners as long as they are wanted, even though they will eventually experience neglect and rejection as their owners grow up. *Finding Nemo* provides another example of difference. Nemo has a disabled fin because of the barracuda attack that resulted in the death of his mother and siblings. Despite his disability, he longs to be regarded as normal, especially by his overprotective father. He risks his life twice to prove that he is overcoming his disability. The main focus of the film, however, is Nemo's father Marlin's search for his son. Pixar films prove successful because children and adults are able to identify with the struggles of the protagonists, be they cutened, primarily adult rats, ants, or fish. These films emphasize the individuality of the characters as they strive to find an accepting community for themselves. Even though viewers can identify with the struggles of the protagonists, the solutions that the protagonists employ in creating an accepting community are not available for the audience. Through the use of anthropomorphism, rather than a child protagonist, Pixar's exploration of difference resonates with the audience without effecting any real change. While Pixar's films do delve into some serious topics, the film's presentation of topics such as ostracism from a peer group and disability provides only a surface treatment of social realities that children experience.

The Pixar films do portray marginalized characters being accepted into the dominant culture, a longing which is a key component of children's film. Richard Dyer states: "Entertainment offers the image of 'something better' to escape into . . . Alternatives, hopes, wishes—these are the stuff of utopia, the sense that things could be better, that something other than what is could be imagined and may be realized" (20). These films extend to children the promise that they, too, will become powerful, celebrated members of their society. These stories may pacify children as they grow towards adulthood, because becoming an adult is the only method children have for entering the majority. This promise of successful integration into the dominant society must resonate with children's desire to be older and have more freedom. When children are given stories where the marginalized character succeeds in becoming integrated into the dominant culture, what do children learn about their own marginalized status?

Upon closer viewing, however, it becomes apparent that several of Pixar's films offer only conditional acceptance into the dominant culture. In *The Incredibles,* for example, superheroes have been banned from society and are forced to relocate and live undercover. After the Incredible family saves the world, they successfully integrate into a previously hostile society. Their acceptance into the dominant society, however, seems conditional. After demonstrating their usefulness, they are readmitted. Still they are forced to modify, though not totally suppress, their superpowers. Dash makes the track team, but his parents tell him not to run his fastest at the meet; he has to come in second. After Remy and his family prove themselves as cooks in *Ratatouille*, a new bistro opens where rats are actually welcomed. The rats and humans, however, have separate dining areas, so while rats are not being actively persecuted in this one safe location, they are not completely integrated into human society: rats are separate but equal. Though Pixar's films seem, upon initial viewing, to portray the acceptance of "the other," some of these films, most notably *The Incredibles* and *Ratatouille*, offer their protagonists only a conditional integration into the dominant culture.

The Bad Kids

Kathy Jackson in *Representations of the Child in American Film* interprets the way children are depicted in films as the cultural shorthand for how American feels about its future since children are so strongly associated with the future. In her study of the history of American cinema, she observed that after World War II, America's confidence in its golden future was shaken, and the images of children became darker and more ambivalent. The family horror film including *Rosemary's Baby*, *The Omen*, and *The Exorcist* emerged from this ambivalence and darkening vision. Jackson states: "Traditionally, children have been the symbol of innocence and confidence in a hopeful future . . . evil children became a filmic representation of much larger social and political problems" (149). Three Pixar films utilize the "demon child" trope. *Toy Story, Toy Story 2,* and *Finding Nemo* have demon or monster children, antagonists who attempt to harm or destroy the protagonists. The inclusion of the "demon child" is fascinating since there are so few representations of any children in this body of films. Having a child figure as the main antagonist is a major deviation from Disney's films. In both Classic and New Disney films, which feature numerous representations of children, the antagonists are typically adults, most frequently wicked stepmothers, witches, and greedy men. Though there are some negative children characters, the stepsisters in *Cinderella* for example, the negative children are always portrayed as the opposite of the good child protagonist. In *Toy Story* and *Finding Nemo*, however, demon children figure as the primary antagonist without the inclusion of a strong positive representation of a child protagonist. Pixar's participation in the demon child narrative and its simultaneous avoidance of positive representations of children may highlight the changing view of children in American and their increasing marginalization. Penelope Leach in *Children First* asserts: "Children are the largest minority group in society and the most subject to discrimination" (12). Pixar's films illustrate one type of discrimination experienced by children as children are unable to participate in the creation of these film texts that they consume. Joseph Zornado in *Inventing the Child* asks, "Whose interests are served when one group determines what another group will read" (or watch)? (42). The "demon child narrative" is a narrative told by the dominant culture (in this case, adults) about the oppressed minority (children) to an audience of children. The Pixar film texts for children's consumption portray primarily negative representations of children.

Sid, Andy's next door neighbor in *Toy Story* and *Toy Story 2*, is Pixar's first depiction of the child-as-demon. Sid strikes fear into all the toys' hearts because he dismembers toys and reassembles them in bizarre forms, drowns them in mud, burns them, and attaches them to fireworks. Compared to Andy's well-lit room full of happy, normal toys, Sid's room is dark, messy, and filled with toys that have been reassembled in bizarre forms. Woody and Buzz are terrified by Sid and, at first, the strange toys he makes from bits of dismembered toys. His room reeks of torture and sadism. He *enjoys* abusing toys. Andy's character as the positive child is not as fully developed as Sid's character. Andy is only in a few scenes of the movie. He is mainly depicted leaving his room, having just finished playing with his toys.

The dentist's niece in *Finding Nemo* strongly resembles Sid. Both children are unattractive. They have braces, wide, cruel smiles, and seem completely absorbed in pursuing pleasure that directly result in pain and death for the film's anthropomorphized characters. The dentist's niece has killed several fish, and Nemo, at one point in the film, looks like he'll be her next victim. Zornado asserts that the "vast majority of children's stories invite children to identify with the adults' idea of what a child should be" (xv), and in Pixar's case, this identification involves children seeing themselves not as the scary child antagonist but instead as the adult protagonist.

Monsters, Inc. provides a thoughtful revisioning of both the "child as demon" tradition and presents a constructive image of reconciliation between groups whose previous interactions have been based on fear and exploitation. *Monsters, Inc.* wittily references this tradition of the "child as demon" (or monster) by creating a world of monsters who are afraid of human children. Their fear results in the "othering" of human children, allowing the monsters to exploit children's fears and nightmares to power their city. Boo (a human child) and Sully (the monster known as the best scarer) are able to overcome their mutual fear and develop a loving relationship. Their friendship directly results in the restructuring of the monsters' energy source, so that children's laughter instead of their screams powers the monster city. One possible criticism of *Monsters, Inc.* is, however, that it simplifies the process of reconciliation between two groups. Can we really believe that one friendship between a child and monster will cause such dramatic changes? This objection, however, could be easily dismissed by asserting that children's films are created for children, so of course the messages need to be simplified.

Conclusion

When I was watching *Toy Story* with William and Robin, they argued about who got to "be" Buzz Lightyear, an adult space ranger toy. They were not able to identify with the children characters in the film, Sid or Andy. Zornado states, "The child is already faced with an adult reification of the world presented as 'neutral' and 'obvious' . . . If we want to understand the way in which a culture envisions itself, we might look no further than the stories adults tell and retell their children" (3). Pixar seems to be telling children that being a child is something to grow out of as quickly as possible. Even the earliest animated Disney movies emphasized the importance of adult-like qualities, but Pixar films give children adult protagonists to relate to. Pixar's films have very few representations of children characters, but these films do investigate the experience of being outside the dominant social group. Children are encouraged to identify with the marginalized characters of Pixar's films. A major shortcoming of Pixar's films, however, is that the solutions employed by the anthropomorphized characters are not viable solutions for the young viewing audience. These films illustrate the experience of marginalization, a theme that resonates with children, without offering strategies for children to use when coping with being outside the dominant culture. Many of the strategies that several of the protagonists in Pixar films use are not available to younger viewers. For example, young viewers cannot organize to preserve a historic town like the adult anthropomorphized characters do in *Cars* or save the world through their superpowers as in *The Incredibles*. As our culture begins to develop awareness about the marginalized status of children, hopefully more texts will be created that adequately reflect the position of children in our society and the strategies they use to navigate the adult-dominated world.

Works Cited

Booker, Keith. *Disney, Pixar, and the Hidden Messages in Children's Films.* Santa Barbara, CA: Praeger, 2010.

——. *Postmodern Hollywood: What's New in Film and Why It Makes Us Feel So Strange.* Westport, CT: Praeger, 2007.

Cohen, Lawrence. *Playful Parenting.* New York: Ballantine Books, 2001.

Cornell, Emma. "The Big Screen and the Big Cover Up: Missing the Female Gaze in *Jane Eyre.*" *Spectator: The University of Southern California Film.* 12.2 (1992), 34–43.

de Certeau, Michel. *The Practice of Everyday Life.* Berkeley: University of California Press, 1984.

Dyer, Richard. "Entertainment and Utopia." In *Hollywood Musicals, The Film Reader.* Ed. Steven Cohan. London: Routledge, Taylor, and Francis Group, 2002. 19–31.

Giroux, Henry. *The Mouse that Roared.* New York: Rowman and Littlefield Publishers, 1999.

Jackson, Kathy. *Images of Children in American Films.* Metuchen, NJ: Scarecrow Press, 1986.

Leach, Penelope. *Children First.* New York: Random House, 1994.

Nodelman, Perry. *The Hidden Adult.* Baltimore: John Hopkins University Press, 2008.

Sammond, Nicholas. *Babes in Tomorrowland.* Durham: Duke University Press, 2005.

Schickel, Richard. *The Disney Version.* Chicago: Elephant Paperbacks, 1997.

Schweizer, Peter and Rochelle. *Disney: The Mouse Betrayed.* Washington, DC: Regnery, 1998.

Wasko, Janet. *Understanding Disney.* Malden, MA: Polity Press, 2001.

Wojcik-Andrews, Ian. *Children's Films.* New York: Garland Publishing, 2000.

Zornado, Joseph. *Inventing the Child.* New York: Garland Publishing, 2001.

Filmography

A Bug's Life. Dirs. John Lasseter and Andrew Stanton. Pixar, 1998.
Cars. Dirs. John Lasseter and Joe Ranfit. Pixar, 2006.
Cars 2. Dirs. John Lasseter and David Lewis. Pixar, 2011.
Finding Nemo. Dirs. Andrew Stanton and Lee Unkrich. Pixar, 2003.
The Incredibles. Dir. Brad Bird. Pixar, 2004.
Ratatouille. Dirs. Brad Bird and Jan Pinkava. Pixar, 2007.
Toy Story. Dir. John Lasseter. Pixar, 1995.
Toy Story 2. Dirs. John Lasseter, Lee Unkrick, and Ash Brannon. Pixar, 1998.
Toy Story 3. Dir. Lee Unkrich. Pixar, 2010.
Up. Dir. Pete Docter. Pixar, 2009.
WALL-E. Dir. Andrew Stanton. Pixar, 2008.

Chapter Twelve
Little Burton Blue: Tim Burton and the Product(ion) of Color in the Fairy Tale Films *The Nightmare Before Christmas* (1993) and *The Corpse Bride* (2005)
by Debbie Olson

Introduction

Color is the language of modern fairytales. Color is also the language of advertising. Children's films, particularly animated films, are constructed around and negotiated within capitalist consumer culture, intricately weaving commodities and consumption with fairy tale lands and utopian spaces. Whenever an animated film hits the theaters it is "part of a package . . . that consists of various commodities attached to it: a program, an illustrated book, a doll, a poster" and many other products that seek to capitalize on children's desire to continue the experience of the film's fantasy world (Zipes 8). How much do children's films influence a child's future consumer choices? For example, do the pastel shades of the Disney palette or the deeply saturated colors of Tim Burton's films help inform, construct, or motivate a child's future consumer tendencies? Though there are numerous studies that seek to gauge the effects of sex and violence on the child viewer, there is much less done on how children negotiate, incorporate, or resist color association that may precondition children as consumers. Are fairy tale films propaedeutical towards creating childhood nostalgia for certain palettes within visual marketing? And do those colors instill and/or inform broader ideological values that then construct future product loyalty? This chapter attempts to answer these questions through an examination of the unique palette in Tim Burton's films and how these films condition children to idealize and commodify their own childhood by creating product identification through color symbolism. In the discussion which follows, the unique palette in Burton's *The Nightmare Before Christmas* (1993) and *The Corpse Bride* (2005) works to associate commodities with childhood utopia.

Childhood as Commodity

Since World War II, film has reimagined childhood into a quasi-Victorian, untainted vision of innocence that works to seduce adults into desiring a nostalgic return to an imagined state of perfection. Cook argues that childhood in the post-Depression era became a "site for commercial activity" (112) with the rise of industrialization and over time evolved in such a way that "a child's value was measured less and less in economic-monetary terms and became constituted increasingly in sentimental-emotional ones" (113). For example, Shirley Temple was the physical manifestation of purity and the social desire for the spiritual innocence that childhood represented—Temple's identity and body commodified in both film and real life.

Most of the Victorian images of perfect childhood are today represented by young cherub-faced girls and are exhibited in a plethora of idealized nostalgia on postcards, in coloring books, picture books, commercials and advertisements, television, and film. As a result, mass media has created a naturalized collective memory of childhood as a "time that refers back to a fantasy world where the painful realities and social constraints of adult culture no longer exist," which is then embellished by advertisers who market a variety of products that promise to help return adults to that whimsical prelapsarian state (Spigel 185). Today, childhood as a site of consumerism has united with its romanticized emotional representation to create products that are marketed effectively to both adults, for nostalgic reasons, and to children, who, by consuming the products that represent "ideal" childhood, become active participants in the creation of their own commodified mythology.

Throughout the postwar years, the media industry increasingly shifted the notion of children as influencing agents used to persuade their parents to purchase goods and services that were marketed to children, to "sovereign, playful, thinking consumers" who are now one of the fastest growing market demographics, particularly in this age of niche markets and kids-only television networks like Nickelodeon, Nickelodeon's TV Land, The Cartoon Network, Noggin, Discovery Kids, and The Disney Channel (Kapur "Television" 125). The advent of children's cable networks affords advertisers "a ripe environment through which to address children as consumers" (Spigel 204) in both programming and advertisements. In early attempts by television and Hollywood films (mainly Disney) to "mass market childhood . . . childhood got branded sweet and cuddly, cute and tiny" and took place in fantasy realms of pure Disney pastel palettes that reinforced the whimsical notion of the perfect childhood (Kapur 57). As Ellen Seiter and Vicki Mayer argue, "Many aspects of children's toy and media worlds have remained unchanged since the 1950s" (Seiter 120) and are the most visible in children's films. The divinity and purity of a prelapsarian state is "at the heart of the bourgeois cult of the beautiful child. . . . [because] childhood itself [is]" one of the most successful products sold to American consumers (49). This chapter argues that the idealization of childhood *through color* in film doubles as a marketing strategy that works to reinforce for the children's desire for goods that allow them to revisit the utopia of the film world, and for adults, to create desire for products—packaged and advertised in the same color palette as the film—that promise a return to that idealized childhood.

In today's niche market, advertisers work through Althusserian interpellation in that the films numerous contrasts of deep saturated colors against drab monochromes unconsciously "hail" the child viewer, who then connects certain product coloring to the fantasy world portrayed within the film's mise-en-scène. Fisk argues that "in responding to the call, in recognizing that it is *us* being spoken to, we implicitly accept the discourse's definition of 'us' . . . we adopt the subject position proposed for us by the discourse" (53), a subject position that is immersed in and shaped by color. Assuming the child viewer is placed in a particular subject position by a film's images and discourse presented through a particular palette, children may become preconditioned to favor certain product colors over others, colors associated with the desired fairy tale utopia in children's film. As a marketing strategy, product advertisers work to "(re) define commodities as beneficial/functional for children. When goods become framed as 'useful' they become means to ends rather than intended for mere consumption" (Cook 115). As color is also one of the primary languages of advertising, Burton's distinctive palette in his fairy-tale films helps children learn to associate, identify, and desire products that are advertised and packaged using similar color palettes. Burton's unusual and highly stylized saturated palette, as a marketing strategy, increases the child viewer's idealization, mythification, and commodification of his own childhood.

The Color of Childhood

Childhood products (toys, games, clothing, etc.) come in a variety of colors and the market has conditioned consumers to associate particular product palettes with childhood. Along with product logos and advertising jingles, "color is one of the many marketing tools that global managers use to create, maintain, and modify brand images in customers' minds . . . companies] strategically use color to communicate desired images and reinforce them to consumers" (Madden, Hewett, and Roth 90) in the hopes of creating long lasting brand/product loyalty, a marketing strategy that is also symbiotically connected to films' use of similar color palettes.

The most dominant marketer of children's films and products is the Disney corporation. Disney's strategic marketing of products based on its films is one example of the film palette used as an advertising tool to guide children towards products that are associated with the images they've seen in a particular Disney film. Media fantasy and fairy tales for children have been the Disney Company's purview since its inception. Disneyland and Disneyworld are the spatial recreation of childhood, structured to reinforce the experience of Disney films fantasy worlds within a cacophony of products. Disney is the symbol of childhood itself and markets a wide range of products to convince consumers they can recapture the essence of the idealized childhood. Disney animated films are a site of consumerism in that the films are the base from which products are then marketed that promise to revisit the experience of the film. Zipes points out that "as commodity, the fairy-tale film sacrifices art to technical invention, innovation to tradition, [and] stimulation of the imagination to consumption for distraction" (8). As Henry Giroux argues, "Disney was one of the first companies to tie the selling of toys to the consuming of movies" (118 n20), and many times, especially in recent years, Disney products associated with a film are sometimes released *before* the actual film itself, relying on film trailers and Internet promotions to communicate the desire for the fantasy world the film delivers. The heavy promotions of children's films are also heavy promotions for the specific palette within the film world.

The Disney film palette is rich with pastel pinks, blues, light reds, greens, yellows: all of the primary shades with just a few marginal colors on the side. Disney products also replicate the palette in the films so as to reinforce product association and identification with the fantasy of the film. For Disney, "art . . . becomes a spectacle signed to create new markets, commodify children, and provide vehicles for merchandizing its commodities" (Giroux 158). The strategic marketing of similar children's products by other companies that adopt the Disney color schemes count on consumer association with the Disney palette to boost their sales: "The meanings associated with different colors are important to marketers because the tools used to communicate brand image are mechanisms of meaning transfer," particularly meanings associated with nostalgia for utopian childhood (Madden, Hewett, and Ruth 91). Products that are marketed to children jump on the color coattails of the Disney palette in order to take advantage of the industry standardization of childhood, which is embodied in Disney colors: "As the fairy tale was 'standardized' so that it could transcend particular communities and interests, it structurally fit into the economic mode of production during the 1930s and 1940s known as Taylorism or Fordism. Films were [are] intended to be mass-produced for profit as commodities" (Zipes 6), including all associated merchandise. The palette of children's products for years has reflected the Disney pastels. Even television cartoons and advertisements marketing children's products were mainly composed of pastels up through the late 1980s. With the advent of new computer technologies and graphics in the mid-90s, however, new colors associated with childhood began to emerge.

Along with today's changing social conditions for children, the palette of childhood is also changing. The pastels of the 40s–50s cult of Victorian childhood innocence are being replaced with bold, gritty, urbanesque, computer-enhanced deeply saturated dark colors that reflect a change in the notion of childhood itself. Today's childhood is no longer viewed as a Victorian utopia; however, the nostalgic *desire* for the Victorian idealistic childhood is still a viable marketing strategy. Today's children are growing up with a new palette that represents a different kind of childhood, and when they reach adulthood, that palette will be used to market childhood, not as a Victorian utopia, but as a return to the fantasy worlds depicted in today's fairy tale films. The advent of computer games and graphics has changed the color scheme associated with childhood—many toys, books, games, and even clothing now reflect the color schemes of popular computer-generated worlds. Disney has been slow to adopt the deep saturated colors and still produces almost all of its films and products in the same pastel colors of the Victorian childhood ideal; however, a new crop of fairytale films has emerged that have been instrumental in changing the palette of American childhood. Tim Burton is one of the top directors of this new style of fairy tale film.

The Burton Hue

Part of Burton's success is his "ability to transform colour into a commodity, to make it the source and content of a vast network of communication, a communication with high visibility in public space," a space that is beyond just the screening of his films (Elliott 5). Burton's highly stylized juxtaposition of deeply saturated colors against bland backgrounds of peachy/beige or his trademark gray/blue work to create a new kind of fantasy realm full of contrasting colors that is then replicated and marketed to children in a variety of products (and not necessarily limited to products based on the film itself). Television commercials and print magazine ads have re-created the saturated colors of the Burton palette as a marketing strategy that entices consumers to associate the colors of the product with the fantasy realm in film. Each new Burton film targeted towards children also brings with it a bevy of products based on the film, but the film's palette alone acts as a tool that preconditions its young audience to associate the films saturated colors, often marginal colors rather than primary, as desirable, thereby reinforcing their future adult tendencies to prefer colors that invoke nostalgia for the fantasy film world that "insinuates itself into their [childrens] lives as 'natural history'. It's as though the film has always been there" (Zipes 8). That naturalization of the film's fantasy world, and its colors, frames later adult product/color associations. According to Elliott, "colour communication—and particularly its standardization—speaks to all . . . visions of communication. Colour itself circulates as a type of commodity and the 'information' contained within Starbucks green, for instance, is easily read by its target audience"(Elliott 1). Though most all of Burton's films utilize the contrast between deep saturated colors and lackluster earth tones to emphasize his themes of dark versus light, this discussion will look closely at the color usage in *The Nightmare Before Christmas* (1993) and *The Corpse Bride* (2005) and how a similar palette has manifested itself in a variety of product marketing.

The Color of Nightmares

In *Nightmare Before Christmas,* color represents warmth, fulfillment, and happiness for Jack, which contrasts sharply with the dull peachy/beige of his Halloween world. Jack is unhappy with his life and just needs *something.* The film tells the audience that something Jack needs is *color* and he finds it on the Christmas tree in the woods. The brightest colored tree in the circle of holiday trees is the Christmas tree, and it is the deep, bright colors that bewitch Jack. As he travels down inside the tree, in rabbit-hole fashion, numerous brightly colored objects whiz past him and then he lands in Christmastown where everything is warmly saturated storybook shades of red, blue, magenta, fuchsia, purple/violet and green against the soft blue/white of the snowy North Pole. Burton's palette incorporates a strategy that was used in *The Wizard of Oz* (1932), which "contrasted color and black and white—color Oz looked exotic; black and white Kansas looked ordinary. In the end, the fantasy land had more presence than the real land ... in these movies color gave the objects pictured a presence of a fantastic type" (Leibowitz 364). To Jack, the colorful world of Christmas town is an exotic, exciting place, full of life and an aura of magic.

The palette in *Nightmare* contrasts the peachy/beige of Jack's Halloween world with the softness and ethereal palette of Christmastown. Christmas in today's postmodern age is more than anything else a holiday for and about commodities; and most are marketed specifically to recapture the fairytale ideal warmth and happiness of a utopian, Dickensian ideal of Christmas. Through color the film highlights the desirability and transformative quality of the Victorian/Dickensian vision of Christmas. Jack's discovery of the brilliant colors in Christmastown works on the audience to demonstrate what Goodwin calls the "motives of displacement," which creates an "invitation to consumers to identify themselves with a fantasy world" (Goodwin 93). Jack is attracted to the *color* of Christmastown, though he has no understanding of the meaning of Christmas itself. As Jack travels through Christmastown he sings, "I want it, oh, I want it for my own!" The goal of the film is Jack's quest to capture (to *own*) the colors that give him such a feeling of warmth and fulfillment, a message that is reinforced by the marketing of products associated with the film as well as conditioning children to associate products similarly colored that promise a return to the warm fantasy of the film. Jack then goes on a mission to discover the meaning of the bright happy colors. But Jack eventually equates ownership of the brightly colored objects to capturing the essence of the feeling they invoke. To own color is the essence of happiness. Jack does not understand Christmas, but when Jack puts on the red Santa suit he believes he then becomes Christmas. It is the *color* of the suit that, for Jack, makes the holiday and brings fulfillment, a message that may condition children's preferences for products in similarly saturated colors that are unconsciously associated with providing the same fulfillment.

The Palette of the Dead

Burton's common theme of light versus dark frequently manifests itself in the juxtaposition of the living versus. the dead. The binary light/dark in *Nightmare* and *Corpse Bride* is also analogous to the juxtaposition of adult versus childhood. In *Corpse Bride*, Burton pits the boring, strictly organized world of the living against the freedom and youthful vitality of the world of the dead. That contrast is reinforced through color. The color of the living (adult) world in *Corpse Bride* is a bland shade of grey/blue and peachy/beige that, in contrast to the brilliant colors of the underworld, reflect the rigid, drab, lifelessness of adulthood. In contrast, the vibrant colors of the underworld and the invigorating liveliness of the inhabitants is punctuated by the deep saturated palette of richly textured shades that weave together objects and (dead) people in a swirling dance of vitality. The *Corpse Bride* palette draws the viewer into a world full of dissent and disruption (nothing in the underworld goes "according to plan" versus the almost neurotic scramble to "stick to the plan" in the world of the living) and makes that chaotic underworld more desirable by its juxtaposition with the blandness of the world above.

The protagonist in Burton films usually arrives at the color-filled world through some kind of transformation or rabbit-hole journey (*James and the Giant Peach, Beetlejuice, Nightmare Before Christmas, Planet of the Apes, Corpse Bride*) where "the descent into color often involves lateral as well as vertical displacement; it means being blown sideways at the same time as falling downward" (Batchelor 41) in a swirl of color and pizzazz, where objects and creatures full of more life and character than those in the real world the protagonist left behind are discovered. In *Corpse Bride,* Victor is whisked away from the drab and stressful adult world and into the lush colors of the underworld through the kiss of his dead bride. Neff argues that "children's filmmaking, which tends to encode its ideas in simplistic, emotionally charged images, provides a spectacular forum" (Neff 56) for expressing the longing for an alternate world. *Corpse Bride* uses "rich colors and textures, a panoply of visual messages [that] entice, exhort, and explain" the desirability of that alternate world (of the dead) using color contrast (Scott 252).

Victor's character is as weak and neurotic as the adults who surround him in the living world, but through his time in the lively underworld he gains both confidence and strength, traits that the characters in the underworld possess in abundance. Socially, the message is a paradox in that death is made to seem preferable to life, and yet, in the end as Victor puts the cup of poison to his lips in order to be a part of the beautiful underworld forever, Emily stops him, allowing him to live. She sacrifices her happiness so that Victor can wed Victoria and live. Yet, the film has constructed an uncomfortable nostalgia for the land of the dead, paradoxically full of color and life.

Though *Corpse Bride* does not feature particular objects as the desired goal, the driving force is still economic. The plots conflict is the result of two families vying for either wealth or status. Victoria's family is titled, but has no money, whereas Victor's family is the "nouveau riche"—no class but lots of cash. Victoria's parents' cold and calculated "desire to commodify and appropriate any aspect of marginalized culture that might be 'useful'" (Neff 54) to the salvation of the family fortunes is the sentiment that drives the frenetic race to marry Victoria to whoever can rescue the family from poverty. In the adult world, Victoria and Victor do not chose their mates, or their life path. They are bound by duty and responsibility and are not free. But Emily, and the other characters in the underworld, are free to choose their own destiny: the film ends with Emily's turning into a flock of (grey/white and colorless) butterflies that soar up in the sky, disappearing into the grey/white moonlight. Burton "make[s] extensive use of the interplay of neutral (black and white) and weighted [color] domains" (Evans 46) to reinforce audience longing for the more colorful underworld in *Corpse Bride*, leaving the viewer saddened at the thought of Victor and Victoria living a long, drab, colorless life in the above world.

The message of *Corpse Bride*, however, is problematic for a child audience in that the film creates a disturbing desire to return to the land of the dead, as opposed to staying with the living. The film sets up a "displacement, then, [which] 'neutralizes' a real hierarchy and substitutes, instead, an inverted, imaginary one" that privileges death over life (Goodwin 96). That privileging is the result of the use of deeply saturated colors that draw the viewer to identify "real" life with color, and hopefully, identify deeply saturated product colors with the imagined fantasy world of the dead in the film. Burton's films have created a new dimension of the idealized visual memory of childhood by "directing the meaning of the visual, anchoring hue to a particular idea, theme, or message . . . It becomes obviously commodified, packaged and sold as a vehicle for increased sales, while verbally rooted in a particular time" (Elliot 8). Burton's frequent juxtaposition of death versus life (as in his 1988 film *Beetlejuice* where the underworld is an infectiously fun place compared to the crazy meanness of the living world) functions to alter the Victorian idealized innocent childhood into a strange reversal of innocence—Burton presents a childhood utopia that is dark, necromantic, gritty, and *knowing*. Burton's protagonists tend to gain knowledge or insight that separates them from adults and the adult world. Gaining special knowledge in Burton films is not from *believing* in magic, but from *experiencing* fantasy or the magical through color in a way that can, ultimately, be more easily associated with products and clothing that are also colored in dark, saturated, urbanesque colors.

Toy Store(y): Conclusion

Though the Victorian ideal of childhood is still very much marketed, the reality of childhood today is nowhere near the utopian innocence it was perceived to be in the 50's–70's. Today's childhood is filled with technology that in some instances replaces socialization and discovery of the world with an internal isolation that relies on stimuli from sources other than human to achieve a sense of adventure, belonging, camaraderie, and culture. Computer games, iPods, television, and film all provide those connections for the modern child, which has resulted in the adultification and, by default, the urbanization of today's childhood. The vision of children innocently dancing through fields of flowers wearing pastel colors and white Keds, watching rainbows and playing in the sand, has evolved into images of children dancing to rap and hip/hop through their iPod earphones, negotiating around traffic and gangs while wearing dark street colors and adorned with a variety of bling. These changes in the conception and experience of childhood are replicated in the changing colors of children's films. These changes in attitudes about the childhood experience are then replicated in products and marketing strategies directed towards children. Marketers "anticipate a viewer who knows certain pictorial conventions and who shares visual experiences with the makers" (Scott 256) in a community of color associations. The dark, deep saturated colors of music videos, TV shows and films also mimic the dark reality of drugs, crime, sex, school shootings, isolation, and technology that inhabit today's childhood. As Elliott argues "between sixty-two and ninety percent of a person's first impression of an item comes solely from its colour" (1). Children learn color preferences through a complex process of association over time. The toys adults surround their babies with also help those children learn to associate comfort, fulfillment, and happiness with the color of the object dangled in front of them. As the child grows and is exposed to visual media of various types, the color associations are expanded, as are the child's experiences while viewing. Depending on the visual media, color association involves a "simple motion of relaxation-tension-release [that] is created by moving from and to points of dynamic symmetry, from one point of visual [color] balance in spatial composition to another" (Evans 46).

And though "reactions to color are considered highly individualized, universal color preferences are thought to exist. For example, blue is the color most frequently chosen by adults" (Madden, Hewett, and Roth 93). A child's experience within the cacophony of media color helps to establish his palette preferences later in life. Films play a large role in establishing those color preferences, especially the highly saturated and stylized color palette in Burton's films.

In the capitalist quest for constant consumers, marketers rely on consumers' "learned vocabulary of pictorial symbols and . . . complex cognitive skills . . . Thus, advertising images can be understood as a discursive form, like writing, capable of subtle nuances in communications or, like numbers, capable of facilitation abstraction and analysis" (Scott 264). As Elliott argues, marketing use of color is a systematic process of developing color associations between product and desired fantasy through certain stages of color association. Color analysts have theorized three types of color consumers According to Elliott these are: Color Forwards, "the twenty percent of the population who are generally younger, attuned to new colour trends and willing to embrace them; Color Prudents" who wait for a color to gain acceptance before adopting it and comprise about fifty-five percent of the population and who "depend on the 'information' conveyed by degrees of display or by high visibility, which might come from a combination of media/marketing use (in retail or the like). . . . As such, the information flow in question is not verbal. . . . but purely visual;" and Color Loyalists, who "comprise twenty-five percent of the population and are profiled as middle-aged with busy lifestyles who have no interest in 'fashionable colour culture'" (Elliot 2). Product manufacturers produce products in the palette of popular children's films to take advantage of children as Color Forwards, who are color malleable—their loyalty to specific colors has not yet been established. As child viewers are presented with the color schemes of utopian worlds within films, such as Burton's, products are then created and marketed in those palettes in the hopes of creating color loyalty that will last through the other two stages of color consumption.

Visual media functions as an advertising vehicle for the cultural production of color and color associations, which influence consumers worldwide. The cultural production of color association is only "one mechanism for creating [brand] logos that are recognizable and evoke positive brand and/or corporate images" (Madden, Hewett, and Roth 103) in relation to products that promise to deliver temporary childhood utopia. Films are another form of the cultural production of color association. And in a consumer culture, that production of color becomes entwined with the ideologically coded desire for eternal youth. That strategy depends on the idealization of childhood, no matter how it changes, which then becomes an "artefact of colour, in short . . . a social phenomenon, a vivid expression of place and space" (Elliott 7) that, in Burton's films, becomes the idealized vision of childhood that young viewers today will desire to return to (through consumption) as they grow into the unfortunate and unmagical condition of Adulthood.

Works Cited

Batchelor, David. *Chromophobia.* London: Reaktion Books, 2000.

Brooks, Peter. *The Melodramatic Imagination.* New Haven: Yale UP, 1976, 1995.

Cook, Daniel Thomas. "The Rise of 'The Toddler' as Subject and as Merchandising Category in the 1930s." *New Forms of Consumption: Consumers, Culture, and Commodification.* Ed., Mark Gottdiener. Lanham, MD: Rowman & Littlefield, 2000. 111–129.

Elliott, Charlene. "Crayoned Culture: The 'Colour Elite' and the Commercial Nature of Colour Standardization." *Canadian Review of American Studies* 33, no. 1 (2003): 37.

Evans, Brian. "Temporal Coherence with Digital Color." *Leonardo. Supplemental Issue, Digital Cinema* 3 (1990): 43–49.

Fiske, John. *Television Culture.* London; New York: Routledge, 1989.

Giroux, Henry A. *The Mouse That Roared* Lanham, MD: Rowman & Littlefield, 1999.

Goodwin, David. "Toward a Grammar and Rhetoric of Visual Opposition." *Rhetoric Review* 18, no. 1 (1999): 92–111.

Kapur, Jyotsna. *Coining for Capital: Movies, Marketing, and the Transformation of Childhood.* New Brunswick, NJ: Rutgers University Press, 2005.

———. "Out of Control: Television and the Transformation of Childhood in Late Capitalism." *Kid's Media Culture* Ed. Marsha Kinder. Durham, NC: Duke UP, 1999: 122–136.

Leibowitz, Flo. "Movie Colorization and the Expression of Mood." *Journal of Aesthetics and Art Criticism* 49, no. 4 (1991): 363–365.

Madden, Thomas J., Kelly Hewett and Martin S. Roth. "Managing Images in Different Cultures: A Cross-National Study of Color Meanings and Preferences." *Journal of International Marketing* 8, no. 4 (2000): 90–107.

Neff, Heather. "Strange Faces in the Mirror: The Ethics of Diversity in Children's Films." *Lion and the Unicorn* 20, no. 1 (1996): 50–65.

Scott, Linda M. "Images in Advertising: The Need for a Theory of Visual Rhetoric." *Journal of Consumer Research* 21, no. 2 (1994): 252–273.

Seiter, Ellen. *Sold Separately: Parents and Children in Consumer Culture.* New Brunswick, NJ: Rutgers University Press, 1995.

Spigel, Lyn. *Make Room for TV: Television and the Family Ideal in Postwar America.* Chicago: University of Chicago Press, 1992.

Zipes, Jack David. "Towards a Theory of the Fairy-Tale Film: The Case of Pinocchio." *The Lion and the Unicorn* 20, no. 1 (1996): 1–24.

Chapter Thirteen
Childhood in War and Violence: *Turtles Can Fly* and *The Kite Runner*
by Lan Dong

Children are pivotal to how a culture defines itself and its future.
—Paula S. Fass (7)

I had gone to Iraq to make an anti-war film.
The film needed to be bitter in order to shock the spectator and not let go of him.
—Bahman Ghobadi (qtd. in Mehrabi 49–50)

Although "histories dealing with war seldom touched on its effects on children" until recently (Reynolds 251), child-aged characters have had a consistent presence in media and literary representations of war. In *The Battle of Algiers* (1966), the section in which a child is eating ice cream before a time bomb goes off is a long, tense scene that "almost forces the viewer to take a stance about the right of the oppressed to use violence in their struggle against their oppressors" (Caviglia 5). In its depiction of a story about the Holocaust as much as about a father-son relationship, the film *Life Is Beautiful* (1997) presents "a fable, a genre with strong connections to both the adult and the child," through which director, screenwriter, and actor Roberto Benigni fuses the child's moral story with the adult's political tale (Kroll 31). More recently there have been several films reflecting the lives and experiences of the child soldier in Africa. Moreover, Iraq War stories such as *The Hurt Locker* (2008) and *The Sandbox* (2010) dramatize the frustrations and complexities that American soldiers have to confront in their missions through the death of children. In *The Hurt Locker*, for example, through the adult characters' eyes, the viewer witnesses a bomb made of explosives implanted in a boy's body.

Consistent with the increasing interest among the general public, there have been scholarly works as well that engage with media and literary representation of the ongoing war in Iraq and Afghanistan. For example, Suman Gupta's *Imagining Iraq* (2011) discusses literary texts published in the United Kingdom and the United States between 2003 and 2005; Stacey Peebles' *Welcome to the Suck* (2011) examines the experience of the Persian Gulf War and the Iraq War from the American soldiers' perspective. As Peebles has pointed out, the central trope emerging from the stories about the Iraq War "emphasizes considerations of agency and trauma in the midst of war" (164). Related to the focus here on children, the accounts about the accidental killing of a child appear repeatedly in these American soldiers' narratives: "The bodies of these children call out as totems of the guilt, helplessness, and frustration felt by soldiers fighting a war in which choices are impossible" (Peebles 164). All these creative and scholarly endeavors present refreshing perspectives and approaches to studying childhood in the war zone.

It is within this context of critically engaging with the impact of war on children's lives and how their presence affects the filmic representations of war that this chapter is positioned. Using two recent films as case studies, this chapter explores how *Turtles Can Fly* (2004) and *The Kite Runner* (2007) document children's daily struggle to survive prior to, after, and in the midst of war while both vehicles call the viewers' attention to politics, ethnicity, and social class that play a significant role in shaping the characters' childhood; this chapter also explores how childhood in a warzone may affect the ways that the stories are depicted on screen. These two films represent the atrocities of war through the lens of Iraqi and Afghanistan children with virtually no direct portrayal of the battle scenes.

Made with a minuscule budget, Kurdish Iranian director Bahman Ghobadi's *Turtles Can Fly* has been successful in Iran as well as at prestigious international film festivals. While shooting the documentary *The War Has Ended* a month after Saddam Hussein's fall from power in Iraq, Ghobadi witnessed some disturbing scenes: children (some of them without arms and legs) working as minesweepers in fields filled with cartridge shells and lands infested with mines. It was these images that inspired him to start writing the screenplay of *Turtles Can Fly* (Ghobadi qtd. in Mehrabi 46). When he returned to Iraq to start filming, Ghobadi enlisted children who had no acting experience to star in the film (including nine-year-old Avaz Latif [Agrin]) who came from a hamlet without electricity and television), beggars he found in a bazaar, and other children who were war survivors (Ghobadi qtd. in Mehrabi 47).

An Iran-Iraq joint production and the first film shot in Iraq after the fall of Saddam Hussein, *Turtles Can Fly* sets the story in Kurdistan at the Iraqi-Turkish border a few weeks before the American invasion in 2003. The film narrative informs the viewer that there are about seventy families in this border-town village: thirty in Iraq and forty in Turkey. This rural village and nearby refugee camps make up the main landscape of the film. Regarding its political stance, the filmmaker has remarked: "It is not the outlook of the Kurds. It is my own personal views and those of some others. I do not use slogans in my film. I show the present lifestyle of the Kurds. Mine is not a political film and if I see things through politics it is because elements such as war and politics have become part and parcel of the culture of the Kurds" (Ghobadi qtd. in Mehrabi 51). It is through the character and presence of children that Ghobadi's film articulates the relationship among witnessing history, traumatic memory, and ongoing struggles for survival. In particular, the child-woman Agrin exemplifies the despair of children in a warzone and the impossibility for them to enter adulthood.

The prelude of the film opens with Agrin in a shapeless plum-colored dress walking to the edge of a cliff, pausing for a moment, and turning around. The camera follows her sight line and cuts to a water surface with what looks like her reflection in it. Then the camera brings the viewer back to the cliff and shifts its angle: first it cuts to a close-up shot of Agrin's expressionless face, next to a long shot of her standing on top of the cliff, and then to another close-up of her feet at the edge. This opening scene, without dialogue or voice-over narrative, ends with Agrin jumping off the cliff. As Karen Lury observes, "The unreadable face of the child is . . . often interpreted or anthropomorphized to fit the political and emotional agenda of the interested adult critic. And the child, as a vivid and emotive presence, is all too often a vehicle for adult concerns and fears, and fails to act or represent its own interests and desires" (Lury 109). Accompanied by the theme song, the caption then introduces the film's title, followed by opening credits. Beautiful as she is, Agrin is not introduced as an idealized child in a sentimental Victorian fantasy. Portrayed as a child/woman in the film, she embodies a combination of beauty and sorrow, innocence and maturity. The image of Agrin standing at the edge of the cliff, as the establishing shot, is not only of significance thematically in the film narrative but it also plays an important role in the formal structure of the film. This image recurs several times in the film, interrupting narrative linearity and troubling the conventional chronology. Through such a strategy, the filmmaker creates gaps, breaks, and breaches that help construct the film's episodic narrative.

Upon first look, Hengov, Agrin, and the blind toddler Riga, who come from Halabcheh, seem to be orphaned siblings struggling to survive in a refugee camp near the Kurdish village. However, the film narrative gradually unveils the truth through flashbacks portrayed in dreamlike scenes: Agrin was raped by a group of soldiers and her child Riga is a constant reminder of the nightmarish past. Amidst daily struggles to survive along with anxiety and uncertainty about the upcoming American invasion, tension emerges in this family comprised of uncle, mother, and child, all of whom are children. Claiming that she does not know what to tell Riga and other people when he grows up, Agrin wants to leave the refugee camp without Riga with the hope that other people will find and look after him. When Hengov adamantly refuses to leave Riga behind, she refers to Riga as "a bastard" and rebuts Hengov's disapproval: "If he is not a bastard, then what is he? Isn't he the child of those who killed our family and *did this* to me?" (emphasis added) (*Turtles Can Fly*, 2004). Their conversation takes place at mealtime when Agrin is feeding Riga and Hengov (who has lost both his arms in a land-mine explosion). Her refusal to acknowledge her motherhood is portrayed as contradictory to her action of assuming the actual role of a motherly figure and taking care of the family.

The film most vividly externalizes war trauma by its use of flashbacks that reveal the pain of Agrin's past and symbolically enact the death of her childhood. Using the recurring images of her walking to the edge of the cliff as juxtaposition to the rape scene, the visual aspects of the film offer an aesthetic pull on the viewer that disrupts the linear narrative. The viewer is barred from direct screen images of the actual rape, which is replaced by visual units shot from shifting camera angles, broken narrative sequences, and sound effects. While standing on the cliff, Agrin recollects on screen chaotic, dark pieces of her memory. The filmmaker has used a handheld camera to shoot this particular scene, which is commonly recognized as an effective device for evasive subjects. The space between the frames in the film allows for another important filmic aspect to take place: sound effects. Agrin's soft footsteps and the sound of blowing wind on top of the cliff during daytime suggest tranquility in her surroundings at the moment. Then the camera abruptly cuts to a dark, chaotic night filled with gunshots, roaming military vehicles, and footsteps of armed soldiers before shifting back to the image of Agrin standing at the edge of the cliff. Next, a girl's piercing scream helps transition the film narrative to the nightly setting again in which a group of soldiers are chasing a girl. While the girl's face eludes the camera, her scarlet dress appears prominently in the scene, the only bright color that stands out visually against the dark night, muddy road, and military uniforms in the frames. Contextualizing both adults' and children's actions, the filmmaker uses lighting and sound to assist the storytelling. Without direct shots of the rape, the film shows Agrin being dragged by the soldiers near a puddle. The absence of visual narrative is replaced by her screaming, the splashing sound of the water, Hengov crying her name, and the soldier's chatter. The image and sound of water in this scene establish a connection to the present in the narrative and foreshadow the climactic ending of the film. The symbolic death of Agrin's childhood takes place in the water; so does the death of Riga. This scene ends with Hengov fishing Agrin out of the water. Her face is completely out of the frame; instead, the viewer sees only a close-up shot of her lifeless hand hanging in the air, which is accompanied by the sound of her frail breathing. Such a narrative structure relays Agrin's blurry and scattered remembering of her wartime experiences and helps produce a framework in which her suffering is glimpsed from the gaps.

As Karen Lury has observed, children generally are "perfect victims" of war because "they are blameless, they make the wrongs of war seem all the more wrong, and the viewer's righteous and explosive response all the more satisfactory . . . The innocence ascribed to children ... often makes them an object, if not the subject, of films about war, in a strategy designed to provoke emotion and moral satisfaction" (105–106). In Ghobadi's film, Agrin's character shows objectivity (being a victim of war and sexual violence) as well as subjectivity (being a mother who takes care of Riga and at the same time rejects him), thus provoking yet suspending the viewer's "moral satisfaction" at the closure of the film narrative. After failing to persuade Hengov, Agrin makes several attempts to abandon Riga with no avail. Toward the end of the film, we see Riga in a pond near the village and turtles swimming by his side, which is presented as one of Hengov's predications. The film employs "images that are full, images that tell more than the story, which hint at possibilities that are not quite spoken or written elsewhere in the film" (Lury 139). When Hengov rushes out searching for Agrin and Riga, he finds Riga drowned at the bottom of the pond. The next shot takes the viewer to another setting, where Hengov stands on the cliff calling Agrin's name before leaving in tears with her shoes in his mouth. As Hengov leaves, he crosses path with American soldiers and military vehicles on the road, suggesting another chapter of life for Kurdish Iraqis, children and adults alike.

Until the end of the film, the U.S. military presence is kept offscreen and functions as a framing apparatus. The film introduces the looming war and American troops through the villagers' anxiety and uncertainty about the near future, another plot line that revolves around a thirteen-year-old boy who is nicknamed "Satellite." In her analysis of popular imagery of the child, Patricia Holland points out:

> Suffering children appear as archetypal victims, since childhood itself is defined by weakness and incapacity. Children living in poverty, children who are the victims of wars or natural disasters, children suffering from neglect or disadvantage: all of these figure in the imagery as the most vulnerable, the most pathetic, the most deserving of our sympathy and aid. This resonant image shows children who appear to be on the receiving end of an oppression in which they can only acquiesce. As they reveal their vulnerability, viewers long to protect them. The boundaries between childhood and adulthood are reinforced as the image gives rise to pleasurable emotions of tenderness and compassion, which satisfactorily confirm adult power. (143)

What is unique about Ghobadi's film is that it complicates the boundaries between childhood and adulthood. On the one hand, *Turtles Can Fly* portrays children living in poverty and suffering from war and dictatorship. Although a child himself, Satellite appears to be the leader of the Kurdish children who support themselves by unloading shells from trucks and disarming and collecting abandoned mines in the fields. These Kurdish children are not portrayed solely as the traumatized witnesses to war and chaos. They also live through the war. Satellite negotiated prices for these children to sell mines to a middleman, who, according to Satellite, would sell them to the United Nations for a much higher price. Working as exploited labor, many children have lost arms and legs, if not their lives, in explosions that take place on a daily basis. To some degree, "one child's experience, or more accurately their presence as a small, emotive figure, can be used to 'stand in' for many deaths. In these instances, the child's narrative function is effectively to act as a metonym for wider suffering" (Lury 107). On the other hand, Ghobadi's film empowers child characters by rendering their abilities to persevere, particularly through the character of Satellite. When this character is introduced to the screen, we see him wearing a polo shirt, blue jeans, military camouflage baseball cap, and glasses. His Westernized dressing style poses a contrastive image to that of others in the film, children and adults alike. He persuades the village elders to pull resources together and buys a satellite dish, manages to negotiate with merchants in the market, and helps to install it. Distinct from youth in other films involving war in which "children are often ciphers for adult anxieties, fantasies and fears" (Lury 106), here Satellite's character, aided by other children, provides an opportunity to resolve the anxiety. Then because of his knowledge in English, albeit limited, Satellite is given the task to translate TV news reports from CNN, Fox News, and other channels for the elders who are very eager to find out information about the upcoming American invasion. In this sense, adults rely on Satellite's assistance in order to gain access to the world outside the village.

Set in a rural Kurdish village with a particular focus on children in war zone, *Turtles Can Fly* presents a myth of "an unconventional survival" (Karimi 58). Except for the close-ups that frame Agrin standing at the edge of a cliff, the film mostly uses medium and long shots to reflect the local landscape and the devastating situation of the children. Through the stories of these Kurdish youngsters—not only orphans of war but also an ethnic minority in Iraq and Turkey—the film makes its strong antiwar statement. Toward the end of the film, American helicopters distribute fliers that promise a bright future: "It's the end of injustice, misfortune and hardship. We are your best friends and brothers. Those against us are our enemies. We will make this country a paradise. We are here to take away your sorrows. We are the best in the world" (*Turtles Can Fly*, 2004). Yet the closing shot of *Turtles Can Fly* is filled with ambiguity and uncertainty as Satellite (whose leg has recently been injured in a land-mine explosion) and Pashow (another child character who has lost a leg in an explosion before the film story begins) stand by the roadside, both leaning on crutches as they watch American troops pass by.

As the War on Terror and the American invasion of Iraq has unfolded, "literature about the Middle East that circulated in the U.K. and USA was variously explored along the lines. A spate of well-publicized 'literary fiction' and memoirs (sometimes balanced on the boundary between those) by émigré writers made their way to the market, those about Iran and Afghanistan circulating most widely" (Gupta 171). Films such as *Kandahar* (2010) and *Osama* (2003) have been "primary vehicles for shaping Western discourse about the rights of Muslim women, the *chadari*, and the nature of Islam as a 'clashing civilization' opposed to Western, supposedly secularist modernity" (Graham 5–6). Such media representations of the Middle East, however, are obviously problematic. As the first Afghan novel written in English that has reached a broad range of readers in America and abroad and has gained widespread recognition, Khaled Hosseini's novel *The Kite Runner* was "a firecracker" (to borrow Louisa Ermelino's metaphor 34) within the Afghani community because of the sensitive issues it addresses: ethnic tension, rape of children, violence of war, and the terror of Taliban. It would not be an exaggeration to say that *The Kite Runner* has become "not only the single most important source of information on Afghanistan for American readers but also the most widely read American story ever written about the modern Islamic world" (Graham 147). Directed by Marc Forster, winner of Best Foreign Language Film at the sixty-fifth Golden Globe Awards, the film adaptation under the same title not only provides a window into Afghan culture, but it also "projects back to the western reader the simple moral absolutes that inform the War on Terror as paradoxically both a 'war,' based on the fulfillment of vengeance or justice, and a humanitarian project of 'sharing' western values, such as democracy and liberalism; for instance, saving oppressed Muslim children/women from misogynist, oppressive Muslim men" (Jefferess 398). Similar to *Turtles Can Fly*, the film version of *The Kite Runner* also complicates the concept of childhood as it becomes entangled with war, violence, and social discrimination.

The film narrative is set in Kabul and California around two friends: Amir Qadiri (a privileged Pashtun) and Hassan (whose father Ali is a Hazara servant and has worked for Amir's family for forty years), who for twenty years have been separated by two continents as a result of war. As the film later reveals, they are half-brothers. Shot in Dari, one of Afghanistan's major languages, and using Afghans to play many roles, the film has aimed to become "a cultural milestone" (Graham 147). The director Marc Forster has made it clear that "the purpose of the film was to 'humanize that part of the world . . . [and] give a face and voice to a country that's been in the news for three decades, and create an emotional connection beyond culture or race" (qtd. in Graham 147–148).

The story portrays Kabul in two eras: the pre-Taliban late 1970s when the main characters are boys growing up together, and the city under Taliban's control in 2000 after Amir has settled in the United States and Hassan has been executed in Kabul. Their narrative gap eclipses both characters' experiences from childhood to adulthood as well as the impact of the Soviet invasion in 1979 and the decade-long occupation of Afghanistan. Born into a well-to-do family, Amir lost his mother as an infant. While he enjoys economic and social privileges as a boy, he struggles to earn his father's approval. Different from the repressive images of *chadari* and the restrictive doctrines regulating people's everyday lives, *The Kite Runner* depicts Kabul as an urban center with prosperity and budding modernity. While Hassan, as a servant's son, wears more traditional Afghan attire such as *chapan*, Amir is dressed in Westernized clothes such as vest, sweater, polo shirt, and padded snowsuit. His liberal father, Baba, wears suits, drinks alcohol, mocks the mullahs, and speaks against communism publicly. "Here for the first time, the Western viewer can watch Afghans who are literate, complex, cosmopolitan, and relatively tolerant" (Graham 148). In particular, the film devotes considerable amount of screen time to feature Amir's extravagant birthday party. In this scene, the camera constantly shifts its angle and uses almost exclusively medium shots, through which to capture a band performing popular songs in the courtyard of the Qadiri residence; men in well-tailored suits consuming alcohol; men dancing with women who are wearing modern dresses, hairdos, and jewelry; and lights decorating the walls together with fireworks accenting the celebratory atmosphere.

The film has aroused much controversy because of the rape scene in which young Hassan was assaulted and the indication that Hassan's son Sohrab has served as a sexual slave. Some believe the plot of rape might actually reignite the interethnic strife and rekindle the tensions between Hazaras and Pashtuns in Afghanistan (qtd. in Haviland). The plot begins in San Francisco, California, in 2000, where Amir has just received copies of his debut novel, *A Season for Ashes*. At the moment of success and celebration, Amir receives an unexpected call from his late father's friend, Rahim Khan, asking him to return to Afghanistan. Khan's words—"There is a way to be good again"—highlights the themes of friendship, childhood, sin, guilt, and redemption, all of which help unfold the film narrative. The camera then follows Amir's sight line outside of the window to a blue kite flying in the San Franciscan sky. The kite is not only of significance thematically but it also plays an important role in the temporal and spatial transition in the film's narrative. From the blue kite, the film seamlessly cuts to kites flying in the sky in Kabul, Afghanistan in 1978.

The boys' friendship, one of the central themes of the film, is introduced by positioning Hassan as a superb kite runner in Kabul and a loyal friend to his master's son Amir. "Too often, our culture imagines childhood as a utopian space, separate from adult cares and worries, free from sexuality, outside social divisions, closer to nature and the primitive world, more fluid in its identity and its access to the realms of imagination, beyond historical change, more just, pure, and innocent, and in the end, waiting to be corrupted or protected by adults" (Jenkins 3–4). When Hassan successfully runs an orange kite and the boys walk home cheerfully against the background of river, bridge, and land, the scenery situates them "closer to nature and the primitive world." *The Kite Runner*, however, does not portray the boys' childhood as a nostalgic paradise; instead, it combines carefree and happy moments of Amir and Hassan's life with violence, discrimination, and malicious lies. Thus, the film quickly presents a twist that breaks the boys' peaceful life: Assef, accompanied by two other boys, stops Amir and Hassan on the street and calls them "faggots." A bully as a boy and a cruel Taliban later in the film, Assef expresses disapproval of the liberal attitude of Amir's family and despises Hassan because of his ethnicity. He states: "Afghanistan is the land of the Pashtuns. We are the real Afghans, not this flat-nose Hazara. His people pollute our homeland. They dirty our blood" (*Kite Runner*, 2007). His remarks refer back to the historical ethnic conflict in Afghanistan as well as foreshadow later plots after the Taliban seizes power. Although Hassan is much smaller in physical size compared to Assef and his aides and is outnumbered, he shows no hesitation; he protects Amir with his slingshot aimed at Assef, which in the end scares him off. Assef's parting words, "We'll deal with these faggots later," help create a suspension in the plot, inviting the viewer to anticipate another confrontation.

An important image thematically and structurally in the film, the kite leads the narrative to the most controversial scene. Before Taliban reshapes the country in multiple dimensions, kite flying has been a popular pastime in Kabul for children and adults alike. Usually two persons team up: one holding the spool and the other flying the kite: "Visually detached from the hands that guide it on the ground, the kite becomes a free and hybrid agent, occupying a luminal space between earth and sky. Such transcendence embodies, paradoxically, domination as well as freedom. Far from being just a colorful toy, the kite functions as a competitive weapon that destroys all the others, taking the sky for its own" (Graham 152-53). For Amir, Hassan, and children of their contemporaries, kite flying is not merely an entertainment; it is also a competition in which their kite needs to cut down others. It takes preparation, practice, and piloting strategy to achieve the goal. The film first uses a pan shot to establish the scene of the city-wide kite flying tournament, which portrays children and adults on rooftops, balconies, and streets, and colorful kites in the winter sky, highlighting the popularity of kite flying. Between shots of kites soaring up the sky and being cut down from their strings and their owners maneuvering their moves carefully, the film subtly shows glimpses of Assef watching Amir and Hassan, who are too occupied to notice his meaningful glances, reminding the viewer of his earlier comment and indicating a brewing, ominous plot.

After cutting down the last competitor, a blue kite, and thus winning the tournament, Hassan tells Amir: "I am going to run the blue kite for you . . . For you, a thousand times over!" Contrasting to children running on the street cheerfully, the film cuts to the establishing shot of the rape scene set in a quiet alley, in which Assef and his lackeys corner Hassan and demand the blue kite as the price for Assef to "forgive" Hassan's "being rude" last time. To keep his promise to Amir, Hassan refuses to give it up and is thrown to the ground and beaten. Although the film does not include explicit direct images of the rape on screen, the fast-shifting shots of Assef trying to pull down Hassan's pants, unbuckling his belt, and the other two boys holding Hassan on the ground facing down leave little doubt of the sexual assault. Afterward, the image of Hassan limping off home with blood dripping on the snow-covered ground further confirms the rape. A series of reverse shots between the confrontation and Amir's face portray the scene from Amir's point of view. He is no more than an observer here. Although Amir has carved "Amir and Hassan, the Sultans of Kabul" on a tree to commemorate their friendship, he now fails to stand up and help upon witnessing the crime, thus betraying his friend. Hence, Hassan is not only physically violated by Assef but also mentally hurt by Amir's betrayal.

The production team is reported to have given substantial consideration and much thought to this rape scene. "The scene has been handled in a very, very discreet and non-gratuitous fashion," said Rebecca Yeldham, one of the producer. "The scene contains no nudity. It's rendered in a very sort of impressionistic way. But it's also important in being faithful to that story—that there's no confusions that the attack in the alley that took place on that child was a sexual violation" (qtd. in Haviland). Yet despite the artistic strategy and planning, the implication of Hassan's rape still proves highly controversial and potentially detrimental to the young actors who star in the film. Twelve-year-old Ahmad Khan Mahmidzada, who played young Hassan, claims that he was not aware of the cultural taboo that the film addresses. He told the Associated Press: "They didn't give me the script. They didn't give me the story of *The Kite Runner*. If I knew about the story, I wouldn't have participated as an actor in this film" (qtd. in Tang). It is said that it was not until Paramount helped the Afghan children who starred in the film and their families to relocate to the United Arab Emirates that the film was released in 2007 (qtd. in Milvy). The author Hosseini has considered the rape scene, despite its short duration of less than a minute, to be pivotal to the plot. He has remarked in one of his interviews: "The scene is necessary, but I think you have to look at the film in a more panoramic way and not let one scene stand for the whole film" (qtd. in Milvy).

After some time lapse, the film shows the blue kite, beautifully framed and hung on the stairway wall in Amir's house. It becomes a constant reminder of Amir's betrayal. To make things even worse, Amir's way of coping with his guilt and the distance between Hassan and himself is to set Hassan up for stealing and eventually driving him and his father Ali out of his household. In December 1979 at the brink of Soviet invasion to Afghanistan, Baba and Amir flee the country to Pakistan and then the United States, leaving Rahim Khan to keep their house and other properties safe. Separated by war, the boys continue with their lives on two continents. Their childhood is suspended in this gap as the film narrative jumps to Amir's graduation from a community college, the writing of a novel, caring for his ill father, Baba, and getting married to Soraya Taheri, daughter of a decorated Afghan general. In contrast, Hassan's life in Afghanistan completely evades the screen. Instead, Khan's brief words and Hassan's letter to Amir comprise all the traces of Hassan's experience growing up in Hazarajat, enduring Soviet invasion and occupation, raising a family, looking after Amir's family house, and being executed by the Taliban. After his death, his son Sohrab is enslaved by Assef, now a Taliban official and a pedophile. The introductory screen image of Sohrab, who is a dancing boy with bells on his ankles and red slippers, reminds the viewer of the violence against Hassan. Portrayed as another victim, Sohrab now provides Amir with the opportunity for redemption.

Despite its portrayal of sophisticated Afghan people and culture, *The Kite Runner* gets trapped in the pitfall of presenting life in America as the safe haven and perfect closure. "When Hollywood has focused on characters between childhood and adulthood, the films tend to follow the dreams of success and popularity that many young people share, and youth culture is portrayed as primarily white, middle class, non-religious, suburban, and fun" (Shary 1). The film closes with a happy ending, in which Sohrab, although traumatized and refusing to communicate verbally, is presented with a promising future in the United States with Amir and Soraya and his presence completes the missing piece of a family for this childless couple.

Both *Turtles Can Fly* and *The Kite Runner* are significant because they refer "directly to the impact of war on a child" and both are informed by the experience of war. Yet both films reflect children's experience during wartime through narrative gaps which mirror the formal gaps inherent in the two films' structure (Lury 113). Focusing on the sexual violence against Agrin, Hassan, and Sohrab, this chapter has focused on how each film explores war and the tensions among different ethnic groups and social classes and their influence on multiple marginalized Kurdish and Afghanistan children. Where these films differ lies with their concluding scenes. The closing shot of *Turtles Can Fly* is filled with uncertainty and leaves the audience wondering about the fate of Kurdish children whose childhoods have been interrupted by warfare and poverty: it shows two crippled children wandering by the roadside while armed American troops pass by. In contrast, *The Kite Runner* renders a relatively "happily-ever-after" ending and closes its narrative with Sohrab's rescue and new life in America. Nonetheless, both films leave the audience with haunting, unforgettable images of childhood in war and violence.

Works Cited

Aubry, Timothy. "Afghanistan Meets the Amazon: Reading *The Kite Runner* in America." *PMLA* 124, no. 1 (2009): 25–43.

Campbell, Jill. "Everlasting Whipcords and Homing Pigeons: Formal Realism in Edgeworth's Children's Tales." *Imagining Selves: Essays in Horror of Patricia Meyer Spacks*. Eds. Rivka Swenson and Elise Lauterbach. Cranbury, NJ: Associated University Presses, 2008. 41–69.

Caviglia, Francesco. "A Child Eating Ice-Cream before the Explosion: Notes on a Controversial Scene in *The Battle of Algiers*." *P.O.V.: A Danish Journal of Film Studies* 20 (2005): 4–19.

Cross, Gary S. *The Cute and the Cool: Wondrous Innocence and Modern American Children's Culture*. Oxford and New York: Oxford University Press, 2004.

Ermelino, Louisa. "Can Hosseini Do It Again?" *Publishers Weekly* (March 19, 2007): 34.

Fass, Paula S. *Children of a New World: Society, Culture, and Globalization*. New York: New York University Press, 2007.

Forster, Marc. Dir. *The Kite Runner*. 2007. DreamWorks Entertainment, 2007.
Frost, Leslie. "Shadows of War: Fascist and Anti-Fascist Representations of Childhood in *Triumph of the Will, A Letter Santa Claus*, and *The Little Princess*." *Children's Literature Association Quarterly* 33, no. 1 (2008): 79–104.
Gabbard, Krin and William Luhr, eds. *Screening Genders*. New Brunswick, NJ: Rutgers University Press, 2008.
Ghobadi, Bahman, Dir. *Turtles Can Fly*. MGM, 2005.
Graham, Mark. *Afghanistan in the Cinema*. Urbana, Chicago, and Springfield: University of Illinois Press, 2010.
Gupta, Suman. *Imagining Iraq: Literature in English and the Iraq Invasion*. New York: Macmillan Palgrave, 2011.
Haviland, Charles. "*Kite Runner* Flies into Controversy." *BBC News*. BBC, September 18, 2007. news.bbc.co.uk/2/hi/6992751.stm (accessed July 9, 2011).
Holland, Patricia. *Picturing Childhood the Myth of the Child in Popular Imagery*. London: I. B. Taurus, 2004.
Jefferess, David. "To Be Good (Again): The Kite Runner as Allegory of Global Ethics." *Journal of Postcolonial Writing* 45, no. 4 (2009): 389–400.
Jenkins, Henry. *The Children's Culture Reader*. New York: New York University Press, 1998.
Junger, Sebastian and Tim Hetherington, dir. *Restrepo*. 2010. National Geographic Entertainment, 2010.
Karimi, Iraj. "Turtles Can Fly: Those Who Have Not Lives Only for Not Having Played." *Film International* 11, no. 1–2 (2004): 58–59.
Kornhaber, Donna. "Animating the War: The First World War and Children's Cartoons in America." *Lion and the Unicorn* 31, no. 2 (2007): 132–46.
Kroll, Pamela L. "Games of Disappearance and Return: War and the Child in Roberto Benigni's *Life Is Beautiful*." *Literature Film Quarterly* 30, no. 1 (2000): 29–45.
Lury, Karen. *The Child in Film: Tears, Fears and Fairytales*. New Brunswick, NJ: Rutgers University Press, 2010.
Mehrabi, Massoud. "Mr. Bush's Coffee-House: A Candid Talk with Bahman Ghobadi, Director of *Turtles Can Fly*." *Film International* 11, No. 1-2 (2004): 46-52.
Milvy, Erika. "*The Kite Runner* Controversy." *Salon*. December 9, 2007. salon.com/2007/12/09/hosseini/ (accessed July 9, 2011).
Peebles, Stacey. *Welcome to the Suck: Narrating the American Soldier's Experience in Iraq*. Ithaca and London: Cornell University Press, 2011.
Reynolds, Pamela. "Afterword." *Under Fire: Childhood in the Shadow of War*. Eds. Elizabeth Goodenough and Andrea Immel Detroit: Wayne State University Press, 2008. 251-53.
Romney, Jonathan. "It's a Small Country." *Sight and Sound* 19, no. 11 (2009): 38.
Shary, Timothy. "Introduction: Youth Culture Shock." *Youth Culture in Global Cinema*. Eds. Timothy Shary and Alexandra Seibel. Austin: University of Texas Press, 2007. 1–6.
Smith, J. E. "Fred Zinnemann's Search (19454848): Reconstructing the Voices of Europe's Children." *Film History* 23, no. 1 (2011): 75–92.
Spaulding, Amy E. *The Art of Storytelling: Telling Truths through Telling Stories*. Landham, Toronto, and Plymouth: Scarecrow Press, 2011.
Tang, Alisa. "*The Kite Runner* Rape Scene Stirs Controversy." *USA Today*. September 24, 2007. www.usatoday.com/life/movies/news/2007-09-23-kite-runner_N.htm (accessed July 9, 2011).
Williams, Linda Ruth. "Kids with Guns." *Sight and Sound* 19, no. 11 (2009): 36-38.

Chapter Fourteen
Spelling Out Racial Difference: Moving beyond the Inspirational Discourses in *Akeelah and the Bee*
by Kathryn E. Linder

Introduction

Akeelah and the Bee (2006) was released in the midst of a spelling bee movie fad that began with the documentary film *Spellbound* (2002) and continued with the film *Bee Season* (2005) based on Myla Goldberg's 2001 novel of the same name. Following the quest of an eleven-year-old black girl as she attempts to win the National Spelling Bee, *Akeelah* received much attention in the press because the film was the first to be produced and promoted by Starbucks Coffee Company. With an adolescent black female protagonist (Keke Palmer) and an almost all-black cast that includes well-known black actors Laurence Fishburne and Angela Bassett, *Akeelah* engages with issues of age, race, and gender throughout. Because *Akeelah* is comprised of the mixed genres of family drama, sports movie, and inspirational inner-city education film, the narrative offers a unique opportunity for an in-depth analysis of how messages about education, privilege, and difference are communicated to diverse audiences.

Of particular interest in this chapter are the ways in which *Akeelah* draws on the conventions of melodrama in order to create a particular narrative of academic success for the film's youthful main character. Although *Akeelah* was labeled by one reviewer as a film with "such a kind heart that it renders itself immune to any real criticism" (*The Washington Times*, April 28, 2006), here I advance an alternative reading. Specifically, I combat the inspirational discourse that surrounds the film and instead acknowledge and critique dominant messages of racial assimilation and white privilege that are communicated to the film's intended audience of young people. After a brief reception study of *Akeelah*, I offer an analysis of how the film engages with standards of melodrama to convey particular messages of age, race, privilege, gender, and difference. Through an application of Linda William's five features of the melodramatic mode, I examine the film's portrayal of the main character Akeelah, her relationships within her black community, and her interactions with the larger dominant (white) society in order to illustrate how the film contains underlying messages of racial assimilation and white privilege.

Spelling as (Melo)Drama

Spelling bee competitions, which have been part of American educational and social culture since the 1700s,[1] have been argued to be "not simply a scholastic game," but rather events that influence Americans "on some level of our cultural psyche and being."[2] In his 1941 article on the spelling bee as a linguistic institution, Allen Walker Read claims that "the attainment of spelling was a symbol of culture" and that spelling bees have historically "rank[ed] among the conservative influences in American speech . . . [they are] a determinant of the course taken by the language."[3] Indeed, American spelling bees "as a genuine folk institution"[4] were one of the mechanisms through which American children both entertained the adults in their communities and also normalized the relationship between knowing how to spell and one's ability to perform a certain level of cultural knowledge and authority through language. According to scholar Sam Whitsitt, author of "The *Spelling Bee*: What Makes It an American Institution?" language is more than a mode of communication between individuals. Whitsitt argues that "language can provide analogies for proper moral behavior, as in expressions such as *minding one's 'p's' and 'q's',* and *being sure to dot one's 'i's and cross one's 't's*."[5] Moreover, Whitsitt claims that "language itself can be the medium" through which "questions of morality, as well as other dramas of a culture" are played out.[6] As I will argue below, the fictionalized spelling bee competition in *Akeelah and the Bee* acts as a platform for a racial melodrama through which ideals of whiteness are reinforced and strengthened.

Melodrama, a complex cinematic term that has been utilized to examine a variety of diverse film genres,[7] has been broadly defined "as a technique or technology for working through ideas, relations, identities, and feelings."[8] While cinematic scholars have postulated a range of comparative definitions of melodrama in order to encompass how the term has changed over time,[9] these same scholars agree that melodrama in film can be broadly characterized through the ways in which melodramas entice audiences with messages of moral uplift, and how melodramas attempt to manipulate audience emotion, especially with appeals to sympathy and pity. Because melodramas depend on the identification of heroes, villains, and Manichaean definitions of right and wrong in order to make particular moral claims, they are ripe for critical analysis.

The relationship between melodrama, moral uplift, and appeals to sympathy may explain why melodramas with young protagonists are so effective. Nancy Lesko, in her book *Act Your Age!: A Cultural Construction of Adolescence* (2001), argues that socially constructed narratives of adolescence are especially engaging for audiences because they often include messages about the future of society and the hope that youth embody. Lesko further claims that "consumers of adolescent narratives are bound emotionally to the story. We are happy, satisfied, and comforted by narratives of fulfillment (conventional adolescent development); we are disturbed and alarmed by precocity and risk."[10] In films that feature youth of color in school settings in particular, anxieties about youth encountering drug use, violence, and rampant sexuality[11] exist alongside arguments about the need for public schooling to educate students about how to be "good" citizens.[12] As I will elaborate below, the education system in *Akeelah* has been simultaneously positioned as both a site of danger and salvation, embodying both the problems of society and the solutions to those problems through the possibility of Akeelah's success. By focusing on an adolescent black protagonist who is fighting to save her school and larger community from funding cuts and urban blight, *Akeelah* is set apart as not only a racial melodrama, but one that is also heavily influenced by societal understandings of youth identity.

Standards of melodrama have been frequently used to examine both historical and contemporary films to better understand filmic representations of racial identity, the concept of passing, and American race relations. This may be, in part, because melodrama has a history of "support[ing] and perpetuat[ing] racist beliefs in white supremacy."[13] Films such as *Uncle Tom's Cabin* (1927), *The Birth of a Nation* (1915), *Imitation of Life* (1934), and *Stella Dallas* (1937) have all been argued to be canonical melodramas that also uphold problematic ideals of whiteness.[14] (Several of these films, it should be noted, also focus on a young, female protagonist.) It is because of the historical relationship between melodrama and messages of white supremacy that film scholar Linda Williams has pointed to the ways in which melodrama has had, and continues to have, an "incalculable influence on American attitudes toward race."[15] In her 2001 book, *Playing the Race Card: Melodramas of Black and White from Uncle Tom to O.J. Simpson*, Williams argues for "the importance of investigating racial melodrama— of understanding the dynamics of melodrama in relation to the stories about race that American popular culture has long been telling itself."[16] Thus, a central goal of this chaper is to identify and critique *Akeelah* as a racial melodrama lest the film become part of an unquestioned national narrative of racial hegemony.

Reviewer Perceptions of *Akeelah and the Bee*

Akeelah and the Bee centers on the story of Akeelah Anderson, a young girl from Los Angeles, who unintentionally wins her school's spelling bee, an event that she participates in at her principal's request after she repeatedly skips school. Following her local win, Akeelah's principal introduces her to Dr. Larabee (Laurence Fishburne), a black English professor who agrees to coach her in the hope that she will be able to advance to the Scripps National Spelling Bee. From the beginning of the film, the odds are against Akeelah. Not only does her impoverished school lack appropriate textbooks and materials to help her train, but her single mother (Angela Bassett) is represented as uninterested in Akeelah's training as she works during the day and at night to make ends meet. Moreover, Akeelah is competing against economically advantaged youths who have been training for years and who are more familiar with the discourses of local, regional, state, and national spelling bees. Throughout the film, Akeelah must overcome a series of obstacles in order to accomplish her goal and prove that a young black girl from a poor neighborhood can succeed in the privileged domain of the spelling bee world.

Viewing *Akeelah and the Bee* as a melodrama that is fashioned after "some gladiator sports event"[17] and that is "reminiscent of many sports movies in which underdogs win the day" (*St. Petersburg Times*, May 7, 2006), it becomes easy to see how film audiences are asked to engage in a cheering on of the young heroine at the expense of critical analysis. The film's main plotline, that of the black community supporting Akeelah to achieve her spelling bee dream, encourages audience members to be just as supportive. To critically question the film's portrayal of Akeelah, her black family, and her black community would mean one is not "playing along." Indeed, scholar Judith Mayne argues about the critical analysis of film that "to be conscious of race and the curious racial politics of the film is to refuse to be a good sport (in several senses of the term)."[18] Throughout *Akeelah*, standards of melodrama both advance issues of race while also encouraging the film's diverse audiences to ignore them in order to be "good sports."

Feminist film scholar Sharon Willis argues that contemporary films are "representations that strive to accommodate diversity through scripts organized around specific identities and intended to capture new identity-based market segments."[19] The corporate support of *Akeelah and the Bee* by Starbucks offers an interesting example of a film about a black community that is marketed across diverse audiences. In part, this marketing occurs through a paradox in which an erasure of issues of race within the film exists alongside a reliance on the film's title, which incorporates the protagonist's ethnic name, to draw both white and black audiences. For example, in a description by Starbucks's chief executive Howard Schultz (*The Independent*, April 25, 2006), *Akeelah* is portrayed as a film with an "inspirational message about a community coming together to support one of its own," which Schultz claims is "emblematic of what Starbucks stands for." In newspaper articles about the film's promotion and reception, representatives of Starbucks do not acknowledge the film's specific racial themes, but allude to the film's "social message" (*Los Angeles Times*, August 27, 2007) and refer to the film as "socially relevant" (*New York Times*, October 22, 2006). *Akeelah and the Bee*'s tagline, "changing the world . . . one word at a time," also offers a vague description of the film's transformative social power, but does not specifically locate this social change as within the black community or as antiracist.

In the remainder of this chapter, I critically analyze the messages of age, race, and privilege in *Akeelah and the Bee* through an application of Linda Williams's five aspects of melodrama: home as a space of innocence, the victim-hero character, pathos and action, realism, and binaries of good and evil. Williams associates each of these standards specifically with racialized melodramas and she presents each standard as a method to more fully understand "a peculiarly American form of melodrama in which virtue becomes inextricably linked to forms of racial victimization."[20] Below, I elaborate on the ways in which *Akeelah and the Bee* is framed as "inspirational" precisely through the film's portrayal of Akeelah's victimization by the black community that surrounds her. Indeed, it is only through pursuing the national spelling bee that Akeelah, her family, and her black community can be redeemed through the idealized discourse of young people's educational success as defined by dominant (white) culture.

Home as a Space of Innocence

For this first melodramatic mode, Williams argues that a melodramatic narrative "begins, and wants to end, in a 'space of innocence.'"[21] Within *Akeelah and the Bee*, however, there is no overt space of youthful innocence for Akeelah to claim as her own. Indeed, the lack of innocence that surrounds Akeelah is highlighted in the film's opening scenes in which the audience is shown shots of her neighborhood with a voice-over introducing Akeelah as a neighborhood misfit. With an opening shot of graffiti and cement buildings, Akeelah states, "You know that feeling, no matter what you do, or where you go, you just don't fit in?"[22] Walking amidst stores with barred windows and signs written in foreign languages, Akeelah explains that she cannot find a word to describe how she feels "all the time" in her neighborhood. Despite having an extensive vocabulary from her hobby of playing a computerized version of Scrabble, Akeelah cannot communicate the relationship she has with her community.

Locating where "this all starts" at her school rather than the home where she resides with her family, Akeelah situates her story in a school space filled with children, a space often constructed as one of innocence, but not in the context of Akeelah's neighborhood. Akeelah's school is a "fragile and fleeting [space] of innocence embedded within larger corrupt social orders"[23] that work to both segregate her school and neighborhood and deny equal academic opportunities to Akeelah and her peers due to lack of funding and institutional support. Rather than opening the film with a nostalgic site of innocence to which Akeelah is trying to return, *Akeelah* instead implies that this innocence never existed. The lack of innocence in *Akeelah and the Bee* immediately calls attention to the racial difference of Akeelah's neighborhood and disassociates innocence from her home and school in distinctly racialized ways.

The first shot of her school is through a layer of chain-link fencing toward a basketball court where children of color are playing. The second shot is from inside the school looking out at razor wire across the top of a fence and is framed in layers of doorways. The third shot is from outside looking in through scratched, grimy windows at children climbing a stairwell. In each shot, the children are trapped within the building or its grounds by fencing. Other shots within the school show dirty lockers, uniformed children sleeping in classrooms, and students' papers with low grades marked in red ink. These opening shots are contrasted with our first view of Akeelah, who is walking down the street toward the school looking unsure of her surroundings and verbalizing the ways in which she feels like she does not fit.

Throughout these opening scenes, the audience is clearly meant to identify Akeelah as someone who does not belong. In addition to her explaining that she does not fit in with her larger community, Akeelah is portrayed as not fitting in with her family. The film's first shot of her home, a shelf of books in her room, is contrasted with a previous shot of garbage on the street. On the shelf are a mixture of word reference books (thesauruses and dictionaries) and classic literature from Hurston, Faulkner, Dickens, L'Engle, and others. This shot is followed by a close-up of a computer screen with a digital Scrabble game, and then a shot of Akeelah playing. Akeelah is interrupted from her game by dinner, which is announced by her sister—a teenage mother holding her child. At dinner, the audience is also introduced to Akeelah's single mother, her soldier brother, and her absent brother who, it is implied, is spending time with a more dangerous crowd in the neighborhood. Through these early scenes of her home, Akeelah is set apart physically in her room as well as academically with her books and computer; she is also placed in opposition to her family who are shown interrupting her efforts to learn words or practice spelling. The film's introduction to her home life ends with Akeelah spelling words to herself in her room with the noise of sirens and helicopters drowning out the sound of her calling out letters

Because a melodrama "ends happily if the protagonists can, in some way, return . . . home,"[24] the audience of *Akeelah and the Bee* may already be expecting a transformation of community that will need to take place by the end of the film for Akeelah to fit in with her neighborhood and family. Following the melodramatic standard, *Akeelah and the Bee* does eventually attempt to redeem the community's innocence so that it will be a place to which Akleelah will want to return. For example, the ending of the film displays a montage of shots that show Akeelah studying with members of her community such as local gang members. The montage (re)presents Akeelah's community without graffiti and with houses now located in a suburban-looking setting with more grass and less cement. For Akeelah to return home now that she has changed, the community must show change as well. The place where Akeelah did not fit in is now a community in which "everything feels right."[25]

The stereotypical representation of the black community throughout *Akeelah* offers the film's audience a nostalgic representation of segregation. The space of innocence in *Akeelah* is not something already present in the film, but rather something outside of Akeelah's community that it must emulate. Indeed, it is the lack of innocence in Akeelah's life that points to the flaws of her black community and home life. The redemption of Akeelah's community at the end of the film when neighbors and family members help her to achieve success at the National Spelling Bee supports Williams's argument that "melodrama offers the hope . . . [that] virtue and truth can be achieved in private individuals and individual heroic acts, rather than... in revolution and change."[26] Rather than interrogate the social obstacles that inhibit Akeelah's success and which she must overcome, the film places individuals in her home and neighborhood as a central barrier to her spelling bee goals. Akeelah becomes a victim of her black neighborhood and can only become a hero through "getting out" when she competes in and wins the National Spelling Bee. The goal of the film is not for the community to revolutionize black education at Akeelah's school, but rather to help one individual achieve an individual success. (Re)locating Akeelah in her community after the final spelling bee returns audience members to a different kind of innocent and unquestioning space: Akeelah has been placed back where she belongs, has accepted her surroundings, and her community has no overt plans for systemic change that might affect the outside (white) world.

The Victim-Hero

By situating Akeelah as separate from her family and her community in her goals and academic efforts, Akeelah is developed early on as an "underdog from the ghetto" who must triumph over "a life of adversity" (*The Gazette*, April 28, 2006). Relying on racial stereotypes, the film identifies Akeelah as a "victim-hero," the character who is developed in the second aspect of the racialized melodrama. According to Williams, "Melodrama focuses on victim-heroes and on recognizing their virtue. Recognition of virtue orchestrates the moral legibility that is key to melodrama's function."[27] Although Akeelah is unmotivated at the beginning of the film, her attendance at the school's spelling bee, despite her reservations, shows her willingness to try. Akeelah, who has skipped a grade, is portrayed as a student who can "show [that Crenshaw Middle School] students can perform" by competing against other students in local, regional, and statewide spelling bees with the hopes of representing the school at the national competition, despite the fact that the school does not have enough money to "put doors on the toilet stalls."[28]

Williams argues that films "need their victim-heroes to suffer in order to purge them of the taint of selfish ambition."[29] In *Akeelah and the Bee*, Akeelah's choice to compete in spelling competitions and to spend all of her summer studying (definitely a form of suffering to the children viewing the movie) is made with the knowledge that her community is counting on her. Her performance in the spelling bee is represented as necessary for the school to argue their need for money for curriculum materials. Without Akeelah, the school will be denied resources and written off as a lost cause. Additionally, Akeelah competes because of her memories of her deceased father. When she initially decides to compete, it is because her brother reminds her that it would be what their father would have wanted. Through each of her motivations, Akeelah is framed as taking responsibility for her own achievements and as representative of her community, this portrayal can be read both positively and negatively. While Akeelah is seen as able to achieve what she puts her mind to, she is also required to take responsibility for her own learning despite significant societal obstacles.

Like Akeelah, her neighborhood can also be characterized through the melodramatic standard of the victim-hero. While Akeelah is victimized by her surroundings, however, her community is seen as being victimized by their own actions (gang activity, older men panhandling on the street, and Akeelah's mother as neglectful and unsupportive of her academic endeavors). The community is redeemed and made heroic at the end of the film when Akeelah is shown studying with the local gang members, older men at the local park, and her mother, sister, and brother on the stoop of her house. Akeelah uses the image of "50,000 coaches"[30] as she envisions her community as study helpers, employing the local grocer and the mail delivery person along the way. By helping Akeelah achieve her individual goal, the community is brought together around one person, but is not shown accomplishing any kind of large-scale change. Akeelah's community is represented as docile and always willing to help achieve a white standard—in this case, success at the national spelling bee. The film's representation of the community's redemption embodies melodrama's "tendency to find solutions to problems that cannot really be solved without challenging the older ideologies of moral certainty to which melodrama wishes to return."[31] Ultimately, the community achieves redemption through its docility, unquestioningly supporting Akeelah as she successfully navigates the (primarily white) spelling bee world.

Pathos and Action

Williams's third aspect of melodrama outlines how an audience's "recognition of virtue [in the victim-hero] involves a dialectic of pathos and action—a give and take of 'too late' and 'in the nick of time.'"[32] This characteristic is also overtly racialized in *Akeelah and the Bee* through the relationship between what is deemed as too late and what occurs just in time for Akeelah and for her community. For example, part of the pressure that Akeelah faces to achieve academic recognition is the pressure to get out of the neighborhood where her father was killed in a random shooting. The danger of getting stuck in Akeelah's neighborhood, represented by repeated shots of metal fencing, are frequently contrasted with the house of Dr. Larabee. Although Dr. Larabee is described as living near to Akeelah (indeed, she questions his importance because he lives so close), his house is surrounded by a tranquil garden and is a place where Akeelah must "speak properly or [she] won't speak at all."[33] Dr. Larabee requires that Akeelah prove herself as someone who can follow orders and leave black culture behind before she can gain entry to his house and become his student. Importantly, their initial meeting takes place outside his home and Akeelah is not allowed entry until she acknowledges needing Dr. Larabee's help to succeed and has shown her efforts to learn Latin roots.

If Akeelah can learn to strip herself of black culture in the nick of time in order to accommodate the expectations of white culture, then maybe she can accomplish her goal of winning the national spelling bee. Dr. Larabee's home represents what Akeelah can achieve if his intervention is not already too late. Akeelah is frequently compared to other children who have been studying and attempting to make it to the national spelling bee for years. In fact, she only has two years left in which she will be eligible to compete, so her time is limited. The various obstacles that Akeelah must overcome, such as the lack of education she receives at her impoverished school, are combined with Akeelah's low self-esteem about her abilities. By not attending school regularly and not turning in assignments, the implication is that Akeelah also thinks that her chance for a transformative opportunity has passed.

The above themes of saving Akeelah in the nick of time from herself and the limited future that supposedly awaits her are amplified by the sporting-event-inspired genre of the film. Several times, Akeelah just makes a deadline to compete or just makes the cut to progress to the next level of spelling bee. At one bee, Akeelah's mother interrupts her spelling and threatens to remove her from a competition. While Akeelah argues with her mother, another contestant whom Akeelah befriends must stall so that Akeelah can return in the nick of time and move forward once again. At another bee, Akeelah loses by one person until her sister identifies another contestant who is cheating, thus allowing

Akeelah to move to the next stage. These repeated situations in which Akeelah barely is able to move forward illustrate the challenges of the bees and also show her need for Dr. Larabee's help in navigating within the spelling bee community.

Realism

Williams argues that the fourth aspect of black and white melodrama is that "melodrama borrows from realism but realism serves the melodrama of pathos and action."[34] This function of melodrama is also evident in *Akeelah and the Bee*. Because the release of *Akeelah and the Bee* followed the documentary *Spellbound* (2002), diverse audiences may have already been aware of the reality of spelling bee competitions. As well, the diverse population of Southern California allows for the possibility that three ethnic children (one black, one Latino, and one Chinese) could compete against one another at the national bee, as happens in the film. Even the stereotypes used throughout the film can be seen as realistic—Akeelah's single mother, her dead father, and her Chinese competitor's verbally abusive father—as these stereotypes are commonly used to portray people of color. However, how the realism within the film is received by white audiences (who may believe the situations with little questioning) versus audiences of color (who may be a bit more skeptical) is significant.

For example, the film plays on realities of black experience in subtle ways that may be read differently by white and black audiences. The ghost of the Ebonics controversy of the late 1990s in Oakland, which validated African American Language as a dialect, is present in Dr. Larabee's demand that Akeelah "leave the ghetto talk outside" before he will allow her in his home or agree to work with her. Larabee's requirement for Akeelah's speech directly contradicts the claim that in spelling bees "what counts in America is not how you say it; you do not have to sound like you come from any higher class to make something count; what counts is how one puts the graphic, material, singular signifiers—the letters—in the correct . . . order."[35] *Akeelah* argues against the idea that the spelling bee "is an egalitarian gathering in which kids from every social class compete in a true meritocracy."[36] In order to begin her training, constraints are immediately placed on Akeelah's vocabulary and pronunciation. As well, the cultural phenomenon of black children's fear of "acting white" in their pursuit of education is present in Akeelah's low self-esteem and in her repeated concern about being called a "freak and a brainiac" by her peers.[37] Although the film never makes direct connections between these historical concerns and the culture of the black community, *Akeelah* clearly relies on contemporary issues of race to drive the film's pathos and action.

A scene in the movie where Akeelah's mother confronts her about a trip to a local school of mostly white children to study words is exemplary of this aspect of black and white melodrama. Akeelah's mother states, "if this spelling thing means sneaking off to the suburbs... I'm calling it all off . . . do you think they care about you in Woodland Hills?"[38] In both this scene and the scene in which Dr. Larabee strips Akeelah of her "ghetto talk," Akeelah is almost thwarted from her goal of participating in spelling bees because of adult perceptions of her racial affiliations. In the case of her mother, it is her white assimilation, while in the case of Dr. Larabee it is Akeelah's embodiment of black culture. Akeelah must overcome both of these perceptions in order to continue toward her goal. She must perform whiteness for Dr. Larabee and the spelling bee officials and also maintain her blackness for her family and neighborhood.

Akeelah's transition into white speech while also maintaining her blackness represents a realistic portrayal of the tension young people of color may feel when forced to accommodate dominant cultural ideas of education and knowledge. Seen through Akeelah's progression through spelling bees as she learns the intricacies of bee rules and regulations, her assimilation is hidden within a spelling bee discourse, but the presence of all-white judges and her all-white competition imply something more disturbing at work in the film that may be more visible to black audiences than white. In the beginning of her spelling bee career Akeelah is asked if she would like a definition and she replies, "That would be cool"; she also does not speak into the microphone when asking questions and asks for definitions saying, "You want to tell me what that means?" Later in the film, Akeelah is much more polished and asks, "Can I have a definition please?" and "Can I have the language of origin please?"[39] This change in Akeelah's language and speech patterns signifies more than her knowledge of spelling bee discourse. On one level, Akeelah's change can be read as her "beating the system" and "playing the game" in order to win. On another level, one must ask, why is this change even necessary? Why does the film have to show this change rather than having Akeelah win the bee while also maintaining a speech pattern inflected by Ebonics?

Some of these questions are addressed by Akeelah's performance of blackness at the National Spelling Bee. Even as Akeelah is performing whiteness for the judges of the competitions, Akeelah performs blackness by jumping rope as a mnemonic device to keep time. The relationship between jump roping and the black community, specifically young black girls, is discussed in Kyra Gaunt's *The Games Black Girls Play: Learning the Ropes from Double-Dutch to Hip-Hop*,[40] in which Gaunt argues that the body-conscious rhythms used in jump rope can be traced back to the times of slavery and are heavily associated with urban girl culture. In addition to Gaunt's book, the metaphors of double-dutch and jumping rope have been used in scholarly works to describe the role of blacks in politics[41] and to discuss black women writers.[42] In the film, Akeelah not only uses jump roping to practice for the competition, but also actually mimics jump roping at the competition itself when she is given a challenging word. Her time onstage is a mixed performance of whiteness for the judges and blackness for her community at home, who are frequently shown watching the live competition on television and cheering her on. Akeelah's balancing of two competing discourses is another component of the film that can be read both positively and negatively. Although at least one reviewer identified Akeelah's jump roping as "a gratuitous racial stereotype" (*The Times*, August 17, 2006), thus representing a clear stereotype of black youth, her use of the jump roping to continue on in the competition also signifies (albeit in a simplistic way) her ability to employ an aspect of historically black culture to engage in the white system. To say that Akeelah's jump roping is either a positive or negative representation of black culture is to ignore that it can be both.

Binaries of Good Versus Evil: White Anxieties in *Akeelah and the Bee*

Williams's fifth and final aspect of the black and white melodrama may be the most important to an interpretation of the racial messages being communicated throughout *Akeelah and the Bee*. Williams states, "The final key of melodrama is the presentation of characters who embody primary psychic roles organized in Manichaean conflicts between good and evil."[43] Throughout the film, clear binaries are drawn between the supportive Dr. Larabee and Akeelah's skeptical mother. Dr. Larabee is perceived as "mythic" (*The Washington Post*, April 28, 2006) and "inspirational" (*The Independent*, April 25, 2006) while Akeelah's mother is perceived as "hostile" (*Today Show*, May 1, 2006) and "embittered" (*Los Angeles Times*, April 27, 2006; *USA Today*, April 28, 2006). Unlike Dr. Larabee, who immediately recognizes Akeelah's potential, Akeelah's mother has doubts about the obstacles that need to be overcome in order for Akeelah to succeed, thus making her the main villain within *Akeelah*. She is demonized by reviewers as a "classic commotion-causing black mom" (*The Boston Globe*, April 28, 2006). Interestingly, Dr. Larabee's association with Akeelah's assimilation into dominant (white) discourses of the spelling bee is not critiqued within the film as much as her mother's lack of support for her educational goals.

In *Playing the Race Card*, Williams draws on the narrative of *Uncle Tom's Cabin* to describe a binary between a "Tom" character and an "Anti-Tom" character, both of which frame black identity in relation to white culture. According to Williams, the "Tom" half of the binary is the "good nigger"[44] who embodies characteristics of "gentle[ness]"[45] and "docility"[46] while also expressing "kindliness, benevolence, dignity, humility, and so on."[47] Unlike the "Anti-Tom" character, the black man who is "an object of white fear and loathing,"[48] Dr. Larabee is dependable and willing to help Akeelah's white principal in his time of need by becoming a mentor and spelling coach for Akeelah. Represented in the film as quiet, reflective, and dedicated to his role as teacher, Dr. Larabee is contrasted with other male figures in Akeelah's neighborhood who are affiliated with gangs or who are poor and without jobs, and also with Akeelah's unsupportive mother. Ultimately, Dr. Larabee, as the main "Tom" character, becomes the catalyst for Akeelah, Akeelah's mother, and Akeelah's community to transition from an "Anti-Tom" portrayal to a "Tom" story. Indeed, Akeelah's success, rather than being attributed to herself or her community, is attributed to the assistance of Dr. Larabee, who Akeelah's mother describes as "generous" when she thanks him for "everything."

In *Akeelah and the Bee*, both Akeelah and Dr. Larabee embody the assimilation of the black community into dominant white discourses of education, language, and larger cultural practices. Throughout the film, a quote from Marianne Williamson's poem "A Return to Love" is repeated by Dr. Larabee to encourage Akeelah. He states, "Our deepest fear is not that we are inadequate. Our deepest fear is that we are powerful beyond measure."[49] Although this quote is meant to illustrate the fears of Akeelah as a young black girl who is unsure of her abilities, it also stands in for white anxieties about people of color. To acknowledge that black people are adequate in their own right would disrupt a hierarchy of racial dominance and submission. In her book on theories of spectatorship, Judith Mayne claims that "one of the most efficient ways to evoke and deny race simultaneously is to make a black character a projection of white anxieties about race."[50] Through *Akeelah*'s focus on the power of Akeelah to succeed through assimilation into whiteness, Akeelah's black identity is disempowered as an equally appropriate method for success.

As scholar James Baldwin argues, "The brutal truth is that the bulk of white people in America never had any interest in educating black people, except as this could serve white purposes."[51] Importantly, although Dr. Larabee repeats the Williamson's quote to encourage Akeelah to fight for her goal, the goal that she is fighting for is located within a particular discourse of educational achievement. The goal of the Scripps National Spelling Bee is, in part, to help young people "develop correct English usage that will help them all their lives."[52] In the film, there is no question that the "correct English" that Akeelah needs to emulate, and that Dr. Larabee already speaks, is a form of English that has been associated with white and middle-upper class culture. As Akeelah works to emulate "correct English" and prove her adeptness at spelling, she, like Dr. Larabee, is portrayed as a special case who is not adequate for who she is, but rather for the dominant discourses of language and education that she can perform.

Like Akeelah, Dr. Larabee's character can also be analyzed in terms of white anxieties about race. By embodying a "Tom" character who can only be trusted and loved rather than feared and hated, Dr. Larabee can be read an a non-threatening black man who has assimilated to white culture and who can be depended on to help assimilate others. Dr. Larabee, who is described by reviewers as "cultured" (*The Gazette*, April 28, 2006), "inspirational" (*The Independent*, April 25, 2006) and "charismatic" (*Mail on Sunday*, August 20, 2006), embodies a phenomenon through which dominant norms of speech and pronunciation are translated into "othered" communities through "othered" individuals themselves. Problematically, Dr. Larabee is portrayed primarily as a positive influence on Akeelah and as an academic mentor; his character is never questioned for the changes that he encourages in her racial identity and performance.

The characters of Akeelah and Dr. Larabee are both used to illustrate how black people can be successfully assimilated into dominant cultural discourses without becoming threats to that dominant culture. Rather than people to be feared, Akeelah, Dr. Larabee, and Akeelah's community are shown adapting to white expectations while remaining segregated and "othered." As within the "Tom" story, the characters in *Akeelah and the Bee* are mostly represented as having "no interest in escape"[53] from societal oppressions and limitations. Akeelah may return to her black neighborhoods more competent in "correct English" than when she left, but there is no sign throughout the film of any kind of lasting change for Akeelah's school or her young peers. The community effort to support Akeelah results in the success of just one individual, rather than in larger changes that are implied to be needed within her school and community.

Conclusion

In her defense of melodrama as a genre worthy of study, Williams states that "melodrama may prove central to who we are as a nation, and black and white racial melodrama may even prove central to the question of just who we mean when we say 'we' are a nation."[54] Used as a tool to define the norm against the "other" while also creating parallel binaries of good versus evil, racial melodramas that employ narratives of youth identity and development allow for virtue to become legible in conjunction with dominant discourses of age, race, privilege, and difference. As Henry Giroux argues, "The racial coding of black youth tells us less about such youth than it does about how white society configures public memory, stability and disorder, and the experiences of marginal groups in America."[55] Problematically, while *Akeelah and the Bee* engages with important social identity issues, the film simultaneously situates these cultural negotiations in a binary construction of success (whiteness) versus failure (blackness). The story of Akeelah's success is merely a mechanism through which racial assimilation is further normalized and white privilege is maintained.

While *Akeelah and the Bee* addresses the need for more films about communities of color, the film also offers a crucial example of how racial melodramas that are meant to inspire can also offer subtle messages that privilege harmful dominant cultural standards and expectations. As the above analysis illustrates, embedded within *Akeelah and the Bee*'s inspirational message there are also some disturbing similarities to historical black and white melodramas with more overt racist messages. Indeed, racial melodrama often offers complex and contradictory messages about both the norm and the other, thus demanding a critical interrogation of racial messages communicated through melodramatic modes. As Williams states, "melodrama is not a static, archaic, stereotyping and non-realist form, but a tremendously protean, evolving, and modernizing form that continually uncovers new realistic material for its melodramatic project."[56] As melodramas adjust over time to incorporate and respond to new realities and racial representations, further analysis of the messages racial melodramas communicate is imperative.

Notes

1. See Allen Walker Read, "The Spelling Bee: A Linguistic Institution of the American Folk." *PMLA* 56, no. 2 (1941): 495–512.

2. Sam Whitsitt, "The *Spelling Bee*: What Makes it an American Institution?" *Journal of Popular Culture* 43, no. 4 (2010): 884; 885.

3. Read, *PMLA*, 512.

4. Read, *PMLA*, 511.

5. Whitsitt, *Journal of Popular Culture,* 884.

6. Whitsitt, *Journal of Popular Culture,* 884.

7. See, respectively: Scott Higgins. "Suspenseful Situations: Melodramatic Narrative and the Contemporary Action Film." *Cinema Journal* 47, mo. 2 (Winter 2008): 74–96; Despina Kakoudaki. "Spectacles of History: Race Relations, Melodrama, and the Science Fiction/Disaster Film." *Camera Obscura* 50, no. 17 (2002): 109–153; Sumiko Higashi. "Melodrama, Realism, and Race: World War II Newsreels and Propaganda Film." *Cinema Journal* 37, no. 3 (Spring 1998): 38–61.

8. Michael Stewart. "Irresistible Death: *21 Grams* as Melodrama." *Cinema Journal* 47, no. 1 (2007): 65.

9. See Dan Flory's explanation of "classical" versus "modified" melodrama in his article "Race, Rationality, and Melodrama: Aesthetic Response and the Case of Oscar Micheaux." *The Journal of Aesthetics and Art Criticism* 63, no. 4 (Autumn 2005): 327–338. Or Ben Singer's differentiation between "action" and "pathetic" melodrama in *Melodrama and Modernity: Early Sensational Cinema and Its Contexts* (New York: Columbia University Press, 2001).

10. Nancy Lesko. *Act Your Age!: A Cultural Construction of Adolescence*. (New York & London: Routledge Falmer, 2001): 132.

11. See Mike Males's *The Scapegoat Generation* (1996) for further explication of these national fears.

12. See, for example, such films as *Dangerous Minds* (1995) or *187* (1997).

13. Flory, *Journal of Aesthetics and Art Criticism,* 330.

14. See Flory, 330; Allison Whitney. "Race, Class and the Pressure to Pass in American Maternal Melodrama: The Case of *Stella Dallas*." *Journal of Film and Video* 59, no. 1 (Spring 2007): 3–18.

15. Linda Williams. "Melodrama in Black and White: Uncle Tom and *The Green Mile*." *Film Quarterly* 55, no. 2 (2001): 20–21.

16. Linda Williams. *Playing the Race Card: Melodramas of Black and White from Uncle Tom to O. J. Simpson.* (Princeton, NJ: Princeton University Press, 2001): 43.

17. Angela Bassett. Interview by Robin Roberts. April 26, 2006. *Good Morning America.* Available from Lexis Nexis (accessed October 28, 2007).

18. Judith Mayne. *Cinema and Spectator.* (New York: Routledge, 1993): 149.

19. Sharon Willis. *High Contrast: Race and Gender in Contemporary Hollywood Film.* (Durham, Duke University Press, 1997): 3.

20. Willis, *High Contrast*, 44.

21. Willis, *High Contrast,* 28.

22. *Akeelah and the Bee*, 2006.

23. Willis, *High Contrast,* 28.

24. Willis, *High Contrast,* 28.

25. *Akeelah*, 2006.

26. Willis, *High Contrast,* 35.

27. Williams, *Playing the Race Card,* 29.

28. *Akeelah*, 2006.

29. Williams, *Playing the Race Card,* 30.

30. *Akeelah*, 2006.

31. Williams, *Playing the Race Card,* 37.

32 Williams, *Playing the Race Card,* 30.

33. *Akeelah*, 2006.

34. Williams, *Playing the Race Card,* 38.

35. Whitsitt, *Journal of Popular Culture*, 889.

36. James Maguire. *American Bee: The National Spelling Bee and the Culture of Word Nerds.* (Emmaus, PA: Rodale Press, 2006): x.

37. *Akeelah*, 2006.

38. *Akeelah*, 2006.

39. *Akeelah*, 2006.40. Kyra Guant. *The Games Black Girls Play: Learning the Ropes From Double-Dutch to Hip-Hop.* (New York: New York University Press, 2006).

41. Elaine Brown Jenkins. *Jumping Double Dutch: A New Agenda for Black and the Republican Party.* (Silver Spring, MD: Beckham house, 1996).

42. Valerie Lee. *Granny Midwives and Black Women Writers: Double-Dutched Readings.* (New York and London: Routledge, 1996).

43. Williams, *Playing the Race Card,* 40.

44. Williams, *Playing the Race Card*, 99.

45. Williams, *Playing the Race Card*, 103.

46. Williams, *Playing the Race Card*, 303.

47. Williams, *Playing the Race Card*, 103.

48. Williams, *Playing the Card, Card*, 99.

49. *Akeelah*, 2006.

50. Mayne, 148.

51. James Baldwin. "If Black English Isn't A Language, Then Tell Me What Is?" *Black Scholar* 27, no. 1 (2001): 6.

52. "About the Bee." www.spellingbee.com/about-the-bee (accessed 16 March 2011).

53. Williams, *Playing the Race Card*, 305.

54. Williams, *Playing the Race Card*, 44.

55. Henry Giroux. *Fugitive Cultures: Race, Violence, and Youth.* (New York: Routledge, 1996): 69.

56. Williams, *Playing the Race Card*, 297.

Works Cited

187. Dir. Kevin Reynolds. Icon Entertainment International, 1997.

"About the Bee." www.spellingbee.com/about-the-bee (accessed March 16, 2011).

Akeelah and the Bee. Dir. Doug Atchison. Spelling Bee Productions2006.

Ayres, Chris. "A Spell of Good Fortune." *The Times* (London) (August 17, 2006): 18.

Baldwin, James. "If Black English Isn't A Language, Then Tell Me, What Is?" *Black Scholar* 27, no. 1 (2001): 5–6.

Bassett, Angela. Interview by Robin Roberts. April 26, 2006. *Good Morning America*. Available from Lexis Nexis (accessed October 28, 2007).

Dangerous Minds. Dir. John Smith. Hollywood Pictures, 1995.

Dominus, Susan. "The Starbucks Aesthetic." *The New York Times* (October 22, 2006): 1.

Errigo, Angie. "OK, It's a Bee Movie but Akeelah Will Leave You Spellbound." *Mail on Sunday* (London) (August 20, 2006): 58.

Fishburne, Laurence and Angela Basset. Interview by Fredricka Whitfield. April 27, 2006. *CNN*. Available from Lexis Nexis (accessed October 28, 2007).

Flory, Dan. "Race, Rationality, and Melodrama: Aesthetic Response and the Case of Oscar Micheaux." *The Journal of Aesthetics and Art Criticism* 63, no. 4 (Autumn 2005): 327-338.

Friedman, Josh. "Disappointing Bean Counters; Starbucks' Efforts to Market Movies Have Had Tepid Results," *Los Angeles Times* (August 27, 2007): C1.

Gaunt, Kyra. *The Games Black Girls Play: Learning the Ropes from Double-Dutch to Hip-Hop*. New York: New York University Press, 2006.

Gumbel, Andrew. "Would You Like a Movie with Your Latte?" *The Independent* (London) (April 25, 2006): 31.

Higashi, Sumiko. "Melodrama, Realism, and Race: World War II Newsreels and Propaganda Film." *Cinema Journal* 37, no. 3 (Spring 1998): 38–61.

Higgins, Scott. "Suspenseful Situations: Melodramatic Narrative and the Contemporary Action Film." *Cinema Journal* 47, no. 2 (Winter 2008): 74–96.

Hornaday, Ann. "'Akeelah and the Bee': One Honey of a Flick." *The Washington Post* (April 28, 2006): C01.

Jenkins, Elaine Brown. *Jumping Double Dutch: A New Agenda for Black and the Republican Party*. Silver Spring, MD: Beckham House, 1996.

Kakoudaki, Despina. "Spectacles of History: Race Relations, Melodrama, and the Science Fiction/Disaster Film." *Camera Obscura* 50, no. 17 (2002): 109–153.

King, Susan. "Loves Got to Do with It; Angela Bassett and Laurence Fishburne Are

Passionate about Their 'Akeelah' Roles." *Los Angeles Times* (April 27, 2006): E4.

Lee, Valerie. *Granny Midwives and Black Women Writers: Double-Dutched Readings*. New York and London: Routledge, 1996.

Lesko, Nancy. *Act Your Age! A Cultural Construction of Adolescence*. New York and London: Routledge Falmer, 2001.

Maguire, James. *American Bee: The National Spelling Bee and the Culture of Word Nerds*. Emmaus, PA: Rodale Press, 2006.

Mayne, Judith. *Cinema and Spectatorship*. New York: Routledge, 1993.

Morris, Wesley. "In a Word, 'Akeelah' Spells Crowd-Pleaser." *The Boston Globe* (April 28, 2006): D1.

Puig, Claudia. "Sit for a Spell with 'Akeelah'; You'll Be G-L-A-D That You D-I-D." *USA Today* (April 28, 2006): 8E.

Shalit, Gene. "Critic's Corner; 'Akeelah and the Bee.'" *Today Show* (May 1, 2006). Available from Lexis Nexis (accessed October 28, 2007).

Singer, Ben. *Melodrama and Modernity: Early Sensational Cinema and Its Contexts*. New York: Columbia University Press, 2001.

Stewart, Michael. "Irresistible Death: *21 Grams* as Melodrama." *Cinema Journal* 47, no. 1 (Autumn 2007): 65.

Stone, Jay. "Student's Hard Work Spells Success for Her Community." *The Gazette* (Montreal) (April 28, 2006): D7.

Toto, Christian. "'Akeelah' Spells a Kind Heart; Family, Community amid National Championships." *The Washington Times* (April 28, 2006): D8.

Waxman, Sharon. "A Small Step at Starbucks from Mocha to Movies." *The New York Times* (May 1, 2006): C1.

Whitney, Allison. "Race, Class and the Pressure to Pass in American Maternal Melodrama: The Case of *Stella Dallas*." *Journal of Film and Video* 59.1 (Spring 2007): 3–18.

Williams, Linda. "The American Melodramatic Mode." *Playing the Race Card: Melodramas of Black and White from Uncle Tom to O. J. Simpson*. Princeton, NJ: Princeton University Press, 2001. 10–44.

Willis, Sharon. *High Contrast: Race and Gender in Contemporary Hollywood Film*. Durham, NC: Duke University Press, 1997.

Wilson, Jon. "Movie Spells Motivation." *St. Petersburg Times* (May 7, 2006): 6.

Chapter Fifteen
See St. Louis and Die: Wartime and the Morbid Child Psychology of *Meet Me in St. Louis*
by Vincent Casaregola

At one point in Carl Foreman's 1963 film *The Victors*, a bitterly critical representation of the U.S. Army in World War II, we witness the execution of an American soldier. The scene is based on actual historical events involving U.S. Army Private Eddie Slovik, who had been convicted of desertion during the fall of 1944. The harsh fighting during that fall had led the court martial to make an example of the soldier and impose the death penalty, a decision then confirmed by higher commanders all the way up to Eisenhower himself (Kimmelman). Slovik was therefore executed at the end of January 1945, the first soldier to be executed for desertion since the Civil War (Kimmelman).[1] To heighten the irony of the execution scene, which is set in a snowy winter landscape and shot mostly at a distance, Foreman undercuts the action with his selection of music, a popular song from that same winter of 1944–1945, "Have Yourself a Merry Little Christmas," originally sung by Judy Garland in the 1944 musical *Meet Me in St. Louis*, produced by Arthur Freed and directed by Vincente Minnelli. Foreman's use of the song provides an obvious, even heavy-handed ironic contrast. The song's gentle melancholy and longing, along with its brave expression of delayed gratification, suggest the desire for a more innocent past represented in that musical. Foreman uses the song to demonstrate the difference between the war itself and the nation's nostalgic self-representation during that war.

Foreman had already established his *bona fides* as an antiwar screenwriter with *The Men* (1950), which starred a very youthful Marlon Brando as a paraplegic war veteran struggling with the physical and emotional consequences of his injury. More importantly, Foreman was cowriter of the Academy Award winning script for *The Bridge on the River Kwai* (1957), based on the novel by Pierre Boulle. However, as a result of his being blacklisted during the McCarthy era, Foreman was not given any screen credit and so did not actually receive the award at the time. On the other hand, after the blacklist was abandoned, he also openly wrote and produced the very popular war film, *The Guns of Navarone* (1961), so rather than demonstrating a general pacifism, Foreman represented complex views of war and rejected simplistic narratives of the World War II experience, especially as they might reflect and support Cold War attitudes.[2] *The Victors* represented his one directing effort, and its dark view of the traditional "good war" narrative likely reflected his concerns about war but even more his bitter experiences with McCarthy-era American politics. His use of "Have Yourself a Merry Little Christmas" as the ironic counterpoint to Private Slovik's execution was Foreman's way of commenting ironically on two mythic American narratives so popular in mid-century film—the "good war" narrative and the complementary narrative of the "good old days" as revealed in stories about turn-of -the-century America. Given both his politics and his personal experience, neither mythic narrative would have appealed to Foreman, and given his skill and insight as a screenwriter, it was clear that the best way to undermine and critique such simplistic narratives was to use their inherent contradictions in high contrast. The scene mentioned above does just this, reminding us that, during the winter of 1944–1945, as Americans at home lulled themselves to sleep with the lullaby-like "Have Yourself a Merry Little Christmas," across the world the brutality of war continued, and continued with a special intensity during the Battle of the Bulge. Some of the men at the front that winter may have comforted themselves with fantasies drawn from such classic Hollywood images as Judy Garland singing from an old-fashioned front porch, but most just tried to find some way to stay alive and keep warm, hoping that someday they would make it home from the war. Garland's voice could, indeed, stimulate their desire for home, but their own home experience was far from the mythic vision of Americana evoked by Hollywood. Also, in many cases, as Foreman recognized, such men would return home far too changed in body and/or mind ever to fit into such a gentle fantasy again.

While Foreman's scene is largely successful in making his point, a further, perhaps unintentional irony emerges from his use of "Have Yourself a Merry Little Christmas," one that points back to the song's original context in *Meet Me in St. Louis*, inadvertently drawing our attention to some less-than-innocent qualities in the original film, where that song leads directly into the climactic sequence. Garland, playing Esther Smith, sings the song to comfort her little sister "Tootie" (Margaret O'Brien). It is Christmas Eve, and the Smith family is about to move from St. Louis to New York because of the father's job. Other than the father, Alonzo (Leon Ames), the whole family is upset by this move, fearing the loss of contact with friends and familiar places in St. Louis, especially just as the 1904 St. Louis World's Fair is about to open the following spring. Being the youngest, Tootie experiences perhaps the strongest reaction and is least able to control her emotional response. Despite Esther's wistfully bittersweet song, Tootie refuses comfort and instead runs outside the house in her nightshirt and begins to attack the group of snow people that the whole family had made earlier that day. It is an extreme act, and certainly the most disturbing moment of the film, so disturbing that it convinces the father to change his mind about the move and keep the family in St. Louis, a decision that provides them with the only Christmas present they really wanted.

For Tootie, however, this incident is hardly aberrant behavior. Indeed, throughout the film she fantasizes about death and enacts numerous morbid rituals related to death and dying—everything from a symbolic killing of the "Braukoffs" on Halloween night, to the burial of her dolls after they succumb to supposedly fatal illnesses. In the aggregate, Tootie's behavior has all along suggested an unhealthy fascination with death and destruction. It seems that Foreman may have unconsciously sensed this quality in the in the musical when selecting "Have Yourself a Merry Little Christmas" as his version of an "executioner's song." Perhaps he picked up on the general feeling of dis-ease that pervades the whole of Minnelli's film, with its supposedly innocent depiction of a simpler and more joyful past. In the end, despite its attempt to provide escape from the stress and horror of wartime, *Meet Me in St. Louis* has been imbued all the more with the unmistakable odor of decay and death. Though trying to suppress the fear, violence, and suffering of war, *Meet Me in St. Louis* still resonates that much more powerfully with these qualities. It is as if the film cannot escape the war from which it was to provide release for its audiences. No matter how hard Minnelli tries to depict innocence, the wartime experience remains embedded in the psychology of characters and relationships to such an extent that it somewhat subverts the intended theme and content of the film, and this morbidity is witnessed most dramatically in the behavior of the apparently charming child Tootie.

In 1944, when MGM producer Freed and director Minnelli began work on *Meet Me in St. Louis*, America had been at war over two years. During that year, the United States would finally deploy armies of the massive scale that would allow the major offensives of the Western Allies to go forward. In the process, American forces would suffer unprecedented casualties. In fact, the vast majority of America's World War II losses occurred during the final fourteen months of the war—from the Normandy landings to the end of the Okinawa campaign—because this is when it had committed truly vast numbers of soldiers to combat across the globe. Even as the country was clearly winning the war, the costs became more and more prohibitive, and the destruction and brutality of the fighting unavoidably obvious. For some time, the Office of War Information—the government agency that monitored everything from journalism and advertising to Hollywood productions—had even begun allowing newspapers to print photographs of dead American servicemen, and allowing advertisers to depict similar scenes in their appeals for war bonds (Casaregola 85, 98).[3] The war, its demands, and its costs, especially its human costs, were on everyone's minds.

At the same time, that war had also made the U.S. economy viable again after over a decade of depression. Factories had expanded beyond the wildest dreams of economic forecasters only a few years before. People had gone back to work, had money in their pockets, and because of rationing and the curtailing of production of consumer durable goods, they could easily buy war bonds and at the same time still have money for discretionary spending on one of the few things that had not been rationed—films. Indeed, Hollywood was undergoing a boom of interest in films, some of which provided support for the war while even more offered escape from its stark realities. This latter venue of escapist fare gave generalized reinforcement to the fundamentally positive myths of American culture, particularly in the idealized iconography of the family, the small town, and the earlier periods of American history viewed as sites of innocence and purity.

It was this venue that Freed and Minnelli chose for the presentation of a major MGM musical that could satisfy the tastes of a public increasingly conscious of and concerned about the growing casualty counts from the war. They also picked the popular "Kenningston Avenue" stories of *New Yorker* writer Sally Smith Benson that recalled her youth in turn-of-the-century St. Louis, Missouri.[4] Bringing to the package the supreme innocence represented by Judy Garland seemed to guarantee that this film would offer a powerful image of normal American life as an antidote to the terror of war, as well as an image of the peaceful environment that all Americans hoped would soon return. Also, while using the 1904 St. Louis World's Fair as the backdrop, the film actually begins in 1903, as the Fair is under development, and so the film can emphasize both anticipation of a better future (a positive wartime theme) and yet still end with the Fair's opening, a dutiful celebration of the American way (a second, positive wartime theme). Thus, the film attempts to provide an escape from the war while it still reinforces the underlying propaganda efforts in support of war aims—patience while waiting for a better tomorrow and confidence that America has the will and means to make a happy future possible.

Despite these well-planned efforts at escapism, it is inevitable that the realities of the most destructive war in human history still lingered in the minds of both the film's audience and its makers. As 1944 grew to a close, more and more "Blue Star" banners on American homes changed to "Gold Star," ironically turning the golden image associated with the top of Christmas trees into a sign of death and mourning.[5] Every day headlines and news stories, film newsreels, and radio broadcasts provided more detailed coverage of a war growing ever more violent and deadly as it moved towards its conclusion. The

Allies' call for unconditional surrender of the Axis powers made total war even more complete, though it is unlikely that Nazi Germany or Imperial Japan would have fought less fiercely without that motivation. Of course, the processes of total war produce horrific casualties, even for the victors, and these human costs of war were evident to the whole American public, even if the news was sanitized through various layers of censorship. Indeed, in the very theaters that showed *Meet Me in St. Louis*, the film may have been preceded by newsreel images of the savage fighting in the Philippines or on the Belgian-German border during the fall of 1944. As a result, the film reveals deep anxieties about the violent conditions of the world through the images of violence in everyday life, albeit images that come in the form of childhood fantasies and games. Though they remain the fanciful acts of children, these actions and images still carry significant symbolic and emotional weight in the film, creating an underlying quality of instability and fear in this otherwise upbeat story of family relations and youthful romance.

Structurally, *Meet Me in St. Louis* focuses on the developing romances of the two oldest sisters of the Smith family—Esther (Garland) and her elder sister Rose (Lucille Bremmer). Rose is already in a long-distance relationship with a local youth who has gone to college in the East. But the central romance involves Esther's love for the proverbial "boy next door," a recent arrival named John Truett (Tom Drake). Esther carries much of the major action, and she provides the vast majority of the musical entertainment, with some of the most popular songs of the era. These include "The Boy Next Door," "The Trolley Song," and, as noted earlier, the still beloved "Have Yourself a Merry Little Christmas." Clearly, Esther is the film's overt emotional center, a role amplified by Garland's growing relationship with director Minnelli (they were married shortly after the film). He photographs and directs her lovingly, carefully blending her traditional image of juvenile innocence with her new potential as a romantic lead.

The structural counterplot involves the career opportunities of the father, Alonzo, well placed in a respected St. Louis law firm. Midway through the film, Smith is offered the opportunity to transfer to New York City to take charge of the firm's office there. His announcement of this opportunity, and of his decision to accept it, comes close upon the comically but still disturbing Halloween sequence. As might be supposed, the father's accepting the appointment without first consulting with the family puts him at odds with the others and introduces an element of genuine instability into the otherwise happy lifestyle. Still, this is a father-run family despite their habit of joking at his expense, and the decision will stand unless he decides to change it. His wife Anna (Mary Astor) serves as a peacemaker, even though she is equally disappointed at the prospect of moving. Under her influence, the family agrees to "soldier on," sadly recognizing that they are in their last few months in their hometown (they will move shortly after Christmas).

While these structural components predictably control the film's actions and relationships on the surface, the film's real emotional power seems to grow more from another source, and that is the youngest child, Tootie. Doted upon and spoiled by the whole family, including by her sometimes stern father, Tootie proves to be a free spirit who introduces her own brand of imaginative and subversive instability into the family and the plot. Her outburst in the early hours of Christmas Day ultimately provokes the father to reject the New York offer and keep the family in St. Louis, where they obviously prefer to stay. But Tootie carries darker emotions into the film than those associated with a mere spritely, innocent child. She is also a strangely morbid child, even if rendered in a comic fashion, and she seems far more like Wednesday Adams (of the Adams Family) than like a Shirley Temple figure. Indeed, it is through the character of Tootie that the emotional consequences of the ongoing war seem to surface unbidden into the milder environment of a nostalgic, period musical. Tootie's emotional condition is the key to the underlying power of the film, and that power comes from her ability to undercut the very hope and cheer that the film's surface seeks to evoke.

When we first meet Tootie, she is riding on a local delivery wagon, amusing the deadpan driver (Chill Wills) with her stories of her current doll's many illnesses. She tells him that the doll has at least four fatal illnesses, to which he quips, "And it only takes one." Tootie does not expect the doll to live through the night, and she obviously relishes the prospect of holding the funeral and subsequent burial. This comic incident is merely the first of many in which Tootie reveals her oddly morbid imagination. Somewhat later, she sneaks into Esther's party, offering a song about drunkenness that opens with the line, "I was drunk last night, dear mother." Here, she again introduces a very negative image that is mitigated by its coming through the appealing voice of this adorable child. No matter the image offered in the song, the motive must be assumed innocent because it comes through the voice of Tootie—these are the assumptions of the family and of the film itself.

Such instances also suggest a particular kind of morbid fascination exhibited by Tootie, one she has likely picked up from long-standing cultural traditions. It is the morbid sentimentality that inspired much vernacular and popular art throughout the mid- and late nineteenth centuries, often associated with a particular kind of middle-class, middle-brow sensibility. This is the very kind of sentimentality that Mark Twain goes out of his way to satirize in parts of the Grangerford episode in *Adventures of Huckleberry Finn*, where he focuses on the deceased teenager Emmeline Grangerford who, as Huck explains, "could write about anything . . . just so it was sadful." He goes on to elaborate:

> Every time a man died, or a woman died, or a child died, she would be on hand with her "tribute" before he was cold. She called them tributes. The neighbors said it was the doctor first, then Emmeline, then the undertaker—the undertaker never got in ahead of Emmeline but once, and then she hung fire on a rhyme for the dead

> person's name, which was Whistler. She warn't ever the same, after that; she never complained, but she kind of pined away and did not live long. (114)

The ultimate fate of the overly sentimental artist is, in Twain's satirical universe, to die from her own excessive sentimentality. Of course, to make sure that we know just how deserving Emmeline is of this fate, Twain allows Huck to go into some detail about her sentimental odes to the local dead, as well as her crayon drawings of heartbroken women expressing their grief at the loss of loved ones (112–113). The drawings, which decorate the Grangerford parlor, come with titles such as "Shall I Never See Thee More Alas" (112). Twain goes so far as to include a complete example of Emmeline's poetry, "Ode to Stephen Dowling Botts, Dec'd," a young man whose death, in her words, made "sad hearts thicken" (113–114). Such obvious sentimentality is an easy target of satire but, for Twain, a necessary one, since it undercuts genuine human sympathy and engagement, replacing it with mere superficial, emotional self-indulgence.

In *Meet Me in St. Louis*, Tootie has obviously picked up on this sentimental tradition in art and narrative, and thus her dolls become opportunities for her to construct fanciful stories of disease and death. Likewise, she has carefully memorized and learned to perform sentimental songs about dissolution and redemption ("I was drunk last night, dear mother"). Original writer Sally Smith Benson and, subsequently, the filmmakers realized that, by the turn of the century, this kind of sentimentality was already self-parodic, and so they could easily lodge it in the character of a young child whose very earnest delivery of the sentimental mini-narratives provides delightfully ironic effects. But beyond this apparently light comic touch lurks something that takes us back to elements in Twain's satire in *Huckleberry Finn*, the connection between this naïve, morbid sentimentality and a hyperbolically violent culture. Recall that the Grangerford episode is one of the most violent in the book because it deals with the very serious consequences of the ongoing feud between that family and the rival Shepherdsons. Huck, who is awestruck at what he sees as the sumptuous lifestyle of the Grangerfords, is equally astounded by their needless and terribly destructive feud, one that leaves several characters dead and convinces Huck that he must flee the place. Twain's more important point, far beyond satirizing sentimentalized art, is to show that such sentimentality is merely one aspect of a culture suffering from broad-based, self-destructive emotional extremism. The same emotional hyperbole that propels the violence also indulges in the sentimental grieving, and for Twain, both deserve critique. In *Meet Me in St. Louis*, the filmmakers wanted to use the character of Tootie to create an innocent but vivacious comedy, and these qualities come out in the morbid tales that seem so at odds with a young child's imagination. Unintentionally, however, the filmmakers also evoke a sense of the hidden experience of extreme violence that is so much a part of 1944. Tootie may seem innocent herself, but her character on film is constructed in and projected through a world that is itself losing more innocence day by day. As Twain recognized, what seems innocent on the surface is often quite a bit more complicated, and darker, beneath.

Subsequently, however, the film's Halloween sequence begins to raise questions about even Tootie's supposed innocence when she engages in two acts of symbolic murder, the latter of which causes genuine danger to real people. On Halloween all the younger neighborhood children dress up as ghostly hoboes, some of them also cross-dressing (girls with charcoal beards and boys in skirts). But these hobo costumes actually represent demons whose charge is to play tricks on the neighborhood residents, acts such as throwing flour in people's faces when they answer the door (symbolizing killing them). As the smallest of the demon crew, Tootie has little choice of assignments, but she bravely decides to take on the feared Braukoff household. Old Mr. Braukoff is described as having committed all forms of horrid offences, including killing cats (acts true only in the children's imaginations). In a mock-suspense sequence, Tootie slowly approaches the house and, at the appropriate moment, "kills" Braukoff by throwing flour in his face. She runs away, narrates her tale, and is proclaimed the fiercest demon of all.

This symbolic murder seems a harmless enough Halloween prank, but if we probe more deeply, we may find something very disturbing in the scene. Unlike the other residents of the neighborhood, the Braukoffs have a foreign-sounding name, and so the children look at them as strangers and therefore as more dangerous. Given the wartime background, this sounds disconcertingly like the kind of xenophobia that leads to violations of civil rights (as in the extreme case of the internment of Japanese Americans). The name can possibly imply a German heritage, and in that case, the "killing" of the dangerous Braukoffs may stand in for the literal bombing campaign against Germany, also killing allegedly guilty civilians in their homes. In contrast, an even more disturbing interpretation emerges if we consider the possibility that the name Braukoff sounds Jewish. In that case, targeting them as the subjects of false narratives of heinous acts, and then engaging in their symbolic murder, offers a set of actions that echo those that went on in early-thirties Germany, when the Nazis were engaged in just this kind of attack on German Jews (not to mention the extension of this type of murder into the systematic genocide of the Holocaust, though Hollywood would not really know about, much less represent the Holocaust until later). But does this scene really reveal some unconscious form of anti-Semitism in the film? That is unlikely; rather, the scene seems to be an unbidden echo of the massive persecutions and genocide at large in the world in 1944. In "innocent" Tootie's Halloween masquerade, we glimpse shadows of the Nazi persecution of the Jews and of so many others, along with shadows of the terrible violence of the war as a whole, where tens of millions died, mostly civilians.

The Halloween sequence continues with a second phase, one which is literally if not figuratively worse than the Braukoff incident. This second phase comes as narration from Tootie after the event itself, followed by further narrative by her slightly older sister Agnes (Joan Carroll) and subsequent explanations by neighbor John Truett. As the family begins gathering for cake and ice cream, Tootie is heard to scream somewhere outside in the distance. After her older sisters find her, they discover that she is crying and has suffered a cut lip. She claims to have been struck by John Truett from next door. At first, Esther refuses to believe this, but after a doctor arrives and confirms that she has hair from someone else clenched in her fist, Esther changes her mind. She runs next door, attacks John without explanation, and runs back home. There she finds that Agnes has returned and is telling the true story. She and Tootie had thrown a Halloween dummy onto the streetcar tracks, causing the conductor to think it was a real body and thus brake so hard as to jump the track. Fortunately, though perhaps to Tootie's disappointment, no real injuries occurred. Seeing their actions, however, John had rushed the girls away so that they would not be caught and get into trouble, but Tootie had struggled away from him because she wanted to relish the aftermath of her morbid stunt. Esther is at first enraged at her youngest sister, but then she forgives her, as do the other family members. Embarrassed by her own behavior, Esther runs next door again so she can apologize to John, who has not taken the matter seriously. He tells Esther that her awkward beating of him was not as bad as the blows he suffers at football practice, but that "it's more fun with a girl" (an oddly sado-masochistic comment). While the whole event is treated as one more of Tootie's imaginative pranks, it could have had serious, real-world consequences, including possible injuries to her or others from the streetcar's derailment. None of this matters to Tootie, who is thrilled at the performance coup she has pulled off. Once more she has transformed her morbid fantasy world into a dramatic event that has made her the center of family attention.

The habit of imagining sensationalistic, gothic, and morbid fantasies is again consistent with a number of nineteenth-century cultural traditions. Much popular fiction of the era appeared in periodicals in serial form, and amongst the most popular forms were those that engaged in extensive use of overly sensationalistic conflict, sometimes involving elements of the gothic or the macabre. These could provide the emotional excitement necessary to keep readers' attention as they awaited the next installment. Certainly some of these elements could emerge in the most artful literary fictions, from Emily Bronte's *Wuthering Heights* to Wilkie Collins's *The Moonstone*. Rendered with skill and insight, such qualities could enhance a novel's revelation of characters' inner emotional lives and conflicts, but these elements frequently invited the poor imitators and self-parodic extremes evident in so much of the popular fiction of the time. They also couple with an overly romanticized sense of sensationalized and sometimes exoticized conflict. Twain himself recognized these qualities in the culture of the antebellum South, and much of the ironic wit of *Huckleberry Finn* is directed against their extremes. Indeed, the novel's ending, with the intricately dramatic but ultimately unnecessary "rescue" of Jim is the best example. Here, Huck's friend Tom Sawyer must orchestrate the events, creating in the process a kind of novella-within-the-novel that goes on for a number of chapters so that he can obtain full emotional satisfaction from the effort (even though Jim is, as we later find out, already freed). Another nineteenth-century novelist, Louisa May Alcott, points a mild satiric finger at her own youthful self for trying to write and/or perform such fantasy narratives/dramas. In *Little Women*, the analog for Alcott, Jo March, spends her young years writing hyperbolic, fantastic stories of adventure and conflict, before she finally learns to write in a more realistic (if still somewhat sentimental) fashion that portrays with authenticity the world she truly knows.

These episodes in Twain and Alcott are but two satirical critiques of what was a common narrative pattern during the nineteenth century, and it is evident that this pattern has shaped Tootie's imagination. Like the young Jo March, Tootie imagines elaborate stories of adventure and danger, but she also transforms these into her own kind of "guerilla theater," especially with the streetcar incident. Also, like Tom Sawyer, Tootie must amplify and extend the sensationalistic possibilities of any event, imagined or real. Tootie lives in an imaginative universe that echoes with the tropes and forms of nineteenth-century popular literature, along with the highly stylized, melodramatic forms of nineteenth-century stagecraft and acting. Thus, in Tootie, we find a character who, by virtue of her young age, becomes a vehicle for comically critiquing the prior century's artistic excesses of morbid sentimentality and sensationalistic narrative.

Of course, Freed and Minnelli, along with Sally Smith Benson, were aware of many of these features of Tootie's character, and they used them to create a combination of subtle pathos and comedy that makes the film emotionally appealing on many levels. It is true that, in the context of 1944, these qualities evoke darker associations than those suggested by the connections with earlier sentimental art, darker than those conceived by the filmmakers. What the filmmakers seemed even less conscious of, however, is how the character of Tootie gradually grows beyond this simplistic form of morbid sentimentality, which reflects nineteenth-century tastes in popular fiction and drama, into a character who reveals a starker and grimmer form of morbid fascination that is expressed in the scene with the snow people, the scene preceded by the singing of "Have Yourself a Merry Little Christmas."

To examine Tootie's dark transformation, we must consider the cultural icon that child actor Margaret O'Brien had become even before the making of *Meet Me in St. Louis*. O'Brien had come to wide public attention when she played an orphaned British girl in the 1942 film *A Journey for Margaret*, the story of American journalist Jesse Davis (Robert Young), reporting from Britain during the Blitz. His wife Nora (Laraine Day) is injured in the bombing, and as a result of her injuries, she suffers a miscarriage and also can no longer have children. This plunges the couple into near despair, but subsequently, while writing a story about the traumatized orphans from the bombing, Jesse meets Margaret and Peter, whose vulnerability and tenderness reawaken his feelings. Of course, the couple finds a new understanding of family by taking the orphans into their hearts and home, ultimately adopting them. O'Brien created such a compelling image of the effects of wartime trauma that she made whole audiences want to adopt her as well (she changed her name to Margaret—it had been Angela—as a result of this film). Thus, for the American public, the sad face of Margaret O'Brien had already become a compelling icon of a child traumatized by the violence of war prior to her role as Tootie.[6]

Minnelli and Freed obviously felt that they could use O'Brien's ability to express pathos, if handled lightly, to produce the necessary comic effects. By and large, they were correct in this assumption. However, the iconography of Tootie's sad-eyed stare called forth a great deal of what O'Brien had already conveyed in *A Journey for Margaret*. While audiences could easily accept the comic situation and its innocently ironic references to earlier sentimental forms, they also sensed a deeper connection to contemporary horrors that were all too real in the daily imagery of the war. On the surface, Tootie becomes a comic figure parodying older morbid sentimentality, both charming and heart-warming at once. In contrast, and less intentionally, she becomes a reminder of all the children, everywhere, who have been traumatized physically and/or emotionally by the war. It is this more contemporary and darker sense of the morbid that pervades the penultimate scene with the snow people.

The Halloween sequence concludes with Mr. Smith's arrival home from the office and his announcement of the move to New York. This incident sobers the family, leading Tootie to mention how she will now have to dig up the graves of her many dolls, but this innocent remark belies the process of actual emotional trauma she has begun to undergo at the thought of leaving behind all that is familiar to her. Since most of the subsequent sequences deal with the developing romances of both Esther and Rose, we see less of Tootie until late in the film. The problems of the forthcoming move create the necessary plot conflicts that structure the remaining action, most of which is concentrated during the Christmas holiday. Close to the film's end, the family members all seem sadly resigned to their fates. Late on Christmas Eve and early into Christmas morning, Tootie sits mournfully at the window seat of her bedroom, waiting to see a Santa Claus who, she worries, may not be able to find them in New York on next Christmas. This concern covers more unspecified but evident anxiety about the loss of any sense of place, a condition shared to some extent with orphans. Of course, one cannot see Tootie's experiences as being anywhere near those of wartime trauma, but they can serve, in this context, as an unintended analog.

Just prior to this scene, Esther has confirmed her love of John and is now even more saddened at the prospect of leaving. Having returned from talking with him after the Christmas Eve dance, she comes to check on Tootie. To allay the young girl's fears and sadness, Esther sings "Have Yourself a Merry Little Christmas," a song that emphasizes patience in adversity while longing for a possible reunion with loved ones in some future Christmas (as the song states, "if the fates allow"). The sentiment must have struck a deep chord with so many in the audience whose husbands, fathers, and/or sons were still off at the war. Tootie's reaction, however, is completely opposite to that expected by Esther. The young girl collapses into sobbing and then runs from the room and downstairs. Propelled by a kind of manic rage, Tootie darts outside, grabs a shovel, and begins hitting the snow figure people that she and her siblings had constructed earlier in the day. Savagely she chops at them, cutting off arms, heads, and other body parts. Esther rushes out to stop her and bring her back in, but she doesn't reach her before Tootie has once again committed a series of symbolic murders.

There is nothing comic in this scene, and Minnelli clearly means for it to be the saddest moment in the film, when even the seemingly innocent Tootie loses complete control. As noted above, the intensity of Tootie's desperate anger leads her father to change his mind and keep himself and the family in St. Louis. The young girl's emotional outburst and symbolic violence are clearly intended to shock the father (and the audience) into seeing what a mistake it would be for them to move away, even if the act is not premeditated by Tootie. But the energy of the scene carries it beyond this limited scope. In one sense, Tootie is behaving almost psychotically, lashing out with violence at whatever targets are available—not unlike those soldiers who, in a near-psychotic state brought on by the extremes of combat, go on a sudden battlefield killing spree involving even disarmed prisoners and civilians. Indeed, in attacking this snow family, Tootie symbolically, though unintentionally, seems to reenact all the senseless violence unleashed against noncombatants and civilians throughout World War II. In this emotional and structural climax of the film, Tootie achieves her ultimate impact on her real-world circumstances, as her symbolic violence carries sufficient shock value to change the course of the family's life.

In one sense, this scene's action follows the logic of a terrorist attack or terror bombing—shock your adversary into changing his mind, and preferably into complete surrender. The British had been pursuing this logic for years with their nighttime saturation bombing of German cities, while within months of the film's release (and even as O'Brien was receiving a special Academy Award for being the best child actor of 1944), American bombers would be pursuing a similar strategy against Japanese cities, culminating in the atomic bombing of Hiroshima and Nagasaki the following August. The Germans and Japanese had done likewise, the former across Europe and the latter throughout Asia, especially in China. As we can see, and as the filmmakers and audience knew intuitively, outside of the fantasy realm of this musical, the war is still raging, raging with a violence that intensified with each passing week. Such violence cannot be kept completely outside of any cultural construction at this point in the war, and so the innocent conflicts of *Meet Me in St. Louis* necessarily take on all the war's powerful energy and terror. Focusing the emotional energy of the film through Tootie, with her childish version of morbid sentimentality, allows these darker cultural forces to emerge in an unexpected and therefore more troubling way. Even in this innocent icon of childhood, and throughout an elaborate effort to escape from and even deny, at least momentarily, the ugly violence of the world at war, Minnelli and Freed have unintentionally unleashed the very horror they sought to hide from their audiences. With the character of Tootie, the filmmakers begin with a collection of comically ironic references to excessive forms of morbid sentimentality in the popular culture of the prior century. But in the course of the film, they allow Tootie to evolve into a new kind of character, one connected more with the traumas that the actor O'Brien had represented in *A Journey for Margaret*. Additionally, they touched on something even more painful and frightening, the change in the character of children for whom the violence of war and the comprehensive insensitivity to the effects of that violence have become cultural commonplaces. Such children will live in a darker world, and the artists, writers, and filmmakers who portray the postwar experience will have an opportunity to explore just how frightening those children and their world can become.[7] This is not usually the stuff of MGM musicals, yet for this brief scene in an otherwise sentimental comedy, the combination of factors brought together by filmmakers, actors, audience, and circumstances managed to evoke a "sneak preview" of the darker world emerging from the war. It was a world in which childhood itself would have been inevitably altered.

The film ends with a brief coda that depicts the Smith family and their friends attending the fair's opening the next spring. They express awe and pleasure at the magnificence of the fair's entertainments and the beauty of its environment, though Tootie cannot resist mentioning some of its more morbid recreations of destruction. The family watches the lights come on and then moves off for dinner at one of the fair's restaurants. But Esther and John linger together at the railing by the reflecting pool, watching the dazzling lights. They marvel that all of this is still "right here in St. Louis," where the family has obviously chosen to stay—a faint echo of Garland, as Dorothy in *The Wizard of Oz*, proclaiming that "there's no place like home." Innocence seems to have been reestablished and now triumphs, and the hoped-for glorious future has been attained. Yet oddly enough, the reflecting pool over which they gaze in this closing scene was also the site at which the Fair reenacted old naval battles, with model ships burning and sinking during the re-creation of old wars. Sometimes, even in a Hollywood fantasy of innocence, there is just no escape from a dark and deadly world.

Notes

1. This court martial, and particularly this execution, came under much scrutiny in later years. It was publicized in the 1954 book by William Bradford Huie, *The Execution of Private Slovik*. In 1974, Martin Sheen stared in a made-for-television version of the work. Benedict Kimmelman was an army medical officer in the 28th Infantry Division, assigned to serve on the court martial. He later changed his mind about his decision to impose the death penalty. Once he had seen combat and then been captured by the Germans during the Battle of the Bulge, Kimmelman found much more sympathy for Slovik. Upon Kimmelman's release at the war's end, he was surprised to learn that the army had actually gone through with the execution.

2. In *Theaters of War: America's Perceptions of World War II*, I discuss at length the ways in which American World War II films of the period from 1949 to the mid 1960s usually offered a World War II story in service of a Cold War ideology. Some film makers—like Foreman in *The Victors,* Robert Aldrich in *Attack* (1956), or Arthur Hiller and Paddy Chayevsky in *The Americanization of Emily* (1964)—ran counter to this overall trend. See my discussion especially in chapters 5, 6, and 7.

3. In *The Censored War: American Visual Experience during World War II*, George Roeder provides a detailed account of how the Office of War Information gradually shifted from censoring all images of dead American servicemen to allowing some images of American dead, though always within specific limits.

4. Specific information about the making of *Meet Me in St. Louis* comes from a documentary, *Meet Me in St. Louis: The Making of an American Classic*, which accompanies some of the commercial VHS and DVD releases of the musical.

5. The "blue star" banner could be displayed by a household with a family member serving in the military, while the "gold star" was the icon for a household member who had died in the war.

6. In 1943, O'Brien played James Cagney's daughter in the patriotic short film *You, John Jones*. Here, Cagney plays an air raid warden in America who must leave home to make his rounds at night. He muses on his safety in America, where he does not really expect to be bombed as have his allies across the world. His prayerful thanks are answered by a divine voice that asks him to imagine his own home and child suffering what others do, so that he might develop greater empathy for those victims. We see him imagining his daughter, O'Brien, in a series of brief vignettes depicting the horrors suffered by allied children from Great Britain to China. The film, while only a short, underlined again the youthful O'Brien's appeal as a child victim of war.

7. Here, one thinks of numerous representations of such postwar, traumatized children who have grown as violent as the war they have survived. One example is Trevor in Graham Greene's 1954 story "The Destructors," an architect's son who leads a gang of fellow children to destroy an eighteenth-century house that is the only building in its area to have survived the bombing of London (the story and its plot figure prominently in the 2001 film *Donnie Darko*). Another example comes in W.H. Auden's poem "The Shield of Achilles," which mocks the elegant imagery of the Homeric original with references to the new barbarism of post-war culture, with particular reference to acts of children. Of course, the main character Alex in Anthony Burgess's *A Clockwork Orange*

(1962) represents perhaps the apogee of this kind of amoral passion for violence in post-war culture.

Works Cited

Alcott, Louisa May. *Little Women.* New York: Grosset & Dunlap, 1947.

The Bridge on the River Kwai. Dir. David Lean. Perf. William Holden, Alec Guinness, Jack Hawkins, and Sessue Hayakawa. Columbia Pictures, 1957.

Casaregola, Vincent. *Theaters of War: America's Perceptions of World War II.* New York: Palgrave/Macmillan, 2009.

The Guns of Navarone. Dir. J. Lee Thompson. Perf. Gregory Peck, Anthony Quinn, and David Niven. Columbia Pictures, 1961.

Kimmelman, Benedict. "The Example of Private Slovik," *American Heritage Magazine* September/October 1987. *American Heritage.* www.americanheritage.com/content/example-private-slovik (accessed July 15, 2011).

A Journey for Margaret. Dir. W. S. van Dyke. Perf. Robert Young, Laraine Day, Fay Bainter, and Margaret O'Brien. MGM, 1942.

Meet Me in St. Louis. Dir. Vincent Minelli. Perf. Judy Garland, Margaret O'Brien, Leon Ames, Mary Astor, Tom Drake, and Chill Wills. MGM, 1944.

Meet Me in St. Louis: The Making of an American Classic. Dir. Scott Benson. Narr. Roddy McDowall. 1994. Turner Home Entertainment, 1994.

The Men. Dir. Fred Zinnemann. Perf. Marlon Brando, Teresa Wright, and Everett Sloane. Stanley Kramer Productions,1950.

Roeder, George H. *The Censored War: American Visual Experience during World War II.* New Haven, CT: Yale University Press, 1993.

Twain, Mark. *Adventures of Huckleberry Finn.* Gerald Graff and James Phelan, eds. Boston: Bedford Books of St. Martin's Press, 1995.

The Victors. Dir. Carl Foreman. Perf. George Peppard, George Hamilton, and Eli Wallach. Columbia Pictures, 1963.

You, John Jones. Dir. Mervyn LeRoy. Perf. James Cagney, Ann Southern, and Margaret O'Brien. MGM, 1943.

Index

About the Authors

Michelle Ann Abate is an Associate Professor of English at Hollins University. She is the author of the books *Tomboys: A Literary and Cultural History* (2008) and, more recently, *Raising Your Kids Right: Children's Literature and American Political Conservatism* (2010). In addition, Michelle is the coeditor, with Kenneth Kidd, of *Over the Rainbow: Queer Children's Literature* (2011).

Katie Elson Anderson is a Reference Librarian and Web Administrator at the Paul Robeson Library, Rutgers University, in Camden, New Jersey. She holds an MLIS from Rutgers University and a BA in anthropology from Washington University, St. Louis, Missouri. Ms. Anderson researches a variety of topics in both library science and popular culture. Publications and presentations include storytelling in the digital age, the philosophy of SpongeBob SquarePants, teaching Generation M and preventing plagiarism. While she thinks her two children are very smart, cute and witty, their videos remain private.

Morgan Genevieve Blue is a PhD Candidate and Assistant Instructor in the Department of Radio-TV-Film at the University of Texas at Austin. She studies representations of childhood, youth, gender, and sexuality in commercial U.S. media, with a specific focus on discourses of girlhood. In addition, she is a coordinating editor of *The Velvet Light Trap* and helped program the 2010 FLOW Conference, hosted by the University of Texas. She has also been a volunteer instructor and programmer for Cinemakids International Film Festival since 2007.

Vincent Casaregola is a Professor of English and film studies at Saint Louis University, where he teaches courses in twentieth-century American literature, film, and popular culture, along with courses in rhetorical theory and cultural rhetoric. His recent book, *Theaters of War: America's Perceptions of World War II*, explores American literary and cinematic representations of that war, from the late 1930s though the first decade of the twenty-first century. He is currently working on a project that examines the history of American representations of business on screen. Professor Casaregola received his PhD from the University of Iowa in 1989.

Drew Chappell teaches at California State University Fullerton. He is a performance studies scholar with research interests in play, globalization, and ideological transfer, as well as visual and narrative research methods. His edited book *Children Under Construction: Critical Essays on Play as Curriculum* was published by Peter Lang in 2010. Drew holds an MFA from the University of Texas at Austin and a PhD from Arizona State University. He is also an award-winning playwright whose work focuses on issues that affect both children and adults.

Vibiana Bowman Cvetkovic is a Reference Librarian at the Paul Robeson Library, Rutgers University in Camden, New Jersey. Her books include *The Plagiarism Plague: A Resource Guide and CD-ROM Tutorial for Educators and Librarians* (Neal-Schuman, 2004), *Scholarly Resources for Children and Childhood Studies: A Research Guide and Annotated Bibliography* (Scarecrow Press, 2007), *Teaching Generation M: A Handbook for Librarians and Educators* (Neal-Schuman, 2009), and *Stop Plagiarism: A Guide to Understanding and Prevention* (Neal-Schuman, 2010). Cvetkovic, a PhD candidate in the Children and childhood studies program at Rutgers University, is the current chair of the Childhood Studies Area of the Mid-Atlantic Popular American Culture Association, a cofounder and technical editor of *Red Feather Journal: An International Journal of Children's Visual Culture*, and the assistant editor-in-chief of *MP: An Online Feminist Journal.*

Lan Dong is an Associate Professor of English at the University of Illinois Springfield. She is the author of *Mulan's Legend and Legacy in China and the United States* (2011), *Reading Amy Tan* (2009), and the editor of *Teaching Comics and Graphic Narratives: Essays on Theory, Strategy and Practice* (2012), and *Transnationalism and the Asian American Heroine: Essays on Literature, Film, Myth and Media* (2010). She has published a number of journal articles and book chapters on Asian American literature and films, children's literature, and popular culture. She is currently editing a two-volume encyclopedia on Asian American culture.

Janet Fink is Senior Lecturer in social policy in the Faculty of Social Sciences at The Open University, UK. Her research is largely focused on mid-twentieth century Britain, exploring how family relationships and practices were constructed in policy and legislation and represented in popular culture. She is particularly interested in how these constructions and representations were deployed and negotiated in film and photography. Her interests also extend into the use of contemporary visual research, where she examines theoretical questions about interpretation, meaning-making and the emotional power of the visual medium. She has published on both these areas in, for example, *Cultural Studies*, *Women's History Review*, *Paedagogica Historica*, and *Sociological Research Online.*

Amy Franzini is an Associate Professor of communication studies at Widener University in Chester, Pennsylvania. She earned her PhD in mass media and communications from Temple University. Her chapter, "Is School Cool: Representations of Academics and Intelligence on Teen Television" was published in Lisa Holderman's (ed.) *Common Sense: Intelligence as Presented on Popular Television* in 2008. Her work has been published in *The Journal of*

Sex Research and *The National Social Science Journal*. Her research focuses on media content representing and/or created for children and adolescents.

Stephen Gennaro is a cultural historian of media and youth. His main area of interest is "perpetual adolescence" which examines the many ways that the culture industries market "youthfulness" to young and old consumers alike. Stephen teaches children's studies at York University in Toronto, Canada and is the editor of pedagogy and teaching for The Society for the History of Childhood and Youth's newsletter.

Lena Lee is an Assistant Professor of early childhood education at Miami University, Ohio. She earned her doctorate of curriculum studies in Indiana University, Bloomington, and D.E.A of women's studies in France. Her scholarly interests are related to the complex relationships between children, education, and society from global perspectives. The specific areas of research include cultural studies, gender studies, multicultural education, teacher education, and comparative/international studies. She has had several manuscripts on these topics published in a wide variety of scholarly journals such as *European Early Childhood Education Research Journal*, *Journal of Early Childhood Research*, and *Teacher Education and Practice*.

Kathryn E. Linder is the Director of the Center for Teaching Excellence at Suffolk University in Boston. She earned her PhD in women's, gender, and sexuality studies from The Ohio State University. Her research interests include cultural studies of education, youth citizenship, feminist and alternative pedagogies, and educational development.

Caryn Murphy is an Assistant Professor of communication at the University of Wisconsin Oshkosh. She holds a Ph.D. in media and cultural studies from the University of Wisconsin-Madison. Her research on the uses of film and television in the construction of social roles and individual identity has appeared in the *Networking Knowledge* journal, as well as the anthologies *Dear Angela: Remembering My So-Called Life* (2007) and *The Business of Entertainment* (2008).

Beth Nardella is an Assistant Professor of writing in the School of Medicine at West Virginia University. She is currently researching the use of skating and other metaphors to teach complex writing concepts across the curriculum. She holds an MFA from the University of North Carolina at Chapel Hill and an MA from West Virginia University.

Debbie Olson, ABD, is lecturer at University of Texas at Arlington. Her research interests include West African film, images of African/African American children in film and popular media, transnationalism, cultural studies, and Hollywood film. She is the Editor-in-Chief of *Red Feather Journal: An*

International Journal of Children's Visual Culture (www.redfeatherjournal.org), and coeditor of *Lost and Othered Children in Contemporary Cinema* (2012). Her articles appear in *The Black Imagination: Science Fiction and Futurism* (2011), *The Tube Has Spoken: Reality TV as Film and History* (2009), and *Facts, Fiction, and African Creative Imaginations* (2009), and many others. She has contributed to such collections as *The African American Biography Project* (2008), *Writing African American Women* (2006), and a variety of others. Her dissertation explores the transnational circulation of the black child image.

Iris Shepard is completing her PhD in English literature at the University of Arkansas. Her area of specialization is children's and young adult literature and film. In addition to finishing her dissertation, she leads an after-school literacy project for middle school students in rural Arkansas. In her free time, she hangs out with her two sons and plays roller derby.